The Convergence of Race, Ethnicity, and Gender

Fifth Edition

Dedicated to my husband and to our beautiful children.

SAGE was founded in 1965 by Sara Miller McCune to support the dissemination of usable knowledge by publishing innovative and high-quality research and teaching content. Today, we publish over 900 journals, including those of more than 400 learned societies, more than 800 new books per year, and a growing range of library products including archives, data, case studies, reports, and video. SAGE remains majority-owned by our founder, and after Sara's lifetime will become owned by a charitable trust that secures our continued independence.

Los Angeles | London | New Delhi | Singapore | Washington DC | Melbourne

The Convergence of Race, Ethnicity, and Gender

Multiple Identities in Counseling

Fifth Edition

Tracy Robinson-Wood
Northeastern University

Los Angeles | London | New Delhi
Singapore | Washington DC | Melbourne

$\circledS$SAGE

FOR INFORMATION

SAGE Publications, Inc.
2455 Teller Road
Thousand Oaks, California 91320
E-mail: order@sagepub.com

SAGE Publications Ltd.
1 Oliver's Yard
55 City Road
London, EC1Y 1SP
United Kingdom

SAGE Publications India Pvt. Ltd.
B 1/I 1 Mohan Cooperative Industrial Area
Mathura Road, New Delhi 110 044
India

SAGE Publications Asia-Pacific Pte. Ltd.
3 Church Street
#10–04 Samsung Hub
Singapore 049483

Development Editor: Abbie Rickard
Editorial Assistant: Carrie Montoya
Production Editor: Bennie Clark Allen
Copy Editor: Renee Willers
Typesetter: Hurix Systems Pvt. Ltd.
Proofreader: Sue Schon
Indexer: Robie Grant
Cover Designer: Janet Kiesel
Marketing Manager: Shari Countryman
eLearning Editor: Lucy Berbeo

Library of Congress Cataloging-in-Publication Data

Names: Robinson-Wood, Tracy L.

Title: The convergence of race, ethnicity, and gender : multiple identities in counseling / Tracy L. Robinson-Wood, Northeastern University.

Description: Fifth Edition. | Thousand Oaks : SAGE Publications, Inc., 2016. | Revised edition of the author's The convergence of race, ethnicity, and gender, 2013. | Includes bibliographical references and indexes.

Identifiers: LCCN 2015040394 | ISBN 9781506305752 (pbk.)

Subjects: LCSH: Cross-cultural counseling.

Classification: LCC BF636.7.C76 R583 2016 | DDC 158.3—dc23
LC record available at http://lccn.loc.gov/2015040394

16 17 18 19 20 10 9 8 7 6 5 4 3 2 1

Brief Contents

Detailed Contents

Preface to the Fifth Edition

Much has been invested in equipping mental health professionals with skills and tools to be culturally competent across contexts. A bounty of beautifully written articles, special editions, guidelines, and handbooks exist on multiculturalism and cultural diversity with the collective aim of enhancing the quality of patients' lives, irrespective of the skin they are in, their personal and political histories, and their multiple identities. While our professions have been strengthened and our teaching, research, and clinical practice enriched, there is so much more we must learn and unlearn.

New to This Edition

In this fifth edition, I have addressed many recommendations from reviewers and students. The following additions are new:

- Updated research literature has been added.
- There are many new clinical case studies that encourage students' growth as counselors-in-training.
- Several new storytelling bars highlight gender, race, ethnicity, and class inequity.
- Text boxes provide the reader with definitions, statistics, demographic data, self-reflection exercises, and other opportunities to be actively involved in this text.
- There are 19 chapters instead of 15.
- This new edition was reorganized to include

  (1) a first chapter that focuses on you, the mental health professional, and provides themes that frame this text;
  (2) a chapter on people of European descent;
  (3) a chapter on people of Jewish descent;
  (4) a chapter on social justice.

- Data from the 2010 Census has been added.
- Dramatic changes throughout the United States have been chronicled and include the 2015 legalization of same-sex marriage in all 50 states, the removal of the confederate flag in front of the South Carolina state house, and the completion of the Army Ranger training program by two women.

Convergence of Race, Ethnicity, and Gender in Counseling

Historically, the multicultural counseling literature has emphasized race. This focus is understandable considering the legacy and current reality of racism in America and the power of social construction given to race as well as to other identities. The expanded focus on discourses, cultural competencies, assessment of competence, whiteness studies, body size, sexuality, and socioeconomic class is crucial to an inclusive cultural paradigm. Convergence requires us to honor race and ethnic identities in our clients while simultaneously incorporating other identities. Resistance to injustice, regardless of the constellation of our identities and even when we have membership in privileged groups, is also a reflection of our commitment to diversity.

Nearly 30 years ago, as a new assistant professor, I began talking about *convergence*. What I meant by convergence was the intersection of race, ethnicity, gender, and other primary identity constructs within the context of counseling. Each of these constructs across contexts informs a person's emotional and psychological development and intersects with other human dimensions. The intersection of identities has been receiving greater attention in the multicultural counseling and psychology literature with increasing emphasis on their fluidity across contexts and over time. A consideration of how multiple identities, visible and invisible, converge simultaneously and affect development, attitudes, values, behavior, and the therapeutic alliance was limited.

This new paradigm for imaging differences, those that are conscious and unconscious as well as those that are visible and invisible, allows us to engage in the never-ending process of self-awareness as human beings with multiple and shifting identities. Differences are celebrated; the structural inequity that assigns power and privilege to immutable characteristics is not. My focus on discourses is due to their pervasiveness, their invisibility, and their enormous power to systemically shape cultural and political attitudes regarding difference and normalcy.

Multicultural counseling and psychology emphasize relational, cultural, ecological, and social justice frameworks. As professionals, we accept our responsibility to be agents of transformation by creating a more just and equitable world that reflects humane distribution of resources and opportunities. Multicultural counseling and psychology also recognize the way in which dominant cultural beliefs and values can perpetuate patients' feelings of inadequacy, shame, confusion, and distrust in both the therapeutic process and within the larger society.

The response to the first four editions from colleagues, instructors, and students has been uplifting. I am grateful to you for your support of my work. As detailed above, this fifth edition offers an updated format with revised chapters, case studies, and storytelling. New and existing research and competencies are discussed. In a spirit of *Umoja* (unity) and *Kujichagalia* (self-determination), I acknowledge and celebrate the contributions of each of us, those who have walked the path before us and cleared a trail, those who journey now and uncover new roads and interpret the map differently, and those who are yet to come who will point us in new directions.

A Message to Students

The material presented in this book is intended to further your development as a culturally competent professional. Some of the information you encounter may provoke dissonance. It is hoped that you will honor your feelings and share them with me, your professors, and your classmates. Through your practica and internships, you will find that your patients will feel dissonance, confusion, anger, and a host of big emotions when exposed to a new insight or technique that will serve them long term but in the short term is hard to take. Once the course is finished and you have your grade, it might be easy to revert to more comfortable discussions about difference. If you are willing to see a different and better way of being in the world, your thoughts, actions, behaviors, and beliefs about yourself and others will undergo transformation as well. The process of transformation is part of a social justice orientation and a lifelong commitment to using your power and privilege for good in the world.

I welcome you to this exploration. Please read the storytelling features and case studies, and listen to other people's stories as well as to your own. Although growth cannot happen without dissonance, trust that you are being prepared to better appreciate the multiple layers and contexts that both you and your patients will bring to therapy. An informed, interrogated, and integrated sense of yourself will help you relate to your patients with greater empathy and flexibility. As you process your own feelings and endeavor to make meaning of new information, I hope you will have communities of support who listen, nurture, and at the same time, challenge your positions. I also encourage you to accept that there may be individuals who will be unable to receive or support some of the new insights that you will take from this text.

A Message to Colleagues

Teaching diversity and multicultural courses is challenging. If successful, students will become aware of unearned skin color privilege and history denied and distorted. Hopefully, they will also become mindful of a dominant culture that esteems white or white-looking skin, masculinity, high-wage-earning persons, an able body, heterosexuality, and athleticism. In coming to understand culture, there will be disillusionment, sadness, and anger—often directed toward you, the messenger. Faculty of color may be perceived as the ones who are best suited to teach diversity-oriented courses. Despite being well prepared and qualified to teach, white professors may be viewed suspiciously by both students and faculty across race and ethnic groups. White students may fear that faculty of color are going to be punitive or make them feel guilty for being white. Students of color may feel the need to carefully weigh their words out of fear that they will offend their white professors and suffer from this power differential with an inferior grade. These matters are contextual. Untenured professors of any race are naturally concerned about student evaluations, which will be a measure of teaching effectiveness during merit, promotion, and/or tenure review. For this reason, I do not advocate junior faculty teaching this class by themselves initially—a coteaching model with a senior colleague is recommended during the first few semesters. Senior faculty and department chairs need to understand these dynamics and protect vulnerable junior and adjunct faculty who are particularly dependent upon good teaching evaluations to progress through academic ranks or to be rehired in subsequent semesters. The politics are fierce and often unspoken, yet they represent the landscape of multicultural work.

With that said, the course is one where teachers are able to bear witness to students being changed at depth. This is a great gift and privilege. It does not, however, come without a price. It is important that you take care of yourselves and do the best work that you can. This is, after all, a calling. Watching students listen to other people's voices and coexist with different ways of being in the world allows us to be the change we want to see and be part of social justice transformation. At the same time, some students will receive excellent grades in their diversity course yet may not appear to be significantly altered by the material. Be prepared to read and hear racist statements from students. You must be prepared to hear that which is difficult to receive when you ask students to speak from their lived experiences. How can the rain of racism fall throughout the land yet miss each and every home, including our own? You have to trust that for some of your students, you are nurturing growth and change that you will not see by the semester's end. I encourage new faculty members who have taken jobs away from home and other communities of support to have a ready list of people on whom to Facebook, call, SKYPE, or text, and confide in after a particularly difficult class that leaves you feeling drained and seriously questioning the decision making that led you to where you are now.

Finally, ask your students to buy world maps or upload a map app on their smart phones. Sometimes, refreshing history and geography lessons can be most helpful to learning. Having a map on the screen can be powerful when describing migration, immigrants (e.g., Sudanese, Syrians) literally risking life and limb to flee a war-torn or uninhabitable place that used to be home, as well as politically driven boundary changes.

Outline of Chapters

The text is divided into three parts: "The Mental Health Professional and Diversity," "Our People," and "Converging Identities." Every chapter has at least one storytelling feature to honor the powerful oral tradition of storytelling that is alive in the world's cultures. To encourage the integration and application of the material, a case study is presented in each chapter.

In this fifth edition, separate chapters are devoted to people of Native American and Alaska Native descent, people of Hispanic and Latino descent, people of African descent, people of Asian descent, people of the Middle East, people of European descent, and people of Jewish descent. The reality of bicultural, biracial, and multiracial people as the fastest-growing demographic in the United States is recognized as well throughout the book.

Part I: The Mental Health Professional and Diversity Chapter 1, "You, The Mental Health Professional, and Diversity in Mental Health Practice," is a new chapter and is focused on you as the mental health professional as you understand the helping profession and acquire the skills to offer support to others. This chapter encourages you to consider the offerings that you present to yourself. The dimensions of diversity, four themes that frame this text, and three skills that are critical—empathy, broaching, and interpretation—are discussed and applied to a case study.

Chapter 2, "Multicultural Competencies: Knowledge, Skills, and Attitudes," focuses on the knowledge, attitudes, and skills, both verbal and nonverbal, which are essential for cultural competence among mental health professionals. The American Counseling Association competencies are reviewed as are competency benchmarks from the American Psychological Association, Board of Educational Affairs, and Council of Chairs of Training Councils. Information is provided on the integration of competencies in various settings and includes the ability to know the limits of one's competence and to consult with others as necessary. The interplay among cultural competence, social justice, and ethics are discussed.

In Chapter 3, "Multiple Identities: Defined," gender, race, ethnicity, nationality, sexuality, religion, ability, disability, and class as sources of differences are defined. The intersections of identities and their contextual nature are discussed.

In Chapter 4, "Identities as Status," a model for socially constructed discourses is presented to reflect dominant society's conceptualization of difference. The intersections of identities and their hierarchal nature across contexts and situations are discussed.

Part II: Our People Chapter 5 is focused on people of Native American and Alaskan Native descent. Chapter 6 explores people of Spanish and Latin descent. Chapter 7 attends to people of African descent. Chapter 8 is dedicated to people of Asian descent, Native Hawaiians, and Pacific Islanders. Chapter 9 celebrates people of the Middle East and of Arab descent. Chapter 10, a new chapter, is dedicated to people of European/Caucasian descent. Chapter 11 is also a new chapter and honors people of Jewish descent. The goal of each chapter is to provide a succinct overview of historical information; migratory and immigration patterns; demographic characteristics; social, psychological realities, including education and class; and cultural values that include information about communication patterns. Intragroup diversity is a primary tenet with an understanding that tremendous differences can be found within groups of people. The terms *people of Asian descent, people of African descent, people of Hispanic and Latin descent, people of Native American and Alaskan Native descent, people of the Middle East, people of European/Caucasian descent,* and *people of Jewish descent* are used for three reasons: (1) to reflect the biracial and multiracial heritages reflected within and across racial categories; (2) to respect the reality that people may live in America, but they and their people hail from other parts of the world, such as the Caribbean or the continents of Europe, Asia or Africa, and South America; and (3) to honor the reality that many people who have resided in America for many generations may not choose to self-identify as Asian American, Arab American, Latino American, Jewish American, African American, or Native American but by a particular ethnicity or ethnicities, such as Korean, Syrian, Jamaican, Venezuelan, Ashkenazi Jew, Nigerian, or Lakota-Sioux.

In 1978, the Office of Management and Budget adopted the term *Hispanic* to describe people who were perceived to have a similar ethnic background. Instead of *Hispanic*, *Latino* is used throughout this text because it is a self-defined term. Latinos can be of any race. Lowercase letters are used for black and white races due to the porous nature of these terms, their inclusivity of continents besides Africa and Europe, their inclusion of people who have dark skin but who are defined as white by the census (e.g., North Africans), and the reliance on social capital for racial identification (e.g., educated or high income dark skinned Latinos who may have referred to themselves as white during the 2010 census).

Part III: Converging Identities Chapter 12, "Converging Race," explores race from sociopolitical perspectives. Race and science are given special attention as they refute socially constructed racial meanings that, although extraordinarily powerful, do not adequately capture basic truths—that all Homo sapiens originated from Africa and, irrespective of phenotypical appearance, Homo sapiens are genetically speaking 99.9% alike. Some relevant research is presented (e.g., recent research on microaggressions). Via the case study, race, gender, acculturation, and assimilation are explored.

Chapter 13, "Converging Biracial and Multiracial Identities," offers clarity through definitions. Research is summarized that addresses biracial identity development as shifting, fluid, and influenced by geography, racial socialization messages, parent's race and/or racial identity development levels. Clinical issues related to multiple racial and/or cultural identities are presented by way of a case study that examines group affiliation and belonging.

Chapter 14, "Converging Gender," discusses gender roles, gender identity(ies), and examines gender briefly from historical and biological perspectives. Sex and sex role typing are explored, and distinctions are made among terms. Female and male models of gender identity are discussed. Attention is given to gender socialization and the construct of physical beauty, emotion, and their influence on power and status.

Chapter 15 is titled "Converging Sexuality." The goal of this chapter is to expose readers to the importance of cultural competence in sexuality, a concept that can be overshadowed by race and ethnicity and tends to be underexplored in a mental health professional's multicultural competence. The importance of clinicians' knowledge of sexuality and the ability to broach this topic in therapy and/or supervision, irrespective of one's sexuality, is emphasized. Greater attention is focused on transgender issues and their intersections with other identities.

Chapter 16, "Converging Socioeconomic Class," focuses on class as a status variable, both in society and within the therapeutic event. Class is inextricably linked to self-worth, perceptions from and treatment by others, social capital, social network, and income. The limited training that graduate students in counseling programs receive is discussed within the context of culture. Questions are provided to help students unravel the role of class in their own lives and with respect to their perceptions and evaluations of others. The intersections of power, powerlessness, gender, and race are considered.

Chapter 17, "Converging Disability," is focused on the definition of disability and its various expressions in daily life and over time. Counseling individuals with disabilities is emphasized, and demographic data are provided with respect to the number of people affected by disability, type of disability, poverty, housing status, and occupational participation. More specifically, the correlation of disability with employment, income, and poverty is discussed along with the U.S. culture and its embrace of normalcy, beauty, and well-being as linked to having an able-body. This chapter contains two new sections—one that discusses veterans and the types of injuries that can contribute to disability and a section on Alzheimer's, a progressive and disabling condition that all American adults either have had some experience with or know someone who is caring for a loved one with this disease.

Chapter 18, "Converging Spirituality," defines religion and spirituality and provides the helping professional with insight into how to competently and comfortably integrate spirituality into the therapeutic event. A case study illustrates a white Jewish therapist's knowledge, skill, and attitudes as he attends to a black Christian patient grappling with a crisis of faith following surgery from a cancer diagnosis.

The last chapter, Chapter 19, is "Converging Social Justice in Diversity Practice," and has returned from the third edition. The definition and spirit of social justice are discussed as mental health professionals seek to advocate for the vulnerable and pursue equity within climates that evidence indifference. A case study exercise is provided for the purpose of applying chapter material to implementable interventions.

Tracy Robinson-Wood
Northeastern University

Note: Instructors, please sign in at **study.sagepub.com/robinsonwood** for additional author-created resources.

Acknowledgments ❖

Twenty-three years ago, Dr. Mary Howard-Hamilton and I approached a publisher in the exhibition hall at an American Counseling Association convention. We told her of our desire and our dream: to write a book on multicultural issues in counseling that incorporated race, ethnicity, and culture as well as the muted topics of gender, socioeconomic class, and sexual orientation. We asked Linda Sullivan, an editor, if we could buy her a cup of coffee. She graciously accepted. Out of that conversation, her scrutiny of us, and our scrutiny of multicultural counseling and of ourselves as women, black Americans, and academicians, an invitation was extended to us to develop a book prospectus that evolved into a signed contract for that first edition. As I present this fifth edition, I thank Mary for her invaluable contributions to the first edition of this text.

My husband and our children are my light and my life. I have precious friends with whom I have the gift of growing old. Thank you for holding me in your hearts and asking "how is the book going?" My angel mother and father have never left my side.

I especially want to thank Kassie Graves at SAGE Publications for sharing her interest in and excitement over my work. I will never forget our first conversation about the possibility of SAGE publishing this fifth edition. I am grateful to Carrie Montoya for her keen attention to details that are critical for such a project. Books do not get to press without good editors. Both of you have been kind and consistently available to me—thank you.

Tracy L. Robinson-Wood

SAGE Publishing gratefully acknowledges the following reviewers:

Mary Olufunmilayo Adekson, *St. Bonaventure University*
Stephanie San Miguel Bauman, *Washington State University*
Angel J. Daniels, *Marymount University*
Josue Gonzalez, *The University of Texas at San Antonio*
John L. Garland, *Alabama State University*
John C. Wade, *Emporia State University*
Bweikia Foster Steen, *Trinity Washington University*
Monique Levermore, *University of Central Florida*
Alberto M. Bursztyn, *Brooklyn College - City University of New York*
Jessica L. Sniatecki, *The College at Brockport, State University of New York*
Grafton T. Eliason, *California University of Pennsylvania*
Richard T. Spears, *Springfield College*

About the Author

Tracy Robinson-Wood is a professor in the Department of Applied Psychology at Northeastern University. She is author of *The Convergence of Race, Ethnicity, and Gender: Multiple Identities in Counseling*. Her research interests focus on the intersections of race, gender, sexuality, and class in psychosocial identity development. She has developed the Resistance Modality Inventory, a psychometrically valid measure of psychological resistance based upon a theory of resistance she codeveloped for black girls and women to optimally push back against racism, sexism, classism, and other forms of oppression. Her research is also focused on parents' racial socialization messages within interracial families and the relational, psychological, and physiological impact of microaggressions on highly educated racial, gender, and sexual minorities. Prior to Northeastern University, Dr. Robinson-Wood was a professor in the Department of Counselor Education at North Carolina State University. A California native, Dr. Robinson-Wood earned her undergraduate degree in psychology and communication from Azusa Pacific University in Azusa, CA. Her graduate degrees are in human development and psychology from the Harvard Graduate School of Education. She and her husband are proud parents of twin daughters.

Part I

The Mental Health Professional and Diversity

1

You, the Mental Health Professional, and Diversity in Mental Health Practice

Harry Stack Sullivan once described the therapeutic relationship as "two people, both with problems in living, who agree to work together to study those problems, with the hope that the therapist has fewer problems than the patient" (as cited in Stiver, 1997, p. 306). Mental health professionals possess knowledge of human development, psychological theories, and an understanding of how to facilitate client empowerment, yet the counseling process is by no means a magical one in which the therapist is free of any personal conflicts and the client is solely dependent on the counselor (McWhirter, 1991).

The Mental Health Profession

The mental health profession is fluid, dynamic, and highly regulated with respect to requirements for ethics, curriculum, practice hours, accreditation, and licensure. Accountability and transparency are coupled with the process of internal and external reviews of students, programs, and institutions with the intention of overseeing, protecting the public, and establishing rigorous criteria for persons who have the privilege of bearing the title as licensed counselor, social worker, and psychologist. Despite this scrutiny, the American Psychological Association is reeling from exposure that it was involved with enhanced interrogation and torture as reflected in the Hoffman report released in July 2015 (American Psychological Association [APA], 2015).

Increasingly, the Council for the Accreditation of Counseling Related Educational Program (CACREP) has been expanding its reach nationwide. What are the implications of this expansion for programs that are and are not CACREP accredited or for programs that wish to become accredited or for those that do not? Social workers and psychologists are allowed to treat patients who are covered by the nation's largest health insurance program, Medicare, whereas counselors are not. Medicare provides insurance not only to people 65 and older but also to the millions of Americans under the age of 65 who have physical and mental disabilities.

There is other news and events for each sector of the very large mental health professional umbrella, which includes Advanced Registered Practicing Nurses, who in addition to providing behavioral health are able to prescribe medications, a privilege that social workers, counselors, and most psychologists do not have. There are states (e.g., Louisiana, New Mexico, and Illinois), however, where psychologists can prescribe if they have received the requisite advanced and specialized training.

Your degree programs have designed their curricula and clinical practice training in conjunction with regulatory bodies (e.g., licensing boards) for articulating degree and licensing requirements. In addition, a required ethics and law course will allow you to mine the professional events and policies, both locally and nationally so that you can be prepared to enter the profession upon completion of your programs.

More states are requiring students to apply for a license as an LPC-A (licensed professional counselor-associate) or other designation prior to becoming an independent practitioner, such as an LPC or LCMHC (licensed clinical mental health counselor).

Students are encouraged to review the state board requirements in the states where they plan to practice prior to graduating so that they can complete specific state requirements while in their graduate programs. For instance, California requires counselors to have a course in psychopharmacology, although most PhD counseling psychology programs do not have such a requirement.

As a mental health professional, people will bring you their stories of woundedness, unfinished business, triggers, stuckness, addiction, trauma, anxiety, depression, and disruptions in interpersonal relationships and employment. You will be called upon to apply the knowledge, skills, and attitudes from your training, clinical experience, supervision, and research that will hopefully provide healing, symptom reduction, insight, and desired change to a behavioral health population. (See Storytelling: Self-Care First.)

Counseling and psychotherapy that is helpful, meaningful, and impactful depend on a sound therapeutic alliance and is at its best when patients feel like they have a holding environment (Kegan, 1982) that is empathic and allows them to tell their stories freely while feeling listened to and validated (Kegan, 1982; Murphy & Dillon, 2008; Rayle, Chee, & Sand, 2006; Vontress, 1986). Your openness to personally consider a therapeutic environment for yourself and to recognize personal strengths as well as areas that need attention and/or healing may complement the therapeutic-alliance with your patients.

❖ STORYTELLING: SELF-CARE FIRST

A client shared her story of being sexually brutalized by her father and "family friends" for years. Her single-parent mother battled with her own addictions and was not emotionally available to protect this defenseless girl child. Her therapist said, "It was not your fault. You deserved better than what you received, and as a little girl, you should have been protected." The patient began to cry. As she did, the raw, but healing skin cut with a razor from the patient's own hands whispered that her heart and soul were healing as well. As mental health professionals, we listen—not distract or silence, but hear our patients' stories. Have you told the painful stories from your life to a therapist or counselor? If yes, did being in the patient's chair support your empathic response to your own patients? For the healers to get help could represent a gigantic step in the direction of a social justice agenda. Mental health professionals bring themselves into the counseling room. They bring their pain, disappointment, success, arrogance, insensitivity, and empathy. They bring their attitudes about race, gender, class, sexual orientation, culture, abortion, gun control, politics, gender roles, immigration, and interracial marriages. Some counselors will find it difficult to bear witness to certain stories or emotions from their clients. The stories themselves are not the problem, nor is it the difficulty that a therapist encounters in hearing accounts of trauma and violence. A problem is the inability or unwillingness to make sense out of how clients' lives contribute to and affect us—our feelings, thoughts, reactions, and sensitivities. The professionals' unwillingness or inability to hear needs an intervention.

As beneficial as psychotherapy can be to reduce patient distress and enhance quality of one's life, stigma is associated with seeking mental health treatment. Owen, Thomas, and Rodolfa (2013) discussed two types of stigma: social and self. Social stigma speaks to the fear of judgment, such as being discriminated against or stereotyped from others within one's social network, whereas self-stigma refers to the internalization of societal messages regarding the stigma related to seeking psychotherapy for a mental health concern. Ironically, there are mental health professionals who have internalized a stigma of therapy and have not sought out therapy or counseling for themselves. Self-knowledge that is needed to identify those places and spaces in our lives that represent triggers and arouse vulnerabilities reflects a gesture of humility and multicultural competence to our patients and to the profession to be as healthy and teachable as we personally can be. (See Storytelling: Giving and Receiving.)

In working with patients across cultural diversity, there are two processes that can be very meaningful: credibility and giving. Credibility refers to the client's perception of the therapist as an effective and trustworthy helper. Giving is the client's perception that something was received from the therapeutic encounter. The client has received a "gift" of some sort from the therapist. Credibility and giving are not new concepts in treatment. They are related to the much discussed notions of expectancy, trust, faith, and effectiveness in therapy (Sue & Zane, 2009).

❖ STORYTELLING: GIVING AND RECEIVING

I heard of a meditation that may be helpful to mental health professionals and to their patients regarding the practice of giving empathy and compassion to others while unconsciously denying it to oneself. Imagine that you are called to the home of a woman who is ill. As you ascend the stairs, you hear the woman's moans of discomfort and pain. As you approach the bed, you see the ill person's face and recognize her as a once dear friend with whom you have lost contact. What do you do? Many people would seek to comfort their friend in the following ways: (1) listen to her story if she wants to share it, (2) offer her some water and/or something to eat, (3) bring her medicine, (4) call her doctor, (5) sit on the edge of her bed, (6) hold her hand, (7) sing to her, (8) tell her that things will get better, (9) pray for her, and (10) read to her. Does your empathy and compassion shift for the ailing person if as you approach the bed, you discover that the person in the bed is actually yourself? Do you experience the same swell of concern and consideration? Do you offer yourself the same understanding, patience, and kindness, or are you critical and dismissive of yourself and your needs? Do you question the authenticity of your illness and feel guilty for lying in bed? Do you practice patience and give compassion toward yourself as you acquire and strengthen skills and become knowledgeable of theoretical orientations, techniques, and interventions that range in effectiveness across clinical contexts? What life scenarios (e.g., not placing at your desired internship site, infertility, loss of wealth, failing a course, failing a licensing exam, permanent disability) would be nearly intolerable for you to hold for yourself? What are the implications of not being able to create a sustaining holding environment for yourself while seeking to create holding environments for others?

A multicultural approach in mental health practice is recognized as essential for therapeutic effectiveness and refers to mental health professionals' knowledge of the many dimensions of psychosocial identity (e.g., race, ethnicity, class, culture, nationality, religion, ability). A multicultural approach also reflects the mental health professionals' awareness of their personal proximity to socially constructed discourses about psycho-social identities as well as insight into how patients have been and can be impacted by these socially constructed discourses. (See Definitions Box 1.1: Discourses.)

❖ DEFINITIONS 1.1

Discourses (Weedon, 1987) are uses of language that

1. represent hidden meanings,
2. are used in place of overtly stated verbal exchanges,
3. operate as forms of social practice, and
4. communicate and perpetuate scripted and particular meanings.

Four themes serve to foreground this text and both define and support a multicultural approach in training you and other mental health professionals.

Theme 1—A Focus on Histories, Voice, and Power (Not on Food, Fabric, and Festivals)

Since its beginning in 1776, the United States has been home to immigrants, documented and otherwise. According to the population clock, there are nearly 322 million documented people living in the United States (U.S. Census Bureau, 2015c). Millions of persons are here illegally and are not among this count. If you are not one of the nearly 5 million Native Americans, then you or your ancestors came to America from somewhere else at some point in time, either by boat, by plane, by train, by car, or on foot. Some of our ancestors came legally; some, illegally, without a government-issued visa, passport, or other document granting entry. Others came voluntarily, and others came against their wills.

The designation "people of color" refers to individuals who are African American, Native American Indian/Alaskan Native (Indian/Native), Asian American, Latinos (who can be of any race), biracial, and multiracial. Sources of diversity include race, ethnicity, gender, sexuality, nationality, physical ability, mental ability, disability, socio-economic status, and religion. In the 2010 census, over 9 million people described themselves as being a member of two or more races (Jones & Bullock, 2012).

The 2010 census reveals that the white population is 77% of the population; however, white alone (non-Hispanic or Latino) is 62.6%. Latinos have increased the most and are 17.1% of the population; African Americans are 13.2% of the population. Asians represent nearly 5.3% of the American population. Native Americans are 1.2% of the population (U.S. Census Bureau, 2015b).

Since the 2000 census, Latinos surpassed African Americans as the largest group of color sometime during the early part of the 21st century (Robinson-Wood, 2013). Much of the racial and ethnic diversity in U.S. society has been influenced by persons from Latin America and Asia, the areas from which the majority of current immigrants originate.

The current work on multicultural psychology and counseling in the mental health professions is inclusive of ethnic, racial, sexual, gender, class, disability, and religious diversity. Native-born people of color, immigrants, white men and women, the lesbian, gay, bisexual, and transgender community (LGBT), and people with disabilities began writing from their lived and clinical experiences. The country has witnessed change in the last few years. When the 4th edition of this text was released in 2012, less than 13 states allowed same-sex marriage. Three years later, as of March 6, 2015, 13 states **did not** allow same-sex marriage. Three months later on June 26, 2015, the Supreme Court ruled that same-sex marriage was legal in **all** 50 states. A seismic shift has taken place in this nation regarding the legality of marriage between people who may be of the same sex, either from biology, identity affirmation, and/or through the transgender transitioning process. This legal and historical paradigm shift reflects a cultural sea change in the social constructions of normal love, marriage, family, and sexuality. America has born witnessed to significant changes in the way society thinks and feels about who is entitled to enter into the legality and sanctity of marriage. Mental health professionals across political and religious ideologies need to know of this legal ruling as it has implications for cultural knowledge, advocacy, and multicultural competence.

America also witnessed a display of different and divisive perceptions among people regarding a flag, as heritage, hate, or history. On July 10, 2015, South Carolina Governor, Nikki Haley, an Asian Indian American and the first female to govern this Southern state, signed legislation to remove the Confederate flag from the state house and place it in a museum. This action followed the shooting deaths of nine African Americans who had gathered at church for Bible study. After the shooter was arrested, a photograph emerged with him holding a Confederate flag.

These two monumental changes are the result of united voices, including those of mental health professionals, across age, gender, sexual, ethnic, and racial diversity, who advocated for justice for all and resisted the status quo. While many people consider same-sex marriage equality and the removal of the Confederate flag from the South Carolina state house to be vivacious and victorious, there are those who do not rejoice but instead mourn and feel their religious rights and personal way of life have been disregarded and trampled.

Convergence asks that we commit to simultaneous incorporation of identities, both visible and invisible, as we work with our patients. Many of the voices behind these and historical changes are from millennials, people like yourself and the majority of students in mental health professional training programs who were born between 1982 and 2000. Millennials, or America's youth born between 1982 and 2000, now number 83.1 million and represent more than one quarter of the nation's population. Their size exceeds that of the 75.4 million baby boomers, according to new U.S. Census Bureau estimates released in late June 2015 (U.S. Census Bureau, 2015a). Overall, millennials are more diverse than the generations that preceded them, with 44.2% being part of a minority race or ethnic group (i.e., a group other than non-Hispanic, single-race white). More diverse than millennials are Americans who are younger than 5 years old. In 2014, this group became majority-minority for the first time, with 50.2% being part of a minority race or ethnic group. Reflecting these younger age groups, the population has become more racially and ethnically diverse in just the last decade, with the percentage minority climbing from 32.9% in 2004 to 37.9% in 2014 (U.S. Census, 2015c).

Millennials are also different from previous generations with respect to their participation in marriage. For example, in 1960, 72% of all adults ages 18 and older were married. Over 50 years later, 51% are married. If these trends continue, adults who are currently married will drop to below half within a few years. Cohabitation, single-person households, and single parenthood are adult living arrangements that have increased over the last few decades. The struggling economy may explain a 5% drop between 2009 and 2010 in the number of new U.S. marriages (Cohn, Passel, Wang, & Livingston. 2011). Other advanced postindustrial societies have also seen declines in marriage that seem to persist through both good and bad economic times. (See Definitions Box 1.2: Social Construction.)

❖ DEFINITIONS 1.2

Social Construction (Gergen, 1985) refers to society's creation of race, gender, class, and sexuality as meaningful categories of privilege and oppression. Society makes sense of these meanings, and difference is created rather than intrinsic to a phenomenon. Deconstruction is taking apart, unlearning, and analyzing the way in which meaning was constructed and engaging in a different process of social construction with different meanings and outcomes.

A multicultural inquiry encourages an analytic that queries: (1) Whose narratives and perspectives are privileged? (2) Whose narratives are denied or undervalued? (3) Which ideologies resonate with you, and to which patients would you be more comfortable providing counseling? (4) What are the values and messages that have helped to shape your sense of comfort and familiarity? (5) And as a seasoned or mental health professional in training, what will you have to learn, unlearn, keep, and release to most effectively do the work that will help you provide multiculturally competent counseling and psychotherapy to people who want the flag up, the flag down, who celebrate same-sex marriage, and who think same-sex marriage is unnatural and an anathema to their religious and political integrity?

Intersectional approaches argue that occupying more than one stigmatized social position leads to experiences with unique forms of discrimination (Friedman & Leaper, 2010) and asks us to think about what it might mean to the therapeutic alliance when mental health professionals are dissimilar from their clients. Dissimilarity is not defined by racial differences but encompasses value orientations about prolonging life extreme measures, fidelity, illicit drug use, the use of blood products in medical treatment, prayer in school, concealed hand gun laws, and more. (See Storytelling: Where Is Patriarchy.)

When clients perceive their therapists as having a multicultural orientation, they are likely to view the therapist as having more credibility. A strong therapeutic alliance is facilitative of improvement in psychological well-being. Researchers have found that clients' perceptions of their psychotherapists' multicultural orientation were positively related to working alliance, real relationship, and psychological functioning. Owen et al. (2013) examined whether 176 clients' perceptions of their clinicians' multicultural orientation were associated with their psychological functioning, working alliance, and real relationship scores. The researchers also tested whether clients' perceptions of the working alliance, and the real relationship served to mediate the relationship between clients' perceptions of their psychotherapists' and psychological functioning.

❖ STORYTELLING: WHERE IS PATRIARCHY?

My students and I were discussing the movie, *When They Leave*, a powerful film by Feo Aladag about a woman (Sibel Kekilli) from Turkey whose traditional Muslim family had immigrated to Germany. We were discussing gender roles and gendered expectations. Several students were critical of the expectation that even in the midst of domestic violence, many men and women believed that it was culturally honorable and appropriate for the film's main female character, as a married woman with a young son, to return to her battering husband. Her refusal to do so created shame for the family, alienated her from her family of origin, and had adverse implications for the family's standing within the community, a component of a collectivistic orientation. To place patriarchy into a cultural context, I mentioned that here in America, patriarchy was more common than many students were able to see given its pervasiveness yet subtle albeit normative nature. There was silence in the room. I asked the predominantly female class, "How many men do you know who are eagerly waiting to take their wives' birth names or step away from their jobs and create gaps in their resumes for several years to raise young children?" I also asked, "Did you know that men will most likely, according to the $.23 hourly pay discrepancy between men and women, make more money than you, even with the same degree or without a graduate degree?" "How many of you, who identify as female, took your boyfriends, husbands, dads, or a male friend with you the last time that you purchased or repaired your car because you knew that their gender-conforming male status would most likely net you a better price for your car purchase or car repairs?" If therapists are unable to recognize when they are professionally and personally challenged by their patients' belief systems or are critical of their patients' values that run counter to their deepest values (e.g., gender equality), the therapeutic event can be compromised.

Theme 2—A Commitment to Feeling Feelings
Amidst Interrogation and Difficult Dialogue

In order to feel our feelings in diversity mental health practice, we need to be able to recognize and name the feelings that are present. Among some of our patients, we have or will come to observe, that they feel feelings but they are unable to identify, name, or understand them. Similar with culture, we are sometimes unable to recognize cultural aspects and values that we resonate with or feel some alienation. Embedded deeply into the fabric of daily life, culture can, ironically, be rendered invisible, largely because it is ubiquitous.

Dominant American cultural values include beauty, competition, control, convenience, gender conformity, democracy, entitlement, educational attainment, equality, heterosexuality, individualism, materialism, meritocracy, productivity, Protestant work ethic, attractiveness, Whiteness, and youth. For some, culture is a dominant identity that informs clothing, prayer, mourning and burial rituals, the Friday and Sunday dinner menus, wedding dress colors, the day of the Sabbath, seating arrangements at the dinner table, the naming of children, circumcision decisions, parent rearing, as well as parent care-taking practices. Others are seemingly oblivious to culture and how it has informed their sense of normalcy, beauty, respect, honor, and justice. Clinicians are encouraged to interrogate the hefty role of culture in shaping the self. Social justice is core to this inquiry, which is undeniably related to power. Socially constructed meanings and discourses are rooted in histories and are relevant to training in diversity and multicultural counseling, in its consideration of voices and perspectives that have been silenced and overlooked yet are part of an important cultural capital narrative with respect to status and stigma. Power interrogates discourses that assume an Asian American is a recent immigrant due to the discourse that Asians are all foreign born and do not look American, yet an immigrant from Albania, a European country, is assumed to have lived in the United States all of her life due to the discourse that white people look like true Americans.

Culture impacts one's assessment of their personal problems. As cultural competence increases among mental health professionals, students might be confused and wonder, "How could I be nearly finished with a graduate degree and have such fear of or inaccurate knowledge about people of color?" Talented students, across race and ethnicity, admit their ignorance about the enormous contributions from people of color to the United States and to the world and are often unable to list three or more inventions that black and Native Americans created or patented? It is not that this information does not exist. It does. However, these are stories that have not been privileged educationally; therefore, the topics are not widely taught.

To uncover obscured stories, students are often required to do their own research or to take the initiative to acquire information about overlooked and understudied groups (e.g., conduct interviews). While it may be interesting to learn the types of food eaten by people from a particular ethnic group, this information may not interrogate power, class, and policy decisions that keep certain business out of certain neighborhoods. For example, the most nutritious and healthy foods are more expensive than foods that are high in oil, sugar, and fat, yet there are higher rates of food insecurity among people of color who also tend to be more obese and have less wealth. The topics

---

| Self-Check Exercise 1.1 |

Detecting Discomfort

How can you tell when you are uncomfortable with material that is being discussed in class? Does your heart beat fast? Do your cheeks feel warm? Do you develop a tremor? Do you feel dizzy? It is helpful to identify the emotion that leads to physiological changes. Is it anger, fear, sadness, confusion, and/or guilt? As an effective mental health professional, you need to know what you feel and be able to assess and coexist with these feelings while simultaneously attending to the feelings of your patients. Feelings are a barometer that informs you of what is going on. Attend to them and commit to sorting out why and when certain feelings are triggered. Doing so will help you to become more emotionally attune to and ready for the varied emotions that your patients will have.

---

of privilege, power, and justice are challenging to engage. In fact, they often contribute to discomfort, feelings of alienation, and students' silence. Being exposed to information about unearned privilege related to socially constructed valued identities, albeit contextually driven, such as white skin color, heterosexuality, physical and intellectual ability, and male gender may appear to some students that they are being blamed for having identities over which they have no control. (See Self-Check Exercise 1.1: Detecting Discomfort.)

Reactions to learning about privilege can lead to a host of emotions, thoughts, and behaviors, including (1) hostility at the messenger (e.g., the instructor/professor); (2) anger and sadness; (3) confusion; (4) guilt, embarrassment, and shame; (5) denial; (6), humor; (7) minimization of the information; (8) rationalization; (9) avoidance of difference; and (10) focus on similarities.

Despite espoused cultural values of democracy, diversity, and equality taught in schools, synagogues, mosques, churches, political structures, and within the family, Americans are socialized into an ethnocentric ideology. Ethnocentrism contributes to misinformation about people who are not legitimized by a culture. Enculturation is both a conscious and an unconscious conditioning process whereby men and women, as children and adults, achieve competence in his or her culture, internalizes his or her culture, and becomes enculturated by internalizing the dreams and expectations, the rules and requirements for the larger society and for each specific demand within society (Grunland & Mayers, 2002).

Theme 3—Inclusion of White People Into the Discussion

U.S. history is a reflection of dominant cultural values and is an institutionalized narrative. Loewen (1995) put it this way: "We are told that White plantation owners furnished food and medical care for their slaves, yet every shred of food, shelter, and clothing on the plantation was raised, built, woven, or paid for by black labor" (p. 95). Most of us also did not hear "America . . . derived its wealth, its values, its food, much of its medicine, and a large part of its 'dream' from Native America" (Gunn Allen, 1994, p. 193).

A discourse related to whiteness is that white people exist as well-meaning but exploratory (e.g., temporary and noncommitted) players in the work of social justice and diversity due primarily to their unearned white privilege. For example, white and heterosexual faculty who teach diversity courses are initially seen, by some students, as dubious. They are met with skepticism regarding their appropriateness, not so much intellectually, but because questions arise regarding their lived experiences and whether such experiences can further understanding about and connections with the material on privilege, inequality, and power.

During classroom conversations, white students often fear that they have little to offer to the conversation about race, particularly when there is more than one student of color in the classroom. These feelings are large and coexisting with them is difficult, intimidating, and for many, uncomfortable for the student and for the classmates. Thoughts that students have during their cultural diversity training include the following: "Will I be perceived as a racist by my classmates?" or "I didn't come from poverty and disadvantage, so I do not have anything to say?" Not all of the racially similar students in a classroom come from the same ethnic and/or class group. There are significant within group racial differences. There are white students, due to their sexuality, family trauma, ethnic status, income, and political orientation who are intensely grounded in the multicultural and social justice literature, whereas there are some black students who are highly assimilated.

What is really challenging for some students is revealing a steady diet of racist statements that they were actually exposed to in their home environment, either from immediate or extended family members, neighbors, and friends. A commitment to feeling our feelings, talking about them, and trusting there are insights from this heart and head work that will contribute to the process of change, discovery, and growth—a process that our chosen profession, the helping profession, requires.

Activism against injustice, regardless of identities, including membership in privileged groups, denotes a reflection of our commitment to the values and convictions that define pluralism, equality, and healthy relationships across difference. Here, differences are celebrated; however, the structural inequity that assigns power and privilege to immutable characteristics is not celebrated. Mining how we benefit from and are disadvantaged by privilege given to some and denied to others allows us to position ourselves in the landscape of honest, meaningful, and admittedly difficult query about difference.

The rain of racism falls on all of the houses in the land. And although this realization is painful and one that people may initially deny, people have no control over phenotype and skin color, typical markers of racial categorization. This text affirms the psychosocial work that mental health professionals, across ethnicity and race, engage in to develop and sustain spaces of justice, cognitive and emotional flexibility and complexity. Cultural competence is not random; it is methodical, informed, measureable, ethical, and habitual practice that displays professional values, both serves and protects the public (Falender, Burnes, & Ellis, 2013) and reflects relational integrity that enhances the quality of patients' lives.

Greater attention has been devoted to multicultural counseling competence and research, indicating that multicultural education produces positive outcomes. How to teach multicultural counseling competence to you and other graduate students in the most effective way possible continues to be explored (Kim & Lyons, 2003). Training and competence models that incorporate participants' ability to both identify multiculturally appropriate strategies and apply these strategies in therapy is important (Sehgal et al., 2011). Students' sensitivity to multicultural issues is not congruent with demonstrating competence, meaning that current training programs may be lacking in their ability to help students take multicultural competence and translate the information into actual clinical practice (Sehgal et al., 2011). Identities are multiple and intersecting, those that are ambiguous, fluid, unidentified, and impact the therapeutic alliance.

Chao, Wei, Good, and Flores (2011) were interested in multicultural training as a moderator of racial differences on multicultural knowledge and the relationship between color-blind attitudes and multicultural awareness. The researchers found in their investigation of 370 psychology trainees that race/ethnicity significantly interacted with multicultural training in its prediction of trainees' multicultural awareness, but not multicultural knowledge. However, color blindness significantly interacted with multicultural training to predict trainees' multicultural knowledge, but not multicultural awareness. At lower levels of training, trainees of color showed significantly greater multicultural awareness than white trainees. The researchers also concluded that multicultural training significantly enhanced multicultural awareness for white trainees, but this was not the case for trainees of color. When white trainees received more training, their awareness levels were enhanced. However, when racial/ethnic minority trainees received more training, their levels of multicultural awareness remained the same.

Among trainees of color, a ceiling effect may exist, and varied as well as additional types of training (e.g., workshops, research teams/projects) are needed for both white and trainees of color. Coursework and frequent and ongoing interactions with people across racial and ethnic diversity may ultimately enhance multicultural awareness for trainees of color. Among white trainees, higher levels of training are important for achieving higher levels of awareness.

Theme 4—Understanding That Privilege and Power Are Not Bifurcations

Unearned privilege need not be connected to power. The lack of unearned privilege need not be a denial of power (see Case Study: Assigning Gender). Consider people who have membership in groups that are socially constructed as having value: white skin, maleness, intellectual developmental and physical ability, physical beauty, wealth, and education yet struggle, albeit unseen or known by others within the general population, with substance issues, gambling addictions, trauma-filled histories, mental illness, life altering losses, interpersonal difficulty, insufficient parenting, and feelings of inadequacy (see Storytelling: In the Beginning).

❖ STORYTELLING: IN THE BEGINNING

Nearly two decades ago, I began talking about convergence. What I meant by convergence was the intersectionality of race, ethnicity, sexuality, gender, and other primary identity constructs and their impact on therapeutic success and outcomes. Fortunately, intersecting identities have received more attention in the multicultural counseling literature. Previously, much of the literature focused on individual aspects of identity (most often race, culture, or ethnicity) and their subsequent influences on a cross-cultural counseling event in which the client was a person of color and the counselor was not. If power is conceptualized from a narrow lens, one either has it or does not, then power belongs to a few and is denied to most, eclipsing the power of resistance, grass root mobilization, and varying dimensions of what constitutes power (e.g., strong family and friendship ties, remembering one's history of struggle and victory, faith in a well-defined relationship with one's higher power, and community collaboration). A new paradigm for understanding an array of differences, allows us to engage in the never-ending process of personal growth, self-awareness as human beings with multiple and shifting identities.

Case Study

Assigning Gender

Justin and Kaitlin are both 25 years old. They live together and are not married. Although earlier than they had planned, both were excited to learn that Kaitlin was pregnant. After nine months of eating well, prenatal vitamins, exercising, and regular prenatal visits, Kaitlin goes into labor. Justin is with her throughout the 17-hour process. When their baby is born, there is silence in the delivery room. Upon inquiring about the gender of their baby, the doctor indicates that a series of tests have to be run. After a harrowing wait, their doctor informs them that their baby was born with ambiguous genitalia, more specifically a micropenis. Because the doctors doubt the functionality of the penis, with respect to urination and having future intercourse, they recommend that their child undergo surgery and be assigned a female gender. In a panic, Katherine calls a local therapist identified through her insurance company. Regina Matthews is a licensed clinical mental health counselor. She is African American. Eager to speak with her, Kaitlin and Justin postpone any surgical interventions until they have had time to enter intensive therapy. They decide to wait until they gather information prior to any surgical interventions and take their child home from the hospital after 2 days. Their child is physically healthy. For 2 weeks, they meet with Regina twice weekly. Their doctors disagree with their decision to leave the hospital without surgery and caution them that they are wasting valuable time that their baby needs for a normal start and chance at life. When friends and family call to inquire about the gender of their baby, they tell everyone they have had a baby boy and that his name is Kaleb. Doctors tell Justin and Kaitlin that if their child undergoes a bilateral gonadectomy and labial skin biopsy prior to puberty, she would need to begin estrogen replacement and have future surgery to create a functional vagina.

Questions

1. Since Justin and Kaitlin have presented for therapy prior to making their decision, what information would be helpful from their clinician?
2. What aspects of culture are impacting Justin and Kaitlin's deliberations?
3. What are your concerns and questions as you read this case study?

Discussion and Integration

Kaitlin and Justin

Kaitlin and Justin, as new and young parents, did not anticipate the outcome they encountered and most likely do not have a frame of reference for dealing with this crisis. Therapy represents a place where these new parents can express their fears and anxieties about the life of their child. Taking time to consider their options, do some research, and secure a second opinion can give Kaitlin and Justin time to make decisions. In addition, in therapy, they have a space to express their concerns about the future. Through a solid and supportive therapeutic alliance, Kaitlin and Justin are able to learn that there is a difference between conditions that on one hand, represent a medical threat, prolong sickness, and interfere with wellness and individual differences that are not indicative of injury, disease, or harm physical health.

During graduate school, Regina was exposed to a brief discussion of intersexuality in her diversity course. Regina defines herself as LGBT affirming and multiculturally competent. However, she does not have any friends who identify as intersexual and has not studied intersexuality for several years. Regina believes that an intersexual designation for children would be confusing and add difficulty to a child's developmental path. Regina once terminated a pregnancy when she discovered that she was carrying a child with Down syndrome. While her personal story is very different from that of her patients, Kaitlin and Justin, Regina does not want her personal material to become an imposition or a distraction. Thus, Regina is aware of the gaps in her knowledge and how she is positioned on this topic. Regina is also mindful of the potential of countertransference, a phenomenon that she seeks to avoid and stems from feelings that the patients' transference can stir within the counselor.

Vontress (1986) defined *countertransference* as psychological transposing. With transference, the therapist is seen as an idealized authority and the patient credits the therapist as having the skills the patient needs (Basch, 1992). Transference can contribute to patient growth (e.g., feelings of validation, heightened ability to act in one's best interest, improved self-esteem, greater insight into affect, behavior, and cognition).

Regina makes two important decisions prior to her initial meeting and following her important phone screening to ensure that she is able to provide effective and relevant services to potential clients. She inquires about contact information, insurance, previous psychiatric hospitalizations, previous therapists' diagnoses, whether a case manager is involved, and so on. Regina consults with a mental health clinician who has published widely on the topic of intersexuality to become more knowledgeable and to recognize her biases. Diversity practice among mental health professionals encourages trainees and seasoned professionals to interrogate their biases related to ethnicity, race, gender, class, ability, and sexuality. While it might be tempting for the novice trainees to assert that they love working with all people, each person has been affected and shaped by cultural discourses about normalcy, desirability, and oppression. Culturally skilled counselors are cognizant of their proximity to discourses that they may hold. Regina understands that intersexuality is fairly common, and yet she has not thought much about the discourses surrounding intersexuality that have influenced her thoughts and feelings.

To acquire additional knowledge, Regina went to the Intersex Society of America website to become familiar with perspectives from intersexuals and their family members. By engaging in these activities, Regina felt that she would be in a better way to confront her biases. Intersexuality was the term used prior to the more frequently used term, disorders of sexual development (DSD; Knott, 2014).

Intersexuality differs from LGBT issues given that conditions known as nonstandard sexual anatomy are frequently exposed at birth, but this way of thinking does not apply universally to all people. DSDs may not be diagnosed until puberty, as a function of failed attempts to reproduce, or after one's death when a person's body is autopsied (Intersexual Society of North America, 2015). Review the Self-Check Exercise 1.2: Values Matter as you become more aware of and apply your feelings and values to the case study.

Nearly 1 in 1,000 to 2,000 newborns are considered ambiguous enough to be candidates for genital surgery (Phornphutkul, Fausto-Sterling, & Cruppuso, 2000). Regina realizes that Justin and Kaitlin are confused concerning their child's situation. They want their child to be healthy, safe, and happy. Dominant cultural values such as patriarchy bifurcate not only gender but also sexuality, including the difference between male and female genitalia. Large clitorises and micropenises are contrary to prevailing meanings of normal genitalia for girls and normal genitalia for boys. Normality and happiness are not synonymous. In addition, Regina is aware of stigma—not just public stigma where the larger public (e.g., doctors, teachers, coaches) may judge them for their choices but also on a more intimate level, social stigma, which comes from judgments within one's social network (Owen et al., 2013).

Upon their first meeting, Regina notices that Justin and Kaitlin appear to be physically exhausted and look like they have been crying. Regina acknowledges their fatigue and asks them how they are sleeping and eating. She is attentive to their thought processes and the impact of this crisis on their mood, comprehension, and communication. Regina takes notes during their session

---

Self-Check Exercise 1.2

Values Matter

Compared to baby boomers (people born between 1946 and 1962), millennials tend to report less religiosity, greater racial and ethnic diversity, and lower marriage rates compared to older generations. How do you feel about Kaitlin and Justin having a child when they are not married? Might your feelings about their nonmarried status impact the therapeutic alliance if you were their therapist? How do you answer this question and what would you do if you discovered that your feelings about their nonmarital status or their decision not to have surgery for their child runs contrary to your beliefs and values? To whom would you feel comfortable speaking?

and sees that Justin and Kaitlin are eager to talk, driven by their love for their child. Both present as vulnerable and frightened. Regina listens attentively. During the time since they brought their son home from the hospital, they have done a great deal of research.

Regina learns that their son has a 46 XY karyotype, that he has descended testicles, and that their son has what is known as a micropenis. Having done her research, Regina learns that their son's condition is an important term within the medical community with respect to normalcy and functionality. Regina asks her patients if they know the size of their son's phallus. They do not know. Among some members of the medical community, a phallus size of less than 1.5 cm at term is considered inadequate for the development of a functional penis. A functional penis is defined as the ability to have intercourse and to urinate standing up. Regina also asks about the medical complications associated with their child's conditions. Kaitlin and Justin do not know. A few days later, Kaitlin and Justin return and report that Kaleb's medical team, comprised of pediatricians, pathologists, urologists, geneticists, and endocrinologists, stated that Kaleb's penis was 1.4 cm and there are no medical problems associated with the primary issue that doctors have identified, namely that Kaleb has a micropenis. While there were no problems currently or problems that they could anticipate in the future, their child may not be able to have a satisfying sex life or be able to urinate standing up like other boys his age. One of the doctors asked Kaitlin and Justin, "Do you want that kind of life for your innocent child?"

Phornphutkul et al. (2000) report that some doctors, in seeking to avoid stigmatization of the patient, believe that gender assignment should be made as quickly as possible and prior to the child's discharge from the hospital. In addition, the future potential for sexual function and fertility are considered. The malleability of gender identity at birth and the long-standing position, supported by the medical community, that ambiguous genitalia should be avoided, have influenced the medical profession's thinking on this topic.

Regina asks Kaitlin and Justin to create two lists, one containing their biggest fears if they did not authorize surgery and one containing a list of their biggest fears if they did authorize surgery. Regina thought that such a list would help her better understand her clients' emotional and psychological concerns in light of the influence of dominant cultural values. For example, Kaitlin wrote that her biggest fear was that her child would not look, feel, or act like other boys and would question his masculinity and his place in society. Kaitlin wanted to know, "Would my son grow facial hair and be able to shave like other boys and men?" "Would he find a nice woman to marry him the way he is?" She wondered out loud, "Would he be able to sire grandchildren for us?" Justin was worried about his son's virility and being "all boy." Regina hears fears that reflect dominant cultural values of masculinity, reproductivity, virility, able-bodyism, strength, heterosexism, and gender conformity. Their biggest concerns were related to the unknown and fears of how a normal male brain already exposed to testosterone might be adversely impacted by a female gender surgical assignment, subsequent female gender socialization, and female hormones.

Regina asked about the procedure that the doctors were recommending. It was their understanding, given their child's genital ambiguity, that doctors were planning to feminize Kaleb's genitalia and have the gender assignment match normal appearing female genitalia. Regina then asked what did Justin envision that the surgery would entail? Justin did not know and squirmed at the thought of future surgeries. He had been told that in the future, estrogen replacement would be necessary—given the absence of female reproductive organs (e.g., ovaries) to produce breasts and to feminize the body in other ways. Eventually, surgery to create a functional vagina would be required. Their daughter, if they decided to go through with the surgery, would never give birth given the absence of a uterus. Regina then asked if the doctors had discussed nonsurgical options. Kaitlin stated that hormone replacement was briefly mentioned but could not guarantee any growth during infancy or during adolescence. "Given that reconstructive surgery aimed at achieving functional female genitalia is considered the more effective alternative, XY intersexual patients with micro phallus and testes are often assigned female gender" (Phornphutkul et al., 2000, p. 135).

There are several principles that guide doctors' decision to perform reconstructive surgery. Phornphutkul et al. (2000) take the position that sexual assignment should be based on the underlying diagnosis "even if sex of rearing may not coincide with size and functionality of the phallus, whenever possible, reconstructive genital surgery should be delayed until the patient's gender identity can be incorporated into the decision making process" (p. 136).

In her work with Kaitlin and Justin, Regina's interventions include a humanistic approach of support, empathy, and listening that involved intentional interviewing. Regina's multicultural competence manifests in her ability to translate knowledge and skills into action and recognize the potential for her biases to influence the therapeutic alliance. Regina asked them to reflect on the following questions:

Therapist to Patient Questions

1. What would it mean for Kaleb's body to be left alone and to live his life as part of a loving family and friends who celebrate him?

2. Do you think it is possible for Kaleb to find meaningful work and satisfying and happy relationships with others who accept him just as he is?

3. What might it mean to Kaleb's mental health, body image, and sexual satisfaction to have, as an adult, the genitals with which he was born?

4. Do you think happiness is possible for Kaleb with the body he has now?

These and other questions posed by Regina reflect four critical skills: empathy, listening, broaching, and interpreting. First Regina exhibits *empathy*. Kaplan (1987) described empathy as a function of both advanced cognitive and affective dimensions. She said empathy is "the capacity to take in the experience and the affect of the other without being overwhelmed by it on the one hand or defensively blocking it out on the other hand" (Kaplan, 1987, p. 13). The therapist must be able to yield (yielding is a traditionally female quality) to the affect of another person while being able to interpret the meaning of this affect within the cognitive domains.

The act of yielding denotes enormous power. In short, the therapist needs to be comfortable with a range of emotions—hers and those of another. While she is neither a parent nor a millennial, Regina exhibits compassion. She demonstrates a capacity to feel deeply with another and join with them where they are without becoming overwhelmed by the emotional complexity of the patient's material. Empathy allows the therapist to be touched, moved, and affected by stories of change and resistance shared by another. The patient is in a position of authority regarding her life, and in collaboration with the therapist, the patient seeks to remove a situation, reduce the adverse effect of the symptoms of the situation from her life, or cope more effectively with it.

Regina's empathy is aided by her teachability as she is aware of her biases and gaps in her knowledge. She does not ignore these gaps, rationalize them, or become defensive about her training. She consults with other professionals, a practice that she has learned is essential, and in her home state, consultation hours are required for renewing her counseling license.

Second, Regina actively *listens* to the client and she mines her personal material as well. She listens to what is said, what is not said, how words are spoken, and to nonverbals (e.g., legs that shake, fingernail biting, muscle tenseness, stammering, and hesitations). As an effective listener, she is able to focus on her patients, summarize what they say, identify contradictions, use confrontation as needed, and request additional information to clarify shared information. Regina is able to sit without speaking while carefully following what her overflowing patients divulge to her. Cognitive empathy or the ability to think about and consider others' perspectives may also be proficient in conceptualizing treatment issues with clients across diversity, including age, marital status, and personal value structure (Constantine, 2001).

Third, Regina is able to *broach* (Day-Vines et al., 2007) difficult conversations by bringing forth questions that are hard to ask and to hear; this deep inquiry is integral to interrupting impasse, indecision, and catastrophizing. Courage is involved in bringing to light controversial and fugitive topics in that a space is created for the patient to give voice to that which has been silenced by others or is even too heavy for the patient to speak on his or her own. Regina says to her patients, "We are from different racial backgrounds and I am not a parent. I wonder what it has been like for you to work with me" (Sanchez, Del Prado, & Davis, 2010).

Finally, Regina is able to accurately *interpret* and capture the meaning of her patients' material—including material not explicitly stated by the patient (Patterson, 1974). For example, Regina observed that Kaitlin and Justin seemed to perceive their child to have something wrong with him, a feeling that filled them with shame and a chronic question of, "What did we do to bring this on?" As long as they felt this way, they were compelled to fix their child's situation. Even with all of their research and confirmation that their child's health was perfect, they continued to think about surgery, as they thought it was a magic bullet. When Regina shared this interpretation with them, Kaitlin wept. She felt relief and less alone—she also felt sadness and anger that she no longer recognized herself or her life. Regina added that Kaleb may feel the same way if exposed to surgery during infancy to feminize his appearance.

With her suggestion of possible interventions, Kaitlin and Justin joined an online support group with parents and family members of intersexual children. They journaled and chose to attend a medical conference on DSD. They also found meditation to be very helpful. The cultural dichotomization of gender through society—from bathrooms, to sports teams, to dressing rooms—is less tolerant of intersexuality and of the trans community than the LGB community. Therapists working with people who have different sexual development or with parents grappling with this trying decision for their children need to be prepared to help patients merge with a support system within the intersexual community as a way of becoming educated, lessening feelings of isolation, and normalizing one's body. Difference is not synonymous with disease. Ultimately, parents want their children to have a good life, to find meaningful work, and to experience love. If they were counseled that such a life were possible without surgical reassignment, they may think differently about the finality of surgical interventions.

Summary

This chapter, which emphasized the individual practitioner and their journey to the mental health profession, defined diversity. Population changes and historical policies include an increase in the numbers of millennials and their racial and ethnic diversity in comparison to older generations, as well as the legality of same-sex marriage in all 50 states. Four themes that are central to this work on diversity in mental health practice were discussed. A case study of an intersexual child ended this first chapter with a focus on the therapist's cultural competence.

2

Multicultural Competencies: Knowledge, Skills, and Attitudes

This chapter explores the development of multicultural competencies in counseling and the guidelines on multicultural education, training, research, practice, and organizational change for psychologists. Strategies for becoming a multiculturally competent mental health professional and guidelines on monitoring dissonance and measuring multicultural effectiveness are reviewed. A case study activity allows for integration and application of the material presented. Prior to a discussion of competencies and guidelines, a distinction is made between cultural competence and multicultural competencies.

According to Chin (2003), cultural competence arose from a systems perspective to evaluate the quality of mental health service delivery programs for children of color. Multicultural competence emerged from a need to move beyond the traditional focus in psychology and mental health, which emphasized and privileged a Eurocentric and Western paradigm. The limitations of this paradigm were particularly apparent with clients of color.

Cultural competency refers to a professional's capacity to use knowledge, skills, and values in the service of the profession, both safely and effectively (Metzger, Nadkarni, & Cornish, 2010). The culturally competent professional possesses the skills necessary to work ethically, effectively, and sensitively with clients from various cultural and ethnic backgrounds, including persons with disabilities, elderly persons, the lesbian, gay, bisexual, and transgender (LGBT) community, racial and ethnic minorities, persons from other countries, and persons who are low income.

Multicultural Competencies

Multicultural competencies (MCCs) have a 33-year history (America Psychological Association [APA], 2003; APA, Board of Educational Affairs & Council of Chairs of Training Councils, 2007; Sue et al., 1982; Sue, Arredondo, & McDavis, 1992; Sue, Ivy, & Pedersen, 1996; Sue et al., 1998; Worthington, Soth-McNett, & Moreno, 2007). There are three competencies recognized by the American Counseling Association (ACA), appearing in bold in the text boxes, labeled as Knowledge Capture (see Knowledge Capture 2.1: Competency 1).

Each competency is followed by parallel components: (1) attitudes and beliefs, (2) knowledge, and (3) skills. Although students are often able to recite the three MCCs along with associated attitudes, knowledge, and skills endorsed by the ACA, they experience difficulty in their ability to clearly apply competencies to a case study and describe the professional and personal relevance of these competencies.

Knowledge Capture 2.1: Competency 1

Counselor Awareness of Own Cultural Values and Biases

Source: Sue et al. (1982).

Competency 1: Counselor Awareness of Own Cultural Values and Biases

Attitudes and Beliefs

The first competency is counselor awareness of his or her own cultural values and biases. Each of us has a cultural heritage story. This story includes information such as where our families came from, how they migrated from one place to the next, and stories of hardship, struggle, war, defeat, success, and victory. Your awareness of your cultural heritage story and the impact of this story on your values, biases, opinions, and preferences are central to knowing who you are and thus critical to your competence in this area. (See Storytelling: Three Wise Men.)

Within this first competency, counselors appreciate the significance and are aware of the core values and beliefs of their own cultural heritage and its impact on them personally, psychologically, and intellectually. Counselors know the limitations of their expertise and are aware when their beliefs and attitudes may hinder service delivery. Culturally skilled counselors recognize their discomfort with differences between themselves and clients in terms of race, ethnicity, culture, and other identities and are mindful of ways to responsibly handle these differences.

❖ STORYTELLING: THREE WISE MEN

When I was growing up, my mother had a picture of three men in a frame together: John F. Kennedy, Martin Luther King, Jr. and Jesus Christ. These three wise men were inspirational and aspirational, and represented core values, such as those held by the Democratic Party, Christianity, social justice, patriarchy, and racial diversity. For mental health professionals to understand and identify their values, they need to know when these values diverge from their families and communities of origin and how these values inform current biases, priorities, and ideals.

Knowledge

Culturally skilled counselors know how their racial and cultural heritage informs their definitions of and biases about normality/abnormality in the process of counseling. (See Case Study: Client Behaviors.) For many students who identify as white, ethnicity is optional or even symbolic since "many do not have knowledge of their ancestral culture or speak the language—a result of broken-down cultural ties to their ancestors through intermarriage, assimilation, and social mobility" (Sanchez, Del Prado, & Davis, 2010, p. 96).

The following questions may help mental health professionals interrogate their cultural and historical lineage:

1. From where in the world did my people come?

2. What are the stories of oppression and privilege associated with their coming to or being in America?

3. What was their social status in America?

4. How did their oppression and/or privilege impact the type of home I grew up in, the food I ate, the clothes I wore, the people who cared for me, the type of schools where I received my education, and the messages that I heard about the inferiority and superiority of me and my people in comparison to others?

It is not unusual for some students to become defensive when they are encouraged to think about their families' migratory story involving grandparents, great grandparents, and other family members that they vaguely remember or never knew at all. That said, culturally skilled counselors have knowledge of privilege and oppression in its many forms and its effect on them personally. They are aware of research on racism, ways to combat racism, racial identity development and measurement, and the relationship of these themes to counselors' professional development (Helms, 2007).

Culturally skilled counselors know how they impact others socially. They are aware of power dynamics and how these interact with difference, across contexts and situations. Counselors are also clear about nonverbal communication styles within and among cultures. When working with people across sources of difference, it is important to know the appropriate terms when referring to ethnic, racial, and sexual minorities that are endorsed by the groups being referenced. For instance, use of the term *Colored, Negro, Oriental,* or *Mongolian* to refer to African Americans and Asian Americans is antiquated and reflects a lack of knowledge about contemporary terminology. Such outdated terms, as well the terms *crippled* and *homosexual* to reference people with disabilities and those in the LGBT community, also suggest that the person using this language is not engaged in current reading and training where appropriate uses of language are widely used. In addition, a lack of sustained interaction with people across race, ethnicity, sexuality, and ability can contribute to the use of antiquated language.

Skills

Culturally skilled counselors seek out educational and consultative training to improve their effectiveness in working with culturally different populations. They desire to understand themselves as racial and cultural beings and know when it is necessary to consult with other professionals about making a referral for their patients to other professionals. Maintaining an updated list of referrals is a critical part of this process.

Culturally skilled counselors pursue experiences that will enhance them educationally. Consultation with colleagues and supervisors, particularly around clinical cases that are ethically complex or when faced with a novel situation, can help trainees and seasoned professionals from making unnecessary errors and avoiding complaints from patients. Novel situations will occur and could include an encounter with a racially and or ethnically diverse patient from a country with which you are not familiar. Experienced counselors benefit from the wisdom gained through consultation with others and know when they may need to integrate a different treatment modality to best meet the needs of their patients. Gaining multicultural competence is an ongoing activity. As such, mental health professionals are interested in understanding themselves as people with racial and cultural identities. Seeking to establish a nonracist identity is core to multicultural competence.

Competency 2: Counselor Awareness of Client's Worldview

Attitudes and Beliefs

The second competency is counselor awareness of the client's worldview.

Worldview (e.g., individualism and/or collectivism; harmony with nature and/or mastery over nature) is deeply influential on people's psychology, decision making, sense of normalcy, and the extent to which religion, informed by culture and history, shape one's existence. Culturally skilled counselors are aware of the range of emotional reactions toward other racial and ethnic groups and are honest about their stereotypes and biases relevant to race, ethnicity, gender, class, sexuality, ability, body size, and immigrant status.

Knowledge

Our patients' cultural values, history, and the ways in which histories have been obscured and/or misrepresented represent important information that mental health professionals need to comprehend. Counselors respect what people have had to do in order to survive oppression and can empathize with, as opposed to judge, the brunt of this oppression on people's personality development, help seeking behavior, career trajectories, coping strategies, and psychological disorders. For example, at the writing of this text, thousands of refugees from the Middle East and Africa have descended upon and are seeking entry into different sections of Europe as they endeavor to escape war, poverty, corruption, human trafficking, and other forms of trauma, often at the risk of injury and/or death. Counselors know about institutionalized racism and sexism, internalized homophobia, and other systemic forces that create psychological vulnerabilities for people and entire communities.

Skills

The culturally skilled are mindful of the research in mental health and career issues that affect different cultural groups. Culturally skilled counselors engage in activities that both challenge preconceived stereotypes and encourage comfort with people across differences. (See Storytelling: Diverse Boston.) Resources, by way of film, narratives, games, learning exercises, role-plays, journaling, and interviews, can assist counselors in challenging previously conceived stereotypes during the process of moving to a place of greater comfort with people across differences.

Knowledge Capture 2.2: Competency 2

Counselor Awareness of Client's Worldview

Source: Sue et al. (1982).

❖ **STORYTELLING: DIVERSE BOSTON**

Several of my students come from small Northern New England towns. Many chose Boston for graduate school because of its urban location and opportunities to interact with diverse groups of people. However, living in Boston will not automatically jumpstart a person's exposure to diversity. There are parts of Boston that are deeply segregated by race. Bus routes, subway lines, neighborhoods, and food stores reflect changes in skin color hue according to the section of the city or zip code. For this reason, some white students have voiced discomfort with taking public transportation to practicum or internship sites; other white students have acknowledged their initial discomfort but have accepted their practicum assignments nonetheless, even when they are one of the few white people on a subway at a particular stop. Our interpersonal relationships can serve as a wonderful opportunity to become comfortable with difference. Perhaps there is a relationship between the fear of or discomfort with diversity that many mental health professionals in training voice and the limited or lack of racial and cultural diversity in people's personal lives?

Knowledge Capture 2.3: Competency 3

Counselors Use Culturally Appropriate Intervention Strategies

Source: Sue et al. (1982).

Competency 3: Counselors Use Culturally Appropriate Intervention Strategies

Attitudes and Beliefs

The third competency is counselor use of culturally appropriate intervention strategies. Increasingly, the importance and relevance of spirituality and religion in patients' lives is being recognized in the mental health professional literature, and counselors are encouraged to identify aspects of spirituality relevant to wellness and healing and incorporate as relevant. For many patients, meditation, prayer, affirmations, crystals, chakras, and visualization are central to healing physical and mental disease. Where appropriate and with the consent of the patient, culturally skilled counselors are able to integrate their efforts with other health professionals, including nutritionists, acupuncturists, physical therapy, psychiatry, and substance use disorders professionals.

Culturally skilled mental health professionals examine the ways in which third-party payers or insurance companies influence the type, scope, and length of interventions that clinicians are able to provide to patients with respect to number of allowed visits per year, co-pay amounts, out-of-pocket maximums, deductibles, and health insurance empanelment challenges by state, town, and/or practitioner's specialty. (See Storytelling: In a Bind.)

❖ STORYTELLING: IN A BIND

Several years ago, I received a call from one of my patients whose antidepressants and anxiolytic medication provider had left the practice. A replacement had not been identified. My patient was out of her medication and was feeling the spiraling effects of a depressed and anxious mood. She called one facility that was willing to be her prescriber but insisted that they also see her for counseling. She did not want to leave my care yet her insurance would not pay for her to see two behavioral health therapists. Her primary care provider, an advanced practice registered nurse, was unwilling to fill the antidepressant medicines because he thought the patient would be better served by seeing a psychiatrist given his discomfort with prescribing for psychopharmacological purposes. Mental health professionals need to be knowledgeable of policies that create hardship for patients to receive the behavioral health services to which they are entitled. In this case, I was able to provide the names of local psychiatrists—one who was willing to be her prescriber of psychological meds without requiring the patient to see clinical staff for professional counseling services.

Knowledge

There are institutional barriers that affect certain groups of people from accessing effective mental health services. These groups include some people of color, women, persons with disabilities, veterans, immigrant populations, people from low-income groups, and LGBT clients.

Culturally skilled counselors are able to interpret assessment instruments in the context of a client's culture and are aware of existing bias in traditional systems of assessment and diagnosis. Counselors are aware of various resources within the community that can assist their clients while recognizing that culture can contribute to a client's decisions that are not culturally consistent with that of the counselor (e.g., making a decision within a collectivistic orientation and although a 32 year old successful career woman, living at home with Jordanian parents until married—because of cultural expectations for single women).

As discussed with multicultural competency 1, some feminist-oriented counselors may perceive certain traditional gender roles to be oppressive when, according to the patient, they represent normative, respected, and valid ways of being in the world. Culturally skilled counselors are knowledgeable of discriminatory practices (e.g., microaggressions) that impact clients' psychological welfare.

Skills

Culturally skilled counselors are able to send and receive both verbal and nonverbal messages accurately and appropriately. For example, among people across cultural and ethnic diversity, the content of the message is not nearly as important as the voice inflection, eye contact, and perceived genuineness.

To effectively confront institutional discrimination, counselors can help clients develop coping and resistance strategies and effective skills. For some patients, involvement with indigenous communities is an important part of the tools and resources relied upon to cope effectively. To this end, counselors are adept at assisting patients in locating resources that provide appropriate language services to clients. Counselors are able to address the need for change, regarding discrimination, on an organizational level. Advocacy and social justice are core to multicultural competence. Clients can benefit from their counselors' education and training with respect to the therapeutic process, psychological theory, therapeutic expectations, legal rights, and the counselor's approach to therapy. There are times when we need to help our patients confront inequity and/or develop and strengthen effective skills to deal with institutional discrimination.

Counselors also educate their clients about the process of psychological intervention, including therapy goals, mental health rights, and the counselor's orientation. For example, patients may want to know how the process of therapy works. More specifically, a patient who is unfamiliar with or perhaps dubious of the benefits of professional counseling may ask, "How will coming to therapy every week and meeting with you help me to feel less stressed out?"

Arredondo and Arciniega (2001) added grounding principles to MCCs, which place the competencies within an ecological framework and encompass multiple systems (individual, family, history) and environmental contexts. The first principle is of the learning organization. Namely, organizations are teachable and open to change by questioning and challenging itself. One of the benefits of undergoing an external review for accreditation, for example, is that outside faculty and other reviewers provide intense review of a program's curriculum, outcome data (e.g., graduation rates, faculty research productivity), faculty–student program philosophy and mission, interpersonal relationships, and commitment to diversity.

The lone cross-cultural class, which characterizes most graduate counseling training programs, was criticized as not being representative of a learning organization or responsive to the research available on the significance of multicultural competence. This second learning organization principle is a competency rationale in that guidelines as well as developmental benchmarks articulate characteristics of competent counselors at different levels of training (e.g., beginning practicum and entry into professional practice after completing the PhD). (See Storytelling: I Fear.)

❖ STORYTELLING: I FEAR

Several years ago, I was talking with a friend, and she asked, "How would our lives be different if we were not afraid?" I loved the question and thought about its relevance for mental health professionals and students in diversity training where there is lots of fear. I asked my students, "Regarding diversity work, what do you fear?" These were some of the answers I received that students anonymously wrote on pieces of paper.

1. I am afraid of people thinking that I am ignorant and don't know anything.

2. I am afraid of saying something insensitive to a person of color.

❖ STORYTELLING: I FEAR

3. I am afraid that people of color will think I am racist.

4. I am afraid of not knowing what to say or do.

5. I am afraid that I won't be able to help someone.

6. I am afraid that I am racist.

7. I am afraid that people think I won't have anything to offer them.

8. I am afraid that people will think I am the enemy because of the color of my skin.

9. I am afraid that I'm more like David (the middle-age man who the whole group spent an inordinate amount of time helping, e.g., *The Color of Fear*) than I dare to think.

10. I am afraid of people's anger.

11. I am afraid of not knowing how to help problems that I've never encountered or have not heard about.

12. I am afraid that people will think that I am not only young but also dumb.

13. I am afraid that white people will assume that I am not competent as a person of color.

My personal concerns about diversity work are listed below:

1. I am concerned, given the central presence of technology in the lives of millennials, that increasingly students have difficulty with face-to-face conversations and are much more comfortable and competent behind a phone or computer screen although working in a human service profession.

2. I am concerned that multicultural competence is much easier to profess than to demonstrate in a climate where seasoned professionals readily avow multicultural competency.

3. I am concerned that race is still a very fugitive topic, particularly between white and black people.

Students in training as well as seasoned clinicians are vulnerable to omitting controversial information or avoid asking particular questions out of fear of being perceived as ignorant, racist, insensitive, or discriminatory. Fear can disrupt the therapeutic event and interfere with the client's growth. Patients depend on the clinicians' awareness and initiative to usher difficult conversations into the room. Is it possible to help patients explore complex issues concerning sexuality, class, race, and cultural differences if clinicians are not actively engaged in this important work themselves? For some, explorations in diversity may not have evolved since the single required diversity course in graduate school.

Personal introspection is a component of multicultural competence. Bringing students face to face with their own stories and feelings is essential to multicultural work. Creating the space for the unspeakable to be reflected upon and perhaps spoken reflects the essential holding environment.

With respect to organizations, not only in the therapy room is the holding environment essential, but also it has relevance in faculty meetings and within the classroom. Checking with students and asking how they are feeling, acknowledging the hard work they are doing, and honoring their emotions, including uncertainty, anger, and apathy, is critical to diversity training. Initially, such awareness can unleash feelings of powerlessness in the mental health professional trainee, yet powerlessness is what many patients feel on a daily basis. Bearing witness to an array of patients' feelings and thoughts is a privilege that, as mental health professionals, we are invited to do.

Competency Guidelines, Benchmarks, and Standards

Six guidelines have been articulated by the APA to provide counselors and psychologists with the rationale and needs for addressing multiculturalism and diversity in education, training, research, and practice (APA, 2003). Basic information, relevant terminology, and empirical research that support these guidelines are also included as are references to enhance continuing education training, research, practice, and organizational change. Paradigms that broaden the purview of psychology as a profession are reviewed.

> Guideline 1: Psychologists are encouraged to appreciate who they are as culturally influenced cultural beings.
>
> Guideline 2: Psychologists are encouraged to understand the interrelationship between stigma and marginalized identities.
>
> Guideline 3: Psychologists are encouraged to become knowledgeable of different learning models and approaches to teaching multiculturally.
>
> Guideline 4: Psychological researchers are encouraged to realize the relevance of culture among racially and ethnically diverse individuals.
>
> Guideline 5: Psychologists are encouraged to apply culturally appropriate skills in clinical and other applied psychological practices.
>
> Guideline 6: Psychologists are encouraged to use organizational change processes to support culturally informed organizational policy development and practices.

Diversity Training

The competency benchmarks provide clear guidelines for entering practicum students, interns, and postdocs. Its purpose is to articulate a model for identifying competencies in professional psychology at different developmental levels: practicum, internship, and postinternship (APA, 2012). By their very nature, the benchmark competencies provide a critical foundation for identifying competencies across all specialties. They are intended to serve as a template and can be modified where necessary by training programs to define competencies of specialties. Referenced below is the Assessment of Competency Benchmarks Work Group (2007) document, which is not the APA benchmark competency document and does not represent the policy of APA. There are six foundational competencies: (1) reflective practice-self-assessment, (2) scientific knowledge-methods, (3) relationships, (4) ethical-legal standards policy, (5) individual-cultural diversity, and (6) interdisciplinary systems. In addition, six functional competencies were identified: (1) assessment-diagnosis-case conceptualization, (2) intervention, (3) consultation, (4) research/evaluation, (5) supervision-teaching, and (6) management-administration.

Delineated below are ready-for-practicum competencies in individual cultural diversity. These include awareness as well as sensitivity to and skills in working professionally with diverse individuals, groups, and communities that represent various cultural and personal backgrounds and characteristics. Essential components of self-awareness include knowledge, awareness, and understanding of one's situation (e.g., one's race and attitudes toward others' diversity); demonstration of self knowledge, awareness, and understanding such as being able to articulate how ethnic group values influence who one is and how one relates to other people; assessment methods (e.g., by faculty, peers, self); and applied knowledge. These are reflected in basic knowledge of and sensitivity to the scientific, theoretical, and contextual issues related to International Statistical Classification of Diseases and Related Health Problems (ICD), as defined by APA policy and as they apply to professional psychology.

The National Association of Social Workers (NASW, 2001) has identified 10 standards for cultural competence. Two important aspects of NASW's standards pertain to the ethics of multicultural standards and the relevance of an ecological framework within the standards. More specifically, the standards reflect the NASW's intentions to be a learning organization as accountable to others, divulging information about diversity (e.g., linguistic diversity), recruitment, and retention of diversity in light of historical systems where specific groups have been dismissed (Arredondo & Arciniega, 2001).

> Standard 1: Ethics and Values: Social workers function with respect to professional ethics; there is a recognition that personal and professional values may conflict with the needs of clients across diversity.
>
> Standard 2: Self-Awareness: Social workers seek to broaden an understanding of their personal and cultural values and realize the relevance of multicultural identities in people's lives.
>
> Standard 3: Cross-Cultural Knowledge: Social workers continue to develop specialized knowledge and understanding about values and family systems of the population groups they serve throughout their personal lives.
>
> Standard 4: Cross-Cultural Skills: Social workers respect the role of culture in helping others.
>
> Standard 5: Service Delivery: Social workers are mindful of the services available in the community and are able to make appropriate referrals for their patients.
>
> Standard 6: Empowerment and Advocacy: Social workers are aware of the impact of social policies and programs on clients across sources of difference and can advocate as needed.
>
> Standard 7: Diverse Workforce: Social workers support recruitment of diversity.
>
> Standard 8: Professional Education: Social workers participate in training that advance cultural competence among social workers.
>
> Standard 9: Language Diversity: Social workers advocate for language appropriate services.
>
> Standard 10: Cross-Cultural Leadership: Social workers communicate information with other professionals about diversity.

Despite the similarity in standards and competencies across counseling, psychology, social work, and curriculum content, there are differences in mental health practice diversity training programs. For example, there has been increased attention to class, spirituality, and disability, yet not all programs expose students equally to these topics (APA, 2003). Greater emphasis has been devoted to gender, sexuality, transgender issues, immigrant populations, gerontology, body size discrimination, and biracial and multiracial populations (Henderson, Metzger, Nadkarni, & Cornish, 2010).

Despite the many handbooks, textbooks, and journal articles that focus on multicultural competencies, faculty grapple with how to best teach multicultural counseling and psychology. Bowman (1996) concluded, "Multicultural instruction should not be limited to one course but should be infused in all aspects of the training" (p. 16). A criticism of a separate multicultural counseling course is that it does not allow the material to be incorporated into other core courses such as history and systems of psychology, psychopathology, and cognitive-affective basis of behavior. That said, there are logistical issues with licensing bodies who expect to see a three credit semester course designated to racial and cultural issues in counseling and psychology.

Mio (2005) suggests that courses build on each other in a heuristic fashion: for example, an introductory multicultural course, a second course on testing in multicultural issues, a third course on research, and a fourth course on clinical interventions.

Society is racially segregated, and with greater emphasis on diversity, the reality of racism can be obscured (Mio, 2005). It is likely that many graduate students and their faculty do not have intimate friendships outside of their racial, sexual, and class groups. Bowman (1996) stated, "Trainees need opportunities to examine the dynamics of establishing relationships with culturally diverse populations and to question how they apply what they know about self and others to successful cross-cultural interactions" (p. 23). To promote self-awareness and empathy, laboratory experiences may be helpful. As students encounter dissonance, they need safe places where they can ask questions and process new information. Faculty need to support students in their efforts at risk taking while encouraging all students to be receptive to new, conflicting, and in some cases, dissonance-provoking ideas from classmates, professors, course readings, and videos.

Exercises can facilitate student introspection and application of multicultural theory. Drawing one's culture with crayons, constructing a genogram (family lineage) to outline family history, the privilege exercise, and the sociocultural wheel are other examples (see Henderson et al., 2010). McIntosh's (1989) article "White Privilege: Unpacking the Invisible Knapsack" can be very thought provoking emotionally, and cognitively challenging. Unearned privileges associated with ability, gender, and sexual orientation can be investigated as well as the intersections of stigmatized identities (e.g., LGBT status, disability, addiction, and low income) amidst white privilege.

Journals, personal narratives, participation in cross-cultural activities as a racial minority, and reading about power and oppression are critical aspects of multicultural training. *Explorations in Privilege, Oppression, and Diversity* by Anderson and Middleton (2004) is an excellent way for students to gain exposure to personal narratives as they think about their own stories. One instructor encourages her students to write a comprehensive racial psychohistory, allowing them to document the role that race has played in shaping their life philosophies, personalities, and coping patterns (Kogan, 2000). A variety of experiential activities, such as role-play, games, and films, are recognized as a means of educating mental health practice students about the counseling process. According to Kim and Lyons (2003), games, in particular, offer "optimal opportunities to gain multicultural counseling competence across attitudes, beliefs, knowledge, and skills" (p. 402).

To guide counselor education and counseling psychology departments in their training efforts, Ponterotto, Alexander, and Grieger (1995) developed a multicultural competency checklist. There are six themes, each with several items:

1. Minority representation

2. Curriculum issues

3. Counseling practice and supervision

4. Research considerations

5. Student and faculty competency evaluation

6. Physical environment

The first four items on the checklist seek to ascertain *minority representation*— whether 30% of faculty, students, and program support staff are visibly racially/ethnically diverse. Bilingual skills are also important. The second theme, *curriculum issues,* is covered across five items that reflect course work, pedagogy, and student assessment. For example, multicultural issues are integrated into all course work. All program faculty members can specify how this integration is done in their courses. Furthermore, syllabi clearly reflect multicultural inclusion. *Counseling practice and supervision* is the third area and contains three questions. The focus here is on students' practicum, supervision quality, and the "Multicultural Affairs Committee," which is recommended as a way to monitor multicultural activities. *Research considerations* have four questions concerned with a multicultural research presence in the program. One item asks if there is clear faculty research productivity in multicultural issues as evidenced by journal publications and conference presentations on multicultural topics. The four items in *student and faculty competency evaluation* emphasize proficiency in multicultural issues. For example, one item asks whether students' "comprehensive exams reflect Multicultural issues." The final two items concern the *physical environment* and whether it reflects diversity in the faculty offices, reception area, and clinic area. The authors of this checklist recognize that very few programs will meet all the competencies in the checklist and suggest the development of one-, three-, and five-year action plans.

Assessment and Research

One of the guidelines for counselors and psychologists affirmed earlier was the importance of conducting culture-centered and ethical psychological research among persons from ethnic, linguistic, and racial minority backgrounds. Multicultural research is defined as "the empirical examination of or inquiry into the experiences of individuals from diverse cultural backgrounds" (Utsey, Walker, & Kwate, 2005, p. 249). Not only are psychometric properties of instruments important to consider, but also flaws in methodological approaches, such as the tendency to aggregate groups instead of disaggregate them. Income, educational, and occupational attainment can contribute to vast differences among racially similarly people. Finally, including people outside of the academy from the cultures being investigated would add to multicultural variety and authenticity (Chang & Sue, 2005).

Sehgal et al. (2011) developed an assessment of demonstrated multicultural counseling competence (DMCCC) of clinical psychology graduate students. DMCCC of clinical psychology graduate students was compared with multicultural competence of experienced psychologists. The researchers also assessed differences between the endorsement of appropriate multicultural competence strategies and the actual use of such strategies in clinical practice. Significant differences were noted between the DMCCC of graduate students and the multicultural competence of experienced psychologists. DMCCC-should reflected the ability to recognize multiculturally appropriate strategies that should be used with clients of color. DMCCC-would referred to participant's willingness to use strategies in actual clinical practice with clients of color. Relative to students, multiculturally experienced psychologists scored significantly higher on both DMCCC-should and DMCCC-would.

In a study, Worthington, Soth-McNett, and Moreno (2007) reviewed and evaluated the content of the 75 articles and 81 studies done on MCCs. Their findings showed that (1) empirical research on MCCs has increased over the past 20 years, (2) a small number of researchers are producing the majority of research, and (3) the methods used in producing empirical research are narrow: 73% are from descriptive field studies and 25% from analogue research. In addition, most of the samples were nonrandom convenience samples, meaning not all potential participants had an equal and fair chance of participating. Sampling has implications for generalizability.

The appropriateness and validity of commonly used psychological and psychoeducational assessment instruments (e.g., assessment of competence), when used with individuals and diverse populations, may be questionable given that many traditional psychoeducational measures used for assessment and research purposes were not initially validated with diverse populations in their original sample groups. Moreover, the measures are based on individual performance or self-report or both. APA (2003) stated, "Culturally sensitive psychological researchers should strive to be knowledgeable about a broad range of assessment techniques, data-gathering procedures, and standardized instruments whose validity, reliability, and measurement equivalence have been investigated across culturally diverse samples" (p. 389). The validity and reliability of assessment tools have implications for research and practice. Culturally insensitive research perpetuates the use of inadequate training models.

One criticism of earlier research on people of color is that important intrapersonal and extrapersonal factors, such as client attitudes, client–counselor racial similarity, communication styles, acculturation, discrimination, and poverty, were virtually ignored (Ponterotto and Casas, 1991). Furthermore, this research had not considered or studied the tremendous heterogeneity in multicultural populations, which serve to foster, and perpetuate ethnic stereotypes and global categorizations. Last, easily accessible subject populations (e.g., white psychology college students from large Midwestern universities) who tend not to be representative of the larger community have typically been selected as research populations. Overreliance on research using analogue designs, "whereby the subject pools have consisted of pseudo-clients (e.g., students) and pseudo-counselors (e.g., graduate students in counseling) instead of 'real' clients and counselors" (Ponterotto & Casas, 1991, p. 78), limits generalizability to actual client and counselor populations.

Researchers such as Ruelas (2003) and Worthington et al. (2007) note limitations with multicultural competency measures, namely, their tendency to utilize self-report, which tends not to be related to observer-rated MCCs. Several instruments have been created to measure MCCs. A study by Kocarek, Talbot, Batka, and Anderson (2001) explored the reliability and validity of three instruments: the Multicultural Counselor Awareness Scale, the Multicultural Awareness of Knowledge and Skills Survey (MAKSS), and the Survey of Graduate Students' Experience with Diversity. With a sample size of 120 master's degree students from seven programs across the country, the reliability and validity of these instruments varied but for the most part held up, except for the awareness subscale of the MAKSS. The authors argue that a lack of consistency exists "between same-named subscales and high correlations between the Knowledge and Skills subscales" (Kocarek et al., 2001, p. 494).

Chao (2013) examined multicultural competence, the counselor's race, ethnic identity, multicultural training, and color-blind racial blind attitudes among 259 high school counselors. She found an association between race, ethnicity, and multicultural training which predicted counselors' MCC. Multicultural training was positively associated with racial/ethnic identity. Chao found that low levels of multicultural competence is associated with high levels of colorblindness and limited multicultural training. With high levels of training and low color-blind attitudes, white students' MCC scores were higher that the MCC scores for students of color. However, with high levels of training and high color-blind attitudes, white students' MCC scores were lower that the MCC scores for students of color. Chao concluded that her findings do not suggest racial/ethnic minority students, as members of underrepresented groups, benefit from additional multicultural training given that they report similar MCC scores at all levels of training.

Concern has also been raised over the validity and applied pragmatic utility of the many research findings appearing in the multicultural literature (Ponterotto & Casas, 1991). Client–counselor process variables (e.g., therapeutic alliance) have been overemphasized, and significant cultural as well as psychosocial variables that might affect counseling have been disregarded, (e.g., learning styles, communication patterns, racism, microaggressions, oppression, poverty). While it may be more difficult to study some process variables, they are vital to understanding the role of counseling with real clients. A high degree of heterogeneity, such as demographic characteristics, class, and attitudes, exists within multicultural populations, yet these intracultural differences tend to be understudied in the research literature.

Qualitative research is also becoming increasingly popular, particularly as it relates to allowing voices to be heard that have historically been overlooked or silenced. In doing so, the researcher is not an objective entity but is actively engaged in the research through ongoing self-examination across multiple contexts (Choudhuri, 2005).

To demonstrate competence in multicultural assessment, conceptualization of presenting problems, establishment of appropriate interventions, development of client treatment goals, and the formulation of multiculturally sensitive research, psychological service providers and academicians will need to acquire cultural knowledge, information, and skills.

Implications for Mental Health Professionals

The aim of multicultural training has been to emphasize knowledge in particular and skills with respect to other people's cultures. One of the challenges with this approach whereby the focus is on the different "Other" is that it may lead to misperceptions of other groups as monoliths, which erroneously supports the notion that these "others" operate according to fixed patterns of behaviors different from one's own. Chao, Okazaki, and Hong (2011) said it beautifully, "Overemphasizing cultural differences, without highlighting the need to be aware of one's own cultural assumptions and beliefs, may inadvertently contribute to the development and maintenance of essentialist beliefs, leading to the endorsement of stereotypes and prejudice against the culturally different 'Other'" (p. 266).

Training programs may be lacking in their ability to help students take multicultural competence and translate it to actual practice with patients. Sehgal et al. (2011) argue that multicultural training has not changed much over the last decade. The result might be mental health professionals who demonstrate sensitivity to multicultural issues but lack multicultural competence.

Professional organizations (e.g., the ACA, APA, and NASW) have voiced a commitment to training students to work competently with populations across sources of diversity. These professional organizations, to which the majority of counselors, psychologists, and social workers belong, have great power, as do the boards affiliated with them that approve and accredit graduate programs according to their adherence to program standards. Professional organizations are accountable to the public, teachable, and a learning organization.

While professional organizations have provided ample multicultural training and educational resources (APA, 2003; 2012), the full benefit of these resources is diminished when educators are unaware of and/or reticent to look at their attitudes and behaviors that perpetuate subtle discrimination. Yet how do accredited graduate programs with all white faculty continue to be reaccredited if racial diversity is more than an espoused value? This concern is an elephant in the room. One of the risks associated with expanding diversity to include other dimensions of identity is that some see this expansion as an opportunity to minimize race, bending diversity to satisfy gender and sexuality diversity yet maintaining whiteness albeit in the service and semblance of diversity. In addition, how is it that students and faculty of color contend with chronic microaggressions within APA and ACA-accredited programs (Robinson-Wood et al., 2015)? The presence of racial and ethnic diversity will allow programs to tick off boxes regarding gender, race, ethnicity, and international status of students and faculty but doing so does not translate into justice, contestations of power, privilege, and demands for equity and justice.

Unlearning practices that distance mental health professionals from themselves, clients, and students is lifelong work. Being honest about the various emotions that reside within mental health professionals, even during the cross-cultural therapeutic event is essential. Abernathy (1995) said, "Minimal attention has been devoted to addressing the anger that frequently emerges in cross-racial work" (p. 96). (See Case Study: Client Behaviors.)

Numerous books, articles, conferences, and associations provide excellent resources for students, professionals, and practitioners who seek to develop their multicultural competence and to connect with others who are like-minded. That said, knowledge of available resources does not supplant authentic relationships—not just with colleagues who we may step out with for a coffee or lunch but with friends who we invite to our homes where honest talk can occur about our lives as racial, cultural, and gendered beings. This type of interpersonal connection allows people to discuss, understand, and ultimately transcend the silence between racially different people around race. At the same time, acknowledging the shame and fear experienced by many clinicians-in-training is a crucial beginning to understanding oppression and inequality. Such feelings are important and should be worked through as part of the multicultural training process (Parker & Schwartz, 2002).

Recommendations from *Guidelines and Competencies for Practice, Research, and Education* (APA, 2003) are provided below as an important resource to mental health professionals:

1. Acknowledge your racial and/or cultural group's history in the oppression of other peoples.

2. Be able to recognize how your religious values affect your views about sex, drugs, death, marriage, reproduction, abortion, birth control, and divorce.

3. Be aware of unearned able-body privilege and how this privilege affects everything from driving, sexual activity, accessing buildings, mobility, and people's perceptions of another's attractiveness, intelligence, and moral character.

4. Know the limits of your multicultural expertise, and seek help (e.g., supervision, consultation, personal therapy) when needed.

5. Acknowledge who is in your circle of friends, and if racial, sexual, and class diversity is lacking, ask yourself why you have been reluctant to develop friendships with people who are not like yourself.

6. Acknowledge feelings of guilt, shame, or resentment that arise as a function of your exposure to different types of diversity.

7. Realize that there are cultures that do not accept your attitudes about individuality, freedom, sexual diversity, choice, and egalitarianism between men and women.

8. Ask yourself what the impact of your culture and ethnicity has been on your education, career, and/or mate choice.

9. Consider how much value you attach to consulting with healers who have not graduated from high school or did not go through a practicum or internship.

10. Understand the potential bias of instruments and the cultural context in which they are normed.

Case Study

Client Behaviors

I routinely ask my students, during their psychosocial narrative assignment, to discuss any client identities that would present a challenge for them within a therapeutic encounter. I get a minority of students who admit to anticipating some difficulty working with someone who is intellectually delayed, a sexual predator, or an elderly person. A few students have discussed their reluctance to work with someone who is blatantly racist (e.g., a Nazi sympathizer) or who does not support women's egalitarianism (e.g., blatantly sexist or an extremely traditional gender-conforming man or woman).

Many students indicate their willingness to work with anyone, despite his or her characteristics. Part of this universal embrace may be a desire to be open and accepting of all people. Certain populations (e.g., forensics, severe mental illness such as psychoses) require specialized training with respect to brain chemistry, defense mechanisms, and appropriate treatment modalities. Multicultural competence encourages awareness of one's personal growth as a gendered, racial, and cultural being who has been shaped by dominant race, gender, and sexuality discourses. Even for the novice trainee who has yet to enter practicum, identification of stuckness and motives for a behavioral health career is important given the biases and belief systems that each of us holds (Sanchez & Davis, 2010). Multicultural competence is ethical through its focus on not doing harm but doing good through a demonstration of skills, knowledge, and attitudes that reflect the clinicians' and training program's accountability to other mental health professionals and to the public. The maxim "mental health professional, know thyself!" is still relevant.

Questions and Discussion

The following is a list of client behaviors. Take the role of therapist. Ask yourself the questions indicated. Think about appropriate interventions for making a meaningful difference in diversity work as you review the guidelines and competencies discussed throughout this chapter. In small groups, add any competencies or standards that apply.

1. *A woman who is emotionally and sexually involved with another person prior to her marriage, denies her involvement to her fiancé, yet plans to go through with the marriage and to continue her involvement with her paramour*
   First, identify your feelings, then ask:
   a. If the client wept in therapy from feelings of guilt yet felt that she truly loved the other person but would not want to hurt the intended with whom she has been in relationship for 5 years, would this admission alter my therapeutic approach?
   b. Would my feelings about working with the client change?
   c. Do I have core values that are in conflict with the patient's behavior?
   d. If so, what might I do to operate from a cultural competence lens?
   e. If the fiancé had terminal cancer and had been given 6 months to live and wanted to marry before death, would my feelings change regarding the partner who is having the external affair?

2. *A transitioning transwoman who is very feminine in dress and mannerisms, is on hormonal treatment, seeing a psychiatrist, and has a very deep male voice*
   First, identify your feelings, then ask:

    a. If the individual was a kindergarten school teacher would my attitude about working with her change?

    b. If she were unwilling to discuss her personal life with colleagues, the principal, or the children, would my attitude about her change?

3. *A man who will not allow his wife to work or leave the house without accompanying her*
   First, identify your feelings, then ask:
   a. If the wife supported her husband's position, would my feelings about working with her change?
   b. If the wife was very beautiful, young, impressionable, and attracted the attention of men whenever she left the house, would my feelings change about the husband's attitude?

4. *A pregnant mother who is abusing alcohol*
   First, identify your feelings, then ask:
   a. If the client's other children did not have fetal alcohol syndrome and she drank throughout her previous pregnancies, would my feelings about working with her change?
   b. If the client knew her baby had a genetic disorder and the child was most likely not going to survive after the first few days of life, would my attitude change?
   c. If the woman planned to give her child up for adoption to a caring and loving family who did not care how extensive the child's disabilities were, would my attitude about her behavior change?

5. *A man on the down low (in a heterosexual marriage but secretly having sex with other men)*
   First, identify your feelings, then ask:
   a. If the client's wife had a neurological disease that prevented her from being sexual with her husband, would my feelings change about working with him?
   b. If the client used condoms faithfully during sexual intercourse with men, would my attitude about his behavior change?
   c. If the client's wife had been badly burned in a house fire and was disfigured, would my feelings about the client's behavior change?

6. *A woman who is planning to leave her husband and two dependent children for another man*
   First, identify your feelings, then ask:
   a. If the client's husband had been beating her, would my feelings about her decision to leave her husband and children change?
   b. If the children were her stepchildren, would my attitude about her decision change?

7. *A man who announces he does not want to work with you because of your race*
   a. If the client had a negative experience in therapy with someone from my same racial group, would my attitude about working with him change?
   b. If the client was dealing with race-related issues that he needed to explore in therapy and he wanted a clinician from his racial group who had expertise in this area, would my attitude about his not wanting to work with me change?

8. *A woman would like her African-born, school-age child tested for learning disabilities prior to finalizing the adoption*
   a. If the client had already adopted an African child with severe learning disabilities, would my attitude about her choice to do testing prior to the adoption change?
   b. If the child's biological mother was developmentally delayed, would my attitude about the client change?

Summary

This chapter offered an overview of MCCs, knowledge, skills, and attitudes. The importance of attending to students' dissonance about their future multicultural effectiveness was discussed through storytelling. The case study activity dealt with various counseling scenarios. Clients' identity profiles can be challenging to our values and beliefs. Our reactions to these identities must be understood, particularly as we develop and strengthen cultural competence with people across sources of diversity.

3

Multiple Identities Defined

❖

Identity constructs include race, ethnicity, gender, culture, sexuality, mental and physical ability, socioeconomic class, age, nationality, body size, and religion. These and other dimensions of identity are sources of difference. Identities co-occur with one another, and they shift over time and across contexts. Some identities have more power than others and can take on different meanings. For example, my paternal grandmother, who had a 4th grade education (before returning to night school), was regarded as a wise, prayerful, and godly woman in her small Baptist church community. Within the larger culture beyond the church, where educational attainment, whiteness, and men, across race were valued, her limited education, and black female status had less power.

Within therapy, the confluence of a patient's multiple identities and his or her socially constructed meanings, affect the client's perspective about and orientation to his or her problem as well as the relationship between the client and his or her therapist.

A primary tenet of this work is that effective mental health professionals acknowledge sources of differences within themselves and among other people. They are aware of their feelings about differences, are mindful of their proximity to the many discourses about differences, and are able to confront themselves on their biases of, fears about, and prejudices against people. The culturally competent clinician receives help to improve his or her multicultural competence and can do so with people across age, ethnicity, ability, disability, gender, race, religion, sexuality, and socioeconomic class. There are discourses (e.g., Asians are good in math and science; Arab men regard women as subordinate to themselves; black women are churchgoing Christians) that mental health professionals hold about people who are different from them. For the therapeutic alliance to be a place of safety as well as a place worth returning to because patients experience the therapeutic event to be beneficial, helpful, and meaningful, mental health professionals are committed to interrogating discourses, honestly and reflexively. In this work, a distinction exists between sources of difference among people and the socially constructed meanings about these differences. Being a 65-year-old college educated woman from the Wampanoag tribe is a source of age, racial, class, and gender diversity. Internalizing socially constructed meanings about older women as unattractive, lonely, and sexless is not the same as being a woman of age who is emotionally and physically healthy and who revels in her life, just as it is.

A limitation of the current state of multicultural counseling and psychology is the lack of clarity about the distinction between stigmatized/marginalized identities and internalized oppression. People possess both privileged and stigmatized identities simultaneously and across contexts. Some of these identities are immutable—people were born into them—and others were acquired. The presence or absence of a particular identity, in and of itself, is insufficient to determine what and how one feels or thinks. Each of us occupies a variety of statuses at any given moment. We may feel that one status is just as or more important than another, yet we do not always get to select which status is most important to others (Ore, 2006). Movements—such as the Asian rights movement, the Chicano moratorium, the civil rights movement, the women's movement, the gay rights movement, immigrant rights movement, the Americans with Disabilities Act (ADA), and the freedom to marry movement—are evidence of the ongoing struggle for human rights, social justice, access, and inclusion. Within a culturally diverse nation challenged by the concept of equity for all, this chapter explores implications for clinicians, counselors, psychologists, social workers, and other mental health professionals engaged in diversity practice. Historically, the focus of multicultural counseling was on race and culture. Over the past few decades, scholars in multicultural counseling and psychology have begun to embrace other dimensions of identity, both visible and invisible. These other dimensions include spirituality, class, disability, sexuality, and body size.

Albeit invisible, unseen aspects of the self can be just as influential as visible identities in the construction of identity. And although race intersects with other dimensions of identity among people of color, sexuality or gender may be the clinical point of focus, representing salient identities for an individual. Race and gender have been socially constructed to function as primary status or master traits with race having grand-master status. Far too often, race eclipses other identities (Robinson-Wood 2010b). Put differently, Cose (1993) argued that race is never irrelevant.

Another primary tenet of this work is that although gender and race are characteristics into which people are born, they are not always visible. A client is done a disservice when the most visible aspect of the self is privileged over other identities. In this work, neither race nor the other dimensions of identity are essentialized. Essentialism boxes people into limiting and restricting behaviors based on preexisting and predetermined definitions that are regarded as natural. As Rosenblum and Travis (2006) said, "For essentialists, the categories of race, sex, and sexuality orientation, and social class identify significant, empirically verifiable differences among people" (p. 3).

Separating people into mutually exclusive racial and gender categories is not what this text is about. This text celebrates and recognizes that each of us has multiple identities that are fluid, sometimes invisible but nonetheless fundamental to personal identity construction. Within a color-conscious society, people are judged initially by immutable characteristics such as skin color and gender conformity rather than acquired traits, such as commitment to justice. Discourses associated with race, gender, and other sources of difference have far-reaching implications for one's income, place of residence, employment opportunity, educational quality, psychological and physical health, and physical safety. This practice among mental health professionals of unconsciously judging by appearances occurs throughout graduate training and creeps into the 50-minute therapeutic hour. (See Storytelling: The Inappropriate Professional.)

❖ STORYTELLING: THE INAPPROPRIATE PROFESSIONAL

Throughout her 30s and 40s, a woman had been receiving medication to treat her bipolar depression condition. She had been suffering throughout her life with this condition and had tried many antidepressants, anxiolytic, mood stabilizers, and antipsychotic medications. A few of them had started working to help her manage her symptoms. The woman struggled with debilitating depression and panic. Consequently, her work performance suffered. She stopped working outside of the home, particularly after she discovered that going to and being at work exacerbated her mood swings and increased her symptoms. The woman, married with children, also provided care to her father who had a diagnosis

(Continued)

❖ **STORYTELLING: THE INAPPROPRIATE PROFESSIONAL (Continued)**

of Alzheimer's. Although the patient had no desire for sexual relations with her husband, she felt obligated to fulfill his needs, due to her religious upbringing. During a scheduled appointment with her psychiatrist, she mentioned her lack of interest in having sex. The psychiatrist leaned forward in his chair and said, "You have an obligation to have sex with your husband." The woman was dismayed by the comment, but believed him to be right; after all, he was her doctor (and a man). She was also dependent on him to refill her psychiatric medications. By taking her medications regularly, she was able to stay out of the hospital. The psychiatrist gave advice to his vulnerable patient based on his personal values. His behavior was dictated by close proximity to discourses about societal gender roles: women are subservient to men and should meet their needs, regardless of their personal feelings. Being multicultural competent means that as mental health professionals, we know when our values interfere with how we listen to our clients. It is also a basic tenet of good psychotherapy not to tell patients what to do. Clearly, it is possible for patients to be harmed (iatrogenic) by psychotherapy; however, patients can be harmed by the decisions that are made about psychotherapy (Dimidjian & Hollon, 2010).

Multicultural Counseling and Psychology Defined

Multicultural counseling and psychology are not new. Often used interchangeably with diversity, "Multiculturalism recognizes the broad scope of dimensions of race, ethnicity, language, sexual orientation, gender, age, disability, class status, education, religious/spiritual orientation, and other cultural dimensions" (American Psychological Association [APA], 2003). Dramatic demographic changes within the United States such as the "browning of America," a term used during the late 1980s, alerted the profession to rethink assumptions about minority and majority status shaped largely by cultural discourses about power and powerlessness.

In naturalizing the world, particular discourses drive orientations to the world. Soza (2014) said the following about discourses:

> Discourses enable individuals to know and act in the world in specific ways; this knowledge can be enabling and at the same time constraining. Discourse structures society and social practices, and it is here that discourse shapes and creates knowledge of the world and how to live in it. (p. 6)

Discourses include text and talk, but more than text and talk are the socially constructed meanings that offer momentum, mobility, and motility to text and talk—rendering discourses representations of normalcy and orienting subjects to their world.

In Chapter 1, discourses were defined and discussed as they are central to this text. As mental health professionals and students in training, we need to ask ourselves the following questions: What are the unconscious and/or unspoken discourses for me that frame or lie beneath socially constructed categories of difference? What do unspoken discourses mean within my therapeutic contexts and/or within my classrooms?

Discourses may be unconscious in that people may not be aware of where they are located within and positioned by certain discourses. Location means "identifying where one resides in this society on a continuum from privilege to oppression in relation to various contextual aspects of the self, such as ethnicity, gender, sexual orientation, religion, and class status" (Vasquez & Magraw, 2005, p. 66–67). Holding enormous power, discourses can be subtle yet pervasive throughout society.

Within the framework of multicultural counseling and psychology, discourses about privilege, oppression, and difference often reflect confusion about meaning and intent. One of the discourses of cultural diversity is that it refers to people who are categorized as diverse: nonwhite, nonmale, and nonmainstream. The disadvantage of this discourse is that it does not encourage people, regardless of race and ethnicity, to acknowledge themselves as racial, cultural, and sexual beings. Because white people exist as persons who are not defined as racial beings, they remain invisible yet define and interpret people of color.

At its core, multicultural counseling and psychology are respectful of multiple epistemological and philosophical perspectives and are to be contrasted with ethnocentrism, a belief that one's own culture and belief systems are superior to those who are culturally different from oneself. Ethnocentrism is in direct contradiction to the goals and aims of multiculturally competent counseling and psychology. Single system or monoculturalism assumes that all people come from the same cultural plane and desire the values of the dominant culture dictated by those with the most racial and ethnic power (McIntosh, 1990). Multicultural counseling and psychology reaffirm comfort with and not mere tolerance of or putting up with people. Differences are viewed as indispensable to a healthy society. Multiculturally competent mental health professionals strive to coexist with similarities and differences without defensiveness or denial but seek to be aware of their biases, values, and trigger points. A dialectical, or both/and, approach to multicultural counseling and psychology supports complexity.

Embedded deeply in the fabric of daily life, culture is often rendered invisible, largely because of its pervasiveness. Dominant American cultural values include assertiveness, competition, convenience, Christianity, control, gender conformity, democracy, entitlement, educational attainment, equality, heterosexuality, individualism, materialism, meritocracy, productivity, the Protestant work ethic, thinness, whiteness, and youth. For some people, culture is a dominant identity. Others are seemingly oblivious to it. Clinicians need to be sensitive to and respectful of culture's role in shaping the self, particularly when patients are not conscious of the impact of culture(s) on their situation or problem in therapy.

Despite espoused values of democracy, diversity, and equality taught by schools, synagogues, mosques, church, political structures, and the family, Americans are socialized into an ethnocentric ideology. Ethnocentrism contributes to misinformation about people who are not legitimized by a culture. Students, across race, admit their ignorance about the enormous contributions from people of color to the United States and to the world. As racial and cultural awareness increase, as well as a social justice orientation, students might be critical of and embarrassed by their limited and inaccurate knowledge about people who do not look like them or who perhaps do. Curriculum materials, including U.S. history, are a reflection of what is valued throughout society and thus part of an institutionalized narrative.

Diversity: An Overview

Population Box 3.1: 2014 Population by Race provides information on the 2014 population. The non-Hispanic white population is the largest, followed by Latinos, blacks, Asians, Native Americans, and Native Hawaiians and Pacific Islanders. In the 2010 census, 53% of Latinos, who vary across skin color hue and are responsible for the largest percentage of population growth, indicated a white race (Ennis, Rios-Vargas, & Albert, 2011). Diversity and whiteness studies are encouraged to query this phenomenon and ask what the motivations and implications are for racial categories when people with white and non-white skin are collapsed into the same racial category. While there is a browning of America and has been since the 1980s with more immigration from Latin America, Asia, and Africa as well as increases in the numbers of biracial and multiracial people, there may be a whitening of America with respect to self-labeling. The Census department contributes to this albeit confusing and racially charged situation by deeming North Africans (e.g., Moroccans and Egyptians) as white irrespective of melanin content in the skin or the fact that their skin color may be darker than persons racially labeled as black.

From 2000 to 2010, Latinos accounted for 56% of the nation's growth (Passel, Livingston, and Cohn, 2012) and five states or equivalents were majority-minority: Hawaii (77.0%), the District of Columbia (64.2%), California (61.5%), New Mexico (61.1%) and Texas (56.5%; U.S. Census Bureau, 2015b).

Population Box 3.1: 2014 Population by Race

1. Non-Hispanic white population: 198 million

2. Asians: 20.3 million

3. Blacks: 45.7 million

4. Hawaii Native and Pacific Islander: 1.5 million

5. Latinos: 55.4 million

6. Native Americans and Alaskan Native: 6.5 million

Source: U.S. Census Bureau (2015b).

Since the recession that hit America in 2007, the workforce has deteriorated for all racial and ethnic groups. Because of factors such as lower average amounts of education, concentration in urban central cities, employment in jobs that tend to have higher levels of unemployment, and discrimination in the workplace, blacks and Latinos have been harder hit by unemployment than other ethnic groups (U.S. Department of Labor, 2010). Compared to the general population and to white people in particular, black people and Latinos have lower levels of wealth. The poverty rates for black people and Latinos are 27% and 23.5%, respectively. For non-Hispanic whites, the poverty rate is 9.6% (U.S. Census Bureau, 2014a). People who are poor experience more chronic health problems, live in crowded and noisy conditions, face job injuries, and are more vulnerable to obesity and violence. There is also greater social isolation (e.g., erosion of family support systems) in high poverty neighborhoods. People have limited neighborhood services (Dominguez & Arford, 2010) and homogenous social networks perpetuate the recycling of the same information (Dominguez & Watkins, 2003). Racial segregation continues to be part of U.S. society.

Regarding workforce participation by gender and ethnicity, Latino men are most likely to work in natural resources, construction, and maintenance or production, transportation, and material movement. Latinas have an employment population rate of 52.9%, with the greatest proportion of women, more so than among blacks, Asians, and whites, working in service-related, sales, or office positions. Asian men had the second highest employment population rate at 72.2%, with half of Asian men working in management, professional, or related occupations. Among women, Asians have the highest employment population rate at 56.7% and are more likely to be in management, professional, and related jobs. Black men, more so than other racial groups of men, are most likely to work in production, transportation, and material movement. Clearly, many aspects of society are largely stratified by race and gender characteristics. Although persons who are more educated are less likely to be unemployed, in 2009 blacks and Latinos at all levels of education were more likely to be unemployed than their counterparts in other ethnic groups (U.S. Department of Labor, 2010).

Gender and sexuality are two other components of the diversity in the United States. Approximately 50.4% of the population is female, and 49% are male—the male–female ratio is dictated by race and age (The World Bank, 2015). This topic will be discussed in greater detail in subsequent chapters.

Human sexuality exists on a continuum and includes heterosexuality, bisexuality, and homosexuality with considerable intragroup and intergroup variation in behavior (Robinson & Watt, 2001). Asexuality has not been given adequate attention in the diversity literature and yet is a phenomenon (Prause & Graham, 2007). The incidence of exclusive homosexuality is estimated to range from 2% to 10% for men and slightly less for women. It is clear that these percentages are not an exact number. People who identify as transgender do not subscribe to a bifurcated male/female dichotomy. A person can be born biologically female and identify as male with respect to gender and sexual identities.

The term *transgender* refers to the full spectrum of persons "whose gender identity transgresses traditional definitions of 'male' and 'female'" (Singh, Boyd, & Whitman, 2010, p. 417). People who are pre- and post-transsexuals may fit under this term or may not depending on identity construction, which is a very personal process. Intersex persons may be born with reproductive anatomy and/or genitalia that do not meet typical definitions of male and female. Prior to any surgical intervention, intersex children are often assigned a gender after physicians have consulted with parents (Carroll & Gilroy, 2002). Some question and contest the rationale of performing surgical interventions on intersexual children particularly if there are no associated health risks. A large clitoris and a small penis are not life-threatening conditions. Ours is an aging population. According to the 2010 census (U.S. Census, 2012), the median age of Americans is 37.2. Between 2000 and 2010, the population 45 to 64 years of age grew 31.5% to 81 million, and this age group comprises 26.4% of the population. Even those 65 and older grew at a faster rate than most of the younger population groups. For example, in the same time period, people under the age of 18 grew 2.6% to 74.2 million comprising 24% of the population. There was .6% growth among those 18 to 44 years of age. Concerning age, race, and/or ethnicity, African Americans and Native Americans have shorter life spans than do white Americans. Latinos and Native Americans have lower median years than whites. The youngest Americans, persons who are younger than 5 years old are, for the first time, majority-minority. Over 50% (50.2%) are part of a minority race or ethnic group (U.S. Census, 2015c).

A B C Dimensions

As a means of conceptualizing human differences, Arredondo and Glauner (1992) developed the Dimensions of Personal Identity (DPI), which recognizes the complexity of all persons across three (A, B, C) dimensions (Fawcett, Briggs, Maycock, & Stine, 2010). *A dimensions* of personal identity refer to the characteristics into which people are born. These include age, culture, sex, sexual orientation, language, social class, accent, outward appearance, and physical disability. *C dimensions* are historical events that affect people's present and future lives and are grounded in historical, political, sociocultural, and economic contexts. Arredondo indicated that the C dimension "suggests there are many factors that surround us over which we have no control as individuals, but which will, nevertheless, affect us both positively and negatively" (Arredondo, et al., 1996, p. 51). The C dimensions also reflect intersectionality of social, political, global, and environmental events that affect clients' life experiences (Arredondo et al., 1996; Fawcett et al., 2010). With this dimension for immigrants, historical events can refer to political events that prompted departure from one's home country, such as war, terrorism, poverty, floods, and earthquakes. The outbreak of diseases (such as polio, SARS, HIV); natural disasters such as hurricanes, tsunamis, and mudslides; and terror are examples of historical events that intersect with A and B dimensions. *B dimensions* are characteristics not necessarily visible to others but influenced by individual achievement; these include educational background, geographic location, income, relationship status, military experience, religion, work experience, citizenship status, and hobbies. The B dimensions may represent the "consequences" of A and C dimensions. Arredondo et al. (1996) said, "What occurs to individuals relative to their B Dimensions are influenced by some of the immutable characteristics of the A Dimension and the major historical, political, sociocultural, and economic legacies of the C Dimension" (p. 52).

Understanding the convergence of multiple-identity constructs (A, B, and C dimensions) is crucial to viewing clients holistically. Throughout this text, the intersections of race, gender, class, spirituality, disability, and sexuality (A and B dimensions) with historical events (C dimensions) and the social construction of difference are given primary focus.

Conceptualization of the Self

A central focus on the individual is not typical of every culture. In many societies throughout the world, the self is conceptualized within the context of the collective or the community, not as a separate entity. What one person does can impact the family's standing, honor, and reputation. The internalization of cultural values is influenced by acculturation, migration status, income, education, generational status, internalized oppression, and racial/ethnic identity development.

Individualism and collectivism have roots in political and economic history, religion, and philosophy (Kagitcibasi, 1997). In individualism, the person is regarded as discrete from other beings and is considered the essential cornerstone of society (Kagitcibasi, 1997). Myers (1991) maintained that because Western society is philosophically oriented to individualism, individuals are the primary referent point and are separate from others. She saw fragmentation between spirit and matter (or *bifurcation of the self*) as an outcome of an individualistic frame of reference.

Enns (1994) stated,

> Consistent with individualistic cultural values, the separate self values personal initiative, self-reliance, and achievement as coping mechanism and tends to take internal responsibility for both success and failure. In contrast, the collectivist is more likely to value making a contribution to a group effort, more likely to express modesty or self-effacement in the face of success and less likely than the individualist to make internal attributions for either success or failure. (p. 207)

Individualism influences and is associated with other core U.S. cultural values such as empiricism. The scientific tradition in academia emerged from a positivistic-empirical model that emphasized quantification, statistical measurement, and validation of reality by use of the five senses. In Western ideology, individualism, measurement, and control are cultural values, exerting powerful influence on the policies, programs, and politics of the United States, both past and present. The visible is legitimate and the invisible is often suspect because it cannot be proved and counted. Yet as Albert Einstein knew, "Not everything that counts can be counted, and not everything that can be counted counts" (Harris 1995).

Strangely enough, individualism may suppress individual expression. For example, external conformity and individualism appear to be in contradiction, yet these are two cultural values in the United States. Americans are encouraged to be autonomous, to be their own persons, and to do their own thing. More specifically to women, a message is given to maintain the status quo and "not rock the boat." U.S. society espouses, "Be all you can be," but conflicting messages are also given about not making people upset with you.

With the difficulty of answering questions of "Who am I?" "What do I want to be?" "What and whom do I want?"—one is vulnerable to adopt others' answers to these questions. Although excessive forms of individualism can interfere with one's ability to function collaboratively, to ask for and receive help, which by the way are intensely feminine traits (Perkins, 2015), individuality can play a critical role in forming an identity.

In addition to socialization factors, structural and economic factors mediate individualism. For example, when the economy of the United States was agrarian based and people were less mobile, interdependence was greater than it is in today's highly technological and mobile society in which people are often physically removed from family of origin, extended family, and community support.

Images of Diversity

Culture

Culture is ubiquitous, central to each of our lives, and shapes the way we see the world. It has been defined as the myriad ways of people to preserve society and meet a range of human needs. Belief systems, behaviors, and traditions make up the essence of culture (Pinderhughes, 1989) as do people's relationships with time, nature, other people, and mode of activity (Kluckhohn & Strodtbeck, 1961). As pervasive as culture is, people are often oblivious to its impact on their and others' lives because of unstated assumptions and shared values that go unrecognized (Bronstein & Quina, 1988).

Enculturation refers to immersion in our own culture to the point where we assume that our way of life is "natural" or "normal" (Ore 2006, p. 3). Dana (1993) identified an *emic perspective* as one that is respectful of and sensitive to the native culture's meanings for phenomena and native language and encourages recognition of persons on their own terms. It holds that the best place from which to help people of color is from their own perspective (Vontress 1986). In contrast, an *etic perspective* emphasizes the observer's culturally driven meanings that are referenced as the standard for interpretation. Here, the focus is on similarities and not cultural differences (Vontress, 1986).

Acculturation appears to be a process of socialization into accepting and adapting to the cultural values of the larger society. Berry and Sam (1997) provided a definition of acculturation from Redfield, Linton, and Herskovits's (1936) definition: "Acculturation comprehends those phenomena which result when groups of individuals having different cultures come into continuous first-hand contact with subsequent changes in the original culture patterns of either or both groups" (pp. 293–94). Acculturation can take place at the expense of one's original cultural values as one internalizes the dominant society's values and traditions. Berry and Sam stated that acculturation is a neutral term in that changes may happen in both groups. Acculturation tends to bring about change in one group, which is referred to as the acculturating group. Two questions clarify the outcome of acculturation strategies:

1. Is it considered to be of value to maintain relationships with the dominant society?

2. Is it considered to be of value to maintain cultural identity characteristics? (Berry & Sam, 1997, p. 296)

Acculturation is not so much identification as it is internalization. Because this process is not always conscious (Sue, 1989), the possibility of cultural alienation from one's traditional culture is high. Berry and Sam (1997) discussed four acculturation strategies: (1) assimilation, (2) traditionality, (3) integration, and (4) marginality. (See Knowledge Check 3.1: Acculturation Model.)

Although a dimension of acculturation, *assimilation* is different and describes those persons who do not desire to maintain their cultural identities and thus seek sustained interaction with other cultures outside their own. Sue (1989) discussed a similar phenomenon when describing assimilation. He said it refers to a conscious process in which the person desires to identify with the traditional society because its art, language, and culture are perceived to be more valuable than the person's own. Persons who are assimilated are viewed as being low in a knowledge of and appreciation for their own cultures while holding the dominant culture in high regard. The original cultures have been lost, subverted or relinquished, and persons have given up most cultural traits of their cultures of origin and assumed the traits of the dominant culture (Berry and Kim, 1988).

Traditionality describes persons who choose to hold on to their cultural connections and avoid interaction with others. Here, people have knowledge of and appreciation for their own cultures while holding the dominant culture in lower regard. When the dominant culture engages in these practices, the term is *segregation* (Berry & Sam, 1997).

Integration describes an interest in maintaining one's original culture while simultaneously seeking interactions with the other culture. According to Berry and

Knowledge Check: 3.1

Acculturation Model

		Culture of Origin	
		High	**Low**
Native Culture	**High**	Integrated	Assimilated
	Low	Traditional	Marginal

Kim (1988), these persons are characterized as being *bicultural.* They are high in knowledge of and appreciation for their own cultures while esteeming the dominant culture as well. An integration of both an original culture and the dominant culture has transpired. Mental health and acculturation modality are related. Berry and Kim (as cited in Dana 1993) stated, "Mental health problems will be least intense with biculturality (e.g., integration) and progressively increase in severity with assimilation, traditionality, and marginality outcomes of acculturation" (p. 112).

Little interest in cultural maintenance and limited desire to interact with others from different cultures is defined as *marginality.* According to Dana (1993), "Marginality will often occur when the traditional culture is not retained and the dominant society culture is not accepted" (p. 112). Emotional and psychological stress is associated with seeking to become acculturated within a given culture. Gloria and Peregoy (1996) discussed how alcohol and other drug abuse may be by-products of acculturation stress among some Latino populations. This connection between substance abuse and acculturation stress seems to apply to Native Americans and other ethnic and racial groups in their attempts to contend with cultural devastation and the ubiquitous, subtle, and overt effects of institutionalized racism (Herring, 1992).

Race

Every human being is a member of the human race, of the species of *Homo sapiens.* Typical conceptions of race often refer to people of color (Christian, 1989); nonetheless, *race* also refers to white people. Race is an extremely volatile and divisive force in America despite the heroic efforts of various movements (e.g., the Asian, Latino, and civil rights movements) that coalesced to create greater racial equality. As has already been discussed, huge variations in income, occupational distribution, educational levels, quality of and access to education, health care, and mortality can be seen between and within racial groups (Anderson, 2003). (See Storytelling: Looking American.)

❖ **STORYTELLING: LOOKING AMERICAN**

Race and skin color affect perceptions of nationality and citizenship. Years ago, I participated in an Asian American literature book club. One of the men in the group, a native New Yorker, talked about how, on a regular basis, people asked him where he was from. He would tell them New York— they would then ask, "No, where are you really from?" He would say, "New York City." "Which country were you born in?" they would continue. "America. I was born in America." Awkward silence and frustration on the part of the interrogator would follow who would then ask where his family was from, and he would say "New York." This man speaks English without an accent. Many people, based on the fact the he is Asian and looks Asian, assume he is a foreigner and not native to America—not American.

What is race? To begin, there is no consensual definition of the term. According to some biologists, *race* (or subspecies) "is an inbreeding, geographically isolated population that differs in distinguishable physical traits from members of the species" (Zuckerman, 1990, p. 1297). Healey (1997) said that race was "an isolated inbreeding population with a distinctive genetic heritage. Socially, the term is used loosely and reflects patterns of inequality and power" (p. 309).

The biology of race is heavily debated (Cornell & Hartmann, 1997; Healey, 1997). In fact, most biologists regard race as a social construct only. Even persons who appear very different from one another by virtue of skin color, facial features, body type, and hair texture are very similar genetically. The Human Genome Project discovered that 99.9% of our 30,000 human genes are shared by everyone (Highfield, 2002). Yet phenotypical properties such as hair texture and the amount of melanin in the skin are typically the dimensions commonly associated with race (Lee, 2001). "Biological racial categories have more within group variation than between group variation" (APA, 2003, p. 1). Of the 0.1% genetic variation among humans, 94% of this exists between people of the same population with 6% among people from different populations (Highfield, 2002). Melanin is responsible for darker skin color hue and represents "an adaptation to a particular ecology" (Healey, 1997, p. 11). Although race is based on phenotype, these variables do not accurately reflect one's race but rather represent a basis for assigning people to a particular racial group. This text recognizes that race is a social construction and not biologically determined (APA, 2003). This issue is explored later in greater depth.

Ethnicity

Race and ethnicity are used interchangeably by some authors and researchers; however, these terms are not synonymous (Sanchez & Davis, 2010). According to Pinderhughes (1989), *ethnicity* refers to a connectedness based on commonalities (e.g., religion, nationality, regions) in which specific aspects of cultural patterns that are transmitted over time create a common history and ancestry. Ethnicity refers to commonality in which unique cultural aspects are shared. Among some racial groups, ethnicity refers more to nationality and country of origin. For others, religion describes ethnicity or values and lifestyle (Lee, 2001). Ethnicity has been defined as the acceptance of group mores and practices of one's culture of origin and having a sense of belonging (APA, 2003). Persons can be of the same ethnicity (e.g., Latino) but represent different racial backgrounds (e.g., white, black, biracial, Asian). Persons can also be of the same racial group (Asian) but of differing ethnicities (e.g., Chinese, Southeast Asian Indian, Cuban, Filipino). When transmitted intergenerationally, language, dancing, dressing, singing, storytelling, ways of worship and mourning, quilt making, weaving, and cooking, for example, are ethnic behaviors (Alba, 1990).

Common discussions of ethnicity in the United States tend to include the "melting pot." This pot has been brewing and bubbling over for generations. Originating in 1910 at the University of Chicago (Steinberg, 1989), the term described the assimilating tendencies of the more than 1 million European immigrants who were entering (immigrating to) the United States each year. Sociologists were interested in knowing how the more than 20 nationalities managed conflict. The melting pot theory differed from the theory of *ethnic pluralists*, who maintained that ethnicity was an enduring factor throughout American life. Yet the loss of native tongues, the decline of ethnic cultures, the dispersion of ethnic communities, the increase in ethnic and religious intermarriage, and the transformation of ethnic-sounding names to white Anglo-Saxon Protestant-sounding names were and continue to be examples of Americanization (Steinberg, 1989). In addition, the melting pot assailed the preservation of individual differences in that the pot was dominated by the majority (the main ingredient) and those with the most power.

The process of assimilation among white ethnics differs greatly from that among people of color. Skin color and other phenotypical characteristics subject people of color to discriminatory treatment. Historical differences exist between race and ethnicity as a function of U.S. policy. The 1790 Naturalization Law, which was in effect for 162 years, stated that only free "white" persons would be eligible for naturalized citizenship. This law meant that general citizenship was denied to Asians through the Walter-McCarran Act of 1952 and even to Native American Indians until 1924 (Takaki, 1994).

When people lack an understanding of history, this misunderstanding can be the basis for ignorance about race and the perpetuation of racism. For example, Loewen (1995) informs us that Pilgrims did not introduce Thanksgiving; the Eastern Indians had been observing autumn harvest celebrations for centuries. Abraham Lincoln, in a move to bolster patriotism, proclaimed Thanksgiving a national holiday in 1863. Alba (1990) also referred to persons from Latin America as "new immigrant groups" (p. 1). During the late 19th and early 20th centuries, Europeans represented the largest group of immigrants to this nation. In the Treaty of Guadalupe Hidalgo (Novas, 1994), Mexico lost half of its national territory, which included Texas, New Mexico, California, Arizona, Nevada, Utah, and half of Colorado (Novas, 1994). Historical accuracy is critical. If not, misinformation and distortion ensue, not only our perceptions of people and their histories but also our perceptions of our own histories.

Gender

Traditional notions of gender reference non-males (Christian, 1989), yet *gender* refers to males, females, and transgendered individuals. Gender has socially constructed categories in terms of roles and behaviors based on a biological given of sex (Renzetti & Curran, 1992). Gender refers to the roles, behaviors, and attitudes that come to be expected of persons on the basis of their biological sex. Despite the advent of the women's and men's movements in U.S. society, men continue to be socialized to restrict themselves emotionally, function independently, value assertiveness and power, and equate sexuality with intimacy, manhood, and self-worth. On the other hand, women are socialized to be emotional and nurturing and are groomed to direct their achievement through affiliation with others, particularly men (Mintz & O'Neil, 1990; Perkins 2015). In truth, men are emotional beings who rely on others, do not always feel strong, and desire to express a full range of emotions, including vulnerability (Perkins, 2015). Women are leaders and providers and can be extremely competitive and harsh with both women and men.

Biological sex refers to the possession of an XY chromosome pair for a genetically healthy male and an XX chromosome pair for a genetically healthy female, along with the corresponding anatomical, hormonal, and physiological parts (Atkinson & Hackett, 1995). Some people are born with a variety of chromosomes, such as Klinefelter's, in which a male person has an extra X chromosome or XXY. According to U.S. Natural Library of Medicine (2015), this condition results in a sexual development where the person may have enlarged breasts, small testes, infertility, and learning disabilities. The clinician's commitment to understanding how the client's life has been impacted by biology as well as by the social constructions of normalcy displays multicultural competence.

Although not often related to chromosomal abnormalities, there are persons who are born with ambiguous genitalia. Physicians, in conjunction with results from appropriate endocrine tests and parental consent, affix a child's gender that corresponds with sexual reassignment. The ethics of this issue are intensely debated by the Intersexual Society of North America.

Sex and *gender* are terms that are easily confused. For instance, lactation and penile erection are sex roles that have biological connection. Canning tomatoes and stacking wood are not sex roles. They are socially constructed gender roles. There are no isolated genes for snow blowing or ironing, yet the arbitrary divisions of labor that society has constructed based on biological sex are stringent and far too often attributed to biology.

Psychological masculinity is not a biological phenomenon, yet it is often equated with characteristics of the U.S. culture, such as rugged self-reliance, competition, and fierce individualism (Robinson & Watt, 2001). The characteristics often attributed to femininity, such as loving children, yielding, and nurturing, are not exclusive to the female sex or to heterosexuals of any gender.

Androcentrism is a traditional systematic construct in which the worldview of men is used as the central premise of development for all individuals, including women (Worell & Remer, 1992). The central image underlying this concept is "males at the center of the universe looking out at reality from behind their own eyes and describing what they see from an egocentric or androcentric point of view" (Bem, 1993, p. 42). The many benefits associated with unearned privilege can distort one's vision of the disadvantages that accompany privilege. Both men and women alike suffer from the constricting consequences of socially constructed gender roles. There is society push-back against traditional notions of gender and yet androcentrism is evident throughout society (see Knowledge Check 3.2: Androcentric Terms). For example, on August 9, 2015, Target announced that it will eliminate its gender specific language throughout its store (e.g., boys' bedding) as well as the gendered pink for girls and blue for boys color scheme.

Knowledge Check 3.2

Androcentric Terms

Mankind, manning the store, man overboard, man-up, men at work, you guys.

Sexuality

Sexuality: There are different expressions of sexuality within and across the sexuality continuum.

All major mental health associations have affirmed that homosexuality is not a mental illness, yet there was a time when the American Psychiatric Association, the publishers of the *Diagnostic Statistical Manual,* viewed homosexuality as an indication of mental illness. *Heterosexism* is the ideological system that denies, denigrates, and stigmatizes nonheterosexual forms of behavior, identity, relationship, or community (APA, 2006). Heterosexism is institutionalized through law, religion, education, and the media and leads to homophobia (Pharr, 1988). Heterosexism has implications for the client–therapist dyad and could limit the type of advocacy a heterosexual therapist might engage in with a gay, transgendered, or bisexual client. This effect is particularly true if the professional is self-conscious about being labeled as gay due to affiliation with or advocacy for gays and lesbians.

Related to heterosexism, *homophobia* is the irrational and unreasonable fear of same-sex attractions and "persons whose affectional and erotic orientations are toward the same sex" (King, 1988, p. 168). It also applies to persons perceived to be gay or lesbian and emanates from the perception of homosexuality as an aberration of the correct social order. The term *homosexual* defines attraction to the same sex for physical and emotional nurturance and is one orientation on the sexual orientation continuum. The terms *gay* and *lesbian* are preferred to homosexual and are used throughout this work. *Homophobia* comes from the Latin *homo,* meaning "same" (in this case, referring to same-gender attraction), and *phobia,* meaning "fear of."

In the fourth edition of this text, which was published in 2012, I wrote,

> The following states now issue marriage licenses to same-sex couples: Massachusetts, Connecticut, Iowa, Vermont, New Hampshire, New York, and the District of Columbia. Delaware, Hawaii, Illinois, and New Jersey allow civil unions. Civil unions provide state-level spousal rights to same-sex couples. (National Conference of State Legislatures, 2011)

Today same-sex marriage is legal in all 50 states.

Disability

Section 504 of the Rehabilitation Act of 1973 and the ADA of 1990 prohibit discrimination against individuals with disabilities. The ADA was signed into law 25 years ago on July 26, 1990. According to these laws, no otherwise qualified individual with a disability shall, solely by reason of his or her disability, be excluded from the participation in, be denied the benefits of, or be subjected to discrimination under any program or activity of a public entity. Disabilities can be physical, mental, psychological, and the result of injury, accident, illness, congenital, or organic.

According to the *Americans with Disabilities Act Handbook* (Equal Employment Opportunity Commission, 1991), an individual with a disability is a person who has a physical or mental impairment that substantially limits one or more "major life activities," or has a record of such an impairment, or is regarded as having such an impairment.

Examples of physical or mental impairments include, but are not limited to, contagious and non-contagious diseases and conditions such as orthopedic, visual, speech, and hearing impairments; cerebral palsy; epilepsy; muscular dystrophy; multiple sclerosis; cancer; heart disease; diabetes; developmental delays; emotional illness; specific learning disabilities; HIV disease (whether symptomatic or asymptomatic); tuberculosis; drug addiction; and alcoholism. According to the U.S. Census Bureau (2012), there are 56.7 million people, or 19% of the population age 5 and over, with a disability.

The nature of disabilities among people varies. The term *disability* is dynamic given the open membership of this identity as a function of the natural aging process, injury, and/or disease. Numerous categories exist in describing persons with disabilities, from mild to moderate to severe. People need not be born into a disability. Whether it exists at birth or occurs at some juncture in life, it is, nonetheless, a biological reality. Persons with physical and mental disabilities continue to face obstacles to access and experience discriminatory attitudes. Some of us have had the experience of going out to eat at a restaurant with a friend who had a visible disability only to find the waiter or waitress completely ignore the person in the wheelchair and ask the person who appears not to have a physical disability what the person with the disability would like to eat. Such attitudes are fueled by a societal perception that persons with disabilities are not worth seeing, dependent, helpless, childlike, and incomplete. When people who are able-bodied disrupt this exchange and say, "Please ask him or her what she would like to eat," the discourse that disabled people are without capacity will be challenged. People with severe disabilities are the least likely to be employed and have higher rates of poverty.

Disability is only one component of a person's overall identity. Fowler, O'Rourke, Wadsworth, and Harper (1992) said the term disabled "conveys a message of inability which overshadows other identity descriptors of the person and becomes the exclusive role for persons who are disabled" (p. 102). When visible, disability can function as a primary status trait and be regarded as the most salient dimension of a person's life. The therapist who associates the experience of being physically able and wealthy with power may perceive an unemployed client with a disability as depressed. Despite the therapist's feelings, the client may feel psychologically empowered with access to emotional and spiritual resources that enable him or her to feel positive about life (Robinson, 1999a) where unemployment is regarded as a transition and an opportunity to regroup.

Socioeconomic Class

Socioeconomic class has traditionally referred to a person's or group's social and financial position relative to rank. Factors that affect one's socioeconomic ranking include educational level, employment stability, wages, marital status, income of spouse and/or other persons in the home, size of household, citizenship, and access to medical benefits. Exceptions exist, but increased education tends to be associated with higher incomes and less unemployment. According to the DeNavas-Walt and Proctor (2014) and Macartney, Bishaw, and Fontenot (2013), the highest poverty rates are among Native Americans, and the lowest are among Asians. (See Population Box 3.2: 2013 U.S. Poverty Rates.)

> ## Population Box 3.2: 2013 U.S. Poverty Rates
>
> U.S. Poverty Rate: 14.5%
>
> Asians: 10.5%
>
> Native Americans: 29.2%
>
> Latinos: 23.5%
>
> Blacks: 27%
>
> Non-Hispanic White: 9.6%
>
> *Source:* DeNavas-Walt and Proctor (2014) and Macartney et al. (2013).

Family constellation helps to explain poverty rates. Female-headed households are more likely to be poorer. For example, in 2009, nearly half (44%) of black families were headed by women compared to 25% among Latinos, 15% among whites, and 13% among Asians (U.S. Department of Labor, 2010). According to the National Center for Education Statistics (2015), the poverty rates among children by race are as follows: black (39%), Native American (36%), Latino (32%), white (13%), and Asian (13%). Class intersects with gender and race. Black, Latino, Pacific Island, and Native American women have higher rates of poverty than do Asian and white women. Having resources to support one's livelihood affects the employee and those who rely on the employee's salary. Sense of worth, access to quality health care, food security, exposure to violence, a sense of personal safety, purpose, agency, and access to fresh air and clean water are all associated with class status and income levels.

Self-construct and feelings of self-esteem and self-worth are impacted by reliable employment and socioeconomic class. It is not surprising that child-rearing practices would also be affected. Storck (1998) suggested that class has to be expanded to include psychosocial characteristics such as a sense of well-being.

In their study of working parents, McLoyd and Wilson (1992) found that parents with fewer economic resources, in comparison to parents who were considered middle class, placed less emphasis on happiness as a goal while they were rearing their children. These parents were less likely to believe that childhood was a protected, care-free, and happy-go-lucky space or that it was their responsibility as parents to create such a climate for their children. The research presented by McLoyd and Wilson plus Storck's call for an expansion of the concept of social class suggest that class is not independent of other dimensions of personhood, such as mental and physical health status, longevity, attention to happiness, and the ability to satisfy need states. Socio-economic status has a substantial influence on health behaviors and health-related psychological processes, including physical activity, smoking, healthy eating habits, access to quality food, sleep quality, depression, cynical hostility, obesity, and chronic stress (Anderson, 2003). The wealth divide between people who are in the 1% and the majority who are in the 99% has increased significantly.

Spirituality

Across all age, race, and ethnic groups, religion and/or spirituality play a part in many people's lives. The United States was founded on Christian principles; however, much religious and faith diversity exists within and between religious and spiritual groups. Christianity is the largest religion worldwide and is purported to have 2.1 billion members, or 33% of the world's inhabitants. Included among Christians are Catholic, Protestant, Pentecostal, Latter-day Saints of Jesus Christ, Jehovah Witnesses, Quakers, and Southern Baptist. Islam has approximately 1.5 billion members, or 21% of the planet's population. Shiite and Sunni are included. Persons who are secular nonreligious/agnostic/atheist number 1.1 billion, are the third largest group, and represent 16% of the world's religious population. Hinduism is fourth, with 900 million followers and 14% of religious followers. Chinese traditional religion is fifth with 394 million people. Buddhism is sixth with 376 million people; primal-indigenous is seventh and represents 100 million people. Included are African/Traditional/Diasporic religions, each representing 6% of the world's religious population (Adherents.com, 2007).

The two largest religious bodies (Catholics at 1.1 billion and Sunni Muslims at 1 billion) account for about 33% of the world's population. The membership of these, the "world's largest religious bodies" among 120 on the list, account for approximately 47% of the world's population. Said differently, nearly half of the world's population can be counted as members of a relatively small number of organized religious entities, if Sunni Islam is counted as a single organization (Adherents.com, 2014). Other world religions include Sikhism, Judaism, Baha'i, Shinto, and spiritism. Religion, spirituality, and their various expressions are affected by race, ethnicity, nationality, culture, gender, tribe, sexual orientation, class, and history.

Religion and spirituality are conceptualized differently. *Religion* may be measured by denominational affiliations (e.g., Baptist, Methodist), as well as by empirical, behavioral, or public indicators, such as churchgoing and avoidance of denounced or sinful behaviors (e.g., alcohol consumption; cigarette smoking; foul language; the revealing of one's face or body; disobedience to one's family, culture, or husband; sexual intercourse outside marriage).

Spirituality is often private and/or internally defined, transcends the tangible, and serves to connect one to the whole (other living organisms and the universe). Spirituality gives life direction and can help people maintain mental health (McDonald, 1990; Swinton, 2001). It is possible to define oneself as spiritual without being religious and to be religious but not spiritual (Burke & Miranti, 2001). Faith was defined by Fowler and Keen (1978) as being connected to but not the same as religion. It is "a person's or a community's way-of-being-in-relation to other persons and groups, and to the values, causes, and institutions that give form and pattern to life" (Fowler & Keen, 1978, p. 23–24).

Implications for Mental Health Professionals

Multicultural counseling and psychology recognize differences exist among people and view the assessment and understanding of one's proximity to discourses as critical. The development of multicultural competence among mental health professionals is a core value and is ethical practice. An inability and/or unwillingness of clinicians to interrogate their competence suggests a fear and/or arrogance that does not serve patients or the profession well. Clients need to be leery of clinicians who would not seek personal therapy. Clinicians are encouraged to acknowledge their cultural and ethnic/racial development since attitudes and beliefs about differences affect the quality of the therapeutic encounter. Clinicians need to communicate effectively with their clients regarding the full range of the clients' values and the relationship between these values and their situations and problem resolution. Because clinicians have biases, it is important to honestly gauge knowledge and feelings about sources of difference and to do this work with others. (See Case Study: Desperation.)

Case Study

Desperation

Mara is a 53-year-old, working-class black woman living on her own in a large city in Maryland. She has been dating Jim for nearly 1 year. Prior to Jim, Mara had not dated anyone since she divorced 14 years ago. Although Mara would like to remarry, Jim has been slow to commit. Upon returning from a vacation with Jim, Mara is unbelievably tired—she is more fatigued now than she can ever remember—getting up in the middle of the night with her infant son years ago was not so fatiguing. After several weeks of catching up on her sleep, Mara continues to be exhausted and feels awful. On the insistence of her adult son, Mara goes to the doctor. Listening to her symptoms and her dating relationship with Jim, her doctor informs Mara that she would like to run a complete blood panel, including Lyme disease and HIV. Mara does not see the need for either test but gives her consent for both. When her doctor inquired if Mara has been practicing safe sex, Mara said, "We are monogamous." "So you use condoms?" asked her doctor. "No," Mara replied. "Jim does not like them." Her doctor then said, "Then you are not practicing safe sex." Later that evening, Mara asked Jim whether he was seeing other people. He became defensive and said, "We are not married, and I don't want to be tied down. Why do you want to ruin a good thing?" A few days later, Mara was asked to return to the office. When her doctor sat down, she somberly revealed that her test was negative for Lyme disease but positive for HIV. Her doctor provided her with prescriptions for medications. In addition, she recommended that Mara seek individual counseling and join a support group for women living with HIV. Mara is devastated by the news, so much that she leaves her car in the parking lot and calls her son to pick her up. After taking several days to call a community agency that provides crisis counseling, Mara is told that she is scheduled to meet with a female clinician. When Mara inquired about the clinician's race, she is told she is white. Mara prefers to see a black therapist and is concerned that a white therapist is going to judge her, accepting the stereotypes about black women being sexually promiscuous. She asks if there is a black therapist available. There is one available, but Mara would have to wait a few weeks for an appointment. In her desperation, Mara reluctantly accepts an appointment to see Dr. Mansil.

Questions

1. Why are black women disproportionately represented among those who are infected with HIV?

2. Where is a good place for the clinician to begin with Mara?

3. Should the therapist address Mara's concern that she initially expressed over the phone regarding her preference for a black therapist, especially if Mara does not bring it up in the therapy session?

Discussion and Integration

The Client, Mara, and the Therapist, Dr. Mansil

Interpersonal relationships are central to human beings' survival and healthy development. Compared to other women, black women across educational levels, have higher never-married rates and higher rates of single parenting. Lower marriage rates, particularly when parenting solo, are associated with fewer economic resources and puts large numbers of heterosexual black women in the unenviable and stressful position of being more likely to be without a mate. Increasing rates of marriage between black men and white women, black men's higher homicide and incarceration rates, as well as higher unemployment and underemployment rates adversely impact black women. Although there are increases in the number of marriages between black women and nonblack men, this social and economic situation with black men translates into fewer marriageable black men (Robinson-Wood, 2009b). Although Mara needs to accept responsibility for her decision not to practice safe sex, Mara's situation needs to be understood within a larger ecological context that respects her racially gendered life. Nationally, black women account for 66% of new HIV cases among women. More than heart disease and breast cancer, HIV is the leading cause of death among black women ages 25 to 34 (Black Women's Health Imperative, n.d.). HIV also impacts older adults. Having unprotected sex with men who have sex with other men or who are intravenous drug users places unsuspecting women in peril. Mara had unprotected sex with Jim who, without her knowledge, was having sex with other men.

Upon meeting Dr. Mansil, or Belle, Mara has many feelings. She is desperate to receive help and afraid to not get help. She fears being judged. She is uncomfortable about having to see a therapist and is embarrassed, frightened, and enraged that she is HIV positive. She is afraid that she is going to die—so afraid that she has been having panic attacks, insomnia, and headaches.

After completing an intake, Belle says to Mara, "This is a very tough road you are on. I would like to walk with you during this rough time. Let's try this first session and see how you feel afterwards. Once our time is up and you decide that you would be better served by a black therapist, I will help you to get an appointment sooner." As a therapist influenced by a narrative therapy approach, Belle desires to listen to Mara's story as Mara desires to tell it. Mara's body language tells Belle that she is terribly uncomfortable, defensive, angry, and ashamed at having to be present. Belle is aware of Mara's initial reluctance to see her from information gathered during the initial phone call that Mara made to the agency. She courageously broached the topic of race. Belle actively listens for the problem saturation in Mara's story and where Mara continues to get stuck and see herself as the problem. After a hesitant start, Mara begins to speak. Belle listens. Mara reiterates that she has HIV, that she can't believe that this has happened to her, that she is so angry at Jim for doing this to her, that she trusted Jim, that she feels so stupid and abandoned by God. Belle shares with Mara that the problem is not Mara; the problem is HIV, and the problem is Jim's dishonesty, and the problem is Mara's struggle with caring for herself. Jim's infidelity and high-risk behaviors along with Mara not protecting herself have infected Mara. Belle sees the benefit of certain psychodynamic techniques in her work with Mara, such as transference. Transference is "the unconscious process by which early unresolved relational dynamics or conflicts are unwittingly displaced or 'transferred' onto the current relationship with the clinician and then reenacted or expressed as though appropriate or 'real' in the moment" (Murphy & Dillon, 2008, p. 313).

Research supports the principle that transference strengthens the therapeutic relationship. In grounded theory research with 26 clients, it was discovered that the "transferential" process was described as positive and appeared to aid alliance building (Levitt, Butler, & Travis, 2006).

Belle validates Mara's emotions, disappointment and rage, fear, and extreme sadness. She also tells her that feeling like a tornado has touched down on only her house while the other houses are left unscathed is part of the avalanche of emotions. Releasing the emotions can keep one sane—yet she asks Mara to suspend the need for now to have insight. Slumped in her chair, Mara cries silently. Belle hands her a Kleenex and puts her hand on her arm. As a multiculturally competent therapist in advanced practice, Belle does not divert her gaze as Mara cries so hard that she chokes and hyperventilates. Belle is unafraid of Mara's emotion—she is able to sit calmly in the presence of it without fearing that she will be overwhelmed or stuck. Belle mines her own racial identity in her work with Mara as well as her emotions while respecting Mara's collectivistic worldview (Sanchez & Davis, 2010). Belle feels compassion and empathy for Mara. In subsequent sessions, Belle, feeling saddened by Mara's story, cries with Mara. While our profession does not require us to be robotic, Belle knows that her tears are not incapacitating and do not render her ineffective. Showing compassion is different from losing professional objectivity.

A theme that has emerged with clients in therapy is that psychologists and counselors should explain to clients that therapy is a place where painful experiences are discussed and that they, the clinicians, do not need to be protected (Levitt et al., 2006). In addition to creating a safe place for Mara, Belle encourages her to find a good lawyer who can help her with legal aspects of her situation, particularly if Jim knew that he was HIV positive and knowingly had unprotected sex with Mara. At some future point, a support group may also be helpful to lessen feelings of isolation and shame. Currently, Mara is too embarrassed of her medical status. After a few sessions, Belle brings to Mara's attention that Mara wanted Jim to protect her and keep her safe. Mara discussed her own childhood with a father who died when Mara was 10—Mara's hunger to be protected and taken care of contributed to her selflessness. Initially, Mara denies Belle's observation and interpretation but in time is able to reflect on and relate to Belle's words. Discourses to which Mara has close proximity include these: "A good man will take care of you and keep you safe"; "If you ask for your needs to be met, your man will become uncomfortable and leave"; "Silence is better/safer and everything will somehow work out on its own." Belle asks Mara for an alternative ending to her situation. Mara says that Jim marries her and together they take their medication and love each other and have very long and happy lives.

Belle helps Mara confront a number of pressing issues such as the social stigma associated with HIV status. Existential concerns, such as loneliness, meaning-making, living life, and dying are on Mara's mind. Mara is in a state of mourning. With the support of her therapist, Mara is not alone in walking a path that she did not plan. After a few years, Mara is eventually able to create an alternative story, an ending where she is healthy due to her medication compliance, is in a support group with other HIV positive women, and helps other women who find themselves newly diagnosed with HIV.

Summary

The various faces of diversity were discussed in this chapter, including culture, race, ethnicity, nationality, gender, sexuality, disability, socioeconomic class, and spirituality. The multiple identities in shaping psychosocial development were highlighted. A case study was presented to illustrate the textured life of a client in crisis and the skills that a racially dissimilar therapist can use to join with clients and help alleviate their suffering.

4

❖

Identities as Status

This chapter explores identities as status. The attitudes that mental health professionals have about clients' identity constructs, particularly those that are visible, greatly impact the therapeutic event. (See Storytelling: Identities as Status.) Via the contextual and social construction of the differences model, the consequences of socially constructed identities within U.S. society are conveyed. Implications for mental health professionals and client populations are emphasized.

❖ STORYTELLING: IDENTITIES AS STATUS

I recently attended a training for mental health counselors. The trainer, a highly educated, influential, and licensed professional, related the story of an "Oriental" woman. The term, *Oriental*, is regarded as highly offensive by many people. Multicultural competence is critical for both students and seasoned professionals. One benefit is the transmission of appropriate terms so as not to insult, minimize, or perpetuate inaccurate terminology to trainees. When we call people out of their name, we render them as other, which is a lessening of people and a statement about respect.

Identities as Status: The Contextual and Social Construction of Differences Model

Seventy years ago, Hughes (1945), a sociologist, addressed dilemmas of occupational and ascribed status. He stated that occupational or vocational status has a complex set of supplementary characteristics that come to be expected of its incumbents. For example, it is anticipated that a kindergarten teacher will be a female. Such expectations are largely unconscious. People do not systematically expect that only certain people will occupy certain positions. Through a process of cultural socialization from the media, educational systems, clergy, and family, people "carry in their minds" (Hughes, 1945, p. 354) the auxiliary traits associated with most positions in society. Persons who newly occupy prestigious positions contend with ongoing suspicions from those who have historically maintained these positions and from those who have observed such people occupying these positions. President Barack Obama contends with this dynamic. Chronic suspicions regarding his U.S. citizenship and Christian religion, despite the presentation of his birth certificate, are largely race based, although some of those who question his legitimacy are likely to publicly deny their suspicions of his authenticity.

At the base of people's thinking is the perception that new incumbents are not as qualified or as worthy as those who preceded them and that their incumbency is due primarily to affirmative action or to other political processes—not a result of education, professional qualifications, hard work, or merit. As new groups occupy positions that have been held almost exclusively by one racial and/or gender group, discourses do not completely disappear. Close proximity to dominant discourses means embodying a belief that quotas, unfair and undeserving advantage, injustice, reverse racism, favoritism, and luck are responsible for occupational success among people with stigmatized identities.

In the society about which Hughes spoke, race membership was a status-determining trait. Race tended to overpower any other variable that might run counter to it, such as educational attainment, which is a component of social class. Because racism, sexism, and homophobia are interlocking systems of oppression, membership in marginalized groups is associated with stigma. *Stigma* refers to "a bodily sign designed to expose something unusual and bad about the moral status of an individual" (Rosenblum & Travis, 2006, p. 27). Hughes's decades-old observations have contemporary relevance.

The model of socially constructed and contextual discourses suggests that human characteristics operate as status variables in society. (See Table 4.1: Model of Socially Constructed and Contextual Discourses.) The model maintains that in the United States, race, gender, and class are socially constructed. From a constructionist perspective, these identities matter because society wants them to—this desire may not be right, but it is so. In both subtle and blatant ways, contextual and socially constructed discourses permit persons who hold membership in particular groups to have status within society, and this status portrays them to be different from persons who do not hold membership in these groups. This stratification of race and other identities is a social construction and not an inevitability, like the rising of the sun each day.

❖ **Table 4.1** Model of Socially Constructed and Contextual Discourses

Visible and Invisible Sources of Difference	Dominant Discourses	Consequences of Socially Constructed Meanings About Difference
Race	Whiteness is unexplored but is the basis by which people of color are evaluated.	Racism; obliviousness about one's status as a racial being, particularly among white people
Skin color	White and white-looking skin is elevated in ways that nonwhite skin is not among white and non-White people.	Colorism; internalized bias for distinct phenotypical characteristics that include lighter skin, Eurocentric facial features (e.g., aquiline nose, thin lips), and "good" hair texture
Sex	The masculine male experience is valued.	Sexism; unrealistic gender expectations for women and men; women treated with less status—paid less money
Sexuality	Heterosexuality is normalized in ways that gay, bisexual, lesbian, or transgendered experiences are not.	Homophobia; homonegativity
Ability	Physical and intellectual ability are esteemed.	Ableism; disability is regarded as imperfection
Class	Upper middle-class status is glamorized. Being working class or poor is undesirable.	Class elitism; celebrity worship
Religion	Christianity is normative and privileged.	Religious bigotry

Source: Author.

Visible and invisible identities (e.g., race, gender, sexuality, religion, ability, and disability) are not oppressive. Racism, colorism, sexism, homonegativity, able-bodyism, class elitism, and religious bigotry are oppressive and discriminatory (Robinson, 1999a, 1999b). A distinction exists between having an identity that is stigmatized (e.g., being a quadriplegic) and internalizing a sense of shame, worthlessness, inadequacy, or inferiority because one is a quadriplegic. The problem is discrimination against the disabled, not having a disability.

According to Reynolds and Pope (1991), a customary norm by which people are evaluated in the United States is based on proximity to being American. A discourse associated with being American is associated with whiteness. Maleness, gender-conforming femininity, upper middle-class status, Christianity, heterosexuality, English speaking, youthfulness, and cognitive/psychological/physical ability have been constructed to mean normativity. Economic exploitation, religious bias, homophobia, racism, able-bodyism, disdain for persons with substance use and mental illness diagnoses are among the sources of discrimination that emanate from this narrow and limiting construction of normalcy. The "other" refers to persons who not only are regarded as different from the norm but also are seen as less than the norm.

Assumptions of Hierarchical Socialization Patterns

The model of socially constructed and contextual discourses presents differences as social constructions. The consequences of these social constructions are also detailed.

Differences between and among people possess rank, have value, and function as primary status-determining traits. Characteristics perceived as normal are thought to be desired by and representative of all. For instance, students often have a difficult time understanding why a woman with a disability would not want to be able-bodied. "Wouldn't her life be easier not having to deal with a scooter, walker, or wheelchair?" Characteristics with less rank (such as being an older or large bodied woman, or a short man) are held in lower esteem, not regarded as desirable, and have less social power (unless wealth, for example, is on board which may trump characteristics deemed to have less social capital). Within this hierarchical framework, the most valued aspect of a person is not an achieved or acquired trait, such as compassion for others, kindness, honesty, or being teachable, but an immutable quality, such as white skin.

Although human beings are more similar than they are different and share 99.9% DNA irrespective of skin color, hair texture, and size of one's nose, a hierarchical framework, where differences have rank, inflates and distorts differences among people. In contrast, a system that honors our humanity deems people as worthy because they are alive and exist with "unique expressions of spiritual energy" (Myers et al., 1991, p. 56).

Racism

Racism involves a total social structure in which one group has conferred advantage over another group through institutional policies. *Racism* is a social construction based on sociopolitical attitudes that demean specific racial characteristics and uses superiority as an answer to discomfort about difference (Pinderhuges, 1989). Pinderhuges (1989) said, "Belief in the superiority of Whites and the inferiority of people-of-color based on racial difference is legitimized by societal arrangements that exclude the latter from resources and power and then blame them for their failures, which are due to lack of access" (p. 89).

Discussing racism is unsettling and dissonance provoking. White people are often reluctant to engage in dialogue about the realities of racism. Racism is a major part of this country's origins, but other terms have been used instead of racism, such as *manifest destiny, progress, discovery, innovation, entrepreneurial,* or *ambition.* Being committed to the process of transformation and social justice means interrogating sanitized histories. Ambition and racial exploitation should not be confused. For example, Christopher Columbus was an ambitious explorer. He also ruthlessly exploited the Arawaks.

It has been said that America was built by taking land from a people and people from a land. Racially discriminatory practices were in progress when Africans built the infrastructure for major cities in the South and were not financially remunerated. White Americans perceived themselves as superior to Native Americans when, for centuries, they stole (there is no more appropriate term) the Native Americans' lands and sought to destroy their way of life. Americans behaved in a racist manner when scores of first- and second-generation Japanese Americans were interned during World War II. Small numbers of German and Italian Americans were interned also, but not to the same extent as were the Japanese. A racist ideology existed when the Southwest, which was once Mexico, was ceded to the United States by the Treaty of Guadalupe Hidalgo in 1848. People of Hispanic ancestry became foreigners in their native land that they had inhabited for centuries. A racist ideology existed when laws such as the 1882 Exclusion Act restricted Chinese from this country while white-skinned European immigrants flooded into America. Racism was practiced when the 1790 Naturalization Law was in effect for 162 years; this policy reserved naturalized citizenship for whites only (Avakian, 2002). While trying to save their lives and the lives of their children amidst mounting Nazi hatred, countless Jews were denied entry into European countries and into the United States. There were acts of violence in countries we occupied, where children—who should never be held responsible for the actions and choices of adults—are vulnerable and live in fear. At various junctures in U.S. history, laws forbade black and white people from marrying and women across racial groups and men of color from voting or becoming literate. Such policies attested to the institutionalization of racism and sexism as blatant devaluations of women and nonwhite people. "The rationale of segregation implies that the 'others' are a pariah people. Unclean was the caste message of every colored water fountain, waiting room, and courtroom Bible" (Loewen, 1995, p. 163).

Racist attitudes portrayed in sentiments against racial intermixing were not simply between races but within ethnic groups as well. In the Nazi publication *Neues Volk,* it was written, "Every German and every German woman has the duty to avoid association with other races, especially Slavs. Each intimacy with a people of inferior race means sinning against the future of our own people" (as cited in Rogers, 1967, p. 19).

Scientific notions about intelligence were developed against a biological and sociopolitical backdrop of racism. The information that is presented below is admittedly dated and yet undergird some prevailing beliefs about the intellectual superiority of white people compared to black people. In *The Bell Curve,* Herrnstein and Murray (1994) examined ethnic differences on intelligence tests. They concluded that "for every known test of cognitive ability that meets basic psychometric standards of reliability and validity, Blacks and Whites score differently" (p. 276). These authors indicated that the differences are reduced once the testing is done outside the South, after age six, and after 1940. Herrnstein and Murray argued that even once socioeconomic differences are controlled for, the differences do not disappear, but class may reduce the overall differences in intelligence testing by about one third.

Grubb (1992) investigated the claim that blacks are genetically inferior to whites on intelligence testing. As a clinical psychologist specializing in the treatment of childhood and adolescent disorders, he examined 6,742 persons with developmental disabilities from three western states. If this argument, that blacks were genetically inferior to whites was true, then he could expect to see a higher proportion of blacks identified as having intellectual delays in comparison with whites. Grubb found that, of the total population included in this project, 0.03% had developmental disabilities. This figure was consistent across racial groups. He concluded that the assumptions regarding heredity among the black race were not upheld in this study, leading him to reject this line of reasoning.

Nisbett (1995) also challenged Herrnstein and Murray (1994). Nisbett argued that comparing high socioeconomic status blacks with high socioeconomic status whites is inherently flawed, given the higher, more stable, and often inherited income levels of whites in comparison with blacks. In addition, Nisbett stated that socialization and social factors affect ability levels and that "g-loaded" (g refers to general intelligence) tests differed between the races, with whites having faster reaction times on complex maneuvers, had been subjectively interpreted. According to Nisbett (1995), "For skills such as spatial reasoning and form perception, the g-loading was relatively low and B/W gap relatively low" (p. 44).

Slavery was a legal institution steeped in dysfunction. There were two forms of psychopathology that were common among slaves. The first, *drapetomania,* consisted of the single symptom of slaves running away. The second, *dysathesia aethiopica,* consisted of numerous conditions such as destroying plantation property, showing defiance, and attacking slave masters. This second condition was also known as "rascality," and both were labeled as nerve disorders by reputable physicians (Bronstein & Quina, 1988).

Explicit in America's charter are liberty and the pursuit of happiness; however, black people's quest for these entitlements during slavery was regarded as pathological. Although black people took care of white people, they were depicted as childlike, incapable of providing for themselves, and dependent upon their benevolent white masters. Clinicians of the day interpreted 1840 census data that reported higher rates of psychopathology among black people to support the belief that "the care, supervision, and control provided by slavery were essential to the mental health of blacks" (Bronstein & Quina, 1988, p. 39). This paradigm supported a false belief that blacks were not only different but also inferior. It was not possible to receive an accurate diagnosis when the psychological community perceived black people to be chattel and inherently flawed. Thus, the current distrust of the mental health community in many communities of color cannot be adequately appreciated without an understanding of this history.

Consequences of Racism for European Americans. Racism, patriarchy, and classism are interlocking systems of both oppression and privilege (Landry, 2007). They operate in tandem with privilege and/or disadvantage people based on their location to immutable characteristics (race and sex). There are consequences of racism for people of color (e.g., stress, high blood pressure, disparities in access to health care) and consequences of racism for white people (Pinderhughes, 1989). It is inaccurate to conclude that white people are not affected by racism. How can there not be consequences, given the pernicious nature of racism that affects all people?

Due to the social construction of whiteness in American society, white people lack understanding about the effects and consequences of race and racism on their own lives, due largely to "race" typically referring to nonwhite people. Not having an identity as a racial being contributes to misperceptions among whites about the reality of racism, racial inequities, and discrimination against people of color. Although white and black Americans believe there is equity for blacks and whites in this country and that blacks are as well off as whites in terms of jobs, incomes, health care, and schooling, white people maintain this belief more than black people (Institute of Medicine, 2003). (See Storytelling: It Had To Be You.)

One way to facilitate a discussion of racism is through an examination of unearned white skin color privilege. McIntosh (1989) maintained that privilege is an invisible knapsack of assets that an entitled group can refer to on a regular basis to negotiate their daily lives more effectively. Unearned skin-color privilege is a fugitive (McIntosh, 1989) subject for two reasons. First, privilege is not something people are meant to be oblivious of and second, nonwhites do not share in the privileges white people tend to take for granted but did not earn. Unpacking privilege produces dissonance among many white people because it assails fundamental Western beliefs of meritocracy and justice while creating confusion about the meaning of being qualified and successful.

One consequence of racism for European Americans is that it limits emotional and intellectual development (Pinderhughes, 1989). Zetzer (2005) discussed her desire not to be a WMWP, or a well-meaning white person—defined as a white person who does not understand the social construction of race, the impact of daily racism on people of color, and their role in the perpetuation of inequality.

❖ **STORYTELLING: IT HAD TO BE YOU**

A black woman was at a park near her home. She sat as her preschool age child played in the busy playground with other children. The woman soon learned that one of the mothers in the park could not locate her cell phone. The woman was asked if she had seen the lost phone. She replied that she had not. She was asked this question repeatedly by the friends of the woman who could not locate her cell phone. The black woman soon realized that the inquiries were not questions but accusations: They thought that she had stolen the phone. Afraid for her and her young child's safety, the woman scooped up her daughter and proceeded quickly to her car. The woman of the lost phone and her friends began following the woman and her daughter, accusing her of stealing the phone. One of them said, "Use my phone to call your number—when it rings, we'll *know* she has it." The number of the lost/stolen cell phone was dialed and its little tune was heard—from the pocket of its owner. No apologies were offered to the black woman and to her daughter who lived in the predominantly white neighborhood. Due to discourses about blackness, the woman, a tenured college professor, was perceived to be guilty of theft.

A growing area of research deals with whiteness and the psychosocial costs of racism to whites. Spanierman, Poteat, Beer, and Armstrong (2007) conducted research with 230 white undergraduate students using the Psychosocial Costs of Racism to Whites (PCRW) scale, with three subscales:

1. White Empathic Reactions Toward Racism, such as sadness and anger

2. White Guilt

3. White Fear of Others

Five distinct cluster groups were also identified:

A. Unempathic and unaware

B. Empathic but unaccountable

C. Informed empathy and guilt

D. Fearful guilt

E. Insensitive and afraid

Spanierman et al. (2007) regard cluster C at the most desirable because participants had the greatest levels of racial awareness (lowest scores on color-blind measures from Neville, Lilly, Duran, Lee, & Browne, 2000, the Color Blind Racial Attitude Scale), which was interpreted to reflect an understanding of institutionalized racism. Furthermore, these researchers see guilt as "not necessarily undesirable" (p. 439). Accountable guilt coexists with empathy and might predict antiracist activism. Later, Spanierman,

Todd, and Anderson (2009) conducted research with 287 white University freshmen. They found that appreciation of diversity and a critical consciousness of white privilege were both important for understanding the psychosocial cost of racism to whites. Diversity appreciation was associated with more desirable PCRW types whereas being unaware of racial privilege was linked to types considered to be less desirable.

The consequences of racism and white skin color privilege may be invisible to white people. Two conditions might intensify obliviousness to unearned privilege. First, there is a lack of awareness about the circumstances that entitle groups to privileges. Second, people have difficulty grasping that others who do not share immutable group membership also do not share privileges. How does obliviousness of skin color privilege impact mental health professionals? Nonseeing can translate into reduced empathy during the therapeutic encounter and within educational and training contexts. Mental health professionals may reveal limitations in their knowledge of systems when they are unable to empathize with others given that empathy and nonjudgment are fundamental tools in counseling.

Each of us has membership in groups that we have chosen: the gym, professional organizations, social media outlets, and so on. Each of us also has group memberships that are not chosen but are nonetheless desired (e.g., being among those who are seeing and hearing). Social justice recognizes that people choose how to respond to earned and unearned privileges and are able to use their privilege in its various forms to address disparities.

McIntosh (1989) identified several privileges that enabled her to negotiate her, a white woman, daily existence more effectively. She could choose not to teach her children about race or racism if doing so would cause them some discomfort. The growing numbers of white women who are mothering nonwhite children are finding that this privilege of not addressing race may support a colorblind orientation not afforded to their children (Robinson-Wood, 2015). She could move to almost any neighborhood, confident that she would be treated well and welcomed (e.g., low-wage earning white people do not have this class privilege). She also knew that her children would be given school curricular materials that testified to the existence of their race.

Clearly there are benefits of privilege, but its absence does not mean a lesser life characterized by unhappiness and an internalized sense of inadequacy. This point is illuminated in the 2001 film *Honey for Ochun* (Lago & Solás, 2001). The primary character is a Cuban man whose father lied to him throughout his child, telling him that his birth mother had abandoned him when he was a child. In truth, the father removed the boy from Cuba and took him to Florida. Years later, the child grew into a man and returned to Cuba in search of his mother, a dark-skinned Cuban woman who is portrayed in the movie as having lower class status. The colorism and classism are evident in the film. The son's persistence is rewarded as he finds his mother in a remote part of Cuba, off of a little lake. The mother knew she had not abandoned her son and believed that she would see him again. Despite the sexism, colorism, and class elitism, the mother resisted internalizing herself as inferior. Here, resistance refers to recognizing demeaning messages and replacing them with empowering messages.

Patriarchy

Patriarchy comes from a hegemonic or a ruling ideology (Rosenblum & Travis, 2006), wherein men have advantage conferred on them because of their prescribed rank or societal status. During the more than three decades of the women's movement, there have been increases in the college attainment rates of women and dramatic increases among women in the workforce. In fact, women under 25 are on par with men in labor participation. Amid these and other advances, gender and racial inequity continues. In the United States, the earnings differences between women and men were widest for whites and for Asians. Asian women and men, in 2010, earned more than whites, blacks, and Latinos. White women earned 88% as much as Asians, while black and Latino women earned 77% and 66%, respectively. In comparison, white men earned 91% as much as Asian men whereas black men earned 68% as much and Latino men earned 60%.

Patriarchy is intertwined with power and privilege. The ascribed status of sex is elevated as a primary status trait over achieved statuses. Biological sex is not chosen but is an extremely powerful determinant of how people have been and continue to be treated. Both women and men are necessary for society's maintenance, yet through an elaborate gender socialization process, expectations and behaviors are disseminated and internalized. These socialization practices, both blatant and subtle, maintain a system not only in the United States but also in other countries throughout the world, where women are not as advantaged because of their less prominent status as females. Haider (1995) viewed this phenomenon globally and historically:

> In many cultures, the notion of male dominance—of man as woman's "god," protector and provider—and the notion of women as passive, submissive, and chaste have been the predominant images for centuries. In many cases, customary practices have been based on a pecking order that has not always been conducive to the well-being and personal development of those lower down the status line (p. 53).

One consequence of patriarchy for men is that it contributes to a skewed emotional existence. Difficulty with experiencing and expressing a full range of emotions, such as fear, vulnerability, and uncertainty, is an outcome of patriarchy and a dichotomizing and polarizing system. Patriarchy is a system of wide-scale inequity to which many people, including women, are oblivious.

Given the potential disadvantages of patriarchy for men, are there possible benefits of patriarchy for women? Patriarchy has its genesis in injustice. If any benefits of patriarchy result for women, they are temporary and elusive, primarily because the benefits would be dictated by women's adherence to the parameters of patriarchy and their compliance with prescribed gender roles. Does equality for women apply primarily to those women who subscribe to at least some but not to too many of the characteristics associated with masculinity (e.g., self-sufficiency, assertiveness, competition)? According to Bem (1993), any such benefits accorded to women are most likely a by-product of androcentrism, or male-centeredness, in which the male standard prevails.

In American society, men generally benefit over women. Male privileges do not bestow power on all men, but they ultimately deny women, particularly women who have less proximity to privileged men. One benefit of the men's movement is that it has called attention to the myth that women's powerlessness translates into men's power. Individual men may feel powerful, but not all men do. Swanson (1993) recognized this phenomenon as the "new sexism" and noted, "Some men, rather than feeling like patriarchs, often feel like workhorses, harnessed with the burden of being family provider, trying to pull the family wagon up a muddy hill of financial debt" (p. 12). Men are conditioned to be providers, protectors, and ready for combat, yet they experience pressure from women to be nurturing, soft, and intimate (Skovholt, 1993). These messages are conflicting. Part of being a protector is not asking for help or appearing to be vulnerable, which is what intimacy and nurturance entail.

Many white men, men of color, or poor, disabled, elderly, and/or gay men do not share the same privileges that some economically privileged, able-bodied, and/or heterosexual men do. Thus, all men do not perceive a sense of personal power in that they do not possess crucial markers that society deems normative and valued. The presence of these critical markers does not ensure that individual men will automatically feel powerful. Because of the underlying assumption that persons who share gender are monolithic, use of the phrase "men in general" is problematic (Carrigan, Connell, & Lee, 1987). Making inappropriate attributions regarding clients' identity constructs is called a *miss*.

Sexism

The women's movement challenged many traditional stereotypes about women, their work, and their place in society. That women wanted equal pay for equal work, respect in a society that too often reduced them to sexual objects, and denied them choice about their bodies and minds was the message echoed across numerous platforms. Women were encouraged to consider seriously the socialization experiences that contributed to their reliance on others for their emotional and financial well-being. *Sexism*, an institutionalized system of inequality based on biological sex, was brought to the nation's attention. (See Storytelling: Colonizing Discourses.) Another identity construct that can mitigate the privileges that certain groups have is sexuality. Some of the privilege associated with maleness has a qualifier of heterosexuality. Despite its association with less privilege, that is, in certain contexts, being gay does not cancel privileges associated with being male or being white. Within a society where white skin is associated with unearned privilege, gay white men mediate the effects of homophobia with their white skin. Gay men of color receive male privilege yet contend with both racism and homophobia (Loiacano, 1989).

Consequences of Sexism for Men. Racism contributes to a dehumanizing stance and limits human development for people, regardless of their race and ethnicity (Pinderhughes, 1989). Sexism also adversely affects all people, men and transgender people included. The male gender role often results in men being restricted in their emotional expressiveness and promotes a limited range of behaviors available to them. "Restrictive emotionality involves the reluctance and/or difficulty men have in expressing their feelings to other people and may be related to their hesitancy to seek help from others"

(Good, Dell, & Mintz, 1989, p. 295). Men are gendered and influenced by rigid and sexist discourses. As such, they are oriented toward success, competition, and the need to be in control (Robinson, 1999a). The danger in the male role is that it has been connected to "Type A" behavior patterns and to depression (Good & Mintz, 1990).

Homophobia emanates from the perception of homosexuality as an aberration of the correct social order. Discourses about gay people are that they are promiscuous, can be marked (e.g., read) according to mannerisms and dress, and may be untrustworthy around young children, due to a perception of aberrant sexual proclivities.

Consequences of Homophobia for Heterosexuals. Men who engage in behaviors deemed "feminine" are suspected of being gay by other men and by women as well. One of the teachings of traditional masculinity is that it is incongruent with femininity. Heterosexual men may feel real fear in expressing emotional or physical affection with another man because of connotations of homosexuality. This concern may explain why upon greeting one another, American men engage in roughhousing, evidenced by vigorous slaps on the back. Such behavior, however, is culturally dictated. In Ghana or in Egypt, for example, it is quite natural to see men holding hands while walking together. European men are often more demonstrative in their affectionate behavior with one another. Cultural expressions of affection and endearment support behavior, yet in the United States, similar behavior might be interpreted among some as suggestive of homosexuality.

Homophobia also interferes with the formation of cross-sexual orientation friendships out of fear that such interaction and proximity would be misinterpreted by others. In this context, heterosexual mental health professionals, may be inhibited in their ability to be allies to lesbian, gay, bisexual, transgender, intersexual, and questioning (LGBTIQ) clients.

❖ STORYTELLING: COLONIZING DISCOURSES

A young woman was at the hairdresser. She and her stylist were talking about an African American pop singer. The stylist, also a young woman in her 20s, said, "She's pretty for a colored girl." The year was 2011, and the young woman who was having her hair done was shocked that this type of statement was made by a millennial well into the 21st century. She was also surprised that the stylist used language that had not been used in over half a century to refer to African Americans.

Able-Bodyism

People with disabilities have a long history of being discriminated against. An understanding of this type of discrimination is enhanced by an assessment of the "mastery-over-fate" orientation descriptive of American society. The U.S. culture places inordinate emphasis on youth and fitness and demonstrates a marked preoccupation with the body beautiful. A disability is seen as an imperfection, which is contrary to the culturally sanctioned values of control and domination.

Smart and Smart (2006) argue that the conceptualization of disability as "an attribute located solely within an individual is changing to a paradigm in which disability is thought to be an interaction among the individual, the disability, and the environment (both social and physical)" (p. 29). Despite this observation, a clear bias in favor of the able-bodied exists. Because most buildings have been constructed for able-bodied persons, persons without disabilities are often oblivious to their unearned privileges. How much thought do able-bodied people give to the accessibility of a house or other buildings? Having disabled friends or family in our lives with a temporary disability (e.g., after foot surgery) or negotiating sidewalks, narrow aisles, and closed doors with children in strollers increases awareness.

Architectural space and design are outgrowths of cultural attitudes and assumptions that are biased against the elderly and persons, in particular, women with disabilities. As Weisman (1992) pointed out, "Placement in barrier-free housing and rehabilitation services favors men . . . Disabled women are not usually thought of as wives and mothers who often manage households with children and husbands. The wheelchair-accessible two- and three-bedroom unit is a rarity" (p. 118).

The myth that people with disabilities are childlike, dependent, and depressed contributes to ignorance from the larger society and denial about the fact that, at any time, able-bodied people can and probably will become disabled if they live long enough. Multiculturally competent professionals have the ability to regard clients with disabilities as whole human beings wherein the disability is understood as a component of identity and not the entire focus of the counseling event or an exhaustive account of the client's essence (Fowler, O'Rourke, Wadsworth, & Harper, 1992). Facility at holding the client's multiple spiritual, occupational, sexual, and social identities is commentary about the professional's multicultural competence across knowledge, skill, and attitudes.

Consequences of Able-Bodyism Among the Able-Bodied. Society was created for persons who are able-bodied. Our society of concrete sidewalks and curbs is uninviting to persons with temporary and permanent disabilities. Discourses abound regarding people with disabilities. One of the most pernicious is that persons with disabilities desire to be able-bodied. This mistaken belief is similar to the belief that people of color desire to be white or that women desire to be men. Equating the experience of having a disability with living a lesser life is problematic for two reasons in diversity mental health practice. First, such an attitude does not embody the spirit of multicultural competence where differences are embraced. Second, this attitude is psychologically restrictive for able-bodied persons. Clearly, having a disability in an able-bodied world can deflate a sense of self and depress self-esteem (Livneh & Sherwood, 1991), yet this is not the experience of all persons with disabilities.

Class Elitism

Much of the formal training counselors receive in traditional counselor education programs emanates from a middle-class bias. This bias is characterized by emphasis on meritocracy, the Protestant work ethic, Standard English, and 50-minute sessions (Sue & Sue, 1990). The difficulty with this type of partiality is that it can alienate mental health professionals from low-income clients. Liu, Corkery, and Thome (2010) discuss social class and classism training in psychology and provide competency benchmark tables relevant to social class. There is acknowledgment that no mental health professional will have complete knowledge of the entire rage of economic cultures among their patients, but they state that it is "incumbent upon the professionals to remain curious about the social class-related expectations and experiences of their clients" (Liu et al., 2010, p. 368). Persons who have limited access to material wealth in a materialistic culture are not perceived as being as viable as those with greater resources. Within our capitalistic culture, a dangerously close relationship exists between self-worth and income. Low-income people, regardless of their work ethic, tend to be perceived as lazy and even immoral (Gans, 1992). Conversely, the rich are esteemed and admired, often independent of their moral or immoral conduct. The relationship between class and power is dubious. Low-income status is not valued by a consumeristic society; having membership in this devalued group can provoke feelings of powerlessness and depression (Pinderhughes, 1989).

Consequences of Class Elitism. Because socioeconomic class converges with gender, race, ability, and personal power, as well as with other identity constructs, it is simplistic to conclude that being able-bodied or male or having a high income is automatically associated with feelings of safety and security or a lesser tendency toward depression and less pain. (See Storytelling: Not Worth More.) It is also faulty to assume that having membership in groups deemed by society to be high status is related to feeling more powerful.

❖ STORYTELLING: NOT WORTH MORE

I was speaking with my 26-year-old babysitter who was also dog sitting and had several babysitting jobs in order to raise money for graduate school that would start in a few months. She told me of an opportunity to puppy-sit over a 24-hour period. I asked her how much money she was going to be making. She said she did not know. I suggested that she contact the owner of the puppy and ask. Not to do so was to depend on the pet owner's good graces as opposed to stating up front what she wanted to earn. We spoke about the difficulty women often have negotiating for pay in contrast with men, who engage in this practice quite frequently. I told her that some people will take advantage of women by paying them much less than what they would pay a man. My sitter called the woman and said that she wanted $5 an hour for the 24-hour period. The puppy had a special dog food that needed to be administered by hand and the puppy had to be let out twice nightly to go potty. The puppy's owner initially agreed but a few minutes later called back and told my sitter that she was asking for too much money. Instead she wanted to offer $50 for the entire 24-hour period, or about $2 an hour. The young woman decided to just stay about 4 hours with the dog, earning $5 an hour (that is all the owners would offer and the young woman needed the $20). She could not believe how little the owner wanted to pay her. She said that she felt proud of herself for asking for what she wanted and would approach future jobs by clearly stating her salary requirements up front.

Ageism

Ageism refers to discrimination against people because of their age. This discrimination is often aimed at the middle aged or the elderly. Ageist terms vary and include primarily negative expressions. Examples are *crotchety, fuddy-duddy, fart, senility, golden-ager, graybeard* (Nuessel, 1982). Atkinson and Hackett (1995) stated that "delineating the elderly as being 65 and over is a purely arbitrary separation" (p. 192). This boundary's genesis is the decades-old Social Security system, which was instituted in 1935, when people did not live as long as they now do.

Ageism is compounded with other layers of discrimination. Until very recently, limited attention had been devoted to the study of breast cancer. On the surface, this lack of focus could be attributed to sexism; however, ageism is also at fault. Does the fact that the majority of women survivors of breast cancer are not in their 20s or 30s but rather in their 40s and 50s contribute to the limited (but growing) research on this disease? Is there a different consequence for a middle-aged woman who is no longer viewed as having or needing beauty?

People, according to their age ought not to be treated as monoliths. Doing so greatly impedes the delivery of effective services. Differences exist between a 65-year-old healthy person and a 90-year-old whose health has begun to decline. Atkinson and Hackett (1995) described the "young-old" and the "old-old" (p. 14). The young-old are in fairly good health with stable financial supports. The old-old may be experiencing deficits in several cognitive, medical, social, and financial resources.

Mental health professionals need to be mindful of the social supports available to elders. Solid social supports with both friends and family can help elders to feel less dependent on others. Part of a professional's assessment should include an examination of an elder's level of involvement in meaningful and purposeful social activity. The elder's sense of personal autonomy or control over life is also an important component of overall wellness. Some illnesses, such as Alzheimer's disease, will require working in sync with other caregivers and integrated levels of support to maximize the quality of living during a stressful and potentially chaotic time.

Age biases contribute to some clinicians seeing little merit in providing psychotherapy to aging persons. For example, one weakness of psychoanalytic theory is that it is not generally regarded as viable when started with persons age 50 or older or for low-wage-earning people who cannot afford analysis several times weekly. Identifying a client's strengths, regardless of the presenting problem, is a crucial step in facilitating growth or bolstering coping abilities.

There is also discrimination against the young, discrimination that occurs with newly minted professionals who are in their early 20s and look it. Older patients may assume that such a young person knows nothing of their life experiences. Young professionals are encouraged to appreciate the need that patients have to be adequately and competently cared for and to show commitment, as opposed to defensiveness, to providing services to patients across the developmental spectrum.

Consequences of Ageism for the Nonelderly. Unlike most traditional cultures in which the elderly tend to be respected and valued, in the U.S. culture, inordinate emphasis is placed on youthfulness. The societal significance attached to doing, productivity, and maintaining mastery over nature may explain this cultural preoccupation with youth and the herculean effort to defy and in some instances, deny or defeat aging. Aging appears to be viewed as a loss of control and of diminishing power and beauty. Discrimination against a segment of the population that is composing a higher percentage of the total and of which all will be members, if they are fortunate, culminates in fear-based discourses about the experience of being an elder. It is heartening to see how a culture of menopausal women is redefining hot flashes as power surges and recognizing the "change" in life as a time of ascendancy and coming into one's own.

Implications for Mental Health Professionals

Not acknowledging the meaning of race, as a social construction, can restrict the development of a racial self. This lack of clarity about a core identity construct adversely affects clinicians' empathy toward their clients. Mental health professionals are encouraged to ascertain whether they are able to work effectively with a variety of clients. (See Case Study: The Difference Class Makes.) Despite an espoused value of diversity, American society socializes people into attitudes that are not honoring of difference. Professionals need to recognize these and other biases within themselves and not allow shame or guilt to fan denial. The process of unlearning these attitudes is ongoing yet possible and reflective of cultural competence.

Although professionals have an ethical obligation to refer clients to other professionals when they are unable to provide necessary assistance, the counselor who is judgmental of a white woman involved in an interracial relationship needs to be concerned if intolerance in one area of her life extends to other persons who, for example, do not support her political ideology.

Case Study

The Difference Class Makes

Ms. Mary Cain is a 47-year-old unmarried white woman who resides in Massachusetts and lives in subsidized housing. She has a history of drug use but has been sober for a few years. Her 31-year-old daughter Ruby resides with her but was recently arrested for her fourth driving under the influence (DUI) and writing bad checks. Ruby does not work and abuses alcohol. Ruby's two teenage daughters, ages 14 and 16, reside in the home with their mother and grandmother. The 16-year-old has a 2-year-old daughter, and the 14-year-old is pregnant. Ms. Cain was referred to a mental health agency by her doctor after he noticed her weight loss, insomnia, and other depressive symptoms. Ms. Cain arrived at her counseling appointment 20 minutes late with her 2-year-old great granddaughter. She travels to counseling via public transportation. She missed the first two counseling sessions she had scheduled with Julie. The agency's policy does not charge a late fee to patients who receive the state's free behavioral health care (i.e., MassHealth). The therapist, Julie, is a 28-year-old Mexican PhD student in clinical psychology. Julie was raised in a working class family that worked very hard and lived from paycheck to paycheck. Both of her parents are certified nursing assistants at a retirement facility. Upon meeting Ms. Cain, Julie warmly refers to her as Mary. After the initial intake questions were asked and answered, Julie asked Mary if she was losing weight because she was depressed about her daughter's unemployment and addiction, as well as her grandchildren having children at such young ages. Ms. Cain responded, "I like a big family and my grandchildren are a blessing to me. I've lost my teeth, but I want to eat. What I need is a dentist, but I don't have dental insurance." Ms. Cain has almost no teeth remaining. Julie asked, "Your place of employment does not provide dental insurance?" Ms. Cain replied, "I get public assistance and disability. With it, I take good care of my family." Julie suggested that Mary reduce her sugar intake and buy Ensure drinks so that she could receive nutrition in liquid form. Julie observes that Mary's great grandchild is obese and has decaying teeth. Ms. Cain said affectionately, "She loves her bottle of fruit punch and macaroni sandwiches at night-night." Later, Julie tells her supervisor during supervision that she feels ineffective with this population and does not want to work with them once she is done with practicum. When asked why, she said they have so many problems and they continue to make choices that worsen their situations. Really, what are they trying to do to help themselves? And when they don't show up, that's my time wasted and the agency won't even bill her for missing a session. I swear, I will only see patients with private insurance once I'm licensed."

Questions

1. Why is Julie so reluctant to work with Ms. Cain and other poor people?

2. What are dominant discourses concerning people who are poor that contribute to Julie's desire not to work with the poor?

3. Do multicultural competencies address Julie's disdain for working with the poor?

4. If Julie chose to work in a private agency where clients paid out of pocket for their mental health services because they could afford it, does this mean she is not committed to social justice?

5. Would a cultural assessment be of assistance to Julie in her work with Ms. Cain?

Discussion and Integration

The Counselor, Julie

There are some discourses that Julie espouses that indicate her struggle with multicultural competency. First, Julie shows that she is having difficulty applying her knowledge of ethics or multicultural competence to practice. While she understands that inequality exists and is aware of the ethics code regarding beneficence and not discriminating against people on the basis of class, Julie is unable to reflect critically on her classism injuries—that her patient is someone she has worked very hard to not be (Liu, Corkery, & Thome, 2010).

One discourse is that in America, people have the freedom to impact their economic lives as they so choose (Robinson-Wood, 2013). Another discourse is that people have the power to change not only their own economic outlooks but also those of their children. Another discourse is that poor people are a burden, are difficult, and are not ideal patients due to the enormity of their problems. Julie believes in and values the myth of meritocracy. In her worldview, all people can achieve if they keep their noses clean, stay out of trouble, and work harder than the next person. Julie does not understand the multigenerational impact of systems on people and the psychological processes that can accompany systems, such as resignation, depression, hopelessness, or patterning one's life after other family members. Julie has knowledge of social inequalities that exist due to class, skin color, gender, body size, age, and more but has a difficult time applying this knowledge to practice. Another discourse is that people who find themselves in chronic poverty have themselves to blame for their lot in life. Julie defines life as being in control over one's fate, delaying gratification, making wise decisions, including when to bring a child into the world, daily exercise, and nutritious foods. She has little patience for people who are not on time (regardless of the reasons) and believes that having to depend on welfare is an embarrassment. Julie seems to believe that mental health is a privilege that low-income people should not have access to, and if they do have access to it, Julie is not the type of clinician to provide care. There is a fundamental lack of empathy and regard for Mary's strengths: sobriety, caring for her family, and commitment to therapy (evident through her travels to counseling via public transportation with a toddler in tow). With quality supervision, multicultural competence training, as well as wisdom gained through life experiences (e.g., sometimes a person can do all the right things and the undesirable still happens), Julie could learn to confront her biases regarding low-income people and became an effective clinician for people across class statuses. Moreover, Julie's biases may reflect unfinished business from her working-class origins.

Currently, Julie's values and attitudes do not evidence openness to interrogating her biases, and she does not have the skills to tolerate ambiguity and uncertainty (Liu et al., 2010). Although a disconcerting thought, it is possible for students to have taken the one required diversity class, even in a doctoral program, without participating in learning processes and activities that encourage exploration of class elitism, power, and privilege.

The Client, Mary

Mary typifies the chronic poor. It is possible to look at her life and say, "Well, if she would just learn a skill, she could get a decent paying job and earn an income that would get her off of welfare—doing so would help not only Mary but her children, grandchildren, and great grandchildren." Mary is actively caring for three generations of family members despite her history of substance abuse, singlehood, and poverty; she is able to love and hope despite a history of adversity and oppression.

Looking at the age of Mary's daughter, it is clear that Mary was a teenage parent like her daughter and granddaughters. Teenage parents are less likely to complete the education required to qualify for a well-paying job. They are also likely to be poor and to remain poor (The National Campaign to Prevent Teen Pregnancy, 2010). Increasingly, women and girls are represented among those incarcerated and yet, as Reid (2011) observes, policy has done little to offer hope for rehabilitation. A therapist needs to address the totality of Mary's life, not just a narrow focus on poverty, addiction, teenage pregnancy, obese children, and tooth decay. Mary needs to be seen as a client worthy of service. Instead of regarding Mary as pathetic, her commitment to a family that depends on her and her delight in her children, grandchildren, and great grandchildren is important to consider.

A cultural assessment that encourages Julie to think about the contextual issues in Mary's life would be helpful to her. Mary is the provider for her entire family, yet her resources are limited. Mary experiences class elitism in a society that blames poor people for not being better off, and if Julie is not careful, the therapeutic event is going to reproduce the dynamic of oppression that many marginalized groups endure on a daily basis (Comstock et al., 2008).

Summary

In this chapter, the presentation of human differences as status variables was explored through an examination of the contextual and social construction of differences model. Hughes's (1945) work on the dilemmas and contradictions of status was foundational to this chapter. The consequences of hierarchical socialization were presented, and the advantages of a model based on cultural pluralism were envisioned. The importance of mental health professionals recognizing systems of inequity was articulated. A case study allowed readers to synthesize the material presented.

Part II

Our People

5

People of Native American and Alaskan Native Descent

Native American and Alaskan Natives refer to people having origins in any of the original peoples of North and South America (including Central America) and who maintain tribal affiliation or community attachment (U.S. Census Bureau, 2000c). The origins of Native American and Alaskan Native people have been greatly debated.

One of the most insightful theories regarding the people who occupied the New World was proposed by Jose de Acosta, a 16th century Spanish Jesuit missionary. De Acosta was also referred to as a pioneer of the geophysical sciences or as one of the Founders of Physical Geography given his novel observations of natural phenomenon and his significant writings, including Historia Natural y Moral de las Indias (i.e., Natural and Moral History of the Indias, published in Madrid, Spain, in 1590; "Jose de Acosta," n.d.).

de Acosta theorized that North America had been settled before the birth of Christ by a group of hunters and their families, who in following large and largely extinct animal herds, passed over a land bridge or narrow strait from Asia. Although the wooly mammoth, giant short faced bear, scimitar cat, and American lion are extinct, the muskox thrives today on Seaward Island in Alaska (National Park Service, 2015).

Proponents of the land bridge theory believe that very low sea levels resulted in a partial drying of the strait and created a land bridge that allowed passage between the two continents. Temporary ice melts for several thousand years most likely created natural passageways in the ice sheets for large game and their spear-wielding human predators (Waldman, 2000). An exploration of the eastern borders of the Russian Empire was chartered by Peter the Great, Russian Czar from 1682 to 1725 who recruited Vitus Behring, a Danish navigator. The Bering land bridge was named after him. It is widely accepted that the first Americans arrived in North America by way of the Bering land bridge, or Beringia. While anthropologists agree with de Acosta's theory, the debate rages over timing issues, as to whether the first people arrived in the Americas more than or less than 15,000 years ago. DNA studies comparing Native Americans with other population groups found three distinct genetic mutations in Mongolia and Siberia, suggesting a separation as early as 30,000 years ago.

Callaway (2014) published an article in *Nature* detailing a story about the remains of a young boy, ceremonially buried 12,600 years ago in what is now known as Montana. The child, under the age of 2, has the ancestry of one of the earliest populations in the Americas, known as the Clovis culture. The boy's genome sequence revealed that Native people, who span North and South America, are all descendants from one population that trekked from Asia across the no longer in existence Bering land bridge. Than (2014) noted that this DNA was compared with other DNA, which showed that it was similar to the genomes of people living in Siberia and East Asian ancestors. The team also discovered a close genetic affinity between the boy's genetic material and those of 52 Native American tribes living in South America and Canada. Native American creation stories tell of being brought into existence by the Great Spirit or having come from the womb of Mother Earth. In writing of these origins, Gunn Allen (1994) honored Woman:

> There is a spirit that pervades everything that is capable of powerful song and radiant movement, and that moves in and out of the mind. The colors of this spirit are multitudinous, a glowing, pulsing rainbow. Old Spider Woman is one name for this quintessential spirit, and Earth Woman is another, and what they together have made is called Creation, Earth, creatures, plants, and light. (p. 13)

History

It was estimated that over 5,000 years ago, the native population was at its highest (Than, 2011). According to Russell (1994), there were approximately 1 million inhabitants within the continental United States (Russell, 1994). Upon his arrival to the new world in 1492, Christopher Columbus thought he had landed in India and thus referred to the Native people as "Indios," "Indien" or "Indianer" (Brown, 1981). According to a genetic study (Than, 2011) that used samples of ancient and modern mitochondrial DNA passed down only from mothers to daughters, the number of Native Americans quickly shrank by roughly half following European contact more than 500 years ago. It did not take long, just a few years after the arrival of Christopher Columbus in the New World, that the decimation of Native people began. This study supports historical accounts that the arrival of Europeans triggered unprecedented losses for indigenous populations across North and South America in the form of ethnic cleansing, starvation, slavery, genocide, war, and disease. Typhus, smallpox, and measles were the greatest killers (Vernon, 2002).

In 1790, the enactment of federal policies with the goal of displacing Native people began. The Bureau of Indian Affairs (BIA) was created in 1824 and is responsible for the U.S. relationship with the 566 federally recognized Native American tribes and Alaskan communities. The job of Thomas McKenney, the first director of the BIA, was to manage Native schools and administer Native trade. For many Native peoples, the BIA represented betrayal: "They made us many promises, more than I can remember, but they never kept but one; they promised to take our land, and they took it" (Brown, 1981).

America's defeat of the British during the War of 1812 had helped create a nation with little concern for European alliances. In March 10, 1821, U.S. President James Monroe appointed General Andrew Jackson as commissioner of the United States to take possession of Florida. In this role, he was given the full powers of governor. Four months later, on July 17, 1821, Spain transferred Florida to the United States (Florida Department of State, 2015). The annexation of Spanish Florida contributed to America's perception of Indians as hindrances to the expansionist interests of the millions of white European immigrants coming to America.

The Indian Removal Act of 1830 was under the leadership of Andrew Jackson, the 17th president of the United States, from 1829 to 1837. The act was intended to relocate Indians to a new Indian country, west of the Mississippi, not to include Missouri, Louisiana, or Arkansas (Hoxie, 1996; Russell, 1994). The cultural and psychological violence is evident in Jackson's Second Annual Message to Congress, given shortly after he became the president of the United States. In this message, he announced the benevolent policy of the government with respect to Native people and its aims, which was to support the millions of Europeans immigrating to the U.S. and to economically advance states. Ultimately this policy removed Native people from Mississippi, the western part of Alabama, and other southern states. Jackson said in 1830, "It gives me pleasure to announce to Congress that the benevolent policy of the Government, steadily pursued for nearly thirty years, in relation to the removal of the Indians beyond the white settlements is approaching to a happy consummation" (as cited in Library of Congress, 2015).

The policy was seen as kindly and Godly, saving Native people from themselves. Jackson said,

> By opening the whole territory between Tennessee on the north and Louisiana on the south to the settlement of the whites it will incalculably strengthen the southwestern frontier and render the adjacent States strong enough to repel future invasions without remote aid. It will relieve the whole State of Mississippi and the western part of Alabama of Indian occupancy, and enable those States to advance rapidly in population, wealth, and power. It will separate the Indians from immediate contact with settlements of whites; free them from the power of the States; enable them to pursue happiness in their own way and under their own rude institutions; will retard the progress of decay, which is lessening their numbers, and perhaps cause them gradually, under the protection of the Government and through the influence of good counsels, to cast off their savage habits and become an interesting, civilized, and Christian community. (U.S. National Archives and Records Administration, 2015)

Jackson considered this act of removal to be benevolent because the government was funding the relocation. To the Native people, it was their "trail of tears" or the westward herding of the "Five Civilized Tribes" (Cherokees, Chickasaws, Choctaws, Creeks, and Seminoles) to Oklahoma. During the cold and brutal winter, people traveled by foot, horseback, wagon, and steamboat. People were hungry, cold, and sick, and hundreds died from starvation, exhaustion, disease, exposure, and accidents (Brown, 1981; Hoxie, 1996). Although Native resistance to removal was fierce, their oppressors were opportunistic, cunning, and destructive. For example, in New Echota (present day Georgia), the capital of the Cherokee nation from 1825 until their forced removal in 1830, the Georgia militia destroyed the printing press of the *Cherokee Phoenix*, a newspaper written in the Cherokee syllabary that Sequoyah had created (Waldman, 2000).

In 1928 and prior to the beginning of the Great Depression, The "Meriam Report" was published; the government study described the intense poverty and living conditions on the reservations, including disease, morbidity rates, terrible care of children attending the Indian boarding schools, and catastrophic aftereffects of the erosion of Indian land caused by the General Allotment Act. President Franklin D. Roosevelt's New Deal policies were designed as a response and focused on relief, recovery, and reform. This context gave rise to passing of the Indian Reorganization Act (IRA) in 1934, also known as the Wheeler-Howard Act or the Indian New Deal. The IRA began a new era of federal government and tribal relations. The most important aspect of the IRA was the promotion of the exercise of tribal self-governing powers (UAF Interior Aleutians Campus, n.d.).

Another goal of the IRA was to end restrictions against Native religions. Today, the Reorganization Act remains the basis of federal legislation concerning Indian affairs. World War II ushered in a period of greater attempts by the government to integrate Native people into American society. As had been typical of the past, more sacred lands were lost during this time and cultures were destroyed. During the 1960s and 1970s, the aims of the act were reinforced by the further transfer of administrative responsibility for tribal lands to Native people. During the 1970s, many traditional Indians were arrested for possessing sacred objects such as eagle feathers or for using peyote in religious ceremonies. Protests against this interference contributed to the 1978 passage of the American Indian Religious Freedom Act. Congress concluded that Native ways of worship were an essential part of Native life and this law sought to protect and preserve such religious liberties (Hoxie, 1996).

Today, Native American and Alaskan Natives are a heterogeneous group, with 252 tribal languages and 566 federally recognized Indian tribes in the United States and in Alaska (U.S. Census Bureau, 2011). There are nearly 80,000 Alaskan Native tribal members that comprise the 229 Alaska region jurisdictions. This area stretches from Ketchikan in the Southeast Panhandle to Barrow on the Arctic Ocean and from Eagle on the Yukon Territory border to Atka in the Aleutian chain (U.S. Department of the Interior Indian Affairs, 2015).

Native American and Alaskan Native tribes have tremendous diversity in customs, language, and family structure (Hoxie, 1996). Aleut, Arapahoe, Arikara, Catawba, Central American Indian, Comanche, Colville, Cree, Crow, Erie, Eskimo, Hopi, Hupa, Inupiat, Kiowa, Lumbee, Osage, Ottawa, Menominee, Mi'kmaq, Mohave, Narragansett, Ottawa, Paiute, Pima, Potawatomi, Seminole, Seneca, Shawnee, Shoshone, Tlingit-Haida, Tununak, Ute, Wampanoag, Winnebago, Yaqui, Yup'ik, and Zuni represent only a fraction of Native American and Alaskan Native tribal groups. (See Population Box 5.1: The Largest Native American Tribal Groups).

Population Box 5.1: Largest Native American Tribal Groups

1. Cherokee: 819,105

2. Navajo: 332,129

3. Choctaw: 195,764

4. Mexican American Indian: 175,494

5. Chippewa: 170,742

6. Sioux: 170,110

7. Apache: 111,810

8. Blackfoot: 105,304

9. Creek: 88,332

10. Iroquois: 81,002

Source: Norris, Vines, and Hoeffel (2012).

Geography and Demography

In 2014, there were 6.5 million Americans who identify as American Indian, Alaskan Native, either alone or in combination with one or more other races (U.S. Census Bureau, 2015b). The nation's Native American and Alaska Native population totaled 6.5 million as of July 1, 2014, up by 93,000, or 1.4%, since July 1, 2013. The increase in numbers among Native people is a reflection of better census methods and wider acknowledgment of mixed ancestry. The 2010 Census revealed that there were 2.9 million people who indicated Native American and Alaskan Native ancestry alone, representing 0.9% of the total population (Humes, Jones, & Ramirez, 2011). Another 2.3 million people indicated American Indian/Alaskan Native with another race. Since the 2000 census, there has been an increase of 1.1 million people in the nation's American Indian and Alaska Native population. This represents an increase of 26.7% compared to a national growth rate of 9.7%.

More than half of the Native American population reported more than one race. Between 2000 and 2010, the Native American population grew 18%, from 2.5 million to 2.9 million. The majority of Native American and Alaskan Natives have mixed backgrounds as biracial and multiracial people and a variety of phenotypic characteristics are found among Native American Indians (Humes, Jones, & Ramirez, 2011).

In 2013, there were 14 states that had more than 100,000 Native Americans and Alaska Natives: California, Oklahoma, Arizona, Texas, New Mexico, Washington, New York, North Carolina, Florida, Alaska, Michigan, Oregon, Colorado, and Minnesota (U. S. Census Bureau, 2014a). California, Oklahoma, and Arizona had the highest percentages among states with the American Indian and Alaska Native population. California had the largest American Indian and Alaska Native population of any state in 2014 (1.1 million) and the largest numeric increase since 2013 (13,000). Alaska had the highest percentage (19.4%). Los Angeles had the largest American Indian and Alaska Native population of any county in 2014 (235,000), and Maricopa, Arizona, the largest numeric increase (4,700) since 2013. Shannon, South Dakota, on the Nebraska border and located within the Pine Ridge Indian Reservation had the highest percentage at 93% (U.S. Census, 2014a). (See Knowledge Check 5.1: The 14 States With More Than 100,000 Native Americans and Alaska Natives.)

Of single race Native Americans and Alaskan Natives, Alaska alone had the largest proportion at 14.3%. Wyoming and South Dakota had 3.4% and 3.2%, respectively, of Native Americans and Alaskan Natives in their populations. All other states combined represented 34% of the Native American and Alaskan Native population (U.S. Census, 2014a).

In 2010, there were 557,185 American Indian and Alaska Native families. Of these, 57% percent were married-couple families, including those with children. The average age of marriage for Native American and Alaskan Native woman was 26.8, and for men, it was 29.6. These data are not significantly different from the general population. In 2004, the greatest percentage of Native American and Alaskan Native adults were married, at 40.1% percent (U.S. Census Bureau, 2011).

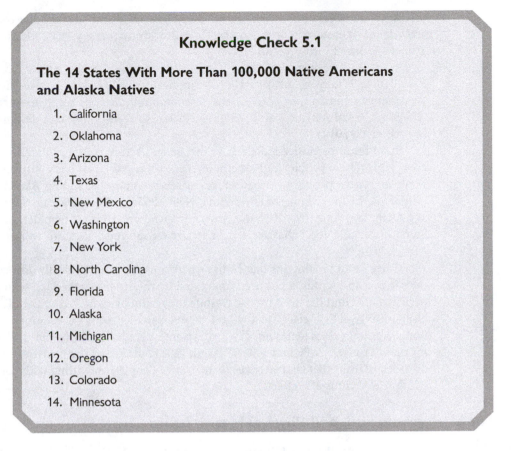

Knowledge Check 5.1

The 14 States With More Than 100,000 Native Americans and Alaska Natives

1. California
2. Oklahoma
3. Arizona
4. Texas
5. New Mexico
6. Washington
7. New York
8. North Carolina
9. Florida
10. Alaska
11. Michigan
12. Oregon
13. Colorado
14. Minnesota

Overall, about 68% of Native Americans and Alaskan Natives live in family households. Twenty percent of these families are maintained by a woman only with no husband present, and 7% were male only with no wife present. Nonfamily households comprised 31.8% (U. S. Census Bureau, 2014a). A *nonfamily household* is defined as people who live alone or people living with unrelated individuals.

Similar to blacks, Native American and Alaskan Natives are also more likely than non-Hispanic whites to live with and care for grandchildren. About 7% of Native American and Alaskan Natives aged 30 and older were grandparents living in the same household with their co-resident grandchildren under the age of 18. More than half of grandparents (58%) were also responsible for the care of their grandchildren. With respect to the age distribution of American Indian and Alaska Native alone-or-in combination population, nearly 65% are 16 to 64 years of age; 28% are under the age of 16, and 7% are over 64 (U.S. Census Bureau, 2011).

About 75% of Native Americans and Alaskan Natives aged 5 and older spoke only English at home, compared with 94% among non-Hispanic whites. Roughly 28% of Native Americans and Alaskan Natives spoke a language other than English at home (U.S. Census Bureau, 2011). The speakers of Inuit-Yupik-Aleut languages are primarily members of First Nations in North America. Some speakers live on the coast and islands of eastern Siberia, Russia. There are approximately 90,000 Inuit, Aleut, or Yup'ik speakers (Sorosoro, 2011).

In 2010, there were 334 federal and state recognized reservations. According to the 2010 U.S. Census, 20% of Native Americans and Alaskan Natives lived inside an American Indian area (i.e., federal reservation and/or off reservation trust land, Oklahoma tribal statistical area, state reservation, or federal- or state-designated area) (Norris et al., 2012).

In addition to earlier federal laws that played a role in the populating of urban areas with Native people, high unemployment on tribal lands has contributed to the move of Native people to urban areas. In several states, including Alaska, Arizona, California, Maine, Minnesota, Montana, New Mexico, North Dakota, South Dakota, and Utah, less than 50% of Native Americans who are 16 years or older and who are living in or near the tribal areas of federally recognized tribes are working (Indian Affairs, 2014).

Horse (2001) maintains that Native Americans are geographically dislocated from their homeland within a culture bombarded by the Internet, the U.S. school system, peer pressure, and the mass media. Despite the reality of some Native people's cultural discontinuity, which refers to the gulf between mainstream expectations and traditional cultural values maintained by many Native people, bicultural survival is a reality for many (Garrett & Pichette, 2000). Arndt (2011) discussed the post-traumatic stress disorder (PTSD) that characterizes many Native people contending with colonization and its deleterious aftereffects.

Social, Psychological, and Physical Health Issues

Compared with the non-Hispanic white population, Native Americans and Alaskan Natives had a larger proportion of younger people and a smaller proportion of older people in 2010. Twenty-eight percent are younger than age 18, whereas only 7% are 65 years or older. The median age among Native American and Alaska Natives is 30.8, which is nearly 7 years younger than the median age for the non-Hispanic white population (U. S. Census Bureau, 2014a).

In 2013, the poverty rate for American Indians and Alaskan Natives was 29.2% compared to 15.9% for the nation. This rate was the highest of other poverty rates for non-Hispanic whites, Asians, Pacific Islanders, and blacks (Infoplease, 2015). For Native American and Alaska Native children, economic conditions have worsened. In 2013, 36% of children lived in poverty, which is seven points higher than it was in 2008 (Kena et al., 2015).

In 2013, the median household income for single-race Native American and Alaskan Natives was $36,252, which is nearly $16,000 less than the median income for the general population. Income is related to status of housing. Although 54% of Native Americans and Alaskan Natives lived in owner-occupied homes, the percentage of renters is 44.5% compared with a national rate of 32.9%. Nationally, 64% of Americans own homes (U.S. Census Bureau, 2014b). Among Native Americans and

Alaska Natives who own their homes, the median value is $95,000, which is $60,000 less than the median value of $154,000 for white owner-occupied homes.

Nationally, 26.9% of single-race Native American and Alaskan Natives in 2013 did not have a usual or normal source of health care and were not regularly seen by a doctor or a clinic that can provide preventive care (U. S. Census Bureau, 2014a). The lack of health insurance among the general population is 14.5%. As a result of treaty obligations, Native Americans receive their health services largely through the federal government and the Indian Health Service. Since 1955, the U.S. Public Health Service was designated to provide federally funded health care to all Native Americans and Alaskan Natives who belonged to federally recognized tribes and lived on or near the reservations throughout 12 service areas (Byrd & Clayton, 2003). Because the majority (78%) of the Native and Alaska native alone-or-in combination population live outside of American Indian and Alaska Native areas, the quality of and access to federally funded health care has been adversely affected by the way in which Native people are scattered throughout the country (Joe, 2003). In light of these and other data that reveal the poor quality of life for unacceptably high numbers of Native American Indian and Alaskan Native people, many First Nation people feel distrust for the dominant culture (Heinrich, Corbine, & Thomas, 1990).

More recently, a total of 3,771 Alaskan Native research participants were recruited in 26 communities across three regions of Alaska to investigate the presence and prevalence of depression. The researchers found higher rates of depression among women. Males who were not married or living together as married and whose highest level of education was below high school had positive odds of depression. Among men, depression was associated with lower levels of income. Among women, odds of scoring positive versus negative were significantly elevated among women aged 34 to 59 years versus 60 and older. Little or no identification with tribal tradition was associated with increased odds of depression in women and decreased odds in men. Stronger acculturation to Western culture, which was more predominant among Alaskan Native males than females, was associated with greater perceived stress and more use of alcohol and drugs as a coping mechanism. Stronger enculturation or Yupik identity, which was more predominant among Alaskan Native women, was associated with less depression and the use of religion and spirituality to cope (Dillard, Smith, Ferucci, & Lanier, 2012). The research is inconclusive regarding cultural identity and substance abuse problems. Venner, Wall, Lau, and Ehlers (2006) reported conflicting findings about the protections against substance abuse that a bicultural identity may offer. However, Dillard et al. (2012) posit that there are aversive consequences of acculturation, namely loss of cultural meaning and viable socioeconomic opportunities.

A vulnerability for Native families is the high incidence of intimate partner violence. Native women are much more likely to be killed by an intimate partner than Latinos and whites and have twice the incidence of rate of rape. There are both immediate and long-term social, economic, and psychological consequence of physical, sexual, and/or psychological threats to Native women (Peregoy & Gloria, 2007).

For many Native Americans, alcohol use disorders affects family life, newborn health, and employment prospects. In 2011, the Centers for Disease Control (CDC) reported that Native Americans along with non-Hispanic white adults were among those with the largest prevalence, frequency, and intensity of binge drinking, compared with other racial/ethnic populations (CDC, 2015). Given the relationship between substance addictions and mental health problems, comorbidity is evident. Among Native people, alcohol abuse is a substantial problem with cirrhosis of the liver in the top 5 of the 10 leading causes of death (CDC, 2015).

Dillard et al. (2012) found binge alcohol use played a positive role in depression for women. More specifically, drinking five or more alcoholic drinks on an occasion one or more times versus never was significantly related to depression among women. In addition to the adverse health effects of alcohol abuse on the body, alcoholism is linked to high-risk behaviors such as unprotected sex because it decreases inhibition, which means greater susceptibility to sexually transmitted infections.

Compared with other racial/ethnic groups, Native Americans ranked fifth in estimated rates of HIV infection diagnoses in 2013, with lower rates than in blacks/African Americans, Hispanics/Latinos, Native Hawaiians/other Pacific Islanders, and people reporting multiple races, but higher rates than in Asians and whites. In 2010, fewer than 1% of the estimated 47,500 new HIV infections in the United States were among Native people (CDC, 2011).

Related to poor diet, diabetes ranges from 5 to 50% among tribes and Native communities, and colon and rectal cancer rates are the highest among any racial or ethnic group in the country (Institute of Medicine, 2003). As major causes of morbidity and premature death, these and other poor health outcomes contribute to nearly one in three Native deaths before the age of 45 (Vernon, 2002).

There are alcohol treatment programs for Native Americans, but empirical, research-based findings on the efficacy of various treatments for alcohol problems in Native Americans is lacking (Thomason, 2000). The term *nativized treatments* refers to standard treatments that have been adapted to be more culturally appropriate for Native populations. These nativized treatments would include, for example, Native American cultural values and traditional healing techniques and ceremonies. A comprehensive program may be the best approach to treating Native clients with alcohol abuse issues. Such a program is descriptive, includes medical care, self-help groups, and purification ceremonies (Thomason, 2000).

Educationally, there have been increases in the high school graduation level, GED, or alternative certificate, now at 82.2% among Native American and Alaskan Natives 25 years of age and older. This percentage compares with 86% for the general population (Infoplease, 2015). Just over 17.6% had completed a bachelor's degree compared with 29.1% of the general population. Nearly 31 different tribal groups have established their own tribal colleges (Horse, 2001). Among Native American people who are more traditional and are not interested in leaving their reservations, lack of educational attainment may be a conscious decision, particularly in light of limited access and economic challenges (Rayle, Chee, & Sand, 2006).

About one quarter (25.9%) of Native American and Alaskan Native workers are employed in management or professional occupations, compared with 38% among non-Hispanic whites. Over 22% of Native Americans worked in sales and office occupations, which is similar to non-Hispanic whites (27%) and 25.2% worked in service occupations (U. S. Census Bureau, 2014a).

Although the available data are dated, the number of Native-owned business has increased in the United States, as has the amount of money that Native people contribute to the U.S. economy. According to the U.S. Census Bureau (2011), in 2007, there were 236,967 Native American and Alaska Native-owned businesses. This represents an increase of 17.7% from 2002. Also in 2007, American Indian and Alaska Native-owned businesses generated $34.4 billion in receipts, representing a 28 percent increase from 2002.

Native people have been overlooked for their inestimable contributions to the Western world. Hoxie (1996) stated that across the Americas, Native people were the first farmers, invented the hammock, the snowshoe, the blow gun, the bulb syringe, the kayak, the rubber boot, herbal oral contraception, bunk beds, petroleum extraction, and pest control. They also wove cloth from feathers, crafted animal and bird decoys for use in hunting, and used acid to etch designs onto shell.

Gunn Allen (1994) reminds us of the irrefutable influence of Native American and Alaskan Native people. Elaborate systems of thought and governments based on egalitarianism, service, pacifism, and freedom characterized many tribal societies prior to the presence of patriarchy. In fact, Iroquois ideas were central to the founding principles of America's Constitution. Portman and Herring (2001) stated,

> Native American Indian women were integral to the economic and social survival of their nations and tribes. They also held positions of political importance. Native American Indians provided guidance and influenced governance decisions and served as leaders and advisers in many Native American Indian tribes and nations. (p. 187)

Acculturation

Most Native adults whose ancestry is both Native and non-Native not only retain their traditional values but also seek to live in the dominant culture (Garrett & Herring, 2001). According to Herring (1992), Native American and Alaskan Native people are "more unalterably resistant to assimilation and integration into mainstream society than are other minority groups" (p. 135); some, however, have become acculturated.

Garrett and Pichette (2000) offered a clear definition of acculturation in their discussion of Native American acculturation. It was stated that acculturation is

> the cultural change that occurs when two or more cultures are in persistent contact... A particular kind of acculturation is assimilation, in which one culture changes significantly more than the other culture and as a result comes to resemble it. This process is often established deliberately through force to maintain control over conquered people, but it can occur voluntarily as well. (p. 6)

Acculturation influences value structures and is important to an understanding of cultural adaptation. Garrett and Pichette (2000) identify five levels of acculturation among Native people: (1) traditional, (2) marginal, (3) bicultural, (4) assimilated, and (5) pantraditional.

These levels exist on a continuum and are a function of a person's life experiences. The traditional Native person may or may not speak English and will hold traditionally Native values, including tribal customs. The marginal person identifies with neither mainstream values nor traditional values. The bicultural person knows and practices both mainstream and traditional values. The assimilated person holds the mainstream American values in high esteem to the exclusion of those Native. Finally, the pantraditional person consciously seeks to return to the "old ways"; he or she attempts to embrace lost traditional values and beliefs and is often bilingual.

Acculturation may take place at the expense of one's original cultural values as one internalizes values and traditions. This process is not always conscious (Sue, 1989), and there is the likelihood of cultural alienation from one's traditional culture because the dominant culture is esteemed over one's own.

One dimension of acculturation is assimilation. Assimilation is different in that it describes those persons who consciously do not desire to maintain their cultural identities and thus seek sustained interaction with other cultures outside their own. The original cultures have been lost or relinquished, and persons have given up most cultural traits of their cultures of origin and assumed the traits, behaviors, and attitude of the dominant culture (Berry & Kim, 1988).

Christianization was one way assimilation was accomplished among many Native Americans. Some Native Americans do not regard the two to be incompatible. In the Native American Church, Christian and Native beliefs coexist (U.S. Department of Health and Human Services, 2001). In addition to the Spanish and French languages, European colonizers brought English to America. Language is a medium of culture, and English functioned as a way to deny the existence and relevance of Native languages. Such a policy existed in the U.S. government-sponsored Indian boarding schools designed to mainstream American Indian youth. The first such school was established in 1879 in Carlisle, Pennsylvania, under the influence of General Henry Pratt. His motto was "kill the Indian and save the man" (Hoxie, 1996; Lesiak & Jones, 1991). In these colonializing contexts, children's hair was cut, traditional clothing was taken away, American Christian names replaced Native names, and only English was allowed to be spoken. The virtues of white American Christian traditions were extolled, and Native ways were denigrated as uncivilized (Cameron & Turtle-song, 2003). Native Americans and Alaskan Natives who possess a strong sense of heritage and honor tradition may be more likely to feel at peace on the reservation, where cooperation with others and respect for tribal values based on ritual are commonplace (Gunn Allen, 1994).

Cultural Philosophies and Values

Despite chronic and contemporary challenges, a commitment to peoplehood, a spirit of resilience, and a strong sense of identity are evident among Native peoples. The tribe is a source of belonging and security for Native American and Alaskan Native people. Personal accomplishments are honored and supported if they serve to benefit the entire tribe or collective. Competition, the hallmark of the educational school system and a dominant cultural value rooted in individualism, is at odds with collectivism, a spirit of cooperation, and sharing of resources that belong to everyone.

Although values vary from tribe to tribe, Native American and Alaskan Native people believe in a Supreme Creator that is considered both male and female and is in command of all the elements of existence. Gunn Allen (1994) said, "There are many female gods recognized and honored by the Nations. Females were highly valued, both respected and feared and all social institutions reflected this attitude" (p. 193). Native Americans and Alaskan Natives also believe that all things in the universe are connected, have purpose, and exemplify personhood "including plants (e.g., 'tree people'), animals ('our four-legged brothers and sisters'), rocks and minerals ('rock people'), the land ('Mother Earth'), the winds ('the Four Powers'), 'Father Sky,' 'Grandfather Sun,' 'Grandmother Moon,' and 'The Red Thunder Boys'" (Garrett & Garrett, 1994, p. 138).

Honoring the Creator is sacred to Native American and Alaskan Native people and is central to Native Americans' and Alaskan Natives' harmonious relationships with nature and all things. Garrett (1998) said that "the wellness of the mind, body, spirit, and natural environment is an extension of the proper balance in the relationship of all things" (p. 78). In these cultures, sharing is valued over materialism because all things belong to Earth. (See Storytelling: Resistance Is Not Futile.)

❖ STORYTELLING: RESISTANCE IS NOT FUTILE

1992 was the 500th anniversary of Christopher Columbus's arrival in the western hemisphere. That year, people across races and nationalities united with First Americans to reject the celebration and glorification of a man who was responsible for genocide, biological warfare, and oppression. The National Council of Churches asked Christians to refrain from celebrating the Columbus quincentennial. One teacher in Portland, Oregon, took a year off from his job to travel the country, helping teachers learn to tell the truth about the Columbus experience. A student climbed aboard a romanticized Columbus exhibit sponsored by the National Endowment for the Humanities called First Encounter. The student held a sign that read, "Exhibit Teaches Racism." Now thousands of teachers are telling the story of Columbus differently as they engage in decolonizing practices.

Among many Native Americans, a leader's influence was based on personal qualities. Authority within a group was derived from the ability to make useful suggestions and knowledge of traditional ways and tribal lore (Waldman, 2000). Elders are valued among Native American and Alaskan Natives "because of the lifetime's worth of wisdom they have acquired" (Garrett & Garrett, 1994, p. 137). Elders are accorded respect, and as they age, there is an increase in sacred responsibility for the tribe and family. They understand that their purpose is to care for and guide young people, yet a spirit of curiosity and openness to life's lessons prevails (Garrett & Herring, 2001).

Native American cultural values emanate from a spiritual center that emphasizes coexisting in harmony with nature. (See Table 5.1: Common Cultural Values Among Native Americans and Alaskan Native People.) This entails a respect for Earth as natural medicine (Peregoy, 1993). Native people have always depended on the land, because it provided life, shelter, food, and medicine. The Paiute boiled sagebrush to relieve headaches and rheumatism. Even dandruff was cured by rubbing boiled willow leaves into the hair and scalp (Ballentine & Ballentine, 1993). "This harmony entails a holistic sensing of the state of continuous fusion among the elements of self with all life, including the creator" (Dana, 1993, p. 84).

❖ **Table 5.1**   Common Cultural Values Among Native Americans and Alaskan Native People

---

Spirituality (Great Spirit)

Nature (Mother Earth)

The sacred

Ritual

Tradition

Balance

Harmony

Explanation of natural phenomena according to the spiritual realm

Noninterference

Cooperation

Sharing

Extended and present time orientation

Hozhq (An expression of happiness, harmonious relationships, the beauty of the land)

Tiospaye (Shared responsibility, extended family, reciprocity)

Oral traditions

The extended family (The tribe)

Selflessness

Deference to and respect for elders

Storytelling

Speak softly at a slower rate

Not holding direct eye contact to show respect

Time is always with us

Source: Compiled by author.

Implicit in this value system is reverence for and acceptance of the gifts from the earth. In their reverence for the earth, a variety of plants, wild and cultivated, were used for both religious and practical purposes, as well as for pleasure. Clearly some Native people, particularly where agriculture was highly developed, used alcohol prior to contact with Europeans, but for the most part, drinking alcohol was a postcontact reality (Waldman, 2000). Native American people believe that to be human is a part of the Sacred, thus there is an acknowledgment that human beings make mistakes (Trujillo, 2000). Nature, in its natural, undisturbed state is respected, and coexisting (not interfering) with nature is paramount as all things have spiritual energy. The universe, or Mother Earth, belongs to all people. For the Indian, the concept of land ownership was foreign and made as much sense as did carving up the sky (e.g., national airspace boundaries).

Honoring traditional ways suggests a respect for the past and the contributions of the ancestral spirits. According to Peregoy (1993), "The traditional Indian/Native's system of life is intertwined with the tribe and extends further into a metaphysical belief system" (p. 172). Native American and Alaskan Natives see the extended family and the tribe as taking precedence over the self (Garrett & Garrett, 1994; Gunn Allen, 1994; Peregoy, 1993). Among many Native American and Alaskan Native people, the concept of self tends to be fluid and includes the individual as well as the tribe, the extended family, and even plants and animal spirits (Dana, 2000). A belief or knowledge in unseen powers and reference to deities and mystery is core to many tribal values, as is the importance of balance (Trujillo, 2000).

Respect for and coexistence with helpful animal spirits are enduring values found in nearly all Native American and Alaskan Eskimo societies. It was believed that the animals made themselves available to humans only for as long as there was respect from the hunters for the animal spirits. This involved ritual treatment of the animals so that the animals would, upon their death, return to the spirit world with a good report, which would ensure the success of future hunters. If a hunter was unsuccessful, it could be stated that the animal spirits had not been treated properly; therefore, proper rituals were needed to restore harmony and to correct the imbalance (Hoxie, 1996).

According to Garrett and Pichette (2000), there are verbal and nonverbal communication style differences between contemporary mainstream American cultural values and those of traditional Native people. More specifically, immediate responses, frequent interruption, and emphasis placed on verbal skills are characteristic of dominant U.S. cultural styles. Delayed responses, less frequent interjection, and emphasis placed on nonverbal skills characterize Native cultural traditions. Some Native children are taught not to establish eye contact with adults as a sign of respect.

Native American Identity

Bryant and LaFromboise (2005) conducted research with 103 Lumbee Indian high school students using the People of Color Racial Identity Attitude Scale by Helms (1995). This instrument was developed to provide a measure of racial identity attitudes among Asians, African Americans, Latinos, and Native Americans. There are four stages. *Conformity* represents conformance to the dominant ideology and a devaluing of a person's own racial group. *Dissonance* reflects confusion about a person's racial group. *Immersion* describes identification and even idolization of a person's racial group. Finally, *internalization* refers to commitment to a person's group and an ability to integrate a person's racial identity into his or her life. Internalization attitudes were dominant among this group, followed by immersion, dissonance, and conformity.

Bryant and LaFromboise (2005) concluded that the internalization findings "suggests they possess a positive American Indian racial identity and also have the ability to acknowledge the positive aspects of White society" (p. 86). In addition, immersion attitudes may suggest some level of psychological as well as physical retreat into the Lumbee American community. Given the students' level of awareness about the impact of race on a daily basis, the conformity and dissonance attitudes may reflect some confusion, albeit minimally, about the sociopolitical constructions of race. Scholl (2006) had similar findings in his research with 121 Native American college students. Internalization attitudes were dominant and conformity (or preencounter) attitudes were least likely to be represented.

Ethics, or the principles or moral values that guide people's actions, provide Horse (2001) with a clear conceptualization of Indian identity. Part of this ethic is within the context of a collective consciousness. Consciousness requires memory, which Gunn Allen (1994) remarked is not encouraged in the West: "The American idea that the best and the brightest should willingly reject and repudiate their origins leads to an allied idea—that history, like everything in the past, is of little value and should be forgotten as quickly as possible" (p. 192). According to Horse (2001), consciousness is influenced by multiple issues: the degree to which someone is grounded in the native language, tribe, family, and culture; the worldview that is embraced; recognition as a member of an Indian tribe by the government of the tribe; and the validity of a person's genealogical heritage as an Indian. Concerns over human-made laws, such as blood quantum amounts (Wilson, 1992), is not as relevant as is someone's consciousness and identity as an Indian.

Implications for Mental Health Professionals

Much of the emphasis in multicultural counseling and psychology has been on helping mental health professionals work effectively with patients who are different with respect to race, gender, class, disability, sexuality, and other sources of differences, however, mental health professionals need to appreciate the tremendous intragroup diversity that exists. Being from the same tribe or family is not an indication that people will endorse similar values, which is the meaning of treating people like a monolith wherein intragroup differences are discounted or minimized. Among Native people, the influences of acculturation, phenotype, identity development, collectivism, and the place of gender play a critical role in psychological and physical health.

Case Study

Success in School

Ocean is 10 years old and in the 4th grade. He is from the Narragansett tribe and lives in Rhode Island with his mother and stepfather. Ocean has been sent to the school's adjustment counselor for difficulty that he has with completing homework on time and participating in class. His teacher has noted that Ocean is a very kind child yet seems to lack confidence, has school anxiety, and seems to feel alienated from school. To improve his academic performance and to help the teacher and counselor personalize interventions for specific students and student groups, Ocean and his parents agree to participate in an online Succeeding in School Program (SIS) program. The program was designed in 1986 as a paper-and-pencil instrument to help school counselors improve the academic performance of fourth and fifth grade elementary school students (Gerler & Anderson, 1986). Used widely in school to assist with retention and mathematics achievement (Zyromski, Bryant, & Gerler, 2011), the program was moved online during the 1990s. Ocean's teacher, aware of lower rates of educational attainment among Native students, decided to focus on helping students negotiate and navigate schools environments that can be culturally alienating for ethnic and minority students as they become more mindful of their cultural and racial identities and begin to experience feeling different from their non-Native peers.

Being comfortable in school and asking for help in school were the program components that she emphasized. Being comfortable in school focused on identifying fears related to school and how to overcome fears surrounding the academic environment. Asking for help in school centered on students' experiences and feelings about asking for help in school. Ocean would panic when called upon—his heart would beat quickly and his cheeks would turn red—he would feel dizzy and stammer, which would create a cycle of feeling more anxious, inadequate, and fearful. Ocean would sometimes cry, which as a boy, was the height of humiliation for him. His teacher would gently come to his desk and reassure him that she was there for him and encourage him to ask for help. Although Ocean felt a bond with his teacher, he did not like feeling so needy and different from the other children. He wanted to be strong and to feel smart. Finally, Ocean is frequently told by his non-Native classmates that he does not look Native. Ocean has fair skin, green eyes, and light brown hair.

Questions

1. What are Ocean's fears?
2. What meaning does Ocean assign to asking for help?
3. How can Ocean's school counselor help Ocean rethink a request for help?

Discussion and Integration

Through a review of Ocean's online entries, it became clear that Ocean was afraid of being wrong, being seen as stupid, and being held back. Understandably, he was concerned about the perceptions that his peers had of him (Zyromski, Bryant, & Gerler, 2009). Ocean was older, taller, and bigger than most of his class peers. His mother made a decision for him to start kindergarten at age 6 instead of age 5. His stepbrother is younger and yet in fifth grade. Because Ocean feels embarrassed at being older, he had previously associated asking for help with not being very smart. Ocean's teacher worked closely with him based on the results of the SIS program. She asked Ocean to find a story online about a Native member who asked for help. Ocean found countless stories of Native people, who as collectivistic people, depended on the tribe to function. Asking for help meant honoring each other's contributions and working collectively as a tribe and a group. Due to her knowledge of collectivism among Ocean's family, Ocean's counselor invites Ocean's parents to an initial school meeting to hear their concerns and share the SIS program with them. Over time, Ocean's confidence in his abilities is seen as he takes greater risks with raising his hand and asking for help, which he now connects with courage and bravery. He also finds that many of his classmates benefit from his questions or often have the same question that he has, helping Ocean to feel like a leader.

Finally, Ocean has been equipped with some behavioral strategies that help him to identify his feelings and respond on his terms. He quietly tells his panic to stop and envisions himself on a horse with a lasso where he captures the panic. Ocean relayed this strategy when his counselor asked him, "What can you do about the panic when it starts to get big and run around?"

His teacher demonstrated multicultural competence in her ability to apply her knowledge of Ocean's culture with interventions that could be relevant to him (Sanchez & Davis, 2010). The image of the horse and the lasso resonated with Ocean and is a source of humor for him that he has learned to use to his advantage. His counselor also helped Ocean to understand that being told that he does not look Indian is referred to as a microinvalidation, which according to Walters (2010), refers to communications that nullify the experiential reality or identity of Native persons (e.g., being told that you do not look or act like a real Indian). Media depictions of Native people, even in the 21st century, are too often demeaning and erroneous. There is tremendous phenotypical diversity among Native people, just as there is with other racial groups, including white people. Ocean is shown pictures of Native people and sees people who look just like him.

Ocean also feels apart from others. His counselor recognizes clearly that "the greatest loss that an Indian/Native can have is the loss of family and community connection" (Peregoy & Gloria, 2007, p. 67). Thus, strong family and community connections are at the heart of what Ocean needs psychologically and academically.

Ocean is not unusual from many children, across age, ethnicity, gender, and race who have personal concerns of competence. According to Garrett and Herring (2001), appropriate uses of humor are critical in integrating Native culture with psychotherapeutic healing. Humor is also a way to maintain Native culture and cope with a difficult situation (Garrett, Garrett, Torres-Rivera, Wilbur, & Roberts-Wilbur, 2005; Mohatt, 2010), which is what Ocean is learning to do through his strategy of using a lasso to subdue anxiety.

Summary

This chapter provided a history of Native American and Alaskan Native people. From an international lens, Western allies, Britain, Canada, and New Zealand are similar to America concerning the shared legacy of colonialism and First Nation indigenous people. Irrespective of the political, historical, and ideological differences across these Western bodies contained in each country's narrative are abuses of power, privilege, and patriarchy. Tribal people's cultural ways of living, languages, land ownership, and humanity have undergone ethnic cleansing and trauma. This chapter focused on the prominent and palpable colonialistic legacy, reflecting cultural violence, the highest of poverty rates, genocide, intragroup violence, educational, and health-related disparities among first nation indigenous people. Representation in the United States, demographic information, history, and common cultural values among American Indian and Alaskan Natives were provided. A summary of these values can be found in Table 5.1. A case study with a school age child was provided for purposes of application of multicultural counseling competencies and SIS, a novel educational program.

6

People of Spanish and Latino Descent

This chapter profiles Latinos, a racially and culturally diverse ethnic group. A brief look at history, cultural values, and demographic trends is included. A case study is provided for the integration of material in a therapeutic context.

The Spanish, Portuguese, Indians, Asians, and Africans

The Western world's Latinos are *la raza,* which means, "the race" or "the people." Places of origin among Latinos are diverse and varied: Puerto Ricans (*Puertorriquenos*), Cubans (*Cubanos*), Central Americans and South Americans, Latin Americans (which include Dominicans [*Dominicanos*]), and Mexican Americans (*Mejicanos*).

The federal government defines *Hispanic* or *Latino* as a person of Mexican, Puerto Rican, Cuban, South or Central American, or other Spanish culture or origin regardless of race (Ennis, Rios-Vargas, & Albert, 2011). Novas (1994) clarified that for many Latinos, Hispanic represents a bureaucratic and government census term." According to Hochschild and Powell (2008), during the 19th century, people who, now in the 21st century are considered to be Latinos and Hispanics, were not regarded by the Census as distinct from whites. In 1930, however, change was evident with an emergent classification of Mexican American. The Census Bureau added "Mexican" to the available color or race choices. Census takers were told that Mexican laborers were somewhat difficult to classify but could be racially located by virtue of their geographic location. The Census director at the time stated, "In order to obtain separate figures for this racial group, it has been decided that all persons born in Mexico, or having parents born in Mexico, who are definitely not white, Negro, Indian, Chinese, or Japanese, should be returned as Mexican" (Hochschild & Powell, 2008).

Increases in the Mexican population, the 1924 Immigration Act, which denied permanent residency to nonwhites, the Great Depression, and racial segregation accompanied by violence were among the weighty factors influencing the discourse about racial classification at the time and led to the Census Bureau's retreat from classifying the Mexican race. In 1936, the census director stated, "'Mexicans are Whites and must be classified as 'White'" (Hochschild & Powell, 2008).

The term *Latino* or *Latina,* depending on gender, is widely used and refers to persons with Spanish ancestry. Many Latinos prefer to be called by their country of origin.

The racial diversity among Latinos is very old and connected to political movements, slavery, family, conquest, defeat, geographic movement, love, and war. The term *Hispanic* comes from España, Spain, the country from which the conquistadors hailed. The Spanish encountered various Native people throughout millennia and across various lands: the Arawaks, Mayas, Aztecs, and Incas. African people who were brought involuntarily to the Caribbean, colonies, and South America as slaves reproduced with the Spanish and First Nation people. In addition to European, Indian, and African ancestries, some Latinos claim an Asian heritage (Santiago-Rivera, Arredondo, & Gallardo-Cooper, 2002). In the Philippines, the Spanish encountered Asian people and made their claim to the land in 1522; thus, Filipinos are categorized as Asian but have Spanish ancestry. Also in 1522, the Spanish infiltrated Central America, including Nicaragua, Honduras, El Salvador, and Guatemala. These countries were conquered two decades later.

Unions between the Spanish and the indigenous Indian people resulted in *mestizos.* Class divisions were connected to skin color in that mestizos were not regarded as equals to the Spaniards but emerged as a higher class than pure Indians. Once African slaves arrived, new class and color configurations appeared. During the colonial period of Spain's reign over these conquered lands, a Spanish elite ruled and others were considered of a lower class. The Spaniards constructed *las castas*, which means the caste system (Montalvo & Codina, 2001). Las castas was a racially stratified system that cast stigma on darker skinned peoples and supported discriminatory treatment. The Spanish Conquistadores along with the Portuguese viewed the caste system as a way to dominate and demean the indigenous and African slaves (Fernandes, 2014). This system also ensured the free labor of indigenous and African people. The new world became a place where Europeans flourished while people with visibly dark skin encountered injustice.

The Latin American social caste pyramid, also known as las castas, ensured Spaniards' power over and privilege in Latin America (Fernandes, 2014). The hierarchical caste system included: *Peninsulares, Criollos, Mestizos, Mulatos, Zambos, Indios*, and *Negros*. The peninsulares and criollos shared Spanish blood, with the later being born in the "new world," Latin America. Although these two groups were similar, native-born Spaniards (peninsulares) held higher-level political positions and had more social capital, power, and privilege over the criollos and the indigenous and African people (Fernandes, 2014).

Beneath the Spaniards were the racially mixed Mestizos, Mulatos, and Zambos. Mestizos were of European and Indigenous ancestries. Mulatos were of European and black ancestries, while zambos were of indigenous and black ancestries. Individuals who were of mixed European descent had more power and privilege over non-Europeans. In a quest to identify as white European, bigoted ideologies and behaviors were at play, such as *blanqueamiento* (whitening) that encouraged the intermarriage with lighter-skinned people (Fernandes, 2014) and an attempt to suppress African or Amerindian bloodlines. People of African descent were deemed as less desirable given that their visible characteristics were likely to manifest in subsequent generations. By appearing physically as Spaniards, individuals aspired to achieve acceptance, elevate their status, and distance themselves from persons with less status (Fernandes, 2014; Montalvo & Codina, 2001).

Whitening policies, were eventually supported by Latin American governments. Consequently, white European immigration was encouraged, which included the recruitment of white prostitutes who were sent to heavily populated indigenous and African areas (Fernandes, 2014). For example, Venezuelans hoped to dilute their darker ancestry by mixing with white people as much as possible and in the process became home to a number of European immigrants from Spanish, Italian, Portuguese, German, French, and English ancestries.

High rates of intermarriage led the Spanish to implement the ideology of *mestizaje*, which deemed that all people, regardless of their ancestry, were of mixed descent. Persons of Spanish, African, and Amerindian descent subscribed to this idea, also believing that it would erase inequality; however, the legacy of mestizaje seems consistent with present day colorblindness in that the racial privilege of lighter and Spaniard looking Latinos was denied (Fernandes, 2014). Nonwhite Latinos experience discrimination that is politically, socially, and racially motivated (Hernandez, 1996).

History informs us that Latinos in Central America and South America can be of any race and represent a range of phenotypical characteristics, including white, brown, red, and black skin color hues. For example, during the 18th century slave trade, Europeans brought black Africans to the Americas. The Garifina people, a group of Africans believed to have come from Ghana, were taken to Central America. African slaves on the island of St. Vincent revolted and led by Marcos Sanchez Diaz, fled to the island of Rotan in Honduras. From there, the Garifina people spread out along the Caribbean to Belize, Guatemala, and Honduras ("Latin America," n.d.).

Migratory Patterns From Mexico

Mexico is one of the largest sources of new immigrants to the United States. A number of push and pull factors influence the migratory patterns of Mexico's people to the United States. During the early 1900s, there was a great need for cheap labor to work in U.S. agriculture. The harsh economic conditions in Mexico and high unemployment, along with Mexico's proximity to the United States, set the stage for large-scale migration (U.S. Department of Health and Human Services [DHHS], 2001).

The land that the majority of Americans now occupy was once Mexico. In 1821, Mexico won its independence from Spain, but this freedom was truncated. In 1848, the Treaty of Guadalupe Hidalgo was the result of Mexico's defeat in a series of wars a decade earlier. Through this formal agreement between Mexico and the United States, Mexico lost 50% of its territory. The cultural and geographic decimation was enormous. Mexicans who had lived on their own land, where their *almas* (souls) resided, now became migrant farm workers. Mexicans who had been landowners found themselves working for white men. Once Texas, New Mexico, California, Arizona, Nevada, and half of Colorado officially became U.S. territory, the Spanish language was ousted, with English becoming the primary and official mode of school instruction.

Demography

In 2011, over half (53%) of all foreign-born persons were born in Latin America and the Caribbean (Grieco et al., 2012). Latinos represent over 17% of the U.S. population, or 55.4 million people as of 2014 (U.S. Census, 2015b). Latinos continue to be the largest group of color; however, this reference is admittedly confusing given that in the 2010 Census, 53% of Latinos, across skin color hues, identified as white (Ennis et al., 2011). More than half of the growth in the United States between 2000 and 2010 was due to increases among Latinos. In this 10-year period, the Latino population grew 43% or 4 times the total U.S. population growth rate of 10% (Ennis et al., 2011). High rates of immigration, low median age, and high fertility rates account for this increase.

Mexican Americans increased the most of the other Latino groups, growing from 20.6 million to 31.8 million in 10 years. Mexicans are the largest group of Latinos, representing 63% of the group. Puerto Ricans grew by 36%, from 3.4 million to 4.6 million and are 9% of Latinos. Cubans grew by 44%, from 1.2 million to

1.8 million and represent 3.5% of Latinos. Central Americans (people from Belize, Costa Rica, El Salvador, Guatemala, Honduras, Nicaragua, Panama) increased 137%, from 1.68 million to 3.99 million and are 8% of Latinos. Of Central Americans, Salvadorians were the largest group at 1.6 million followed by Guatemalans at 1 million (Ennis et al., 2011).

South Americans (people from Argentina, Bolivia, Brazil, Colombia, Chile, Paraguay, Peru, Uruguay, Venezuela) increased 105%, from 1.35 million to 2.76 million. Among Latinos, South Americans are 5.5%. Colombians were the largest group at 909,000, followed by Ecuadorians at 565,000 (Ennis et al., 2011). (See Population Box 6.1: Percentage of Latinos in the United States by Ethnic Subgroup.)

Although Latinos can be of any race, in the 2010 census, over half of Latinos reported their race as white alone (Humes, Jones, & Ramirez, 2011). Over one third (36.7%) stated they were some other race. Very small percentages of Latinos identified as one of the other racial groups: 3% identified as black; 1% identified as Native American and Alaskan Native; .4% as Asian alone; and .1% as Native Hawaiian, other Pacific Islander (Ennis et al., 2011).

Among Latinas, the total fertility rate is 2.4. For non-Hispanic whites and for non-Hispanic Asians, it is 1.8. Non-Hispanic blacks (2.1) have higher fertility than whites but lower fertility than Latinas (Passel, Livingston, & Cohn, 2012). Compared with non-Hispanic white women, Asian women, and black women, Latinas are least likely to have not married between 25 to 29 years of age. The rate of never marriage for Latinas is 36.8% compared to 70.5% among black women, 52% among Asian women, and 43% among white women (Kreider & Ellis, 2011).

There were considerable within-Latino group differences with respect to marriage and divorce data from the 2000 census. Divorce and widowed rates were lower at 7.5% and 3.3%, respectively, compared with 10.2% and 6.1%, respectively, in the general

Population Box 6.1: Percentage of Latinos in the United States by Ethnic Subgroup

Mexicans: 63%

Other Hispanic or Latino: 8%

Dominican: 2.8%

Puerto Ricans: 9%

Central Americans: 8%

South Americans: 5.5%

Cubans: 3.5%

Source: Adapted from Ennis et al. (2011).

population. Rates of separation were slightly higher, at 3.5% compared with 2.1%. Cubans have the highest rate of divorce, compared with Guatemalans who have the lowest: 12.4% and 4.1%, respectively. Cubans were also the least likely to have never married at 25%, whereas Hondurans and Salvadorans were the most likely to never have married, both at 40% (Therrien & Ramirez, 2001).

Struggling with transition from one cultural context to the next and working long hours to support self and family back in the home country can interfere with dating and family formation regardless of specific group. Latinos tend to have larger household sizes at 3.4 compared with 2.6 for the general population. Guatemalans had the most people in their households at 3.9 (Therrien & Ramirez, 2001).

The median age of non-Latinos in the United States is 37. Among Latinos, the median age is 27 years (Pew Research Center, 2012). Mexicans have the lowest median age, 25.3 years, and Cubans had the highest, at 40.6 years. In fact, one third of Mexicans, Puerto Ricans, Dominicans, and Hondurans are children. In 2000, the largest 5-year age group among Latinos was children under the age of 5 (Therrien & Ramirez, 2001).

Geography

Brazil is a South American country where the official language is Portuguese. Millions of Latinos from countries such as Argentina and Costa Rica are not of Spanish or Indian descent but rather descend from European or Antillean nations (Beals & Beals, 1993). Some British left England during the 18th century, and other Europeans fled to Latin America to escape Nazi oppression (Santiago-Rivera et al., 2002).

Latinos in the United States are united by the Spanish mother tongue. There are dialect differences. Beals and Beals (1993) stated that the majority of Spain's citizens speak Castellano, whereas the majority of Chicanos (Mexicans) speak Pocho. According to Carballo-Dieguez (1989), many Latinos are fluent in both Spanish and English, others know very little English, others have limited knowledge of Spanish, and others speak Spanglish, a mixture of both languages.

One of the discourses about Latinos is that they are brown, speak with an accent, and are foreign. (See Table 6.1: Discourses About Latinos.) The 20th century witnessed the mass migration of Latinos to the United States, with most foreign-born Latinos entering in 1990 or later (U.S. Census Bureau, 2007d). Their points and periods of entry have differed from legal to nondocumented, from post-Castro for Cubans to citizenship status issues for Puerto Ricans, to the illegal and extralegal status of Mexicans and other Latinos en route to America. America has been enhanced, enriched, and transformed as a function of the presence of Latino people (Sanchez, 2002). Immigration reform has been led by President Obama who experiences considerable conflict with Congress over this issue.

In 2010, 41% of Latinos lived in the West, and 36% lived in the South. California had the largest Hispanic population of any state in 2014 (15.0 million). However, Texas had the largest numeric increase within the Hispanic population since July 1, 2013. New Mexico had the highest percentage of Hispanics at 47.7% (Ennis et al., 2011).

❖ **Table 6.1**   Discourses About Latinos

Low-income/poor

Lots of children

Brown

Non-English-dominant

Catholics

Gang member

Foreign born

Illegal/immigrant

Sexism among men

The Northeast and the Midwest accounted for 14% and 9% respectively of the Latino population.

Over half of the Latino population resides in three states: California, Texas, and Florida. New York, Illinois, New Jersey, and Colorado are among the states that have Latino populations of 1 million or more. Mexicans are most likely to live in California, Texas, and Arizona; Puerto Ricans have the highest representation in New York, Florida, and New Jersey. Cubans are most likely to live in Florida, California, and New Jersey (Ennis et al., 2011).

Social, Psychological, and Physical Health Issues

The diversity among Latinos is tremendous. Latinos are descendants of the oppressed and the oppressor with a history marked by social oppression, conquest, liberation, and struggle (Garcia-Preto, 1996). Among the diverse group of Latinos, differences exist across geography, country of origin, racial identity, skin color hue, class, social capital, traditions, acculturation, and the time and sociopolitical circumstances in which persons entered the United States (Beals & Beals, 1993; Nicolau & Santiestevan, 1990). Stavans (1995) said, "We Latinos have an abundance of histories, linked to a common root but with decisively different traditions. At each and every moment, these ancestral histories determine who we are and what we think" (p. 20).

Variations are striking among ethnic groups with respect to educational attainment. More than one quarter, or 27%, of Latinos have a 9th-grade education or less compared with 5% of non-Hispanic whites (Schneider, Martinez, & Owens, 2006). The high school graduation rate for all Latinos is 60% compared with 88.6% for non-Hispanic whites. South Americans (Peruvians, Colombians, and Ecuadorians) have much higher graduation rates (84.5%) than Central Americans (Guatemalan, Honduran, Salvadoran) with an average of 53%. Puerto Ricans have the next highest graduation rate at 71%. Compared to other groups, Mexicans have a lower educational attainment rate. The college attainment rate among Latinos is 10% compared with 21.3% of non-Hispanic whites (Schneider et al., 2006).

The percentage of eligible Hispanic students attending college appears to be on the rise, at least at the community college level (Nora & Crisp, 2009). For many Latino youth and adults, being a linguistic minority represents a real barrier to education and employment. Arbona and Nora (2007) examined the likelihood of Hispanic high school graduates attending either a 2- or 4-year college. The researchers found five significant factors. These factors were (1) the student's gender, (2) students' perceptions of their parents' educational expectations, (3) the student's English self-concepts, (4) enrollment in high school calculus, and (5) the perception that most of the student's peers planned on attending college. Male Latino students were more inclined to enroll in a 2-year college. Female Latina students were much more likely to attend a 4-year postsecondary institution. Choice of institutional type also depended on parents' expectations that their children would attend college. Students whose parents had low expectations that their children would attend college were twice as likely to enroll in a community college as opposed to a 4-year higher education institution. Finally, the more positive a Latino student's academic self-concept in science, the more likely he or she would enroll in a 4-year university. The two most influential factors that predicted enrollment in a 4-year college were taking a precalculus or calculus course while in high school (3.98 times more likely) and knowing that most, if not all, of a student's peers also planned on going to a 4-year institution. Advanced degrees are on the rise among Latinos. The proportion of doctorates awarded to Latinos rose from 3.4% in 1993 to 6.3% in 2013 (National Science Foundation, 2015).

In addition to geographic diversity, income varies as well. Latinos are more likely to be unemployed at 6.8%, compared with 3.4% of non-Hispanic whites. Puerto Ricans have the highest unemployment rate at 8.1%, with 5.1% among Central and South Americans. When employed, Latinos are more likely to work in service occupations, at a rate of 19.4%, or in operator or labor positions, at 22%. Compared with non-Hispanic whites, their rates in these positions are 11.8% and 11.6%, respectively. Non-Hispanic whites are more than twice as likely to work in managerial positions at a rate of 33.2%. Many of the male Latino workers who newly arrive in the United States now work in construction. These workers were also older and thus less likely to be low-wage earners. Nonetheless, many Latinos who are foreign born are in poverty (Kochhar, 2007).

The poverty rate among Latinos is more than twice that of the non-Hispanic White population (U.S. Census Bureau, 2014a). Among Latino children under the age of 18, 30% live in poverty. Among Latinos, Dominicans, Puerto Ricans, and Mexicans have the highest poverty rates at 28, 24, and 24%, respectively. Colombians have the lowest poverty rate at 11%. The poverty rate among Central Americans is 18%, which is higher than it is for South Americans at 13% (U. S. Census Bureau, 2007d).

High poverty rates contribute to Latinos having the highest probability of being medically uninsured (Institute of Medicine, 2003). Despite the high poverty rates among Latinos, which actually fell from 25.6% in 2012 to 23.5% in 2013, substantial income gains have been made. In 2013, the median household income for Latinos was $40,963, or nearly $10,000 less than the median income for the general population (DeNavas-Walt & Proctor, 2014).

Income is related to status of housing. Latinos are more likely to own their homes than to rent them, but there is tremendous variation across ethnic groups. More than half, or 52%, of Latinos owned their homes in 2004 compared with 48% who rented. Only 25% of Dominicans own their own homes, whereas 61% of Cubans are home-owners. The median value of owner-occupied homes was $152,000, which was similar (a few dollars higher) to the general population. The median value of homes among Mexicans was $136,468 compared with nearly $300,000 among Ecuadorians. Latinos also have extremely high uninsured health rates, 34% compared with 16% in the general population (DeNavas-Walt, Proctor, & Smith, 2007).

Along with African Americans and Native Americans, Latinos have a 50 to 100% burden of illness and mortality due to diabetes compared with white Americans (Institute of Medicine, 2003). In addition, high blood pressure and obesity rates are also higher among this group (U.S. DHHS, 2001).

The Epidemiologic Catchment Area Study investigated rates of psychiatric disorders in five communities. Los Angeles was one of the sites studied, and Mexicans were oversampled. Mexican Americans born in Mexico were found to have lower rates of depression and phobias compared with those born in the United States. Another study examined rates of psychiatric disorders in a large sample of Mexican Americans residing in Fresno County, California. Lifetime rates of mental disorders among Mexican American immigrants born in Mexico were remarkably lower than the rates of mental disorders among Mexican Americans born in the United States. The length of time that Latinos spent in the United States was a factor in the development of mental disorders. Immigrants who had lived in the United States for at least 13 years had higher prevalence rates of disorders than those who had lived in the United States fewer than 13 years (U.S. DHHS, 2001). "Recent immigrants of all backgrounds, who are adapting to the United States, are likely to experience a different set of stressors than long-term Hispanic residents" (U.S. DHHS, 2001, p. 133). Acculturation, according to some epidemiological studies, may even lead to an increase in mental disorders.

Vulnerabilities among youth have been reported as well. A large-scale survey of primarily Mexican American teens in both Texas and Mexico found higher rates of depression, drug use, and suicide among Texas-based youth (U.S. DHHS, 2001). Living in the United States was related to a higher risk of mental health difficulties than not living here. Texan youth were more likely to report high rates of depressive symptoms than Mexican youth, 48% compared with 39%. Youth residing in Texas who reported illicit drug use in the last 30 days was also higher among Texas-based youth as was suicidal ideation compared with youth who lived in Mexico. Latino youth are at higher risk for poor mental health outcomes, and they are more likely to drop out of school and to report feelings of depression and anxiety. Latino youth also represent 18% of juvenile offenders in residential placement (U.S. DHHS, 2001). The number of Latino college students is growing, however, an understudied area is the examination of acculturative stress and psychological distress (Crockett et al., 2007).

The HIV/AIDS epidemic is a major threat to the Latino community. According to the Centers for Disease Control (2013), 1 in 36 Latino men will be diagnosed with HIV and 1 in 106 Latina women. In 2010, HIV was the sixth leading cause of death among Hispanics/Latinos aged 25 to 34 in the United States and the eighth leading cause of death among Hispanics/Latinos aged 35 to 54. In 2010, Latinos accounted for 21% of the new AIDS diagnoses in the United States. Latinos are most likely to be infected with HIV as a result of sexual contact with men. Latino men who have sex with men represent 79% of new infections among all Latino men. The estimated new HIV infection rate among Hispanics/Latinos in 2010 in the United States was more than 3 times as high as that of whites. In addition, poverty and language barriers may contribute to Latino HIV infection rates among Latinos. Latina women may not be aware of their male partner's risky behavior and ultimately how they are unwittingly being impacted. In several studies of gay and bisexual Latinos in the United States, Latinos had the highest rates of unprotected male-to-male sexual contact.

Migration and Acculturation

Given the disproportionately higher levels of poverty, stress, and trauma of immigration and adapting to a foreign culture, and cultural isolation upon arrival, multiculturally competent mental health services for Latinos are critical. Adjusting to a new environment, acquiring a new language, and contending with a host of internal and external demands, the stress may be much greater than previously thought, with chronic acculturation stress having enormous psychological implications (Santiago-Rivera et al., 2002). On average, Latinos have relatively low educational and economic status. Despite the fact that the United States is referred to as the second largest Latin American country in the world (Arredondo & Rodriguez, 2005), migration experiences and the psychological impact of these on mental health and well-being is an area of research that needs further exploration (Santiago-Rivera, 2003).

To have access to economic opportunity and to give their children a good life are the dreams of immigrants, regardless of their country of origin. Political instability, unemployment, wars, terrorism, and devastation of a country's infrastructure compel people in search of a better life to leave their homes. Although their homelands are rich in beauty, culture, and natural resources, economic and social development opportunities are often lacking (Suarez-Orozco & Paez, 2002). Feelings of personal loss and grief are part of the experience even when a person's and/or family's economic outlook improves. Political turmoil may prevent some families from returning to their homeland. For some, there are fears of deportation if they return home. These circumstances can heighten a person's longing for home and the family and friends left behind (de las Fuentes, 2007). (See Storytelling: I Quit).

Acculturation or the process of adjusting to a nonnative culture (Miranda and Matheny, 2000) is a form of stress for many Latinos and there are multiple factors that contribute to this stress. The degree of acculturation, amount of coping with stress resources, facility with the English language, the degree of cohesiveness with family members, and the length of time that people have resided in the United States all impact acculturation stress for Latinos (Miranda & Matheney, 2000). Since September 11, 2001, xenophobic attitudes have increased, and Latinos are vulnerable to such personal attitudes as institutional structures impinge upon their lives. Acculturation stress is the emotional, physical disharmony, and spiritual imbalance that is part of the acculturation process following immigration. Lack of a solid social network, not having facility with the English language, intergenerational conflicts, overcrowded and unsafe living conditions and neighborhoods have been documented as part of the acculturation process (Arredondo & Rodriguez, 2005).

In working with Latinos, it is important to consider the client within the broader context of the family. (See Case Study: Oblivious.) A multidimensional ecological comparative model may help mental health professionals devise a relevant and respectful treatment approach. There are four domains to the model (Falicov, 1995):

1. The impact of migration and cultural change

2. Family organization

3. The current ecological environment and the family

4. The family life cycle or transitions

Colorism refers to differential and often inequitable treatment because of skin color hue (Robinson & Ward, 1995). As with African American communities, colorism affects Latino communities. Sue and Sue (1990) indicated that "the more a person resembles an Indian, the more prejudice and discrimination he or she will encounter" (p. 298). A variety of hues—white, tan, black, brown, and red—compose the Latino population, attesting to roots from Africa, Asia, the Caribbean, Spain, and other parts of Europe, and an indigenous (first people) Native heritage. Research is needed to investigate the role of colorism among brown and black Dominicans, Mexicans, and Puerto Ricans, Latino subgroups with higher rates of poverty.

Cultural Orientation and Values

Cultural heritage commonalities are strong. Among most Latinos, cooperation rather than competition is stressed. The extended family and friendship networks are held in high esteem and are the basis of Latino culture (Gloria & Peregoy, 1995). (See Table 6.2: Common Cultural Values Among Latinos.) Family members feel a sense of obligation to provide for, and receive support from, one another both emotionally and materially (Vasquez, 1994). *Familismo* (familialism) is considered to be one of the most important cultural values that Latino people have (Santiago-Rivera, 2003) and "involves the strong identification and attachment to nuclear and extended family. Loyalty, reciprocity, and solidarity among members of the family are associated with this attachment" (p. 50).

Latino cultures tend to be collectivistic, which means individual goals are subordinated to the larger group. Relationships in collectivistic cultures also tend to be

❖ **Table 6.2**   Common Cultural Values Among Latinos

Personalismo (intimacy)

Dignidad (personal honor)

Familismo (faith in friends and family)

Respeto (respect)

Confianza (the development of trust and intimacy)

Simpatia (being a nice, gentle person)

Carino (a demonstration of endearment in verbal and nonverbal communication)

Orgullo (pride)

Loyalty to family

Collectivism

Service to others

Education as a means of development

Religion (for most, the Catholic Church—but not for all)

Personal communication that reflects personalismo

more stable and even involuntary "because they arise from the fewer, yet closer knit, in-groups that permeate this orientation" (McCarthy, 2005, p. 110).

In many Mexican American families, the extended family is strong and includes *compradazgo,* or godparents, and among Puerto Ricans, *compadres,* or special friends who often act as co-parents and receive a high place of honor, affection, and respect in the family (Santiago-Rivera et al., 2002). Gloria and Peregoy (1995) stated that more status is given to a person who honors family than to someone with material possessions.

Family structure and personal honor are highly valued. *Dignidad* is linked to both personalismo and respeto. Personalismo is an orientation in which the person is more important than the task. Warm and interpersonal relationships are valued (Santiago-Rivera, 2003). Respeto refers to "sensitivity to a person's position and creates a boundary within which conversations should be contained to avoid conflict" (Santiago-Rivera et al., 2002, p. 113). Dignidad encourages actions that cultivate pride for people independent of their position and refers to a strong sense of self-worth and personal dignity. A focus is also placed on being in the moment, with emphasis on the present.

Family structures are often formal and hierarchical, in that deference to elders and males is practiced. Although often misunderstood as related to men's sexual prowess and women's objectification and subjugation, *machismo* is a part of Latino culture that describes stoicism, the need for dignidad, or dignity, respeto, or respect, and in some instances, dominance within the family (Vasquez, 1994). Adherence to family roles, such as males outside the home and females inside, represents another value orientation practiced by some traditional Latino families (Arredondo, 1992). Preserving the Spanish language within the family is a common practice in many Latino homes.

In Latino culture, a premium is placed on personal relationships. *Personalismo*, or a desire to be close, to know one another intimately, and to communicate personally rather than impersonally, represents a value orientation common to many Latinos (Arredondo, 1992; Gloria & Peregoy, 1995). Communication styles represent a significant part of the way meanings are expressed and interpreted. Many Latinos tend to speak softly, avoid eye contact when listening to or speaking with persons perceived as having high status, and interject less. Often, the manner of expression is low-key and indirect (Sue & Sue, 1990). *Simpatia* refers to the value of smooth and harmonious interpersonal interactions (Gloria & Peregoy, 1995). It also speaks to the importance of harmonious and polite interactions (de las Fuentes, 2007). Latino families are more likely to live within family units and similar to Asian Americans and Pacific Islanders, are least likely to live alone. Children also tend to remain with the family (especially girls) until they marry (U.S. DHHS, 2001).

❖ STORYTELLING: I QUIT

I went to college in southern California. One summer, I needed to find work to pay tuition. I found work in a factory where we made the telephone cords that went to landlines. We also detangled the cords and used a chemical on the cords to clean them. This cleaning is what I and the other women in my particular area did all day long. Feeling bored, I decided to wipe these cords down while studying Italian—this subversive move did not go over well with the supervisor, who told me to stop. Although I needed the money, I quit this job (I suspected that I was close to being fired). The smell of the chemical gave me a headache and made me nauseous. I was alarmed by the numbers of pregnant Mexican women subjected to this toxic chemical hour after hour every single day. I spoke quietly to one of the women and told her that her job might be dangerous to both her health and to her baby's health. I remember that she looked at me like I was crazy. She said she liked working, and that she had a family. I soon came to realize that many of the women who worked at this factory were not in California legally. I was an American citizen, a college student, and although I needed summer work, I had no children to support. These women were not in a position to think about safety given their focus on survival.

Demonstrated through loyalty for one's family, cultural pride is significant (Rendon & Robinson, 1994). According to Comas-Diaz (1993), the concept of respeto "governs all positive reciprocal interpersonal relationships, dictating the appropriate deferential behavior toward others on the basis of age, socioeconomic position, sex, and authority status" (p. 250). Within the concept of respeto, parents desire to raise children who are polite and well mannered (*bien educados*) as opposed to children who are not well behaved (*malcriados*), which is an indication of poor parenting that reflects on the family (Arredondo & Rodriguez, 2005).

For most Latinos, the bond to Catholicism is strong. In fact, the concept of *Marianismo* "is based on the Catholic cult of the Virgin Mary, which dictates that when women become mothers they attain the status of Madonnas and, accordingly, are expected to deny themselves in favor of their children and husbands" (Vasquez, 1994, p. 202). Clearly, conflicts can emerge within this cultural value system, particularly for Latinas who may be more acculturated. Overall, the church and faith play a crucial role and shape core beliefs, such as the importance of sacrifice, charitability, service to others, and long suffering, even in the face of adversity (Sue & Sue, 1990).

As is consistent with other groups who are more oriented toward collectivism than individualism, there is a holistic connection between the mind and body. *Curanderos,* or spiritual and herbal folk healers, who are primarily women, practice an ancient Native American art (Novas, 1994). They hold special status in many Mexican and Mexican American communities and often work in consultation on psychiatric cases with priests and other religious authorities (Arredondo, 1992). *Espiritistas* are spiritual guides, and *Santeros* (a reference to worshipers of Catholic saints and African gods) are consulted to diagnose conditions, both physical and psychological. Oils, prayers, holy water, candles, and special herbs are items used to perform rituals (Santiago-Rivera, 2003). Aztecs have a rich history as herbalists, healers, botanists, and medical doctors (Padilla, 1984). That some of their descendants would have the gift of healing is understandable.

Families gather to celebrate holidays, birthdays, baptisms, first communions, graduations, and weddings. Latino families teach their children the importance of honor, good manners, and respect for authority and the elderly. Importance is given to physical appearance as a sense of honor, dignity, and pride. Formal attire is commonly worn to church, parties, social gatherings, and work (Clutter & Nieto, n.d.)

Culture-bound syndromes are defined as "recurrent, locally specific patterns of a typical behavior and troubling experiences that may or may not be linked to a particular *DSM–IV* diagnostic category" (Shiraev & Levy, 2004, p. 244). Folk illness such as *empacho*, which is a bad upset stomach, *nervios* (nerves), and *mal de ojo* (evil eye) are often related to supernatural causes, particularly among Puerto Ricans, Cubans, and Dominicans. *Susto* refers to fright, and it originated from and is a combination of medieval Spanish, African, and indigenous beliefs (Santiago-Rivera, 2003). An expression of distress commonly linked to Latinos and Mediterranean groups is *ataques de nervios* or attack of nerves. Symptoms of an *ataque de nervios* include screaming uncontrollably, crying, trembling, heat in the chest rising to the head, and verbal or physical aggression. Death of a loved one, divorce, or interpersonal conflict can bring about this syndrome (Shiraev & Levy, 2004). Dissociative experiences, seizures, or fainting as well as suicidal gestures are known to occur in ataques (U.S. DHHS, 2001).

Personal identity for Latino Americans is sociocentric in nature, with the self and self-interest often subordinated to the welfare of *la casa* and *la familia* (Becerra, 1988). The balance of group and individual prerogatives, however, depends on the individual manner of dealing with the culture in traditional, bicultural, nontraditional, or marginal terms. For traditional and bicultural persons, the balance will often be in favor of needs in the extended family. For nontraditional and marginal persons, the balance may favor more egocentric decisions and actions.

Traditional sex roles are clearly defined by machismo for men and marianismo and *hembrismo* for women (Becerra, 1988). Machismo is more than male physical dominance and sexual availability. It includes the role of a provider responsible for the welfare, protection, honor, and dignity of his family. Marianismo refers to the spiritual superiority of women and their capacity to endure all suffering, with reference to the Virgin Mary. After marriage, the Madonna concept includes sacrifice and femaleness, or hembrismo, in the form of strength, perseverance, and flexibility. These hembrista behaviors ensure survival and power through the children.

Personal identity is also associated with being strong. Strong refers to inner strength, or *fuerza de espiritu*, characterized by toughness, determination, and willpower (Dana, 1993). A strong person can confront a problem directly and be active in resolving it, thereby delaying the admission that help may be needed. *Controlarse*, or controlling oneself, is the key to being a strong person and includes *aguantarse*, or being able to withstand stress during bad times; *resignarse* refers to resigning oneself and accepting fate. *Sobreponerse* speaks to imposing one's will or overcoming circumstance. A weak person will have little or no self-control and be less able to exercise responsibility or to display orgullo, or pride, and *verguenzza*, or shame. As a result, he or she is more easily influenced by people or events and is relatively unable to become strong.

The family name is very important to Latinos; a man, along with his given name, adopts both his father's and mother's names. It is often expected, as well as encouraged, that family members will sacrifice their own needs for the welfare of the family (Goldenberg & Goldenberg, 1996). Thus, the family constellation is loyal, committed, and responsible to each other and has a strong sense of honor.

Latino Ethnic Identity Development

That Latinos can be and are of any race is often confusing and difficult for students to grasp. When students are told that Latinos are not a racial group but an ethnic group with different ethnic and racial subgroups, the confusion magnifies. When I make the point to students that sharing race does not mean sharing ethnicity and sharing ethnicity does not mean sharing race, I often draw a Venn diagram or say something like, "A white-skinned woman with blond hair and blue eyes might identify herself ethnically as Cubana but racially she considers herself to be white she Latina?" Yes! At the same time, a sister Cubana may have African roots, dark skin, and very curly hair. Ethnically, she is also Cubana but considers herself black. "Is she also Latina?" Yes! I refer to my experience in Cuba by using the aforementioned example. Cubans hail from Africa, Europe (Spanish), or Asia (Chinese), and/or are indigenous (Indian). The difficulty with understanding Latinos both racially and ethnically is related to the dichotomization of racial categories. An inaccurate and limited bifurcation of people—"you are either this or that"—has had implications for a racial/ethnic identity development model for Latinos. A dialectic embraces a "both/and" way of being in the world and is needed to appreciate multiple identities within and across groups of people. In addition, the existing models of racial identity may not aptly apply to Latinos who are racially diverse and are Latinos across different ethnic groups.

According to Ferdman and Gallegos (2001), there are key dimensions involved in defining a nonlinear Latino identity: (a) how a person prefers to identify himself or herself, (b) how Latinos as a group are seen, (d) how white people are seen, and (d) how race fits into the equation.

Latino Integrated. Persons who are Latino integrated are able to embrace the fullness of their Latino identity and integrate this into other identities, such as class, profession, and gender. A dialectic, as mentioned earlier, is characteristic of the Latino integrated. This person is comfortable with all types of Latinos as there is a broad lens used to see himself or herself, white people, and others.

Latino Identified. This group has more of a pan-Latino identity, with a view of race, la raza, as uniquely Latin. There is a deep and abiding understanding of a history of political struggle and a desire to be united with other Latinos in racial unity. Despite the awareness of and vigilant stand against institutional racism, Latino-identified persons may see whites, blacks, and other groups in rigid ways.

Subgroup Identified. Persons of this group see themselves as distinct from white people but do not necessarily identify with other Latinos or with people of color. The broad pan-Latino orientation discussed in the previous orientations is not reflected here. Other Latino subgroups may be viewed in an inferior way. People's allegiance to a particular subgroup is nearly exclusive. Race is not a central or clear organizing concept, but nationality, ethnicity, and culture are primary.

Latino as "Other." Persons with this orientation see themselves as people of color. This may be a function of biracial or multiracial status, ambiguous phenotype, or dominant constructions of race. In certain contexts, persons see themselves as minorities and not white. There is no identification with Latino cultural norms or with white culture, and an understanding of Latino history and culture is missing.

Undifferentiated. Persons with this orientation regard themselves as simply "people" with a color-blind eye. The emphasis on racial classification is not a part of their framework. The desire to associate with other Latinos is not prominent because contact with others is distinct from a person's race or ethnic identity. Life is lived apart from attention to and thoughts of difference.

White Identified. White-identified persons perceive themselves as white and thus superior to people of color (nonwhite-skinned people). Assimilation into white culture is a possibility as is connection primarily to only one other group (e.g., light-skinned Cubans) while denying connection to other subgroups. There is an acceptance of the status quo and a valuing of whiteness to the extent that marrying white is preferred over marrying dark. Latinos with this orientation are majored la raza (i.e., improve the race).

The strength of this model is that it helps mental health professionals and clients ascertain identity development for Latinos who differ greatly across acculturation level, skin color, education, class, national origin, and political ideology. This model is also not linear; nonetheless, it is clear that there are orientations more conducive to unity with others across race and skin color wherein people are valued because they are human and not because of what they look like.

Umaña-Taylor (2004) studied ethnic identity and self-esteem among 1,062 Mexican-origin adolescents who attended one of three schools: predominantly Latino, predominantly non-Latino, and balanced Latino/non-Latino. Phinney's Multigroup Ethic Identity Measure was used to assess ethnic identity. Rosenberg's Self-Esteem Scale measured self-esteem. A significant relationship emerged between ethnic identity and self-esteem for adolescents attending the predominately non-Latino school, the balanced school, and the predominantly Latino school. This finding suggests that the relationship between self-esteem and ethnic identity may not be context specific. Maternal education was higher among students at the predominantly non-Latino school. Students attending the predominantly non-Latino school were more likely to have been born in the United States than students at the balanced school. Finally, students at the predominantly non-Latino school reported higher levels of ethnic identity than teens at the predominantly Latino and balanced schools. These data suggest that "ethnic identity appears to be more salient for Mexican-origin adolescents when they are in a minority context than in a majority context" (Umaña-Taylor, 2004, p. 144). However, the relationship between self-esteem and ethnic identity did not differ across schools. Predominantly Latino school students are a minority in the larger society, irrespective of their majority presence at school, which may account for this finding.

Implications for Mental Health Professionals

Among many collectivistic cultures, mental health services are not sought because in-group members' reliance for help comes from family or church. Persons who are members of the out-group might be viewed with mistrust and suspicion (McCarthy, 2005). Other barriers to psychotherapy services for Latinos include mental health services that are culturally insensitive and a lack of Spanish speaking behavioral health providers. In addition to having Spanish language skills, being an effective listener, engaging in intentional questioning, having empathy, and strong diagnostic skills, can make a big difference. For example, there is such informality in Western culture where people, regardless of age and status, are on a first-name basis. Some clients of color as well as some white people are put off by a casual air that may feel disrespectful. This is a basic concept when working with clients who are older than the clinician. The concept of *falta de respeto* (lack of respect) is considered to be a major cause for breakdowns in communication across a number of relationship dyads (Santiago-Rivera et al., 2002). The Western view of the nuclear family is limiting for many Latinos and is connected to the cultural tendency to bifurcate and separate the self into discrete categories. Among many Latinos, family need not be defined through blood. It is important for mental health professionals to assess the clients' relationships within and outside the nuclear family (Schoulte, 2011).

An understanding of collectivistic frameworks and their influence on people's problem orientation and resolve can help a clinician serving Latino individuals. Many Latino families value close and intimate communication styles in which there is greater emphasis on the group and less on the individual acting as a lone agent, where the husband is the primary and only breadwinner and gender roles are well prescribed.

Latino consciousness and solidarity should never be presumed for all subgroups. For many Latinos, identity labels that are linked to a country of origin are preferred (Fernandes, 2014).

Case Study

Oblivious

Zoe is a 23-year-old graduate student who has traveled to Guatemala with her college professor and other college students. Zoe was adopted as an infant from Guatemala. Through her travels, she is struck at the beauty of the country. She also encounters the blinding poverty that many Guatemalan people experience daily; the skin color differences are striking to her as well; she is aware that had she stayed in Guatemala, many opportunities might not have been available to her because of her dark skin color. Gender roles are well prescribed, and many women her age do not have an opportunity to get educated at the university. Zoe is angry at not knowing more about her country of origin, sad at the discrimination, and confused at how she has remained oblivious to class, gender, and skin color issues, not only in Guatemala but in the States. Zoe has always resented being mistaken for an African American. Her adopted sister, who is also from Guatemala, looks European. Zoe has always wanted her sister's appearance over her own. Zoe never mentioned this desire to her mother, and they never spoke about race or skin color in their home. Zoe resented when people wanted to connect with her because of her race. Throughout her life, Zoe emphasized softball (she won a scholarship to college because of her talents). She also emphasized her academic strengths, religion, and being an animal lover (she has two cats and a dog at home with her mother and sister). The trip has been life changing for Zoe who enjoyed long conversations with her professor, local women, and some of the students of color with whom she has been traveling. Zoe observed the women in Guatemala see themselves within the context of their relationships. She is eager to return in order to find out more about herself, her birth mother, and her birth father.

Questions

1. Why was Zoe so unaware of her country of origin?
2. How could a therapist be effective with Zoe's confusion, anger, and sadness?

Discussion and Integration

Zoe

According to Falbo and De Baessa (2006), Guatemala is divided between Indian (40%) and non-Indian groups. The Indian groups are considered to be descendants of the ancient Mayans, who dominated the area during the first millennium AD. Beginning in 1523 and typical of the colonizers who were determined to extinguish the indigenous peoples' language and ethnic identities, the Indians were compelled to assimilate into the Spanish colonial system. *Ladinos*, a term used to describe non-Indians, refers to a mix of the descendants of the ancient Mayans and Spanish colonists—who are part of the dominant national culture. *Ladinization* is the process of shifting from

Indian to Ladino. Although a diversity of experiences exists, Ladinos on average have higher social status than Indians (Falbo & De Baessa, 2006).

Like other Latinos, Guatemalans have a variety of phenotypes. There were African slaves in Guatemala, and many, due to their African roots, have dark skin and other Negroid features. Guatemala is home to more than 6,000 black Guatemalans. Prior to her trip, Zoe knew that Guatemala was a Central American country. She also knew that Spanish was spoken, the dominant language of the conquistadores. She did not know about the Garifina people or that Indian languages are spoken as well, namely Kiché and Q'eqchi' (Falbo & De Baessa, 2006). Zoe knew that poverty rates were very high in Guatemala, but she was unaware of the class/caste/color differences. Q'eqchi people tend to have less formal education and lower earnings than other Indian groups (Falbo & De Baessa, 2006). Her upbringing did not emphasize her country of origin where the focus is family and community centered. Although in her family, respect for elders, hard work, and honesty were transmitted values, she cannot recall a conversation with her white mother about racism, racial pride, or racial socialization.

A skill in multicultural competence is to wait and listen for valuable information that the client may reveal, which could be a reflection of how the client is positioned by her or his culture, acculturation, and identity development. It appears that Zoe is largely defined as undifferentiated where colorblindness (e.g., not seeing color) is part of how she exists in the world. Persons with this orientation regard themselves as simply a person. Multicultural competence could be built with the learning exercise of a sociocultural identity wheel where she lists the various components of her identity (Metzger, Nadkarni, & Cornish, 2010). An instructor could point out the absence of any mention of being Guatemalan or a person of color or nonwhite, or adopted.

If Zoe ever entered therapy with a multiculturally competent mental health professional, there would be a need to listen to the range of conflicting emotions (gratitude from being adopted, sadness from not knowing her birth parents, envy of her white-skinned sister, feelings of alienation from a predominantly white culture that sees her as nonwhite, sense of safety with people of color). Confusion regarding her multiple identities as a dark-skinned and Guatemala-born American woman, as well as internalized racism and colorism, are the issues that tug at her yet are developmentally on task for this young woman.

Summary

This chapter focused on Latinos as a heterogeneous group. A demographical snapshot was provided and included information about representation in the population by ethnic group, the most populated states where Latinos reside, and educational attainment. Immigration was discussed, as were push and pull factors contributing to immigration. A case study was included, and cultural elements were discussed. An adopted Latina child and the confusion of learning about the meaning of race, color, and gender differences were addressed through the case study, including ways in which multicultural competence could be assessed and improved.

7

**People of
African Descent** ❖

This chapter is about people of African descent. The majority of black people in this country are descendants of African slaves. The term *people of African descent* is used to recognize this majority as well as refer to people who have origins in any of the black racial groups of Africa.

History, 500–1500 AD

The skeletal remains of the earth's earliest human come from East Africa, representing all Homo sapiens' ancestors. According to social historian Bennett (1982),

> Civilization started in the great river valleys of Africa and Asia, in the Fertile Crescent in the Near East and along the narrow ribbon of the Nile in Africa . . . Blacks, or people who would be considered Blacks today, were among the first people to use tools, paint pictures, plant seeds, and worship gods. (p. 5)

Between 500 and 1600 AD, Africa had empires, governments, and systems of trade throughout the continent. The West African empires of Ghana, Mali, and Songhai emerged in the western Sudan and were in existence during that time (Christian, 1995). Each of these three states had a powerful king and was wealthy, with an abundance of gold, thriving agriculture, manufacturing, and successful international trading efforts. Ghana dominated the Sudan for three centuries and reached its peak in the early part of the 11th century. Mali rose in the 13th century, and Songhai was a formidable power in the 15th and 16th centuries. During this time, Timbuktu represented one of the world's greatest cities, with a reputation as the intellectual center of the Songhai Empire.

The Slave Trade

The majority of black people in America, including people who trace their ancestry to the Caribbean where slave ships took Africans from Africa, can trace their ancestry to the slave trade. The slave trade operated for 4 centuries. In 1501, for instance, the Spanish government authorized the use of African slaves in the Americas. Portugal was actually the first country to land a cargo of slaves in the Western Hemisphere (Christian, 1995) and remained the dominant slave trader well until the end of the 16th century (Stewart, 1996). In 2010, the ship São José Paquete was found in the Cape of Good Hope, having left Mozambique in 1794 for Maranhão Brazil's sugar plantations, with nearly 500 African slaves on board. Buffeted by violent weather, the ship came apart on two reefs not far from Cape Town. The Portuguese captain, crew, and half of the slaves survived (Cooper, 2015).

In addition to the Portuguese, the Spanish, Dutch, British, and the colonies provided fierce competition for this lucrative industry in which human beings were traded for gold, salt, sugar, wine, and tobacco. Nations that controlled most of the American waters controlled most of the trade. With an estimated 60,000 voyages (Cooper, 2015), that could take anywhere from 60 days to 4 months, slaves were shipped to Cuba, Europe, the West Indies, South America, and to the colonies. The first American slave ship bound for Africa was called the Rainbow and sailed from Boston.

During the slave trade throughout Europe, the Americas, and the Caribbean, nearly 12 million people were taken out of Africa, mainly from West and Central Africa. Slave ships brought kidnapped Africans to the Western Hemisphere, which included the colonies, Brazil, and the Caribbean. Most slaves came from an area bordering a 3,000-mile stretch on the West Coast of Africa. They hailed from different tribes, including the Hausas, the Mandingos, the Yorubas, the Efiks, the Krus, the Ashantis, the Dahomeans, the Senegalese, and the Fantins (Bennett, 1982). Royalty, African merchants, and the poor were among those who were abducted for trade.

It is estimated that as many as 2 million people perished at port, at sea, or upon arrival during the slave trade. The *middle passage* typically refers to the journey from Africa to the Americas, Europe, or the Caribbean. From roughly 1450 to 1600, about 367,000 Africans were removed from Africa, with this number increasing dramatically to more than 6 million during the 18th century.

Africans played a role in capturing other Africans for sale to white slave traders. Prior to European enslavement of Africans, slavery existed in the African states. This historical reality was used to justify the use of African slaves among Europeans. Although enslavement of any human being is morally reprehensible, there were two important differences between the slavery of Africans by other Africans and the slavery of Africans by Europeans. African slavery was not plantation or mining slavery. It did not strip African people of family linkage, nor was it based on racial hatred that reduced people's humanity. African slaves owned by other Africans would sometimes marry, own property, and become a member of the family (Zinn, 2003). The extent of Africans' participation in the selling of other Africans to Europeans depends on which version of history we read. According to Bennett (1982), there has been an attempt to overemphasize the degree of African involvement. Bennett said, "It is true that some Africans, corrupted by Europe's insatiable desire for human flesh, sold their countrymen. But many Africans, like King Almammy and Captain Tobba, loathed the whole business and forbade their subjects to take part in it" (p. 47). According to Stewart (1996), "Most of the Africans who became slaves were sold into slavery by other Africans . . . A lucrative trade for European goods, especially weapons, facilitated the selling of slaves to the Europeans" (p. 10). Africans captured by other Africans and sold to white slave traders who sold them to the highest bidder in Virginia became part of the social structure of the colony (Christian, 1995).

The year 1619 is designated as the date when the first African settlers reached North America on a Dutch man-of-war ship in Jamestown, Virginia. This group of African indentured servants was not regarded as slaves. In exchange for their passage over, people sold their labor for a period of time. Thousands of whites used this method as a means of coming to the colonies, and life for them was often similar to that of black indentured servants. They worked alongside each other farming, clearing forests, and cutting tobacco. For these first 40 years, black settlers moved about with relative ease, had voting rights, and even—after surviving indentured servitude—purchased other black people. This system began to erode with the arrival of greater numbers of Africans, which made the profits from the slave trade escalate for both the slave trader and slave owner.

These servants were not, however, the first Africans to arrive in North America. Estevanico was the most important African explorer of America and the first foreigner to discover New Mexico. He was born in Morocco around 1500 and left Spain in 1527 as the slave of Andres Dorantes. These two were members of the expedition of Pánfilo de Narváez, the Spanish governor of Florida. Estevanico became the first foreign explorer of the southwestern United States and explored the area that became Arizona and New Mexico (Christian, 1995; Stewart, 1996). In 1539, Estevanico was murdered by Zuni Indians who were protecting their land.

During the latter part of the 1700s, southeast Native American tribes, such as the Choctaws, Seminoles, and Creeks, were slave owners, with the Cherokees having the largest number of slaves. Prior to Native people's removal to Indian Territory, Native Americans used black slaves on their plantations in Georgia and Tennessee.

The slave trade was outlawed in the United States in 1808. At that time, there were approximately 1 million slaves. By 1860, there were close to 4 million, with Virginia leading all other states followed by Georgia, Alabama, and Mississippi. These states, along with Texas, Louisiana, Tennessee, and Arkansas, were the cotton kingdoms, and half of the black population worked in these states.

Resistance to Slavery

A history of resistance and revolt characterize the African slaves. In 1526, in the San Miguel settlement, now known as present-day South Carolina, slaves set fire to the settlement and fled to live among the Native Americans. Those slaves who managed to make it safely to the Gracia Real de Santa Teresa de Mose settlement founded by escaped slaves were granted their freedom by the King of Spain.

The resistance to slavery was multifaceted: It was political and literary, and it appeared on the podium as preachers spoke against this abomination to humankind. Many slaves ran away, often seeking to be reunited with loved ones and risking life and limb to escape their enslavement. Frances E. W. Harper, a black poet, was born to free blacks in Maryland. Some thought her to be a man or a white person with a black painted face given how intelligent and articulate she was. She protested the unequal treatment of people on the basis of gender and race. Her poem "The Slave Auction" appeared in her 1854 *Poems of Miscellaneous Subjects:*

And mothers stood with streaming eyes,

And saw their dearest children sold,

Unheeded rose their bitter cries,

While tyrants bartered them for gold.

Slavery was a barbaric institution supported by the government and often sanctioned by the Christian church. The impact on and implications for black people's mental health, self-image, psyches, and earning potential can never be truly assessed.

The ways in which black people coped or resisted took on a number of different forms, with religion and spirituality being critical. "In the slave quarters, African Americans organized their own 'invisible institution.' Through signals, passwords, and messages not discernible to whites, they called believers to 'hush harbors' where they freely mixed African rhythms, singing, and beliefs with evangelical Christianity" (Maffly-Kipp, 2000, p. 2). Negro spirituals (e.g., Wade in the water; wade in the water children; wade in the water. God's gonna trouble the water) had double meanings of salvation and freedom/escape. It was in this context that Negro spirituals were created and remain to this day.

Although the slave trade had been outlawed, slavery itself continued in the South until Abraham Lincoln, out of military necessity, signed the Emancipation Proclamation in 1863. The purpose of this document was to deplete the South of its slave labor power. Lincoln had no authority to free slaves in the loyal states, only in the states of rebellion. In 1865, on June 19th, a day better known as "Juneteenth," slavery was outlawed in Texas. Later that year, on December 18, slavery became illegal with the passage of the 13th Amendment to the U.S. Constitution.

The only way for many blacks to gain access to opportunity was to leave the South. Baltimore was considered a border city and represented a popular place for newly freed slaves to start a new life, after looking from town to town for displaced loved ones. In the same year the 13th Amendment was ratified, the Ku Klux Klan was organized in Pulaski, Tennessee. Its purpose was to undermine racial equality through acts of terrorism, which often went unpunished and in some municipalities, were sanctioned by political officers who were also Klan members.

The 14th Amendment in 1868 extended citizenship to African Americans, whereas the 15th Amendment ensured the right to vote. Poll taxes, grandfather clauses, and literacy tests prevented blacks from voting. *De jure* (by law) *segregation* replaced slavery—also known as Jim Crow. This inferior status of blacks was supported by law, requiring blacks to ride at the back of the bus, sit in different sections of movie theaters and sports stadiums, drink at separate water faucets, live in separate neighborhoods, and eat at separate restaurants.

After passage of the 13th Amendment, many blacks sharecropped. Sharecroppers worked the landowner's land for a share of the profit once the crop went to market. Landowners kept the accounts. Keeping landowners honest was very difficult for sharecroppers who had little power or literacy.

The majority of blacks in the United States reside in the South. This percentage declined during the 20th century. World War I created a huge demand for unskilled labor in the urban North; recruiters went to the South to bring black workers to northern cities such as Pittsburgh, Chicago, Detroit, and Indianapolis. Between 1916 and 1919, 500,000 African Americans migrated north (Stewart, 1996). After World War II, between 1940 and 1960, nearly 5 million blacks went north.

Demographic Trends

As the second largest group of color in the United States, the 45.7 million people of African descent come from diverse cultures, including Africa, Haiti, Dominican Republic, Jamaica, central Europe, and North and South America. African Americans

Knowledge Check 7.1

The Black Immigrant Population

1. The black immigrant population accounts for 8.7% of the U.S. black population and is nearly triple their share in 1980.

2. Black immigrants come from various parts of the world with half from the Caribbean.

3. Jamaica is the largest source country with about 682,000 black immigrants and accounts for 18% of the national total.

4. Haiti follows with 586,000 black immigrants, or 15% of the U.S. black immigrant population.

Source: Anderson (2015).

---

are 13.2% of the population (Humes, Jones, & Ramirez, 2011; U.S. Census Bureau, 2015b). Outside of the white population, the black population had the smallest percentage growth between 2000 and 2010, growing by 4.3 million people, and grew slower than most of the major racial groups. (See Knowledge Check 7.1: The Black Immigrant Population.)

Much of the recent growth, however, in the size of the black immigrant population has been fueled by African immigration. Between 2000 and 2013, the number of black African immigrants living in the U.S. rose 137%, from 574,000 to 1.4 million. Africans now make up over one third (36%) of the total foreign-born black population, up from 24% in 2000 and 7% in 1980 (Anderson, 2015). In Massachusetts, one in four black people is foreign born.

The majority of blacks in America reside in 10 states: New York, Florida, Georgia, Texas, California, Illinois, North Carolina, Maryland, Virginia, and Louisiana. In 2010, 55% of blacks lived in the South, with 18% residing in the Midwest, 17% living in the Northeast, and 10% living in the West (U.S. Census Bureau, 2011).

States in the West have low proportions of blacks in the population. Blacks were less than 5% of the population in the West, and blacks were less than 1% in Idaho, Utah, Wyoming, and Montana. A similar situation exists in New England states, where blacks are less than 1% of the population in Vermont, New Hampshire, and Maine. In Washington, D.C., 57% of the residents are black, and in Mississippi, Alabama, Louisiana, Maryland, Georgia, and South Carolina, more than 25% of the state's residents are African Americans (U. S. Census Bureau, 2011). (See Knowledge Check 7.2: Top 10 States Where Black People Reside.)

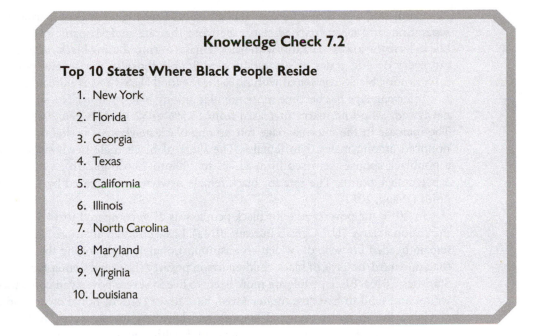

Knowledge Check 7.2

Top 10 States Where Black People Reside

1. New York
2. Florida
3. Georgia
4. Texas
5. California
6. Illinois
7. North Carolina
8. Maryland
9. Virginia
10. Louisiana

Social, Psychological, and Physiological Health Issues

In 2010, the median age of the nation was 37.2 years (Howden & Meyer, 2011). The geographical areas with the lowest median ages are along the United States and Mexico border. Persons with the lowest median age are Latinos/Hispanics. The highest median ages are among nonwhite Hispanics in Maine, Vermont, West Virginia, New Hampshire, and Florida. African Americans, although older than Latinos, are younger, by about 9 years, than the median age of non-Hispanic whites. Persons between the ages of 18 to 44 are 39.1% of the population, followed by children under the age of 18 at 31.2%. Persons 45 to 64 are 21.4% of the population, with people 65 and older at 8.2% (U.S. Census Bureau, 2007c).

In 2004, black women had higher rates of fertility than white women. Over 60% (62.4%) of the black women who gave birth in 2004 were unmarried, compared with 20.5% of white women. Black women are the least likely, compared to other women, to be married, particularly in the childbearing years. The greatest percent of black people were in nonfamily households at 35%. A nonfamily household is defined as people who live alone or people living with unrelated individuals. Thirty percent of black households had women only with no male present, 29% were married couples, and nearly 6% were male only. Blacks are also more likely than whites to live with and care for grandchildren. About 7% of blacks aged 30 and older were grandparents living in the same household with their co-resident grandchildren under the age of 18.

Compared with the population at large, blacks have higher rates of marital divorce, separation, and never-married status. Between the race and Hispanic-origin groups, blacks have the lowest sex ratio, with black females outnumbering black males throughout every decade. Rates of separation were double those in the general population: 5.1% among blacks compared with 2.1% for the total (U.S. Census Bureau, 2007c).

Intermarriage has become more popular among black people. The share of black newlyweds who intermarry increased from 15.5% to 17.1% between 2008 and 2010. The increase in the intermarriage rate among black newlyweds is slightly more pronounced among males than females. The share of black male newlyweds marrying a nonblack spouse increased from 21.7% in 2008 to 23.6% in 2010, a rise of nearly 2 percentage points. The rate for black female newlyweds increased by 1 percentage point (Wang, 2012).

In 2013, the poverty rate for black people was 27% compared to 14.5 percent for the nation at large (U.S. Census Bureau, 2014a). Black children are more likely to live in female-headed households, which are disproportionately high among the poor. More than one third, or 39%, of black children live in poverty (National Center for Education Statistics, 2015). Black people are more likely to live in severe poverty in comparison to whites and tend to have less money saved, have lower rates of home ownership (54% of blacks live in renter-occupied homes), and have few investments (DeNavas-Walt, Proctor, & Smith, 2007; U.S. Department of Health and Human Services [DHHS], 2001). In addition, black children are more likely to be exposed to violence. As Boyd-Franklin (2003) stated, "Many are acquainted from an early age with violence in their homes in the form of child abuse, sexual abuse, drug overdose, and AIDS" (p. 266).

Among black people who own homes, the median value of their homes is $104,000, which is $50,000 less than the median value of white owner-occupied homes. There is another side, however, to black economic conditions. More than 30% of blacks in America have incomes between $35,000 and $75,000. Nearly 32% live in the suburbs (U.S. DHHS, 2001). Although there is a discernible middle class among African Americans, regardless of income, black people in America tend to have fewer resources (e.g., public services, access to health care), tend to be segregated in neighborhoods, and have higher levels of health risks (Institute of Medicine [IOM], 2003). Compared with whites, black people are more likely to use public transportation to commute to work (12% of blacks compared with 3% of whites).

There have been increases in the high school graduation level, now at 80% among blacks 25 years of age and older. This compares with 83.9% for the general population (U.S. Census Bureau, 2007d). Just over 17% had completed a bachelor's degree (U.S. Census Bureau, 2007c). Less than 30% of employed blacks are employed in management or professional occupations, compared with 39% among non-Hispanic whites and 49% among Asians (Bureau of Labor Statistics, 2013). Nearly 24% of blacks work in sales and office occupations, similar to non-Hispanic whites, 27%. Nearly one quarter of blacks work in service occupations, with 6% in construction jobs. Among non-Hispanic whites, 14% are in service, and 10% work in construction jobs. Higher percentages of blacks are in production and transportation in comparison with whites, 13.1% and 11.7%, respectively. (See Table 7.1: Discourses About People of African Descent.)

❖ **Table 7.1**   Discourses About People of African Descent

Urban

Dangerous (particularly men yet includes women)

Representation of diversity

Affirmative Action byproduct

Poor or low income

Christian and black church attending

Good entertainer (dancer and singer)

Good at sports

Not good in math and science

Emotional

Compared with the general population, black people are more likely to be exposed to violence, which has implications for mental illness symptoms such as depression and post-traumatic stress disorder (PTSD). In 2013, nearly 18% of blacks did not have health insurance (Centers for Disease Control, 2015).

Access to mental health care is limited. Among blacks who have health insurance, treatment-seeking behavior for mental health services does not automatically increase. Reluctance to seek mental health services is related to the stigmatizing attitudes that exist regarding mental health care. One study found that the number of blacks who feared mental health treatment was 2.5 times greater than the proportion of whites (U.S. DHHS, 2001). Other research found that blacks were less likely than whites to be properly diagnosed when suffering from affective disorders, such as depression. The tendency of clinicians, both black and white, was to diagnose blacks with schizophrenia (Good, James, Good, & Becker, 2003). Parham (1992) noted that among some African Americans, depression manifests not as psychomotor retardation but as increased activity in order to "keep on keeping on." Much of the black experience in America is coping and surviving. In 2010, black men were more than 6 times as likely as white men to be incarcerated (Drake, 2013). Black women are 2 and 4 times more likely to be incarcerated compared to Latina and white women, respectively (Harrison & Beck, 2005).

The higher rates of nonmarriage and female-headed households among black people need to be understood in context of socioeconomic data (high poverty rates) and the experiences of so many black men in America who are incarcerated, underemployed, unemployed, and unskilled.

Health outcomes are related to lifestyle choices, such as smoking and nutrition. Black people have a myriad of health challenges that warrant an examination of experiences with poverty, substandard housing, underemployment, unemployment, unequal access to quality health care, and chronic racial discrimination. Blacks have diabetes at a rate more than 2 times than that of whites. Stroke, obesity, cigarette smoking, prostate cancer, HIV/AIDS, and infant mortality are disproportionately higher among blacks compared to whites (National Center for Health Statistics, 2015). Relative to whites, African Americans (along with Latinos) are less likely to receive appropriate cardiac medication (e.g., thrombolytic therapy, aspirin, and beta blockers) or to undergo coronary artery bypass surgery even when insurance status, income, co-morbid conditions, age, and symptom expression are taken into account (IOM, 2003).

According to the National Survey of Life (Williams et al., 2007), the largest psychiatric epidemiologic study of black people in the United States, the prevalence of depression is higher for African Americans (56.5%) and Caribbean blacks (56%) than it is for white people (39%). Despite this data, only 7% of black women will receive some type of mental health treatment (Beauboeuf-Lafontant, 2007). Cultural and religious reasons fuel a belief held among many black women that they must resolve problems, including microaggressions, on their own (see Case Study: Microaggressions). With rates of depression among black people higher, and the likelihood of receiving mental health treatment lower, the adverse implications of microaggressions (subtle yet chronic racialized discrimination) are apparent. Nearly 60% of black women are obese and are disproportionately represented among people with stress-related mortality and racial health disparities, such as diabetes, high cholesterol, hypertension, and HIV disease (Centers for Disease Control, 2015; Dingfelder, 2013; Robinson-Wood, 2013).

Physical Appearance

Skin color has social power and status within the African American community (Okazawa-Rey, Robinson, & Ward, 1987; Ward, Robinson-Wood, & Boadi, in press). Mullins and Sites (1984) found that the inheritance of light skin color, which generally came from the mother, who tended to be lighter than the father, along with the mother's education, occupational attainment, and income, served to bolster a family's social position over time. Within a society preoccupied with skin color and where white skin is valued, the desirability of lighter skinned women stems from their closer proximity to European beauty standards. Research has found that skin-color hue affects income, educational attainment, and perceptions of success (Rockquemore, 2002).

Intraracial conflict around *colorism*, or stereotyped attributions and prejudgments based on skin color, has been documented in the literature (Okazawa-Rey et al., 1987; Robinson & Ward, 1995; Rockquemore, 2002; Ward et al., in press). As children, many African American women remember being cautioned by their mothers that unless their newly washed hair was done (which meant being pressed and curled or braided), they could not go outside. The implicit and sometimes explicit message in this statement was that a female's natural state was synonymous with not being presentable and looking unkempt. Among black Americans, appearance is not solely linked to skin color but to a variety of phenotypical traits, such as body shape, facial features, and hair texture (Rockquemore, 2002).

Colorism is often manifested as a preference for lighter skin tones over darker ones. Color consciousness is rooted in the social, political, and economic conditions that existed during and after slavery (Hall, 1992; Hall, 2005). During slavery, persons who were lighter in skin color received privileges that darker skinned blacks did not. Privileges included working inside of the house instead of outside or having educational opportunities. The color hues differences were due to mixed-race offspring who had white slave owning fathers and black slave mothers. Colorism in the black community may be a double-edged sword, affecting those who are seen perhaps as "too black" and those who may be seen as "not black enough." Discrimination against persons with lighter skin tones occurs as well. Robinson and Ward (1995) reported that African American adolescents reported high levels of self-esteem, yet students who were at the extremes of skin color, lighter or darker than most African Americans, were less satisfied with skin color than students who were somewhere in the middle. Skin color attitudes are connected to several variables, including the particular ethnic group, group cohesiveness, the group's status in society, and family, school, peers, and majority vs. minority status (Phinney, 1992). For instance, Harvey, LaBeach, Pridgen, & Gocial (2005) found that at a predominantly black university, students placed more emphasis on skin tone than students at a predominantly white university. According to Ward (2000), unhealthy strategies of surviving racism include adopting hairstyles for the sole purpose of looking white and discriminating against other African Americans on the basis of skin color. Ward (2000) maintains that black children and arguably adults must be taught to value their bodies for their strength and to appreciate the diversity of beauty found in black people.

Cultural Orientation and Values

There is great diversity among people of African descent in country of origin, language, ethnicity, class, education, acculturation level, point of entry into America, and religious orientation. Despite struggle and hardship, values that transcend intragroup diversity are spirituality, persistence, forgiveness, resistance, humor, wisdom, and resilience (Exum & Moore, 1993). Spirituality is typically cited as a primary value in helping men and women survive prostate and breast cancer diagnoses and endure the strains of caregiver burden (Dilworth-Anderson, Boswell, & Cohen, 2007; Hamilton, Powe, Pollard, Lee, & Felton, 2007; Halbert et al., 2007). Black people are united by strong and rich spiritual traditions that infuse educational systems, cultural values, kinship networks, and political revolutions. Cultivating the spirit and maintaining a strong connection with the church represent a foundation for the experience of most blacks in America. Black people may not go to church or even have a church home, but they may still "pray to the Lord" (Boyd-Franklin, 2003, p. 270) when confronted with difficult times, such as illness, death, loss, and bereavement. (See Storytelling: She Didn't Really Love Him.)

❖ STORYTELLING: SHE DIDN'T REALLY LOVE HIM

Nearly 15 years ago, an almost 40-year-old black woman married a man whom she met online. She didn't really love him, but he said he loved her. He wanted to be a father, and she wanted to be a mom. In her mind, her time was running out to find someone. She was overweight and did not feel good about her physical appearance. She wondered who else could love her and when would she ever have another opportunity at marriage and motherhood. Her aunt said to her before the wedding, "You do not have to go through with this if you do not want to—it is never too late." The woman married the man anyway. They had a child and loved her dearly. The woman was not truly happy in marriage. Her husband was extremely critical, and she felt controlled.

Although she was college educated, she felt small, dumb, and insignificant in his presence. She eventually filed for divorce. The woman vowed to always, in the future, listen to her inner voice and not expect others to love her more than she was willing to love herself. This story puts a face on the census data that documents the very high rates of nonmarriage among black women, across educational levels. Black women receive the same messages in society as do other women regarding the significance of marriage, leading some women to make desperate choices born more of fear than of true love. A college education may mediate or attenuate the effects of sexism and other forms of oppression, but higher education does not indemnify one from discrimination.

Historically, the black church has been a focal point in the African American community and a place where advocacy and social and political change have taken hold. The black church played a prominent role in the civil rights movement, voter registration, fund-raising for college students, health promotion, and personal and spiritual development. Many musicians and other celebrities had their talents recognized and nurtured by participating in the choir, youth programs, and leadership forums.

Although the majority of blacks in American regard themselves as Christians, growing numbers of blacks are counted among Islamists, Buddhists, Jews, and agnostic. Neal, McCray, Webb-Johnson, and Bridgest (2003) discussed critical elements of African American culture, including movement, harmony, verve, and affect that are connected to a West African cultural tradition. Furthermore, Neal et al. (2003) stated that the psychological health of black people is connected to "the interweaving of movement, rhythm, percussion, music, and dance" (p. 50). Values common among many blacks in America include the extended family and others who are not blood relatives. Collaborative relationships are valued over highly individualistic styles (Sue & Sue, 1990). Education as a means of self-help and a strong work ethic are often taught to children from a very early age.

Communication patterns are not limited to verbal dialogue or to standard English—the black dialect has survived rather well as has a sense of humor when dealing with injustice and all things ludicrous. Most black people depend on nonverbal modes of communication patterns—how something is said rather than what is actually verbally spoken. Body movement, postures, gestures, and facial expressions represent dominant patterns of communication within the black community. These tend not to be strictly linear as in Western society (Exum & Moore, 1993).

Another value that is manifested in the black community is giving people status as a function of age and position. A present-time orientation is seen at church, parties, and other events. The event may formally begin at one time, but the majority of people may arrive at a much later time. This fluid relationship with time varies by individual differences and acculturation levels. Value is also placed on the use of proverbs (e.g., "every goodbye ain't gone") and spiritual wisdom ("if a door closes another one opens") to not only cope but to resist and to thrive. (See Table 7.2: Common Cultural Values Among People of African Descent.)

According to Nobles (1972), African Americans' cultural traditions have been derived from several cultural and philosophical premises shared with West African tribes. Myers (1991) states,

> Afrocentricity refers to a worldview that believes reality is both spiritual and material at once . . . with highest value on positive interpersonal relationships between men/women; self knowledge is assumed to be the basis of all knowledge, and one knows through symbolic imagery and rhythm. (p. 19)

❖ **Table 7.2** Common Cultural Values Among People of African Descent

Oral traditions

Reliance on proverbial wisdom

Spirituality and faith

Firm child-rearing practices

Education as a means of self-help

Collateral interpersonal relations

Formal communication styles with elders and authority figures

Respect for elders and authority figures

Nonverbal modes of communication

Extended family based on blood and strong ties

Unity and cooperation

Resistance

Purpose

Creativity

Fluid time orientation

Within Africentric thought, the self is extended in unity with others and emphasis is on the collective. An African proverb, "I am because we are and since we are, therefore I am," summarizes the saliency of the collective. Among some African Americans, *consubstantiation*, or the sense that everything within the universe is connected as a part of a whole, is a way of seeing the world (Parham, 1992). Myers (1991) stated that, in the Africentric paradigm, spirit and matter are one and are a representation of one spirit manifesting good.

The *Nguzo Saba*, or classical African values, also provide insight into African American values (Karenga, 1980). The first and third principles are *Umoja* and *Ujima* and refer to unity and collective work and responsibility, respectively. These principles endorse solidarity, harmony, cooperation, and connection with others toward a common destiny. The second principle, *Kujichagalia*, means self-determination and naming for the self who the self will be, despite others' definitions. *Ujaama*, the fourth principle, refers to cooperative economics, in which resources are shared for the good of all. *Nia*, or purpose, is the fifth principle and benefits not only the self but also the collective for which everyone has responsibility. The sixth principle is *Kuumba*, or creativity. Creativity is inextricably linked to imagination, ingenuity, and leaving the world a better place than it was when you first arrived. *Imani*, or faith, is the last principle and encompasses the past, present, and future.

Worldview refers to the way people make meaning. Adapted from Hilliard's work, Exum and Moore (1993) summarized elements of African American worldview. These elements include emphasis on the whole as opposed to the parts, preference for approximations over accuracy, focus on people rather than things, and acceptance and integration with the environment. In addition to these values is a respect for nature and emphasis on the group.

A theory of resistance is based on the Nguzo Saba principles (Brookins & Robinson, 1995; Robinson & Kennington, 2002; Robinson & Ward, 1991). The goal of resistance theory is to empower marginalized groups with optimal tools to name, confront, repudiate, and replace dominant and demeaning messages with knowledge of self and community (Ward, 2000). Resistance theory is an important response to the chronic stress of racism. There is limited research related to the use of specific modes of coping with perceived racism (Clark, Anderson, Clark, & Williams, 2002). African tradition includes a strong tie between the living and the world of the dead in defining the scope of community. J. A. Opoku (personal communication, April 3, 1994) said about Ghanaian culture, "The dead are still with us."

Robinson-Wood (2009b) conducted research with 80 black college women, 18 to 25 years old from a private, predominantly white university in Massachusetts. They were administered the Africultural Coping Systems Inventory (ACSI). Of the ACSI's four coping modalities: cognitive emotional, ritual, collective, and spiritual centered, collective coping was utilized most. Collectively centered coping reflects a reliance on the group and appears to be most similar to problem-focused/approach coping. It involves an awareness of what and how others have dealt with similarly difficult situations. Among many black people, collective centeredness is central to being in the world.

There is great diversity among black families, yet there are similarities independent of place within the Diaspora. According to Black (1996), people of African descent are set apart from other ethnic groups by the following:

1. The African legacy rich in custom and culture.

2. The history of slavery and its insidious attempts to destroy people's souls while keeping their physical bodies in servitude.

3. Historical and contemporary racism and sexism.

4. The victim system in which people are denied access and then blamed for their marginalized positions.

Black families have demonstrated a stability and cohesive functioning that is often culture specific. Competence among intact inner-city African American families includes shared power, strong parental coalitions, closeness without sacrificing individual ego boundaries, and negotiation in problem solving. Many of these competent families are at risk because of economic conditions, appalling neighborhood conditions, violence, and uncertainty in employment status (Ingrassia, 1993).

As a result of economic conditions, families often do not include only blood relations but may have uncles and aunts, cousins, "big mamas," "play sisters," and "home boys and girls." In many black American families, there is a three-generation system. The extended families encourage an elastic, kinship-based exchange network that may last a lifetime. These families exhibit spiritual strength, role flexibility, and interchangeability in which male–female relationships are often egalitarian because of the presence of working wives, mothers, and grandmothers (Hines & Boyd-Franklin, 1996; Staples, 1988). Members of the extended family may also exhibit "child keeping," using an informal adoption network.

Despite a feminist perspective that characterized large numbers of black homes prior to women's liberation, black American men have identity as the nominal heads of households, tied in to their ability to provide for their families. Women often socialize their daughters for strength, economic independence, family responsibility, and daily accountability (Boyd-Franklin, 1989). Many black mothers also raise their daughters with the responsibility of educating them about racism and sexism (Turner, 1997). Wilkinson (1997) said, "In the racially structured and multicultural evolution of this country, sex and gender alone have not been the principal determinants of the experiences or self-definitions of Native Americans or American Indians, Mexican Americans, Japanese, and certainly not of African Americans" (p. 267).

Women are identified as possessing fortitude, perseverance, and strength during adversity. As such, women are also generally more religious than men and function to tie the family into a complete church-centered support system of persons in particular roles, activities, and social life (Boyd-Franklin, 1989; Hines & Boyd-Franklin, 1996). This is especially notable in black Christian (e.g., Baptist) churches. Other major religious groups with similar functions include the African Methodist Episcopal, Jehovah's Witnesses, Church of God in Christ, Seventh-Day Adventist, and Pentecostal, as well as the Nation of Islam sects to which more black people are converting (Black, 1996).

This culture-specific description of the African American family is not intended to suggest that all families are extended and nonconsanguineous in composition. Increasing numbers of blacks are single, and many marriages have an increasing fragility as reflected in the higher rates of divorce and separation when compared with the general population (Boyd-Franklin, 1989; Ingrassia, 1993). Many African Americans are acculturated, have opted for identification with the dominant European American culture, and are more egocentric in lifestyle and less communal in orientation.

African American Racial Identity

Cross's (1991) theory of racial identity development, called the Negro-to-black conversion experience, or Nigresence, is the most widely used racial theory about African Americans. It presumes a sociopolitical perspective and refers to the process of developing healthy racial collective identities as a function of discrepancies in sociopolitical power across racial groups. In Cross's work, a distinction is made between personal identity and reference group orientation. The former refers to self-esteem and interpersonal competence; the latter refers to racial identity and racial self-esteem. Cross's work on black racial identity has been extremely influential in the development of models related to other aspects of identity, including racial and cultural identity models for other groups of color and the womanist identity model (see Ossana, Helms, & Leonard, 1992).

Within Cross's (1991) theory, identity development is a maturation process whereby external negative images of the self are replaced with positive internal conceptions. Cross's (1991) five-stage Nigresence model—preencounter, encounter, immersion and emersion, internalization, and internalization and commitment—refers to "a resocializing experience" that "seeks to transform a preexisting identity (a non-Africentric identity) into one that is Africentric" (p. 190). Robinson and Howard-Hamilton (1994) discussed Africentricity as a conscious ideology with a strong connection to spirituality and kinship via African culture, culminating in the shared belief: "I am because we are and since we are, therefore I am." An optimal Africentric worldview can be measured by an instrument called the Belief Systems Analysis Scale, developed by Fine and James-Myers (1990). Africentrism involves an awareness of black identity, knowledge of cultural customs and traditions, liberating psychological resistance strategies, and an understanding of oppression and strategies to resist it (Dana, 1993; Robinson & Howard-Hamilton, 1994).

Cross developed the Cross Racial Identity Scale (Vandiver, 2001) to measure the revised dimensions of his 1991 Nigresence model. Vandiver reviewed the Cross Racial Identity Scale (CRIS), a 40-item, 7-point Likert-type inventory, to measure Cross's revised theory of Nigresence. Reference group orientation and race salience are also assessed. There are six scales: Preencounter Assimilated (PA), Preencounter Miseducation (PM), Preencounter Self-Hatred (PSH), Immersion/Emersion Anti-White (IEAW), Internalization Afrocentricity Black Nationalist (IA), and Internalization Multiculturalist Inclusive (IMCI). The psychometric properties of the CRIS report acceptable Cronbach alphas: PA = .85, PM = .89, PSH = .85, IEAW = .85, IBN = .79, IMCI = .76.

At preencounter, the acculturated African American views the world through the lens of the white dominant culture. Essentially, race has low salience. When people are asked to describe themselves, identifiers other than race, such as work, church, profession, and club affiliation, surface as key descriptors. Cross (1991) maintained that many preencounter African Americans are psychologically healthy and that anti-black attitudes among African Americans in this stage are rare, although they do exist. Despite indices of psychological health among African Americans at this initial stage of racial identity, Cross (1991) stated, "Preencounter Blacks cannot help but experience varying degrees of miseducation about the significance of the Black experience" (p. 192). African Americans in this first stage are more likely to operate from a Eurocentric cultural perspective in evaluating beauty and art forms.

According to Jones, Cross, and DeFour (2007), the assimilation subscales measure pro-American and assimilationist attitudes (e.g., "I think of myself as an American, and seldom as a member of a racial group"). The miseducation subscale taps into the extent to which the respondent adheres to negative stereotypes about black people as group (e.g., "blacks place too much importance on racial protest and not enough on hard work and education"). Racial self-hatred assesses racial self-hatred attitudes (e.g. "When I look into the mirror at my black image, sometimes I do not feel good about what I see").

At the encounter stage, a person's new view of the world, as a result of a shocking personal experience, is inconsistent with the old. According to Cross (1991), the two aspects of this stage are experiencing an encounter and personalizing it. In every year of a black person's life, myriad encounter experiences could encourage movement from preencounter to encounter. If the experiences are not internalized and personalized, however, movement along to this next stage cannot occur. Other identity constructs, such as religion, class, and education, may delay racial identity formation, particularly when similarity with the referent group (e.g., being Christian, middle class, academically gifted) is encouraged and differences (e.g., race) that may be perceived as threatening or divisive are ignored (Robinson, 1999b).

In the immersion and emersion stage, the focus is on being black to the exclusion of others, particularly whites. Cross (1991) indicated that this is a transitional stage with respect to identity transformation: "The person's main focus in life becomes a feeling of 'togetherness and oneness with people'" (p. 207). The antiwhite subscale assesses dislike for white people and culture (e.g., "I have a strong hatred and disdain for all white people").

The fourth stage of Cross's model, internalization, is characterized by more peace and calm. At this juncture, dissonance regarding an emerging identity has been resolved, evidenced by high salience attached to blackness.

Internalization and commitment persons seek to eradicate racism for all oppressed people. According to Cross (1991), this stage is similar to the internalization stage but is reflective of sustained long-term interest and commitment, as opposed to a brief period in that person's life. Here, the African American is more able to reconceptualize the self across multiple identities. At initial stages, the African American has little awareness of racial oppression because race has minimal importance. The Afrocentric and Multicultural subscales assess this internalization stage. The Afrocentric subscales measure Black Nationalist attitudes characterized by empowerment (e.g., "I see and think about things from an Afrocentric perspective"). The multicultural subscale measures blacks' acceptance and connection with others from diverse cultural contexts (e.g., "As a multiculturalist, I am connected to many groups").

Jones et al. (2007) administered the CRIS, the Rosenberg Self-Esteem Scale, the Schedule of Racist Events, and the Center for Epidemiologic Studies Depression Scale to 118 African American and 144 self-identified Caribbean women. They discovered that racist stress events and racist stress appraisal play a role in negative mental health, particularly depression. In their sample, multicultural identity attitudes lessened the negative mental health impact of racist stress events and racist stress appraisals, particularly as they related to depression. There was an increase in depression scores as racist stress appraisals increased, but "not to the same degree as those with multicultural identity attitude scores 1 standard deviation below the mean" (Jones et al., 2007, p. 222).

Implications for Mental Health Professionals

Multicultural competence requires knowledge of the psychological stress that is born of racism and oppression as well as clinical skills to improve mental health outcomes. Sutherland and Moodley (2010) discussed historical hostility that describes the collective psychology of black people due to exposure to slavery, discrimination, and fears about unequal treatment. It is this historical context as well as contemporary realities of the ongoing and pervasive nature of racism that helping professionals need to be aware of and have the ability to integrate this information into assessment, diagnosis, treatment planning, and implementation of interventions.

It is also relevant for mental health professionals to know of black parents' preparation for and resistance to racism. To prepare children to face a racially hostile world, black people have long engaged in racial socialization practices in an effort to interrogate race for survival purposes as well as to resist racial oppression (Ward, 2000). In doing so, black parents have talked to their children about how to survive and thrive in a society where race matters. Such messages are delivered in conversations about the type of clothing to avoid so as not to be viewed as unkempt and lazy, stereotypes that have assailed black people. Parents have also provided explanations regarding the importance of staying in school so that a child could make something of himself or herself and how to interpret blatant racism so it does not destroy their child's self-worth. Thomas (1999), a black woman, gave an example of racial socialization. Her parents told her "she would have to work twice as hard as her white peers to be successful and not to be frustrated by that challenge" (pp. 35–36). Here, reference is made to the protective nature of racial socialization from racism's harmful psychological effects (White-Johnson, Ford, & Sellers, 2010).

Part of our multicultural competence as mental health professionals is to realize our limitations. It is important not to get overwhelmed by the magnitude and sadness of clients' narratives. Listening, advocacy, attending, and empathy are valuable skills, particularly in times of crisis. These skills allow patients to feel cared for and held within a stable and nonjudgmental therapeutic environment. Such environments are not dictated by racial similarity between the patient and counselor but from a connective and relational capacity. There is tremendous ethnic diversity among black people. Some people of African descent do not identify as African American or black but instead wish to identify according to their country of origin (e.g., Jamaican, Nigerian, Dominican, Haitian, Cape Verdean).

Case Study

Microaggressions

Shannon is 24 years old and is Dominican American. She is a Massachusetts Institute of Technology (MIT) graduate and is currently in medical school. Her field of study is pathophysiology. She grew up in a working-class neighborhood (Dorchester) with parents who taught her the importance of studying hard, avoiding the wrong crowd, and making something of herself. Her high school friend, Diane, is also Dominican American. When visiting together (Shannon and Diane come from the same neighborhood), Diane confides that she has been having difficulty at work. Diane is an investment banker with an MBA from Harvard. Diane was told by a colleague that the primary reason she was hired was to fill a racial quota; recently she was told by her supervisor that her hair was "bewildering." Diane wears her hair natural—in a neat, large-sized afro. She has not been asked to be a team leader and does not get invited to the informal weekend parties on Cape Cod that her supervisor hosts. Diane asked a white coworker why she thinks she has not been invited; her colleague asked, "Do you even enjoy the beach scene? We do a lot of water sports and hang out in the sun to get tanned, something that you wouldn't want to do, right?" Shannon tells Diane the following: "It is 2016, not 1966. Race is not the big issue that you and so many minorities make it out to be. America is open to everyone. You just have to work hard, know what you want, and go for it. It's your choice. You didn't listen but remember when I told you your wild hair would get you in trouble at the bank? Just straighten your hair." At work, Diane begins to withdraw from colleagues. Some have mentioned to Diane's supervisor that Diane seems disinterested and hostile. What Diane actually feels is loneliness and sadness. She has insomnia, has begun to doubt her competence, and feels like she is in a cognitive fog. She has gained 15 pounds in 6 weeks and eats late at night when she is unable to sleep, which is most nights. At her recent checkup, her doctor told her that although she was only 25, she was prediabetic, had high blood pressure, and needed to exercise. Diane turns to you for counseling.

Questions

1. Diane asks you, what is happening to her at work and why? What do you say?
2. Choose a relevant model reflective of your current racial/cultural identity. Indicate if you have any concerns about being Diane's counselor based on your racial/cultural identity. If so, what are these concerns and what can you do about them? If you have no concerns, discuss this as well. Integrate chapter material.

Discussion and Integration

The Client, Diane

Diane is contending with multiple issues as a black woman. Suboptimal resistance, such as excessive eating, is associated with short-term solutions that offer immediate gratification and are soothing but do not serve women well in the long run. In a study that examined microaggressions among highly educated black women, including PhD students, faculty, and professionals, all 17 women stated that microaggressions were descriptive of their experiences. Women spoke of other people's knowledge being legitimized over their own and their capabilities being questioned and underestimated by peers, students, and faculty. Microaggressions are insidious, chronic, and traumatizing. An accumulation of microaggression stressors has debilitating psychological impact, including reduced self-efficacy, heightened feelings of vulnerability, feelings of powerlessness, anger, hypervigilance, distancing, and isolation (Robinson-Wood et al., 2015).

Microaggressions are experienced as ridiculous, offensive, frustrating, unbelievable, and sad. School and work can be alienating and harsh places for most highly educated black people to negotiate, due largely to racial discrimination expressed through microaggressions. Robinson-Wood et al. (2015) found that young black women in their 20s, compared to women in their 30s, 40s, and 50s, were more vulnerable to isolation from communities of support and to chemically altering natural hair for the purpose of appeasing others, characteristics of suboptimal strategies.

Diane is contending with microaggressions, which target people on the basis of their phenotype, are stressful, sometimes traumatic, pervasive, and associated with psychological and physiological health conditions (Sue et al., 2007, 2011). Diane is presumed to be less intelligent than her white peers and is considered to hold her job because of affirmative action policy. She is also objectified by meanings surrounding her natural hair and is experiencing colorism.

As intensely relational human beings, microaggressions are particularly injurious to women when they occur within workspaces and classroom environments. Within these contexts, people coexist together as colleagues, classmates, students, program faculty, and cohort members (Robinson-Wood et al., 2015). Because microaggressions can be subtle and ambiguous, multicultural competency training, particularly for professionals who already perceive themselves to be multiculturally competent, is needed.

The Counselor

Diane's therapist needs to feel racially competent in his or her own racial identity development in order to hold Diane's material and emotions. Race has enormous power to create discomfort and inflame tension, particularly when black women name racism to white people who seemed reluctant to recognize racism as real, were not mindful of their white privilege, and/or denied individual racism (Sue et al., 2007, 2011).

The relevance of race in the explanation of black women's differential treatment or negative experiences can often be met with disbelief and invalidation, primarily, by white classmates and coworkers. Sue et al. (2007) referred to this phenomenon of nullifying people's racial experiences as a microinvalidation.

Martin (2007) encourages therapists to do the following to increase their cultural competence with black patients: (1) Review the literature concerning black women (Martin, 2007). Good sources are *Journal of Black Psychology*, Patricia Hill Collins's work titled *Black Feminist Thought*, and workshops dealing with black women. (2) Use intentional interviewing skills and query: "Do you believe you have experienced any racial prejudice or has discrimination had an effect on your life" (Martin, 2007, p. 42). A patient's response would be a source of clinical information. (3) Become familiar with African-centered psychotherapies (e.g., Myers et al., 1991) on optimal psychology. (4) Personally explore racial identity, which for some white therapists is not a task that seems relevant due to colorblindness and/or white privilege. A therapist who has not explored his or her own racial identity is not an appropriate candidate for Diane who is impacted by gender and race oppression and needs a therapist who can competently broach these difficult topics with her.

Strategies of coping, resistance, multiple jeopardy, acculturation, and racial identity are critical to Diane's specific situation as a professional black woman with an immigrant history (Sanchez & Davis, 2010). Diane's immigrant history needs to be considered with respect to the messages she received about herself and other black people. For example, a practice among some black Caribbean parents to distinguish themselves and their children from native-born black Americans, due to their low social status and perceptions of undesirable characteristics, has been documented in the literature. This practice speaks to the promotion of mistrust, defined as teaching children to be cautious of people from different racial, ethnic, or cultural backgrounds based on perceived barriers to success or experiences of discrimination (Priest et al., 2014; Waters, 1994).

While Diane has earned an advanced degree at a highly reputable university, she is dogged by perceptions that she is inferior in an environment where subtle racism occurs. Power dynamics exacerbate a difficult situation given that Diane is supervised by those who she deems to be unsupportive or untrustworthy. Individual therapy, a therapeutic group with other black women, bibliotherapy, journaling, and sitting with the question, "Why should I be ashamed of myself and where did I learn to be ashamed of myself?" may help Diane's gender and race personal explorations as she developmentally evolves. Diane may also benefit from consultation with a nutritionist for support with and insight into her food choices.

Summary

This chapter provided history, geographic data, demographic data, and cultural values for people of African descent. A case study was presented for students to gain practice with integrating multiple issues: a professional young black woman contending with racial and gendered microaggressions that contribute to her depression. Counseling with people of African descent is discussed in the case study.

8

People of Asian Descent, Native Hawaiians, and Pacific Islanders

❖

TOPICS COVERED IN THIS CHAPTER

- **History**
- **Demography**
  - Native Hawaiians and Pacific Islanders
- **Social, Psychological, and Physical Health Issues**
- **Acculturation and Experiences in America**
- **Cultural Orientation and Values**
- **Asian American Identity Development**
- **Implications for Mental Health Professionals**
- **Case Study**
- **Summary**

This chapter is a focus on people of Asian descent. The diverse ethnic groups among Asians are highlighted. Demographic information, history, and cultural values are also presented.

Tremendous diversity is found within the Asian community. According to Hoeffel, Rastogi, Kim, and Shahid (2012), "Asian" refers to a person having origins in any of the original peoples of the Far East, Southeast Asia, or the Indian subcontinent, including Cambodia, China, India, Japan, Korea, Malaysia, Pakistan, the Philippine Islands, Thailand, and Vietnam. It includes people who indicated their race(s) as "Asian" or reported entries such as "Asian Indian," "Chinese," "Filipino," "Korean," "Japanese," "Vietnamese," and "Other Asian" or provided other detailed Asian responses (p. 3).

Compared with the Chinese, Japanese, Koreans, Filipinos, and Asian Indians, the Vietnamese are the most recent immigrant group to arrive in the United States. Between April and December 1975, 100,000 refugees from Vietnam and Cambodia were admitted to the United States as parolees, as announced by the U.S. attorney general (Avakian, 2002). Southeast Asia represents the Asian subcontinent south of China and east of India. Persons from Vietnam, Laos, and Cambodia are neighbors. Indonesia, Malaysia, Thailand, Burma, Bhutan, and Bangladesh are also included. According to Sandhu (1997), more than 40 cultural groups comprise Asian and Pacific Islander Americans. Many of these groups are less researched and perhaps less well known than other groups who have lived in the United States for several generations.

Asian newcomers speak hundreds of languages and dialects and practice a broad array of religions. Many ethnic Asian newcomers are more likely to identify with specific national or regional ties (e.g., Vietnamese, Korean, Hmong, Punjabi Sikh, Cantonese, Taiwanese). The Pacific Islands include 22 islands, including Micronesia (Guam, Belau, and the Carolines, Marianas, Marshalls, and Gilberts) and Melanesia (Fiji).

Uba (1994) observed, "The term 'Asian culture' is technically a misnomer. The tenets of these belief systems are shared by many cultures—there are also significant differences among Asian cultures" (p. 12). More than 100 languages and dialects are spoken, and in some communities such as the Hmong and Cambodians, high rates of linguistic isolation exist, which explains the phenomenon of persons over the age of 14 not speaking English "very well" (U.S. Department of Health and Human Services [U.S. DHHS], 2001).

Ethnicity, nationality, migration or generational status, assimilation, acculturation, facility with the English language, political climate in country of origin, religion, socioeconomic status, occupation, transferability of skills, foreign credentials to the United States, and educational level provide some of the many sources of differences within the group (Sue & Sue, 1990; Tsai & Uemura, 1988).

History

Geneticists have discovered through DNA analysis of a small child's remains in Clovis, New Mexico, and the remains of a female teenager found in a Yucatan cave, from respectively 12,600 and 13,000 years ago, that Asians have ancestral linkage to Paleo Americans or the first Americans who are Native Americans (Hodges, 2015).

The Chinese are the Asian ethnic group with the longest history in the United States and were the first Asian ethnic group to be recruited to the West Coast during the 1840s. At that time, there was a need for cheap labor to work on the transcontinental railroads (Tsai & Uemura, 1988). U.S. policymaker Aaron H. Palmer predicted that with a connection to the East Coast, San Francisco would become the "great emporium of our commerce on the Pacific" (Takaki, 1993, p. 192). Chinese were perceived to be more suited for "cleaning wild lands and raising every species of agricultural product" (p. 192).

In 1863, Congress authorized construction of the U.S. transcontinental railroad. The eastward track was laid from Sacramento, California, through the Sierra Nevada, and eventually into Utah. During the winter months, working conditions were often brutal, and snowdrifts would bury entire work crews. When spring arrived, their frozen bodies would be discovered. The westward track was built mainly by Irish immigrants and started in Omaha, Nebraska. Both the Irish and Chinese received a monthly wage of $31. Unlike the Irish, the Chinese worked longer days and slept in tents near the side of the road. The Irish worked 8-hour days and resided in boarding rooms.

Despite the harsh realities of work on the railroad, many Chinese were motivated to come to America. In China, floods were making it difficult to harvest crops. Political instability, such as taxation and ethnic conflict, was also a factor. Between 1865 and 1869, the total number of Chinese railroad workers increased from 50 to almost 12,000 (Avakian, 2002). Finding gold in California was also a dream of many Chinese (Cao & Novas, 1996).

Life in America was difficult not only for Chinese men, but also for Chinese women. In 1860, it is estimated that more than 80% of Chinese women were prostitutes (Hirata, 1979) and many were teenage girls aged 15 and 16. As a result of slavery, kidnapping, and deception, Chinese girls found themselves on the auction block, where they worked as concubines or prostitutes, sexually serving both white and Chinese men (Avakian, 2002).

Hirata (1979) spoke of two periods of prostitution concerning Chinese women in California. The first period was considered a period of free competition where the woman is said to have control over her "body service." This timeline was estimated to be around 1849 to 1854. The second period was 1854 to 1925 and was considered to be a time of organized trade where women were involved in a web of slavery similar to today's trafficking and exploitation of girls and women for sex work throughout America and the world. Prior to the arrival of other Asians into the United States, Congress passed the Chinese Exclusion Act of 1882, which barred the "immigration of all Chinese laborers, lunatics, and idiots into the United States for a 10-year period" (Avakian, 2002, p. 51). This act enabled "only women who were native born, married, or born overseas to domiciled merchants to immigrate to the United States" (Hirata, 1979, p. 11) and was the first and only law in U.S. immigration that ordered an entire group of people of a specific nationality to be banned from the United States (Avakian, 2002).

In 1868, 141 Japanese men, women, and children arrived in Hawaii. The Japanese were recruited to work on the Hawaiian sugarcane plantations, along with the Koreans, Filipinos, and Puerto Ricans who came later, near the turn of the 20th century. The Japanese migrated to the United States during Japan's period of rapid modernization known as the Meiji Restoration (after Emperor Meiji). Because of tax increases levied to pay for sweeping reforms, Japan's peasant farmers suffered greatly from economic hardships and lost their land. Persons from the districts of Yamaguchi, Hiroshima, and Kumamoto were hit hardest by poverty and comprised the majority of immigrants hailing from Japan (Avakian, 2002).

Between 1885 and 1925, 200,000 Japanese left for Hawaii, and another 180,000 went to the U.S. mainland. By the turn of the 20th century, 70% of Hawaii's sugar plantation labor was from Japan. In 1900, with the passing of the Organic Act, the U.S. Congress voted to create the Territory of Hawaii. Despite the fact that Chinese and Japanese Hawaiians represented more than half of the population, they were not allowed to vote. Whites, the minority, represented the elite and ruling class. Laborers toiled in the sugarcanes within a paternalistic system characterized by oligarchy and suppression. To organize and to protest substandard living conditions, many laborers joined unions (Roffman, 1974). Such resistance, led by the Japanese, encouraged planters to look for new labor sources, primarily from Korea and the Philippines.

On December 7, 1941, Pearl Harbor, a major base of the U.S. Navy on the Hawaiian island of Oahu, was attacked by the Japanese. Bases in the Philippines, Guam, Midway Atoll, and other ports in the Pacific were also attacked. Nearly 3,000 soldiers, sailors, and civilians were killed. This surprise attack fueled existing anti-Japanese sentiments. With the passing of Executive Order 9066, signed by Franklin D. Roosevelt, wartime curfew and internment measures were enacted primarily against 110,000 West Coast Japanese Americans, three quarters of whom were *Nisei*, or second-generation, American-born Japanese. The other fourth, the *Issei*, were born in Japan and thus barred from becoming American citizens (Zinn, 2003). Small numbers of Germans, Italians, and Eastern Europeans were also relocated to camps to safeguard the security of the United States. Although the order was a constitutional violation as well as a legal violation of due process (there were no warrants, indictments, or hearings), Japanese Americans were forced to leave their homes and move to cramped internment camps for 3 years (Zinn, 2003). The notice of Japanese Internment stated, "All persons of Japanese ancestry" are given 2 to 5 days notice to dispose of their homes and property and report to the "camps" (Chang, 2002).

The construction plans used for housing were for unmarried army recruits, thus up to six families resided in long army barracks with very little privacy. The traditional diet of many Japanese people, such as fresh vegetables and fruits, was not available, and waiting in lines for meals and bathroom facilities was commonplace (Avakian, 2002).

A century ago, most Asian Americans were low-skilled and low-wage laborers. Today they are the most likely of any major racial or ethnic group in America to live in mixed neighborhoods and to marry across racial lines. During the last 50 years, the number of foreign born from Asia increased rapidly in the United States, from about 0.5 million in 1960 to 11.6 million in 2011 (Gryn & Gambino, 2012). Their points and periods of entry have differed and have been largely influenced by work, including the railroads, cotton, sugarcane, technology, medicine, and war—namely World War II, Korea, and Vietnam.

Demography

The 2010 Census question on race included 15 separate response categories and three areas where respondents could write in detailed information about their race. The response categories and write-in answers can be combined to create the five minimum Office of Management and Budget (OMB) race categories plus some other race. In addition to white, black or African American, American Indian and Alaska Native, and some other race, 7 of the 15 response categories are Asian groups, and 4 are Native Hawaiian and Other Pacific Islander groups. The seven Asian response categories are Asian Indian, Chinese, Filipino, Japanese, Korean, Vietnamese, and Other Asian (Hoeffel et al., 2012).

In the 2010 Census, 5.6% of all people in the United States identified as Asian, either alone or in combination with one or more other races representing. The Asian population increased 4 times faster than the U.S. population (Hoeffel et al., 2012). Even at a faster rate, the multiple-race Asian population grew by 60% in size since 2000, from 1.65 million to 2.65 million (Hoeffel et al., 2012).

This group experienced the second largest numeric change, by 4.4 million, going from 10.2 million in 2000 to 14.7 million in 2010. Another 0.9% or an additional 2.6 million people reported Asian in combination with one or more other races. Together, these two groups totaled 17.3 million people (Hoeffel et al., 2012).

"Other Asian" is a category that includes Bhutanese, Burmese, Indochinese, Iwo Jiman, Madagascan, Maldivian, Nepalese, Okinawan, and Singaporean (U.S. Census Bureau, 2007e). In 2010, examples were added to the "Other Asian" response category (e.g., Hmong, Laotian, Thai, Pakistani, Cambodian; Hoeffel et al., 2012).

Native Hawaiians and Pacific Islanders

In 2010, 540,000 people reported being Native Hawaiian or other Pacific Islander, representing 0.2% of the U.S. population. The Native Hawaiian and Other Pacific Islander population includes people who marked the "Native Hawaiian" checkbox, the "Guamanian or Chamorro" checkbox, the "Samoan" checkbox, or the "Other Pacific Islander" checkbox. It also includes people who reported entries such as Pacific Islander; Polynesian entries, such as Tahitian, Tongan, and Tokelauan; Micronesian entries, such as Marshallese, Palauan, and Chuukese; and Melanesian entries, such as Fijian, Guinean, and Solomon Islander (Hixson, Hepler, & Kim, 2012). The total U.S. population grew by 9.7%, from 281.4 million in 2000 to 308.7 million in 2010. Another 685,000 people reported "more than one race," for a total of 1.2 million people who identified themselves as either Native Hawaiian/Pacific Islander or in combination with other races; therefore, 0.4% percent of the U.S. population identify as Native Hawaiian/Pacific Islander (Hixson et al., 2012).

In comparison, the Native Hawaiian and other Pacific Islander alone population increased more than 3 times faster than the total U.S. population, growing by 35% from 399,000 to 540,000 people. In 2010, more than half (56%) of the Native Hawaiian/Pacific Islander alone-or-in-combination population reported more than one race. Most of the growth among Native Hawaiians and other Pacific Islanders who reported multiple races was due to combinations that included white and/or Asian (Hixson et al., 2012).

In 2010, 1.6 million people reporting Asian and some other race were Asian and white, representing 18% of persons reporting two or more races. High rates of intermarriage between Asians and whites, particularly among Asian women and white men, help to explain respondents' report of their biracial heritage. More than one third (37%) of all recent Asian American brides wed a non-Asian groom (Pew Research Center, 2013). According to Wu (2002), "Among Asian Americans under the age of thirty-five who are married, half have found a spouse of a non-Asian background" (p. 263). In 2008, 30.5% of Asians had married someone outside of their racial group. Two years later, this rate had slightly declined to 27.7%. White/Asian couples have higher combined earnings than either white/white or Asian/Asian couples (Wang, 2012).

With respect to ethnicity among Asians, there is considerable diversity. Sixty-one percent of Asians are Chinese, Filipino, and Asian Indian. The largest proportion of Asian in combination with another race(s) was for respondents who identified as Filipino (24%). The Chinese alone-or-in-any combination population is the largest detailed Asian group at 4.0 million or 23% of the population. Filipino and Asian Indian were the second- and third-largest detailed Asian groups at 20% and 18.4% respectively. Vietnamese, Korean, and Japanese were fourth, fifth, and sixth largest at 10%, 9.9%, and 7% respectively (Hoeffel et al., 2012).

Although the Japanese were the second group of Asians to enter America, more recent newcomers have surpassed this group in numbers. Moreover, Japanese had the highest proportion reporting multiple detailed Asian groups and/or another race(s) relative to the largest detailed Asian groups and are the only Asian ethnic group who are most likely to be U.S. born (Hoeffel et al., 2012). The Bhutanese population experienced the fastest growth from 2000 to 2010, growing from about 200 in 2000 to about 19,000 in 2010, a percentage change of 9,699%. Other sizable groups are the Cambodian/Khmer, Pakistanis, Laotians, Hmong, Thais, Taiwanese, and Bangladeshi.

The distribution of Asians depends on ethnicity. More specifically, nearly half (49%) of Chinese and Vietnamese live in the West; however, only a quarter of Asian Indians live in the West, 30% of Asians live in the South, another 30% of Asians live in the Northeast, and 16% of Asians live in the Midwest. Over 70% of Japanese live in the West. Koreans have the lowest percent in the West (43.7%) with 20.5% in the Northeast and 24% in the South. Despite the regional diversity among Asians, California was the top state for each of the six largest detailed Asian groups. In the 2010 Census, of all respondents who reported Native Hawaiian and other Pacific Islander alone or in combination, 71% lived in the West, 16% lived in the South, 7% lived in the Northeast, and 6% lived in the Midwest (Hixson et al., 2012). In 2011, over one fourth (29%) of the foreign born were born in Asia (Gryn & Gambino, 2012).

Nearly three quarters (74%) of Asian American adults were born abroad; of these, about half say they speak English very well and half say they do not (Pew Research Center, 2013). After Spanish, Chinese was the most widely spoken non-English language in the home. Tagalog, Vietnamese, and Korean were each spoken at home by more than 1 million people.

Milestones of economic success and social assimilation have come to a group that is still majority immigrant. Asians recently passed Hispanics as the largest group of new immigrants to the United States. The educational credentials of Asians are striking. More than 6 in 10 (61%) adults ages 25 to 64 who have come from Asia in recent years have at least a bachelor's degree. This is double the share among recent non-Asian arrivals and it is likely that recently arrived Asians are the most highly educated cohort of immigrants in U.S. history (Pew Research Center, 2013).

Social, Psychological, and Physical Health Issues

The demographics of Asian ethnic groups differ on many measures. Indian Americans lead other groups by a significant margin in their levels of income and education. Seven in ten Indian American adults ages 25 and older have a college degree, compared with about half of Americans of Korean, Chinese, Filipino, and Japanese ancestry, and about a quarter of Vietnamese Americans (Pew Research Center, 2013).

On the other side of the socioeconomic divide, Americans with Korean, Vietnamese, Chinese, and other U.S. Asian origins have higher shares in poverty than does the U.S. general public, while Asians with Indian, Japanese and Filipino origins have lower shares (Pew Research Center, 2013). More specifically, in 2013 the poverty rate for Asians was 10.5%. There are variations by ethnic group: Among the Vietnamese, the poverty rate is 14.7%, 15% among Koreans, and 5.8% among Filipinos (Pew Research Center, 2013). Asian children are more likely to live in married-couple households, although 13% of Asian children live in poverty (National Center for Education Statistics, 2015).

Rates of divorce among Asians are less than half of those in the general population: 4.7% among Asians compared with 10.2% for the total population (U.S. Census Bureau, 2007e). Approximately 10% of Asians are separated, widowed, or divorced compared with about 19% among non-Hispanic whites. There are interethnic group differences. Asian Indians were most likely to be married, about 69%. People who were biracial (Asian and white) had the highest never-married rates, at 50.5%, as well as higher divorce rates, nearly 7% compared with less than 5% among Asian-only groups (U.S. Census Bureau, 2007e). In the east, it has been said that people first marry then love, whereas in the west, it is people first love then marry (National Healthy Marriage Resource Center, 2008).

Although Asians as a whole tend to exceed the non-Hispanic white population with respect to educational attainment and income, a different picture exists for Native Hawaiians and Pacific Islanders compared with other Asians. In 2004, one third of Pacific Islanders had never married. In addition, about one of every eight Pacific Islanders was separated, widowed, or divorced, compared with about one in five of non-Hispanic whites (U.S. Census Bureau, 2007b). (See Table 8.1: Characteristics of Pacific Islanders).

❖ Table 8.1   Characteristics of Pacific Islanders

Characteristic	Whites	Pacific Islanders
Total poverty rates	12.5%	19%
High School Graduation Rate	91.5%	86%
Bachelor's degree	32.5%	14.4%
Graduate Degrees	12.0%	4.0%
Percent Uninsured	10.4%	14.1%
Median Income	$56,565	$52,865

Source: Adapted from Hoeffel et al., 2012; Ogunwole, Drewery, & Rios-Vargas, 2012.

The greatest percentage of Asians lived in family households at nearly 75%. A nonfamily household is defined as people who live alone or people living with unrelated individuals. Sixty percent of households were married couples, 26% were nonfamily, 9% were female households only with no male present, and nearly 5% were male only with no female present. Unlike blacks and Latinos, Asians were not more likely than whites to live with grandchildren; however, Pacific Islanders were. About 10% of Pacific Islanders were living in the same house with co-resident grandchildren (U.S. Census Bureau, 2007b).

Overall, Asians tend to have higher rates of home ownership at 58% in owner-occupied homes. Koreans were less likely than other Asian groups to own their homes (U.S. Census Bureau, 2007c). Among Asians who own homes, the median value of their homes is $306,000, which is nearly twice the median value of white owner-occupied homes ($154,000).

The poverty rate for Pacific Islanders was much higher at 19% (Hoeffel et al., 2012). (See Table 8.1: Characteristics of Pacific Islanders.) One quarter of Pacific Island children live in poverty. Among white children, the rate is 11% in married-couple households (U.S. Census Bureau, 2007f). Pacific Islanders have lower rates of home ownership compared with other Asians, or 46.4%. Among Pacific Islanders who own homes, the median value of their homes is $230,000, which is higher than the median value of white owner-occupied homes ($154,000) (U.S. Census Bureua, 2007f).

Asians are among the most highly educated groups of color in the nation. Among Asians age 25 and older, 85% have graduated from high school. This percentage compares with 86.5% for the general population. Among Asians, 7% have a 9th grade education or less (U.S. Census Bureau, 2012). Half of all Asians (50%) have completed a bachelor's degree, and 20.3% of single-race Asians 25 and older had a graduate (e.g., master's or doctorate) or professional degree in 2009 compared with 10% for all Americans 25 and older (Ogunwole et al., 2012).

Educational attainment among Pacific Islanders is very different. Among Pacific Islanders age 25 and older, 86% have graduated from high school, whereas 14.4% of Pacific Islanders have completed a bachelor's degree and 4% had a graduate degree

(Ogunwole et al., 2012). Nearly half, or 46%, of Asians are employed in management or professional occupations compared with 38% among non-Hispanic whites. Nearly 24% of this group work in sales and office occupations, a number similar to non-Hispanic whites (27%). Comparable to the total in the general population, 15.5% of Asians work in service occupations, and very low numbers of Asians are in construction jobs (4%). Among non-Hispanic whites, 14% are in service and 10% work in construction jobs (Ogunwole et al., 2012).

Sue and Sue (1990) cautioned against acceptance of well-known myths and stereotypes concerning Asians in America as "model minorities" who do not face difficulties that other groups of color experience. (See Storytelling: Activism and Peace.) The model minority myth also denies the tremendous diversity that exists among individual Asian Americans.

❖ **STORYTELLING: ACTIVISM AND PEACE**

I met a black woman recently who was a native of the Solomon Islands, which is in the South Pacific east of Papua New Guinea and northeast of Australia. Solomon Islanders are Melanesians, one of the broad groups of Asian peoples. In 1999, a militia group called the Isatabu Freedom Movement, made up of indigenous Isatabus from Guadalcanal, expelled more than 20,000 Malaitans, or people from Malaita. The Malaitans had migrated to the Solomon Islands in search of employment. Many had jobs in Guadalcanal, leading to resentment from the indigenous people, the Isatabus. The Malaitans formed their own group in response to the ethnic tensions. They were called the Malaita Eagle Force. Over the years, there was unrest, corruption, and instability. This woman became a peacemaker. Although it was dangerous to speak to the men, many of whom saw women as subordinate and inferior, she was courageous in her actions, taking her brother with her not only for protection but to have the status of a man with her. This resistance and activism is part of the experience of Asian diversity among the world's Asian people. Many young Asians, including the Maori people in New Zealand, were inspired by the struggles of people in America to develop a sense of ethnic pride and self-esteem. One example is when black power movement leaders encouraged black people's empowerment (Avakian, 2002).

Asian American success has emerged as the new stereotype for Asians. While this image has led many teachers and employers to view Asians as intelligent and hardworking and has opened some opportunities, it has also been harmful.

The model minority cannot be broadly applied. Wong and Halgin (2006) observed that the label cannot acceptably capture "the lives of all Asian Americans subsumed in this panethnic category" (Wong & Halgin, 2006, p. 41). The model minority myth interferes with economically disadvantaged Asian American communities receiving the necessary emotional and financial resources and creates division among groups of color as one group is pitted against another

(Wong & Halgin, 2006). Some suffer because of unemployment, and some newly immigrated groups, such as the Vietnamese, have very high poverty rates and difficulties with social adjustment due to the trauma they experienced prior to immigration. In fact, Vietnamese Americans have an average family income that is about half that of Asian American Pacific Islander populations as a whole (Byrd & Clayton, 2003).

Pacific Islanders tend to have higher rates of poverty than other Asian groups, with Tongans and Samoans having some of the highest rates. Because of autonomous governments with a variety of political relationships with the United States, varying levels of health and health care exist for Pacific Islanders. For instance, Guam has a relatively high level of health care, with the Republic of Belau and the Federated States of Micronesia having older hospitals that provide a "generally poorer level of care" (Byrd & Clayton, 2003, p. 480).

Much of the literature that is available would suggest that Asian Americans, in comparison with the general population, consume less alcohol and drugs (Mercado, 2000). The myth of the model minority fuels this assumption. The truth of the matter is that Asians, like other groups, contend with substance addictions as well. There is research to suggest that substance abuse among Asians is on the rise (Zane & Huh-Kim, 1998). To best treat substance abuse issues, Mercado (2000) suggests a family counseling/therapy intervention. Respecting cultural values and understanding the extent of acculturation are critical to treating the client, even if the client is being seen alone (Chang, 2000).

Among refugees, such as Cambodians, Laotians, and Vietnamese, post-traumatic stress disorder (PTSD) and depression are common, given a history of war and poverty. Between 1975 and 1979, Pol Pot, leader of the Khmer Rouge, a communist guerilla organization, presided over Cambodia's "killing fields," an inhumane period of genocide during which one third of Cambodia's population, or between 1.5 and 2 million Cambodians, were slaughtered. Anticommunists, students, intellectuals, the wealthy, and doctors were considered to be enemies of the state and tragically lost their lives (Avakian, 2002). One study found that Cambodian high school students had symptoms of PTSD as well as depressive symptoms. Among Cambodian adults who had been resettled in Massachusetts, 43% reported the deaths, while in Cambodia, of between one and six children (U.S. DHHS, 2001). This distress produced an intense but invisible sadness. Asians also suffer discrimination on the job, and career choices are skewed because of racial inequities. Educationally, some Asians have problems with the English language on standardized tests, and conflicts exist between American and Asian values. The stereotype of the model minority permeates the culture. Asian students who internalize this myth may find it extremely hard to ask for needed assistance or feel increasingly isolated in their attempts to achieve academic success (Gloria & Ho, 2003).

Asian Americans are frequently viewed as a model minority who have made it in this society and experience little in the form of racism (Wong & Halgin, 2006). Despite the long documented history of racism toward Asian Americans, there has been a lack of attention paid to prejudice and discrimination directed against them (Sue,

Bucceri, Lin, Nadal, & Torino, et al., 2007). Sue identified microaggression themes experienced by a qualitative sample of Asian Americans that include: (a) alien in own land, (b) ascription of intelligence, (c) exoticization of Asian women, (d) invalidation of interethnic differences, (e) denial of racial reality, (f) pathologizing cultural values/communication styles, (g) second-class citizenship, and (h) invisibility. There has also been insufficient attention devoted to family dysfunction, including verbal, sexual, and emotional abuse of children, communication problems, harsh parenting practices, and the adverse impact that this has on children. In 2009, young Asian American women had the second highest rate of suicide among those aged 15 to 24 of all racial groups (Hahm, Gonyea, Chiao, & Koritsanszky, 2014). The authors argued that women develop a fractured identity—on one hand, wanting to honor their families and on the other hand, feeling enormous pressure to measure up with the ideal of the perfect Asian woman. Facility with the English language is one of the factors, from a study of Chinese Americans in the Bay Area of California, found to be associated with a more positive attitude toward help seeking for a nervous or emotional problem (Ying & Miller, 1992). In a study by Lin (1994) with 145 adult Chinese Americans, when qualified ethnic and language-matched therapists were provided, sample participants stayed in therapy as long as the general American public.

According to Dana (2002), "Somatization constitutes an attempt to communicate an experience of bodily symptoms and distress in response to psychosocial stressors often associated with depression and anxiety disorders, or worry and preoccupation with well-being" (p. 37). Research suggests that some groups of Asians may have higher rates of somatoform issues compared with the general population. Headaches are one way in which somatization is manifested.

Asian Americans typically have patriarchal families with authority and communication exercised from top to bottom, interdependent roles, strict adherence to traditional norms, and minimization of conflict by suppression of overt emotion (Kitano, 1988; Min, 1988; Tran, 1988; Wong, 1988). Guilt and shame are used to control family members, and obligations to the family take precedence over individual prerogatives (Kitano, 1988; Sue & Sue, 1990; Wong, 1988). Under the aegis of the family, discipline and self-control are sufficient to provide an impetus for outstanding achievement to honor the family. Negative behaviors such as delinquency, school failure, unemployment, or mental illness are considered family failures that disrupt the desired harmony of family life. In addition is the belief in external control, a fatalism that allows an equanimity and acceptance without question of life as it unfolds.

In China and the United States, absolute control by the family as a major ingredient in the formation of a traditional self-concept has not only diminished but also is being openly questioned (Wong, 1988). Despite questioning of traditional filial identity, strong evidence suggests, at least among Hong Kong Chinese students, the continued presence of an extended self or collective orientation. Similarly, in Japan the emphasis on the importance of collectivity has been increasing, particularly in the form of corporate family effectiveness instead of intrafamily lineal authority or filial piety (Goldenberg & Goldenberg, 1996; Kitano, 1988). However, this collectivity may also be expressed in humanistic or socialist terms.

The primary tradition is *filial piety*, which is the dedication and deference of children to their parents (Goldenberg & Goldenberg, 1996). In the United States, problems faced by first- and second-generation Chinese may differ as a result of inability to express this tradition properly (Sue & Sue, 1990; Wong, 1988). Although first-generation men in particular are required to achieve and to be good providers for their families, sufficient achievement to fulfill family expectations has not always been possible for them. Second-generation individuals also may fail to be unquestioningly faithful to the traditional values of their parents. Their self-worth is increasingly defined either by dominant culture values or by pan-Asian values, in which a common response to racism and personal pride may take precedence over filial piety. As a result, individuals in both generations may experience considerable guilt and anxiety. It may be argued that the locus of loyalty within the Chinese community is in the process of shifting from the family, including ancestors, to other collectivities, including the pan-Asian community in the United States. Overall, the traditional Asian American family believes in loyalty and devotion to its values (Goldenberg & Goldenberg, 1996).

Acculturation and Experiences in America

There are differences in the values expressed in Asian cultures and in the United States. Much of this difference, in addition to personality, is related to acculturation. Length of time in the United States, access to resources, English-language fluency, educational level, and employment status are factors that affect adjustment. Other moderator variables include generational status, age, neighborhood ethnic density, country of birth, kinship structures, and purposes of immigration. Two different immigrant streams are associated with huge diversity within the Asian and Pacific Island populations. The first stream represents people from countries that have large populations in the United States and tend to have better health. Included are Chinese, Filipinos, Koreans, and Asian Indians. The second stream consists of lower socioeconomic groups. Many refugees are included in this number (Frisbie, Cho, & Hummer, 2002).

Cultural maintenance refers to cultural identity characteristics that are considered important and for which people strive. *Contact and participation* refers to the extent to which groups deem it important to become involved with other cultural groups or remain primarily among themselves. *Assimilation* is defined as what takes place when persons internalize the dominant culture and rejects the indigenous culture. *Separation* refers to the maintenance of proficiency in the dominant culture but does not adapt to the dominant culture. *Segregation* is the term used to describe the dominant group's stance with respect to the non-dominant group. *Integration* refers to the maintenance of cultural integrity while seeking to participate in the larger social network of a multicultural society. *Marginalization* occurs when a person rejects both the indigenous and dominant cultures.

According to Zhang and Moradi (2013), a bilinear perspective of acculturation and enculturation allows for a more comprehensive and nuanced perspective with respect to acculturation and enculturation among Asian Americans. (See Storytelling: Next Life.) Such a perspective speaks to a relationship between adoption of the original culture and the host culture "whereby it is possible for individuals to maintain a positive relationship with both cultures and to shift their behaviors as needed across contexts to fit into these cultures (Zhang & Moradi, 2013, p. 754). More specifically, intraindividuality is emphasized over generalizing a person's level of acculturation or enculturation in one dimension to the other dimensions (e.g., behaviors, knowledge, and cultural identity).

❖ STORYTELLING: NEXT LIFE

In class some years ago we were discussing lower rates of divorce among Asians. I stated that given the challenges that impact human beings in intimate relationships, Asians are no different from others from feeling like they may have come to the end of their current marriage. One of my students said some Asians may not be happy in their marriages; however, cultural expectations (see Table 8.2: Discourses About Asians) and to some extent discourses influence thoughts and behavior. Although most people may not leave unhappy marriages, they hope in their next life they will find greater happiness. We discussed the values of looking to the next life for happiness, collectivism, and acceptance of fate, values that differ from dominant American values.

Research conducted by Chae and Foley (2010) looked at three separate Asian groups: Chinese, Koreans, and Japanese. The constructs of ethnic identity, acculturation, and psychological well-being were investigated. Among all groups, ethnic identity was a strong predictor of psychological well-being. Overall, bicultural identity had the greatest relationship with psychological well-being, more so than low or high

❖ **Table 8.2**   Discourses About Asians

Successful
Model minority
Emotionally restrained
Perceived not to be angry like blacks and Latinos
Brilliant in math and science
Smarter than white people
Buddhists
Studious, hardworking
Foreign-born
Scientists
Women as exotic
Enduring marriages

acculturation. There were ethnic group differences with respect to acculturation and psychological well-being. Among Koreans, there was a significant inverse relationship between acculturation and psychological well-being. For this group, but not for Japanese where acculturation added little to the regression model or Chinese, high acculturation may be linked to lower levels of psychological well-being.

Lee and Ahn (2011) were interested in the relationship between racial discrimination and mental health. They found in their meta-analysis of 23 independent studies concerning Asian Americans that the relationship between racial discrimination and mental health was statistically significant. More specifically, racial discrimination had significantly stronger correlations to depression and anxiety than to psychological distress. In relation to racial discrimination, Asians were equally as likely to suffer from depression and anxiety. (See Storytelling: Not to Speak.) Contrary to the emphasis on the collectivistic values of Asian people, this research found that individualistic forms of resources (e.g., personal constructs and strengths, coping strategies) appeared to have equal or stronger correlation to racial discrimination and mental health in comparison to collectivistic forms (e.g., social support and cultural identity).

Prior to arrival in the United States, most Asian immigrants and refugees have primary exposure to their own culture. Upon arrival, cultural adaptation is required, and a relinquishing of native aspects of their culture to function in school and work contexts is part of this process. In addition to the factors cited earlier that affect adaptation, age of migration (before or after the age of 12), reason for migration (economic development or political refuge), and mode of migration (with or without parents or family members) are critical issues (Tsai & Chensova-Dutton, 2002).

Among many Asians, arranged marriages are still practiced. Another practice is that of Asian-born children being adopted by primarily white American parents. During the Korean War, there were growing numbers of children in Korean orphanages. After the passage of legislation that made the adoption process easier, the practice became increasingly common in the 1970s. In addition to Korea, India, Vietnam, the Philippines, and Cambodia experienced upheaval that exacerbated poor living conditions. Vulnerable families relinquished their children for adoption. Between 1989 and 2003, according to the U.S. Department of State, China sent 7,044 children to the United States, followed by Russia with 5,865, and South Korea with 1,716 (Le, 2008).

The successes and creativity of many newly migrated groups from Asia have been attributed largely to the informal network system of valuing the group, being a member of the group, and attending to the needs of others through sharing financial and human resources, from employment information to housing, for the betterment of all (Chang, 1996; Sue & Sue, 1990). Among some Asian groups, even among newly arrived immigrants, a substantial number have higher education and extensive career experience. Much of the success in business noted among many Korean Americans can be explained by a system called *kae*, which is similar to the Chinese concept of *woi* and the Japanese system known as *tanomoshi*. These systems enable successful people to help newcomers through a lending and borrowing system. In addition, many of the Korean banks in America are under the authority of banks in Korea. In this way, newcomers face less discrimination than would be seen at an American bank (Avakian, 2002).

❖ **STORYTELLING: NOT TO SPEAK**

A colleague of mine who is Chinese told me of a family member whom she suspected of being depressed but was uncomfortable speaking with the relative's parents. Doing so would be a source of embarrassment for the highly successful parents and for my colleague's parents who would be ashamed of any discussion from their child about a close relative's mental health problems. Such problems would be perceived as a weakness. I asked if a referral from a respected medical professional would make a difference. She thought about this recommendation and decided it was worth a try since medicine was more understood and respected compared to mental health professionals who only studied the mind and not the brain.

Cultural Orientation and Values

Confucianism, Taoism, and Buddhism underlie many Asian cultural values. Founded in the 5th and 6th centuries BC by followers of Siddhartha Gautama, later known as Buddha (Avakian, 2002), the basic teachings of Buddhism maintain that there is suffering, the first noble truth. Understanding the roots of suffering, the cessation of suffering, and being on the path to refrain from that which causes suffering are also emphasized (Nhat Hanh, 1998). Hinduism is older than Buddhism and dates back to 1500 BC. Hindu beliefs are presented in two sacred books, the *Vedas* and the *Upanishads*. People are ranked into caste systems from the Brahmans (priests) at the top to the Shudras (peasants and laborers) on the bottom. Confucius, born in about 551 BC, was China's most influential philosopher and emphasized family loyalty, hard work, and respect for parents and elders. Like Confucianism, Taoism was also a religion in addition to being a philosophy. It emphasized harmony in nature and contemplation (Avakian, 2002). Such a philosophy is seen in the eighth chapter of the *Tao Te Ching*: "In dwelling, be close to the land. In meditation, go deep in the heart. In dealing with others, be gentle and kind. In speech, be true. In ruling, be just. In business, be competent. In action, watch the timing. No fight: No blame" (Lao Tsu, 1972). *We wei*, which literally means "doing nothing" or inaction, was emphasized, but it could also refer to modesty, simplicity, and absence of ambition for power (Hong & Domokos-Cheng Ham, 2001).

The religious identities of Asian Americans are quite varied. According to the Pew Research survey, about half of Chinese are unaffiliated, most Filipinos are Catholic, about half of Indians are Hindu, most Koreans are Protestant and a plurality of Vietnamese are Buddhist. In total, 26% of Asian Americans are unaffiliated, 22% are Protestant (13% evangelical; 9% mainline); 19% are Catholic, 14% are Buddhist, 10% are Hindu, 4% are Muslim, and 1% are Sikh. Overall, 39% of Asian Americans say religion is very important in their lives, compared with 58% of the U.S. general public (Pew Research Center, 2013).

Values common to Asian ethnic groups include emphasis on harmony in relationships, emotional restraint (emotional expression may be interpreted as a sign of immaturity), precedence of group interests over individual interests, extended family, deference to authority, obedience to and respect for parents, emphasis on hard work, fulfilling obligations, and high value associated with education (Sandhu, 1997; Uba, 1994). (See Table 8.3.) According to Ying (2002), "The primary objective of socialization is *tsuo jen* (which literally means to make/become human), that is, to teach a child proper social rules of conduct and submission of personal desires to that of others in order to avoid interpersonal conflict and social disapproval" (pp. 174–175).

Among the Chinese, selflessness, obedience to authority, or deference to the collective unit is a primary value and is manifested in relations with elders or those in authority. Body parts are used to describe intimate relationships. For instance, biological children are referred to as bone and flesh, and siblings are referred to as hand and foot (Ying, 2002). The concept of *jen*, or personhood, is emphasized. Jen is a Confucian virtue and is written with two strokes. Each represents one person and refers to responsibility for kin as expressed through respect, loyalty, and love (Dana, 1993). (See Table 8.3: Common Cultural Values Among People of Asian Descent.)

Among collectivistic people, the self is conceptualized in a social way (Ying, 2002). In the West, the self is primary and exerts influence on expectations concerning

❖ **Table 8.3** Common Cultural Values Among People of Asian Descent

---

Enryo (reserve, constraint)

Jen (benevolence, personhood, humanity)

Yuan (the influence of past relationships on present social relationships)

Face (concern for maintaining face)

Thrift

Interpersonal harmony in relationships

Ren qing (social favors exchanged in the form of money, goods, information—according to an implicit set of social rules)

Precedence of group interests over individual interests

Educational attainment and achievement

Obedience to authority

Marriage

Emotional self-control

Honor given to elders

Modesty and humility

Patriarchy

---

psychological well-being. For instance, personal happiness is considered an inalienable right and an essential goal, almost an entitlement. In many Asian cultures, including Chinese but also Southeast Asians, achievement of personal happiness may be a less salient goal and constructed within a collectivistic framework because appraisal of the self is based on external social standards (Tsai & Chensova-Dutton, 2002). Kim (2007) added that the ability to resolve psychological problems and self-effacement are salient value dimensions among Asians.

Despite diversity among Asians, certain ethnic groups share some similarities, such as the Chinese and the Japanese. According to Sue and Sue (1995), in both cultures, the families are patriarchal and communication styles tend to be formal, well defined, and flow from the top downward. Relationships among family members are highly inter-dependent, with one person's actions reflecting on the entire family unit. Control of the children is maintained by fostering feelings of shame and guilt. Although parenting children in this manner may characterize many Asian families, it also applies to other cultures as well. Hsu (1953) observed that the most important issue to Americans is what parents should do for the children; to Chinese, what children should do for their parents is of greatest importance.

Family is given respect and honor. Among the Vietnamese, it is not uncommon for multiple generations to reside collectively in one home. Elders are honored, respected, and cared for because of the importance of family. Compared with other groups, Asian Americans are more likely to live in households comprised of family members only. They are less likely to live on their own and are characterized by low percentages of female-headed households. Pacific Islanders are also more likely to have larger families than most Asian Americans and non-Asian Americans (Byrd & Clayton, 2003; U.S. DHHS, 2001).

According to McFadden (1993), Asians tend to believe that marriage is the most important event that can occur in a person's life and is perceived to be long lasting, until the end of the person's life, with divorce being considered the greatest possible tragedy that could occur. "Most Asian cultures are historically patrilineal and patrilo-cal and favor male offspring over female. Consequently, women often grow up feeling devalued and suffer emotional and psychological consequences from these sexist customs throughout their lives" (Chang, 2000, p. 201).

Restraint of emotions represents a value for many Asian Americans. This value is not to be confused with the absence of a sense of humor; however, *enryo*, or reserve and constraint, is important and represents a primary mode of communication. Uba (1994) said, "This syndrome may be manifested in a number of ways, as in a hesitancy to speak up in class or to openly contradict a person in a position of authority . . . Another part of the *enryo* syndrome is a modest devaluation of oneself and one's possessions" (p. 18).

Humility is a cultural value, as is the notion of loss of face. Self-effacement and modesty are highly valued and reflect wisdom and function to increase social harmony (Ying, 2002). Leong, Wagner, and Kim (1995) stated that communication styles among Asians allow participants to maintain face. Therefore, direct communication styles, reflective of a Western style and involving confrontation and challenges, tend to be less desirable.

Asian American Identity Development

As a heterogeneous group, myriad challenges face Asians in America. One of the most pervasive is related to the psychological conflict around racial identity. This conflict is connected to the experience of institutional racism, which is often subtle but damaging nonetheless to people who are targeted as different from a standard of white acceptability (Kim, 2001). According to Kim, "At some point in their lives, many Asian Americans have either consciously or unconsciously expressed the desire to become White, and tried to reject their identity as Asians" (p. 70).

Very few studies exist on Asians and ethnic and racial identity development. Lee (2003) concluded from his research studies on two types of perceived discrimination (minority group discrimination and personal ethnic discrimination) that ethnic identity did not moderate or mediate the negative psychological effects of personal ethnic discrimination or minority group discrimination. He surmised, "It is possible that ethnic identity functions primarily as a psychological asset that contributes to well-being but it does not—in and of itself—protect against the effects of discrimination" (p. 139).

Chen, LePhuoc, Guzman, Rude, and Dodd (2006) conducted research on 344 self-identified Asian American adults recruited through Asian American electronic mailing lists, professional organizations, and snowballing. The study authors investigated racial identity profiles, racial attitudes, and racism-related stress among Asian Americans using the PCRIAS, the CoBRAS (a measure of Color-Blind Racial Attitudes), and the ASRRSI (or the Asian American Racism-Related Stress Inventory). Within the context of other groups of color, the social construction of race is such that Asians occupy an intermediary position in the racial hierarchy, with whites on the highest rung and blacks on the lowest (Chen et al., 2006).

Kim (2001) identified grounding principles of an Asian American identity development model:

1. The predominance of white racism and its impact on Asian American identity development must be acknowledged.

2. Internalized racism has to be unlearned unconsciously.

3. A healthy identity requires the transformation of a negative racial identity into a positive and healthy one.

The proposed stage model is sequential, not linear. This model is influenced by other racial identity development theories, yet takes into consideration the unique experiences of Asian Americans.

Stage 1: Ethnic Awareness. This first stage represents the period prior to children's entry into the school system. The social environment and reference group consists largely of family. The extent of participation in Asian-oriented activities can bolster a sense of positive ethnic awareness.

Stage 2: White Identification. This stage is marked by children's painful awareness that they are different from white people and that this difference is not regarded as a good thing.

Feeling a sense of shame for being Asian can result in desperate attempts by Asian children to fit into white society. To compensate for feelings of inferiority, many Asian children will seek leadership in organizations and excel academically. Active white identification refers to the Asian student not consciously perceiving himself or herself as different from whites, thus there is a desire to alienate himself or herself from and not be regarded as Asian. Passive white identification Asians enter this stage during their later years and are buffered by early exposure to predominantly Asian communities that nurtured self-esteem. The distancing from Asians and seeking to pass for white is not evident here, but fantasizing, (e.g., "I wish") about being white does occur.

Stage 3: Awakening to Social Political Consciousness. A shift from personal to social responsibility for racism allows Asian Americans to understand racism and transform their negative sense of self into a positive one. At this stage, white people are no longer the reference group and Asians do not regard themselves as inferior. The person essentially asks the question, "Why should I be ashamed of who I am?" There is a connection to other people of color.

Stage 4: Redirection to an Asian American Consciousness. In this stage, the sense of self as a minority is crystallized into a sense of being Asian. There is often an immersion into the Asian experience, and the ego is centered on things/people Asian. Racial pride is experienced as is a positive self-concept. In addition to pride, people feel angry at the way in which the dominant white culture perpetuates racism and cultural violence.

Stage 5: Incorporation. A person's racial identity is blended into other social identities. The self is seen as whole, with race representing only one aspect of social identity. The immersion of the previous stage is relaxed. A clear Asian American identity has been achieved, yet people in general are the person's reference group.

Implications for Mental Health Professionals

There is tremendous diversity among Asians with respect to nationality, language, immigration status, educational and occupational levels, push and pull factors for immigrants, and income. Despite this heterogeneity, the myth of the model minority for the entire group of Asians prevails. Ignoring this level of diversity among Asians is problematic. Monolithicizing a group reflects racism in its failure to honor important intragroup differences. In addition, the unique challenges and concerns that do not reflect success and achievement are obscured. Poverty, mental illness, gang affiliation, school failure, domestic violence, incest, addiction, and racism are realities among Asians. The stereotypes of Asians—China doll, Tokyo Rose, savage, mysterious, Charlie Chan, dragon lady, exotic, insolent, diminutive, mail order bride, and little brown brother (Zia, 2000)—are still with us today.

Although the median value of homes among Asians homeowners exceeds that of whites, there was a time in this country when Asians could not own land. Known as the Alien Land Law, this law prohibited anyone of Asian ancestry from owning land. Internalized racism was also part of the experience of many Chinese after Pearl Harbor was bombed. Signs were seen posted in stores that announced, "This is a Chinese shop." Some people wore buttons that said, "I am Chinese" or "I hate Japs worse than you do" (Zia, 2000). Despite discourses that Asians are passive or politically safe, Asians have a long history of oppression and resistance to it. (See Case Study: Denial of Tenure.)

The Japanese American Citizens League and the Chinese Consolidated Benevolent Association were centers of organization for equal rights and social justice. In a study investigating the benefits of Asian cultural values to Asian clients in counseling, Kim, Li, and Liang (2002) found that Asian American clients who had high adherence to Asian cultural values, as measured by the Asian Values Scale, perceived greater client–counselor working alliance and counselor empathic understanding than did clients who had low adherence to Asian cultural values. Such values representing related aspects of Asian cultural values included collectivism, conformity to norms, emotional self-control, family recognition through achievement, filial piety, and humility. Kim et al. (2002) concluded, "Asian Americans who adhere to Asian cultural values try to be understanding, accommodating, conciliatory, and not directly confrontational, and they expect the same from others" (pp. 351–352). In providing mental health services to Asians, consider acculturation, facility with English, religious and cultural values, generational status, and social supports as part of diagnoses and treatment.

Case Study

Denial of Tenure

Jenny is a single, 36-year-old Japanese American. She is an Assistant Professor in Pharmacy at a large university in Georgia. She was born in California and so were her parents and grandparents. Jenny comes from a family of professionals in health sciences. She has heard stories of her family's internment during World War II due to their Japanese ancestry. Her family has worked hard and has dealt with racial discrimination. Her parents sacrificed to put Jenny and her siblings through school. Her sister is a nurse, and her brother is a pharmacist. Her father is a physician's assistant, and her mother is a physical therapist. Jenny has recently learned that she has been denied tenure and promotion. Because of this denial of tenure, she will need to find employment elsewhere within the next year. Jenny is devastated and feels very ashamed. She does not know how to tell her parents the truth. They assume she had been awarded promotion and tenure and want to know when she is coming home to celebrate. Jenny has been extremely prolific and has presented the results of her research throughout the world. She was told that although she received many small grants, the university did not see the amount of money she brought in as adequate. Jenny has appealed the denial of tenure, but her appeal was rejected by a faculty committee. Jenny is a lesbian. She has not dated much during the last few years due to some rejections in dating and relationships. Jenny has not revealed her sexuality to her parents although her father caught her kissing a girl when Jenny was a teen. Her father beat her with a belt and told her that if he ever caught her doing that again, she would receive worse. She is concerned that such a revelation would contribute to distress and disappointment from both her parents and her married-with-children heterosexual siblings. When Jenny was younger, her parents asked for grandchildren but have lately slowed their requests as Jenny ages. On the suggestion of a friend, Jenny seeks therapy. She has been weepy and irritable and suffers from insomnia, vomiting, and hair loss. Jenny's long-standing but secret bout with bulimia and cutting concern her enough to seek therapy. Jenny's therapist is Naomi, a 40-year-old psychologist who is Filipino.

Questions

1. From a cultural lens, why is it so difficult for Jenny to tell her parents about her denial of tenure?

2. What is the influence of culture on Jenny's silence about her sexuality, professional, and personal life?

Discussion and Integration

The concept of talk therapy is foreign to many Asian American clients (Hong & Domokos-Cheng Ham, 2001). Asian Americans may be hesitant to discuss their feelings and problems openly and question the effectiveness of counseling. Some of the same attitudes that discourage Asian Americans from seeking mental health services discourage them, once in therapy, from discussing their problems. In spite of a lack of familiarity with psychotherapy, many Asian Americans might expect quick relief from their symptoms. Deferring to nonprofessionals, elders, and older relatives within the community (Yeh & Wang, 2000) is a way that Asian American communities deal with mental health challenges.

In addition to concerns about traditional coping strategies, there are other reasons that explain the reluctance among Asian Americans to discuss their problems. According to Uba (1994), it is not uncommon for Asian Americans to perceive talking about themselves or disclosing private personal information to a stranger as reflective of low maturity and lack of discipline.

Naomi listens to Jenny, who is rather verbal during her initial intake. Naomi assumed that Jenny was reluctant to tell her parents about her sexual orientation due to the heightened stigma of homosexuality that many lesbian and gay people of color face. Although this fear is true for some, Moradi, DeBlaere, and Huang (2010) conducted research that indicated similar levels of perceived heterosexism between lesbian, gay, and bisexual (LGB) people of color and white LGB. They stressed the importance of exploring perceived heterosexism among LGB people of color on an individual basis as opposed from a group perspective.

Jenny is a woman of color and a sexual minority. According to Friedman and Leaper (2010), lesbian, bisexual, and queer women experience discrimination based on their positions as sexual minorities and as women. The authors argue that "gendered heterosexism emphasized that sexual-minority women may experience discrimination that is qualitatively different from either sexism or heterosexism" (p. 153).

Jenny has been discreet regarding disclosure of her sexuality, which was consistent with findings from Moradi et al. (2010) that people of color who are LGB have lower levels of outness. In particular, LBG people of Asian descent are often invisible with respect to cultural norms relative to privacy about sexuality and intimacy (Sanchez-Hucles & Jones, 2007). Jenny wonders if being out to a few colleagues at work has cost her tenure. Naomi asks if Jenny thinks racism was involved in her denial of tenure. Naomi evidences the ability to broach the topic of racism and ascertain its applicability to Jenny's perception of her situation. Jenny sighs and says that she does not know, but she has wondered this for a while. Jenny had some dating experiences with white LGB members that felt very racist—some people were interested in her as a commodity. One woman she briefly dated said she "wanted to know what it was like to be with an exotic girl from the orient." Jenny also found that LGB people of color (mainly African Americans and Latinos) were surprised to find a "nice, smart, good, and quiet Asian gay girl" in their midst. According to Syzmanski and Sung (2010), LGBT (lesbian, gay, bisexual, and transsexual) Asian Americans experienced racism from the white LGBT community as well as internalized racism from LGBT communities of color. Both types of encounters are psychologically distressing.

Chow (1994), identified four cultural dilemmas facing Asian American women: (1) obedience versus independence, (2) collective (or familial) versus individual interest, (3) fatalism versus change, and (4) self-control versus self-expression or spontaneity (p. 186) that help Naomi in her approach to Jenny, particularly collective versus self-expression or spontaneity. When exploring this topic with Jenny, Naomi discovered that Jenny wanted to be a science fiction author, but her family, siblings included, thought such dreams were adolescent, unrealistic, and inconsistent with the health science trajectories of her immediate family members.

Naomi aided Jenny in getting in touch with her disappointment and anger at the tenure decision, the discrimination she has experienced from white people, and the dismissal from people of color in the LGBT community. She is also angry at her family for being so prescriptive regarding her life choices. Her work with Naomi helped her to clarify future career steps as well as finding peace about her practice of not sharing her sexuality with her family but with supportive others from inside and outside of the LGBT community.

Jenny is not alone in feeling the burden of the inordinate emphasis on being thin, which translates into being pretty, that exists in American society. Phan and Tylka (2006) conducted research on 200 Asian American women to examine whether several variables and paths included within one empirically supported model of eating disorder symptomatology were supported. More specifically, researchers examined ethnic identity, self-esteem, pressure for thinness, eating attitudes, and body shape. They found that Asian American women's perceived pressure for thinness slightly predicted their self-esteem and moderately predicted their body preoccupation both directly and indirectly. It was also found that Asian American women's body preoccupation strongly predicted their eating disorder symptomatology. What was most interesting and contradictory to previous research was that ethnic identity actually intensified the pressure for thinness. More specifically, "Pressure for thinness and body preoccupation were strongly related for women with high ethnic identity but moderately related for women with low ethnic identity" (Phan & Tylka, 2006, p. 45). It was hypothesized that within collectivism, a value often espoused by women who have high ethnic identity, Asian American women are more likely to be concerned about how their weight may have an adverse impact on significant others, which can then lead to body preoccupation.

Although Jenny espouses collectivism and strong ethnic identity, she struggles with disordered eating and her culture's dictates about whom she loves and what she does vocationally. It is important that Naomi not assume that because of Jenny's sexual orientation, long held desire to pursue a science fiction writing career, and push back of family expectations regarding marriage and children, that she is not enculturated. The best treatment strategies may be a combination of psychotherapeutic techniques and indigenous healing practices, such as acupuncture (Kim, 2007). Naomi shows cultural competence regarding skills, attitudes, and interventions and knows that racism, sexism, and homophobia can interfere with trust in the therapeutic alliance. As such, listening intently, not writing down excessive information, and proceeding cautiously with a request for private information too prematurely (Sanchez-Hucles & Jones, 2007).

Due to her knowledge of the research literature that has clinical implications, Naomi sees Jenny as having a "fractured identity." Hahm et al. (2014) defined a fractured identity among Asian women as a function of exposure to multiple negative parenting types that paralyze women who are stuck between an intense desire to fulfill their parents' and society's expectations while seeking to resist or rebel against the image of "the perfect Asian woman" (p. 56). A fractured identity is the foundation for unsafe coping strategies, isolation, self-harm, and suicidal behaviors.

Naomi asks Jenny what her plans are as she seeks new employment. Jenny says, "I am not sure, but I have told my parents that I did not receive tenure. As I anticipated, they were ultra critical of me. My mother said my father is sick, and I should come home to care for him since I have no job and no husband. I told her that I would not be doing that." Jenny tells Naomi of a recent job offer with tenure that she has received but is not sure she wants to move to the cold Midwest. Naomi observes that Jenny appears to be coping well by attending therapy weekly, writing science fiction, and doing yoga. Part of Jenny's question that she is discussing in therapy is whether she wants to stay in academia at all.

Naomi also has a history with bulimia, and she was rightly concerned about possible countertransference. To respond ethically, Naomi interrogates her own history and recovery so as not to contaminate the therapeutic event and has had personal therapy. She meets annually with her psychologist for a mental health checkup where she can continue to examine the multiple forces in her own life—cultural, familial, and institutional—that contribute to her disordered eating as an Asian woman.

Summary

This chapter focused on people of Asian descent. A case study provided insight for counseling, where an Asian professor who is lesbian with a history of bulimia and cutting has recently been denied tenure. Her therapist is Filipino who also has a history of an eating disorder. The therapist's negotiation of the therapeutic relationship required her to examine her own history with bulimia and the meaning of her patient's experiences with racism from both white and LGBT communities of color.

9

People of the Middle East and Arab Descent

❖

In 2011, the Middle East experienced the Arab Spring, a series of uprisings, demonstrations, gatherings, and revolutions that began in Tunisia and spread to Egypt, Yemen, Bahrain, Syria, Jordan, and Libya. Three years ago, Libyan rebels (a group of students, bus drivers, doctors, and expatriates) took control of their country from Muammar Gaddafi, who ruled the nation for over four decades. Gaddafi is now deceased. Young people (ages 15–29), who represent 30% of the population in the

Middle East (Assaud & Roudi-Fahimi, 2007), were pivotal to the uprisings, but people across age, nationality, race, and class were united. By word of mouth, the airways, the internet, poetry, and rap, voices of protest were lifted regarding a desire for democracy, decrying food inflation, low wages, high unemployment, state of emergency laws, corruption, police brutality, and censorship. In Egypt, the outcome was victory, and Hosni Mubarak was ousted. The world witnessed the power of civil unrest. Tragically, lives were loss and there were injuries; however, the protests were largely peaceful yet transformative. Countries in the Middle East (e.g., Syria and Iraq) contend with extremism and terror, which has uprooted people and families who have fled to other countries such as Lebanon, Turkey, Hungary, Bulgaria, Slovenia, and Germany. The situation is a humane crisis.

This chapter profiles people of Arab ancestry and other people of the Middle East. A brief look at history, cultural values, and demographic trends is included. A case study is provided for the integration of material within a therapeutic context.

The Africans, Asians, Europeans, and Arabs

The Middle East represents a region that encompasses southwestern Asia and northern Africa. It spans from Morocco to Pakistan and includes the Caucasus Mountains, which is a mountain system between the Black and Caspian seas that separates Europe and Asia. For example, Western Asia includes many countries discussed within the context of the Middle East and references Armenia, Azerbaijan, Bahrain, Cyprus, Georgia, Iraq, Israel, Jordan, Kuwait, Lebanon, Oman, Qatar, Saudi Arabia, Syria, Turkey, United Arab Emirates, and Yemen (Hoeffel et al., 2012).

Spanning two continents, Africa and Asia, the Middle East is home to the beginning of civilization and all three monotheistic religions. The region's history has been influenced by Persians, Greeks, Romans, Crusaders, Mongols, Mamluks, Ottomans, Europeans, and many others. The majority of the countries that comprise the region only gained independence in the last century. The Middle East has been transformed by the discovery of oil, the creation of the state of Israel, the revival of Islam, the Iranian Revolution, the Iran-Iraq War, the Arab-Israeli conflict, the Persian Gulf War, America's wars in Afghanistan and Iraq, and ISIS. The future of the Middle East is uncertain as it struggles to balance the importance of religion, development, and stability in an ever-democratizing global world (Middle East Institute, 2004; Dwairy, 2005).

The term *Arabs* originally applied to the Semitic peoples of the Arabian Peninsula. It is now used for populations of countries whose primary language is Arabic. Arabic was named as the sixth official language of the United Nations and is currently ranked as the fourth most widely spoken language in the world. A good command of the Arabic language is highly valued, as it is extremely difficult and grammatically complex (Dwairy, 2005).

The Arab League of Nations includes 21 countries: Algeria, Bahrain, Comoros, Djibouti, Egypt, Iraq, Jordan, Kuwait, Lebanon, Libya, Mauritania, Morocco, Oman, Palestine, Qatar, Saudi Arabia, Somalia, Sudan, Tunisia, United Arab Emirates, and

Yemen. Due to uprisings in Syria and their government's inhumane method of dealing with political opposition and its unwillingness to comply with the league's demands to stop the violence, the league suspended this member state.

Representatives of the first six member states—Egypt, Iraq, Jordan, Lebanon, Syria, and Saudi Arabia—that initiated the league's formation signed the agreement in Cairo, on March 22, 1945 (Arab League, 2015). Its charter was intended to seek close collaboration on matters of economics, communication, culture, nationality, social welfare, and health. Violence was renounced for the settlement of conflicts between members and empowered league offices. Signatories agreed to collaborate in military affairs. In 1950, the pact was strengthened with a commitment among members to treat acts of aggression on any member state as an act against all (Masters & Sergie, 2014).

Aided by the use of advanced technology, according to the Arab League of Nations (See Knowledge Check 9.1: The Arab League of Nations), interest has been demonstrated in resolving modern day issues: (a) encouraging and promoting their young talents, (b) supporting women in their struggle for equality, (c) improving child welfare, and (d) seeking to solve decades-old problems such as the conflict between Palestine and Israel (Arab League, 2015).

Iran, although located in the Middle East, is not one of the countries in the Arab League; its official languages are Farsi and Persian. Bedouins are Arabs who reside primarily in Israel and who, until a few decades ago, had lived in the desert in a tribal social system. Now many reside in small villages (Dwairy, 2004).

According to de la Cruz and Brittingham (2003), inclusion in the category of Arab is based on self-report as Egyptian, Iraqi, Jordanian, Lebanese, Middle Eastern, North African, Palestinian, and Syrian, as well as other Arab countries. Some people from these countries may not define themselves as Arab, whereas people who identify as Arab may not have their country listed. Based on responses from the American Community Survey, 2006–2010, the U.S. Census included the following groups to be of Arab ancestry: Algerian, Bahraini, Egyptian, Emirati, Iraqi, Jordanian, Kuwaiti, Lebanese, Libyan, Moroccan, Omani, Palestinian, Qatari, Saudi Arabian, Syrian, Tunisian, and Yemeni (Asi & Beaulieu, 2013).

That said, three of these groups considered to be Arab are also considered to be white according to the U.S. Census, which include Egyptians, Lebanese, and Syrians (Hixson, Hepler, & Kim, 2011).

Knowledge Check 9.1

The Arab League of Nations

Algeria, Bahrain, Comoros, Djibouti, Egypt, Iraq, Jordan, Kuwait, Lebanon, Libya, Mauritania, Morocco, Oman, Palestine, Qatar, Saudi Arabia, Somalia, Sudan, Syria (delisted), Tunisia, United Arab Emirates, and Yemen.

Mauritania, Somalia, Djibouti, Sudan, and Comoros are also part of the Arab League; however, they are not counted in the American Community Survey as Arab in its focus on select Arab ancestry groups (Asi & Beaulieu, 2013).

The term *Palestinian* refers to people whose ancestors originated in Palestine prior to the establishment of the State of Israel in 1948. The majority of Palestinians, who are Muslims, are of the Sunni sect, whereas the majority of Christian Palestinians are Orthodox (Abudabbeh, 1996). Palestinians identify as Arabs and speak a dialect of Arabic that is shared with Syria and Lebanon.

The Arab homeland covers 5.25 million square miles. By comparison, the United States is 3.6 million square miles. Nearly three quarters, or 72%, of the Arab homeland is in Africa, with 28% in Asia. Long coastlines give it access to vital waterways and include the Atlantic Ocean, the Mediterranean Sea, the Arabian Gulf, the Arabian Sea, the Gulf of Aden, the Red Sea, and the Indian Ocean (Dwairy, 2005). Another way to think about it is that 15% of Muslims live in the Arab world. One quarter live in Africa.

Muslims and Arabs: Differences and Similarities

Islam is a younger religion than Christianity. It is the second largest in the world following Christianity with more than a billion followers and had its beginnings in the early 7th century (AD 610) in Mecca, a town in the western Arabian Peninsula. According to Islamic tradition, *Allah* (God) conveyed to Muhammad, a tradesman, a series of revelations that form the basis of Islam. *Islam* means submission to the will of God and comes from the Arabic word meaning "peace" and "submission" (Dwairy, 2005). A Muslim believes in the Islamic tradition, has submitted himself to *Allah*, and acknowledges Muhammad as His prophet.

The Prophet called upon the people of the Arabian Peninsula to submit to God's will as expressed in the Qur'an. The Qur'an represents the "direct instruction from Allah and articulates the message that family members are expected to fulfill rules of behavior and family roles, such as husband, wife, child, etc. without dissonance or disobedience" (Hall & Livingston, 2006, p. 144). For Muslims around the world, Islam is a way of life requiring absolute submission to the will of God. The Qur'an provides guidance to Muslims, just as the Bible provides guidance to Christians. A large percentage of the Arab world practices Islam, yet there is considerable overlap between Arabic and Muslim cultures (Nassar-McMillan & Hakim-Larson, 2003).

Sharia, or Islamic law, guides all aspects of Muslim life. Meaning "path" in Arabic, Sharia has influence on daily life and on familial, financial, and religious obligations. It is primarily derived from the Qur'an and the Sunna (the sayings, practices, and teachings of the Prophet Muhammad). Although there are varying interpretations of what Sharia law actually means, Sharia's impact on criminal law and personal status law is a source of controversy, as some interpretations are used to justify cruel punishments as well as the unequal treatment of women with respect to wealth, dress, interpersonal relationships, and autonomy (Johnson & Sergie, 2014; Johnson & Vriens, 2011).

The three main Islamic sects are the Sunni, who comprise about 85% to 90% and the Shi'a (Shi'ite) who comprise approximately15% of Muslims (Arab American National Museum, 2009). The Sufis are also a sect. The Sunni are the largest branch in Islam and are sometimes referred to as "Orthodox Islam." Their full name is Ahlus Sunnah wal-Jamaa'h. Although a fundamental creed is shared with the second largest division of Islam, the Shi'ite, the two divisions split regarding leadership after the death of Muhammad. The Shi'a of Ali, which literally means "the party of Ali," insisted that it was the Prophet's intention for his son-in-law, Ali, to succeed him. In contrast, the Sunni accept the legitimacy of the first four caliphs or successors to the Prophet. They maintained that the caliph should be elected and did not have to belong to the Prophet's family. Shi'ite legal tradition is generally regarded as more conservative than Sunni. Ali's followers insisted that a *caliph*, or Imam, be a lineal descendant of Ali and his wife, Fatimah. There are also numerous small sects and subsects, such as Ahmaddis, Alawites, and Wahhabis, that differ in degrees of orthodoxy and practice. The Five Basic Obligations of Muslims are the Pillars of Islam: (1) The first pillar is oral testimony that there is only one God and that Muhammad is his prophet, (2) the second pillar is that ritual prayer must be practiced 5 times a day with certain words and certain postures of the body, (3) the giving of alms is the third pillar, (4) the fourth pillar is keeping a strict fast including no liquid or food from sunrise to sundown during Ramadan, and (5) the fifth pillar is the holy pilgrimage to Mecca once in a lifetime at a specific time of the year (Dwairy, 2005). Sawy (2005) saw the beauty of Islam and refers to it as a peaceful religion, saying there is an "element of poetry in a Muslim's everyday life. One says, 'Allah' or 'ma sha'a Allah' (as God wills) upon seeing something beautiful, like a sunset or a newborn baby" (p. 571).

Many of the world's people who consider themselves to be Arabs are also Muslims, but being Arab does not mean the person is Muslim. Being Muslim does not mean the person is Arab. Substantial parts of Asia are predominantly Muslim. For example, the largest population of Muslims in the world is in Indonesia, which is also the fourth most populous nation in the world. Indonesia is located in Southeast Asia and is not part of the Middle East. In addition, Indonesian, a standardized dialect of Malay, is the official language, not Arabic.

Arabic script is used today in Indonesia, Afghanistan, Malaysia, sections of China, and in the Muslim areas of the Philippines and in the former Soviet Union. Millions of people throughout Africa and Asia write their languages in the Arabic alphabet. Farsi, the language of Iran, and Urdu, the language of Pakistan and some parts of India, are written in the Arabic script. There are also significant Muslim populations in Europe and in the Americas.

One of the dominant discourses in this country is that to be Arab means to be Muslim. The term *Arab* refers to a person's language and culture (Abudabbeh & Nydell, 1993). Much to the surprise of many students, the majority of Arab Americans are Christians, not Muslims. Approximately 14 million Arabs follow the Christian faith. Forty percent of Arab Americans are Catholic (Roman Catholic, Maronite, and Melkite); 23% are Orthodox, 23% are Muslim, and 12% are Protestant (Arab American Institute, 2006). Arab American Muslims represent the fastest growing segment of the Arab American community (Arab American Institute, 2012). The largest Christian denomination in the Middle East is the Coptic Orthodox Church. Orthodox denominations also include Antiochian, Syrian, and Greek. Lebanon contains the largest Christian population in the Middle East, as nearly half of that nation's citizens are Christian (Abudabbeh, 2005a).

It is estimated that approximately 15% of the 1 billion plus Muslims worldwide are Arab. According to the *Muslim Journal*, 30% of Muslims live in the Indian subcontinent, 20% live in sub-Saharan Africa, 17% live in Southeast Asia, and 10% live in the former Soviet states. It is also estimated that there are 50 to 70 million Muslims in China, alone (*Frontline*, 2014).

Awad (2010) conducted research with 177 people from the Middle East who identified as Arab Americans. He looked at the constructs of acculturation, ethnic identity, and religious affiliation. Awad found that ethnic identity was a predictor of perceived discrimination. Persons who were Muslims also reported higher levels of discrimination than did Christians. It was also found that Muslims who were more highly acculturated to dominant society were more likely to perceive discrimination whereas Christians who were highly acculturated were less likely to perceive discrimination. Nassar-McMillan and Hakim-Larson (2003) maintain that Arab Muslims have a more difficult time assimilating into mainstream society than Arab Christians.

Migratory Patterns From the Middle East

The first wave of people from the Arab homeland came to the United States between 1890 and 1940. Merchants and farmers emigrated for economic reasons from regions that were part of the Ottoman Empire. Ninety percent of this first wave were Christians from Syria and Lebanon. Lebanese families, like many other Arab families, are "traditionally patrilineal, endogamous, and extended, with wide and complex kin relationships that help to sustain traditional functions of the culture" (Simon, 1996, p. 365). Simon also pointed out, "Identity for the Lebanese does not exist apart from the family. In fact, the proper introduction of a Middle Easterner does not end with the announcement of his name—his family group must also be established" (p. 365).

The second wave came after World War II, following the creation of the State of Israel in 1948, which for Palestinians was a loss of their homeland and a push factor in migration. Palestinian migration was comprised of the highly educated and/or was politically motivated. Immigrants from the Middle East came with an Arab identity and were from regions of post-European colonization as well as from sovereign Arab nations.

The third wave to the United States came after the 1967 Arab-Israeli War and included people from various Arab countries. Like many immigrants from around the world, people were seeking refuge to escape political unrest in their home countries. Lebanese immigrants and Iraqis following the Gulf War were also included.

Demography

According to Asi and Beaulieu (2013), the population among people who reported Arab ancestry on the American Community Survey, 2006–2010 is 1.52 million. The Lebanese are the largest at nearly 486,000 followed by Egyptians at 180,000. Syrians are the next largest group at 147,000, followed by Palestinians at 83,000. Moroccans numbered 75,000, and people from Iraq at 74,000.

Research by the Arab American Institute and Zogby International suggest that the Census Bureau estimates of Arab Americans is considerably lower than the actual number of Arab Americans in the country, which is estimated to be 3.6 million. Several factors contribute to this discrepancy in numbers. First, the American Community Survey selects a segment of the Arab population vis-à-vis an ancestry question on the census long form. The undercounting is related to: (1) the placement and limitations of this ancestry question, which is different from a question about race and ethnicity; (2) a statistical phenomenon regarding the effect of the sample methodology on small and unevenly distributed ethnic groups; (3) high outmarriage rates among later (e.g., third and fourth) generations; and (4) distrust of government surveys among newly arrived (Arab American Institute, 2012). (See Population Box 9.1: Largest Arab Ancestry Groups in the United States.)

Arabs live in all 50 states, and unlike blacks, Latinos, and Asians, Arabs are evenly distributed across the country with 25% living in the Northeast, 27% in the Midwest, 24% in the South, and 23% on the West coast (de la Cruz & Brittingham, 2003). New York, Los Angeles, Dearborn, Chicago, and Houston are the top five metropolitan areas with Arab American populations (de la Cruz & Brittingham, 2003). Large numbers of Arab Americans reside in Florida, Texas, New Jersey, Ohio, Massachusetts, Pennsylvania, and Virginia (Arab American Institute, 2012).

Arabic is one of the top 10 languages spoken in the home with the majority of English speakers speaking very well. German, French, and Tagalog are the three languages that had higher rates of speaking English very well in the home (Ryan, 2013). In addition to Arabic, Arab Americans speak many languages, including Farsi, Persian, Urdu, French, and Kurdish (de la Cruz & Brittingham, 2003). The Arab American

Population Box 9.1: Largest Arab Ancestry Groups in the United States

1. Lebanese: 485,917

2. Egyptians: 179,853

3. Syrians: 147,426

4. Palestinians: 83,241

5. Moroccans: 74,908

6. Iraqi: 73,896

7. Jordanians: 60,056

8. Yemini: 29,358

Source: Asi & Beaulieu (2013).

population is also diverse, with people claiming ties to 22 countries and various religious backgrounds (Krogstad, 2014).

U.S. Census Bureau Classification as White

The U.S. Census Bureau will test a new Middle East-North Africa (MENA) classification for possible inclusion on the 2020 Census, if it receives enough positive feedback about the proposed change once the public comment period ends. Arab Americans, who make up the majority of those who would be covered by the MENA classification, have previously been classified by default as white on the Census. Today, white as defined by the federal government U.S. Census is a person having origins in any of the original peoples of Europe, the Middle East, or North Africa. Included are people who indicate their race as white or report entries such as Irish, German, Italian, Lebanese, Near Easterner, Arab, or Polish.

A challenge with the designation of white, despite white privilege, is that some Arab Americans feel that it overlooks their needs and denies the racial and ethnic identities of Arab Americans. Data collected about race by the Census helps determine congressional district boundaries and impact how billions of dollars in federal funding are allocated. People advocating for the MENA classification state that it would more fully and accurately count them, thus increasing their visibility and influence among policymakers.

Samer Khalef, who is the national president of the American-Arab Anti-Discrimination Committee, stated, "We're counted as 'white,' but we're not treated as 'white.' We have the 'no-fly' lists; we're subjected to heightened security wherever

❖ **Table 9.1** Dominant Arab Discourses

Muslim
Monied
Terroristic
Conservative, suspicious, sneaky
Closed off from non-Arabs
Intelligent
Muslim extremists
Terror suspect
Foreign born
Subordinated women
Sexist men

we go. Yet we're considered 'white.' That's our problem. We are considered 'white' without the privileges of being 'white'"(Wiltz, 2014). U.S. Middle Eastern communities have been pushing for the new Census classification, which could also allow people to self-identify under subcategories such as Assyrian, Chaldean, Berber, or Kurdish (Karoub, 2015). Nassar-McMillan (2007) aptly said, "Over their 100-plus history, Arab Americans have been classified as being 'from Turkey in Asia,' 'Syrian,' neither white nor of African descent and thereby negligible for citizenship, 'colored' and 'white'" (p. 87). Not being viewed as a minority or protected group can lead to a dismissal of their issues with discrimination and stigmatization.

The U.S. Census Bureau will sponsor focus group discussions with people who would be affected by the proposed change. There are also Arab Americans serving on the U.S. Census's National Advisory Committee on Racial, Ethnic, and Other Populations with respect to this issue (Karoub, 2015). Congress would have to sign off on the proposal before the change could be added to the 2020 Census. Some Republican lawmakers are generally critical of the expense and intrusion of the Census and have sought to eliminate the community surveys, which are not constitutionally mandated. Only the main decennial count is mandated. Generational issues impact decision making on racial classification among Arab Americans. Some older Middle East immigrants or their descendants recall the legacy of U.S. laws in the early 20th century whereby Asians were excluded from entry and included Syrians and others from the eastern Mediterranean for a time. Whiteness meant being allowed to become a citizen.

Not all Arab Americans who identify as Middle Eastern or North African support the proposed Census change (Karoub, 2015). In a post-9/11 world, some Arab Americans have expressed concern about sharing information about nationality with the government and some have said that keeping the status quo would allow them to feel more American (Karoub, 2015).

Yalla 2020 is the push for the MENA Census designation. Yalla is a common expression and refers to "let's get going." It comes from and is an abbreviation of classical (traditional) Arabic words "Ya Allah" (in Arabic الله اي) literally meaning "O God" or "My dear God."

A move to be conceived of and counted as something other than white is contrary to over century ago. In the early 20th century, people from the Middle East argued within the court to be counted as white instead of Asian. Anti-Asian legislation was in existence and denied Asians U.S. citizenship (e.g., The Chinese Exclusion Act of 1882; Jacobson, 1998). An example of this battle between Arab Americans and the courts over racial designation took place in 1909. George Shishim, a policeman living and working in Venice, California, fought to claim U.S. citizenship. Because he was born in Lebanon, he was deemed by the United States to be of "Chinese-Mongolian" ancestry and thus ineligible for citizenship. The Syrian-Lebanese community joined with him and retained a lawyer. Ethnographic studies were done to prove the "white" bona fides of the Arab population. Finally, a Superior Court judge agreed, and Shishim was sworn in as a citizen (Jacobson, 1998).

Social, Psychological, and Physical Health Issues

In America, race is a fluid concept. There are people today who are classified as white but would not have been during a different time. Racial classification stakes are high. For a long time in America, nonwhite persons were not eligible for citizenship. From the 1890s through the 1930s, an African American family with mixed-race heritage could be coded, depending on the year and the person doing the classifying, as "quadroon" to "mulatto" to "black" to "Negro," (See Storytelling: Ralph Johns).

❖ STORYTELLING: RALPH JOHNS

Largely an unsung hero, Arab American Ralph Johns played a major role in igniting America's civil rights movement in the 1960s, specifically the Greensboro, North Carolina, Woolworth sit-ins. Johns was born in the early 1920s to Syrian immigrants. He was the owner of a clothing store and could not understand why such a large percentage of the population could not eat at a local restaurant because they were black. In a spirit of resistance, Johns, a former football player, placed signs in his store window, such as "God Hates Segregation." He also frequently hired black employees to work at his business. On February 1, 1960, the Greensboro, North Carolina, sit-in at Woolworth's took place. Dr. George Simkins, president of the National Association for the Advancement of Colored People (NAACP) Greensboro chapter for 25 years, said about Johns, "He was the sit-in. There's no question about it, it was his idea" (Arab American Institute, 2015b). Johns was also the first nonblack person to join the local chapter of the NAACP. Johns's courage in the face of the racism and segregation did not come without consequence. Throughout his time in Greensboro, Johns received more than 25 bomb threats and was repeatedly beaten. His store was also defaced with racist slurs. In time, Johns's store went out of business, and he was forced to move. During the Vietnam War, the patriotic Johns made international headlines by offering to be exchanged for American pilots being held by Ho Chi Minh's regime. Johns's act of courage inspired 1500 other Americans to offer themselves for American prisoners of war. Later in life, Johns continued in his passion to promote equality, as he regularly delivered blankets to the homeless in Los Angeles. Johns exemplifies the history of Arab Americans' involvement in racial equality and justice.

Source: Adapted from the Arab American Institute (2015b).

There is rich diversity among people of Arab ancestry and people of the Middle East as a function of gender, education, level of acculturation, income, phenotype, and geography. For example, life expectancy is lower in poor Arab (e.g., Somalia) and Muslim (e.g., Afghanistan) countries compared with rich Arab (e.g., Kuwait and United Arab Emirates) and Muslim (e.g., Malaysia) countries.

Arab countries have the highest level of extreme poverty in the world, with one out of five people living on less than $2 per day, with Saudi Arabia, Qatar, United

Arab Emirates, and Bahrain being wealthy countries because of the oil that was discovered in the middle of the 20th century. Although Arabs in America are more likely than the general population to have a college education, two thirds of illiterate Arabs are women. Adult literacy in the Arab world is about 60%, compared with 79% in the world at large. Approximately 85% of Arab Americans have a high school diploma, and more than 4 out of 10 Arab Americans have a bachelor's or higher degree—this number is compared with 24% of the American average. Twice as many Arab Americans as non-Arab Americans have postgraduate degrees (Abudabbeh, 2005a).

According to a Pew Research Center (2011) survey of 1,033 Muslim Americans, 59% of adult Muslims are between the ages of 18 and 39, compared with 40% of adults in the general public. Twelve percent of Muslim adults are ages 55 and older. These data are compared to 33% of all U.S. adults who are 55 or older. Foreign-born Muslims are somewhat older than native-born Muslims. In general, immigrants tend to arrive as adults and then start families in the United States.

Nearly two thirds (64%) of Arab Americans are in the labor force. Among workers, 42% are in management and professional positions; 31% are in sales, office, and administrative support; 12% are in service industries; 10% are in production, transportation, and material moving; and 5% are in construction, extraction, and maintenance (Arab American Institute, 2006).

The general public's perceptions of Muslims differ from reality. For example, a majority (56%) of Muslim Americans say that most Muslims who come to the United States want to adopt American customs and ways of life. Only 20% say that Muslims in this country want to be distinct from the larger American society. The general public, however, said that just a third (33%) of Muslims in the United States today want to assimilate. The take away message is that Muslim Americans embrace the American Dream more so than the general public. Nearly three quarters (74%) of Muslim Americans endorse the idea that most people can get ahead if they are willing to work hard. Only 26% say hard work is no guarantee of success. Among the general public, somewhat fewer (62%) say that most people who work hard can get ahead.

U.S. Muslims are about as likely as other Americans to report household incomes of $100,000 or more (14% of Muslims, compared with 16% of all adults). They also reported similar levels of satisfaction with their financial situations. Nearly half, 46% say they are in excellent or good shape financially; among the general public, 38% report excellent financial condition. Muslim Americans are as likely as the public overall to have graduated from college (26% of Muslims vs. 28% among the general public). About one in three (33%) say they have worked with other people from their neighborhood to fix a problem or improve a condition in their community in the past 12 months, compared with 38% of the general public.

The Pew Research Center (2011) survey also found that Muslims in the United States continue to reject extremism by much larger margins than Muslims in most other nations surveyed this year by the Pew Global Attitudes Project. Muslim Americans expressed concern about the possible rise of Islamic extremism, not only in the United States but also throughout the world. (See Table 9.2: Pew Research Survey on Attitudes of Muslims and the General Public.)

❖ Table 9.2   Pew Research Survey on Attitudes of Muslims and the General Public

	Muslims	General Public
Perception that Muslims wish to be distinct from larger society	20%	33%
Hard work can lead to success	74%	62%
Worked with others to fix a problem/improve community	33%	38%
College graduation	26%	28%
Household incomes of $100,000 or more	14%	16%
Excellent financial shape	46%	38%

Arab Americans have a tendency to display emotional distress in terms of physical complaints. This somatization may be partially explained by the mind–body connection descriptive of many people from collectivistic cultures. Many Arab Americans come from Middle Eastern countries where tobacco use is high. On average, 45% of the men and 5% of the women in the Middle East smoke cigarettes. Tobacco use by women in the Middle East was traditionally very low, but it is now on the rise. The Middle Eastern nations with the highest adult cigarette-smoking rates include Iraq (40%), Yemen (45%), Lebanon (58%), and Tunisia (60%; World Health Organization Tobacco Free Initiative, 2005).

According to Abudabbeh and Nydell (1993), some of the mental health problems presented clinically by the Arab immigrant population are physical abuse, identity confusion, loss of extended family support system, adjusting to a lower social and economic status, intergenerational value conflicts, changes in the role of family members, and parenting problems.

Given that sexuality discussions are regarded as taboo for many people of the Middle East, where does the Arab homeland stand in the fight against HIV/AIDS, since sexual transmission remains one of the primary ways to contract the virus? The Middle East and North Africa (MENA) region have one of the lowest HIV prevalence rates worldwide, at .1%. In 2013, an estimated 230,000 people were living with HIV in this part of the world. However, since 2001, new HIV infections have increased by 35% and between 2005 and 2013, AIDS-related deaths increased by 66% in comparison with a worldwide fall of 35%. This region has the lowest antiretroviral treatment (ART) coverage of any region in the world, at 11% (Avert, 2015). The most recent estimate of the number of people living with HIV/AIDS in the Middle East and North Africa is a half million. It has been suggested that the low prevalence of HIV in these regions is linked to Islam and its influence on the behaviors that affect the transmission of HIV (Obermeyer, 2006). Traditional Muslim approaches tend to be conservative; some even regard HIV as divine punishment for deviance, whereas religion is regarded as a protection.

Certain risk factors increase the spread of the epidemic such as unprotected extramarital sex, war, migration, and the population of intravenous drug users who may constitute a "bridge" to the general population. Compared with sub-Saharan Africa,

HIV rates in the Middle East and North Africa are relatively low. Low alcohol intake as well as male circumcision may also account for this low prevalence rate. Governments in several countries are breaking the silence and allowing information about prevention and treatment to be disseminated.

A cultural context exists where marriage is universally expected. A high value is placed on virginity; therefore, unmarried young women are subject to judgment and stigma from health workers if they try to obtain contraception (DeJong & El-Khoury, 2006). Moreover, women are pressured to have children as soon as they marry. Tunisia is cited as the only Middle Eastern country that has legalized abortion; however, unsafely induced abortion occurs throughout the Arab world.

Following the events of September 11, 2001, many Arabs were personally subjected to discrimination or knew someone who had experienced discrimination because of anti-Arab attitudes. In research with 108 Arab Americans, the constructs of discrimination, self-esteem, and personal control were examined. A direct link was found between perceived discrimination events and psychological distress (Moradi & Hasan, 2004). This study also found that "perceived discrimination events were related to lower levels of perceived control over one's life and lower perceived control in turn was related to lower self esteem and greater psychological distress for Arab American individuals" (p. 425). (See Storytelling: Racial Profiling.) Islamophobia, which is a form of intolerance defined as "prejudice against, hatred or irrational fear of Islam and Muslims," has a long history (Arab American Institute, 2015a).

Discourses associated with Arabs or people from the Middle East include potential Muslim extremist, terror suspect, foreign-born and foreign looking, oppressive toward women due to patriarchy and sexism, and non-Christian. Research suggests that such discourses are damaging and affect the psychological well-being of Arab Americans, who represent an understudied group. As multicultural competence is developed through workshops, classes, supervision, and continuing education, clinicians will hopefully become mindful of their proximity to these and other discourses and acquire the knowledge and skills needed to do good work.

❖ STORYTELLING: RACIAL PROFILING

Her son is now 22. Prior to his arrival into the world in 1991, his mother, a very pregnant African American Christian woman in her last trimester, was dressed in a head scarf and a long coat. As she walked alone down the street, a white man in a business suit quickly approached her. Upon passing her, he stared directly into her face and angrily uttered the words "sand nigger bitch!" He then spat on her. Terrified, she stumbled away as quickly as her body would allow. This impeccably dressed stranger had verbally and physically abused her. Due to her light skin and head wrap, the man assumed she was Muslim and an Arab; therefore, she was something to be hated during America's involvement in the Persian Gulf War. There are countless stories like this one that happen to Latinos, African Americans, Asians, Indians, and Arab Americans since 9/11, illuminating the terror and threat surrounding groups who are marked and targeted.

Cultural Orientation and Values

According to Abudabbeh (2005a), the Arab family can be described as "patriarchal, pyramidically hierarchal with regard to age, sex" (p. 427). (See Table 9.1: Dominant Arab Discourses.) Communication styles are restrained and formal, making it difficult for an Arab client in therapy to disclose personal feelings and problems to someone outside of the family. Persons who are subservient to authority by virtue of age or gender communicate accordingly. In terms of communication between parents and children, Abudabbeh (2005a) maintains that children respond to parental authority by censoring themselves, crying, or withholding information. An Arabic saying goes, "To satisfy God is to satisfy parents" (Hall & Livingston, 2006, p. 144).

For the majority of Arab people, the family is the primary means of support. The family is described as the body and is the cornerstone of Arab American culture. *Umma* is the Arabic translation for the word nation; families are given importance as units. The concept of umma also refers "to solidarity based on common language, territory, economic interests, culture, history, and destiny" (Barakat, 1993, p. 35).

Men have specific duties toward their wives and children. Similarly, wives are given instructions regarding the proper treatment of their husbands and children. Muslim law allows a woman to be contracted for marriage by her guardian. In most cases, this guardian is the woman's father (Abudabbeh, 2005a). The more education a woman has, the older she is likely to be when she marries. A collectivistic orientation prevails in that the good of the family is elevated above the fulfillment of personal and individual needs and wishes. Talking negatively about the family is unacceptable. Sexuality is a taboo subject (Abudabbeh, 2005a). (See Table 9.3: Common Cultural Values Among Arab Americans.)

Cultural values recognized by the Qur'an include hospitality and generosity in giving and spending, respect for elders and parents, wealth and preeminence of male children, subordination of women to men, modesty, intensive religiosity, equality of all human beings, and health and strength (Hall & Livingston, 2006). In addition, final authority rests with the father. Individualistic pursuits in the West, such as when and where to go to graduate school and who to marry, are seen as selfish. Privacy is primary and is connected to honor and the good name of the family. Family structures are often formal and hierarchical, in that deference to elders and males is practiced. Because of the central place of family, going outside the family to seek help for personal problems may be seen as disloyal or a threat to group honor. Most Arabs believe in modesty, in intrafaith marriage, and gender and familial relationships (Nassar-McMillan, 2007). There is a concern of being seen as *manjun* or crazy (Shiraev & Levy, 2004).

Muslim Women

According to Dwairy (2004), women's treatment is inferior in the Arabic world. More specifically, their freedom is limited, as is their mobility, social behavior, and decision making. A premium is placed on the family as a core unit. Gender socialization and

❖ **Table 9.3** Common Cultural Values Among Arab Americans

Hospitality and generosity in giving and spending

Family honor

Respect for elders and parents

Wealth and preeminence of male children

Subordination of women to men

Modesty and privacy

Intensive religiosity

Marriage

Group values over individual interests and career

Equality of all human beings

Health and strength

Communication patterns dictated by authority, age, and gender

Family cohesion

Loyalty

roles are often prescribed with the fathers having a level of authority and centrality in the home. Girls are raised to exercise discretion and modesty in their interactions with others and through their styles of dress. Boys are socialized to be leaders in the home and to be head of their household by showing strength and Godly direction.

Currently, women are not allowed to drive in Saudi Arabia. Domestic violence at the hands of brothers, husbands, and fathers is a reality for many. In countries struggling to keep their integrity because of war, famine, upheaval, and corruption, mental health needs are not a priority for women or men (Souter & Murthy, 2006).

Most traditional Muslim women will cover their head or hair. According to Tolaymat and Moradi (2011), the hijab has different names and manifestations depending on context and can be understood as existing on a continuum from least to most covering (Tolaymat & Moradi, 2011). (See Knowledge Check 9.2: Head, Hair, and Body Covering for Muslim Women.)

Traditional Islamic law allows men four wives; however, polygamy is rare in modern Arab societies. Men are also instructed by the Qur'an to not marry more than one woman unless they are able to treat all wives equally. Tunisia forbids the practice of polygamy, whereas some Arab countries, for example, Iraq, require the man to secure a court's permission to take on a second wife. In some countries, such as Lebanon and Morocco, a woman can insist on a premarital contract that allows her to divorce her husband if he decides to marry a second wife (Abudabbeh, 2005a).

Knowledge Check 9.2

Head, Hair, and Body Covering for Muslim Women

Hijab: Head and body coverings for Muslim women.

Shayla: Popular in the Gulf region, is worn as a loose-fitting head scarf set in place at the shoulder, leaving the neck visible.

Khimar: A long veil that covers the body just above the waist, leaving only the face visible.

Chador: A large open fabric held together at the chin to cover the body and leave the face visible.

Burqa: The most conservative form of the hijab and covers the body in its entirety, including a gauze like cover over the eyes.

Source: Tolaymat & Moradi (2011).

Implications for Mental Health Professionals

The Western view of the nuclear family is limiting for many Arabs and other groups of color in that there is a cultural tendency to separate the self into discrete categories. Interventions with Arab clients need to be considered within the context of the family, the extended family, community, and even tribal background (Al-Krenawi & Graham, 2000). At the same time, it is important that clinicians view Arab Americans as individuals rather than as a group to avoid treating people as a monolith, and to provide a more culturally competent therapeutic interaction (Nassar-McMillan, 2007).

Al-Krenawi and Graham (2000) identified that clients of Arab origin tend to have a negative view of mental health service delivery and may even mistrust it. This theme of mistrust is rather common among people, both with stigmatized identities and nonstigmatized identities. Clients may even expect the therapist to provide them with solutions to their problems and see the mental health provider as an authority figure. Treatment can be enhanced if the therapist is willing to relinquish traditional approaches (Abudabbeh, 2005a).

Therapists are encouraged to use didactic and structured therapies, calling other family members personally if they refuse to present for therapy, and be willing to accept gifts and invitations to their homes. Refusal may be perceived as rude. Therapists should also remember that some topics are taboo, such as sexual problems or homosexuality. Flexibility to accommodate the patient and the family's needs is an important therapeutic skill. Among Arab Americans, distrust of outsiders is not uncommon.

Many Arab clients tend not to see the origins of illness from a biomedical point of view but rather as stemming from an external locus of control. The intervention of supernatural elements such as spirits and angels is a belief held by some within the culture, as is a belief in fate. Thus, some Middle Eastern clients turn to fortune-tellers, priests, imams, physicians, and Koranic healers for assistance with mental health issues (Nassar-McMillan & Hakim-Larson, 2003).

Informality is an aspect of Western culture. For example, children and adults are on a first name basis. Some Arab clients as well as members from white European groups may be put off by a casual air that can feel disrespectful. Al-Krenawi and Graham (2000) maintain that "an assessment of the client's personal background and level of acculturation will alert the sensitive practitioner to potential cultural conflicts with regard to treatment" (p. 12).

Among first-generation immigrants who are attempting to adjust to a new environment, acquire a new language, and deal with a host of internal and external demands, the stress may be much greater than previously thought, with chronic acculturation stress having enormous psychological implications. Finally, an Islamic concept of predetermination or fate can make primary prevention a challenge (Nassar-McMillan & Hakim-Larson, 2003).

A myriad of factors have been found to predict the mental health of Arab Americans and include age, gender, income, and education, age at migration, length of time in the United States, religion, and discrimination experiences. It is important that counselors assist Arab American clients to develop skills for recognizing and confronting the negative effects of racial and religious discrimination (Aprahamian, Kaplan, Windham, Sutter, & Visser, 2011). (See Case Study: Perceptions of Dangerousness.)

Case Study

Perceptions of Dangerousness

Yasin Ahid is a 19-year-old college student. For many years, Yasin's parents lived in Morocco before immigrating to Illinois where Yasin was born. His parents are Palestinian; however, they encourage Yasin to identify as Moroccan. They are keenly aware of the vilification of Palestinians as terrorists and suicide bombers. He and his family are Muslims. Yasin is very active in college—he is involved with the psychology club and is president of the Middle Eastern club. His girlfriend, Amina, is also from Morocco—he grew up with Amina (her parents immigrated to the states shortly after his parents did). Yasin is fluent in Arabic, English, and French. He has been accepted to be a resident assistant next year, and is very excited about being a student leader. Yasin was attending an orientation for future resident assistants. The group facilitator presented a case of a male student with alcohol problems, poor academic performance, and behavioral problems (e.g., getting into arguments and fights with other males). The facilitator asked attendees to discuss methods of effective intervention. One student said that it is important to show empathy and a willingness to listen to the students' problems and to know when to refer the student to the campus counseling center. Yasin stated that one of his concerns when dealing with combative residents was related to how his religion and physical appearance might intensify existing feelings of anger that the student may already have. Yasin has brown skin with dark eyes and dark curly hair—he likes to say with a smile that he looks like a very handsome Middle Eastern man. A few of the students, including an African American woman and a Chinese man, stated that Yasin's concerns were unfounded and that students only care about the quality of leadership. Yasin stated that he has personally experienced racism on and off campus. He recalled an encounter when he was at a local pub with other students. Some of the patrons appeared uncomfortable with his presence and kept giving him negative looks. One man began hurling racist comments at him, particularly after the CNN news commentator discussed the recent death of American troops in Afghanistan killed by insurgents who used a rocket propelled grenade to bring the American's helicopter down. The same students who dismissed Yasin's claims of discrimination blamed the man at the pub's behavior on too many beers and a loss of inhibition. Yasin said that he is not imagining racism, but it is a reality and that people who don't experience racism should listen to those who actually experience it. A few of the white group leaders now have concerns about Yasin's appropriateness given his inability to tolerate multiple and diverging perspectives. They also have concerns about his claims of racism, particularly in light of the denial of racism from students of color who were in attendance.

Questions

1. What are the factors that influence Yasin's outlook about racial and religious discrimination?
2. What prevents students and administrators from validating what Yasin is saying?

Discussion and Integration

Yasin

Yasin's identity and orientation have been shaped by multiple influences. These include his nationality, acculturation levels, skin color, U.S. citizenship, his parents' immigrant status, religion, education, and personality. Yasin has a high ethnic identity—in that who he is as an Arab American is important to his self-concept as is his involvement with other Arab Americans (e.g., he is president of the Middle-Eastern club and yet appears to be rather integrated in his ability to function in the dominant culture, e.g., resident assistant).

Yasin is a Muslim man from a collectivistic and pyramidic culture. A person from a collectivist culture is likely to define himself or herself as the following:

> In an interdependent fashion; the self may vary across situations or contexts. Rather than emphasizing personal distinctiveness, this person is likely to stress his similarity to a group, view roles and obligations to a group as central aspects of self definition, and value restraint and harmony. (Enns, 1994, p. 206)

That said, Yasin represents a young Arab American millennial who is open-minded and cognitively flexible in his thinking about Arab identity, nationalism, history, and injustice.

It is not surprising that some of the students of color could not relate to Yasin's claims of racism. They have asserted that we are all Americans here. Yasin, although not born in Palestine, identifies with his parents' homeland and mourns his parents' sense of loss. He recognizes that they have accepted America as home but struggle at times with negotiating what they have lost by leaving Palestine, what they have gained in America, and the realization that the Palestine they left is not the same. They cannot return home (Inman & Tummala-Narra, 2010).

Not all students of color perceive discrimination. This inability to perceive discrimination does not mean the discrimination is not occurring; it just means people are unable to detect it, an inability that could be a function of various factors, including racial identity levels that reflect obliviousness or the salience of other identities at a particular time in a person's life. Regarding the group facilitators present, it is not uncommon for white people to not understand the reality of racism, if they do not have people of color in their lives who are racially aware.

Unfamiliarity with the multicultural psychology literature that addresses racism in the 21st century would also inhibit knowledge, skills, and attitudes that indicate multicultural competence. Yasin could be encouraged to use his cultural competence with the class and suggest a learning experience. For example a sociocultural learning wheel (Metzger, Nadkarni, & Cornish, 2010) could provide students with an opportunity to see the identities that are most salient for themselves and others. They could be discussed and analyzed according to their inclusion of race or ethnicity. What does it mean to live in the world without including race and/or ethnicity as part of your identity? What are the implications for this absence when working as a student leader or mental health professional with those who perceive race and ethnicity to be critically important to their lives and to the lives of people from their same ethnic and/or racial group? Yasin is encouraged to show teachability and a willingness to receive feedback from his group leaders. If there are educational resources (e.g., film, journal articles, authors) that could be helpful to the group in structuring discussions about race, difference, and ethnicity, Yasin could suggest these.

Yasin's group leaders have concerns about Yasin's flexibility. The difficulty with this case is that people in positions to evaluate others who are limited in multicultural knowledge, attitudes, and skills can, themselves, fail to be flexible or just. Because students of color (e.g., non-Arab Americans) deny racism, their position is privileged over Yasin's—naming racism always changes the group dynamics in the room and is awkward. And yet, Islamophobia is a reality for Yasin and other students of Arab ancestry who are regarded as Muslim, irrespective of their religion. Yasin is vulnerable because of an imbalanced situation. In addition to the suggestions above, he may want to speak to his faculty adviser as well as with other student leader supervisors. Due largely to a power differential, students often do not realize that there are advocacy and support options available to them (e.g., Office of Inclusion and Diversity, International Student Groups, and the Counseling Center).

Summary

This chapter focused on Arab Americans and people of the Middle East. A demographic snapshot was provided and included information about the Arab homeland, distinctions between Muslims and Arabs, religion, and the most populated areas where Arab Americans are from and now reside. The three dominant waves of immigration were discussed, as were the factors contributing to immigration. A detailed case study was included that featured a Muslim college student leader who shared his experiences of racism with other student leaders who were dismissive of his experiences. Emphasis was on understanding the reality of racism among people from the Middle East, particularly those who are Muslim and have high levels of ethnic identity.

10

People of European Descent

This chapter is dedicated to an examination of people of European descent. According to the U.S. Census, "White refers to a person having origins in any of the original people of Europe, the Middle East, or North Africa. It includes people who indicated their race(s) as 'White' or reported entries such as Irish, German, Italian, Lebanese, Arab, Moroccan, or Caucasian" (Hixson, Hepler, & Kim, 2011).

History and Immigration

In 2008, an ancient human skull fragment was found in Israel and might provide clues as to the first modern day humans to colonize Europe (Choi, 2015). From 150,000 to 200,000 years ago, modern humans in Africa first arose. Scientists suggest that migration out of Africa began about 60,000 to 70,000 years ago. Due, however, to a lack of fossil evidence, much is unknown regarding the dispersal of Africans. The skullcap is similar to recent Africans and Europeans but differs from modern residents of the Levant (eastern Mediterranean). Scientists believe that humans and Neanderthals lived together and interbred around this time when this skull was found.

The 250 year history of Europe in the Americas is a long one, yet it is clear that the energy that kept battles raging for land, people, sugar, tobacco, ore, fur, and cotton was the desire for power—getting, keeping, losing, and recovering it (National Humanities Center, 2006). Historians tell us that in 1607, Jamestown, Virginia, was the first permanent English settlement. Of the 104 English colonists who landed in the New World, just 30% survived through the first winter, and within the first 15 years, 20% of the over 10,000 who had left England for the New World were still alive.

Several years later, in 1614, the Dutch established a permanent settlement in present day New York prior to the Mayflower's settlement 6 years later in 1620. A year before, in 1619, African slaves had arrived in Virginia (National Humanities Center, 2006).

Over a century earlier in 1496, Isabella (Hispaniola or present day Dominican Republic) was the "first of the Indies" permanent (e.g., colonization) settlements of the Spanish. Mexico City, which was built on the site of the destroyed Aztec city, Tenochtitlan, had been thriving for some time and was the site of New Spain. The French had been established in Newfoundland, Canada, for centuries in the cod fishery business; their presence in the New World occurred in the middle part of the 17th century as fur traders (National Humanities Center, 2006). In the late 17th century, there was rivalry between the French and the Spanish for land, including support from French King Louis (XIV) to build a settlement (e.g., Louisiana) in the lower Mississippi valley. By the time the colonists had established the 13 colonies (Connecticut, Delaware, Georgia, Maryland, Massachusetts, New Hampshire, New Jersey, New York, North Carolina, Pennsylvania, Rhode Island, South Carolina, and Virginia), the Dutch, Russians, Spanish, and French were largely represented in the Americas (History, 2015c). Due to interference from the British with respect to taxes and colonists' dissatisfaction with representation and the demand for rights similar to those that other British subjects had, the Revolutionary War erupted. With the help of the French, the colonists won their independence from Britain in 1781. Five years earlier, in 1776, the Continental Congress moved to adopt the Declaration of Independence.

During the middle half of the 19th century, steamers took Irish emigrants to Liverpool where their transatlantic voyage began. More than one half of the population of Ireland immigrated to the United States, as did an equal number of Germans. American immigration affected almost every city and almost every person in America. From 1820 to 1870, over 7.5 million immigrants came to the United States, more than the entire population of the country in 1810 (U.S. History.org, 2014). Nearly all of the immigrants during this time came from northern and western Europe. About one third came from Ireland, and almost a third came from Germany. Expanding companies were capable of absorbing all who wanted to work. Immigrants built canals and constructed railroads and became involved in almost every labor-intensive endeavor in their new homeland (U.S. History.org, 2014).

Due to their poverty and living on farms that produced little income, most Irish people depended on potatoes for food. When this crop failed 3 years in succession, it led to the Irish potato famine. Over 750,000 people starved to death. Seeking relief from these deplorable conditions, over 2 million Irish eventually moved to the United States. Unable to purchase property, the Irish congregated primarily in northeastern part of the United States. The push factors were related to civil unrest, severe unemployment, and desperate living conditions (e.g., famine), which followed the Irish to America. Greedy landlords, poverty, crowded living conditions, and disease (e.g., cholera) reduced many Irish to the grinding task of eking out a living (Ignatiev, 1995).

Although fully integrated in America now as white people, the Irish were often referred to as "Negroes turned inside out" and "Negroes as smoked Irish"; despite this discrimination, many collaborated in the oppression of Africans in America (McDonald, 2015). Becoming white for Irish meant losing their greenness (e.g., Irish cultural heritage and the legacy of oppression and discrimination in Ireland).

Between 1845 to 1855, more than a million Germans fled to the United States to escape economic hardship and political unrest caused by riots, rebellion, and war (U.S. History.org, 2014). Outside of the United States, there were few countries that accommodated a German request for immigration. Unlike the Irish, many Germans had financial resources to travel to the Midwest in search for farmland and for work. The largest settlements of Germans were in New York City, Baltimore, Cincinnati, St. Louis, and Milwaukee.

With the vast numbers of German and Irish coming to America, hostility, based largely upon religion, erupted. The Irish and many of the Germans were Roman Catholic. Part of the opposition was political. Most immigrants living in cities became Democrats due to the party's focus on commoners and their needs. Part of the conflicts occurred because Americans in low-paying jobs were threatened and sometimes replaced by groups willing to work for almost nothing in order to survive (U.S. History.org, 2014), similar to the dynamic occurring now in the United States.

Signs that read, "No Irish Need Apply" or "NINA" could be seen throughout the country (Jacobson, 1998). A desire to repeal naturalization laws and a prohibition on immigrants from holding public office were in effect. Ethnic and anti-Catholic rioting occurred in many northern cites. In 1844, the largest riot occurred in Philadelphia during a period of economic depression. Protestants, Catholics, and local militia engaged in street battles fought where people died and were injured. Over 40 buildings were destroyed (U.S. History.org, 2014).

Nativist political parties quickly emerged. The most influential of these parties, the Know Nothings, was anti-Catholic and wanted to extend the amount of time it took immigrants to become citizens and voters. They also wanted to prevent foreign-born people from holding public office. The economic situation stabilized after the 1844 depression and reduced the number of serious confrontations for a period as workers were needed.

Nativism returned in the 1850s and in 1854 elections. Nativists won control of state governments in New England (e.g., Massachusetts, Connecticut, Rhode Island, and New Hampshire), as well as in California (U.S. History.org, 2014).

In February 1861, Jefferson Davis was the first president of the newly formed Confederate (e.g., slave) states (Alabama, Florida, Georgia, Louisiana, Mississippi, and South Carolina). Later that same year, Texas seceded from the Union and joined the Confederacy. In April 1861, the Civil War erupted with Arkansas, North Carolina, Tennessee, Texas, and Virginia also joining the Confederacy (History, 2015a).

In 1865, the Southern Confederacy was defeated. All racial and ethnic groups fought in this extremely high stakes and immensely bloody battle: the Chinese, the Irish, Latinos, Jews, Irish, German, and blacks. Women were involved as spies, activists, nurses, owners, and managers of farms and plantations (History.net, 2015). Slavery of black people ended in 1865.

Geography and Demography

The 2010 Census revealed that the documented U.S. population totaled 308.7 million people (Humes, Jones, & Ramirez, 2011). Out of the total population, 223.6 million people, or 72%, identified as white alone. In addition, 7.5 million people, or 2%, reported white in combination with one or more other race (Hixson et al., 2011). While the white population continued to be the largest race group, representing 75% of the total population, it grew at a slower rate than the total population. The majority of the growth in the white population was due to the growth among Hispanic whites. The increase in the multiple-race reporting of groups that included white, specifically the white and black population and the white and Asian population, also contributed to the growth of the white population. The white population has become more diverse as evidenced by the growth of the Hispanic white population and the multiple-race white population (see Storytelling: Why White).

Since Latinos may be any race, Latinos overlap with data for race groups. Whites who identified as being of Hispanic origin increased by 56% between 2000 and 2010. White people who reported one race and identified as Hispanic accounted for 70% of the growth of the white alone-or-in-combination population (Hixson et al., 2011).

The non-Hispanic white population share of the total population decreased. Non-Hispanic whites are projected to become a minority of the population (47%) by 2050, according to Pew Research Center Population Projections (Passel, Livingstone, & Cohn, 2012). However, the non-Hispanic white alone-or-in-combination population increased numerically from 198.2 million to 201.9 million and grew by only 2% over the decade.

The German and Irish represent the largest two white ethnicities in the United States. In the 2000 Census, 42.8 million people or 15% of the population considered themselves to be of German (or part German) ancestry. More than 30 million people (30.5) stated they were Irish (Brittingham & de la Cruz, 2004).

Increased immigration has resulted in gains for some language groups (e.g., Vietnamese, Russian, Persian, and Armenian). Other groups experienced aging populations and diminishing immigration into the United States. The languages that declined in use since 1980 include Italian. Italian had a net decline of about 900,000 speakers (55% decline). Polish, Yiddish, German, and Greek languages also saw decreases (Ryan, 2013).

The tremendous growth in other groups such as Latinos and Asians contributed to the non-Hispanic white alone-or-in-combination population's proportion of the total population to decline from 70% to 65% (Hixson et al., 2011). Being Hispanic was reported by 14.2% of white householders who reported only one race; 4.6% of black householders reported only one race, and 2.6% of Asian householders who reported only one race (DeNavas-Walt, Proctor, & Smith, 2013).

Hispanic whites and non-Hispanic whites reported different multiple-race groups. Among non-Hispanic whites who reported more than one race, the top combinations were white and black (32%), white and Asian (29.5%), and white and American Indian and Alaska Native (24%). These three race combination categories accounted for the vast majority of all non-Hispanic whites who reported multiple races.

The largest multiple-race combinations reported by Hispanic whites were white and some other race (65%), white and black (10%), and white and American Indian and Alaska Native (9%) (Hixson et al., 2011).

White Americans show variation with respect to their representation around the country; however, the numbers are comparable between the white-alone population and the white in combination with other races. The largest percentage of white Americans not in combination with other races are mainly located in the South, at 68 million followed by the Midwest at 52 million, the Northeast at 38 million, and the West, also at 38 million (Hixson et al., 2011).

Among white Americans in combination with other races, 36% lived in the South (District of Columbia, Florida, Georgia, Kentucky, Louisiana, Maryland, Mississippi, North Carolina, Oklahoma, South Carolina, Tennessee, Texas, Virginia, and West Virginia); 24% lived in the Midwest (Illinois, Indiana, Iowa, Kansas, Michigan, Minnesota, Missouri, Nebraska, North Dakota, Ohio, South Dakota, and Wisconsin); 22% lived in the West (Alaska, Arizona, California, Colorado, Hawaii, Idaho, Montana, Nevada, New Mexico, Oregon, Utah, Washington, and Wyoming), and 18% lived in the Northeast (Connecticut, Maine, Massachusetts, New Hampshire, New Jersey, New York, Pennsylvania, Rhode Island, and Vermont; Hixson et al., 2011).

Although there is similarity between the geographical location of the white-alone population and in combination, the distribution of white people who reported multiple races was very different. Multiple-race whites were much more likely to live in the West (38%) than other regions. More than half of the top 10 places with the highest percentage of whites were in the West. Six of the ten places with the highest proportions of whites alone or in combination were in the West, three in the Midwest, and one in the South. The highest proportion of whites was in Hialeah, FL, at 94%. In Hialeah, 95% of the population was Hispanic, indicating a large white Hispanic population, which is unique among the other top 10 places with the highest proportion of whites in 2010. (See Knowledge Check 10.1: Top 10 Places in America for White People to Live Alone and in Combination With Other Races).

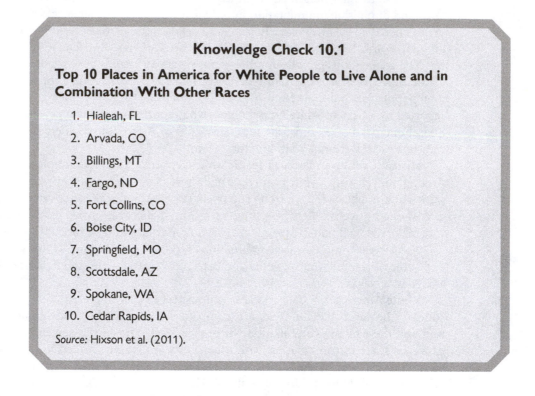

Knowledge Check 10.1

Top 10 Places in America for White People to Live Alone and in Combination With Other Races

1. Hialeah, FL

2. Arvada, CO

3. Billings, MT

4. Fargo, ND

5. Fort Collins, CO

6. Boise City, ID

7. Springfield, MO

8. Scottsdale, AZ

9. Spokane, WA

10. Cedar Rapids, IA

Source: Hixson et al. (2011).

Social, Psychological, and Physical Health Issues

In 2011, non-Hispanic whites have the oldest median age of 42.3, according to the population estimates (Passel et al., 2012). In 2010, the median income for white (non-Hispanic) people was $54,620. In comparison, the highest median income was among Asians at $64,308. Median incomes vary by race, at $37,759 among Latinos across race, and $32,608 among blacks (DeNavas-Walt, Proctor, & Smith, 2011). (See Knowledge Check 10.2: 2010 Income by Race.)

White women have benefited richly from movements (e.g., Suffrage, Feminist, and Affirmative Action). People of color, individually and as groups, have been helped by Affirmative Action; however, data and the research studies suggest that white women in particular have structurally benefited disproportionately from these movements and policies such that they share more in common with white men than they do with black or Latina women (Daniels, 2014).

Social class, within the context of Affirmative Action, is multifaceted and complex. In the social sciences, there has been a tendency to minimize race issues and emphasize class, particularly in light of increasing numbers of middle-class families of color;

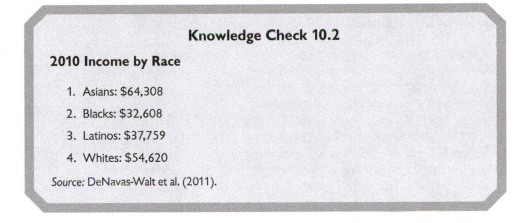

Knowledge Check 10.2

2010 Income by Race

1. Asians: $64,308

2. Blacks: $32,608

3. Latinos: $37,759

4. Whites: $54,620

Source: DeNavas-Walt et al. (2011).

however, such increases tend to be more fleeting given the wage gap between black and white people with equal levels of education.

❖ **STORYTELLING: WHY WHITE?**

In a diversity class, we were talking about the 2010 Census, which indicates that 54% of Latinos identified as white. Given that there is a variety of racial groups among Latinos, I stated that identification as a white person need not be dictated by skin color. More specifically, there may be brown and black skinned people who claim a white identity.

A white student sincerely asked, "Why would someone want to be white when they are not?" We had a good discussion about race as a social construction, social capital, white privilege, historical meanings, perceptions of white inclusivity (e.g., the Irish have not always been considered white in the United States), colorism, and racial entitlement.

The Meaning of Whiteness

Racial groups are invented and are fluid categories with designations and perceptions coined for the purpose of grouping and separating people along the lines of presumed difference (Jacobson, 1998). Caucasians are created, not born. (See Storytelling: Who Identifies as White?) The Irish, Greeks, Hebrews, Syrians, Poles, Sicilians, Finns, and Italians who came to the United States as free white persons, according to the existing naturalization laws at the time, eventually became Caucasian. However, these persons were different from the old stock, Anglo-Saxons who, in Massachusetts, were descendants of English Puritans, and as such, white European immigrants did not lay claim to the proprietary documents and to its stewardship (Jacobson, 1998).

❖ STORYTELLING: WHO IDENTIFIES AS WHITE?

I ask this question every semester, "Who identifies as white?" Increasingly, there are U.S. born and students with immigrant histories who are visibly brown and identify as white. North Africa, Latin America, Europe, and U.S. born white/SOR biracials describe the areas from which people and their families hail. What does it mean to be white? I have also been asking this question to my students for nearly 30 years. Many white students do not answer this question; instead, they respond cerebrally to ideals about justice and equality. Those students who answer the question say the following:

1. Not having to think about being white
2. Fitting and blending in—not being different
3. Being in the majority
4. Regarded as normal
5. Being an individual
6. Presumed to be safe, nice, smart, and nonthreatening
7. Having power
8. Having choices
9. Not being stigmatized

White Racial Identity Development

Traditional, albeit incorrect, conceptions of race refer to people of color. European Americans are also racial beings and experience racial identity development. As racial beings, white people are shaped by the construct of race in their own and other people's lives and are affected by both skin color privilege and the adverse consequences of racism (Robinson, 1999a).

It is an infrequent experience or encounter that would encourage a white person to assess his or her attitudes about being a racial being (Pope-Davis & Ottavi, 1994). In a society where unearned skin color advantages are conferred, European American mental health professionals need to develop a positive racial identity that does not emanate from oppression and domination. This transformation may be difficult for two reasons:

1. It is possible for white people to live in U.S. society without having to acknowledge or give much consideration to the meaning of being white.

2. Denial about one's own race impedes self-awareness, a crucial factor in racial identity development.

Leach, Behrens, and LaFleur (2002) make a distinction between white racial identity and white racial consciousness. They define white racial consciousness as the ways that white people think about people who are not white or the racial out-group. The model "attempts to identify commonly held constellations of attitudes and attempts to determine, which, if any best characterize the racial attitudes held by White individuals" (p. 69).

Seven types of attitudes have been grouped into two categories: achieved, which is the result of personal consideration and commitment to some set of attitudes about racial material (four types), and unachieved, or lack of exploration or commitment or both with respect to racial attitudes (three types). Unachieved attitudes include the following:

1. Dependent, or attitudes determined by a significant other.

2. Dissonant, or uncertainty about attitudes.

3. Avoidant, which is attitudes that ignore and/or minimize racial issue.

Achieved attitudes include the following:

1. Conflictive, which describes fairness but where rugged individualism is strong.

2. Dominative, which describes ethnocentric or prowhite attitudes.

3. Integrative, which reflects positive and pragmatic attitudes.

4. Reactive, which are strong progroups of color attitudes.

Helms (1995) and Helms and Parham (1984) have been the predominant voice in the development of white racial identity theory. Hardiman (1982, 2001) developed the white identity development model, which was the first model on white racial identity development. Helms's (1984, 1995) white racial identity development model has six statuses. The term *status* is preferred over *stage* in that the latter is more reflective of a fixed state. Helms believed that people could be characterized by more than one status at a given time. These statuses are contact, disintegration, reintegration, pseudo independence, immersion-emersion, and autonomy. Helms's revised model includes information-processing strategies for each of the six statuses.

A white person enters the *contact* status from encountering the idea or actuality of black people. Family background and environment affect whether the attitude toward black people is one of trepidation or naive curiosity. In contact, the European American automatically benefits from institutional and cultural racism without the conscious awareness of doing so. The identity ego status and information-processing strategy for contact is obliviousness. White people are satisfied with the status quo and are fairly oblivious to the role of racism and their involvement in it.

White people in the contact status tend to have positive self-esteem. They are idealistic about the equal treatment of black people; however, in actually interacting with blacks, they may experience some anxiety or arousal. Through interaction with African Americans, the European American realizes that, independent of economic conditions, clear distinctions exist in the treatment of people across race.

Continuing to have socialization experiences will move the person into Helms's second status, *disintegration*. Entry into disintegration is characterized by conscious conflict that has its origins in dissonance. Here, the white person realizes that people are treated differently as a function of race. The identity ego status and information-processing strategy for disintegration are suppression and ambivalence. White people in this status are truly confused by anxiety-provoking racial moral dilemmas that require them to choose between own-group loyalty and humane behavior.

The third status is *reintegration,* which is entered as the white person realizes that, within the dominant culture, the covert and overt belief of white superiority and black inferiority exists. The desire to be accepted by the white racial group is very strong. It is important in reintegration that a racial identity be acknowledged. Here, white privilege is protected even though it is unearned. People of color are not entitled to privilege because they are morally, socially, and intellectually inferior. Because honest dialogue about race between racially different people does not often take place, it is fairly easy for a person to fixate here. A jarring event can trigger movement into the fourth status, *pseudo independence.* The identity ego status and information-processing strategies for reintegration are selective perception and negative out-group distortion. White people are idealized and other groups are not tolerated well.

According to Helms (1990), "Pseudo independence is the first stage of redefining a positive White identity" (p. 61). This status is primarily one of intellectualization, wherein the person acknowledges responsibility for white racism. The negativity of the earlier stages does not exist; nonetheless, white norms continue to be used to interpret cultural or racial differences. Socially, the person is met with suspicion by both whites and blacks. Discomfort with their ambiguous racial identity may move the person into the fifth status. The identity ego status and information-processing strategies for pseudo independence are reshaping reality and selective perception. The commitment to racism is largely intellectual. The goal is to reach out and assist other racial groups.

This fifth status, *immersion-emersion,* is characterized by the replacement of old myths and stereotypes with accurate information. It is a period of unlearning. Here, the person may participate heavily in white-consciousness groups in which the goal is to help the person abandon a racist identity. The focus is not on changing black people but rather on seeking to change white people. The successful resolution of this status requires that the individual recycle or reexperience earlier emotion that was distorted or repressed. The identity ego status and information-processing strategies for immersion-emersion are hypervigilance and reshaping. There is a diligent search for the personal meaning of racism and the ways in which people can benefit from racism.

Autonomy, the sixth and last status of Helms's model, is an ongoing process. In this status, a primary goal is internalizing and experiencing new ways of being racial that were learned from previous stages. Race, your own and other people's, is not a threat. The identity ego status and information-processing strategy for autonomy are flexibility and complexity. Internal standards are used for defining the self, and there is a capacity to relinquish the privileges of racism. Helms (1990) stated that the second phase, development of a nonracist white identity, begins with the pseudo-independent status and ends with the autonomy status.

One's race impacts the quality of the college environment. For example, Ancis, Sedlacek, and Mohr (2000) studied 578 African American, Asian American, Latino, and white college student responses to a questionnaire assessing perceptions and experiences of the Campus Cultural Climate Questionnaire. This scale has 100 statements regarding campus climate. The 11 factors include racial tension, fair treatment, cross-cultural comfort, racial pressures, comfort with own culture, and lack of support. Racial differences were found among respondents. Black students reported more negative experiences in comparison with Asian American, Latino, and white students. More specifically, black students experienced "greater racial-ethnic hostility, greater pressure to conform to stereotypes, less equitable treatment by faculty, staff, and teaching assistants, and more faculty racism than did the other groups" (p. 183). The Asian American and Latino students reported experiences of stereotyping and prejudice. They indicated limited respect and unfair treatment by faculty, teaching assistants, and students as well as pressure to conform to stereotypes. Compared with other racial groups, Latinos experienced the least racism and a campus climate relatively free of racial conflict. White students reported less racial tension, few expectations to conform to stereotypic behavior, an experience of being treated fairly, a respectful and diverse campus climate, and the most overall satisfaction.

Watt, Robinson, and Lupton-Smith (2002) conducted a study of ego identity and black and white racial identity among 38 graduate students (30 white, 6 black, and 2 Middle Eastern) at the beginning, middle, and end of their counseling training in a program that included student counseling, community agency, and school counseling tracks. The researchers used the Washington Sentence Completion Test to measure ego identity and used black and white versions of the Racial Identity Attitude Scale. It was hypothesized that the ego developments of students enrolled in prepracticum (a second-year class) would be higher than the ego development of students enrolled in theories and cross-cultural (both first-year classes). It was found that students in theories had lower ego development than students in cross-cultural and prepracticum; however, there were no differences in ego development between students in cross-cultural and students in prepracticum. It was also found that students enrolled in Theories had a lower mean score at the pseudo independence status than did the prepracticum students. In addition, the racial identity status of students enrolled in cross-cultural was higher than the racial identity status of students enrolled in theories. These data are important in understanding ego and racial identity development for students at different developmental stages in their programs. The study needs to be updated given it was conducted 15 years ago and replicated with a much larger and racially and culturally diverse sample.

White Privilege and Colorblindness

Jacobson (1998), a whiteness scholar, queried, "Why is it that a white woman can give birth to black children but a black woman cannot give birth to white children"? Race is clearly not a monolith but is ladened with history, perception, designation, and is fluid. Within the discourse of diversity, who is included? The current discourse suggests that it is not white people. (See Storytelling: Will You Be My Friend.) Although whiteness is unremarkable and unexamined (Newman, 2007), it is against whiteness that discussions about diversity occur yet it is in the context of nonwhiteness that whiteness is shaped. Lipsitz (2005) said, "Whiteness is everywhere in American culture, but it is very hard to see . . . As the unmarked category against which difference is constructed, whiteness never has to speak its name, never has to acknowledge its role as an organizing principle in social and cultural relations" (p. 402).

Interrogation of skin color privilege by white people is differently perceived when compared to interrogation by people of color of skin color privilege. Despite white people's reliance on their white skin color privilege to escape speaking out against oppression, white privilege is a social construction, structural, in that it is systemically embedded in Western society and confers unearned dominance (Dressel, Kerr, & Stevens, 2010). When white people critically examine their skin color privilege, they are likely to be perceived by other whites as well as by some people of color as honorable and thus are exalted in ways that people of color may not be when they tackle similar issues. The embedded discourse is that whites are admirable when they challenge racism, particularly because they do not have to and are going above and beyond what is required of them.

Conversely, a discourse regarding people of color is that they would understandably focus on race, women would logically be interested in gender, and gay and lesbian people would reasonably devote their scholarly pursuits to LGBT (lesbian, gay, bisexual, transgender) issues. Regardless of the constellation of our identities, a commitment to social justice is a reflection of multicultural competence, social justice, and ethical behavior.

❖ STORYTELLING: WILL YOU BE MY FRIEND?

Years ago during a summer school class on understanding diversity, I made the point about the importance of having racially conscious and racially diverse people in our personal lives as a way of becoming less afraid of and more comfortable with differences while becoming more aware of our biases. Several white women in the class acknowledged that they had no black friends. After class one evening, some white women cornered my black graduate teaching assistant and asked her if she would be their friend. It was a touching request and spoke to their perceived difficulty with connecting with black people as well as their inexperience with cross-racial relationships.

One way to facilitate a discussion of racism is through an examination of unearned white skin color privilege. McIntosh (1989) maintained that privilege is an invisible knapsack of assets an entitled group can refer to on a regular basis to negotiate their daily lives more effectively. Unearned skin-color privilege is a fugitive subject for two reasons. First, privilege is something about which people are meant to be oblivious. Second, nonwhite people may not share in the privileges that white people take for granted but did not earn. Unpacking privilege produces dissonance among many white people as it assails fundamental Western beliefs of meritocracy, individualism, hard work, and justice while creating confusion about the meaning of being qualified and successful.

❖ **Table 10.1**   Discourses About White People

Middle-class

Qualified

Oblivious about whiteness

Unsure allies in ending racism

Smart, capable, successful

Beneficiaries of God's grace

Hardworking

Normal Americans

Necessary

In-charge, powerful

How do discourses about whiteness and other race discourses manifest and affect the profession, our students, clients, and clinicians? Where do white people who are not gay, female, or disabled go to explore their whiteness? More importantly, what is the motivation for doing so? (See Table 10.1: Discourses About White People.) Without being named in the dialogue, white people who do not have a socially constructed marginalized identity are given a message that it is not necessary for them to be engaged in and embraced by the work of diversity. We know this to be untrue.

Implications for Mental Health Professionals

Several dynamics support noncolorblindness, particularly within the context of multicultural competence. First, interrogating blackness and whiteness against the backdrop of a racially stratified society, as opposed to colorblindness, may help white clinicians to broach race within therapy (Day-Vines et al., 2007).

According to Neville, Spanierman, and Doan (2006), colorblindness is defined as the "denial, distortion, and/or minimization of race and racism" (p. 276) and is a dominant racially based framework used to justify and explain away racial inequalities in the United States.

The view of people that "race should not and does not matter" (Neville, Lilly, Duran, Lee, & Browne, 2000, p. 60) appears admirable and seems to embrace multiculturalism; however, ignoring race distorts the reality of racism and upholds the status quo. Colorblindness appears to protect white people from recognizing and addressing racial inequalities in society, alleviates cognitive dissonance, encourages inaction, while preserving the privileges that many white people receive from the current system (Neville et al., 2000). Thus, colorblindness, may not equip white clinicians with skills that could help their patients, across racial diversity, traverse racial terrain in a world where race and skin color really do matter.

Lower levels of white fear (of people of color) have been associated with more interracial friendships (Spanierman & Heppner, 2004). Therefore, it is possible that when white students have low white fear, they have strong personal connections with people of color and may be able to connect their awareness of racial privilege to the impact on their friends of color. Researchers (Todd, Spanierman, & Aber, 2010) encourage faculty who teach diversity to be aware that students' levels of white fear vary. Psychosocial assignments of independent reflection may lead to more affective participation for some but not for others.

The consequences of racism, as discussed in Chapter 4, apply to people of color and for white people. Cultural competence would have clinicians respect this reality for themselves personally and for their patients. As a function of growing up in a culture where race tends not to designate whiteness, white people have not been required to interrogate, unpack, and personalize the meaning of whiteness for themselves. Mental health professionals need the skills of deconstructing racism and broaching race; otherwise race as a fragile and fractured topic among racially different people will continue. The history of legal slavery of black people by white people established a system of white superiority and black inferiority that manifests today and has implications for racially segregated friendships, timidity with cultural competence, white people's fear of people of color, and mistrust of white people among people of color.

Fortunately, racial status (e.g., racial categorization and designation, typically based on phenotype, over which people do not have control) and racial identity development (e.g., one's cultivated racial awareness and consciousness) are dissimilar concepts and mental health professionals need knowledge of this distinction as part of their tool kit.

Noncolorblind dialogue about race and racism between clinicians and their racially different patients is possible when race, as an important and navigable construct, is openly discussed. That said, there are times when patients may request a clinician who they perceive to be ethnically and racially similar to themselves. Such a request need not reflect negatively on the patient (e.g., a resistance/immersion/radical identity status). For a variety of reasons, ethnic and racial groups often function as a protective buffer and include racially diverse, allied kin, and social networks (Darity, Mason, & Stewart, 2006; Dominguez & Watkins, 2003; Twine, 2010).

What White People Can Do About White Privilege

1. Accept the discomfort of contending with racism

2. Look for your perpetuation and acceptance of white privilege

3. When you see white privilege in action, say something

4. Do not get stuck in guilt

5. Take responsibility for your privilege and be a strong ally

(Adapted from Dressel et al., 2010)

White skin is not the same as whiteness. With respect to cultural values among people of European descent, the list might be consistent with the list of dominant U.S. values: individualism, educational attainment, gender equality, achievement, competition, meritocracy, wealth, control, and convenience. Ethnicity, however, does inform cultural values and must be considered.

Research is needed on the intersections of white skin, privilege, ethnic, and racial identity development. For example, there are black, Latino, and Native people who appear phenotypically white but have ethnic and racial identities that are discounted if only white skin is emphasized and treated as the same as a white race only designation. Research is also needed to ascertain similarities and differences in racial socialization messages transmitted by black women in interracial black and white families, compared to white women within interracial black and white families. Finally, the meaning and impact of whiteness and white privilege on all family members who reside in interracial families would add to the research (Robinson-Wood, 2015). (See Case Study: Two Different Worlds.)

Case Study

Two Different Worlds

Liz is 37 and a second generation white Irish American. She is the mother of two biracial children, Dolan, a 15-year-old son, and Delaney, a 13-year-old daughter. Their father, Tim, is black. Liz and Tim have been divorced for 5 years and met in college. While together, Tim rarely spoke about race. He privileged other aspects of his identity, such as school and sports. The children reside with Liz in the same rural and largely white New England town in which she was born. Tim resides about 8 hours away and sees his children 3 to 4 times yearly. Delaney looks like her paternal grandmother and has brown skin, dark eyes, and coily hair. Dolan resembles his maternal side of the family and has green eyes, is tan colored, and has wavy hair. Dolan, who is nearly 6 feet tall like his father, has mentioned to his mother that lately he has noticed white women clutching their purses when he approaches them. Liz has told him to hold his head high and treat people the way he would want to be treated. Recently, Dolan was in the mall with his friends. He noticed that he was being watched in ways that his white friends were not. He mentioned this incident to his mother who told him that large crowds of teenagers at malls always make store personnel nervous. Dolan told his mother that he feels that he is being racially profiled because of the way he looks. Liz told Dolan that when her Irish immigrant grandfather came to America with no money and a thick accent, he worked hard to make a better life for himself. Liz encouraged Dolan to do the same and to remember he is just as good as anybody else. Delaney would like hair extensions so that she can look like Beyoncé. Her friends told her that she would be prettier with longer hair. Extensions cost over $300. Liz says that kind of money is not in the budget and does not know anything about extensions and has no one to ask. There are no local hair salons that provide services for ethnic hair. She tells Delaney that she is beautiful just as she is. Peers have asked Delaney, "Why are you so much darker than your brother?" Delaney is angry with her mother that she will not drive her to Boston (nearly 3 hours away) to get her hair done. Liz is not in regular communication with Tim's family although her children see their father's family of origin each summer.

Questions for Consideration

1. What could help Liz understand Dolan's or Delaney's experiences from their perspectives?

2. What are the consequences for Delaney and Dolan not receiving help in interrogating their gendered and racialized experiences?

3. How could a counselor help Liz help her adolescent children?

Discussion

A dominant issue that surfaces among white women who are raising daughters of African descent is hair. Natural black hair and white hair tend to be different in terms of texture, hair care, hair products, and styling. Often white women do not know how to care for their daughter's curly or coily hair unless they have been exposed through relationships with the black community (e.g., black women).

Among white women raising black sons, the core issue is related to run-ins with police due to ascriptions of criminality from the public (Sue, 2010). Robinson-Wood (2010a) found that mothers of visible males of color in New Zealand and in America reported their sons' negative encounters at school, with the police, and the legal system. At 6 feet tall, Dolan looks more like a man than a sweet little boy.

Liz

Liz seems colorblind in that she minimizes race and racism. When her children initiate talk about race with her, Liz's colorblindness manifests, reflecting and informing the content of her knowledge about race and racism. There are ethnic capital benefits available to Dolan as a descendent from an Irish immigrant. Liz encourages a Protestant work ethic of overcoming adversity. However, she references her Irish grandfather's success without the concurrent ability to interrogate her grand-father's white skin color privilege as playing a role in his success within a society that valued his whiteness. Liz values her Irish ethnicity, yet is unable to hear and hold Dolan's observations about being racially profiled as a visible young man of African descent. Regarding racial socialization, there is no direct teaching about racial discrimination.

Dolan is affected by others' apprehensions and fear of him. Feelings of loneliness, sadness, and anger are common reactions to discrimination (Sue, 2010). Despite his mother's silence about race and her lack of understanding that black men are often perceived to be dangerous and threatening, Dolan has learned, perhaps from the media, that a melanin tax (Robinson-Wood et al., 2015) has been levied upon him and he is being racially profiled. Dolan is experiencing forms of racism similar to monoracial black adolescent males.

To the extent that Tim is able to personalize his experiences growing up as a black teen and coping with discrimination, he could lessen his son's isolation by affirming his observations and feelings. The case study, however, does not evidence Tim being racially literate. A big brother might be helpful to Dolan. A possible resource is local colleges. Even those located in rural areas have a population of racially and ethnically diverse students of color in attendance. Travel may be required, but a racially mixed religious congregation may provide Dolan and Delaney with an opportunity to be around other teens of color and learn of resources (e.g., hair salons, youth groups, magazines, books, blogs, films, appropriate social media sites, the YMCA, and the YWCA). Sharing experiences with other ethnically and racially diverse youth as well as with white allies in an effort to recognize, name, confront, and replace racial discrimination is a critical skill (Ward, 2000).

As an adolescent girl, Delaney wants to step into greater maturity with a different hairstyle. While her request is developmental appropriate, she is influenced by a culture that attaches girls' and women's worth and status to unattainable beauty norms. Moreover, colorism dominates perceptions of hair and skin color (Ward, Robinson-Wood, & Boadi, in press). For example, Delaney has been told through media images and her peer group that longer, lighter, and straighter hair would make her more attractive. It would be helpful for Liz to detect colorism, which drives the sociopolitical nature of hair among black girls and women. Relationships with adult black women would be a valuable resource for Delaney, particularly if they are capable of engaging in dialogue about the external pressures and internal motivations for black women's various hair style choices.

The social construction of race in Western contexts has contributed to Liz, although once married to a black man, not having to think about the personal meaning of being white and not understanding the relevance of race in the lives of her biracial children. Growing up, Liz did not interact with black people, is not in contact with Tim's family, and does not have black friends. Her white habitus (e.g., racial residential segregation from black people) appears to reflect limited racial literacy.

Twine (2010b) conducted an extensive ethnography of more than 40 white British mothers in relationships with men of African descent and also interviewed black partners, friends, and extended family members. Her work introduced the concept of *racial literacy*, which refers to "discursive, material, and cultural practices in which parents train themselves and their children to recognize, name, challenge, and manage various forms of everyday racism" (Twine, 2010b, p. 8). Twine found that white women in interracial families who had racial literacy skills were different from those who did not, with respect to (1) racial composition of friendship networks as children and adults, (2) informal education from friendship networks and experience in antiracist political groups, (3) exposure to overt racism and immersion in multicultural communities as children, (4) relationships with black women, and (5) the racial consciousness of the children's black father (p. 259).

To participate in informed, open, and honest talk about race with black and white biracial children, racial literacy seems critical for white women. Racial literacy is cultivated through interpersonal relationships and psychosocial work with racially different people where racial meanings are explored, experienced, and contested. For most white people, working collaboratively with people of color to discover white privilege and reshape racial identity is work that has not been required given the social construction of whiteness, which seems to coincide with and is in support of color-blind talk and the minimization of race.

For most white people, including Liz, parenting biracial black and white children means not having to interrogate race, uncover whiteness, or choosing to racially segregate one's residential location and interpersonal relationships from black people are consequences of white privilege. And yet Liz's path is not an easy one. Uncovering whiteness within interracial families is psychosocial work that relies on social networks and sustained connection to others, more specifically with people of color (Spanierman, Todd, & Anderson, 2009). Liz cannot do this work on her own. Doing so, however, could reveal the enormous impact that racism has on Liz, Delaney, Dolan, and Tim.

Multicultural Competence

Facing multiple stressors such as divorce, solo parenting, and father absence (Robinson-Wood, 2010a), Liz needs support in raising children who have a different set of realities than she experienced while growing up as a middle class white female. A multicultural competent counselor needs to be aware of the literature on whiteness, white racial identity, racial literacy, and white privilege (Dressel et al., 2010). To help Dolan and Delaney, who are looking to Liz for direction as they interpret racialized issues, a clinician may also suggest interventions that encompass the community.

It might be helpful for Liz to cultivate community with members from Tim's family, particularly those who are able and willing to be in community with Liz and her children and help her acquire skills that could prepare her for conversations about race with her children.

Other interracial families who have skills and knowledge about race could be beneficial as well. Learning that one's children are targets of discrimination, because of the color of their skin, can instill feelings of powerlessness, sadness, and rage. Such feelings do not translate into the tools to skillfully converse about and effectively intervene in racism.

Being in interracial relationships with black people does not indicate proximity to dominant discourses or racial awareness. Lack of insight into race has been documented among white women, including those in intimate relationships with black men and who mother children conceived from these unions (Rockquemore, 2002).

Rockquemore (2002) conducted semistructured qualitative interviews with 16 black and white biracial individuals who were taken from a larger research sample of participants from the American Northeast, the South, and the Midwest. She found that more of her biracial interviewees were raised by white women than by black women. The biracial adults who had been raised by white mothers frequently reported being aware of their white parents' explicit racism and experienced their mothers' racist views of their black father.

A multiculturally competent clinician has knowledge of the isolation that many white birth mothers of biracial children experience and the misperceptions that swirl with respect to who they are as women and mothers. Verbian (2006) noted that white birth mothers of black and white biracial children are subjected to discourses about their sexuality and maternal competence. In addition, they are publicly scrutinized in ways that white women within monoracial heterosexual unions are not (Verbian, 2006). Twine (2010a) identified discourses regarding white women who coexist in relationship with black men, including white women as (1) sexually adventurous, (2) an economic and social asset due largely to the symbolic nature of her white skin, and (3) a cultural threat to the black family.

Liz's acknowledgment of her white privilege is important to transmitting information about negotiating racism and empathizing with her visibly black children. Any clinician who would work with Liz would need to have considered the question, "Can I choose to consider what makes me who I am?" Openness to analyzing assumptions around identity and self-perception is critical to gaining the knowledge/awareness, skills, and values that can lead to competency in white privilege and identity (Dressel et al., 2010).

Summary

This chapter on people of European descent explored historical, demographic, and shifting notions of whiteness in America. Whiteness studies are increasing as researchers explore definitions and meanings of whiteness. The case study addressed a single and divorced white mother of biracial black and white children, each struggling with race issues. Cultural competence was described for clinically effective work with white people.

People of Jewish Descent

his chapter is focused on people of Jewish descent and encompasses racial, ethnic, age, and religious diversity (see Storytelling: Say Something).

History of Migration and Acculturation

According to Khazzoom, (2015), regardless of where Jews live most recently, all Jews have roots in the Middle East and North Africa. She reminds us that Sarah and

❖ STORYTELLING: SAY SOMETHING

In class one night, one of my students noted that my textbook (4th edition) did not mention Jews. She said she went through the entire book and found nothing. I acknowledged what she observed and thanked her for her honesty and bravery for speaking to me. I also stated that if there was a fifth edition that I would not be silent about the Jews. I then asked her what she would like to see included. She stated that she did not know, but to say something.

Abraham came from Mesopotamia, the land that is today Iraq. Some Jewish communities in Africa date back more than 2,700 years and are among the oldest. There is tremendous ethnic and religious diversity among Jews and Judaism in Africa. The Beta Israel of Ethiopia are generally recognized as historically Jewish by the majority of world's Jewry. Although many Ethiopian Jews have immigrated to Israel, France, Brazil, Canada, and to the United States, Sephardic Jews and Mizrahi Jews (descendants of Jews from North Africa and the Middle East) live in Morocco, Algeria, and Tunisia (North Africa; "Jews in Africa," 2015).

Throughout time, there have been numerous periods where Jews have been in search for a home as they have been expelled and exiled. For example, during the Spanish Inquisition, which lasted from 1478 under Ferdinand and Isabella to until the early part of the 19th century, Jews were a primary target as were Christian heretics. Although thousands of Jews were expelled from Spain, lost their lives, or converted to Catholicsm, many Jews practiced Judaism in private and kept their Judaism confined to the synagogue and maintained an acculturated identity (Rich, 2011a).

In America, the majority of Jews are Ashkenazi. (See Knowledge Check 11.1: The American Jewry). Ashkenazi Jews (Ashkenazim is plural for Ashkenazi) can trace their ancestry to Germany, France, and Eastern Europe and arrived from the mid 1800s to the early part of the 20th century (Rich, 2011a). The first Jews to arrive, however, in what would eventually become America were Sephardic as they could trace their ancestry to Spain and Portugal.

There were three significant periods of Jewish immigration in American history: Sephardic, German, and Eastern European. Each wave left their homeland for different reasons and experienced different levels of welcome and acceptance by Americans (American Jews and the Holocaust: History, Memory, and Identity, n.d.) Jewish immigrants sought the United States as a place of refuge and freedom. During each period of immigration, immigrants were not solely of any one origin. For example, some Germans came during the "Sephardic" period. In addition, there were Jews from Eastern Europe who arrived during the "German" era. Nonetheless, the character and culture of Americans Jews were influenced by the dominant immigrant group (Rich, 2011a).

The first wave (Sephardim) began with the first colonists, who in 1654, arrived from Brazil in New Amsterdam (which later became New York). In fact, the first

---

Knowledge Check 11.1

The American Jewry

1. **Ashkenazi:** Descendants of Jews from German, French, and Eastern European ancestry (largest group in America)

2. **Sephardic:** Descendants of Jews from Spanish, Portuguese, North African, and Middle-Eastern ancestry

3. **Mizrachi:** Descendants of Jews from North Africa and the Middle East

Source: (Rich, 2011).

Jewish congregation (Shearith Israel) was founded in 1684 in what is now current day New York (Rich, 2011a). Emma Lazarus, the author of the "New Colossus," the poem that poignantly tells the immigrant's dream of America ("give me your tired, your poor, your huddled masses . . .") was a descendent of Jews from Shearith Israel (Gerber, 2009).

For several decades, Sephardic and Ashkenazi merchants established homes in American colonial ports, including Newport, Rhode Island; Philadelphia, Pennsylvania; Charleston, South Carolina; and Savannah, Georgia (Zollman, 2015).

Within 100 years, by 1730, there were more Ashkenazi Jews than there were Sephardic Jews in the colonies. Speaking of the world's Jewry, South African Jews are mostly Ashkenazi and pre-Holocaust immigrants who descended from Lithuanian Jews (Jacobson, 1998).

Through the American Revolution, the character of the American Jewish community remained Sephardic. Colonial American synagogues adhered to Sephardic ritual customs and administered all aspects of Jewish religious life. Albeit a departure from the Old World in Europe, the synagogue did not seek to oversee the economic activities of its (mostly mercantile) members by taxing commercial transactions. In this manner, colonial synagogues set a precedent of compartmentalization—a division between Jewish and worldly domains in American Jewish life (Zollman, 2015).

Colonial American Sephardic synagogues sought to balance modernity with traditional Judaism. Synagogues established rules of order so that deference and decorum were evident. There was assigned seating according to gender; these seats were related to social capital (e.g., the best seats went to the prestigious congregational families who paid the highest dues). Subsequent waves of Jewish immigrants came as Germans and Eastern Europeans struggled to build the Reform and Conservative movements in America (Zollman, 2015).

In 1840, Jews exited Germany and came to America due to persecution, restrictive laws, and economic hardship. As with other immigrants, Jews saw America as a social and economic opportunity. Prior to World War I, more than 250,000 German-speaking Jews came to America. This sizeable immigrant community with less capital compared to the first wave of Jews established in smaller cities and towns throughout the Midwest, West, and the South. German Jewish immigrants often started out as peddlers, settled in one of the towns on their route (e.g., Cincinnati), and started a small store there that helped to establish American Judaism as a national faith (Zollman, 2015). The Gimbel Brothers, the Macy family, and Levi Straus are all examples of Jewish families that were successful (American Jews and the Holocaust: History, Memory, and Identity, n.d.).

Cincinnati became the seat of American Reform. German Jewish immigrants also created institutions, such as B'nai B'rith, the American Jewish Committee, and the National Council of Jewish Women.

After 1880, Eastern European Jews began to immigrate to the United States in large numbers, but they were pushed out by European overpopulation, political strife, anti-Semitism, and poverty. Between 1880 and the onset of restrictive immigration quotas in 1924, over 2 million Jews from Russia, Austria-Hungary, and Romania came to America (Robinson, 2000). This period was the end of large-scale Jewish immigration to the United States. The character of the American Jewry was transformed given that Eastern Europeans were now the majority. Unlike the first and second wave, immigrants were more likely to settle in poorer sections of major cities, such as New York, Philadelphia, Boston, Baltimore, and Chicago. Living conditions were often poor, dense, and squalid (American Jews and the Holocaust: History, Memory, and Identity, n.d.).

Jewish immigrants found work in factories, especially in the garment industry, but also in cigar manufacturing, food production, and construction. They supported the labor movement's struggle for better working conditions. In addition, Yiddish culture, drama, journalism, and prose flourished in American Jewish immigrant neighborhoods. The plight of the immigrant worker was acknowledged and esteemed as important. Some Eastern European Jews had ideological principles that would influence American Jewry. For instance, many workers supported socialism as a way to secure economic equality and had unprecedented support for Jewish nationalism (Zollman, 2015).

The presence of Eastern European Jews ushered in religious diversity among Jews. While this group was not comfortable with Reform Judaism, there was a desire to uphold tradition, albeit within the context of modernity, a desire that contributed to the establishment of Conservative Judaism and infused Orthodox Judaism (Zollman, 2015).

Defining Judaism

Approximately 5 million of the world's 13 million Jews live in the United States. There are three main Jewish sects: Orthodox, Reform, and Conservative. (See Definitions Box 11.1: Main Jewish Sects/Movements.) Some people also include a fourth movement, the Reconstructionist movement, which is substantially smaller than the other three (Rich, 2011b). While Jews have never been a monolith and have reflected differences (e.g., the Samaritans, the Sadducees, the Pharisees, the Sephardic, and the Ashkenazi), for about 1500 years, the basic choices were Rabbinic Judaism or exclusion (Robinson, 2000). There was no such word as Orthodoxy given that everyone was traditional and Torah observant or they were an apostate.

DEFINITIONS 11.1

Main Jewish Sects/Movements

1. **Orthodoxy**: Orthodox Jews seek to follow traditional laws that were given to Moses on Mt. Sinai, including observing the Sabbath and dietary laws.

2. **Reform**: Reform Judaism does not believe the Torah was written by God. Accepts the Bible as written by separate sources. Greater flexibility regarding personal observance. Less emphasis on commandments yet retains values central to Judaism with service to others being primary.

3. **Conservative**: Grew out of the tensions between Orthodoxy and Reform. Conservative Jews believe God gave the Torah to the Jews who interpret God's word within the context of both history and contemporary society.

4. **Reconstructionism**: Founded in America in 1922 by Rabbi Mordecai Kaplan, Reconstructionists believe that Judaism is an evolving religious civilization and do not believe in a personified deity active in history. They introduced the idea of a Bat Mitzvah for girls, the idea of Jewish community centers, and the idea of Havurot, which are small Jewish fellowships.

Sources: Loup (2013); Rich (2011b); Robinson (2000).

Although ideological differences have existed for 2000 years (Freeman, 2015), Orthodox and sometimes Conservatives are described as "traditional" movements. Reform, Reconstructionist, and sometimes Conservative are described as "liberal" or "modern" movements that have occurred during the 20th century.

The different sects or denominations of Judaism are generally referred to as movements. The differences between Jewish movements today are not so much a matter of theology but more a matter of how literally the scriptures are interpreted and include thoughts regarding the flexibility and the extent to which biblical requirements are mandatory (Freeman, 2015).

Prior to a discussion of the major sects of Judaism, the Pew Research Center Survey of U.S. Jews (2013) Research survey data on religious affiliation among Jews is relevant. Reform Judaism is the largest Jewish denominational movement in the United States. One third (35%) of all U.S. Jews identify with the Reform movement; 18% identify with Conservative Judaism; 10% with Orthodox Judaism, and 6% with various smaller groups, such as the Reconstructionist and Jewish Renewal movements.

Approximately 3 in 10 American Jews (including 19% of Jews by religion and two thirds of Jews of no religion) do not identify with any particular Jewish denomination.

Orthodoxy

Orthodox Jews observe traditional religious beliefs and practices. During the 18th century, Orthodox Jews became differentiated as traditional Jews, were distinguished from Reform Judaism, guided by the 613 *mitzvot*, which are laws dictated by God to Moses on Mount Sinai concerning all aspects of life (see Definitions Box 11.2: Select Hebrew Terms). Orthodox Jews seek to follow them strictly, including the dietary laws and honoring the Sabbath (Loup, 2013).

In most Orthodox services, men and women sit separately in the synagogue and are separated by a divider called a *mekhitza*. The service is conducted primarily in Hebrew. In traditional Judaism, gender roles influence behavior. Women have primary influence in the home and in rearing children. Men are involved in the public realm of religious services (Loup, 2013).

Although rejected by the Conservative, Reform, and Reconstructionist movements, specific missions are assigned to respective groups of people. As such, men who follow Orthodoxy thank God for not having made them women so that they are obligated to carry out all commandments at a designated time for performance, mitzvot, from which women are excused by traditional Jewish law "on the assumption that their traditional household duties may make it difficult for them to perform them in a timely fashion" (Robinson, 2000, p. 30).

In Israel, only Orthodox rabbis are considered official representatives of Judaism. Among Orthodox Jews, there is diversity with respect to observance, from modern to strictly traditional (Loup, 2013), and include the modern Orthodox, who have largely integrated into modern society while maintaining observance of *halakhah* or Jewish Law. The Chasidim live separately and dress distinctively (commonly, but erroneously, referred to in the media as the "ultra-Orthodox"), and the Yeshivish Orthodox are neither Chasidic nor modern (Rich, 2011).

❖ DEFINITIONS 11.2

Select Hebrew Terms

1. **Mitzvot:** *613* Laws dictated by God to Moses on Mount Sinai concerning all aspects of life. Orthodox Jews seek to strictly follow these, including dietary laws and honoring the Sabbath.

2. **Mekhitza:** A divider in the synagogue that separates men and women

3. **Halakhah:** Jewish law

4. **Torah:** First five books of the Bible: Genesis, Exodus, Leviticus, Numbers, and Deuteronomy

5. **Haskalah:** Jewish Enlightenment

6. *Yarmulkes:* Yiddish word for skullcap

7. *Havurah:* Jewish fellowships and prayer groups

Source: Robinson (2000).

The Orthodox all believe that G-d (written in this manner due to English translation and out of respect for the sacred name of the most high) gave Moses the whole Torah at Mount Sinai. The "whole Torah" includes both the written *Torah*—which are the first five books of the Bible: Genesis, Exodus, Leviticus, Numbers, and Deuteronomy—and the Oral Torah, an oral tradition interpreting and explaining the Written Torah. They believe that the Torah is true, that it has been transmitted intact and unchanged, and that the Torah contains 613 mitzvot binding upon Jews but not upon non-Jews (Rich, 2011b).

Traditional Hasidic Jews dress in the clothing of their European ancestors: the men wear long black coats and hats, and married women wear head coverings (Loup, 2013). As an eternal document, however, the Torah provides for change with built-in adaptability with some Orthodox Jews not wishing to be defined as Orthodox but as Torah Observant (Freeman, 2015).

Reform Judaism

Throughout history Jews have contended with anti-Semitism and segregation from the larger society. With the annexation of most of Poland, Catherine the Great, born Sophie von Anhalt-Zerbst of Prussia (Maranzani, 2012), inherited 1 million Polish Jewish subjects that she did not want. History tells us that for 300 years, Russia had excluded Jews. In 1795, Catherine's new Jewish subjects were confined to the Pale of Settlement—in time, some Jews were allowed to live outside of this rectangular piece of land but were required to have written permission and would need their papers with them at all times. This system forecasted the institutionalized racism of Nazi Germany and South African apartheid (Robinson, 2000).

The Enlightenment, during the 18th century, was inspirational for European Jews during a period of innovation and ambition. Judaism experienced *Haskalah*, its own Enlightenment, which gave rise to the beginning of the Reform Judaism movement that was started by Jews who were interested in a modern view of their religion that would fit more easily into the world (Loup, 2013). With the rise of the middle class in Europe, many Jews desired to look more similar to their neighbors.

Within Reform Judaism, the local vernacular in synagogues was encouraged during prayer rather than in Hebrew (Robinson, 2000). There were also many opportunities for women to participate in public religious life as equal to men. By the 1970s, the Reform Movement in the United States welcomed women as rabbis and cantors. English was added to the prayer service, and long Hebrew prayers were shortened (Loup, 2013).

Prior to Reform Judaism had been a theological shift. The Torah was seen as divine inspiration but not as divinity or the actual word as understood by Orthodox Jews. The 613 mitzvot were not as important as the underlying values that were being taught (Loup, 2013). Reform Judaism does not believe that the Torah was written by God. The movement accepts that the Bible was written by separate sources and redacted together. More flexibility and freedom were available to people regarding the extent of one's observance. Reform Jews do not believe in observance of commandments but retain many values central to Judaism, along with some of the cultural practices (Rich 2011b). Social justice, community service, and service to others are foundational to Reform Judaism (Freeman, 2015; Loup, 2013).

Since the Second World War, the Reform movement has made many major thrusts back toward tradition, and in more recent years, the movement has reembraced ritual and spirituality. The original basic tenets of American Reform Judaism were set down in the Pittsburgh Platform. There are plenty of Reform Jews who are religious in a Reform way (Rich, 2011b).

Conservative Judaism

Conservative Judaism grew out of the tension between Orthodoxy and Reform (Rich, 2011b). In reaction to the dramatic changes of the Reform movement, the Conservative movement arose during the 19th century. American Jewish leadership was shocked by the Reform movement's rejection of kosher food laws, circumcision, not working on Shabbat, and other laws of Torah; therefore, the Conservative movement began. It was intended to conserve certain rituals they felt were critical elements of Judaism, while allowing those reforms that were deemed necessary to make it appealing to the Jews of their times (Freeman, 2015).

It was the opinion of some Jews that Reform Judaism had gone too far, that far too many rituals had been dismissed, and that traditional ways had relevance and importance. Conservative Jews believe that Jewish law is the law by which people need to govern themselves. Change is allowed but more slowly and with caution among followers of the Conservative movement. While there is a place for modernity and allowance for innovations in Jewish law, Conservative Jews believe God gave the Torah to the Jews who interpret God's word within the context of both history and contemporary society. Most Conservative Jews have accepted women as rabbis and cantors since 1985, albeit this issue has been divisive (Freeman, 2015; Loup, 2013).

Conservative Judaism maintains that the truths found in Jewish scriptures and other Jewish writings come from G-d, transmitted by people and reflect a human component. Although Conservative Judaism generally accepts the halakhah as binding, they believe that the Law should be adaptable and amenable to the press of culture while adhering to Judaism values (Rich, 2011b).

Freeman (2015) also states that there is considerable variation among Conservative synagogues. Some are indistinguishable from Reform, except for the use of more Hebrew, and others are nearly Orthodox, except that men and women sit together. This flexibility is deeply rooted in Conservative Judaism.

According to Freeman (2015), Reform and Conservative are recent interpretations of Jewish tradition. At first, there was only the Torah. Jews were those who held to a tradition that their ancestors had witnessed an amazing revelation at Mount Sinai, something that transformed the way they perceived the world and lived within it. They had a written account, pristinely preserved to the detail, as well as a vast oral tradition that explained that written document. While there have been detractors who questioned the authority of the oral tradition and of the rabbis who made decisions based on Torah tradition, the foundation of Judaism, unanimously for 3000 years, was that revelation given to Moses and its implications.

Reconstructionism

Although Reform and Conservative movements were born in Germany, the Reconstructionist movement began in the United States in 1922 by Rabbi Mordecai Kaplan, who had been a prominent rabbi in the Conservative movement but broke away because he felt a new definition was required. The entire idea of God needed to be reworked. He believed that God was not an all-powerful being but the power of our ethics and beliefs for good (Loup, 2013). Because Reconstructionism emerged from the Conservative movement and retained attachment to many traditional practices (e.g., dietary laws, Hebrew in the liturgy, men in yarmulkes—Yiddish word for kippot or skullcap), Reconstructionist practice looks like Conservative practice (Robinson, 2000, p. 62).

For Kaplan, Judaism was an evolving civilization based in religion and the sum of its ethical teachings, literature, history, ideals, and ways of life. Kaplan rejected the belief that a Messiah would come to save the Jews. The construction of God needed to be revisited. He believed that God was not omnipresent, but a reflection of our ethical beliefs and behaviors.

Reconstructionists are few in number. There are about 100 synagogues worldwide compared to 900 among Reform Judaism and 750 among Conservatives and yet they have contributed in significant ways. Reconstructionists, despite their small numbers, receive quite a bit of attention and have a disproportionate number of Reconstructionists serving as rabbis to Jewish college student organizations and Jewish Community Centers (Rich, 2011b). Reconstructionists believe that Judaism is an evolving religious civilization (Robinson, 2000). They do not believe in a personified deity that is active in history, and they do not believe that God chose the Jewish people to promote change and progress within the Jewish community (Rich, 2011b).

According to Kaplan, the sacred texts are not the product of divine revelation but are the creation of the Jewish people (Robinson, 2000, p. 62). However, Reconstructionism lays a much greater stress on Jewish observance than Reform Judaism. They introduced the Bat Mitzvah for girls. Kaplan said that he had four reasons for instituting the Bat Mitzvah: Judith, Hadassah, Naomi, and Selma, his four daughters (Scult, 2015). Jewish community centers, and *havurah*, or Jewish fellowships and prayer groups, were also outgrowths of Reconstructionism.

The Reconstructionists believe that ritual can help knit a community and connect it to the larger Jewish community (Loup, 2013). Although most Jews do not have any theological objections to praying in the synagogues of other movements, liberal services are not "religious" enough or "Jewish" enough for traditional Jews, and traditional services are too long, too conservative, or incomprehensible to liberal Jews given that traditional services are primarily, if not exclusively, in Hebrew. Some Orthodox will not attend liberal services because of the mixed seating arrangements and because the liberal prayer book cuts many required prayers (Rich, 2011b).

The Meaning of Being Jewish

A survey of Jewish Americans was conducted by the Pew Research Center Survey of U.S. Jews (2013) and is considered to be the most comprehensive national survey of the Jewish population since the 2000-2001 National Jewish Population Survey. More than 70,000 screening interviews were conducted to identify Jewish respondents in all 50 states and in the District of Columbia. Longer interviews were completed with 3,475 Jews, including 2,786 Jews by religion and 689 Jews of no religion.

If Jewish refers only to people whose religion is Jewish (Jews by religion), then the survey indicates that the Jewish population is nearly 2% of the total U.S. adult population, or 4.2 million people. If one includes secular or cultural Jews, which includes people who say they have no religion but were raised Jewish or have a Jewish parent and who still identify as Jewish although not religiously, then the estimate grows to 2.2% of American adults, or about 5.3 million (Pew Research Center Survey of U.S. Jews, 2013).

In the Pew Research Center Survey of U.S. Jews (2013) report, these two groups comprise the "net" Jewish population. The estimate that Jews by religion make up nearly 2% (1.8%) of U.S. adults is consistent with the results of Pew Research Center Survey of U.S. Jews (2013) Research surveys over the past 5 years.

The percentage of U.S. adults who say they are Jewish when asked about their religion has declined by about half since the late 1950s and currently is a little less than 2%. Meanwhile, the number of Americans with direct Jewish ancestry or upbringing who consider themselves Jewish, yet describe themselves as atheist, agnostic, or having no particular religion, appears to be rising and is now about 0.5% of the U.S. adult population (Pew Research Center Survey of U.S. Jews, 2013).

When asked whether being Jewish is mainly a matter of religion, ancestry, or culture, 6 in 10 (62%) cite either ancestry or culture (or a combination of the two). Fewer than one in five (15%) say being Jewish is mainly a matter of religion. Roughly one quarter of Jews (23%) say being Jewish is a matter of religion as well as ancestry and/or culture. More than half of Jews (55%) by religion say being Jewish is mainly a matter of ancestry or culture, while 17% say it is mainly a matter of religion, and 26% say it is a combination of religion and ancestry and/or culture (Pew Research Center Survey of U.S. Jews, 2013).

Roughly 8 in 10 Jews of no religion (83%) say being Jewish is mainly a matter of ancestry or culture, while just 6% say it is mainly a matter of religion. The survey asked Jews whether each of nine attributes and activities is essential to what being Jewish means to them, is important but not essential, or is not an important part of what it means to be Jewish (Pew Research Center Survey of U.S. Jews, 2013).

In response, roughly 7 in 10 U.S. Jews (73%) say remembering the Holocaust is an essential part of what being Jewish means to them. Nearly as many say leading an ethical and moral life is essential to what it means to be Jewish. And a majority of U.S. Jews say working for justice and equality in society is essential to being Jewish (Pew Research Center Survey of U.S. Jews, 2013). (See Table 11.1: What Being Jewish Means to Jews.)

One notable difference between Jews of religion and Jews of no religion is the importance they attach to caring about Israel. About half of Jews by religion (49%) indicated that caring about Israel is essential to what it means to them to be Jewish. Among Jews of no religion, 23% expressed this view. Compared to caring about Israel as essential, Jews of no religion are more likely to see having a good sense of humor as

❖ **Table 11.1**   What Being Jewish Means to Jews

	Net Jewish %	Jews by Religion %	Jews of No Religion %
Remembering the Holocaust	73	76	60
Leading an ethical and moral life	69	73	55
Working for justice and/or equality	56	60	46
Being intellectually curious	49	51	42
Caring about Israel	43	49	23
Having good sense of humor	42	43	40
Being part of a Jewish community	28	33	10
Observing Jewish law	19	23	7
Eating traditional Jewish foods	14	16	9

Source: Pew Research Center Survey of U.S. Jews (2013, Q. E5a–i).

essential to the meaning of being Jewish (40% compared to 23%; Pew Research Center Survey of U.S. Jews, 2013).

The changing nature of Jewish identity is seen when the survey's results are analyzed by generation. Nine in ten (93%) of Jews in the greatest generation identify as Jewish on the basis of religion (called "Jews by religion" in the Pew Research Center Survey of U.S. Jews, 2013, report). Only 7% describe themselves as having no religion ("Jews of no religion"). By contrast, among Jews in the youngest generation of U.S. adults, the millennials, 68% identify as Jews by religion, and 32% describe themselves as having no religion. Identification as Jewish is on the basis of their ancestors, ethnicity, or culture (Pew Research Center Survey of U.S. Jews, 2013).

The survey also found generational differences with respect to the importance attached to caring about Israel. Among Jews who were 65 and older, 53% stated that caring about Israel is essential to what being Jewish means to them. Among Jews under age 30, 32% expressed this view. Compared to younger Jews, older Jews also are more likely to say remembering the Holocaust, working for justice and equality in society, and having a good sense of humor are essential to their Jewish identity (Pew Research Center Survey of U.S. Jews, 2013).

Remembering the Holocaust is essential to what it means to be Jewish and is shared by majorities in all of the large Jewish denominational groupings. There are, however, sizable differences across denominations in the importance attached to Israel. Half or more of Conservative Jews (58%) and Orthodox Jews (55%) say caring about Israel is essential to what being Jewish means to them. Among Reform Jews, 42% express this view (Pew Research Center Survey of U.S. Jews, 2013).

Among Jews with no denominational affiliation, nearly one third (31%) say caring about Israel is essential to their Jewish identity. Eight in ten Orthodox Jews (79%)

say observing Jewish law is essential to what being Jewish means to them. This view is shared by just 24% of Conservative Jews, 11% of Reform Jews, and 8% of Jews with no denominational affiliation (Pew Research Center Survey of U.S. Jews, 2013).

Shoah (the Holocaust)

Over 6 million Jewish babies, children, and adult men and women were murdered (e.g., liquidated), during the Holocaust. U.S. President Roosevelt condemned the activities of Kristallnacht (Night of Broken Glass) where Jewish people and their homes, synagogues, and businesses were attacked, burned, and destroyed by Nazis on November 9 and 10, 1938. Nonetheless, Roosevelt was reluctant to relax immigration policy that would allow German Jews to immigrate to America in an effort to flee excessive taxation and societal ostracism, but primarily to save their lives and the lives of their children from increasing Nazi violence and murder (History, 2015c).

A few days prior to Kristallnacht, 17-year-old Herschel Grynszpan shot a German diplomat (Ernst vom Rath) in Paris upon learning that the Nazis had exiled his parents to Poland from Hanover, Germany—Herschel's birth place. Vom Rath died a few days later from a gunshot wound. After Kristallnacht, more than 30,000 young Jewish men were arrested and sent to German concentration camps that were specifically constructed to house Jewish people (History, 2015c).

According to Jacobson (1998), The Immigration Act of 1924 enforced quotas by origin of country and provided immigration visas for 2% of the immigrant population based upon the 1890 census rather than a later census. Congressman Johnson of Washington and president of the Eugenic Research Association, 1923 to 1924, "argued that a formula based on the 1890 census rather than on a more recent one 'would change the character of immigration and hence of our future population by bringing a preponderance of immigration of the stock which originally settled this country'" (Jacobson, 1998, p. 83). More immigrants from Western Europe and England were included, decreasing the number of visas available to people (e.g., European Jews) from Eastern Europe.

While Shoah was not the first genocide in modern history, it exemplifies genocide committed by an industrialized nation with technical skills. The question of Western civilization is raised given the barbaric and uncivilized actions of the Nazis against their fellow human beings and citizens. Jews were not murdered because of their belief in Judaism but because they had at least one grandparent who was a Jew, perhaps not even a religious Jew. Irrespective of their affiliation, Jews were not offered an option of conversion, and Jewish children, in particular, were targeted for murder (Robinson, 2000).

Demography

According to the Pew Research Center Survey of U.S. Jews (2013), Jews are disproportionately represented in the Northeast (43%), compared with 18% of the public as a

---

Population Box 11.1: Geography and Jewish Americans

Jewish Inhabitants by Region

1. Northeast: 43%

2. South: 23%

3. West: 23%

4. Midwest: 11%

Jewish Inhabitants by City

1. New York City, New York: 750,000

2. Miami, Florida: 535,000

3. Los Angeles, California: 490,000

4. Philadelphia, Pennsylvania: 350,000

5. Chicago, Illinois: 248,000

Source: Pew Research Center Survey of U.S. Jews (2013).

whole. Roughly a quarter of Jews reside in the South (23%) and in the West (23%), while 11% live in the Midwest. Half of Jews (49%) reside in urban areas, 47% reside in the suburbs, and 4% of Jews reside in rural areas. According to Robinson (2000), New York City has the largest population of Jewish people, at 750,000, followed by Miami, Florida (535,000); Los Angeles, California (490,000); Philadelphia, Pennsylvania (350,000); and Chicago, Illinois (248,000). (See Population Box 11.1: Geography and Jewish Americans.)

Most Jews have high levels of educational attainment: 58% are college graduates; 28% have earned a postgraduate degree. By comparison, 29% of U.S. adults say they have graduated from college, including 10% who have a postgraduate degree. One quarter of Jews (25%) say they have a household income exceeding $150,000, compared with 8% of adults in the public as a whole. By contrast, 20% of U.S. Jews report household incomes of less than $30,000 per year. About 6 in 10 Jews in this low-income category are either under age 30 or 65 or older (Pew Research Center Survey of U.S. Jews, 2013). (See Storytelling: Simple Pine Box.)

Roughly 4 in 10 U.S. Jewish adults (39%) say they live in a household where at least one person is a member of a synagogue. This percentage includes 31% of Jewish adults (39% of Jews by religion and 4% of Jews of no religion) who say they personally belong to a synagogue, temple, or other congregation (Pew Research Center Survey of U.S. Jews, 2013).

❖ STORYTELLING: SIMPLE PINE BOX

A friend of mine went to the funeral of a colleague. He was Jewish. She is Christian. She stated, with sadness, that her renown and prestigious colleague was buried in just a pine box. She was confused by this fact given his prestige and wealth. According to Robinson (2000), because American laws require the use of a casket, "The casket used should be a simple wood box, made without nails; nothing must be done to impede the return of the body to the earth" (p. 188).

The plainness of Jewish burial arrangements are designed as a reminder that in death, all people are created equally. Jewish practice is against embalming and cremation. Cremation shows disregard for the body that is created in the image of God. My friend was struck that the funeral happened so quickly after her colleague's death, which was rather different from her experience with Christian friends and relatives who were buried up to 10 days following death.

Social, Psychological, and Physical Health Issues

According to Schlosser (2008), the experience of Jews in America needs to be described in terms of microaggressions. Microaggressions have been frequently ignored in the multicultural literature, particularly among certain groups (e.g., Jews, Native Americans, Asians, and people with disabilities). Microaggressions are commonplace verbal, behavioral, and environmental indignities that are hostile, whether intentional or unintentional, and communicate putdowns that have harmful psychological and physiological impact on targeted individuals or groups. An accumulation of microaggressions reduces self-efficacy and increases feelings of vulnerability and powerlessness, anger, sadness, hypervigilance, and isolation from others.

Discourses fuel microaggressions. (See Table 11.2: Dominant Discourses About Jewish People.) A microaggression occurs when one is told to hire a Jewish lawyer, for example due to discourses that Jews are regarded as pushy, aggressive, powerful, miserly, and at the same time wealthy. He argues that Jews are treated as second class citizens when Christians are given preferential treatment over Jews and when Jews are not seen as an ethnic minority group. Forty-three percent of Jews face discrimination with 15% of Jews stating that in the past year they personally have been called offensive names or snubbed in a social setting because they are Jewish (Scholosser, 2008).

Ascription of intelligence is ascribing intelligence to a person on the basis of his or her race (Sue, Bucceri, Lin, Nadal, & Torino, 2007). Schlosser (2008) argues that Jews were the first model minority, a term that currently refers to Asians.

Another microaggression refers to the premier place that dominant white values hold over all others within the American culture. An example would be referring to Jews as pushy or JAPS (Jewish American Princesses). Jews endure the stigma/microaggression of being an alien in their own land, as traitors who are disloyal to America, because part of Jewish nationalism is assumed allegiance to Israel.

❖ **Table 11.2** Dominant Discourses About Jewish People

Calculating

Miserly

Pushy

Greedy

Entitled

Wealthy

White

Jewish looking (curly dark hair, brown eyes, Jewish nose)

Non–ethnic minority

Jewish Nationalism

Religious

In charge, powerful

Colorblindness invokes the minimization of skin color and refers to Jews. Although the ethnic minority status of Jews may be invisible, particularly among non-Orthodox Jews, European Jews are regarded as white in America (Jacobson, 1998) and are ethnic minorities. (See Storytelling: Whose Sabbath.)

❖ **STORYTELLING: WHOSE SABBATH?**

I know of an Orthodox PhD student in clinical psychology who faced discrimination at his internship site, which was located within a college counseling center. The intern, due to his Sabbath being on a Saturday, was not available to participate in student activities. He began to notice some tension from other interns and from his supervisor. Although nothing was overtly stated, he perceived the work environment to be critical and weary of his chronic absence from Saturday activities.

He then learned that a new policy was put into place for next year's interns, requiring Saturday participation. Is this new policy descriptive of religious discrimination, in that it may exclude certain groups from participating in this internship match due to religious conviction? From a social justice perspective, would it not be inclusive and fair to alternate weekend activities on a Sunday? How might Sunday church going Christians feel about a requirement to work on their Sabbath?

A number of genetic diseases exist for which persons of Jewish heritage (at least one grandparent) are more likely to be carriers of than the general population. Carriers are healthy individuals, unaffected by the disease for which they carry. If both parents are carriers of a gene mutation for the same condition, there is a 25% chance with each pregnancy of having an affected child. These diseases are all serious and can be fatal and or life altering to children born with them.

There are different genetic concerns for people of Ashkenazi Jewish background (German, French, or Eastern European) and people of Sephardic (Mediterranean) or Mizrahi (Persian/Iranian or Middle Eastern) background. It is estimated that nearly one in two Ashkenazi Jews in the United States is a carrier of at least 1 of 38 Jewish genetic diseases. There is no single preconception carrier-screening panel for people of Sephardic or Mizrahi background. Carrier screening is dependent upon country of origin. Regardless of specific Jewish background, all Jewish and interfaith couples are encouraged to seek preconception genetic counseling.

Cultural Orientation and Values

There is a diversity among Jewish people with respect to age and Jewish identity, religion, and cultural values. For example, according to Schorsch (2015), Conservative Judaism manifests a cluster of discrete and unprioritized core values that fall into two sets: three national and three religious, which are grounded and joined to each other by the overarching presence of God, who represents the seventh and ultimate core value. (See Table 11.3: Common Values Among Jewish People.)

Rabbi Wine wrote the following about values, both good and bad, and their presence across cultures:

> Good values are universal. They are to be found distributed among all cultures. Love, loyalty and compassion are very Jewish. But they can also be very Greek and very Chinese. Bad values are also universal. Hate, bigotry, and greed have no single national home. They are welcomed by people of many cultures. They have even been welcomed by Jews. (as cited in Chalam, 2013)

Implications for Mental Health Professionals

There is tremendous diversity among Jewish people, and yet according to Robinson (2000), Judaism is a belief system based on certain key ideas: There is one God who created the world ex nihilo; God is omnipotent, omniscient, omnipresent; God is just and merciful; God made a covenant with Jews, choosing them to be "a light unto the nations" (p. 492).

Non-Jews are encouraged to be familiar with the Holidays (e.g., Yom Kippur—the Sabbath of Sabbaths/Day of Atonement) in terms of planning the calendar and excusing absences from school and work as needed for observances. Just as other religious groups acknowledge holidays, including Muslims, Christians, and people of the Ba'hai faith, Yom Kippur is a day of fasting. Jews are not to work, eat, drink, wear leather shoes, engage in sexual relations, wear cosmetics and lotions, or "to wash any part of the body other than the fingers and eyes" (Robinson, 2000, p. 98).

As discussed earlier, Jews vary by religion, movement, and generation. There are also ethnic and racial differences among Jewish people; therefore, they are not a

❖ Table 11.3   Common Values Among Jewish People That May Be
Movement Influenced

The centrality of modern Israel

Hebrew: The irreplaceable language of Jewish expression

Devotion to the ideal of *Klal Yisrae* (The unfractured totality of Jewish existence and the
ultimate significance of every single Jew)

The defining role of Torah in the reshaping of Judaism

The study of Torah

The governance of Jewish life by Halakhah

Study of the Torah

Faith

Belief in God

Humor

Remembrance

High holidays

Educational attainment

Social justice

Honoring tradition

Progress

Communication patterns influenced by authority, age, and gender (orthodoxy)

Simple burial

Source: Robinson (2000); Schorsch (2015). Compiled by author.

monolith or cannot be spotted according to "looking Jewish or not appearing Jewish."
(See Case Study: A Jewish Woman's Multiple Religious and Racial Identities.)

Multiculturally competent professionals understand the history of anti-Semitism
and climates where derisive attitudes and behaviors toward Jewish people continue
to exist.

Case Study

A Jewish Woman's Multiple Religious and Racial Identities

Marsha is a 25-year-old PhD student. She was raised by her Jewish mother. Her Puerto Rican
father died when she was 7. Marsha was raised in an all white community, went to predominantly
white schools, and identified as white and Jewish, although at times she felt different from other
Jewish people, particularly during summer camp when her tan was darker than other children
and her hair much curlier when wet. Most of her friends assumed she was Italian unless Marsha

mentioned her deceased father. Marsha did not spend time with her father's side of the family during her childhood. In graduate school, Marsha met Jacob, a Mexican male PhD student who identifies as Christian. Despite the differences in their faiths, their interpersonal connection transcends religious differences and embraces their faiths. His parents have been married for 29 years and raised him to love God and to be proud of his Mexican heritage. Jacob came to the United States from Mexico when he was 12. Marsha's mother is a widow, having lost her husband (Marsha's father) 18 years ago to cancer. Through Marsha's and Jacob's many talks and budding friendship, a romantic relationship developed much to Marsha's surprise. She had never dated immigrant men of color and was comfortable with Jewish men only. Marsha has spent most of her life ignoring her identity as a person of Puerto Rican ancestry. In addition to not spending time with her father's side of the family, she was not exposed to Latinos through family outings, school, summer camp, vacations, or at her synagogue. Through meeting Latinos and from diversity training, Marsha has come to understand that she was actually afraid of Latinos, seeing them as illegals, loud, emotional, and dismissive of any religion besides Catholicism. Prior to graduate school, Marsha did not identify with Latinos. Her new racially diverse friends, cultural exposure, immersion into multicultural competence, and Jacob's unrelenting pursuit of her for over a year—although initially she rebuffed his obvious interest in being more than her friend, were critical to reshaping her racial identity development. Marsha's mother and grandmother are discouraging of her dating relationship with Jacob. They tell Marsha that she will come to regret marrying a Latino man even though he is college educated and pursuing a PhD. Marsha asked her mother why she had such negative thoughts about Latino men given that she married a man who was Puerto Rican. Marsha's mother then confides that she never married Marsha's father but accidentally became pregnant, tried to maintain the relationship with her father for Marsha's benefit, but struggled with her father's mental health issues (bipolar depression) and alcoholism. This significant portion of Marsha's history had never been shared with her. Marsha begins to understand her fear of Latino and black men as she reflects on the many racist comments she has heard from her mother and society in general. And yet, her mother was heavily involved in their synagogue with outreach to low-income communities. To sort out her relationships with Jacob, her deceased father, and her mother, Marsha seeks the assistance of a mental health professional. Marsha loves Jacob and is seriously contemplating his marriage proposal. He has promised to raise any future children as both Jewish and Christian with bar mitzvah and/or bat mitzvah ceremonies. Jacob suggests that Marsha seek out a therapist who can help her dialogue about race related identity issues. Marsha states she is more comfortable with a therapist who identifies as Jewish. Prior to his proposal to Marsha, Jacob found the following statement in his research on Judaism and interfaith marriage:

> The Central Conference of American Rabbis declares that the child of one Jewish parent is under the presumption of Jewish descent. This presumption of the Jewish status of the offspring of any mixed marriage is to be established through appropriate and timely public and formal acts of identification with the Jewish faith and people. The performance of these mitzvot serves to commit those who participate in them, both parent and child, to Jewish life (Central Conference of American Rabbis, 1983).

To Jacob, it is important that his children be faith-filled and religious people, participate regularly in church and in temple, and that he and Marsha commit to their respective faiths, to the Torah, to the Bible, and to the holidays.

Questions

1. What are the implications for therapeutic effectiveness when the patient is reeling from a secret from her childhood, that her parents never married, and that her father had a substance abuse and bipolar depression diagnoses?

2. What are the factors that contribute to Marsha's confusion about her Puerto Rican and Jewish heritages? How do we make sense of Marsha's request for a Jewish therapist?

Discussion and Integration

The Client, Marsha

Part of Marsha's difficulty with reconciling her Puerto Rican ancestry may be due to the centrality of her Jewish identity amidst the absence of any Latino involvement with Latino culture, history, art, music, or with Christianity. Robinson-Wood (2010a) found that some biracial children had difficulty racially identifying with a parent who was absent from the family or who had been violent within the family.

The Therapist, Ruth

Ruth is Jewish and follows Orthodoxy. She is a licensed mental health counselor. Marsha notes that Ruth wears a wig and although the psychological group with which Ruth is affiliated sees patients on Saturdays, Ruth does not. She is however, available on Sundays, which has interfered with Jacob's desire to have Marsha accompany him to his Sunday morning worship services. Marsha becomes self-conscious as she talks to Ruth about her non-Jewish Latino father who was an alcoholic and who had mental illness. She also feels anxious about discussing her interest in Jacob, a non-Jewish Mexican man who has proposed marriage.

Ruth attends to Marsha's increasing discomfort as she listens to her story. Ruth indicates that she is able to support Marsha as she makes the best decisions for herself, and not judge her. This statement reassures Marsha and contributes to her relaxation as she talks openly without censure. In therapy, Marsha's sensitivity to judgment or rejection from Jewish women is interpreted in the context of her "never happy with me" mother.

Ruth engages in skillful questioning with Marsha as she learns of her conflict with her multiple identities. She asks her, "If Jacob were white and Christian, do you think you would have a conflict with marrying him?" Marsha answers by saying that she always envisioned her life with a Jewish man—a white Jewish man since she has never met a nonwhite Jewish man. Ruth then asks Marsha, "If Jacob was an Ethiopian Jewish graduate student, would you have any conflict with marrying him?"

Ruth and Marsha were able to untangle Marsha's reticence to marrying Jacob—the man of her dreams was Jewish, preferably Israeli-born, fluent in Hebrew, just as she was, and white. Ruth engaged in the skill of broaching, of bringing out of the shadows a discomforting question but doing it delicately and empathetically while attending to the relational quality of the therapeutic encounter.

With Ruth's help, Marsha realizes that her dreams were based on a construction of internalized colorism that excluded dark-skinned Latinos and black people. Her expanded friendships and the knowledge that accompanies different ideas and realities have enabled her to see the world differently. Marsha also came to see that her criticism and rejection of Jacob was an extension of her mother's rejection of Marsha and of her father. Marsha was afraid, that due to her perceptions of

Ruth's conservatism as an Orthodox Jew, Ruth would devalue a Jewish woman who would marry outside of Judaism.

The intermarriage rate among Jews has grown significantly through the decades. According to Goldstein (2013), intermarriage among Jews has reached a high of 58% for all Jews, and 71% for non-Orthodox Jews. These statistics represent a major change from before 1970 when only 17% of Jews married outside the faith. One third had a Christmas tree in their home last year. The Pew Research Center Survey of U.S. Jews (2013) Research Trust also tells us that among Jews with a non-Jewish spouse, 20% say they are raising their children Jewish by religion, 25% are raising their children partly Jewish by religion, and over one third (37%) of intermarried Jews say they are not raising their children Jewish. That Jacob wants to raise future children to embrace both their Jewish and Christian heritages is meaningful to Marsha.

Summary

People of Jewish descent were discussed within the context of European history, immigration to America, racism, and anti-Semitism throughout time. The different movements of Judaism were also reviewed along with a discussion of the Holocaust. A biracial Puerto-Rican-Jewish woman who historically identified as white was discussed in the case study, as were some psychodynamic roots to her conflict with a Mexico-born Christian man who has proposed marriage to her.

Part III

Converging Identities

Converging Race

Race intersects with other dimensions of identity and across situations and contexts. For most patients, including some people of color, race does not exist as a primary source of clinical exploration. Throughout this chapter, racial identity theory is discussed. The discussion expands race beyond the limiting and essentializing dimensions of phenotype and skin color and includes greater focus on race and science.

The Social Construction of Race

Defining and demarcating race is shifting, as are race discourses. Some white college students claim a Native or white identity to improve their chances of getting into college. There are biracials who claim a black identity to get into college but otherwise would not, despite knowledge of African ancestry. For some, depending on the context, place, and people assembled, racial identification is fluid. Some Latinos claim a white identity although they have brown skin. The U.S. Census defines North Africans as white, irrespective of melanin content, and yet a black American who may have lighter skin is not designated as white.

Historically, the multicultural counseling and psychology literature has emphasized race. This emphasis is understandable considering both the legacy and current reality of racism in America and the power that society gives to racial differences to privilege, stratify, and stigmatize. Omni and Winant (2006) argued that although particular meanings, myths, and stereotypes about race can indeed change, "the presence of a system of racial meanings and stereotypes, of racial ideology, seems to be a permanent feature of U.S. culture" (p. 23).

Written predominantly by heterosexually identified and racially diverse men, the initial writings on cross-cultural counseling and psychology emphasized race, ethnic, and cultural identities. As U.S.-born women and people of color, racially and ethnically diverse immigrants, transgendered people, gay people, and people with disabilities began writing from their personal and clinical experiences, gender, sexual, and disability identities were added to the literature. Increasingly, this is much needed emphasis on spirituality and body size. This expanded focus on disability, spirituality, sexuality, and socioeconomic class is crucial to a more integrated cultural paradigm.

To what extent are recently added identities perceived to trespass on the terrain and turf of race and ethnicity? It is important to ask if and what the socially constructed legitimate and illegitimate dimensions of diversity are. Convergence asks that we honor race and ethnic identities in our clients while simultaneously incorporating other identities that are just as legitimate in the never-ending process of meaning-making (Robinson-Wood, 2010b).

Despite the tremendous heterogeneity within racially similar groups and homogeneity across different racial groups, race functions as a master status in society. As a social construction, race has the power to eclipse other identities that are just as potent to identity construction. It is even powerful enough to challenge scientific data that stipulates race as a biological entity. Race is not only a master status but functions as grandmaster status.

The social construction of race is sociopolitical and looms large. Racial categories contribute to race labeling. *Race labeling* is a function of phenotype and skin color characteristics to assign people to categories that are caste-like in nature. *Race* typically refers to appearances, such as skin color, hair type (straight, curly, kinky), skin hue, eye color, stature, body size, nose, eyes, and head shape. Clearly, these characteristics alone do not accurately assign a particular racial classification or negate the larger biological similarities that Homo sapiens are destined to share.

Representations of race are used by police, mortgage lenders, judges, teachers, employers, potential suitors, health care professionals, and the public at large to categorize people into racial groups. (See Storytelling: Silence Is Not Benign.) Socially constructed discourses about race contribute to differential and discriminatory treatment. Compared with whites within a similar income bracket, blacks and Latinos are given loans with higher interest rates and are not provided the same quality of health care treatment. In sum, race and ethnicity discourses affect the nature of people's daily experiences.

Research on microaggressions among 114 Native American young adults indicates that a stronger identification with Native or indigenous ethnic identity was related to more experiences with microaggressions, especially among males who reported greater Native identity affiliation than females. Women, in turn, reported higher affiliation with white identity and culture (Jones & Galliher, 2014).

Among Native American young female adults, *microinvalidations* (actions that exclude or negate the psychological thoughts, feelings, or experiences of people of color) were more upsetting than *microinsults* (verbal, nonverbal, or environmental actions that subtly convey insensitivity or directly demean a person's racial identity or heritage; Sue, 2010). Ascription of intelligence or being regarded as less intellectually equipped in comparison to others (e.g., non-Natives) was most challenging for the women in this study.

Other case research examining the impact of racism among Native American women and Chicanas pursuing doctorates reinforces the physiological and psychological effects of microaggressions and emphasizes culturally aligned beliefs and practices, including health and spiritually related responses and resources (Cueva, 2013; Huber & Cueva, 2012). This emergent body of microaggressions research is contextualized in the established literature on historical and intergenerational trauma among Native and indigenous people. Moreover, it specifically draws attention to the growing urgency on addressing trauma-related disease and health disparities among Native people (Craddock, 2015).

Native Americans contend with invisibility due to the longstanding and systematic dismissal and distortion of Native culture and indigenous people. The consequences of this aggression manifest in multiple health issues and suboptimal ways of coping, including substance abuse, suicide, and depression—all of which are ranked highly among Native people.

Racial discrimination has been found within federally funded agencies. One study found that African Americans were less likely than whites to receive grants from the National Institutes of Health (NIH). Stark differences were found between scored and non-scored proposals. About 16% of applications from black applicants were approved, compared with about 29% of those from white applicants. Asian applicants appeared to be slightly less likely than whites to get grants (25%). Kaiser (2011) reported that "black Ph.D. scientists—and not other minorities—were far less likely to receive NIH funding for a research idea than a white scientist from a similar institution with the same research record. The gap was large: A black scientist's chance of winning NIH funding was 10 percentage points lower than that of a white scientist."

❖ STORYTELLING: SILENCE IS NOT BENIGN

A former student of mine taught cultural diversity courses for years. Although she knew the material and was very committed to teaching, she was often met with suspicion from students. My former student was white, and among some students, her skin color contributed to their doubts about her legitimacy or whether her lived experiences as a white woman provided sufficient insight into the topics germane to a diversity course: inequity, experiences with racism, power imbalance, and privilege. When she spoke with me about this dynamic, I asked her how she came to know what some students were thinking and feeling. She said that some students, each semester, mentioned this during their anonymous evaluation of her course. I asked if she raised this issue in class. She said she did not because she did not know how and she was annoyed that some students would feel that way about her given her academic qualifications. I told her that there are students who question a faculty member of color's capacity to teach certain course material, such as statistics. I told her that not speaking to the issue did not allow her to bring this unsettling but substantive topic out of the shadows. This silence was not fair to her or to the students. I reminded her of Audre Lorde's quote: "Your silence will not protect you."

In an effort to address racial and gender inequity, affirmative action was created through the provision of opportunity for groups that had been targets of historical discrimination. Takaki (1994a), a scholar on race and ethnicity, stated,

> Affirmative action is actually designed to address the legacy of past racial discrimination and existing inequality by training and identifying qualified individuals of excluded racial minorities and allowing them greater access to equality and opportunity in education and employment. (p. 7)

That affirmative action seeks to impose quotas, which results in unqualified people (meaning people of color and women) taking jobs away from those who are qualified, meaning white males, is a myth, although there have been challenges to affirmative action in college admissions from white and nonwhite students who claim they are being unfairly disadvantaged due to their race. The goal of affirmative action was to encourage college admissions and employers to create opportunity for people of color, given their exclusion throughout history and in current-day America. Eventually, this provision extended beyond racial classification to include gender, sexual orientation, physical disability, and religion.

Race and Science

It is clear that in America race has long been and is currently a big deal—too big, especially when we consider race from a scientific lens. Fujimura and Rajagopalan (2011) examined the population designators "race" and "genetic ancestry" and the relationship between these two concepts in current day biomedical genetic research.

They interviewed population geneticists who accept the theory that modern day humans originated relatively recently in Africa and then dispersed to different migratory treks across the globe. These researchers are interested in conducting genome-wide association studies and are among those who critique the use of race in their search for the role that genes contribute to diseases. In their view, race categories do not correspond well to genetic groupings and are not the best tools to use when searching for disease-related genes. These researchers found that the practice of invoking race bore the marks of history and were sociocultural in nature and yet, the two are not the same.

An understanding of ancestry is derived from contexts and their meanings, and can also refer to lines of descent, hierarchical inheritance relationships, such as found in genealogy trees. Instead of race (e.g., Asian, African, European), some medical geneticists are adamant about the use of technical definition for populations based on genetic similarity (Fujimura & Rajagopalan, 2011).

In 1967, nearly 50 years ago, Rogers, a historian, wrote, "For us of the present day, the earliest history of all peoples and nations is lost in a fog" (p. 21). It appears that Spencer Wells (2002), a population geneticist, has lifted this fog referred to by Rogers. Wells has provided scientific information obtained in the blood of indigenous people throughout the world with a history book of the origin of the human species.

Through an analysis of DNA, a manual of life from thousands of blood samples, Wells (2003) stated that about 50,000 to 60,000 years ago, all ancestors of the world's people were living in southern Africa and a group of African hunters left armed with tools, that included hunting/navigation skills, environmental language skills, and tool making skills. What this means is that we are all African originally in our ancestry.

In a 2007 TED talk, Wells said, "The reason you're alive today is because of those changes in our brains that took place in Africa, around 60, 70 thousand years ago, allowing us not only to survive in Africa, but to expand out of Africa." After this small group of Africans left Africa but subsequently populated the earth, they arrived in Australia, via an early coastal migration, along the south coast of Asia, leaving Africa and reaching Australia within 10,000 years. Wells' research shows that Africans do not have Australian markers in their blood; however, Australians have African markers in their blood—indicating that Australians came from Africans. Africans did not come from Australians.

Male chromosomes are needed to search for markers found in the Y chromosome. On the way to Australia, African ancestors passed through India. Then 45,000 to 50,000 years later, a second group of African travelers travelled to the Middle East and another went to China. It took about 10,000 years from migration to Europe from the Middle East as people made their way around the Mediterranean.

Weather conditions allowed Africans to leave when they did. About 60,000 years ago, according to Wells (2003) was the worst part of the last ice age with the last ice age starting around 120,000 years ago and began accelerating around 70,000 years ago according to evidence from sediment cores, pollen types, and oxygen isotopes. He went on to say in this TED talk, that the last glacial maximum occurred around 16,000 years ago. For example, most of Britain and all of Scandinavia were covered by ice several kilometers thick. The ice age trapped the Africans who had made it to Europe, which over time led to phenotypical changes in hair color, shape of nose, and height (e.g., large body core/short limbs preserve heat in the midst of extremely cold weather). In contrast, Homo erectus had a tall and lean body useful in a hot and dry African environment (Smithsonian, 2015b).

The first Americans, as discussed in Chapter 5 on Native Americans, came over the Beringia land bridge into the New World between 12,000 and 15,000 years ago. It is believed that within 800 years, North and South America had been populated. There are seven species that are considered to be in the Homo group, which refers to other humans, prior to Homo sapiens, who had large brains and used tools. (See Knowledge Check 12.1: The Homo Group.) These individuals were the first to expand beyond Africa (Smithsonian, 2015i). This list, however, does not include Ardipithecus (four species), Australopithicus (four species), or Paranthropus (three species) who are not classified in the Homo group but are regarded as earliest and early humans. For example, Ardipithecus are the earliest humans and our closest link to other primates. Sahelanthropus tchadensis (Ardipithecus genus) is one of the oldest known species in the human family tree and lived about 6 to 7 million years ago. Australopithicus had both ape and human features. Australopithicus anamensis lived 4.2 to 3.9 million years ago. Paranthropus aethiopicus lived 2.7 to 2.3 million years ago (Smithsonian, 2015i). Paranthropus had large teeth and powerful jaws that enabled them to eat a variety of food. (See Knowledge Check 12.2: Early Hominins.)

Homo habilis lived about 2.4 million to 1.4 million years ago in eastern and southern Africa and is one of the earliest members of the genus Homo. It had a slightly larger braincase (e.g., hence the ability to make tools found in the Olduvi Gorge of Tanzania) and a smaller face and teeth than older hominin species yet apelike features, (e.g., long arms and a moderately prognathic [projecting jaw] face; Smithsonian, 2015d).

A fossil of Homo rudolfensis, who lived from 1.9 to 1.8 million years ago, was found in the Lake Turkana basin, Kenya, in 1986. It had a braincase size of 775 cubic centimeters, which is considerably above the high end of Homo habilis' braincase size. Homo rudolfensis was originally thought to be Homo habilis but differences were clarified. In Homo rudolfensis, the brain is larger, the face is longer, and the premolar and molar teeth are larger. The jury is out and some scientists want to refer to this species as Australopithecus with a big brain (Smithsonian, 2015g).

The science is evolving and different opinions exist given that there is still much to learn regarding the evolution of Homo sapiens and who its direct ancestor is. Agreement among reputable historians, population geneticists, and archaeologists is that the color of primitive humans was black. Zuckerman (1990) wrote, "Although there is considerable speculation on the origin of races, little can be proved other than that a species, *Homo sapiens*, gradually evolved from its predecessor *Homo erectus* about 200,000 years ago in East Africa and spread through Africa and Eurasia" (p. 1297).

According to the Smithsonian, Homo erectus (sometimes called Homo ergaster), lived in northern, eastern, and southern Africa; western Asia (Dmanisi, Republic of Georgia); and east Asia (China and Indonesia) between approximately 1.89 million and 143,000 years ago. Thus Homo habilis and Homo erectus may have been sister species, coexisting for 500,000 years.

Homo Neanderthals lived in Europe and southwestern to central Asia about 400,000 to 40,000 years ago. They are known to be Homo sapien's closest extinct relative. Their brains were just as large if not larger than ours (they are the first to be

Knowledge Check 12.1

The Homo Group

1. Homo habilis lived about 2.4 million to 1.4 million years ago in eastern and southern Africa. One of the earliest members of the genus Homo. Fossils were found in Olduvai Gorge in Tanzania.

2. Homo rudolfensi lived from 1.9 to 1.8 million years ago. Fossil was found in the Lake Turkana basin, Kenya, in 1986.

3. Homo errectus (sometimes called Homo ergaster) lived from 1.9 million to 143,000 years ago in northern, eastern, and southern Africa; western Asia (Dmanisi, Republic of Georgia); and east Asia (China and Indonesia). Fossils were found in 1891 in Indonesia.

4. Homo heidelbergensis lived in Europe, possibly in China and eastern and southern Africa about 700,000 to 200,000 years ago. Fossils were found in Germany in 1908.

5. Homo Neanderthalis lived in Europe and southwestern to central Asia about 400,000 to 40,000 years ago. Fossils were first discovered in Belgium in 1829.

6. Homo floresiensis were discovered in 2003 in Flores, Indonesia, and are believed to have lived from 95,000 to 17,000 years ago.

7. Homo sapiens lived from 200,000 years ago to present.

Source: Smithsonian (2015b, 2015c, 2015d, 2015e, 2015f, 2015g, 2015h).

known to make symbolic and ornamental objects and buried their dead and marked graves with flowers). They are also known to have had angled cheekbones and a very large nose for humidifying and warming cold, dry air. Their bodies were shorter and stockier than ours, which is regarded as another adaptation to coexisting in very cold environments. Neanderthals made and used a variety of complex tools, made and wore clothing, were skilled hunters of large animals and also ate plant foods and occasionally made symbolic or ornamental objects (Smithsonian, 2015f).

Remains of Homo floresiensis were discovered in 2003 in Flores, Indonesia. It is thought that they lived from 95,000 to 17,000 years ago. Nicknamed the Hobbit, individuals were diminutive in stature (e.g., 3 feet, 6 inches tall) with small brains, large teeth, shrugged-forward shoulders, no chins, receding foreheads, short legs, and large feet. This group made and used stone tools, hunted small elephants and large rodents, and coped with predators such as giant Komodo dragons. They may have also used fire (Smithsonian, 2015c). The diminutive stature and small brain of Homo floresiensis may have resulted from island dwarfism—an evolutionary process that results from long-term isolation on a small island with limited food resources and a lack of predators. Pygmy elephants on Flores, now extinct, showed the same adaptation. The smallest known species of Homo and Stegodon elephant are both found on the island of Flores, Indonesia. However, some scientists are questioning if the ancestors of Homo floresiensis may have been small when they first reached Flores.

Knowledge Check 12.2

Early Hominins

1. **Ardipithecus Group**: Earliest humans and Homo sapiens' closest link to other primates.
   a. Sahelanthropus tchadensis lived about 6 to 7 million years ago in West and Central Africa. Fossils were discovered in 2001.
   b. Orrorin tugenensis lived about 6.2 to 5.8 million years ago in East Africa. Fossils were discovered in 2001.
   c. Ardipithecus kadobba lived about 6.2 to 5.8 million years ago in East Africa. Fossils were discovered in 2001.
   d. Ardipithecus ramidus lived about 4.4 million years ago in Ethiopia. Fossils were discovered in Ethiopia in 1924.

2. **Australopithicu Groups**: Species that walked upright regularly but still climbed trees.
   a. Australopithicus anamensis lived 4.2 to 3.9 million years ago in East Africa. Fossils were found in 1995.
   b. Australopithicus afarensis lived 3.85 to 2.95 million years ago in East Africa. Fossils were found in 1994.
   c. Australopithicus africanus lived 3.3 to 2.1 million years ago in South Africa. Fossils were found in 1924.
   d. Australopithicus garhi lived 2.5 million years ago in Ethiopia. Fossils were found in 1990.

3. **Paranthropus Group**: Species with both ape and human features; they had large teeth and powerful jaws enabling these early humans to feed on a variety of foods.
   a. Paranthropus aethiopicus lived 2.7 to 2.3 million years ago in East Africa. Fossils were discovered in 1967.
   b. Paranthropus boisei lived 2.3 to 1.2 million years ago in Ethiopia and East Africa. Fossils were discovered in 1959.
   c. Paranthropus robustus lived 1.8 to 1.2 million years ago in South Africa. Fossils were discovered in 1938.

Source: Smithsonian (2015i).

Rogers's writing preceded Wells and yet agreed with Wells. Wells's mentor was Luca Cavalli Sforza, who began studying the blood of the world's people during the 1950s. Rogers (1967) maintained that early humans are thought to have been of "small stature, probably from four and a half to five feet tall. Their nearest living descendants are believed to be the Bushmen of South Africa; the Mincopies of the Andaman Islands off the coast of India; the hill-folk of Southern India; the Tapiro of New Guinea; and the Negritos of the Philippines" (pp. 28–29).

Given that the origins of the human race are black, the white race (a scientific fact that is still difficult for some students to accept) is a function of lack of pigmentation, lost over time because it was not needed in cold environments.

Sergi (as cited in Rogers, 1967) of the University of Rome, stated that European man was African man, *Eur-African*, transformed by European environmental effects. There are three categories of Eur-African: "(a) The African with red, brown, and black pigmentation, (b) the Mediterranean or brunette complexion, inhabiting the great basin, including part of Northern Africa . . . and finally, (c) a Nordic variety of blond skin and hair, blue or gray eyes, most universally represented as Scandinavia, North Germany, and England" (as cited in Rogers, 1967, pp. 29–30).

A question remains as to Homo sapiens' direct ancestor. Some paleoanthropologists believe that our direct evolutionary ancestor may have been Homo heidelbergensis (Smithsonian, 2015e). Fossils were discovered in 1908 near Heidelberg, Germany. It is believed that Homo heidelbergensis lived in Europe, possibly in China, and eastern and southern Africa about 700,000 to 200,000 years ago. Homo heidelbergensis had a flatter face and a larger braincase. It was the first early human to live in colder climates. They lived at the time of the oldest definite control of fire and wooden spear use, and they were the first to routinely hunt large animals, build shelters, and create dwellings out of wood and rock. This species had short and wide bodies, which scientists believe was an adaptation to heat conservation (e.g., reduces overall skin surface area and heat loss; Smithsonian, 2015e).

There are many scientists who believe that the direct ancestor of our genus is Australopithecus afarensis (albeit in the hominin family, but not in the genus Homo or the species sapien). Known as "Lucy" who lived about 3 million years ago in Ethiopia, this hominin walked upright and had a small brain (Shreeve, 2015). The Smithsonian (2015a) dates australopithecus afarensis even further back to have lived from 3.85 to 2.95 million years ago. Fossils were discovered in 1974 in Ethiopia, Kenya, and Tanzania. Australopithecus afarensis had ape and human characteristics. Face proportions were apelike (flat nose, projecting jaw, and a small brain, which is less than one third the size of a modern human brain). The arms were long and the fingers were curved for climbing trees.

A substantial portion of the dialogue about race includes conceptual frameworks that attribute inferior yet inherent biological deficiencies to African and Semitic people. In 1758 Swedish naturalist Carolus Linnaeus published *Systema Naturae*, where he essentially described physical and personality characteristics of four major racial groups. Homo sapiens americanus were described as having good posture, red skin, black and thick hair, harsh faces, and were ill-tempered, obstinate, and governed more by custom than by formal law. Linnaeus was referring to Native Americans. Homo sapiens europeaeus (Caucasians) had white skin, long flowing hair, and blue eyes. They were smart, sanguine, and their political and social relations were governed by formal law. Homo sapiens asiaticus had yellow skin, black eyes, and black hair. Linnaues described Asians as melancholy and greedy. Their relations were governed more by custom than by formal law. Finally, black people, Homo sapiens afer, had black silky skin, frizzed black hair, broad noses, and bulging lips. They were crafty, lazy, and were ruled by caprice (Ossorio, nd). It is against this centuries-old classification system that current discourses have their roots. Charles Darwin's (1859) work *The Origin of Species by Means of Natural Selection* was used to support the genetic intellectual superiority of whites and the genetic inferiority of nonwhites, who were referred to as the "lower races."

In October 2007, James Watson, a 1962 Nobel Prize recipient for his role in discovering the structure of DNA, found himself in trouble for making statements that were interpreted as racist. He stated that he was "inherently gloomy about the prospect of Africa because all our social policies are based on the fact that their intelligence is the same as ours, whereas all the testing says not really" (as cited in Nugent, 2007). Watson later apologized for his remarks.

There are claims regarding racial purity and racial superiority, but these are bogus and represent a false hope (Cooper, 2002). Everyone comes from the same source (Zuckerman, 1990). Human beings are products of migratory patterns and world conquests throughout the centuries; thus, the argument of a pure race does not exist (Dobbins & Skillings, 1991).

Scientists studying the human genome have announced that the genetic difference between individual humans today is extremely small, about 0.1%, on average. In other words, the DNA of human beings is 99.9% alike. We are all one species (Smithsonian, 2015j). The recently completed Human Genome Sequencing Project has confirmed what scientists have known for a very long time—humans do not fit into the biological criteria that define race. The widely held belief in the biological differences between racial groups is simply incorrect (LaVeist, 2002). "Any way you measure, the amount of divergence between people is essentially zero," according to Joseph L. Graves, an evolutionary biologist; he went on to say, "The scientific case for the nonexistence of human race is overwhelming" (as cited in "Genetic Research Confirms," 2003). (See Storytelling: Can You Imagine?)

❖ STORYTELLING: CAN YOU IMAGINE?

I was speaking to a woman recently while at the library. She was telling me about her church and the Christian school associated with it. She mentioned that my daughters, who were wearing dresses with long leggings, would not be able to wear that outfit because girls have to wear dresses below the knees. "Even though they have leggings on?" I asked.

She said yes. "How do you teach science?" I asked. She said that they teach and believe the Bible, that God made the world in 7 days. "But how do you treat science, evolution, fossil remains, DNA evidence?" She leaned forward and said, "We teach the Bible. Do you think I would ever believe that I actually came from an ape?"

Origins of Racial Groups

In 1790, the first decennial census was taken (Jones & Bullock, 2012). At that time in U.S. society when the U.S. Census Bureau listed five races, to be *colored* (black or mulatto) was not just a source of difference. Race functioned as a status variable. More specifically, the experience of being colored meant no voting rights, no educational access to predominantly white institutions, inexistent or woefully inadequate health care, extreme vulnerability to being lynched, and no legal protection under the law. Yet the mere classification of race was not solely responsible for differential treatment. Attitudes about race were pivotal to the creation of a social structure in which institutional policy bestowed privilege and conferred disadvantage on persons because of race (Cornell & Hartmann, 1997; McIntosh, 1988; Pinderhughes, 1989).

As early as 1870, the U.S. Bureau of the Census divided the U.S. population into five races: white, colored (black), colored (mulatto), Chinese, and Indian (Root, 1992). One hundred and thirty years later, the 2000 U.S. Census, for the first time, enabled people to select more than one race as a way of describing themselves. Of the 309 million Americans who responded to the 2010 Census, 2.9% indicated that they belonged to more than one race—that is over 9 million people (Grieco et al., 2012).

Since 1870 when the Census divided people into five races and in present day, controversy among biologists, anthropologists, and other scholars has surrounded the topic of number of races. Zuckerman (1990) sought to clarify misconceptions surrounding racial similarity and difference. He reported that, in his analysis of 18 genetic systems (blood groups, proteins, and enzymes) in 40 populations within 16 subgroups around the world, "the major component of genetic diversity is between individuals in the same tribe or nation; it accounts for 84 percent of the variance. Of the remaining variance, 10 percent is accounted for by racial groupings and 6 percent by geographic regions" (p. 1300). The existence of definable groups or races is not self-evident, although human variation is (Cooper, 2002).

Alan Goodman, dean of natural science at Hampshire College, said that depending on which trait is used to distinguish races, "You won't get anything that remotely tracks conventional race categories" (as cited in Begley, 1995, p. 67). Spickard (1992), a scholar on biracial identity argued, "The so-called races are not biological categories at all. Rather, they are primarily social divisions that rely only partly on physical markers as skin color to identify group membership" (p. 17). (See Storytelling: Introjected Racism.)

❖ STORYTELLING: INTROJECTED RACISM

In Henry Louis Gates's *Blacks in Latin America* video, the ruler of the Dominican Republic from 1930 to 1961 was featured. Although General Rafael Leonidas Trujillo Molina had Haitian ancestry, he ordered the army in 1937 to murder Haitians living on the Dominican side of the border. This event was known as the Parsley Massacre. It is estimated that over 15,000 Haitians were killed over a 6-day period. To hide their murders, the soldiers used machetes, hence the term *el corte* (the cutting) in the Dominican Republic. The soldiers interrogated persons with dark skin, using the shibboleth *perejil* (parsley) to distinguish Haitians from Dominicans. The 'r' of *perejil* was difficult for haitians to pronounce. As a result of the massacre, the Dominican Republic agreed to pay Haiti U.S. $750,000 which was later reduced to U.S. $525,000. Trujillo was assassinated in 1961. In a museum to honor his memory, white powder was found—he used powder to whiten his appearance.

Despite the intimate relationship that all humans have with one another genetically, scientific notions about intelligence were developed against a biological and sociopolitical backdrop of racism similar to Linnaeus and the racial hierarchy that he created in his seemingly subjective elevation of white people and his devaluing of people of color.

Interrogating the assumptions of race is essential to a social justice framework. Nisbett (2009) found that young black children in Milwaukee who were suspected of being at risk for having some cognitive disability and were randomly assigned to intensive day care and enriched education improved significantly over children who received traditional schooling.

IQ scores can provide a partial explanation for academic success, however, they do not explain academic success completely. By age 5, the children exposed to the intensive program had an average IQ score of 110 whereas children in the control group had an average IQ score of 83. Benefits of early intervention were seen as long as 10 years later.

On Race, Ethnicity, and Difference

The importance of and a search for racial and cultural understanding is a tenet of racial identity development. Nonetheless, the importance of racial identity development is its connection to cultural competence (Henderson et al., 2010).

Racial identity theory assumes that individuals at initial levels of development have the potential to change over time as they encounter dissonance to existing cognitive schema (Robinson, 1999b). The models reflect movement and change over time. By integrating racial identity with a discussion of race, a focus is placed on development, an achieved characteristic, and not solely on skin color, an immutable one.

Until recently, within the past 15 years, the racial identity development literature has focused primarily on white, black, and other monoracial groups. Helms's (1995) work on a model of racial identity for people of color and the earlier racial/cultural identity development model (originally called the minority identity development model) by Atkinson, Morten, and Sue (1983) are exceptions. A problem with traditional racial identity models is their failure to include people who are biracial and/or multiracial. Increasingly, researchers are applying multicultural competence to specific groups of people across identities (Henderson et al., 2010). In addition, a focus on identity moves the discussion of race beyond the narrowness of phenotype traditionally associated with race.

Racialized experiences differ among groups of color and within groups of color. A number of factors may moderate the experience of racism for people of color such as physical appearance or skin color hue and class markers (e.g., income, occupation, country of origin, and facility with the English language). What the research reveals is that qualitative and quantitative studies are being conducted across racial groups and ethnic groups.

In a qualitative study by Chang (2015), 27 Latino American and 31 Asian American undergraduate students ages 18 to 22 years old were compared on social support as a means of coping with stressors. The study also explored how support-seeking behaviors relate to cultural factors. Study results revealed that participants in both groups believed that support seeking behaviors would make matters worse for the self and the group, rather than decrease their stress because they felt they would be burdening others with their problem. Asian American participants, in particular, anticipated that if they sought support from parents then they would receive advice to exercise emotional restraint, which implies an element of control. They further anticipated that their parents' reactions would not be useful or helpful. When compared with their Latino American counterparts, Asian American participants more frequently noted the importance of upholding family honor, which as a result lessened their use of family support (Chang, 2015). This study illustrates how family honor within collectivistic societies may connote a sense of control that could limit speaking freely.

Pieterse and Carter (2007) conducted research with 220 black American men, recruited primarily from barbershops in New York and Washington, DC. The purpose of the study was to examine the influence of perceived racism-related stress on psychological health and to explore the predictive quality of racism-related stress on psychological health when controlling for general life stress. All of the men reported experiencing some type of racist incident in the prior month and year. Although racist events were stressful, racism-related stress did not seem to influence the well-being of working-class men. The researchers concluded that for black men in particular, "social mobility encompasses hidden costs, one of which could be a greater sensitivity to experiences of racism and discrimination" (p. 106).

While research has addressed the cumulative health impact of racism on people of color, Torres, Driscoll, and Burrow (2010) highlighted the resulting stressors and health effects of racial microaggressions given frequent behavioral and environmental encounters with inferiority. This longitudinal mixed-method study of 107 black doctoral students and recent graduates found that assumptions were made about criminality and second-class citizenship within the academy. An underestimation of abilities was particularly salient for graduate students and impacted mental health. Cultural and racial isolation and alienation in predominantly white academic settings exacerbated other stress. Racial microaggressions can increase the perception of greater life stress, which may explain the enduring nature of racial disparities in mental health (Torres et al., 2010).

Rowley, Burchinal, Roberts, and Zeisel (2008) investigated changes in racial identity, cross-race friendships, same-race friendships, and classroom racial composition on changes in race-related social cognition from 3rd to 5th grade for 73 African American children. Three major findings were reported. First, there was a decline in expectations for discrimination from 3rd to 5th grade. Second, having more African American friends was associated with expecting more discrimination in cross-racial interactions from 3rd to 5th grade. Third, increases in racial centrality were related to increases in discrimination expectations. Increases in public regard were associated with decreases in discrimination expectations. Racial identity includes the extent to which a person defines himself or herself in terms of race (racial centrality). A person's sense of pride in group membership and evaluation of the merits of the group refers to private regard. Public regard involves beliefs about how others view the group.

Because there are conceptual differences between ethnicity and race, it makes sense for there to be a difference between racial identity and ethnic identity. *Representations of race* typically refer to phenotype or genetic heritage, whereas *ethnicity* is defined as sociocultural heritage. There has not traditionally been a difference in the psychological literature between racial and ethnic identity.

Cokely (2005) argued that confusion exists among racial identity, ethnic identity, and Africentric beliefs. Ethnic identity refers to the extent to which a person identifies with his or her ethnic group: "It is the meaning, strength, and salience of one's ethnic identity" (Cokely, 2005, p. 517).

In the early days of ethnic identity, Phinney (1990) acknowledged that there was no widely agreed upon definition of ethnic identity. At the same time, the components of ethnic identity include self-identification as a group member, a sense of belonging to the group, attitudes about group membership, and ethnic involvement social participation, cultural practices, and attitudes (Phinney, 1990).

Ethnicity is often presented as a subset or is subsumed under race, although people can be of the same ethnicity while representing different races. An example is Dominicans, an ethnic group. There are dark-skinned Dominicans whose ancestors came from Africa and Spain whereas the ancestors of some Dominicans were African, European, and Native/Indigenous. People can be from the same race and have different ethnicities. For example, there are people of African descent who are Nigerian, some are Cape Verdean, some are Canadian, others are Jamaican, and others are African Americans.

At adolescence, ethnic identity has particular relevance given the pressure of peer groups and the upheaval associated with identity search across multiple levels of identity, including sexuality, gender, and race. In her study of 669 American-born African American, Latino, and white high school students, Phinney (1997) found that ethnic identity was clearly an important contribution to an adolescent's sense of self and that this finding was consistent across ethnic groups. Among black and Latino teens, being an American was not closely tied to the sense of self. American identity had no contribution to their self-esteem. For white students, however, ethnic identity and American identity were strong predictors of global self-esteem. Many African American and Latino teens may feel ambivalent about being American given their uncertainty about the meaning of American and the discourses about Americans actually referring to white people.

A challenge with the concept of ethnic identity is its confusion with acculturation. *Acculturation* "deals broadly with changes in cultural attitudes, values, and behaviors that result from contact between two distinct cultures" (Phinney, 1990, p. 501). In other words, acculturation speaks to changes that occur over time when two cultures not only come into contact but stay in continuous contact (Phinney &

Flores, 2002). Acculturation is mentioned with ethnic identity due to the importance of considering the ethnic group member's relationship with the dominant group. Ethnic identity can be approached as a state in terms of the self-defining labels that a person may use to label himself or herself at a given point in time. Stages of ethnic identity chart changes over time in a person's way of identifying as an ethnic group member.

In path-making research, Phinney (1989) was instrumental in providing a framework of ethnic identity development. Ninety-one American-born Asian American, black, Hispanic, and white 10th-grade students, all from integrated urban high schools, were interviewed. The subjects were also given questionnaire measures of ego identity and psychological adjustment. On the basis of the interviews, the minority subjects were coded as being in one of three identity stages: diffusion/foreclosure, moratorium, and identity achieved. Among children of color, nearly one half of the subjects had not examined their ethnic identity, which was conceptualized as diffusion and foreclosure. *Diffusion* referred to a lack of interest in or concern with ethnicity. *Foreclosure* reflected the views and opinions held by others (Phinney, 1990). In Phinney's (1989) work sample, about one quarter were considered to be in *exploration* or *moratorium*, understood as seeking to understand the personal meaning of ethnicity for oneself. One quarter were identified as *ethnic identity achieved* in that they had explored and were committed to an ethnic identity and had a clear and confident sense of their own ethnicity. This last group had the highest scores on a measure of ego identity and psychological adjustment. Although identity development was similar across the three groups of color, the issues specific to each group differed.

Myers et al.'s (1991) optimal theory applied to identity development is discussed in the following sections. More differences exist within groups rather than between them. As such, differences in racial identity and value orientation are to be expected among racially similar individuals. Racial identity development theory underscores the reality of psychological differences within monoracial and ethnic groups.

Optimal Theory Applied to Identity Development

Myers et al. (1991) developed a theory of optimal identity that is neither linear nor categorical. In criticizing some psychosocial identity models, they observed that the models have limited the role of the individual in the identity process, did not consider people with multiple identities, and were based on a Eurocentric worldview. Myers et al. maintained that the dichotomy of the spirit world and matter within American society make it difficult to attain a positive self-identity in the United States, regardless of race, because self-worth is based primarily on external validation. Persons who turn outside themselves for meaning, peace, and value have adopted a suboptimal worldview. According to Myers et al., within an optimal perspective, self-worth is intrinsic in being. Thus, the purpose of life is becoming clearer about how the self is connected with all of life. Spiritual development is an integral part of identity development.

In Phase 0, known as *absence of conscious awareness,* the person lacks awareness of being. This is regarded as an infancy stage. Phase 1 is *individuation.* Here, the world is the way it is in that people simply lack awareness of any view of self other than the one to which they were initially introduced. They rarely assign meaning or value to the various aspects of their identity. Phase 2 is *dissonance;* persons begin the exploration of their true self and effectively explore dimensions of the self that may be demeaned by others. In Phase 3, *immersion,* persons' energy is focused on those who are regarded as similar. Phase 4, *internalization,* occurs as people feel good about who they are and have successfully incorporated feelings of self-worth. Phase 5, *integration,* happens as people's deeper understanding of themselves allows them to change their assumptions about the world. The self is more secure internally, and peaceful relationships are a manifestation of this security. The final stage, Phase 6, is *transformation.* The self is redefined toward a sense of personhood that includes ancestors, the unborn, nature, and community. The universe is understood as benevolent, orderly, and personal.

Implications for Mental Health Professionals

In a survey conducted by the Kaiser Family Foundation (U.S. Department of Health and Human Services [U.S. DHHS], 2001), it was found that 12% of African Americans and 15% of Latinos, compared with 1% of whites, felt that a doctor or health care provider would judge them unfairly or treat them with disrespect because of their race or ethnic background. There is a climate of mistrust around race. Low-income black families are often stigmatized as disorganized, lazy, and deprived (Boyd-Franklin, 2003).

Part of multicultural competence is knowledge of these sociopolitical dynamics and resources for counteracting them. Day-Vines et al. (2007) introduced the concept of *broaching,* which refers to the initiation on the part of the clinician to bring issues of race and diversity, often regarded as fugitive topics, into the therapy room. The purpose of doing this is to encourage the client's exploration of these difficult topics. Due to fear of being perceived as incompetent, insensitive, or racist, counselors will avoid asking particular questions. This fear can paralyze the therapeutic event and interfere with the client's growth. Leadership requires therapists to introduce conversation about difficult and sensitive topics. If students and mental health professionals do not challenge themselves to grow and think critically, although they have taken the required graduate-level cross-cultural diversity course, there may be resistance to broaching race/racism and other sensitive topics.

The therapeutic relationship is influenced by a client's racial identity development in that it can directly affect the client's preference for a counselor. Clients of color in initial phases of racial identity development may be more likely to prefer a white counselor over a counselor of color. The belief exists that "whites are more competent and capable than members of one's own race" (Sue & Sue, 1990, p. 108). In this scenario, if the counselor is white, the patient will typically be overeager to identify with the counselor. If the counselor is nonwhite, then the counselor will experience feelings of hostility from the client even if the client and the counselor are of the same race.

Independent of the counselor's race, the counselor has a responsibility to help reeducate the client as they work together through the client's conflicts. Regardless of race, counselors who choose not to face their biases with humility and courageous introspection may be inappropriate candidates for the mental health profession.

During the encounter and dissonance stages, clients are preoccupied with questions concerning the self and identity. They may still prefer a white counselor; however, counselors can take advantage of clients' focus on self-exploration toward resolution of identity conflicts. During the immersion/emersion and resistance and immersion stages of racial/ethnic identity, clients of color tend to view their psychological problems as an outgrowth of oppression and racism. In this stage, clients of color are prone to prefer counselors of their own race. In fact, people of color may tend to perceive white counselors as enemies. Thus, it is important for counselors to not personalize or pathologize resistance from clients but instead determine if this data have clinical relevance with respect to assessment and diagnosis. Statements regarding the unjust sociopolitical nature within the United States have legitimacy. It is also wise for counselors to anticipate that resistance/immersion clients may test their clinicians, as this stage is one of great volatility.

Clients of color at more integrated phases of racial identity often experience an inner sense of security. They are able to choose therapists, not necessarily on the basis of race, but on the basis of the professional's ability to be empathic and understanding of the issues clients bring to counseling. Sue and Sue (1990) stated that "attitudinal similarity between counselor and client is a more important dimension than membership-group similarity" (p. 112). Nonetheless, clients at more advanced stages of racial identity may accept a counselor of a different race while preferring one of their own racial, ethnic, or gender group. This preference need not be an indication of discriminatory attitudes but may instead reflect a desire or need for a cultural connection that may occur or may not occur. (See Storytelling: Requests for Same-Race Therapists.)

Mental health professionals need to acknowledge their biases and assess their personal readiness prior to engaging in counseling across sources of diversity. Not to do so is to place the patient in jeopardy. If need be, licensed professionals may want to contact a supervisor at parallel or more integrated levels of racial identity to facilitate their racial identity progression (Ladany, Brittan-Powell, & Pannu, 1997). Collaboration groups may also be a source of professional and personal development. In some states (e.g., New Hampshire), collaboration hours are required for counselor and psychologist license renewal.

Richardson and Molinaro (1996) found that the reintegration therapist may be impatient toward clients of different races and less likely to establish rapport with these clients. Cook (1994) suggested that white counselors may also engage in ethnocentric behavior if they operate at Helms's reintegration stage and recognize their own race as standard for "normal" behavior of the client. Not until the immersion/emersion stage do white clinicians acknowledge clients' race, respect cultural influences, and examine the sociopolitical implications. At the pseudoindependence stage, the white counselor will discuss racial issues but only when interacting with persons of color (Cook, 1994). Ethnocentric assumptions still frame people's thinking.

Ultimately, our beliefs and attitudes will inform the quality of our listening and our talking. Delpit (1997) eloquently said, "We do not really see through our eyes . . .

but through our beliefs. To put our beliefs on hold is to cease to exist as ourselves for a moment—and that is not easy . . . but it is the only way to learn what it might feel like to be someone else and the only way to start the dialogue" (p. 101).

❖ STORYTELLING: REQUESTS FOR SAME-RACE THERAPISTS

I recently received two requests from colleagues looking for black clinicians to work with black women, one a graduate student and the other a working adult. These women specifically asked for professionals of color. Fortunately, there were licensed professionals available to whom I could refer these women. It does not surprise me that some black clients prefer other black professionals, particularly when issues of racism or mircoaggressions are at the core of the presenting issue. Preference for a counselor on the basis of race can and does occur. An agency or practice or group may not have an appropriate match but may have gender compatibility. The literature is inconclusive regarding the link between racial identification and counselor preference (Pope-Davis, Liu, Toporek, & Brittan-Powell, 2001). Being a therapist of color or a woman or both does not ensure that one is able to work effectively with women clients of color. Wilkinson (1997) pointed out that educators and mental health professionals, across racial and ethnic diversity, are vulnerable to believing dominant class discourses. The consequences of having close proximity to dominant class discourses can have a number of impacts. For example, it can contribute to black professionals' lack of knowledge about class discrimination and its influence on people's lives, leaving people unable to relate to others of the same race who are of a lower income bracket. Despite this reality, a same-race counselor has often had "similar emotional and physical experiences with racism, and more of a willingness to confront this external barrier" (Washington, 1987, p. 198).

It is important for multiculturally competent white therapists to broach the topic of race and explain to their clients that discussions of race and racism are welcomed—that the focus of therapy is on the clients' healing, not on protecting the therapist from topics of white racism. Part of the everyday experience of black people is comporting and/or censuring themselves so as not to offend in order to get along. Therapy should not be a site of reproducing inequity. Multicultural competence is an awareness of sociopolitical issues such as structural inequalities that affect people's attempts to be agentic and have control over their psychological and economic lives. Knowledge and assessment of proximity to race and ethnic discourses, broaching skills, referral, and advocacy, as well as an understanding of racial identity development and multicultural terminology are all reflections of multicultural competence (Holcomb-McCoy, 2000).

Case Study

Teaching Privilege to the Privileged

There are a host of emotions that accompany undergraduate and graduate students' awareness of unearned white skin-color privilege. Guilt, anger, minimization, rationalization, humor, sadness, and confusion are common emotions. The following themes are intended to assist instructors with teaching privilege to the privileged. This discussion is relevant for skin-color privilege as well as gender, ability, class, religious, and sexuality privileges.

Questions and Discussion

1. Realize that unawareness of unearned privilege and entitlement go hand in hand. Entitlement is the belief that one has the right to be acknowledged, protected, respected, and rewarded. When denied any of these, shock and anger emerge.

2. Respect the difficult feelings that accompany the unpacking of the invisible knapsack. Allow feelings, knowing that such feelings are necessary for change and growth.

3. Democracy and justice are dominant U.S. cultural values.

4. Although race, gender, class, and sexuality are identity constructs that have status, race in America is a grandmaster status and can eclipse other identities, such as class.

5. Working-class whites may invoke their modest class origins and attempt to compare their class oppression with racism. Skin color is an immutable characteristic and is not as fluid as is class. Universities are filled with white professors whose families of origin were low-wage earning, immigrant, and working class. Unless people identify this history, they are physically indistinguishable from those whose parents and grandparents were academics and/or who came into tremendous wealth. Working-class status among whites and working-class status among blacks and other groups of color is different. Being low income and black represents two marginalized identities.

6. Not having white skin-color privilege or other sources of privilege does not render a person powerless. Having white skin-color privilege does not result in people feeling and being powerful, competent, well, sober, healthy, or peaceful.

7. "Counselors need to enhance themselves personally and professionally by reading and exposing themselves to various artistic art forms" (Lee, 2001). Reading journal articles, blogs, attending films, and cultivating quality relationships with others can inform a professional's sense of another person's culture.

8. Engage in an inventory of your life. Who are the people you invite into your home? What level of comfort do you feel with certain groups of color compared with others? Culture-free service delivery does not exist; therefore, it is impossible to help clients examine cultural identity and self-esteem issues if counselors and psychologists have not done this important work for themselves (Pinderhughes, 1989).

9. Encourage narrative with students as well as their exposure to others. Psychosocial narrative questions that I ask students include the following:
   a. What does it mean to be the race(s) you are?
   b. What impact has spirituality had on your development as a counseling professional?
   c. What did your parents teach you about race and skin color?
   d. What are the privileges and oppression in your life?
   e. How do you feel about the presence and/or absence of privilege and oppression in your life?
   f. Tim Wise (2005) suggests this question for white students, "What does it mean to be White, especially in a nation created by people like you, for people like you?" (p. 2). There is a distinction between a nation created and a nation built—the latter done by unremunerated African slaves and their descendants.

10. Healing racism is an evolving but important process. Ellis (2004) wrote that healing promotes self-discovery, people discovery. Healing also provides a person with the rest needed when involved with race-based information from a personal and historical onslaught of racial inequity.

11. Multicultural competencies and guidelines encourage counselors and psychologists to understand how gender, race, class, sexuality, ethnicity, and nationality intersect in the lives of their clients (Salazar, 2006).

12. Diversity has become a marketing tool—most universities have smiling and happy students, staff, and faculty of color on glossy recruitment brochures. Racial and ethnic diversity does not mean that interpersonal relationships reflect justice, fairness, or have been analyzed according to power, privilege, and inclusion.

Therapists attempting to develop a process that will take into account the impact of culture could follow Hanna and Brown's (1995, p. 101) assessment questions of racial and cultural factors:

1. How does your racial/cultural/religious heritage make your family different from other families you know?

2. Compared with other families in your cultural group, how is your family similar?

3. What did your parents teach you about gender, race, sexuality, immigration, and class?

4. What are the values that your family identified as being important parts of your heritage?

5. At this particular time in your (family's) development, are there issues related to your cultural heritage that are being questioned by anyone?

6. What is the hardest part about being a person of color in this culture? In your family?

7. When you think of living in America versus the country of your heritage, what are the main differences?

8. What lesson did you learn about your people? About other people?

9. What did you learn about disloyalty?

10. What are the privileges and/or oppressions in your family? How does your family feel about their presence and/or absence of privilege/oppression?

11. What were people in your family negative about?

12. Does your spirituality and religion differ from your family's?

13. What might an outsider not understand about your family's racial/cultural/religious background?

Summary

This chapter examined race as a social construction and as a status variable. Other constructs were considered in relationship to race in an effort to provide an understanding of the saliency of race as an identity construct that intersects with other multiple identities. The case study focused on teaching privilege to the privileged, and emphasis was on the instructor in terms of strategies that might facilitate learning and cultural competence development.

13

Converging Biracial and Multiracial Identities

This chapter on converging biracial and multiracial identities explores race as a shifting construct in American society. In doing so, demographic data reflecting increases in biracial and multiracial populations are reviewed. Greater emphasis is given to the foreign-born population. A case study is provided, relevant research is discussed, and stories are presented that emphasize the narrative tradition.

❖ STORYTELLING: MUM

One of the New Zealand mothers in my research with white mothers of nonwhite children witnessed racism in New Zealand that her Maori-white daughter was facing. Her daughter was about 21 at the time and looking for a flat. Her daughter was also pregnant and single. She had brown skin, curly hair, and dark eyes. One day her daughter approached her mother and said, "Mum, you come with me so that I can get the flat." The mother accompanied her daughter to look for an apartment. Her daughter was offered the first apartment she and her mother looked at together. Prior to this, the daughter had searched day after day looking for an apartment but could not get one. The daughter knew that having her mother with her as she looked for an apartment would result in success. The mother, however, had no idea that her daughter was being discriminated against in this way. She wept bitterly as she told this story of injustice.

Definitions

Racial purity is myth. For the purpose of clarity, definitions are provided. The child described in Storytelling: Mum is *biracial*; she is of Maori (Polynesian) and New Zealand/Pakeha (British) heritage. Her mother is white and her father is Maori. As a group, biracial people are also referred to in the literature as "biracials." There is considerable *intraracial* diversity among people from the same racial group. The daughter and her mom are part of an *interracial* family. Their college student neighbors are *monoracial*. One of the men is white—from Australia. His roommate is from Fiji and considers himself to be one of the indigenous Melanesian people; he has dark skin. This student is *bicultural* in that he speaks Fijian, which is an Austronesian language. He also speaks English and some Hindustani because of the large Punjabi population in Fiji. He celebrates his Fijian culture as well as the cultures of many immigrant groups, including Punjabi and Chinese. His girlfriend is Chinese and white. If he marries his girlfriend and they have children, their children will be multiracial, with African, Asian, and Caucasian ancestries.

People may choose an identity that may be inconsistent with others' perceptions. In addition, identities are fluid and can change over time. It is our hope that the world in which these children live will become increasingly *multicultural*. (See Definition Box 13.1: Biracial and Multiracial Definitions.)

Demography

The U.S. Census Bureau documents the reality of increasing numbers of persons who are biracial and multiracial. For the second time since the 2000 Census, in

Biracial and Multiracial Definitions

❖ DEFINITIONS 13.1

1. *Biracial:* A person who has parents from two different racial groups (e.g., a white parent and an Asian parent).

2. *Intraracial:* Within the same racial group.

3. *Interracial family:* A family comprised of people from different races (e.g., a black mother, white father, and biracial children).

4. *Monoracial:* A person who identifies as being from one racial group (e.g., a person who identifies as white).

5. *Bicultural:* A term that is also used to describe one of the acculturation strategies. Can refer to a person who may be bilingual (e.g., speaks Arabic and Hebrew as well as French) (e.g., lives in Montreal, Canada) and practices traditions from more than one culture (e.g., Ramadan and Hanukkah).

6. *Multiracial:* A person with multiple races (e.g., Asian, white, black, and Native American).

2010, people were asked to report one or more of the following races: white, black or African American, American Indian or Alaskan Native (AIAN), Asian, Native Hawaiian or other Pacific Islander, and some other race (SOR).

There were 9.1 million, or 2.9% of the U.S. population, reporting more than one race. About 92% of the people reporting more than one race reported having two races. Eight percent reported three or more, and less than 1% reported more than four races (Humes, Jones, & Ramirez, 2011).

The largest multiple race categories were among four groups: white and black at 20.4%, white and SOR at 19.3%, white and Asian at 18%, white and Indian or Alaskan Native at 15.9%. Nearly half of the American Indian and Alaskan Native population (43.8%) and more than half of the Native Hawaiian and other Pacific Islander population (55.9%) had the highest percentages reporting more than one race (Jones & Bullock, 2012). (See Table 13.1: Two or More Races Population by Combination: 2010.)

People who reported more than one race were considerably younger than the total U.S. population. As stated previously, in 2014, Americans under the age of 5 became majority-minority for the first time (U.S. Census Bureau, 2015a). The median age for two or more races was 23.4 compared with 35.4 for the total U.S. population. Among those reporting two or more races, 25.2% were under the age of 10 compared with 14.1% in the total population. White and black races were particularly young, with 71% of the population under the age of 18 compared with 25% in the general population. More than 2 million Hispanics, or nearly one third of two or more races in the population, reported more than one race; 43% were under 18. Among non-Hispanics, the comparable rate was 24% (Jones & Symens Smith, 2001). The median age for white and black races was 9.7 years. The next youngest was white and Asian, with a median age of 18.1 years.

❖ **Table 13.1**   Two or More Races Population by Combination: 2010

Two or More Racial Groups	Population Total	Population %
White and black	1.83 million	20.4%
White and some other race (SOR)	1.74 million	19.3%
White and Asian	1.62 million	18.0%
White and Indian/Alaskan Native	1.43 million	15.9%
Black and SOR	314,571	3.5%
Black and Indian/Alaskan Native	269,421	3.0%
Asian and SOR	234,462	2.6%
Black and Asian	185,595	2.1%
White and Hawaiian/Pacific Islander	169,991	1.9%
Asian and Hawaiian/Pacific Islander	165,690	1.8%

Source: Jones & Bullock (2012).

About 27% of the total population 15 years of age and older had never been married. Among two or more races, 37.3% had never been married. The group with the lowest never-married rates was white and Native American/Alaskan Native, at 28.3%. Among two or more races, 45.6% were married, compared with 54.4% in the total population. Asian and Native Hawaiian/Pacific Islanders and whites and SOR had higher than average rates of marriage among this group, 50.6% and 50.4% respectively (Jones & Symens Smith, 2001).

More than one half (52.5%) of all households in the United States were maintained by a married couple, compared with slightly less than one half (46.6%) of households with two or more races (Jones, 2005). Two or more races had slightly lower than average separated, widowed, and divorced rates than the total population, 17.1% compared with 18.5%. There was, however, a greater likelihood of female householder families among two or more races compared with the total population. The average is 11.8% compared with 16.3% among two or more races. White and Asian races have lower female householder rates, at 10%. The highest is among black and American Indian/Alaskan Native (29.8%), black and SOR (26.5%), and white and black (25.6%).

People who reported two or more races were more likely to be foreign-born at 24%, compared with 11% of the U.S. population that is foreign-born. About 46% of foreign-born people who reported more than one race entered the United States between 1990 and 2000 (Jones, 2005).

Over the last four decades, there has been a definite increase in interracial and interethnic marriage. Much of this growth is attributed to the number of foreign born people living in the United States, particularly from Asia and Latin America and the Caribbean (Larsen & Walters, 2013).

Between 1980 and 2010, the foreign-born population increased from 14.1 million to 40.0 million. About two thirds (65%) of that increase was due to the growth in the foreign-born population from Latin America and the Caribbean. Over one third of this growth is due to the foreign-born from Asia. More than half (54%) of the foreign-born who arrived before 2005 and 53% of those arriving from 2005 through 2007 were born in Latin America and the Caribbean (Larsen & Walters, 2013). Of the newly arrived foreign-born population, from 2008 or later, only 41% were born in this region (Walters & Trevelyan, 2011). (See Population Box 13.1: Place of Birth of the Newly Arrived Foreign-Born Population.)

Clearly, the foreign-born population has contributed to the racial and ethnic diversity of the United States. This growth has expanded the group of potential spouses for interracial and interethnic marriages, thus increasing the proportion of interracial and interethnic marriages (Larsen & Walters, 2013). It is also possible that this growth has influenced the rate of intermarriage between native and foreign-born people. Researchers have analyzed intermarriage among different racial and ethnic groups, however, much less is known about patterns of intermarriage between persons born in the United States and persons born outside of the United States (Larsen & Walters, 2013).

Nearly 20% of people who reported two or more races had attained a bachelor's degree or higher compared with 24.4% of the total population. White and Asian races had the highest percent, 34.8% with a bachelor's degree or higher. Asian and SOR were the only group with 25% or more of people in the same group with less than a high school diploma and 29.5% with a bachelor's degree or higher. American Indian and SOR had the highest rates of less than a high school diploma at 43.8%, compared with 19.6% in the total population (Jones, 2005).

Compared with the U.S. population 16 and older, the two or more races population had a larger proportion employed in service occupations but a smaller proportion employed in management, professional, and related occupations. White and Asian and white and black and American Indian/Alaskan Native individuals were the most

Population Box 13.1: Place of Birth of the Newly Arrived Foreign-Born Population

Africa: 6.6%

Asia: 40.3%

Europe: 9.1%

Caribbean: 9.4%

Central America: 25.2%

South America: 6.1%

Other regions: 3.3%

Source: Walters & Trevelyan (2011).

likely to hold management, professional, and related occupations at 36.8% and 35.7% respectively. The group with the highest proportion working in service occupations was black and SOR at 27% (Jones, 2005).

A range of median annual earnings exists between the two or more races population and gender. It should be noted that the following data are dated, and while income data are available on persons who report a single race, such data does not appear to be available for people who report two or more races. Although the average earnings for all working males were $37,057, they were $31,035 among men of two or more races, $37,055 among white and Asian men, and $24,665 among American Indian/Alaskan Native/SOR men. The average earnings for all working females were $27,194, about $10,000 less than for men. They were $25,399 among women of two or more races, $29,973 among white and Asian women, and $29,988 among American Indian/Alaskan Native/SOR women (Jones, 2005). White and Asian households had a median family income of $52,413, which was higher than the average for the total population. The next highest were Asian and Native Hawaiian/Pacific Islander at $51,664 and white and Native Hawaiian/Pacific Islander at $45,758.

Surprisingly, in 2014, the poverty rate increased for people with a bachelor's degree or more and married-couple families. For related children under the age of 18 in a household, the poverty rate was 21%. (DeNavas-Walt & Proctor, 2015). (See Table 13.2: Characteristics of Two or More Races and Total Population.)

For people aged 65 and over, the poverty rate was 16.9% for the two or more races population, compared with 10% for the U.S. population (DeNavas-Walt & Proctor, 2015; Jones, 2005). Among children, black and American Indian/Alaskan Native and black and SOR combinations had higher poverty rates than children in other race combinations. White and Asian was the only population in which a larger proportion of the elderly than children lived in poverty, 16.6% compared with 7.5% among white-Asian children.

In the United States, about two thirds of occupied housing units were owner occupied, compared with 46.6% of those occupied by individuals who reported more than one race. Four of the race combinations had home ownership rates of 50% or higher, which is greater than that of the total two or more races population: white and American Indian, 59.6%; Asian and Pacific Islander, 51.9%; white and Pacific Islander, 51.4%; and white and Asian, 50.5%. Black and SOR and white and black householders were the most likely to be renters, at 69.3% and 65.1%, respectively (Jones, 2005).

Because race is a social construction, it is possible that the 2010 Census might have yielded a different estimate of the size of the biracial and multiracial population had an alternative measure been selected than the one given, which was to report one or more of the following races: white, black or African American, Native American or Alaskan Native, Asian, or Native Hawaiian or other Pacific Islander (Harris & Sims, 2002). In other words, who in the household completed the census? Who identifies as multiracial on a daily basis? Whose ancestors come from more than one racial group?

In the 2010 Census, just over one third of the U.S. population reported their race and ethnicity as something other than non-Hispanic white alone. The states with more than 40% minority populations were Arizona, California, the District of Columbia, Florida, Georgia, Hawaii, Maryland, Mississippi, Nevada, New Jersey, New Mexico, and Texas (Humes et al., 2011).

❖ **Table 13.2** Characteristics of Two or More Races and Total Population

Characteristic	Two or More Races	Total Population
Median age	23.4 years	35.4 years
Native born	76.5%	88.9%
Poverty rates of elderly	16.9%	9.9%
Poverty rates of children	21.0%	21.1%
Bachelor's degree	19.6%	24.4%
Never married	37.3%	27.1%
Marriage	45.6%	54.4%
Divorce	17.1%	18.5%
Median-income women	$25,399	$27,194
Median-income men	$31,035	$37,057
Owner-occupied homes	46.6%	66.2%

Source: Adapted from Jones (2005); U.S. Census Bureau (2015b).

California led the nation with the largest minority population (22.3 million), including being the key destination state among the foreign born population (see Population Box 13.2: Traditional Immigrant Destination States). Other states with high numbers of the minority population are as follows: Texas (13.7 million), New York (8.1 million), Florida (7.9 million), and Illinois (4.7 million); (Humes et al., 2011). People with two or more races were most likely to reside in the West, at 40%, with 27% residing in the South, 18% in the Northeast, and 15% in the Midwest.

Population Box 13.2: Traditional Immigrant Destination States

1. California: 10.2 million

2. New York: 4.3 million

3. Texas: 4.1 million

4. Florida: 3.7 million

5. New Jersey: 1.85 million

6. Illinois: 1.8 million

Source: Walters & Trevelyan (2011).

Increases in biraciality are largely linked to reproductive increases in interracial marriage and relationships. Among all newlyweds in 2008, 9% of whites, 16% of blacks, 26% of Hispanics, and 31% of Asians married someone whose race or ethnicity was different from their own (Wang, 2012). Gender patterns in intermarriage vary widely: 22% of all black male newlyweds in 2008 married outside their race, compared with just 9% of black female newlyweds. Among Asians, the gender pattern is altogether different. Forty percent of Asian female newlyweds married outside their race in 2008, compared with just 20% of Asian male newlyweds. Among whites and Hispanics, by contrast, there are no gender differences in intermarriage rates (Wang, 2012).

Among Asians, Japanese American women have the highest rates of outmarriage to whites (Le, 2007; Wang, 2012). More than 38% of Japanese women have white spouses, compared with 27% of Filipino women, 23% of Korean women, 14% of Chinese women, and 11% of Vietnamese women. Asian Indian women at 4.3% are the least likely of all Asian groups to have a white spouse (Passel, Wang, & Taylor, 2010).

The One-Drop Rule

The one-drop rule emerged in the South during slavery and is traditionally understood as disallowing a white identity to anyone who had one-sixteenth black ancestry, regardless of physical appearance. People were considered black or Negro not only if either of their parents was black but also if their only black ancestor was a great grandparent. People who were not considered to be white were classified as Negroes and other races. During this time, race was not simply a social construction, but was steeped in biology. Spickard (1992), a scholar on biracial identity, argued, "The so-called races are not biological categories at all. Rather, they are primarily social divisions that rely only partly on physical markers as skin color to identify group membership" (p. 17).

A caste-like naming system existed. Whites had the most social power, followed by mixed-race and often light-skinned blacks: mulattos (one black parent and one white parent), quadroons (one black grandparent and three white grandparents), and octoroons (one black great grandparent and seven white great grandparents). Darker-skin blacks were on the bottom rung of this ladder (Brunsma & Rockquemore, 2001). Mulattos had one black parent and one white parent, usually a black mother and a white father. Quadroons had one-quarter black blood with one black grandparent.

Social privileges such as indoor housework instead of field work in the hot sun and educational opportunities were provided to offspring of white fathers, which served to create division in the black community and gave rise to colorism. Octoroons had one-eighth black blood or a black great grandparent. They were classified as nonwhite regardless of their phenotypical presentation. Passing was an option, that is, presenting as white, as long as the person did not maintain contact with family members who were counted as and/or identified as black.

Sharfstein (2007) argues that the one-drop rule did not automatically make all mixed-race people black. Communities coexisted with contradiction and allowed people to cross over the color line—not because they were liberals or abolitionists, but because the individual doing the crossing may have held segregationist and antiblack attitudes as well.

Despite changes, the one-drop rule is still alive; however, it is not as pervasive as it used to be (Rockquemore, 2002). Increases in biracial and multiracial populations are different; hybrid identities of race in a post-civil rights movement age contribute to the lessening grip of this antiquated way of defining people's racial identities. Nonetheless, society has difficulty with multiracial individuals' alignment with more than one racial identity. Rigid and binary notions of race are being contested, and the cultural dimensions of race in the United States are shifting (Brunsma, 2006). Biracial and multiracial identities do not obfuscate the construct of race, but they do challenge the one-drop rule that denies a claim to a white identity if a person is also black.

For some, a denial of multiple aspects of their racial and ethnic identities is likely to occur when a monoracial identity is claimed. Within the black community, biracial and multiracial identities have existed since slavery. The one-drop rule, which is cloaked in a racist ideology that assumes racial purity, disallowed other than a Negro identity for people with both white European and black African ancestry.

Mulattos were considered black due to the concept of *hypodescent*, or the process wherein biracial people were assigned to the social group with less social status (e.g., the black mother during slavery). Due to the violence of slavery, black-white offspring conceived during this time were predominantly between black slave women and white slave-owning men, but such was not always the case.

Biracial and mixed-race identities have existed in the black community for centuries. What has not always existed, and is still highly contested, is whether black-white biracial identities occupy a space that is different but not altogether separate from blackness. Claiming a biracial identity is neither a rampant negation of African ancestry nor an unbridled introjection of whiteness, but this fact is not collectively known or believed. Today, there are white people and people of color who resist multiracial identity claims among black-white people.

The elevated social status associated with lighter skin, a characteristic among many monoracial and biracial people, has served to pit black people in this country, and arguably throughout the world, against one another. Some people of color believe that a single racial definition reflects unity and power, while some political groups oppose a multiracial category. There is concern that allocations for school and social-based programs will be adversely affected by a multiracial designation (Schwartz, 1998), that a biracial identity might lead to further divisions among black people, result in a loss of political clout, or be interpreted by the dominant society as biracial people's rejection of blackness in a racist world that already does that.

The Fluidity of Race

Confusion exists as to who is considered multiracial. How past generations racially identified, phenotype, and self-identification have all been used to define multiracial people. Among Native Americans, blood quantum has been considered. The concept of race as fluid suggests it—like class, social experience, and custom—is not static; is shaped by social circumstances, politics, and immigration laws; and extends throughout the developmental life (Hall, 2001; Jacobson, 1998).

Shih and Sanchez (2005) maintain that several approaches exist for understanding multiracial people. One approach is the problem approach, which sees non-monoracial groups as marginal and susceptible to poor psychological outcomes such as low self-esteem and an inferiority complex, lability in mood, and hypersensitivity. The equivalent approach argues that after 1970, there were social movement shifts in the form of civil rights and racial politics. Racial pride was invoked and miscegenation was outlawed. Although racial identity models for monoracial groups were in development, their application to biracial people was deemed appropriate; in reality, this limited applicability to biracial people was shortsighted and did not account for simultaneous identification with more than one racial group.

The variant approach is the most recent approach and views "multiracial identity as a unique category, separate from any monoracial category (e.g., Asian, white, or black)" (Shih & Sanchez, 2005, p. 571). It seems that it is interdisciplinary in focus; draws on sociology, psychology, anthropology, literature, and feminist studies; and encourages the perspective that multiracial people have multiple understandings of their racial identities (Brunsma & Rockquemore, 2001).

Race as a fluid construct is fundamentally different from passing. What would the fluidity of race mean, across contexts (home, school, and work) if biracials neither denied any one identity nor chose to pass as something they were not but were free to racially identify according to context? Would such freedom reflect not just the fluidity of race, but also the fragility of race?

Harris and Sims (2002) examined data from Wave 1 of the National Longitudinal Study of Adolescent Health (Add Health), a school-based, longitudinal study of health behaviors for youth in Grades 7 through 12 collected in 1994 and 1995. More than 83,000 in-school interviews were conducted with students from 80 high schools and 52 middle schools. In addition, this study was conducted in the home with more than 18,000 youth from the school sample. Finally, in-home interviews were conducted with a primary caregiver of each of the youth interviewed at home. All children who identified as Hispanic were excluded, as Hispanicity is deemed separate from race. The sample was also restricted to youth sampled both at school and at home.

Great variation in patterns of expressed internal race for multiracial populations was found. Among white-black, 0.6% identify as white and black at home and at school. White and Asian students did not differ between the school and home interviews in terms of their identities. However, white-Native American youth were different. More than 2% identified as white and Native American at school, yet a smaller share (1.5%) claimed a white-Native American identity at home. The researchers concluded that with "respect to racial self-identification, there is not a single multiracial experience" (Harris & Sims, 2002, p. 618). That racial identities are fluid was concluded: 87.6% of adolescents expressed identical racial identities across contexts. Furthermore, 8.6% of youth reported being multiracial at home and 1.6% identified as multiracial in both contexts, across home and school. Geographical context is important to consider. In the South, white-black youth were less likely to select white as their best single race.

Other people's interpretations and evaluations of a biracial person's appearance may place parameters on racial self-understanding (Brunsma & Rockquemore, 2001).

Racial Socialization

Previous research has revealed that talk focused on coming from a good family, getting a good education, being a good person, and possessing a belief that one is just as good as anyone else characterizes white mothers' discussions with their nonwhite children (Robinson-Wood, 2010a; 2011). Black parents deliver similar humanistic/egalitarianistic messages to their monoracial black children; however, racial content is often at the center due to the daunting task among black parents of helping children contend with racial inequality.

Historically, the majority of racial socialization research has occurred with black American families (Frabutt, Walker, & MacKinnon-Lewis, 2002; Hughes et al., 2006; White-Johnson, Ford, & Sellers, 2010). In addition to statements from parents given to children about their minority status, Hughes et al. (2006) addressed the presence of egalitarianism (e.g., orienting youth toward developing skills and characteristics needed to thrive in mainstream and dominant settings) among black parents where children are taught to develop skills and embody characteristics (e.g., hard work, self-regard).

Racial socialization and cultural socialization overlap and refer to racially and ethnically diverse parents' practices whereby children are taught about and encouraged to promote their heritage and cultural traditions. Examples include relevant books, stories, ethnic foods, and learning and speaking the family's native language (Hughes et al., 2006). The research on the relationship between racial socialization and youth behavioral outcomes is modest, although cultural pride, an aspect of racial socialization, may have a positive effect. Strategies that focus primarily on racial barriers are associated with negative outcomes (Hughes et al., 2006; Rodriguez, McKay, & Bannon, 2008).

In their analysis of maternal race and racial socialization messages, Rollins and Hunter (2013) employed a quantitative methodology. There were 73 biological mothers of biracial children in their sample taken from a 1991 public-use subsample (Wave I) of the longitudinal Maryland Adolescent Development in Context Study. Forty-two percent of mothers racially identified themselves as black, 40% as white, 11% were Asian, 4% were Latino, 1.4% were Native, and 1.4% identified as other. Nearly 1,500 families with a 12- or 13-year-old child attending public schools were in the original sample. From their thematic analysis of mothers' racial socialization messages, Rollins and Hunter (2013) identified three approaches. These approaches were labeled *promotive*, *protective*, and *passive*. With promotive racial socialization, mothers emphasize equality and encourage a color-blind worldview. There is no preparation for or direct teaching about racial discrimination. A protective racial socialization approach prepares children for racial discrimination; children are encouraged to be the best they can be. Children are given a sense of self as a member of a racial group and are taught to stand up for their rights but to be respectful. Mothers characterized by a passive racial socialization approach either do nothing to prepare their children for discrimination or did not answer the question posed by the interviewer. Although racial socialization approaches did not vary by maternal race, mothers of black and white biracial children engaged least frequently in silent racial socialization messages.

Rollins and Hunter (2013) concluded that black parents of biracial children may be more aware of the role that skin color plays in society whereas parents of non-black biracial children (e.g., Eurasian or Latino) may not have encountered negative racial experiences with their child. Black parents seemed to have awareness of their children's racialized experiences, an awareness that may not have been present among parents of racially ambiguous children (Robinson-Wood, 2015).

Research on ethnic socialization began with the lived experiences of immigrant populations (Latinos, Asians, and to some extent African and Caribbean groups residing in America). The focus was on children's maintenance of culture and group affiliation given assimilation pressures in the United States (Hughes et al., 2006). A tendency for some black parents from the Caribbean to distinguish themselves and their children from native-born black Americans due to lower social status and perceptions of undesirable characteristics has been documented in the literature and speaks to a promotion of mistrust as part of the ethnic-racial socialization process (Hughes et al., 2006; Waters, 1994).

Multiracial and Biracial Identity Development

Brunsma and Rockquemore (2001) conducted research with 177 white and black biracials (people with one black parent and one white parent) to assess racial identification. Four identities were identified in previous research by Rockquemore (1999):

1. Singular identity (singular black and white)

2. Border identity (exclusively biracial)

3. Protean identity (sometimes black, sometimes white, sometimes biracial)

4. Transcendent identity (no racial identity)

In Brunsma and Rockquemore (2001, p. 32), respondents were asked, "Which of the following statements best describes yourself exclusively?"

1. I consider myself Black (or African American).

2. I sometimes consider myself Black, sometimes my other race, and sometimes biracial depending on the circumstances.

3. I consider myself biracial, but I experience the world as a Black person.

4. I consider myself exclusively as Biracial (neither Black nor White).

5. I consider myself exclusively as my other race (not Black or biracial).

6. Race is meaningless; I do not believe in racial identity.

7. Other

Phenotype (skin color), appearance, and interactional experiences (preadult racial composition and negative treatment from whites and blacks) were queried. The majority of respondents (56.2%), despite a variety of skin color hues, defined themselves as "ambiguous though most people assume I am black," (Brunsma & Rockquemore, 2001, p. 38). Seventeen percent stated they "appear black, most people assume I am Black" and nearly 17% stated, "Ambiguous, most people do not assume I am black." Ten percent said they "appear White, I could pass as white."

The majority of the sample considered themselves to have border identities, in that they understood themselves as neither black nor white but as exclusively biracial. Although this identification is the case, most of the border biracials said they experience the world as a black person. Their experience as exclusively biracial is not validated by others in interactions. Only 14% of the sample saw themselves as exclusively black. The same percentage did not apply racial labels to themselves and is considered to be a transcendent identity or with no racial self-understanding. Five percent saw themselves shifting among black, white, and biracial identities, depending on the circumstances. This way of casting one's identity is referred to as a protean identity. Nearly 4% saw themselves as singularly white.

Wijeyesinghe (2001) presented a factor model of multiracial identity developed from a qualitative study of African American–European American multiracial adults. This model is nonlinear and represents factors or dimensions of identity. These dimensions include the following:

- Racial ancestry or family tree
- Early experiences and socialization, which includes exposure to culture, such as food, music, holiday, dialect, and language
- Cultural attachment that may influence racial designation
- Physical appearance, which includes skin hue, body shape, and hair texture
- Social and historical context, such as the presence of other multiracial people or the 2000 census allowing people to choose more than one box to designate themselves racially/ethnically
- Political awareness and orientation, which is connected to the awareness of race and racism within a larger sociopolitical context
- Other social identities, such as sexual orientation and social class
- Spirituality or being guided by spirit, which fosters connection to others and allows people to transcend the divisions of race and ethnicity

Kich (1992) developed a three-stage biracial model for Japanese and white Americans from semistructured interviews with 15 biracial adults. The first stage is awareness of differentness and dissonance between self-perceptions and the perceptions from other people. Biracial people are seen as different. Dissonance or discomfort about this difference can occur when the comparison process is regarded as devaluation. The second stage, struggle for acceptance from others, can extend into adulthood and often occurs in the context of school or community settings. In cases where a biracial person is the only one in a particular context, the question "What are you?" may be asked, especially in light of differences in the person's name or phenotype. The final stage is self-acceptance and assertion of an interracial identity. Kich

(1992) says, "The biracial person's ability to create congruent self-definitions rather than be determined by others' definitions and stereotypes may be said to be the major achievement of a biracial and bicultural identity" (p. 314).

Kich (1992) also discussed the ways in which biracial Japanese Americans achieved a sense of identity development. Some traveled to Japan and learned the language. Others met and spoke with extended family members who may have been less emotionally available in the past. Others who had endorsed the European American community exclusively may have explored their Japanese heritage anew or for the first time.

It is not uncommon for biracial persons to struggle with reconciling their various identities. (See Storytelling: Birthday Party.) According to Mass (1992), Japanese people in Los Angeles had higher rates of outmarriages compared with other Asian groups. In a study conducted among interracial Japanese Americans, Mass (1992) sampled 53 college-age white and Japanese respondents and 52 monoracial Japanese American college students. She measured ethnic identity, acculturation, self-concept, and the Japanese American ethnic experience and then administered a personality inventory. No differences in the psychological adjustment and self-esteem of the two groups were found. However, it was discovered that interracial Japanese Americans showed less identification with being Japanese than monoracial Japanese Americans. Japanese Americans who were raised in parts of the country (Hawaii and certain California communities) where there were larger numbers of Japanese Americans tended to have few or no problems with race.

❖ **STORYTELLING: BIRTHDAY PARTY**

A 7-year-old is invited to a classmate's birthday party. She had a lovely time. When the party was over, the child's black mother picked her up. In class on Monday, the little boy, from Argentina, said to the biracial child (black mother and Puerto Rican father), "I would have never invited you to my birthday party if I had known you were black."

Source: Adapted from Rivera (1999).

Poston (1990) proposed a model of biracial identity development with five linear stages: (1) personal identity, (2) choice of group categorization, (3) enmeshment/denial, (4) appreciation, and (5) integration. Stage 1 is the initial step in the identity process and is seen among young children who have not developed group self-esteem. Choice of group categorization (Stage 2) consists of persons choosing a racial group to identify with. Ethnic background, neighborhood, and social support are factors that can influence this choice. Stage 3 represents upheaval and confusion about choosing a group with which to identify. Feelings of being betwixt and between can characterize people who may not feel acceptance from either group. Learning to accept their multiple identities describes Stage 4, and Stage 5 is an integrated place where people are able to celebrate all of who they are.

Research and Biracial and Multiracial Populations

Although more research is being conducted, there is a dearth of empirical research on multiracial populations (Herman, 2004). Shih and Sanchez (2005) observed that much of the work done was on investigating the psychological impact of having a multiracial identity and the difficulty that multiracial people had in defining a racial identity. There have been difficulties with sample size, methodological issues such as randomization in sampling, and problems with self-report inventories (Herman, 2004). Qualitative research may be best suited for research on biracial and multi-ethnic populations given that it allows the researcher "to enter the subjective world of other people and groups through interviews and rich descriptions, which is not achieved through quantitative methods" (Jourdan, 2006, p. 330).

George and Ward (2013) conducted qualitative interviews with 23 white mothers of Chinese-born adopted girls. Mothers discussed the contours of their daughters' lives in China prior to adoption: poverty, draconian albeit now eliminated One Child Family Policy, and patriarchy, despite the fact that the mothers had very little biographic information on their daughters. In an effort to establish solidarity with their Chinese daughters, mothers invoked their ethnic differences (European-born, being Jewish, dark-haired, large bodied, and being too tall). Seeking to connect with their daughters, mothers seemed to reinforce similarities between themselves and their phenotypically-visible Chinese girls, which may contribute to daughters' learning not to see or minimizing their experiences with difference as Chinese adoptees in a white family. George and Ward encourage mothers to realize that Chinese girls have been denied the privilege of telling their own adoption story due to the visible racial difference between themselves and their white mothers. Together, mothers and their daughters can construct a narrative that integrates the various components of their story.

Ho, Sidanius, Levin, and Banaji (2011) examined whether the rule of hypodescent, whereby biracial individuals are assigned the status of their socially subordinate parent group, would govern perceptions of Asian-white and black-white targets. Across five experiments using speeded tasks, a face morphing program, and a family tree, the researchers confirmed the rule of hypodescent that reflected the racial hierarchy in the United States.

Theoretical sampling is a critical concept in qualitative research and refers to the research participants' contribution to the study with less emphasis on numbers. Qualitative methodologies, such as semistructured interviews, are ideal for research with multiracial populations in that they allow for a broader and more in-depth exploration of mixed-race people's life experiences while allowing the researcher to develop hypotheses for future studies from a contextual and cultural perspective (Collins, 2000).

Biracial Identity Development

The majority of the research conducted on biracial populations has focused on children and teens. Until recently, this literature has been scarce. Concerns about identity diffusion, low self-esteem, academic difficulties, and heightened risk of problem behaviors among multiracial children have been feared, found, and/or predicted (Choi, Harachi, Gillmore, & Catalano, 2006; Kerwin, Ponterotto, Jackson, & Harris, 1993; Gibbs & Hines, 1992).

Although the focus was on adults, Miville, Constantine, Baysden, and So-Lloyd (2005) conducted a qualitative investigation with 10 self-identified biracial and multiracial individuals. People were asked to describe their experiences with growing up, a time when the person first became aware of racial group membership, general observations about monoracial and multiracial people, and joys and hardships related to being multiracial. Four essential themes related to identity development were found:

1. Encounters with racism

2. Racial identity label and/or reference group orientation

3. The "chameleon" experience

4. Identity development in context

Encounters With Racism. This research found that all participants had encounters with or experiences of racism that facilitated their understanding of racial group membership. Being asked the question "What are you?" was common fare for these participants, as were encounters with "monocultural" racism through work or other contexts.

Reference Group Orientation. Participants discussed their racial or ethnic label, such as Puerto Rican or Asian, but also saw themselves as multiracial. Identification as a person of color facilitated community building, racial intimacy and pride, and social support networking. Some participants also talked of feeling alienated by groups with whom they were unable to fit.

The Chameleon Experience. The importance of strategies to negotiate their multiple racial identity was a finding from this research. The ability to be flexible across rigid social boundaries was seen as an advantage, although a sense of not belonging to any group was echoed by some.

Identity Development in Context: Critical People, Critical Places, Critical Period. Parents were cited as the most influential people in participants' lives regarding the expression of their racial identity. The authors said, "In general, it seemed that participants adopted the racial-ethnic label of the parent to whom they felt emotionally closest or whom they viewed as most dominant in the household" (Miville et al., 2005, pp. 512–513). Social settings were identified as possibly playing a major role in the development of a positive racial identity with respect to acceptance or tension. Critical periods were connected to elementary school, high school, and college.

Rockquemore (2002) conducted in-depth, loosely structured, qualitative interviews with 16 black-white biracial respondents. The primary theme that emerged was negative interactions with monoracial African Americans. (See Storytelling: Assumptions.) Women were more likely than men to report negative interactions. The content of these encounters was typically related to physical appearance, such as skin color, body size, and eye color. Competition for black men was discussed. That black women have fewer eligible suitors given that successful black men are just as likely to marry inside and outside of their race has to be considered within the context of this finding. The internalization of negative messages among some of the biracial women in the sample was identified. Black people were broadly characterized as being on drugs, without jobs, and ill-mannered. Many of the respondents were raised by white women.

❖ **STORYTELLING: ASSUMPTIONS**

One of the mothers in my research with white mothers of nonwhite children, along with her husband, had adopted two black-white biracial children. She was at the grocery store one day with her children and noticed that the checkout clerk, a young black woman, seemed to be hostile toward her. She chalked it up to her having a bad day. The same experience occurred when she took her children to buy school clothes. She reflected on these events during our interview and said that it actually happened a lot. I asked her if she thought the women had made an assumption that she was the biological mother of these children, which meant their father was a black man. She nodded and concluded that this may explain their attitude. While many white mothers speak of close family ties, negative interactions from black and Maori women toward them, even women who have adopted children or single lesbians, has been discussed in my research.

Skin color is no small issue within society and impacts dating, mating, money, and politics. Hochschild and Weaver (2007) noted that Americans across and within racial or ethnic groups attribute more favorable characteristics to people who have lighter skin tones and often believe that others also deem light skin as more attractive than dark skin. They also note that dark skinned blacks in the United States have "lower socioeconomic status, more punitive relationships with the criminal justice system, diminished prestige, and less likelihood of holding elective office compared with their lighter counterparts" (Hochschild & Weaver, p. 643).

Implications for Mental Health Professionals

Two identity tasks face biracial people: (1) distinguishing how others see them from how they personally experience themselves, and (2) developing a sense of belonging (Gillem, Lincoln, & English, 2007). Some of the early research suggested that biracial children had a high incidence of academic and behavioral problems presumed to be connected to identity conflicts and related challenges (Gibbs, Huang, & Associates, 1989). Santiago-Rivera, Arredondo, and Gallardo-Cooper (2002) encouraged parents of bicultural children not to impose their culture on the child, particularly adolescents. It is suggested that children will internalize a variety of experiences and beliefs into their own value system that encompasses multiple identities and worldviews.

Shih and Sanchez (2005) cautioned researchers who study clinical samples to apply these findings to nonclinical samples. In their review of multiracial literature, multiracial persons in the general population were not more dissatisfied, unhappy, or uncomfortable with their racial identity. In their analysis of Add Health data comparing mixed-race adolescents to single-race adolescents, Udry, Li, and Hendrickson-Smith (2003) concluded adolescents who identify with more than one race were at a higher health and behavior risk when compared with adolescents identifying with only one race. The risk may be related to the stress associated with identity conflict. Without direct evidence, the researchers cautioned against jumping to conclusions.

Schwartz (1998) observed that the racial identity development of multiracial youth is more complicated than for monoracial youth. Herman (2004) affirmed the ethnic identity research, which suggests there are opportunities associated with identity development. Although there is societal racism (negative feelings about interracial marriages) and families that do not emphasize race, children come to see prejudice and racism in society. In addition, some children may feel enormous conflict about choosing one racial identity over another based on the child's phenotype, neighborhood, or, in the case of divorce, the race of the custodial parent. Socialization of children to embrace a biracial or multiracial identity communicates to a child the value and importance of all of his or her racial and ethnic identities.

Although more complicated, the experience of identity formation can be a positive and affirming experience (Herman, 2004). Treating race as a social construction as opposed to a biological one was found by Shih, Bonam, Sanchez, and Peck (2007) to help buffer people from stereotype threat effects.

Being biracial or multiracial is not equivalent with having emotional difficulties or interpersonal challenges. Nurturing homes with emotionally involved parents can provide a foundation for stability, self-cohesiveness, and attributes associated with a healthy sense of self (Hud-Aleem, Countryman, & Gillig, 2008). People who are biracial or multiracial may contend with intrusive questions, such as "what are you?" as well as with stares. Moreover, among school age children, unfavorable reactions from classmates and even teachers can exacerbate a child's sense of not belonging or difference from others, particularly in areas where racial and ethnic diversity are less common, such as in parts of the midwest and in New England.

Case Study

A Child's Abandonment, Sadness, and Anger

Hayden is an 11-year-old boy who lives with his father, Len. His mother, Shera, lives elsewhere with two of her other children. She told Len that he needed to take care of Hayden; Shera has other children she is raising. Hayden's siblings have a different father. Len is biracial (Cuban and Haitian) and was born and raised in Florida. Shera is Eurasian (White and Chinese). She was born and raised in New York. Len took Hayden to counseling because his behavior changed dramatically once his mother stopped caring for him. Hayden's grades have fallen—to the point where the teacher has told Len that Hayden will most likely have to repeat sixth grade. Hayden has also been caught speaking negatively about some of his Asian classmates. Hayden resents when he is mistaken as Latino. When asked about his race, he says he is Italian. Some children at school have accused Hayden of lying about his race. Hayden begins to cry when he speaks about his mother during therapy and yet does so with disdain and anger. Ama, the counselor, is Japanese American. Ama's husband is white, and their children are biracial. Len was attracted to Ama as a counselor given her clinical emphasis on biracial children, interracial families, and identity development. Ama senses hostility from Hayden. Len reacts with embarrassment when his son behaves rudely to Ama. Len says he acts like this with his teachers. Hayden interjected, "Not all of them" as he glares angrily at Ama. Len mentioned that Shera has a problem with alcohol and was told that if she kept drinking, she would eventually lose custody of her younger children as well. Len stated that Shera's alcohol problem was responsible for their relationship failing.

Questions

1. What are the implications for therapeutic effectiveness when the counselor is the same race as the young client's mother with whom he has an estranged relationship?

2. How does the multiculturally competent therapist discuss race related issues when in therapy with children?

Discussion and Integration

The Client, Hayden

There are multiple issues in Hayden's life. He feels rejection from his mother. He is understandably saddened and angry at his mother for choosing to raise her other children over him. He may have difficulty identifying with his mother from whom he feels alienated and estranged. Robinson-Wood (2010a) found that some biracial children have difficulty racially identifying with a parent who had abandoned the family or who had been violent within the family. While a history of physical violence does not apply to Hayden, he elevates whiteness and appears to harbor negative feelings toward Asians.

According to Spencer (1985), this tendency of elevating whiteness has been found in black preschool age children but tends to change as children age. Ama realizes that underneath Hayden's anger is confusion and sadness—from feeling abandoned by his mother while desiring a relationship with her. His hostility toward Ama can be used clinically by Ama in understanding Hayden's conflict with his mother. Although Hayden is young, he can be helped to explore his feelings about race. Ama senses that his bullying of Asian children is connected to his anger at his Asian mother and the disruption of the maternal bond when Shera sent Hayden to be raised by his father.

The term *double* is not applicable to Hayden. "Double denotes those who have a positive reflection of their identity based on the coexistence of their ethnicities" (Collins, 2000, p. 126). Hayden has not yet created an identity that is more than the sum of its parts regarding his multiracial identities as white, Asian, Latino, and black. Lee and Beal (2007) conducted interviews and found that multiracial blacks were not as likely as Asians and Latinos to identify multiracially largely because of other people's ascriptions of them as black only.

Choi, Harachi, Gillmore, and Catalano (2006) found that multiracial youth are at greater risk for substance use and engaging in violence than monoracial youths. Perceived racial discrimination may be an additional risk for multiracial youths. However, stronger and more positive ethnic identity may function as a protective factor, particularly as it relates to the frequency of substance use and violence. These findings are important to consider clinically, given that Hayden is a preteen, multiracial boy who looks like a person of color with a family history of substance use and maternal neglect.

The Therapist, Ama

To competently respond to clients' issues associated with race as a personal identity and social construct, Ama's awareness of her own racial identity is a benefit. Her understanding of the literature regarding biracial children and clinical issues that can arise for them is also a plus to Hayden and Len and the other families she serves—many who are interracial families with biracial and multiracial children. For example, Ama knows that the racial identity development of biracial people is more complicated than for monoracial youth. Some biracial children are psychologically conflicted about choosing one racial identity over another based on the child's phenotype (e.g., skin color, hair texture, shape of facial features), neighborhood, or in the case of divorce, the race of the custodial parent (Poston, 1990).

Hayden's bullying behavior and racial name calling of Asian children could be a reflection of his displaced anger toward his Eurasian mother. A parent's silence about race and racism will not protect a child from experiencing racism (Robinson-Wood, 2010a) or in Hayden's case, perpetuating racism.

Ama has a developed sense of her multiple identities as a Japanese woman, a mother, wife, both in professional communities and in her interracial marriage. Collins (2000) found in her qualitative research with Japanese-white individuals who grew up in predominantly white neighborhoods, that they did not acknowledge their Japanese ethnicity, did not have the opportunity to socialize with other biracial children, and their self-definition was thus devalued. As children grow and seek to belong to others, exclusion from groups may become an issue. Physical appearance, stereotyping, or being given a message that you are excluded from a desired group can provoke dissonance about where a person belongs and even encourage attempts to belong to the excluded group (Ahnallen, Suyemoto, & Carter, 2006). This information is helpful to Ama as she processes Hayden's relationship to race.

Root (1998) investigated 20 sibling pairs. She found that hazing was reported as an experience among many of these siblings. Root (1998) referred to hazing as "an injunction to prove one is an insider through a demeaning process of racial and ethnic authenticity testing" (pp. 242–243). Although children are believed to benefit when parents discuss race as a component of identity, Root (1998) stated that there are times when family dysfunction (abuse and addiction) result in racial themes not being salient. Addiction is part of Hayden's family dynamic.

Ama's children are biracial and are being raised to be bicultural. Biculturally identified people take pride in cultural traditions from both ethnic and racial groups. Despite differences in her sons' appearances, Suzuki-Crumly and Hyers (2004) state that Asian-white biracials may be less noticeably nonwhite and more ambiguous in their appearance than black-white biracials. Ama notes that Hayden looks like a child of color, which makes his attestations of being Italian, despite the dark features of many Italians, to be a source of confusion for some of the children at his school. In time, Ama plans to disclose to Hayden that she, too, has children who have parents of different races.

The following recommendations from Hud-Aleem et al. (2008) may be helpful to Hayden and to other biracial or multiracial children: (1) The creation of a cultural genogram with coping strategies, child-rearing practices, strengths, and challenge from both sides of Hayden's families; (2) establish a sense of identity as an interracial family; (3) Len's recognition that his bicultural identities as a Cuban-Haitain man differ from his son's multiracial identities; (4) encourage Hayden to interact with other children who are biracial or multiracial; and (5) support Hayden's development of a sense of pride of his rich quadruple heritages.

As a multicultural competent therapist, Ama is aware of her Asian enculturation as well as her white and Asian children's biraciality. She keeps a copy of Maria P. P. Root's (1993) *Bill of Rights for Racially Mixed People* on her wall, which begins as,

I have the right

not to justify my existence in this world

not to keep the races separate within me

not to be responsible for people's discomfort with my physical ambiguity

not to justify my ethnic legitimacy

I have the right

to identify myself differently than strangers expect me to identify

to identify myself differently than how my parents identify me

to identify myself differently than my brothers and sisters

to identify myself differently in different situations

Summary

This chapter provided several definitions, including definitions for biracial, multiracial, bicultural, intraracial, and interracial. Research on biracial and multiracial populations was highlighted, and a discussion of research methodologies was examined. The political nature of the topic of race and biracial identities was a theme throughout the chapter. A case study of an 11-year-old multiracial child was presented as a means of integrating relevant literature on multiple identities as well as the clinical literature.

14

Converging Gender

❖

TOPICS COVERED IN THIS CHAPTER

- **Gender Definitions**
- **Gender and Biology**
- **The Social Construction of Gender**
- **Undoing Gender**
- **Sex and Gender Roles**
- **Gender and Emotion**
- **Gender and the Body**
- **Gender and Experiences in Therapy**
- **Gender Identity Models**
  - ○ **The Womanist Model**
  - ○ **White Male Identity Development Model**
- **Implications for Mental Health Professionals**
- **Case Study**
- **Summary**

Black men and women brought to the Americas as slaves suffered an oppression that lasted for 4 centuries and continued after slavery was abolished. White women suffered oppression as well. Legally, albeit immorally, they were denied their own wages, unable to vote, and were objects. It was even against the law to have a child outside of wedlock. Women were not allowed to speak publicly and were encouraged to be compliant, to entertain their men, and to be chaste. Laws from the English that were unduly influenced by Christian doctrine dictated women's place. Women won the right to vote in 1919, but their cries regarding their inequality were heard in the 18th century. Women resisted their subjugation and demanded to be seen as equals, spoke out in churches, refused to take their husband's name, organized meetings, received medical degrees, resisted slavery, founded schools, created clothing for women (e.g., bloomers), and wrote books and poetry. It was a long struggle of resistance and persistence. Lucy Stone, Elizabeth Cady Stanton, Lucretia Mott, Elizabeth Blackwell, Dorothea Dix, Harriet Tubman, and Sarah and Angelina Grimke were some of the courageous heroines who resisted society's refusal, from men and women alike, to honor their voice and vote.

According to Zinn (2003), the wife of one of the early presidents asked him to recognize women and give them the vote. It is said that he reminded her of the constitution, that all *men* were created equal. The majority of today's college students are women who often have no sense of the struggles that women have endured in order for them to vote, wear shorts, choose who they wish to marry (if at all), buy a home in their own names and live in it by themselves.

Gender is a social construct and a status characteristic. It is acknowledged that gender differences exist among people and within groups of people. This truth is neither refuted nor regarded as problematic. However, the way gender inequity is perpetuated as a primary status characteristic within society is examined. Selected literature is presented that examines relationships with the self and others as a function of gender, gender roles, and sex role typology. The subsequent impact on gender identity is also investigated, as is gender from a biological perspective.

Gender Definitions

Sex roles and *gender roles* differ. Typically, sex roles are behavioral patterns culturally approved as more appropriate for either males or females (Worell & Remer, 1992); however, in this work, sex roles refer to roles related to the function of one's biology, such as erection, ejaculation, menstruation, ovulation, pregnancy, and lactation. Gender roles are a consequence of society's views regarding appropriate behavior based on one's biological sex, such as diaper changing, snow removal, leaf blowing, bill paying, and primary breadwinning. Gender labels are applied to people, and once done, people behave toward an individual based on a set of expectations held for persons who have the same label. A role is a cluster of expectations for behavior of persons within a specific category.

The meaning of *gender* varies among different cultures and changes throughout time (McCarthy & Holiday, 2004). The most common definition is the culturally determined attitudes, cognitions, and belief systems about females and males. Haider (1995) said, "The focus of gender is on social roles and interactions of women and men rather than their biological characteristics which is sex . . . gender is a matter of cultural definition as to what is considered to be masculine or feminine" (p. 35). The male gender role affirms masculine identity around qualities such as self-reliance and success. For women, it is feminine characteristics traditionally associated with noncompetitiveness and care of others. The negative consequences of gender role restriction is termed *gender role conflict* (Lane & Addis, 2005) and "describes the detrimental consequences of gender roles either for the person holding them or for those associated with this person" (Mintz & O'Neil, 1990, p. 381).

Masculinity refers to traditional societal roles, behaviors, and attitudes prescribed for men, whereas *femininity* references traditional societal roles, behaviors, and attitudes prescribed for women (Mintz & O'Neil, 1990). Masculinity is construed with hegemonic power and men's dominance over women; however, men are dependent on women and perceive women as having expressive power over them or the power to express emotion (Pleck, 1984). Another form of power that women are perceived to have over men is *masculinity validating power*, or men's dependence on women to affirm their masculinity and validate their manhood. A system of this nature reinforces heterosexism in its dependence on rigid adherence to gender and sex role—appropriate behaviors that operate exclusively in the context of heterosexuality, or the semblance of heterosexuality, and gender conformity. West and Zimmerman (1991) said, "Not only do we want to know the sex category of those around us (to see it at a glance, perhaps), but we presume that others are displaying it for us in as decisive a fashion as they can" (p. 21).

Androcentrism refers to males at the center of the universe, looking out at reality from behind their own eyes and describing what they see from an egocentric—or androcentric—point of view (Bem, 1993).

Gender and Biology

In each human body cell, chromosomes are the genetic material carried. Except for the reproductive cells (sperm and ova) and mature red blood cells, each cell has 46 chromosomes arranged into 23 pairs. Twenty-two pairs of chromosomes, called *autosomes*, are matching sets in both males and females. The 23rd pair, called *sex chromosomes*, differs between the two sexes. Among "genetically normal" males, the sex chromosomes are XY; among "genetically normal" females, they are XX (Moir & Jessel, 1991).

From conception to about the 6th week in utero, all human embryos are anatomically identical. During the 6th week, sexual differentiation begins. The genetic information in the Y chromosome stimulates the production of a protein called *H-Y antigen*. This protein promotes the change of the undifferentiated gonads into fetal testes. The fetal testes synthesize myriad hormones known as *androgens*. Two important androgens are *Mullerian inhibiting substance (MIS)* and *testosterone*. MIS is involved in the degeneration of the female duct system (Renzetti & Curran, 1992). Testosterone promotes further growth of the male Wolffian duct, the duct system that leaves the testes. Testosterone is often referred to as the aggression, dominance, and sex hormone (Moir & Jessel, 1991).

In the 8th week, the hormone dihydrotestosterone encourages the formation of external genitals. It is suggested that, for the female, the lack of testosterone may prompt the undifferentiated gonads of an XX embryo to transform into ovaries around the 12th week of gestation (Renzetti & Curran, 1992).

The Social Construction of Gender

Gender is a crucial part of our daily lives. It takes deviation from gender conformity to get people to notice the undoing of gender. Gender influences what we believe about ourselves and others. Across race, class, culture, disability, and sexuality, common gender themes seem to exist for men and women. Among people of color, gender is often obscured by race, in that race vies for more attention as the salient identity construct.

Gender is a status characteristic that manifests in dominant and multiple ways (See Storytelling: Caring for Children). For the most part, males tend to enter into the world as the preferred sex and are accorded power within a patriarchal society. Because gender intersects with sexuality, class, and race, some men in society have more power than others and less power than some women. Clearly, not all men feel powerful and exert power over all women within a system of male supremacy. There are women, who by virtue of their race, nationality, skin color, able-body, and class privileges, exert power over some men and other women. Men operate as both the oppressed and the oppressor (McCarthy & Holliday, 2004). An androcentric culture exists and dictates for both women and men images and standards of acceptability, which influence body image and self-esteem. And there are people who do not identify as either male or female.

The devaluation of women and the esteem given to men is culturally rooted. Saucier (2004) noted that "women are set up to fail in a system that defines success for men in terms of productivity and accomplishment and designates beauty and sexiness as the measure of success for women" (p. 420). The process of preparing boys to be masculine men and girls to be feminine women is largely an unconscious one within the culture. The family influences children in their most important identity formation, the gender role. Socializing influences include parents, grandparents, the extended family, teachers, the media, other children, and textbooks. Evans and Davies (2000) found in their examination of first-, third-, and fifth-grade literature textbooks that despite publisher's guidelines and Title IX, males are still portrayed in stereotypical ways: to be aggressive, argumentative, and competitive.

❖ **STORYTELLING: CARING FOR CHILDREN**

I know a woman who hired a babysitter to care for her young children while she was attending a staff meeting. The sitter sat with the children in the hallway near the woman's meeting. One of the children was fussy, so the mother brought the child into the meeting. The child played quietly. Eventually, the mother returned the child to the sitter, but the other child began to fuss, so the woman brought this child in.

The sitter was in the hallway with the other child. Several of the woman's coworkers commented on how quiet the children were. This staff meeting was the 2nd of nearly 50 that the woman had brought her children to. The woman received the following e-mail from her male supervisor 2 days later. The year is 2011:

I would like to give you some feedback regarding child care during meetings, and

❖ STORYTELLING: CARING FOR CHILDREN

I hope that you will take my feedback as constructive, rather than critical. I believe it must be a challenge balancing child care and work responsibilities. I noticed that you have brought your child or children to several meetings on campus (e.g., meeting with me or more recently staff members). I think in general it is a good practice to communicate about your child care plan with the faculty members with whom you are meeting, or at least the chair of the meeting, prior to bringing your child(ren) to the meeting. The advance communication and request will be respectful for all. As for me, I would prefer not to have children present when I am having formal meetings with staff. I also think that it is not appropriate to have children at our monthly staff meeting. I hope that you are able to find child care help during those meetings, and I suggest that you look into what the company has to offer regarding child care. I understand that this feedback likely is not pleasant to hear, when you have to juggle so many things. I do hope you understand that meetings involve other people, and we want

to be mutually respectful and productive in meetings. Please let me know if you have any question or concern. Thank you for listening.

In sharing the e-mail with others, the woman heard stories. One woman had been criticized for taking too much time for prenatal visits; she eventually resigned her job. Another woman, during her third trimester of pregnancy, asked her professor if he would get a laptop and video Skype her in so that she could participate in classroom discussions. Her doctor did not want her traveling the lengthy distance between home and school. The professor stated that the department did not have the resources to accommodate her request, and he neither tried to help nor did he offer solutions. A fellow student helped the woman by skyping her in for every class. Another woman talked about how a colleague of hers brought her young child to meetings. She said, "Nobody minded—we understood that she was taking care of her child and working. We supported her—the child didn't bother anything or anybody."

An individual's personality develops through the interplay of both biological inheritance and social experience. At birth, males and females are ascribed certain roles, characteristics, and behaviors associated with explicit values and expectations according to a constructed gender role that is socially generated (Haider, 1995). Society places men's work on a higher level for remuneration and recognition. (See Storytelling: Maiden Name.) Even in female activities, male involvement reflects their expertise.

Historically, parents have ensured that children were exposed to games, activities, and household chores compatible with children's gender. Children were rewarded for acting appropriately and punished when there was deviation from a standard. Rewards may be in the form of toys, accolades, encouragement, playing with other children, or actually offering advice and instructions. Punishments may be in the form of ridicule, denial of privilege, or removal of an offensive object (e.g., a Barbie doll for a little boy).

Pressure is put on girls to be obedient, good mothers, selfless, dependent, and trustworthy (McBride, 1990). A relationship exists between these types of gender socialization experiences and girls' tendency to attribute their success to luck as opposed to skill (Sadker, Sadker, & Long, 1993). In a study of 392 college women, a lack of problem-solving confidence predicted depressive symptoms, which predicted eating disorder symptoms (VanBoven & Espelage, 2006). (See Storytelling: No Choice.)

❖ **STORYTELLING: NO CHOICE**

I was flipping through *National Geographic* recently and saw a picture of a newborn baby being washed in a bucket by a young girl. A toddler was sitting next to her. What caught my eyes was how very small this newborn baby was as well as how young the girl was who was taking care of it. As I read on, I came to understand that the young girl was actually the mother—of the newborn and of the toddler playing nearby. This 14-year-old girl had just given birth to her second child. Still ill from the delivery, weak, and bleeding, she was responsible for taking care of her brand new baby and her toddler. She had no education regarding how to care for herself. This girl was one of many in Haijah (Northwest Yemen) where children are required to marry at a very early age.

Dealing with novelty or the unexpected can be a challenge for girls because they tend to be protected and sheltered. Boys are taught to be outgoing, independent, and assertive. However, not all boys are assertive and feel powerful and not all females do not feel powerful. Race, class, sexuality, disability, and immigrant status are all factors that mediate the impact of privilege and oppression on people's gendered lives. Fortunately, the study of femininity and masculinity is increasingly more focused on cross-cultural contexts (Wester, Kuo, & Vogel, 2006). For instance, immigrant women in the United States experience oppression from xenophobia, racism, class discrimination, and sexism (Yakushko & Chronister, 2005). (See Storytelling: No One Says Anything.)

❖ **STORYTELLING: NO ONE SAYS ANYTHING**

I was talking with a woman from the Middle East about Paris and the tragic events that occurred on November 13, 2015. We talked about how very sad we were that people were killed and wounded. We commented that the news coverage was nonstop. I stated that you couldn't watch anything else on CNN. "Where is the news about all of the Palestinians who die?" she asked. "No one says anything!" Whose stories are told? Whose stories are not told? Why do some stories receive the light of day and others stay silent?

Research was done with 60 male participants at a school in Massachusetts and 45 male participants at a large public university in Costa Rica. The research was investigating culture, gender role conflict, and likelihood of help seeking for two different problems from a variety of potential help providers. The Costa Rican men were more likely to report higher levels of restrictive affectionate behavior between men and lower levels of conflict between work and family than were U.S. men. The researchers surmised that the two groups of men might experience similar levels of success, restrictive emotionality, power, and competition, but the meaning and importance of these constructs might vary between the cultures (Lane & Addis, 2005).

Leaper and Brown (2008) conducted research with 600 preteen and adolescent females, ages 12 through 18. What they found was disturbing. Nearly all of the sample (90%) of girls experienced sexual harassment at least once. Few girls reported sexual harassment that had occurred several times. Most frequently cited were inappropriate and unwanted romantic attention, demeaning comments related to gender, teasing about one's appearance, and even unwanted physical contact. The results are concerning given that sexual harassment can make girls vulnerable to developing negative images about their bodies; self-esteem can also be adversely affected. Finally, many girls expect demeaning behaviors to be normative in heterosexual relationships. Thus, they may be at risk for future abusive relationships. The study found that male peers were the most likely perpetrators of academic and athletic sexism. Girls can become rather conflicted when boys are disapproving of their technical skills or athleticism. Consequently, because some girls may minimize their competencies in athletics and/or math and science, subsequent achievement can be hindered. Other girls were another common source of perpetrators of sexism. Same gender peers are powerful players in gender socialization. Sadly, "Teachers were among the most common sources of negative comments about girls' academic abilities" (Leaper & Brown, 2008, p. 697).

Good and Mintz (1990) found that boys' games, although rule governed, rewarded creativity, improvisation, and initiative and involved teams comprised of a larger number of peers while encouraging both cooperation and competition. Although their research is dated, it is relevant more than two decades later. Boys are also prepared to engage in the world and explore it and to play by themselves. In doing so, they develop improvisational and problem-solving skills and are given important practice in the art of negotiation. Achievement and success are emphasized for boys, possibly explaining why boys enter an activity with a premise that they should master, create, and make a difference.

The instrument commonly used to measure masculine role conflict is the Gender Role Conflict Scale (GRCS). It is based on the notion that the traditional gender socialization of boys asks more than what is possible to give. To be regarded as masculine, men are expected to have power, compete with one another, demonstrate control over themselves and their environment, and show power over women (Perkins, 2015). Vulnerability is frowned upon, as is weakness and irrationality. The inability to shoulder all of these expectations ushers in distress. Gender role conflict was associated with psychological distress, such as paranoia, psychoticism, obsessive-compulsivity, depression, and interpersonal sensitivity.

One consequence of the male socialization pattern that emphasizes strength, self-reliance, and independence is *restrictive emotionality*. Restrictive emotionality, the socialized practice of men not expressing their emotions, is one of the subscales on the GRCS. According to Good, Robertson, Fitzgerald, Stevens, and Bartels (1996), four behavioral patterns emerge when men experience gender role conflict. The first behavioral pattern is restrictive emotionality, which refers to men's reluctance or difficulty in expressing their emotions. *Alexithymia* describes symptoms that include a decreased ability to label and communicate affect, confusion of affective and somatic symptoms, and externally oriented thinking. Alexithymia may be linked to a variety of both psychological and physical disorders, including depression (Carpenter & Addis, 2000).

The second behavioral pattern is *restrictive affectionate behavior between men*. Men may be afraid of sharing a full range of emotions for fear of being seen as gay (Good, Dell, & Mintz, 1989). Gertner (1994) said that men may also be limited in how they express their sexuality and affection to others.

Obsession with achievement and success is the third behavioral pattern, which references a disturbing and persistent preoccupation with work, accomplishment, and eminence as a means of demonstrating value. Seeking help may be experienced and perceived as the antithesis of being in control and having power. This perception may explain why men remain less likely than women to seek therapeutic assistance (Gertner, 1994). It is not that women are more psychologically disturbed than men; it is that men's socialization patterns do not encourage them to seek needed psychological help. Feeling sad or depressed may be seen as unmanly (Good et al., 1989).

There has been greater emphasis in the past few decades on *coaching*, defined as an ongoing professional relationship that helps people produce extraordinary results in their lives, careers, businesses, or organizations (McKelley & Rochlen, 2007). Coaching may appeal to men, particularly to those who are adverse to receiving professional help. Its emphasis on a collegial relationship (perhaps less of a power differential) and on the teaching of human relationship skills to successful executives over addressing psychological deficits has been cited as the appeal.

Balancing work and family relations is the fourth behavioral pattern. Because men are socialized to focus on achievement, other areas of life, such as home and leisure, can easily be ignored or sacrificed or both. These four behavioral patterns have been related to depression (Good & Mintz, 1990). Gertner (1994) added homophobia and health care problems to this list as well.

A study was done involving 103 master's- and doctoral-level male interns in Association of Psychology Postdoctoral and Internship Center. The main finding, which investigated gender role conflict and the supervisor working alliance, was that men high in restrictive emotionality tended to deal with less power by turning against themselves in the form of negative perceptions of their own counseling efficacy. This study revealed that counseling students were not immune to internalizing gendered behavior, even if it had negative consequences (Wester, Vogel, & Archer, 2004).

Another way of understanding restrictive emotionality on men's lives is by comparing an underused muscle to the difficulty many men have in receiving assistance during emotional stress or accepting responsibility when necessary. In a study with

207 college students (17% nonwhite), men were found to experience shame prone-ness, guilt, and externalization (Efthim, Kenny, & Mahalik, 2001). *Externalization* was defined as the act of shifting blame outward for negative events and is a defensive maneuver in dealing with shame and guilt (Skovholt, 1993). Men's tendency to avoid expressing affection toward other men is associated with increased likelihood of depression, as is their reluctance to seek psychological help.

❖ STORYTELLING: MAIDEN NAME

When you call the credit card company and speak to a representative to check on your balance, request a credit line increase, or request a lower interest rate, the password is your mother's *maiden* name. Every time I get asked this question, I complain—ultimately to the representative who has no power to make or change policy but only to enforce it. Heterosexist, racist, and sexist discourses are loaded in the question. First, it is assumed that people's mothers married—growing numbers of women have a child or children without marrying the father. Nonmarriage is not a negation of a child's birth. A large percentage of women across race, but particularly among black women and Latinas, are single parents. Second, it assumed that a woman is hetero-sexual, married a man, renounced her birth name, and took her husband's name. This practice is antiquated. It will be interesting to see if the legalization of same-sex marriage will amend this policy.

The psychological distress experienced by women occurs within the context of unfair treatment due to their biological sex (perceived discrimination) and subsequent and negative personal views of women as a group (private collective self-esteem) and of themselves as individuals (personal self-esteem; Fischer & Holz, 2007).

Undoing Gender

Western philosophy dictates the construction of masculinity and femininity as mutu-ally exclusive or dichotomous. Common language used when referring to the two genders is "the opposite sex," or reference is made to one's partner as "the other half." Masculinity in the Western worldview is associated with an instrumental orientation, a cognitive focus on getting the job done, or problem solving. Femininity, in contrast, is associated with a concern for others and harmony with the group. Until gender roles ascribed by society change and the inherent sexism is transformed, men and women alike will be constricted to and suffer from the consequences of inequities based on biological sex and socially constructed roles (Gertner, 1994). Although there are seri-ous consequences associated with rigid sex-based gender roles that limit the range of affect, behaviors, and cognitions perceived to be available to people, they are adopted and perpetuated. This issue was explored by psychologist Sandra Bem, who developed the concept of androgyny. She also designed the Bem Sex Role Inventory (BSRI), which has been used in hundreds of research studies on *gender role socialization* and *androgyny.* Androgyny is from the Greek *andro,* meaning "male," and *gyne,* meaning "female" (Bem, 1993). Androgyny is consistent with the notion of people as gendered beings fully developing without restricting and confining sex roles.

Androgynous refers to persons who are high in both feminine and masculine psychological and behavioral traits, not to persons' biological, male or female, physical characteristics. According to Bem (1993), an individual can be both masculine and feminine; expressive, instrumental, and communal; and compassionate and assertive, depending on the situation. Limiting oneself to one domain could be costly to human potential in that individuals may be required to mitigate agency with communion and strength with yielding. Bem stated that balance is necessary because extreme femininity untempered by a sufficient concern for one's own needs as an individual may produce dependency and self-denial, just as extreme masculinity untempered by a sufficient ability to ask for help from others may produce arrogance and exploitation. An individual with both masculine and feminine characteristics would arguably be more flexible and function more productively than a sex-typed individual. Androgynous persons demonstrate a lack of statistically significant differences between masculinity and femininity scores, thus showing a blend of both dimensions.

Psychological differences between the sexes are not biological destiny but rather are learned after birth through the sex role socialization process (Cook, 1987). Although true, a uniformity myth tends to make sex synonymous with gender roles. Men are connected with masculine characteristics that are instrumental, agentic, and goal oriented in nature. Emphasis is placed on self-development and separation from others. Masculine characteristics are associated with goal directedness, achievement, and recognition by others for one's efforts. Highly valued traits within the culture of the United States are also deemed masculine—competitiveness, assertiveness, high achievement, and individualism (Burnett, Anderson, & Heppner, 1995). Saucier (2004) observed that most positive traits associated with masculinity increase with age (e.g., competence, autonomy, self-control, and power). Not only are males elevated, masculinity has greater "social utility" than does femininity. This privileging, according to Burnett et al. (1995), is known as the masculine supremacy effect. "This position suggests a cultural bias toward masculinity such that individuals who are masculine receive more positive social reinforcement and hence develop higher self-esteem" (Burnett et al., 1995, p. 323). Masculinity was viewed as more valuable not only for men but also for women. Women who were low in individual masculinity were at greater risk for decreased self-esteem. There is, however, a flip side. Women who demonstrate too much masculinity are regarded as aggressive, difficult, and bitchy, whereas boys and men who exhibit an excess of feminine qualities are ridiculed and called derogatory names, such as fag and sissy (Haddock, Zimmerman, & Lyness, 2003). Femininity may influence how others respond to a person, but masculinity is strongly related to various indexes of psychological health (Burnett et al., 1995). Masculinity had a more positive impact on how one sees oneself. Conversely, women are associated with the feminine characteristics of expressiveness and communality, with a focus on emotionality, selflessness, sensitivity, and interpersonal relationships. The traditional masculine role, which has been found to be unhealthy on many indexes of functioning, is related to status, toughness, success, achievement, emotional stoicism, and antifemininity (Lane & Addis, 2005).

The challenges with measurement of masculinity and femininity were echoed by Hoffman (2001):

> There are numerous instruments that are widely used today by a range of individuals from researchers in counseling, psychology, and education to human resource personnel. Unfortunately, what is being assessed is often given only cursory consideration by researchers and consumers alike. (p. 472)

Masculinity and femininity are popular within the culture. Sex role typology, which references a psychological dimension, is not predicated on biological sex. Masculinity or femininity refers to behaviors, not physical makeup. Men can be psychologically feminine, and women can be psychologically masculine. Sex-typed persons (e.g., men ascribing to a strictly masculine role, women to a feminine role) have internalized society's sex-appropriate standards for desirable behavior to the relative exclusion of the other sex's typical characteristics.

Sex role rigidity contributes to narrow and restricted behaviors. An example of this effect was seen in research conducted by Stevens, Pfost, and Potts (1990). They found that "masculine-typed men and feminine-typed women reported the most avoidance of existential issues, with sex-typed persons indicating the least openness to such concerns . . . the findings also complement evidence of behavioral rigidity among sex-typed individuals" (p. 48).

Spence and Helmreich (1978) developed the Personal Attributes Questionnaire (PAQ). Like the BSRI, the PAQ identified four groups: feminine, masculine, androgynous, and undifferentiated. This model recognized that masculinity and femininity coexist to some degree in every individual, male or female. The androgynous person, less bound to the restrictive, sex-appropriate standards for behavior, is theoretically able to develop psychologically to the fullest and respond receptively to a wide range of situations, perhaps in ways that the less integrated person is unable to do.

Cross-culturally, the concepts of masculinity and femininity have been represented as complementary domains, traits, and behaviors for thousands of years. The yin-yang theory of the harmony and balance of forces in nature is based in Confucian thought and Chinese cosmology. Uba (1994) said that the yin is representative of feminine—negative, inferior, and weak—whereas the yang is symbolic of masculine—positive, superior, and strong. "If this supposedly natural balance is upset (e.g., if a wife domineers over her husband), the equilibrium within the family would be disrupted" (Uba, 1994, p. 29). Good and Sanchez (2010) investigated gender conformity, self-esteem, and affect among 401 women and men. It was found that investment in living up to a societal gender ideal (feeling that it is important to be like society's ideal man or woman) was associated with pressured motivation for gender-conforming behavior—this need negatively impacted self-esteem. Private regard was defined as a subset of collective self-esteem that captures positive feelings regarding one's particular gender group or having a sense of pride in being a woman or a man. It predicted autonomous motivation for gender-conforming behavior that positively predicted self-esteem. Valuing one's gender was not shown to be costly for the person directly but instead it influenced self-esteem through a motivation to actually engage in gender-conforming behavior.

Sex and Gender Roles

Several models describe women's development (Enns, 1991). These models seek to highlight the relational strengths that women embody and according to Enns, attempt "to correct the inadequacies of mainstream theories and conceptualize women's experiences in their own terms" (p. 209). Evans, Kincade, Marbley, and Seem (2005) reviewed the historical aspects of feminism and feminist therapy in women and men's lives. Feminist therapy skills, an emphasis on social justice and change, and the relationship between the client and the counselor were all highlighted.

Erikson (1968), one of the early and essential voices in identity development, has been criticized for focusing the majority of his attention on the masculine version of human existence. However, the primacy of men in the human life event reflects the sexism of the time (Horst, 1995). Women's psychosocial development is different from men's. Gilligan (1982) criticized major identity development theorists who depict women as inferior to men because of important gender differences. According to Gilligan, women's development "relies more on connections with others, on relatedness rather than separateness" (p. 271). Recently, other psychologists have written about the unique experience of womanhood on development. Jordan (1997c) and Nelson (1996) commented that relational skills are highly functional and involve a complex array of competencies essential to preserving family and culture.

Compared with men, women may emphasize relationships and the importance of autonomy for women cannot be underestimated. McBride (1990) argued that *autonomy* refers to being able to define oneself, rather than being defined by others. This definition is not seen as an isolated and extremely individualistic self. Rather, autonomy refers to interdependence, mutual cooperation, and individuation. McBride stated that *instrumental autonomy* refers to the ability to act on the world, carry on activities, cope with problems, and take action to meet one's needs. *Emotional autonomy* is the freedom from pressing needs for approval and reassurance. Women are often unaware of how much energy they invest in doing things for others versus developing healthy interdependence. The capacity to commit to concrete affiliations and partnerships and to develop the ethical strength to abide by such commitments, even though they may call for significant sacrifices and compromises, is a source of strength. It is questionable as to whether such commitments and mutuality can be achieved when there is a considerable power differential (Haddock et al., 2003).

Gender and Emotion

The history of gender relationships in this country is steeped in patriarchy and inequality. Elizabeth Cady Stanton, one of the cofounders of the first Women's Rights

Convention held in 1840, observed the burden of caring for everyone other than oneself on the faces of women. She said,

> The general discontent I felt with women's position as wife, mother, housekeeper, physician, and spiritual guide, the chaotic condition into which everything fell without her constant supervision, and the wearied, anxious look of the majority of women, impressed me with the strong feeling that some active measures should be taken to remedy the wrongs of society in general and of women in particular. (as cited in Zinn, 2003, p. 123)

This socialization process of being selfless contributes to women equating self-care with being selfish. Women who sacrifice their own development to meet the needs of others often inhibit the development of self-expression, self-knowledge, and self-esteem (McBride, 1990). Yet the culture encourages women to sacrifice their development and needs for the benefit of others' needs, usually men's needs. Depression is associated with the behavior of women constantly putting others' needs first and discounting their own needs. It is important, then, not to pathologize women for behaving in this manner. Women who are selfless and sacrificial have had cultural, institutional, and relational reinforcement (Lemkau & Landau, 1986). Choosing to care for the self might be perceived as an unacceptable proposition because it is likened to the denial of others (McBride, 1990). When women feel that they have failed to be in nurturing and sustaining relationships, there is a sense of shame. Gender socialization is riddled with shame for women and men. There is not enough room in this book to address the shame heaped upon transgendered people due to nonconformity with gender socialization processes and practices.

Researchers found that shame proneness among women was the dominant affective response related to living up to female gender role norms (Efthim et al., 2001). For shame to be experienced, a person appraises the self as having violated group norms or as having failed to live up to the standards of the social group. Five factors of the Female Gender Role Stress Scale examined women's gender role stress:

1. Emotional detachment (e.g., having others believe that you are emotionally cold).

2. Physical unattractiveness (e.g., being perceived by others as overweight).

3. Victimization (e.g., having your car break down on the road).

4. Unassertiveness (e.g., bargaining with a salesperson when buying a car).

5. Failed nurturance (e.g., having someone else raise your children).

In the Efthim et al. (2001) study, five factors of the Male Gender Role Stress Scale examined men's gender role stress and reinforced the dimensions of masculinity:

1. Physical inadequacy (e.g., losing in a sports competition).

2. Emotional inexpressiveness (e.g., admitting that you are afraid of something).

3. Subordination to women (e.g., being outperformed by a woman).

4. Intellectual inferiority (e.g., having to ask for directions when lost).

5. Performance failure (e.g., being unable to become sexually aroused when you want to).

Many men leave intimacy to women. Consequently, the requirement for intimacy in adult relationships, to join in mutuality and to surrender to another, is a tremendous source of conflict and anxiety for men (Jordan, 1997c). Men need to be educated on the benefits of emotional expression. As human beings, men have basic needs to love and to be loved, to care and to be cared for, and to know and to be known, but socially prescribed gender roles tend to require men to be inexpressive and competitive with one another. Evaluating life success in terms of external achievements rather than interdependence is emphasized.

In the Newman, Fuqua, Gray, and Simpson (2006) study, the relationship between gender, depression, and anger was investigated in a clinical sample. There were 65 men and 74 women in the study, with a median age of 31. People were in the low-to-moderate income range and were predominantly white. Despite previous research that women are more likely to be depressed than men, this study found no difference between men and women on any of the affective scales, including depression. Both men and women had high Beck Depression Inventory scores. A significant finding was that 38% of the variance in depression was related to the five anger scales used in the study: state anger, trait anger, anger-in, anger-out, and anger control. The relationship between anger and depression was substantial for both men and women. The emphasis on quantitative methodologies and homogeneity in race and ethnicity represent severe limitations to this research, and yet the findings help us see the benefit of focusing on clinical samples and not relying on and applying findings from nonclinical samples.

Wester, Vogel, Wei, and McLain (2006) provide one of the first studies to examine race and male gender role conflict. In their sample, 130 black male college students completed the GRCS, the Cross Racial Identity Scale, and the SCL-90 to measure psychological distress. A Bonferroni correction was done to address the multiple independent t tests performed on gender role conflict subscales. Black men's GRCS scores were predictive of their psychological distress. Black men who internalized a racist understanding of themselves as men of color suffered more from their attempts to navigate the male gender role than did men whose racial identity reflected appreciation of their African American heritage. Internalized racism served as a vehicle through which internalized sexism (gender role conflict) affected quality of life. Racial identity partially mediated the effects of gender role conflict on psychological distress. The negative consequence of internalized racism was associated with racialized gender behavior.

Healthy male development can be accomplished with the expansion of gender roles. Skovholt (1993) said that "this narrow funnel of acceptable masculinity may give males a solid sense of gender identity, but it can, in time, also become a prison that constricts personal growth and development" (p. 13). Men are fearful of being perceived as or labeled feminine, which is part of the narrow funnel through which they must conduct their lives. From a psychosocial perspective, this fear stems from the arduous task men must complete: separate from their mothers toward developing their male identities (Skovholt, 1993). This particular socialization process dictates that men should never engage in opposite-sex behaviors and attitudes.

Men travel through their developmental paths unduly conflicted yet trying to maintain power over women and other men (Perkins, 2015; Pleck, 1984). Perkins (2015) conducted a study with 177 men, analyzing the constructs of attitudes toward seeking help and male role norms inventory (MRNI-R). He found a negative and significant relationship between these two constructs. He also found that younger men (18–24) scored lowest on the MRNI-R, a result he attributed to a gradual progression toward greater gender equality in the United States and less gender role polarization. A key task of the men's movement was to articulate the male experience of power and powerlessness, which assumed that female powerlessness translates into male power (Swanson, 1993). It is clear that the wounds of patriarchal power and control are damaging to men and women (Brown, 1994). The roles for men need to be transformed so that men become "acutely aware of their power to influence self and to break the bonds to patriarchy, emotional handcuffs in the form of assumptions and interpretations that favor patriarchal values above the worth of human beings and the meaning of their experiences" (Brown, 1994, p. 118).

Gender and the Body

Cultural values of independence, thinness, physical strength, and athleticism pervade U.S. society. Both print and audiovisual advertisements are a primary medium for the transmission of images. Chronic dieting and preoccupation with bulk and speed among men and women to the point of damaging the health of one's body with steroids and from anorexia and bulimia are epidemic within the culture. Cultural values must be considered when tracing the etiology of gender-based practices. (See Storytelling: Barbaric Practice or Cultural Rite?) For instance, health behaviors may manifest masculinity. Men "anticipate their world from the experiences of being males in their respective cultures (e.g., being told to be tough, self-reliant, violent, promiscuous) and take (or not take) certain actions based on their understanding of their world (e.g., ignore pain, refuse help, become violent, engage in risky sexual practice)" (Mahalik, Lagan, & Morrison, 2006, p. 192). These behaviors have their genesis in culturally laden images that privilege physical power.

❖ STORYTELLING: BARBARIC PRACTICE OR CULTURAL RITE?

When traveling in Tanzania, our group had the privilege of staying with the Masai—a nomadic people who eschew modern conveniences like electricity and plumbing. We were told that circumcision for women and men is a prerequisite for marriage, and girls know they will not be marriageable (deemed worthy of a Masai man's hand in marriage) without doing so. We were told that women did not fear circumcision; they anticipated it as part of the marriage preparation. Chung (2005) cites that the Western-coined female genital mutilation for circumcision is a standard cultural practice in preparing for marriage and adult status in sub-Saharan Africa, Egypt, United Arab Emirates, Bahrain, Oman, Indonesia, South Yemen, Pakistan, Malaysia, and some parts of Russia. It also occurs in immigrant and refugee communities in the Americas and in Europe.

Pursuit of the thin beauty ideal has meant different things for women. One percent of the 10- to 20-year-old American female population has anorexia nervosa (self-starvation). It is estimated that 4% of college-age women have bulimia nervosa—this number could be higher given the secret nature of binge eating. Ten percent of anorexics and bulimics are men. About 72% of alcoholic women under the age of 30 also have eating disorders (ANRED, 2006). Disordered eating is far too often associated with becoming or remaining thin. Large numbers of young women in high school report that they use maladaptive weight control techniques such as fasting (39.4%), appetite suppressants (8.1%), and skipping meals (33.5%) to lose weight (Tylka & Subich, 2002).

Adolescents are particularly vulnerable to eating disorders because anorexia nervosa has its highest incidence at the beginning of adolescence and bulimia nervosa has its highest incidence at the end (Emmons, 1992). From a psychodynamic perspective, the earlier scripts that are set in motion will have a powerful impact on behavior and cognition unless early information is replaced with new information. Arrival to adulthood does not ensure clarity about the existence or elimination of dysfunctional tapes. Thus, one task of adulthood is to unlearn many of the negative tapes received during childhood and adolescence and to replace them with messages that affirm the self and are more reflective of who the individual has sculpted the self to be. The media, church, educational institutions, other women, family members, and men create an environment wherein men "construct the symbolic order" within which gender inequity and male supremacy are reproduced.

In this system, women and men (due to the price associated with the privilege of defining reality) become at war with their bodies. This effect is particularly true when a gap exists between body image perception and proximity to the socially constructed standard. Learning to define oneself as acceptable amid the aging process where one may no longer fit the ideal of beauty is essential in combating appearance anxiety or fear-based thoughts that one's aging body is betraying them in a youth-obsessed culture (Saucier, 2004). Intense body dissatisfaction and a sense of disembodiment can ensue when one's body does not conform to the standard. Hutchinson (1982) stated, "The body is experienced as alien and lost to awareness . . . The body has broken away or has been severed from the mind and is experienced as a foreign object, an albatross, or a hated antagonist" (pp. 59–60).

Alienation from the body hampers appreciation and acceptance of multiple identities. Perceptions of the body amid parts that cause pain, create difficulty, or are defined by society as unattractive and unacceptable can be transformed through paradigm shifts. New discourses or ways of bringing meaning to bear on the value of the body can emerge and take root interpersonally.

Oppressive stereotypes about women of color continue to be pervasive throughout the media, although more visible women of color with non-European features are being seen. For instance, Root (1990) identified that

Women of color are either fat and powerless (African American and Latina women); fat, bossy, and asexual; corrupt and/or evil (Asian/Pacific Island Americans and

African Americans); obedient, quiet, and powerless (Latinas and Asian/Pacific Americans); exotic (Asian Americans, mixed race); or hysterical and stupid. (p. 530)

Gunn Allen (1992) observed that American society would be different if various traditions from Native American culture were followed, saying, "If American society judiciously modeled the traditions of the various Native Nations, the ideals of physical beauty would be considerably enlarged to include 'fat' strong-featured women, gray-haired, and wrinkled individuals, and others who in contemporary American culture are viewed as 'ugly'" (p. 211).

Race and skin color are variables in the beauty business. American standards of beauty are based on white or white-approximating ideals. The physical features of many white women, as well as those of women of color, differ from socially constructed rigid and often unattainable beauty standards. In an effort to conform to accepted standards of beauty, many women of color will seek to fulfill Eurocentric beauty standards equated with status, acceptance, and legitimacy. Some Asian women have undergone plastic surgery to make their eyes appear more round or double-folded, as opposed to single-folded, for a more Western look. This drastic physical change may be fueled by Uba's (1994) statement, "There is evidence that Asian Americans have lower self-concepts than Euro-Americans do when it comes to physical appearance" (p. 83).

Rhinoplasty is a surgical procedure many Jewish women have undergone to obtain a smaller, narrower, and finer nose. Black women spend an inordinate amount of time, psychic energy, and money on the monumental issue of hair. Many, along with their Jewish sisters, have for decades been relaxing their hair by applying chemicals or a hot metal comb to naturally curly and coily hair to make it straight. Alice Walker (1987) refers to this relaxing process as oppressing the hair.

Emmons's (1992) research points to an erroneous assumption about eating disorders—that they are rare among people of color. She found that African American teenage girls were more likely than any other race and gender group examined to use laxatives as a dieting ploy. In contrast, European Americans were more likely to vomit to lose weight. Cultural factors, values, and institutional variables such as racism and religious discourses all converge to influence the presence and diagnosis of eating disorders in women. Among black women, stress associated with the struggle to deal with acculturation, success, racism, and family responsibilities may trigger bingeing and purging behavior in some who did not evidence disordered eating during adolescence.

Mastria (2002) maintains that cultural components of Latina culture predispose girls to defer and sacrifice themselves. She said, "From childhood, females are taught to repress sexual desires, and conditioned to be extremely modest and 'virginal' in terms of their bodies, which may cause conflict and shameful feelings about their bodies" (p. 71). Research conducted by Lester and Petrie (1998) on 139 female Mexican American college students found evidence of bulimia nervosa among 1.4% to 4.3% of the sample. Despite strongly entrenched beliefs about the protective aspects of ethnic/racial minority status, a relationship may exist between increasing opportunities for social mobility for women of color and increasing vulnerability to disordered eating (Root, 1990).

The desire to bring honor and not disgrace to the family, coupled with the model minority myth, may contribute to disordered eating among Asian American girls (Mastria, 2002). The changing roles of women within the family and workforce have to be considered when understanding the etiology of eating disorders and its relationship with power and control. Family of origin plays a pivotal role in the life of a young woman who has an eating disorder. Brouwers (1990) reported that negative attitudes toward the body begin in the family and that, after self-body evaluation, the daughter's belief that the mother was critical of the daughter's body was the second biggest predictor of bulimia in female college students.

College campus factors or values may influence a young woman's vulnerability to eating disorders. Kashubeck, Walsh, and Crowl (1994) discovered that the literature on one college website emphasized physical appearance, attention to fashion, and participation in the sorority-fraternity system. Another college, a liberal arts institution, emphasized political activism and intellectual talent. The rate of eating disorders did not differ between the two schools, but the study found that at the first school, the factors associated with eating disorders were the perceived pressure to dress a certain way, to be smart, and to have a marginal grade point average. At the second school, being female and having low masculine gender role identity were the strongest predictors to disordered eating behaviors.

Research by Rogers and Petrie (2001) found that among 97 college women (27 nonwhite), dependency and assertion of autonomy were important in explaining the variance on the Eating Attitudes Test. It appears that symptoms of anorexia are characterized by dependency on and need for approval from a significant relationship, as well as the need to deny this reliance. Restricting food intake may be a way to assert one's sense of individualism within the gender role. Women's power comes from their beauty and physical allure as approved and esteemed by others.

In research with 200 Asian American college women, self-esteem, perceived pressure to be thin, ethnic identity, body shape, internalization of society's emphasis on appearance, and eating disorder symptomatology were assessed. The following were found: Asian American women's perceived pressure for thinness slightly predicted self-esteem and moderately predicted body preoccupation, self-esteem predicted body preoccupation, and body preoccupation strongly predicted eating disorder symptomatology. Although ethnic identity predicted self-esteem, ethnic identity did not predict internalization of the thin ideal, body preoccupation, and disordered eating. Ethnic identity only influenced internalization of the thin ideal and body preoccupation through its association with self-esteem (Phan & Tylka, 2006).

There is enormous pressure on people, including white people, to look according to European ideals. Teens as well as adults may feel compelled to change hairstyles, dress, skin color, noses, lips, body size, and makeup to be accepted in an effort to access opportunity. Among many African American women, disordered eating, which can lead to obesity, may be a quick-fix resistance strategy to negotiate the pressures and frustrations of daily racism and sexism (Robinson & Ward, 1991).

Women of African descent bleach their skin, yet skin-color issues are connected to broader themes of identity and awareness of the sociopolitical context of race in

America. As people of African descent celebrate various hues, skin color as a status variable may take on less prominence.

Balogun (2015) conducted critical research with 230 African women, largely from Nigeria and Kenya. She examined several constructs including body image, objectified body consciousness, and internalization of white beauty ideals. She found that African women with high levels of objectified body consciousness (body surveillance and body shame) were more likely to endorse more pathological eating behaviors. She also found that body shame significantly influenced eating pathology. Moreover, internalized white beauty ideals significantly predicted body shame as well as body surveillance. Finally, body surveillance significantly predicted body shame.

Gender and Experiences in Therapy

Qualitative research was conducted with 16 counselors to address how counselors conceptualize and address privilege and oppression within counseling and understand their perceptions of their training with respect to these constructs. Specifically two research questions were asked: How do practitioners see privilege and oppression influencing and interacting in counseling, and what changes in training and practice related to these constructs do they see as necessary to better serve clients? Two themes emerged from the data: (1) the intersection between counselor process and cultural power and (2) transitions in counselor training practice. More specifically, interactions with clients were facilitative in counselors' awareness of privilege and oppression. In addition, counselors felt they lacked a sense of preparedness to address power issues in counseling (Hays, Dean, & Chang, 2007).

Bernardez (1987) found three specific reactions to women in therapy: (1) the discouragement and disapproval of behavior that did not conform with traditional role prescriptions, such as mother; (2) the disparagement and inhibition of expression of anger and other "negative" affects, such as hatred and bitterness; and (3) the absence of confrontation, interpretation, and exploration of passive-submissive and compliant behavior in the client. Despite these reactions from therapists, Bernardez reported that female therapists showed greater empathy and ability to facilitate self-disclosure than males. There are exceptions; male therapists may be more inclined to reproduce the dominant-subordinate position by unconscious encouragement of the female's compliance, submissiveness, and passivity.

Fauth and Hayes (2006) investigated the applicability of a transactional theory of stress to understanding countertransference with male clients. Therapists' positive appraisals were linked with more positive diagnostic evaluation of their client. Negative appraisals were linked with increased distance from and hesitance with the client. "Counselors who felt more efficacious in managing their feelings and value conflicts with the client tended to avoid him less" (Fauth & Hayes, 2006, p. 436). The authors did not find that counselors' male gender role attitudes and male clients' gender role conformity interacted to predict the counselors' stress appraisals and countertransference.

A problem for both sexes is the strong gender role prohibition against female anger, criticism, rebellion, or domination. Anger is often equated with hatred, destructiveness, or bitterness. Helping clients realize that they have the right to take care of themselves, even if those in their environment tell them they are hurting others, is an important step on the road to self-mastery. Some clients "may exclude information that they assume the counselor will not understand or include details designed to counteract the counselor's presumed prejudices" (Hays, 1996, p. 36). The very exploration of bitterness and resentment can lead to the identification of sources of dissatisfaction.

The female counselor–male client dyad represents the typical caregiving pattern in society. Most men would feel very challenged entering therapy and abdicating power to a woman. If a woman is uncomfortable with her power, given her proximity to discourses that sing the power-of-men-over-women song, she may acquiesce her power and view men as greater authorities than herself.

Female counselor–female client is probably one of the most emotionally intense dyads. This dyad was found to allow for a fuller exploration of childhood experiences. Female clients, because of socialization, may challenge the female counselor and question her competence. Because of gender role socialization, therapists of both genders have difficulties with a whole array of aggressive behaviors in their women clients (Kaplan, 1987). When both the client and counselor are lesbian, the therapeutic relationship is shaped by the intersections of gender and sexuality in that both parties attempt to honor the mutuality inherent in empathic counseling (Slater, 1997). The very process of the counselor "coming out" to her client is an act of mutuality, and yet lesbian therapists should not be the only therapists engaging in this type of self-disclosure. It is also the task of the heterosexual counselor to disclose. Robinson and Watt (2001) summarized this point and stated, "The socially endorsed experience of heterosexuality and the unconscious and unearned privilege afforded heterosexuals often deems them unaware of the importance to transition through sexual identity formation. It is presumed that sexual identity formation pertains to gay people only" (p. 594). People who are heterosexually identified are sociopolitically advantaged and privileged (Mohr, 2002). Hoffman (2004) argued that lack of attention to identity development for majority group members is the inadvertent perpetuation of the need for minority group members to explain their realities.

Regardless of the gender of the counselor and the client, empathy is the key ingredient in therapy (Pinderhughes, 1989). *Empathy* is the ability of the therapist to surrender himself or herself to the affect of another while cognitively structuring that experience so as to comprehend its meaning in terms of other aspects of the client's psyche (Pinderhughes, 1989, p. 13). It requires that the counselor be comfortable and familiar with the world of affect and the nature of connections between people (Kaplan, 1987). Empathy allows for a merger of people's experiences and understanding—not toward enmeshment but attunement. "In true empathic exchange, each is both object and subject, mutually engaged in affecting and being affected, knowing and being known" (Jordan, 1997b, p. 15). There are power differentials within counseling that are part of the professional relationship, yet empathy and mutuality are impeded by unacknowledged hierarchies within the counseling event when they reinforce hegemonic power dynamics (Mencher, 1997).

Therapists may disapprove of women who show power and controlling, competitive, and autonomous behavior while disliking behavior typically regarded as feminine (e.g., self-depreciation, submissiveness). Some male therapists may subconsciously dread women dominating them and fear their own vulnerability to female aggression. Female therapists may also fear the eruption of their own anger toward men, a result that may or may not have an adverse impact on the therapeutic relationship. It is also possible that some therapists are afraid to experience the powerlessness that comes with examining social injustice, racism, and oppression (Bernardez, 1987).

Independent of race, ethnicity, and sexual orientation, male and female children and adolescents receive similar gender-appropriate messages. Poor white men and upper-class men of color are socialized to function and be in positions of control (whether they actually *are* is a different matter). For this reason, seeking help is incompatible with the masculine role. Middle-class white women and low-income women of color are socialized to emphasize the needs and wants of others, usually before their own. Despite the similarities, more research is needed on the specific effects of class and other sources of differences as mediating traditional gender role messages.

Depression among college men and the low likelihood of their seeking out psychological services suggests that college counseling centers are in a prime position to do outreach (e.g., residence halls, orientations, classrooms, student development). Helping people reclaim the parts of themselves they have forfeited to conform to society's role expectations, both at home and at work, is a form of healing. In addition, men can be encouraged to reframe their notions of counseling. Good and Wood (1995) said that "changing men's view of counseling might consist of efforts to emphasize that participating in counseling is an activity involving personal courage and strength that is displayed through facing and sharing one's concerns" (p. 73).

A primary theme articulated throughout this work is that more differences are found within groups than between them. The need for mental health professionals to be aware of the salience of physical attractiveness as a status variable in everyday life is crucial to understanding clients as whole beings. Narrow definitions of physical attractiveness have implications for mental health attitudes, body validation, and the development of coping strategies to cope meaningfully with both unanticipated and normal maturational changes in physical appearance and ability. Integrated into this discussion is an examination of the culture's clear preference for the able-bodied and intolerance for persons with disabilities.

Gender Identity Models

The Womanist Model

Ossana, Helms, and Leonard's (1992) womanist identity model, adapted from Cross's four-stage Nigresence model, is helpful in illuminating the process of self-awareness. The first stage in the womanist identity model is *preencounter,* which maintains that women at this stage accept traditional or stereotypical notions of womanhood. Such notions are often steeped in women's reliance on others for approval and legitimation. Naturally, the locus of control for women in this stage would be external. The second stage, *encounter,* occurs when a woman has an experience wherein she begins to question notions of womanhood and becomes aware of the prevalence of sexism in society. A woman's discovery that her male colleague with less education and experience is paid significantly more than she is could be described as an encounter. In the third stage, *immersion/emersion,* the woman surrounds herself with other women and literature about and by women. She is critical of the patriarchal context of society and may experience turbulent emotions, such as guilt and anger, toward herself for having been selfless for so long and at society for its history of promoting gender inequity. During the fourth and last stage, *internalization,* the woman defines womanhood on her own terms and is not bound by external definitions or dictates about what it means to be a woman. Research conducted by Carter and Parks (1996), using the womanist scale on black and white women, found a relationship between womanist identity attitudes and mental health. No relationships were found among African American women, but they were found among European American women. More specifically, white women ($n = 147$) who were not at the highest or internalization stage of womanist identity were more likely to feel depressed, anxious, and scrutinized or under attack. These findings suggest that white women pay a psychological tax for pushing back against the dictates of hegemony. They also pay for their dependence upon hegemony.

White Male Identity Development Model

Scott and Robinson (2001) presented a circular white male racial identity model. According to the model, movement occurs in multiple directions; however, one type, a term preferred over stage, is most descriptive. It is a theoretically driven model and influenced by Helms (1995), Myers et al. (1991), and Sue and Sue (1990). This model addresses "the convergence of race and gender attitudes that White men exhibit as a result of socially constructed attitudes regarding appropriate displays of manhood" (Scott & Robinson, 2001, p. 418). It could be used when counseling white men to help them gain insight into how race and gender intersect and contribute to problem presentation.

Type I, noncontact, describes men who represent the status quo, deny racism, and seek power and privilege. Type II, the claustrophobic, characterizes the man who feels that other races are closing in on him. Men whose lives are characterized by this type are disillusioned by the American Dream. There is a feeling that power and privilege are going to other races. Type III, conscious identity, describes the man who is in dissonance and feels this dissonance between existing belief systems and realities. The Type IV empirical man questions his role in racism and oppression. Finally, Type V, optimal, describes the man who understands how his struggle for power and privilege has contributed to racism and oppression.

Implications for Mental Health Professionals

One reverberating point throughout this text is that U.S. society is highly gendered and has rather rigid notions about appropriate modes of being for men and women (Kaplan, 1987). Thus, the power of the therapeutic event is found in the interpersonal relationship between client and therapist. The importance of clinical skills and training is not being minimized; however, the relational bond based on mutuality and trust is primary.

Over time, women and men maintain and modify their sex role–related perceptions, attitudes, and behaviors. Sex role typology is complicated. Individuals play a determining role in shaping and contesting sex roles. It can be therapeutically meaningful to incorporate gender socialization in our work with patients. For instance, educating women about the relationship between perceived discrimination, collective self-esteem, personal self-esteem, and psychological distress may provide tools for understanding their own experiences (Fischer & Holz, 2007).

Gender dyads have an impact on the counseling event. Often, the male and client roles are rather discontinuous. For instance, the personal characteristics of the male role often focus on physical strength and accomplishment, whereas the client role emphasizes acknowledgment of weakness. In the male role, men are often punished for seeking help, whereas in the client role, help seeking is reinforced (Skovholt, 1993).

More researchers are conducting rich qualitative research to better understand gender themes. Phillips and Daniluk (2004) tape-recorded interviews with seven women between the ages of 30 and 57 who had been sexually abused as children. Women were asked questions such as

> How would you describe your recovery process?
>
> What aspects of who you are as a person do you feel have remained constant or stable throughout your life?
>
> In what ways do you think your past abuse experiences inform your sense of who you are today? How has this changed over time?
>
> Several themes emerged: (1) An increasing sense of visibility, congruence, and connection; (2) an emerging sense of self-definition and self-acceptance; (3) a shift in worldview; (4) a sense of regret over what has been lost; and (5) a sense of resiliency and growth.

Kaplan (1987) found that women with male therapists saw themselves as less self-possessed, less open, and more self-critical than did women with female therapists.

In examining the constructs of race and gender among college students, Cokely (2001) conducted research on academic self-concept, racial centrality, and academic motivation of 257 African American college students. Ninety-two were male and 165 were female. Packets were given to students during summer school at two historically black colleges. The purpose of the study was to examine gender as an important variable in understanding the psychosocial development of African American students. The researchers found that women scored significantly higher on one of the extrinsic motivation scales (the Extrinsic Motivation Identified Regulation scale). Men had significantly higher scores on the Atrinsic Motivation scale, which represents neither intrinsic nor extrinsic motivation. The researchers concluded that black female students were more motivated about being in college than were black male students, who evidenced a lack of motivation. In tandem with the larger society, the college experience for many black males is perceived as alienating. The number of black males enrolling in and graduating from college has fallen off sharply over the years (Cokely, 2001). The lack of difference in race centrality scores between males and females may suggest that for both genders, race is a central and dominant construct.

The socialization differences for men and women have been widely documented. Men continue to be socialized toward assertiveness, power, and independence—to restrict emotion. Women are socialized toward nurturance, compliance, and direct achievement through affiliation with others, particularly men (Mintz & O'Neil, 1990). Such socialization patterns in early childhood have implications for relationships and can enhance a client's vulnerability to selflessness or excessive individualism. Because humans have myriad emotions, it is important for therapists to confront clients' beliefs about rigid gendered emotions while having the ability to hold women's intense anger and men's overwhelming sadness and fear (Brown & Gilligan, 1992).

The role of women in multicultural counseling and psychology is being explored in greater depth. Initially, the literature took a monolithic approach to counseling that failed to show how gender interacts with other identities as well as with forces such as racism, sexism, class elitism, and homophobia. Gender similarities do not negate racialized realities, nor do racial similarities negate gendered sexism.

Case Study

Building Rapport

Alena is 15. She is Mexican America and lives with her parents who brought her to counseling because Alena appears anxious and often has panic attacks. Her mom says she cries at the drop of a hat. Alena enjoys her therapist, Lima. Alena confides in Lima that she enjoys smoking and that although she is a virgin, she has been pressured by her friends (boys and girls alike) to have sex. Lima asks Alena if she is personally interested in being sexually active. Alena replies that she does not know. Lima explores Alena's relationship with her parents to assess the connections that are there and to ascertain what might be driving Alena's restlessness and feelings of insecurity. Alena says that her father is rather sarcastic with her and that she feels "stupid" in his presence. She says her father smokes but would be livid if he found out she smokes. Alena remarks that her mother is mousey and does not stand up to her father when he yells at either one of them. Alena wishes that her mother were not such a wimp when it came to dealing with her husband. Alena feels bored a lot—she and her parents don't really spend time together. She likes a boy at her school who is 2 years older than she is. Lima asks Alena what she likes about him. Alena is not sure, other than she thinks he is cute. Lima discovers over several therapy sessions that the boy Alena likes does drugs and drinks. He has been pressuring Alena to have sex with him. Alena comes into one of her sessions during July with a turtleneck on. Lima asks why she is wearing a turtleneck when it is so hot out. Alena shrugs her shoulders. Lima lets the issue go. During the session, Alena inadvertently moves the turtleneck down, and Lima sees hickies on her neck as well as bruising. When she inquires, Alena blushes—she's deeply embarrassed. Alena says that she and Doug, the guy she has had a crush on, are having sex. Lima asks Alena why she decided to have sex. Alena said that she did not mean to, but Doug said they did it because Alena got him so excited that he couldn't stop himself.

Questions

1. What appear to be the critical issues facing Alena?
2. What are some of the gender dynamics operating in Alena's life?
3. What does cultural competence look like for Lima?

Discussion and Integration

Alena and Lima

A major gender script that both males and females receive is that men are entitled to their sexuality in ways that women are not. Part of this entitlement absolves men of responsibility, given the enormity and legitimacy of their desire. A huge burden is heaped on the woman to control the man's sexuality (Jordan, 1997c). Prior to Alena's leaving the office, Lima needs to ascertain the meaning of Alena's statement about her initiation into sexual intercourse. Was Alena forced into unwanted sexual activity? Wilkinson (1997) said, "In the racially structured and multicultural evolution of this country, sex and gender alone have not been the principal determinants of the experiences or self-definitions of Mexican Americans," (p. 267). And while this is true, the question becomes, How would communities of color be transformed if gender were more central to the analysis or if the intersections of race and gender were seen as relevant to the improvement of both men and women's lives (Cole & Guy-Sheftall, 2003)?

Although white women contend with sexism, race and racism are constructs that most do not think about (Robinson, 2001). Among white people, race is often not the most organizing construct in their lives. For girls and women of color, race, culture, social class, and urbanization interact with gender and create female responses and positions that are diverse and fluctuating (Abrams, 2002). It is critical that clinicians conceptualize their patients' stories within the context of female gender and as other (Smart, 2010).

Often adolescents who are depressed exhibit irritable behavior that is mistaken for behavioral misconduct (e.g., oppositional defiant disorder) but is actually deep sadness. In some instances, there is a combination of anxiety and a mood disorder; however, the context and the length of time that the child has had the symptoms needs to be known. Alena could be sad and anxious for many valid reasons: She has a fractured relationship with her father and thus feels rejected by him; she lacks a circle of women with whom to confide about her multiple identities, she is 15, and she has questions about sex and boys and relationships, yet she feels silenced by both of her parents. It is highly possible that Lima, a therapist who is old enough to be Alena's mother, is able to hold Alena's sadness. Lima asked Alena's mother about Alena's early childhood. As a young child of 7, Alena was reserved yet tended to be oversocialized with somewhat negative appraisals of herself (intropunitive). Block and Block (2006) indicated in their 30-year longitudinal study that depressive tendencies identified in young adulthood are related to prior observer-based evaluations from parents and teachers.

Alena's parents love her. There are, however, narratives that Alena needs to share that may be hard for her parents to hear. Even with all of the strides that women have made, women tend to be socialized not to express anger; sadness and fear are more readily tolerated. Alena needs to learn that anger is an acceptable emotion, but there are positive and nondestructive ways to release it. Thus, Lima demonstrates multicultural competence by being aware of her own sexist biases and the mental health issues that often impact women in particular. Brown (2003) is critical of the culture and its suppression of girls' strong feelings. To mediate their frustrations, fears, marginalization, and anger, girls will fight with other girls. Alena's feelings of rejection and betrayal from her father contributes to her emotions as does her frustration with her mother's lack of autonomy.

Alena's parents and other wise people can offer her a place to go and to be as healing occurs. Alena would benefit richly from a mentor, someone who can nurture her development and focus on the communal aspects of being in community with others (Portman & Garrett, 2005). May Alena experience what Duerk (1994) envisions when she asks:

> How might your life have been different if, through the years, there had been a place where you could go? A place of women . . . who understood your tiredness and need for rest? A place of women who could help you to accept your fatigue and trust your limitations and to know in the dark of winter, that your energy would return, as surely as the spring, women who could help you to learn to light a candle and wait? (p. 60)

Summary

In this chapter, the construct of gender in women's and men's lives was considered. The socialization process, as well as biological dimensions, were explored. Mental health professionals need to be aware of the consequences of gender socialization on their personal lives and on those of their clients. Not to do so is to ignore the role of gender in life. Implications for the development of a healthy relationship with the body were presented. Multiple components of physical attractiveness exist and encompass facial beauty, skin color, body size, strength, visible signs of aging, height, weight, and hair length and texture. A case study examined multiple themes in the gendered, cultural, and clinical life of an adolescent teen.

15

Converging Sexuality

❖

This chapter focuses on sexuality. From the beginning, it should be noted that language is in flux and has changed over time. Terms in this chapter will be defined including more recent terminology. Sexuality exists on a continuum representing variations within and between homosexuality, bisexuality, and heterosexuality. There are people who have lived part of their lives with a particular sexual orientation and have come to question this identity construction. Persons who are transgendered, including people who identify as lesbian, gay, and bisexual may or may not fit into the binary of woman or man, gay or straight. This chapter recognizes the fluidity of sexuality over the developmental cycle and recognizes sexuality as part of a developmental system. A person's "sexual landscape might change, thus creating new opportunities for self description while transforming or eliminating existing possibilities" (Rust, 2006, p. 174). A possible outcome of this discussion is that the reader will become more conscious of a heterosexual bias that continues to exist in the societal culture at large and the profession in particular. An assumption of heterosexuality can be silencing and offensive to lesbian, gay, bisexual, transgender, and questioning clients. As clinicians increase their awareness of their biases and their proximity to heterosexist discourses, service delivery will hopefully improve. Far too often, graduate counseling programs do not provide adequate training in transgender issues, in particular. Unpacking personal biases and receiving knowledge about gay, lesbian, bisexual, intersexual, and transgendered clients provides therapists with the knowledge, skills, and competencies needed for this and other sexual minority populations. A case study concludes the chapter.

Definitions and Terminology

Definitions are provided to enhance understanding and to stay current with evolving terms associated with the lesbian, gay, bisexual, and transgender (LGBT) community. Hunt (1993) said, "As with any group, language has a strong impact on gay and lesbian culture. As times change and as words develop new connotations some words fall out of favor" (p. 2).

Current terminology in the multicultural literature includes the following terms. The relevance of these terms will vary according to an individual's personal preference: gay man, transman, transwoman, lesbian woman, bisexual, pansexual, asexual, transfeminine, transmasculine, gender queer, zer, and *they* (Davis, Henise, & Galupo, 2014; Weber, 2015). *They* reflects the fluidity and multiplicity of gender and sexuality within an individual's life. (See Storytelling: Language.) Mental health professionals have a responsibility to be informed of the current language so as not to be insensitive or misinformed.

Heterosexism is the belief that everyone is heterosexual and that heterosexual relationships are preferred and necessary for the preservation of the family, particularly the nuclear family. Heterosexism is institutionalized through religion, education, and the media and leads to homophobia (Robinson & Watt, 2001). It describes the institutionalization of antigay, antilesbian, and antibisexual beliefs, attitudes, and behaviors. Heterosexism is the deeply ingrained notion that heterosexuality is the superior sexual orientation (Wall & Evans, 1992). Pharr (1988) stated that heterosexism has been defined as a worldview, a value system that prizes heterosexuality, that assumes it is the only appropriate manifestation of love and sexuality, and that devalues homosexuality and all that is not heterosexual. Dines and Humez (2002) described heterosexism as the heterosexual predisposition that is encoded into and characteristic of the major social, cultural, and economic institutions of our society.

❖ STORYTELLING: LANGUAGE

The terms *transsexual, transgender, cross-dressers,* and *gay* are not well understood. Transgender is an umbrella term that can be used to refer to anyone for whom the assigned sex at birth does not apply and/or is incomplete (Nadal, Skolnik, & Wong, 2012). As I lectured in class one night, I mentioned that the majority of men who were cross-dressers were not gay but heterosexual and that people can be transgendered but not gay. There was silence, and the confused looks on students' faces told me that they did not understand what I had just said. Another way to look at transgender was defined by Towle and Morgan (2002), who said that the word *transers* "has sometimes replaced third gender to designate gender roles and practices which are not definable in terms of local understandings of gender normativity"

(p. 473). *Trans* is short for transgender or transsexual, although there are people who are transgender who do not regard themselves as transsexual. The term *third gender* was introduced in 1975 by M. Kay Martin and Barbara Voorhies and drew attention to the ethnographic evidence that gender categories in some cultures (as well as our own here in the West) could not be adequately explained in a two-gender framework. The man who loves his body and has a girlfriend refers to himself as transgendered because he does not always feel male; sometimes *they* (his preferred pronoun) feels female. *They* wear skirts, do not regard this traditionally female garment as similar to cross-dressing, and have no intention of making medical changes (e.g., the use of hormones is not an option).

Although the term *transvestite* has been in existence for a long time during an era prior to the legalization of same-sex marriage, it has been replaced with cross-dressers due to the negative connotations associated with transvestite ("GLAAD Media Reference Guide," 2015). Cross-dressers are often heterosexual males who do not wish to change their sex or live permanently as women but choose to dress in culturally defined women's clothing and other accessories as a form of gender expression, to experience the inner feminine, with or without sexual arousal (Boyd, 2003; "GLAAD Media Reference Guide," 2015).

According to the U.S. Census Bureau (2014c), there are 783,100 same-sex couples in America, which is vastly lower than the numbers (901,997 same-sex couples) reported by demographer Gary Gates in 2011. The majority of the same-sex couples (52%) are female (405,197). According to the U.S. Census Bureau (2014c), same-sex male couples number 377,903. (See Population Box 15.1: Demographic Characteristics of Married and Opposite-Sex and Same-Sex Couples.)

Albeit surprising, due to the religious and political conservatism, demographer Gates (2011) states that it is in the deep south and mountain west regions that child rearing among same-sex couples is most common. Speaking to the developmental nature of sexuality, people may come out later in life as LGBT and have children from a previous relationship with a partner of a different sex or gender identity.

Population Box 15.1: Demographic Characteristics of Married and Opposite-Sex Couples and Same-Sex Couples

Married Opposite-Sex Couples	*Same-Sex Couples*
Total Number: 55,779,842	Total Number: 783,100
Average Age: 51.9	Average Age: 48.4
65 years and older: 21.9%	65 years and older: 15.2%
55 - 64: 21.3%	55 - 64: 17.1%
45 - 54: 22.2%	45 - 54: 26.6%
35 - 44: 20%	35 - 44: 19.7%
25 - 34: 13.3%	25 - 34: 17.3%
15 - 24: 1.3%	15 - 24: 4.1%
White alone: 73.4%	White alone: 75.7%
Hispanic (of any race): 12.4%	Hispanic (of any race): 11.7%
Black: 6.9%	Black: 7.4%
AI/AN: 0.6%	AI/AN: 0.7%
Asian: 5.6%	Asian: 3.1%
NHPI: 0.1%	NHPI: 0.2%
SOR: 3.2%	SOR: 2.5%
2 or more races: 1.5%	2 or more races: 2.5%
Interracial couples: 6.8%	Interracial couples: 14.8%
Householder/bachelors: 38.2%	Householder/bachelors: 48.6%
Both partners employed: 47.8%	Both partners employed: 59.5%
Children in home: 39.6%	Children in home: 17.3%

Source: U.S. Census Bureau (2014c).

There are people who are transgendered who may also identify as gay or bisexual or questioning their sexuality. Transgendered does not mean gay. Transgender refers to persons who have a female or male gender assignment at birth but may experience a different gendered reality from the gender assignment at birth. People may refer to themselves as transgender and still consider themselves gay, lesbian, bisexual, or heterosexual. A male-to-female transsexual (e.g., trans female) might put it this way, "I see myself being with a man, but I do not see myself as a man with a man. I see myself as a woman with a man." (See Storytelling: Living Authentically.)

Transsexuals may not define themselves as gay but have had or plan to undergo gender-affirming surgery that may include hormone treatments or electrolysis for assigned males at birth who are transitioning to the female gender.

The term *cisgender* is used by some to describe people who are not transgender. *Cis* is a Latin prefix, which means "on the same side as," and is an antonym of trans.

Homosexual defines attraction to the same sex for physical and emotional nurturance and is one orientation on the homosexuality, bisexuality, and heterosexuality continuum. This term has become associated with the historical belief that homosexuality is unnatural, a sin, and a sickness. For this reason, females who are homosexual/gay often prefer the term lesbian to describe their sexual orientation. The difference in terminology, which arose during the feminist movement, reflects the difference between gay men and lesbians. The term lesbian gets its origins from the Greek poet Sappho (c. 600 BC), who lived on the Greek island of Lesbos in the Aegean Sea. Sappho's poems are exclusively about women.

Although similar to heterosexism, *homophobia* is regarded as a sense of dread of being in close quarters with people who are lesbian, bisexual, or gay (Worthington, Dillon, & Becker-Schutte, 2005). Homophobia comes from the Latin *homo,* meaning "same" (in this case, referring to same-gender attraction), and *phobia,* meaning "fear of"; thus, the term's original application to individuals was an extreme and persistent fear and loathing of homosexuals (Pharr, 1988). Fear, hatred, and dislike tied to cultural socialization, political, and/or religious beliefs are often present with homophobia. *Homonegativity* has been defined as negative feelings and thoughts about lesbian, gay, or bisexual orientations or individuals (Worthington et al., 2005). Someone who acknowledges their homoerotic orientation and incorporates this knowledge into their identity and carries this identity into interpersonal relationships is defined as gay. The term gay signifies more self-awareness, self-acceptance, and openness than the term homosexual. Often, in developmental literature, the process of coming to terms with one's sexuality involves moving from being homosexual to becoming gay. One consequence of homophobia is *internalized homophobia*. It is produced by the negative messages about homosexuality that people hear throughout their lives. Because gay men and lesbians are stereotyped, uninformed, or fed inaccurate, distorted information about homosexuality, the messages are internalized and may result in low self-esteem. Internalized homophobia can lead to self-hatred and other psychological problems (Dworkin & Gutierrez, 1991).

Rust (2006) aptly pointed out that people sometimes misrepresent their identities to avoid judgment and disapproval. She said, "Lesbians and gay men often misrepresent their sexual locations when in heterosexual contexts, and bisexual women often misrepresent their location when in lesbian contexts" (p. 179). *Bisexuality* represents a shifting and dynamic sexual landscape that can be misunderstood, not only among heterosexually identified people but also among gay men and lesbian women.

❖ STORYTELLING: LIVING AUTHENTICALLY

I once knew someone who had a wife and three children. This person, who I'll refer to as Cedar, served many years in the military. Although Cedar had an outward appearance that was masculine, in terms of style of dress, mannerism, and voice, Cedar felt that being male was not accurate, that an error had occurred. Cedar also was attracted to men, but as a person who identified as female. Cedar felt paralyzed. On one hand, Cedar loved the woman with whom Cedar had three children and had shared a life together for a long time. On the other hand, Cedar felt that the secrecy and hiding were a death sentence. Denial was no longer an option. Cedar decided to get therapy to explore sexuality and identity as well as how to live authentically. Cedar has always felt different because there had been an attraction to men, but not as a gay man—as a woman attracted to a man. Cedar did not want to hurt anyone and said in therapy, "My wife has always been good to me, and she is such a kind soul." It took Cedar a while to find a suitable counselor. The first therapist, upon learning Cedar was struggling with transgender issues, suggested Cedar see another counselor, citing her Catholicism and Cedar's LGBT issues as conflicting with the counselor's religious values. Feeling deflated and defeated, Cedar waited before searching again for a suitable professional with whom to work. After nearly a year, Cedar found a skilled and nonjudgmental clinician. After therapy for almost a year, Cedar decided to tell the truth: that a divorce was necessary and that to live authentically meant living life as a female. Therapy helped Cedar realize that no one was going to emerge from this situation without being hurt, including herself.

Cedar had spent so much of her life hiding and denying what she knew to be true. Because she started to feel her own hurt and pain, she was able to recognize that her coming forward would be hurtful to her wife and children. Sadness was one emotion but altogether different from deception. Therapy also helped Cedar think about what it meant to be transsexual. Not only had Cedar been battling heterosexism throughout her life, but sexism as well. At the same time, she was committed to being honest, answering people's questions, and staying connected to family.

For as long as Cedar could remember, she felt different, and yet words failed to fully express the nature and extent of this difference, which contributed to Cedar's sense of isolation and confusion about who she was and who she was not. Not having people in whom Cedar could confide contributed to her loneliness. It was a significant step for Cedar to disclose her struggles with a therapist. In doing so, words again failed her in that she did not have the language to explain who she was: a medically "normal" XY person assigned to the male gender at birth who felt that her gender assignment was wrong but did not identify as gay because she saw herself as a female who was attracted to men. Growing up in rural West Virginia fueled Cedar's self-perception that she was abnormal. Therapy helped Cedar understand the stigma associated with not aligning with the gender binary. Therapy also helped her see how she had internalized oppression and that racism, sexism, and homophobic attitudes were prevalent throughout her life. Cedar's authenticity was noted in deciding to no longer live a lie. Fortunately, Cedar's

---

❖ STORYTELLING: LIVING AUTHENTICALLY

therapist was attentive to her multiple identities, particularly within the context of multiple sources of discrimination (Greene, 1994).

While mental health professionals are not supposed to function outside of their scope of training or competence, counselors are encouraged to "gain knowledge, personal awareness, sensitivity, and skills pertinent to working with a diverse client population" (American Counseling Association, 2005, C.2.a). Cedar's first counselor clearly exhibited biased and inappropriate practice (Garnets, Hancock, Cochran, Goodchilds, & Peplau, 1991).

Hermann and Herlihy (2006) caution counselors about not treating sexual minority clients because of the counselor's religious convictions. In citing the case of *Bruff vs. North Mississippi Health Services, Inc.,* in 2001, they explained that "the most significant legal aspect of the Bruff case is the court's holding that an employer's legal obligation to make reasonable accommodations for employees' religious beliefs does not include accommodating a counselor's request to refer homosexual clients who ask for assistance with relationship issues" (p. 416). In short, counselors cannot use their religious practices and beliefs to defend discrimination based on sexual orientation.

Intersexual refers to people who are (pseudo) hermaphrodites (Kitzinger, 1999), or persons born with genitalia that is different or ambiguous enough to raise concerns because it deviates from a normative appearance. However, intersexuality is not always evident from an external evaluation. A newborn might have genitalia that resemble a very large clitoris and/or male genitalia that have a more masculine appearance. Intersexuality may be caused by congenital adrenal hyperplasia, mixed gonadal dysgenesis, androgen insensitivity syndrome (complete or partial), 5-alpha reductase deficiency, and many other conditions (Chase, 2003). The narrow construction and bifurcation of gender, which translates into males having a designated penis size and testicles and females not having a clitoris that is too large and a vagina and uterus, does not apply to all children born in the United States and throughout the world (Sterling, 1992).

Queer theory is a field of gender and sexuality studies that emerged in the early 1990s out of the gay/lesbian and feminist studies, drawing attention to the social construction of categories of normative and deviant sexual behavior. Queer theory rejects the idea that sexuality exists as an essentialist category determined by biology and/or judged by eternal standards of morality. Among queer theorists, sexuality is complex, and includes social codes, forces, individual activity, and institutional power, which interact to shape the ideas of normativity and deviance at any point in time which then operate under the rubric of what is natural, biological, or god-given (Klages, 2005). Deconstructionists influenced this field, which is a critique of gender and sexual identities. Queer language exists as a form of resistance to imposed structures from dominant cultures.

When gay men and lesbians come to accept being gay or lesbian as a salient component of their identities, it is descriptive of the process of *coming out*. Numerous developmental models describe the stages of the coming-out process, such as those of Cass (1979) and Coleman (1982). Gay and lesbian people have struggled throughout history with the notion that their sexual identity was a choice—and the wrong choice. Because of socialization, some gay men and lesbians have behaved heterosexually although their identity was gay or lesbian. Many remember feeling different at a very early age and see this difference as stemming from their gay and lesbian orientation. For this reason, the term *sexual orientation*, rather than *sexual preference*, is used. By owning this orientation, gay men and lesbians make a conscious choice to allow their behavior to conform to their orientation.

Heterosexism affects everyone, covertly and overtly, in this society. It is harmful not only to the victims but also to the perpetrators. According to Smith (1982), heterosexism is intimately associated with other discriminatory practices (e.g., classism, sexism, racism, ageism) in our society. She stated that verbal and behavioral expressions of heterosexism are acceptable and go uncontested in contexts where other discriminatory comments or gesticulations (e.g., racist, sexist, or anti-Semitic remarks) would be challenged or prohibited.

Sexual politics ensures the dominance of males over females and the dominance of heterosexuals over persons who are gay and lesbian (Pleck, 1984). Within a system of *hegemony* (a historical situation in which power is won and held) and androcentrism (in which the complementarity of women and men implies women's subordinate social position to men), homosexuality becomes a threat for heterosexual men. Heterosexual men are socialized into believing that to reject anything that remotely resembles homosexuality, they must oppress women. For this reason, "any kind of powerlessness, or refusal to compete among men becomes involved with the imagery of homosexuality" (Pleck, 1984, p. 84). Sexual inequality and heterosexuality cannot be discussed without addressing sociopolitical power dynamics within society, such as the suppression of women's sexuality, forced sexuality through incest and rape, the idealization of heterosexual marriage, and the contradicting and confusing roles of motherhood.

Traditionally, a healthy or ideal personality has included a concept of *sexual identity* with three basic components:

1. A sexual preference for members of the opposite sex.

2. A sex role identity as either masculine or feminine, depending on one's gender.

3. A gender identity that is a secure sense of one's maleness or femaleness.

Bem (1993) challenged these components by stating that the terms heterosexual and homosexual should be used to describe acts rather than persons.

Narrative Questions

It is often through exposure to other people's personal narratives that students gain insight into the lived experiences of others. Gaining insight into one's own personal stories and histories is essential to self-knowledge. Consider your responses to the following questions (Falco, 1991, p. 174):

1. What was the first reference to gay men or lesbian women that you remember hearing?

2. What do you remember about the first person you ever saw or met who you identified as gay or lesbian?

3. What did your parents teach you about people who are gay and lesbian?

4. What type of treatment did gay and lesbian clients receive in your therapy or counseling course?

5. How were gay or lesbian student therapists treated in your training program? Gay or lesbian supervisors or instructors?

6. Do you currently have friends or acquaintances who you know to be gay or lesbian? If not, why do you think this is so?

7. What is the most memorable same-sex experience of your life? The most traumatic? The most meaningful and/or eye-opening?

8. What were you taught about people who were transgender?

9. How helpful or problematic do you think reality show images are of transfeminine transwomen, particularly within the context of being monied and glamorous? Are such images accurate depictions of the lives of people who identify as transfeminine or transmasculine transsexuals?

The Importance of a Focus on Gay, Lesbian, Bisexual, and Transgender Issues in Mental Health Diversity Practice

To be effective, therapists need to receive adequate training in counseling persons who are LGBT. First, they must understand the terms briefly discussed earlier. Rudolph (1990) projected that approximately 25% to 65% of the gay, lesbian, and bisexual population seeks psychotherapy, a percentage 2 to 4 times higher than in the heterosexual population. Moreover, a significantly larger percentage of gay men and lesbians report dissatisfaction with their treatment, compared with heterosexuals.

Although there is a need to provide psychotherapy in the gay/lesbian community, many mental health professionals have not been provided the appropriate training to assist gay men, lesbians, and bisexuals effectively through their coming out or identity development process. Beals and Peplau (2006) found in their study of 144 gay men and lesbians that they have better relationships with people they have directly told about their sexuality compared with people with whom they have not disclosed. Clearly, disclosure of a stigmatized identity can have profound and lasting implications for relationships; nonetheless, this finding suggests that relationship quality is adversely affected when people have not revealed core information about their identity.

Survey and anecdotal literature reveals that the source of dissatisfaction often is the counselor's ignorance or prejudice toward people who are gay (Bell & Weinberg, 1978).

Just as clinicians must be aware of their racial biases regarding cultural and racial groups, they must also assess their biases as they relate to gay, lesbian, and bisexual clients (Pope, 1995). Clinicians have been influenced by living in a society that socializes people toward racist and homophobic attitudes. For example, Caroline Pace (1991) conducted an in-depth study on the attitudes of mental health professionals and graduate students in training programs toward gay men and lesbians. She found that "counselors, like other individuals socialized by heterosexist institutions in the United States, hold negative attitudes toward lesbians and gays" (p. 73). The mental health professionals and counselors-in-training scored in the "low grade homophobic" range of the Index of Attitudes toward Homosexuals Scale.

LGBT people experience homophobia not only in the counselor's office, which should be a safe place to explore identity issues, but also from the general public. In a study of 1,669 students, staff, faculty, and administrators at 14 private and public colleges and universities, 29% of respondents reported that they had been harassed because of their sexual orientation or gender identity (Rankin, 2002). Harassment was defined as "conduct that has interfered unreasonably with your ability to work or learn on this campus or has created an offensive, hostile, intimidating working or learning environment" (Rankin, 2002, p. 26). The harassment was most likely, at 57%, to occur in public space on campus or while people were walking or working on campus. The harassment most frequently occurred through derogatory remarks, at 89%; verbal harassment or threats, 48%; graffiti, 39%; and pressure to be silent about sexual orientation/gender, 38%. This study also found that the majority of respondents, 71%, perceived transgender people to be the most likely to be harassed on campus. The actual percentage of harassment that occurred against transgendered people was 41%. In an environment that should support the universe of expression, ideas, and exploration, colleges and universities have been bastions of heterosexist and homophobic activity.

Other crucial issues that face the LGBT population are substance abuse, depression, running away, HIV and AIDS, partner abuse, and attempted suicide. Researchers maintain that substance abuse among lesbians and gay men is high. The gay bar may be the most accessible and visible place to persons who are "out" to interact with others who are also "out" (Rothblum, 1994). Gay men and lesbians attempt suicide 2 to 7 times more often than heterosexual comparison groups (Durby, 1994; Hammelman, 1993). Gay youth have a plethora of problems during adolescence, such as intensified feelings of isolation, depression, and lack of healthy role models (Browning, Reynolds, & Dworkin, 1994). School counselors should be aware of, and be prepared to work with, a diversity of youth because an estimated 3 million adolescents across the country are gay, lesbian, or bisexual. Unfortunately, because of the lack of role models and sympathetic support systems, another 20% to 35% of these young individuals attempt suicide (O'Connor, 1992). Gay youth are vulnerable and need caring adults. Racism and other sources of discrimination heighten this vulnerability among gay youth (Greene & Herek, 1994).

Asian American gay people find themselves "caught between two conflicting cultural values, between Asian and Western influences" (Chan, 1992, p. 116). Asian American and Native American Indian gay men and lesbians also contend with strong traditional family roles, subsequent expectations, and community values that are often collectivistic, as opposed to individualistic, in orientation (Greene, 1994).

Developmental Processes

Sexuality interacts with other aspects of the self, such as race, age, class, and geography. The need to develop a clear sense of one's sexuality is not limited to GLBTIQQ (gay, lesbian, bisexual, transgender, intersexual, questioning, and queer people) only. Robinson and Watt (2001) argued, "The socially endorsed experience of heterosexuality and the unconscious and unearned privilege afforded heterosexuals often deems them unaware of the importance to transition through sexual identity formation" (p. 594).

Not thinking about oneself as a sexual being (even if one self-identifies as asexual) is similar to not thinking about oneself as having race and has implications for therapists' ability to hear their clients talk about matters related to sexuality. Several themes of identity evolution, which is different from formation as it suggests an endpoint, have been identified by Eliason and Schope (2007): differences, confusion, exploration, disclosure, labeling, cultural immersion, distrust of the oppressor, degree of integration, internalized, oppression, managing, stigma, identity transformation, and, authenticity. (See Storytelling: Living Authentically.)

Several linear models of gay and lesbian identity development exist. There are limitations associated with these models. Not all people progress through the stages as prescribed in that they may skip a stage or recycle back through them in the face of a significant event. There are older adults who experience their sexuality differently from youth. Some of the models do not account for development after adolescence. In addition, the experience of being bisexual and/or transgender is different from being gay or lesbian. Being a lesbian is a very different experience from being a gay male.

Erwin (2006) argues that lesbians are frequently overlooked by researchers, except when they are open about their identity, do not conform to societal gender role expectations, or have concerns about their sexual orientation. Being a feminine lesbian does not describe the experience of a woman who is butch in her appearance or lesbian woman of color (Eliason & Schope, 2007). Despite the limitations of stage models, they do provide some understanding of where people might be in their evolution. This model can also help therapists and student development professionals with understanding the questions and themes that describe certain stages or phases. Cass's model is described below.

Cass's Model of Gay, Lesbian, and Bisexual Sexual Identity Formation

Vivian Cass (1979) developed a model to assess the growth, development, and awareness of gay, lesbian, and bisexual individuals. Most counselors will work with a gay, lesbian, or bisexual client at some juncture during their professional careers. The Cass model is provided as a guideline for assessing a client's level of development. It is important to note that the client may foreclose at a given stage, skip certain levels, or regress from a higher stage to a lower stage, depending on the events that occur in his or her life, or the significance of other identities in the person's life.

Coping strategies vary for LGBT clients. Often, a therapist can assess the gay client's level of identity development in the coming-out process. According to the Cass model (1984), the gay identity formation process occurs in six stages, beginning with the individual having a sexual self-portrait that is heterosexual. For example, if the client were talking about a female, the female would see herself and her behavior as heterosexual as well as perceive others to view her as heterosexual. For the most part, the person's sexual self-portrait is consistent or congruent with heterosexuality. At some point in life, however, a change occurs. It might happen in childhood, in adolescence, in early adulthood, in middle age, or even very late in life.

Stage 1: Identity Confusion: Identity confusion is characterized by a growing awareness of thoughts, feelings, or behaviors that may be homosexual in nature. These self-perceptions are incongruent with earlier assumptions of personal heterosexuality and constitute the first developmental conflict of this model. Entrance into this stage begins with the conscious awareness that information regarding homosexuality is somehow personally relevant. When the continuing personalization of this information can no longer be ignored, the individual's sexual self-portrait feels inconsistent, or incongruent. The process of gay identity formation has begun.

Examples of questions a person in Stage 1 may be asking are "Who am I?" "Am I homosexual?" and "Am I really a heterosexual?" The individual sometimes feels, thinks, or acts in a homosexual way but would rarely, if ever, tell anyone about this behavior. The individual is fairly sure that homosexuality has something to do with him, her, or *they* personally.

With continuing personalization of information regarding homosexuality, the person begins privately to label their behavior (or thoughts or feelings) as possibly gay. Publicly, the person maintains a self-image as heterosexual and perceives others as maintaining the same image. To deal with this incongruity, the person adopts one or more of the following three strategies (Berzon, 1988). The first is the *inhibition strategy* and describes the person who regards the definition of their behavior (thoughts, feelings) as correctly gay, but who finds this definition undesirable and unacceptable. Several actions are taken: the person restricts information regarding homosexuality (e.g., I don't want to hear, read, or know about it) or inhibits behavior (e.g., It may be true, but I'm not going to do anything about it). Denying the personal relevance of information regarding homosexuality is also an action taken (e.g., It has nothing to do with me). Other possible behaviors include becoming hypersexual (e.g., within the context of heterosexual interactions) or becoming asexual, wherein the person seeks a "cure." Another action is to become an antigay moral or religious crusader. If the inhibition strategies employed are successful in enabling the person to inhibit, redefine, or disown responsibility for gay behavior, a foreclosure of gay/lesbian identity will occur at Stage 1.

Personal innocence strategy is a second strategy. Here, the person rejects either the meaning or the context of the homosexual behavior so as not to have to own it but then redefines the meaning or context of the behavior. For example, in U.S. society, genital contact between males is acceptable in a variety of situations without the participating individuals being defined as gay. Little boys have "circle jerks." Men confined for long periods of time without access to women, such as in prison or other confined situations, have genital contact with one another, and they are not necessarily defined as gay. The shift occurs in the contextual meaning when males develop emotional attachments to the other males with whom they are having sex or when they have repeated contacts with the same male, increasing the possibility of emotional involvement.

For females in U.S. society, just the opposite is true. Girls can be inseparable, experience deep emotional involvement with one another, and spend more time with each other, even into adulthood, than they do with the men in their lives, and this behavior is not regarded as gay or unusual. For this reason, it may be easier for girls and women to hide their lesbian behavior or identities longer. The shift occurs when they have genital contact in addition to their emotional involvement, which is more likely to be considered lesbianism but may not be. Quite a bit of same-sex sexual experimentation occurs in adulthood among persons who had been or currently are in heterosexual marriages. Qualitative research is needed in this area.

Another personal innocence strategy is categorized as redefining context. The individual disowns responsibility for their homosexual behavior by redefining the context in which it occurred. Examples of these rationalizations are "I was just experimenting," "I was drunk," "I just did it for the money," "I did it as a favor for a friend," "It was an accident," and "I was taken advantage of."

Success in the use of the inhibition and personal innocence strategies depends on the individual's ability to avoid provocative situations and to employ the psychological defense of denial. It is impossible to avoid erotic dreams and physiological responses to persons of the same sex to whom the individual is attracted. In this instance, these strategies will be only partially successful, and the individual may very well experience the beginning of a negative or self-rejecting sexual identity.

The person in the *information-seeking strategy* is likely to adopt this third strategy if the meaning attributed to their homosexual behavior is perceived as correct, or at least partially acceptable. Now the individual seeks more information in books, in therapy, or in talking with anyone who might have expertise or experience related to this topic. The question being addressed is "Am I homosexual?" How individuals perceive these characteristics or behaviors will influence the way they seek to resolve the incongruence, either through repression (identity foreclosure) or by moving into Stage 2. This strategy of seeking more information moves the person along to Stage 2.

Stage 2: Identity Comparison: Individuals begin to investigate those qualities first experienced in Stage 1. As they begin to gather information and seek out contacts with gay others, there is increased congruence between self-perceptions and behaviors but increased conflict with others. Stage 2 statements of *identity comparison* would include "I feel like I probably am gay, although I am not definitely sure." "I feel different. I think I may want to talk with someone, maybe someone gay about feeling different, but I'm not sure if I really want to or not."

As the person accepts the possibility that he, she, or they may be gay, the individual begins to examine the wider implications of being gay. Whereas in Stage 1 the task was to handle the self-alienation that occurs with the first glimmerings of homosexuality, the main task of Stage 2 is to handle the social alienation that is produced by feeling different from peers, family members, and society at large. With the letting go of a perception of a self that is heterosexual, one can experience confusion or a sense of loss. Here people may see a gap between the identity of which they themselves are aware and the identity presented to others.

Certain conditions heighten the feeling of alienation from others, such as living in geographic isolation with no other gay people or resources available and being from a family that is deeply religious and with strong convictions about homosexuality as a sin.

Here are four strategies the individual may employ to reject homosexual self-definition while continuing homosexual behavior:

1. *Special case.* The person characterizes what is happening as the product of the liaison with one person and this one person only.

2. *Ambisexuality.* The person says he, she, or they can be sexual with anybody; it doesn't matter what gender the other person is.

3. *Temporary identity.* The person regards being gay as only temporary: "I could be heterosexual again any minute."

4. *Personal innocence.* The person blames being gay on anyone or everyone else.

As conflict heightens, individuals may move to Stage 3.

Stage 3: Identity Tolerance: *Identity tolerance* is marked by increased contact with the gay community, leading to greater empowerment. At this point, individuals hold an increasingly strong gay self-image but continue to present themselves (outside the community) as heterosexual. There is dissonance, and the person is characterized as reluctantly adopting a gay self-concept based on the stigma associated with this identity and their own internalized oppression: "I'm gay and I tolerate (put up with) it." "I see myself as homosexual for now, but I'm not sure about the future." These are statements that a person would make at this stage. It occurs when the person has come to accept the probability that he, she, or they is gay and recognizes the sexual, social, and emotional needs that come with being homosexual.

With more of a commitment to a gay identity, the person is now free to pursue social, emotional, and sexual needs. Meeting these needs accentuates the difference between the person and heterosexuals even more. To deal with the increased social alienation from heterosexuals, the person seeks out gay people and the gay subculture. Involvement in the gay/lesbian community has distinct advantages in terms of movement toward a more positive gay/lesbian identity. According to Berzon (1988), it (1) contributes to a ready-made support group that understands and shares the individual's concerns, (2) provides opportunities to meet a partner, (3) gives access to positive gay and lesbian role models, and (4) provides opportunities to practice feeling more at ease as a lesbian or a gay man. However, if the person has poor social skills, is very shy, has low self-esteem, has strong fear of exposure (of sexual identity), or has a fear of the unknown, positive contacts are made more difficult.

A negative experience may occur if the person encounters gay men and lesbians who are still employing the inhibition and denial strategies of Stages 1 and 2. These lesbians and gay men will be perceived as unhappy, self-rejecting individuals with whom one would not want to be affiliated. However, individuals at this stage will be empowered by people who are accepting of their own gay and lesbian identities. A shift occurs when the individual's significant others are gay rather than heterosexuals.

If the contacts made are experienced as negative, a reduction of involvement with gay subculture is probable, resulting in a foreclosure at Stage 3. If contacts are perceived as positive, it is likely that the strategies employed have broken down and that the individual will want to explore further. This breakdown of strategies will result in movement into Stage 4. In any case, the commitment to gay identity is now sufficient for the person to say, I am gay.

Stage 4: Identity Acceptance: At this point, the conflict between the self and non-gay others' perceptions is at an intense level. This conflict may be resolved through passing as "straight," having limited contact with heterosexuals, or selectively disclosing to significant (heterosexual) others. A person at this stage may say, "I am quite sure that I am gay/lesbian." "I accept this fairly happily." "I am prepared to tell a few people about being gay/lesbian (e.g., friends, family members), but I carefully select whom I tell." Identity acceptance occurs when the person accepts, rather than tolerates, a gay self-image and contact with the gay/lesbian subculture continues and increases.

The individual now has a positive identification with other gay people. The questions of earlier stages (What am I? Where do I belong?) have been answered. Attitudes toward sexual orientation of the gay men and lesbians with whom the person becomes associated are crucial at this point. If these individuals regard being gay as partially legitimate (being gay is okay in private, but being public about it is not okay), then the person is likely to adopt this attitude as their own philosophy and to live a compartmentalized, "passing," gay life.

To reduce the stress involved in interfacing with a homophobic society, the person has less and less to do with heterosexuals. Some selective disclosure of gayness to nongay family, friends, and coworkers occurs, but as much control as possible is exercised over the potentially discrediting information. The emphasis is on fitting into society and not making waves. If, on the one hand, this strategy is successful, the person forecloses at this identity acceptance stage. If, on the other hand, the person comes to associate with people who regard being gay as fully legitimate (in private and public), this attitude is likely to be adopted. Greater acceptance of one's gay orientation tends to increase the distance the person now feels from a society that is still homophobic. Homophobic attitudes are now particularly offensive to the person characterized by this stage.

To deal with the anger toward a rejecting society, in combination with the increasing self-acceptance that is occurring, the person moves into Stage 5. Those who find that the strategies described effectively manage the conflict may stay at this level comfortably; otherwise, the continuing conflict pushes them onward.

Stage 5: Identity Pride: Identity pride is marked not only by strong pride in the gay community and in identity, but also by intense anger directed toward, and isolation from, the heterosexual society. The conflict is managed through fostering a dichotomized homosexual (valued) and heterosexual (devalued) worldview. How others, particularly those who are not gay, respond to the expression of these feelings influences whether individuals move to the final stage. Persons who have arrived at this stage may say, "I feel proud to be gay/lesbian." "I am prepared to tell many people about being gay/lesbian and make no attempt to hide this fact." "I prefer to mix socially with other gay men/lesbians because heterosexuals are typically antigay." This stage occurs when, accepting the philosophy of full legitimization, the person becomes immersed in the gay/lesbian subculture and has less and less to do with heterosexual others.

As identification with the gay/lesbian community deepens, pride in accomplishments of the community increases. Daily living still requires continuing encounters with the heterosexual world and its homophobic attitudes. These encounters produce feelings of frustration and alienation. The combination of anger and pride energizes the person into action against the heterosexual establishment and creates "the activist."

Confrontation with the heterosexual establishment brings the person more into public view, and earlier strategies to conceal sexual orientation must be abandoned. Doing so precipitates disclosure crises with significant heterosexuals, such as family and coworkers.

What becomes crucial at this point is whether those significant heterosexuals in the gay person's life react negatively to the disclosure as expected or react positively. If the reaction is negative, confirming the person's expectations that it would be so, the view of the world as being divided into gays (who are okay) and nongays (who are not okay) gets reinforced. In this instance, the person forecloses at the identity pride stage. If the reactions of the heterosexuals to whom the person discloses are positive and inconsistent with their negative expectations, the person tends to change those expectations, which moves one to Stage 6.

Stage 6: Identity Synthesis: Movement to identity synthesis most likely occurs when individuals experience positive reactions from heterosexual others. The need to dichotomize the world into gays who are okay and nongays who are not is gone. The gay/lesbian aspect of one's identity can now be integrated with all other aspects of self.

Sexuality is regarded as one part of the individual's total identity. There is some conflict, but it is at the lowest and most manageable point. The person at this stage says, "I am prepared to tell anyone that I am gay/lesbian." "I am happy about the way I am but think that being gay/lesbian is not the most important part of me." "I mix socially with fairly equal numbers of gay men/lesbians and heterosexuals and anyone who is accepting of gay men and lesbians." The individual now acknowledges that some nongay people are as supportive of their gay identity as other gay people are. Because heterosexuals as a class are no longer seen as hostile, it is no longer necessary to sustain the high level of anger seen at Stage 5. Increasing contact with supportive nongays produces more trust.

Counseling LGBT Racial and Ethnic Minorities

A tremendous amount of oppression and isolation exists within communities of color around homosexuality. A man's expression of interest in another man is construed as homosexuality. In a heterosexist society, homosexuality is often feared. Kimmel (2006) said homophobia is interwoven with sexism and racism. Cedar, as a young man (from earlier Storytelling), exaggerated his masculinity and interest in traditional markers of masculinity: fighting and hypersexuality. Persons of color who are transsexual differ from white people who have similar experiences.

Within generally supportive gay and lesbian social communities, people of color who are LGBT are often oppressed and do not receive the affirmation that white LGBT people receive (Loiacano, 1989). Chae and Walters (2009) found in their cross-sectional investigation of 447 gay, lesbian, bisexual, and other sexual-minority American Indians/Alaska Natives that the effect of discrimination on self-reported health varied by actualization levels. Specifically, the negative influence of discrimination on self-reported general health may depend on levels of actualization: among two-spirit (LGBT) Native American/Alaska Natives with low levels of actualization, discrimination was associated with worse self-rated health, and among those with high levels of actualization, discrimination had little relationship with self-rated health.

Battle, Cohen, Warren, Fergerson, and Audam (2002) conducted a study in conjunction with the National Gay and Lesbian Task Force with 2,465 black LGBT people—58% men, 43% women, and 3% transgendered. They found that two thirds indicated that homophobia was a problem within the black community. Half of the respondents agreed that racism is a problem for black LGBT people in their relations with white LGBT people. Gender differences were found regarding the most important issues facing black LGBT people. Approximately 72% of the men stated that HIV/AIDS was the most important issue facing black LGBT people, while 55% of the women responded the same way. Women were more likely, at 50%, to say that hate crime violence was the most pressing issue; less than 40% of the men responded in this way. In addition to contending with hate crime, there is the pressing issue of domestic violence in same-sex relationships, which the National Coalition Against Domestic Violence estimates at 25% to 33% (Peterman & Dixon, 2003). Gay families struggle with many of the same issues that heterosexual families contend with and need support and appropriate intervention (Laird, 2003).

The racism and oppression faced by gay men and lesbians of color often urge them to turn to their same-race communities for the development of coping techniques, help with maintaining a positive identity, and potential support (Icard, 1986). Because of the level of homophobia, few gay men and lesbians of color actually find needed support psychologically and socially. The African American community often reflects the attitude that homosexuality is inconsistent with being black (Riggs, 1994).

Black gay males are faced with a problem of complying with male role expectations that include propagating the race and holding allegiance to the African American community, which generally maintains an antigay attitude (Icard, 1986). Similarities are found within the Native American Indian and Asian American cultures. Greene (1994) said that "bearing some similarity to Asian cultures, gender roles are clearly delineated among Indian families, and obedience to parents is expected" (p. 247).

In working with Native American Indian gay clients, the devastation of colonialism and Western influences need to be considered in interpreting sexuality. It is crucial that Spirit, and not the material world, be held as sacred in traditional Native American Indian cultures. Gunn Allen (1992) talked about the gynocentric societies, which value the centrality of women, honor the young, and revere all of life that is part of the whole. In traditional society, there were sacred places for men and women who were embodied by Spirit and did not want to marry persons of the other gender, and there were men who dressed and lived like women. Among Native Americans, the term *berdache* has been misapplied to both gay men and lesbians. It is an Arabic word meaning "sex-slave boy" and has no relevance to American men or women (Gunn Allen, 1992). Concerning contemporary Native American Indians who are gay, Greene (1994) stated that acceptance may be less on reservations than in large urban centers. Gunn Allen (1992) pointed to acculturation and fundamental Christianity as major influences on homophobic attitudes among some Native people.

The Policy Institute of the National Gay and Lesbian Task Force interviewed 912 Latino gay men drawn from New York, Miami, and Los Angeles as part of a project called Nuestras Voces (Our Voices). The men reported widespread experiences with oppression (homophobia, racism, and poverty). Sixty-four percent were verbally insulted as children for being gay or effeminate, 31% reported experiences of racism in the form of verbal harassment as children, 35% reported having been treated rudely as adults on account of their race or ethnicity, and 61% experienced a shortage of money for basic necessities, with 54% borrowing money to get by during the last 12 months before the interview (Diaz & Ayala, 2002). The report found that men who were high risk (less likely to use protection when engaging in anal intercourse with a non-monogamous partner) had higher rates of oppression when compared with low-risk men. To survive or cope with the pain of societal oppression and accompanying feelings of powerlessness, many men turn to drugs or alcohol as aids and comforters. Diaz and Ayala (2002) stated, "Substances are used to cope not only with homophobic messages but also with the anger and frustration caused by poverty, racism and many other forms of social discrimination and abuse" (p. 16). The authors proposed that HIV prevention programs must also help men learn to cope with (*and resist—* emphasis mine) the toxic forces of racism, poverty, sexism, and homophobia because these social forces weigh heavily on Latino gay men's lives. It is important for therapists who work with gay immigrant, ethnic, and other clients of color to ask themselves the following questions:

1. Is the client an immigrant or American born?

2. To what ethnic group does the client belong?

3. What are the specific cultural values of this group? Of the client's family? Of the client?

4. How strongly does the client follow traditional customs?

5. What is the client's socioeconomic status?

6. What is the client's level of bilingualism?

Implications for Mental Health Professionals

Exposure to people perceived to be threatening, such as lesbians and gays, can in turn reduce antigay attitudes (Moradi, van den Berg, & Epting, 2006). Personal exposure as well as exposure to information about this diverse population would be helpful. Gender prescriptions normalized by heterosexuals extend to LGBT populations. In addition, the social construction of race is evident within the LGBT community. LGBT individuals of color experience more psychological distress, financial instability, limited access to culturally competent care, and housing inequality than their white counterparts. Discrimination occurs among most LGBT older adults as, however, vast intragroup differences exist and are related to disability, age, gender status, race, income, the quality of aging, and identity development. For example, a 66-year-old adult who is transgender, single, working class, a person of color, and residing with non-related friends in an apartment, lives in a society where his or her gender, sexuality, and marital status are inconsistent with cultural values such as patriarchy, heterosexual marriage, home ownership, economic success, and reproduction. Conversely, the 48-year-old middle-class gay male who is married to and living with his husband, their children, and owns a home, occupies identity statuses that are culturally privileged and valued (Robinson-Wood & Weber, 2015).

According to Grant et al. (2011), who surveyed 6,540 transgendered and gender nonconforming individuals in all 50 states, Puerto Rico, and Guam, discrimination was pervasive throughout the entire sample. The combination, however, of antitransgender bias and persistent, structural racism was particularly evident and devastating. In general, people of color in general fared worse than white participants across the board. African American transgender respondents fared worse than all others in many areas examined. Income was adversely affected in that respondents lived in extreme poverty and were four times more likely to have a household income of less than $10,000/year compared to the general population. Forty-one percent of respondents reported attempting suicide compared to 1.6% of the general population. Vulnerability to attempting suicide was heightened by other losses and conditions such as losing a job due to bias (55%), being harassed/bullied in school (51%), low household income, or being the victim of physical assault (61%) or sexual assault (64%).The American Psychological Association (2006) has issued 16 guidelines for psychotherapy with lesbian, gay, and bisexual clients organized across four areas: attitudes, relationships and families, diversity issues, and education. Guidelines 1 through 4 stipulate that psychologists recognize bisexuality and assessment and treatment of LGBT populations, that homosexuality is stigmatized in society, and that psychologists' prejudicial attitudes can adversely affect the LGBT clients' level of disclosure. The second four guidelines state that psychologists strive to respect the important role that relationships have for LGBT people, that parenting can be particularly challenging, that family ties need not be defined by biology only, and that sexuality can have an impact on relationships and communication within one's family of origin. Guidelines 9 through 13 encourage psychologists to understand the struggles that many LGBT people experience, particularly youth, people with disabilities, and persons of color, and that the population as a whole is very diverse. The last three guidelines pertain to education and state that psychologists support training and knowledge development on LGBT issues and are aware of community resources for this population.

Moradi et al. (2006) conducted research with 175 heterosexual persons. It was found that the level of lesbian gay threat (which is defined as the self, and LG [lesbian and gay] as "fundamentally incompatible" [p. 58]) was positively correlated with antilesbian and antigay attitudes.

Several helping strategies that counselors can employ in their work with LGBTIQQ people are as follows:

1. Be aware of personal feelings toward gay men, lesbians, and people who are transgendered.

2. Validate confusion.

3. Provide a safe, supportive environment conducive to the exploration of this struggle and confusion.

4. Explore what it means to be gay.

5. Dispute myths about homosexuality and bisexuality.

6. Suggest readings.

7. Help the client move beyond the grief by acknowledging and expressing the loss of a heterosexual blueprint for life.

8. Become familiar with local resources for gay men, lesbians, bisexuals, and transgendered people, and suggest supportive organizations to assist the client in building a support structure within the gay community.

9. Assist the client in overcoming barriers to positive socialization.

10. Be sensitive to the impact a gay/lesbian, bisexual, or transgendered identity may have on the context surrounding the problems and issues faced by the individual.

11. Encourage the client to create a support system within the LGBT community before coming out to heterosexual significant others.

12. Have some type of gay, lesbian, or bisexual literature on the bookshelf.

13. Display something as small as a pin (one pin available for heterosexuals says "Straight but not narrow"), a poster, or a quote that depicts a multicultural and nonbiased view of the world.

14. Attend workshops on counseling gay men, lesbians, bisexuals, and transgendered people.

15. Stay informed of local gay events that can serve as a resource to clients.

16. Personally and honestly assess one's level of sexual identity development.

17. Be aware of sexual identity models for heterosexuals as well as models for LGBT clients.

There are gay and lesbian clients who feel cautious about entering therapy because they are aware of the homoprejudice among society at large and even among members of the helping profession (Rothblum, 1994). Gay, lesbian, or bisexual persons are disadvantaged when the helping professional is ignorant of sexual orientation, developmental processes, identity development, counseling techniques, and overall challenges with which this population contends on a daily basis. Referring a client to a different mental health professional who can be more effective may be an option, particularly when the first mental health professional is unable or inadequately trained to provide the necessary support to the client. Yet counselors need to ascertain whether their unwillingness to work with persons who are gay and lesbian is indicative of an intolerance for other sources of diversity, such as race, class, and, ability.

Case Study

Trans Man

Hanna is a white American, 43-year-old licensed psychologist in Georgia. She is a devout Catholic and the clinical director of a mental health practice located in an upper-middle-class community. Many of Hannah's patients struggle with eating disorders, substance use disorders, and body image issues. Hanna supervises several doctoral students who are doing their advanced fieldwork at her site. One of her first-year PhD practicum students, V, who comes highly recommended by faculty, is a black 29-year-old biological female (XX karyotype). V comes from rural Georgia and is the first in the family to graduate high school. When V (known then as Vela) interviewed for practicum in February 2015, Vela was gender conforming in appearance as a female. Outside of school and work, Vela now (October 2015) openly identifies as a transgendered male and has an intersexual partner. At the practicum site, V insists people refer to V as V and not Vela but does not explain why. After the first session with V, most of V's patients request a different therapist or stop receiving therapy at the agency. One patient told Hannah, "It creeps me out receiving therapy from someone who looks like a guy but sounds just like a girl—I thought I had problems." V needs practicum hours from face-to-face contact to complete the PhD program. Patient terminations are working against V's need and desire to provide quality psychotherapy services to patients. During supervision, Hanna asks V if there is something that V would like to talk about. V responded, "No. Is there a problem?" Hanna then states that V's patients are terminating at a higher rate than she has seen in the past with other practicum students. She then asks V if V has a sense of why patients are terminating? V said, "I did not know there was a problem. Maybe some people are not accepting of everybody." Hanna then asks V to be aware that patients are terminating and that Hanna is there for V if V would like to talk. Three weeks later, the terminations continue with more patients coming to Hanna saying that they are uncomfortable with V looking more like a guy but sounding like a woman. During supervision, Hanna asks V how V's cases are coming. V says, "I think they are going well." Hanna then says, "It appears that your physical transition appears to be disquieting to many of your patients and to some it seems to be clinically disruptive. What are your thoughts?" V is quiet, looks down, with the right foot shaking vigorously. Hanna says, "I wonder would you be willing to plan and/or facilitate a session for clinical staff and practicum students on body image issues among lesbians? In this way, we could offer an in-service for patients later." V then responded defensively, "I am not a lesbian!" and then begins to cry. Hanna then apologizes and says, "I am very sorry, V. Is there anything you would like to speak with me about? I am concerned about you." V does not answer. Hanna asks, "Would you be willing, then, to plan and/or facilitate a session for staff and practicum students on body image issues among the bisexual community? I also wonder if you would be willing to return to the appearance that you had when you first interviewed earlier this year?" V gets up abruptly and storms out of the agency. Hanna calls V. There is no answer. Hanna sends V an e-mail asking V to return and that she would like to invite her faculty supervisor and clinical instructor to meet with them both. V does not respond. Hanna reassigns V's cases for the remaining week to other practitioners. V's faculty adviser and instructor call Hanna to request an emergency session and indicate that V said the practicum site discriminates against transgender people and against black people.

Questions

1. Would you be comfortable working with V as V's counselor?
2. Do you think V could have done anything differently to reflect cultural competence?
3. Do you think Hanna could have done something differently to reflect cultural competence?

Hanna does not appear to evidence knowledge of people who are transgender. This is evident when Hanna confuses V with lesbianism and bisexuality. Hanna also does not seem to appreciate that being transgendered involves a process of identity development that is more complex than choosing to wear different attire. Knowledge of the differences among lesbian, transgender, transsexual and the differences between biological sex and gender identity is consistent with cultural competence and would have helped Hanna understand why it was problematic to suggest that V revert to a previous expression of identity that was more gender conforming.

Was Hanna discriminatory for asking V to return to her former physical appearance approximately 8 months earlier? Context has to be considered. As director of a mental health agency, Hanna has a responsibility to run a mental health center that is oriented to the health and healing of the vulnerable patients who come to her with their own psychological issues and challenges.

It is unfortunate that Hanna was unable to acknowledge V's commitment to his consolidated identity as a transgendered person. It would have been appropriate for Hanna as a supervisor and mentor to speak to V about any challenges related to his female to male transition. Hanna sees that patients are confused and disturbed by V's drastic appearance. Suggesting that V could simply revert to his former physical experience is reflective of Hanna's limited knowledge and awareness and is not in the service of multicultural competence.

The patients' reactions are understandable. Many people do not understand what it means to be transgendered and the importance for transgendered people, as they move through developmental stages, to have consistency between their physical appearance and the internal identity work they have been doing. Does this mean transgendered counselors are not appropriate providers of quality mental health services? Transgendered counselors can be very effective clinicians. However, irrespective of one's sexuality, cultural competence is ethical practice. From the case study, it appears that V did not demonstrate cultural competence in his unwillingness to consider how showing up as a trans man could be source of confusion and alarm to patients who struggle with body image and substance use issues. At the same time, there are tremendous hardships for transgender people during the transition phase, such as worries about being accepted, struggles with feelings of hopelessness, and not being in control (Budge et al., 2013).

A conversation with Hanna or individual disclosure to each of V's patients is characteristic of one possible approach. Doing so would have demonstrated V's understanding of multicultural competencies (Sue et al.,1982) wherein the counselor is aware of the client's worldview and the way in which clients' development and notions of normalcy are shaped and influenced by race, sexuality, and class.

The Effect of Heterosexism on the Development of Multicultural Competence

Heterosexism allows counselors to minimize information about sexual minorities. As discussed earlier, research shows that people who engage in any type of same-sex sexual behavior as well as those who experience same-sex sexual attraction is much higher than persons who actually claim an identity as a gay or lesbian person. The bifurcation of sexuality into two groups, heterosexuals and nonheterosexuals is inconsistent with sexuality as existing along a continuum.

Hanna may not be cognizant of her proximity to gender and sexuality discourses. Ineffective supervision is characterized by supervisors' unawareness of multicultural issues in counseling, particularly when they avoid or shy away from the topic due to their discomfort (Ladany, Mori, & Mehr, 2013). One discourse is that prettiness in a woman is incongruent with a lesbian identity. Pretty and gender-conforming lesbians are often told, "Gosh, you don't look like a lesbian." Transgendered need not mean gay and although V is a biological female, he does not identify as female. Transsexuals may not define themselves as gay but have had or may plan to undergo gender-affirming surgery to complement hormone treatments or biologically born males may use electrolysis during their transition to women.

V's partner is intersexual (a disorder of sexual development). As such, some intersexual persons may not subscribe to a gender binary. It is important that as multiculturally competent mental health professionals, we understand the meaning of intersexuality. Intersexual refers to persons born with genitalia that are different or ambiguous enough to raise concerns as they deviate from a typical appearance. Mental health professionals can deconstruct their fears about people often deemed as the other. Professionally trained supervisors/consultants; education; film; literature; quality relationships with people who are racially, sexually, and culturally different from oneself; and/or a personal therapist can serve to close the knowledge, skill, and intervention gap. Humility is also needed to recognize the limits of our multicultural competency and expertise. Engaging in a variety of professional growth experiences to address these limitations is essential (Arredondo et al., 1996).

Singh, Boyd, and Whitman (2010) suggest participation in community events, such as the Transgender Day of Remembrance and Intersex Awareness and peer consultation groups. Mental health professionals are capable of learning what fuels their fear of people because of their skin color, or gender, or sexuality. Hanna's difficulty with V is driven by a lack of familiarity and openness to personal change. It is essential to show a willingness to look at oneself.

Even multiculturally oriented and experienced psychologists have difficulty with multicultural competence. Knowing what one should do is not necessarily consistent with what one would do (Sehgal et al., 2011). More research is definitely needed to understand the reasons and conditions that therapists may or may not choose to employ strategies that seem to be consistent with multicultural competence.

How do mental health professionals address their fears of difference when they live in rural or small towns where diversity is less of a feature? It is important to remember that transgendered people are everywhere. Hanna does not know anyone who is transgender and, until V, has never met a transgendered person. She does not have the benefit of living in a large city center, which may reflect a greater diversity of people across race, nationality, and sexuality. In addition to not knowing anyone who is transgender, it would be helpful for Hanna to ask herself why she does not have any friends who are gay or lesbian. How might her religion or cultural assimilation shape her social circle? Did V's multiple and stigmatized identities overwhelm Hanna's ability to competently supervise? Because Hanna is no longer being supervised but is the supervisor, it is likely, albeit unfortunate, that there will not be much impetus for Hanna to interrogate herself regarding transgender issues.

Collaboration groups could be helpful to Hanna in improving her cultural competence. Her difficulty with broaching difficult topics is evident. It would also be helpful to Hanna's cultural competence with people who are transgender to review The Association of Lesbian, Gay, Bisexual, and Transgender Issues in Counseling competencies (Burnes et al., 2009).

Summary

This chapter examined sexual orientation and acknowledged that it exists on a continuum. Definitions were provided, and developmental processes, identity models, and implications for mental health professionals working with gay, lesbian, transgender, and bisexual clients were discussed. A case study that dealt with transgender issues exposed readers to an issue that may not be covered as thoroughly as lesbian, gay, and bisexual issues are.

16

❖

Converging Socioeconomic Class

This chapter is dedicated to an examination of the intersections of socioeconomic class with other aspects of identity such as race, sexuality, gender, education, disability, and ethnicity. A case study is provided to facilitate the integration of the material discussed throughout the chapter. The implications of a middle-class bias on the training of students in graduate counseling programs are discussed.

The Invisibility of Class as a Variable in Counseling

Class is ubiquitous, and yet it is largely understudied, particularly as it relates to counseling and therapeutic effectiveness (Liu et al., 2004). Social class position is largely determined by income, education, and occupation. According to Liu et al., "Social class may be defined as an individual's position within an economic hierarchy that is determined by his or her income, education level, and occupation; the individual is also aware of his or her place in the economic hierarchy and of others who may share a similar position" (p. 8). A primary component of social class is power, which exists across individual, institutional, and societal levels (Appleby, Colon, & Hamilton, 2001).

Disciplines such as sociology, public health, medicine, feminist psychology, and anthropology have devoted ample attention to class issues, particularly because class affects educational equity, access to health care, racial disparities, and collectivistic versus individualistic societies (Fine, 1991; Lareau, 1997; Ogbu, 1997; Institute of Medicine, 2003). In counseling, the investigation of class as a status variable is increasing but had been largely neglected. Researchers are bridging this gap. Liu et al. (2004) conducted a content analysis of the frequency of use of social class in the empirical and theoretical literature in three counseling journals: *Journal of Counseling Psychology, Journal of Multicultural Counseling and Development*, and *Journal of Counseling and Development*. Results of social class were typically reported in the method section. In fact, of the empirical articles that used social class, 31% did so in the method section of the article, and only 4% used social class in the data analysis. Liu et al. (2004) stated, "Although social class may have been regarded as an important demographic variable to measure in the method section, few studies analyzed the participant data or incorporated social class findings into the discussion section" (p. 15). It was concluded that social class is an infrequently used variable in empirical counseling research.

Myths about class might contribute to this neglect. One myth states that we are a classless society and a second that we are a middle-class nation. The third myth is that we are all getting richer and everyone has an equal chance to succeed (Appleby, Colon, & Hamilton, 2001). Meritocracy, fairness, equality, and beating the odds is part of the cultural fabric regardless of one's indebtedness or income; however, greater attention on political and social levels is being given to income equality, college student debt, minimum wage, and gender disparities in Hollywood.

Data on class, income, and poverty challenge prevailing discourses about justice and a level playing field for all Americans. Millions of Americans live below the poverty line. In 2014, the official poverty rate for the nation was 14.8%, which translates to 46.7 million people in poverty. People between the ages of 18 to 64 had a poverty rate of 13.5%, and people 65 and older had a poverty rate of 10%, which is half of the rate seen among children.

Children under the age of 18 have a poverty rate of 21.1%. Children suffer because of the economic situations of their parents, particularly among single mothers. Higher unemployment, underemployment, and incarceration rates among men of color adversely affect black and Latina women who are most likely to be in relationships with black and Latino men. It is imperative to examine children's poverty in light of the events and circumstances occurring in the lives of their mothers, fathers, and caregivers. Not to do so is to blame them for circumstances over which they have no control.

The poverty rate among Hispanics is 23.6%, 26.2% among blacks, 12% among Asians, and 10.1% among non-Hispanic whites. Rates for Native Americans were not reported in this report; however, poverty rates among Native Americans tend to be the highest of any group (DeNavas-Walt & Proctor, 2015). (See Knowledge Check 16.1: People in Poverty by Selected Characteristics.)

Knowledge Check 16.1

People in Poverty by Selected Characteristics

Poverty rate in families: 12.7%

Poverty rate in unrelated subfamilies: 42.9%

National poverty rate: 14.8%

Asians: 12%

White, non-Hispanic: 10.1%

Blacks: 26.2%

Hispanics: 23.6%

Under age 18: 21.1%

18 to 64: 13.5%

65 and older: 10%

Male: 13.4%

Female: 16.1%

With a disability: 28.5%

With no disability: 12.3%

No high school diploma: 28.9%

Bachelor's degree or higher: 5%

Midwest: 13%

Northeast: 12.6%

South: 16.5%

West: 15.2%

Source: DeNavas-Walt & Proctor (2015).

The data tell us that gender drives wealth. Womanhood varies considerably according to educational status and occupational position, which influences neighborhood safety and the presence of gang and gun violence, access to cancer-fighting fruits and vegetables (the healthier food is more expensive), and access to a doctor when one is sick. People who live in poverty experience more chronic health problems, live in crowded places, contend with noise and injury on the job, and are more likely to engage in behaviors associated with chronic disease. Over time, these experiences contribute to lower life expectancy (Newman, 1999). Class status does not negate the effects of discrimination yet can minimize these effects (Chae & Walter, 2009).

In 2011, the poverty rate of custodial mother families (31.8%) was about double the poverty rate for custodial father families (16.2%; Grall, 2013). Put differently, the poverty rate for families in 2014 was 11.7%. When the family data are disaggregated, we find that among married couples, the poverty rate was 6.2%. Among female headed households with no husband present, the poverty rate was 30.6%, but nearly half, at 15.7% among male householders with no wife present (DeNavas-Walt & Proctor, 2015).

The Intersections of Class

Social class is multifaceted and complex. In the social sciences, there has been a tendency to minimize race issues and esteem class, particularly in light of increases in the numbers of middle-class families of color. Class, particularly for people of color, does not operate as a primary status trait because race and gender tend to be more conspicuous than class and can override it. (See Storytelling, Cutting Hair, Death of a Dream.) "In the race-class-gender-nexus, race constitutes more than a social construction. It is a permanent and salient identity marker, self-indicator, and status locator that defines one's being, along with gender, sexuality, and class" (Wilkinson, 1997, p. 270).

❖ STORYTELLING: CUTTING HAIR, DEATH OF A DREAM

I recently heard a story of a young black American woman who had long and straight hair. Her hair was beautiful. One day she arrived home to her mother and aunt. Immediately upon seeing her much shorter hair, they wailed and cried and screamed, "What did you do to your hair; what have you done to yourself; what have you done to this family?" Atop this woman's head was socially constructed "good" hair. On it were pinned the family's dreams of her attracting not just a good man but a better man endowed with the social capital (e.g., wealth, power, and status) to transform the family's social and economic situation. This young woman's unearned but most powerful asset was now gone, although it would grow back. This story speaks to the intersections of patriarchy, sexism, heterosexism, classism, and hegemony. It also speaks to the wretched vulnerability of classism that crushes low-income people as they search for anchors of stability and progress on which to grab hold.

Within a materialistic and consumeristic society, the structural inequities that can work against a person's best efforts to be successful can be overlooked. It is perhaps easy to blame people for failing to transcend their situations despite structural and institutional forces. For instance, women systematically earn less money than men. Often, men in nontraditional jobs (e.g., nursing) earn more money than their female counterparts (Chusmir, 1990).

Ogbu (1997) argued, "The inequality between Blacks and Whites is one not of class stratification but of racial stratification" (p. 766). *Racial stratification* is "the hierarchical organization of socially defined 'races' or groups on the basis of assumed inborn differences in status, honor, or material worth, symbolized in the United States by skin color" (Ogbu, 1997, p. 768).

Race and gender intersect and are reflected in poverty data. In 2012, the poverty rates for white, non-Hispanic women was 10.8%, compared to Hispanic women, who had a poverty rate of 27.9%, and African American women, who had a poverty rate of 28.6%. Although data were not available, it is anticipated that the poverty rates for Native women are the highest among all women given that poverty rates for Native people are the highest than for any other group. The poverty rates were lower for Asian women at 12.3% (Ahmad & Iverson, 2013). (See Knowledge Check 16.2: 2012 Poverty Rates by Race and Gender.)

Compared to white women, women of color are confronted with greater occupational segmentation and increasingly higher rates of unemployment compared to white women. For example, unlike the large numbers of white women newly entering the workforce, black women have a history as workers, slaves, servers, domestics, field, and factory hands (Jones, 1985). This identity is imprinted on the American psyche and influences the perception that society at large may have of black women, particularly when they newly occupy class positions initially reserved for white men.

Wage disparities impede women of color from experiencing economic stability by depressing their lifetime earnings: Estimates show that women lose an average of

---

Knowledge Check 16.2

2012 Poverty Rates by Race and Gender

1. White, non-Hispanic women: 10.8%

2. Hispanic women: 27.9%

3. American women: 28.6%

4. Native women: Unavailable

5. Asian women: 12.3%

Source: Ahmad & Iverson (2013).

$434,000 in their lifetime from the gender-based wage gap. Women of color are hit harder by this loss. Overall, they have lower-wage jobs and higher rates of unemployment (Ahmad & Iverson, 2013). As a consequence of poverty, women of color are more likely to suffer from inadequate access to medical and mental health services.

In 2014, people with lower household income had lower health insurance coverage rates compared to people with higher income. More specifically, 83.4% of people in households with annual household income of less than $25,000 had health insurance coverage, compared with 89.3% of people in households with income ranging from $50,000 to $74,999 and 94.7% of people in households with income of $100,000 or more (Smith & Medalia, 2015).

Race also impacts uninsured rates. In 2014, non-Hispanic whites had a higher rate of health insurance coverage (92.4%). This rate was higher than it was for other racial groups. The health insurance coverage rates for blacks and Asians were lower than for non-Hispanic whites, at 88.2% and 90.7%, respectively. Hispanics had the lowest rate of health insurance coverage in 2014, at 80.1% (Smith & Medalia, 2015).

In addition to higher rates of health insurance coverage, non-Hispanic whites and Asians were most likely to have had private health insurance in 2014, at 72.9% and 72.1%, respectively. Hispanics, who had the lowest rate of any health insurance coverage, had the lowest rate of coverage by private health insurance, at 48.7%. Among blacks, 54.1% had private health insurance coverage (Smith & Medalia, 2015). (See Population Box 16.1: Health Insurance Rates and Private Insurance [PI] Coverage by Race, 2014.)

In American society, success is defined and measured by material acquisition. Homes, cars, boats, jewelry, and other "things" are indicators of income, success, and occupation; wealth suggests attributes such as being hardworking, smart, savvy, special, and morally good. Manhood is tied to being a provider and having success in one's chosen career (Swanson, 1993). The inability to be successful in this fashion has and continues to have far-reaching implications for men who, for a variety of personal and systemic reasons, are unable to attain or maintain success. (See Storytelling: I Fed America But. . . .)

Population Box 16.1: Health Insurance Rates and Private Insurance (PI) Coverage by Race, 2014

1. Non-Hispanic Whites: 92.4%, PI: 72.9%

2. Blacks: 88.2%, PI: 54.1%

3. Asians: 90.7%, PI: 72.1%

4. Hispanics: 80.1%, PI: 48.7%

Source: Smith & Medalia (2015).

I was recently in a grocery store and overheard a white man talking with a customer about the years that he spent driving trucks and delivering food to the nation's grocery stores. He suffered an injury that left him disabled and unable to continue trucking. He lamented, "I fed America, but I can't even afford to eat." He bought some store brand American cheese that was on sale. I later saw him in another part of the store, talking to another customer and heard the same refrain, "I fed America but I can't

afford to eat." I debated as to whether to put this story in the chapter on class or disability. I decided to place it in the class chapter, given that class and disability are intertwined. What does it mean to work hard all your life and then to feel discarded due to an injury that interferes with your ability to be productive, feel purposeful, and function as a provider? Feelings of inadequacy, anger, and a sense that one is being treated like surplus may, for some, be a consequence.

Class: An Identity Construct

Wealth does not translate to feelings of power, security, and privilege, or lower class to feelings of anxiety, depression, and low self-esteem. Low-wage earning does not translate to feelings of powerlessness, insecurity, and low self-esteem. Class has psychological effects on people's lives. For instance, McLoyd and Wilson (1992) found that working- and lower-class parents placed less emphasis on happiness during the rearing of their children. In the case of these parents, survival issues took precedence over happiness. Robinson (1990) found in her analysis of black student persistence that the students who were most likely to graduate from college in 4 years came from two-parent households and had participated in anticipatory socialization experiences such as Future Teachers of America and Future Business Leaders while in high school. These variables, associated with persistence and success, and as measured by graduation, are representations of class but not necessarily income and support the effects of class on career commitment and vocational identity.

Race affects gender- and class-linked messages. Renzetti and Curran (1992) cited research that stated black boys and girls tend to be more independent than white boys and girls. Parents' strong emphasis on hard work and ambition and the less frequent gender stereotyping and exposure to strong mothers that characterizes the lives of many black children may explain this finding (Cole & Guy-Sheftall, 2003).

Storck (1998) proposed that the definition of social class be expanded to include psychosocial class, which is "defined by a person's education and occupation, and correlated behaviors, thoughts, and feelings" (p. 102). Storck also observed that a working-class person tends not to be defined as college educated and is typically employed as a factory worker, with thoughts such as, "life starts after working hours," or "psychotherapy means that they will lock you up." Storck also stated that "both 'lower' and 'higher' ranking individuals and groups may feel disadvantaged or disempowered, in different contexts" (p. 101). Yet a person from a lower psychosocial class may have higher feelings of marginalization or feel ignored and denied access. These class-determined feelings, according to Storck, are important contributors to depressive symptoms.

People can have similar jobs, incomes, and educational levels and have a different perspective about money as a function of environment and context. (See Storytelling: Small House.) Mental health professionals are encouraged to take a contextualized approach to patients and consider multiple issues: (a) sociohistorical, or the ways in which people's histories have been silenced and misrepresented; (b) sociostructural, which includes legal, economic, and educational systems; and (c) sociopolitical, or the distribution of power (Liu & Arguello, 2006).

❖ **STORYTELLING: SMALL HOUSE**

A friend of mine was talking about her school age daughter who was the only child of color in her school. I asked her if her daughter struggled with being the only brown child. She said, "Somewhat—in the beginning, the children would want to touch her hair or asked her why her skin was so dark." My friend noticed that her daughter was mostly influenced by class. She had taken her child to visit a classmate, and after the visit, her child asked, "Mommy, why is *their* house so small?"

Middle-Class Bias and Counselor Training

Counseling students receive very little information about socioeconomic class as it relates to influences on identity development and subsequent implications for counseling. Moreover, the training caters to the haves, as opposed to other social classes (e.g., working and lower classes). A client's discussions about economic exploitation and oppression can be extremely difficult for a counselor to hear if the counselor is a member of the very group that the client is discussing (Cardemil & Battle, 2003). The therapist's inability to hear should not be the client's problem, but it becomes the client's problem when the counselor is unavailable emotionally.

Part of middle-class bias is related to the nature of graduate education, which is steeped in privilege. Graduate students are college graduates who have distinguished themselves from others in the general population as capable of meeting the rigors of an academic program. Having status as a graduate student is an esteemed position in society that carries middle-class connotations, independent of students' class-linked childhood socialization experiences or their current state of poverty.

The graduate school environment acculturates its members to a middle-class orientation given the emphasis on success, competition, control, and individualism. In addition, there is an expectation of future employment and class mobility. Graduate students are preparing themselves for positions that will designate their middle-class social standing and prestige. It is hoped that students' future salaries, note that the majority of mental health professionals today are female, will reflect justice.

Despite the privileged status of graduate school, some students make considerable financial sacrifices (e.g., working and going to school, borrowing money from family, securing substantial school loans) to attend school. Currently at my institution, each credit is approximately $1,300.00. It costs master's students close to $80,000 for their 2-year master's degree.

The majority of graduate students in the United States could be described as embodying traditional values anchored within a middle-class framework, which include delayed gratification, success, educational attainment, motivation, perseverance, self-reliance, Standard English, indebtedness, and hard work. For some first-generation college and graduate students, the delayed gratification and financial indebtedness may not make sense to working-class family members. The family member who has received an education and physically moved away from the family of origin may be perceived by working-class siblings or parents as not belonging anymore due to different ways of speaking and life experiences.

What does it mean for a middle-class bias to pervade the training of mental health providers? Is it possible that the effects of socioeconomic class on psychosocial identity have been neglected in the counseling literature because the middle-class bias is so pervasive and has rendered the profession oblivious to itself? Sue and Sue (1990) identified two aspects of middle-class bias within counselor training. The first pertains to the emphasis on Standard English within society at large. The second refers to the 50-minute counseling sessions that typically characterize the counseling event.

Standard English represents a class issue because dialect, accent, and use of English are often used in drawing conclusions about a person's educational, occupational, income, intellectual, legal, and ultimately class status. Accent modification training is offered as an attractive means of changing how some people sound when they speak (e.g., foreign-born and/or U.S. regional accents). Standard English operates as a form of power and access within society. Delpit (1997) discussed the power embodied in language and dialect. She argued against obliterating the unique cultural or speaking style of a group, yet she advocated educating people about the sociopolitical context in which standards and rules regarding the status quo exist. She advocates speaking honestly to children about the beauty and value of their language and cultural style while helping them understand the political power games at stake. Delpit demonstrates the dialectic: a "both/and" perspective in which on the one hand the cultural style is embraced and esteemed, while on the other hand students understand that others perceived as powerful (e.g., teachers, prospective employers) may disparage it. This both/and perspective means having knowledge of two realities: the appropriate contexts in which one's language can be celebrated and contexts where it will not.

Cultural encapsulation, or defining reality on the basis of a limited one-dimensional cultural orientation (Wrenn, 1962), contributes to counselors' bias toward normative standards: being white, able-bodied, and heterosexual and using Standard English (Reynolds & Pope, 1991). Schofield's (1964) use of the acronym YAVIS (young, attractive, verbal, intelligent, and successful) may enable counselors to see their tendency to favor this type of client due to the counselor's perception that the YAVIS patient is more similar to the counselor's actual or imagined sense of self.

Noticeable differences in communication and behavioral styles (e.g., the use of slang, street talk, or non-Standard English) between the client and counselor can contribute to counselors' discomfort with clients from lower socioeconomic groups. If the mental health professional is bothered that the client is on a sliding scale, counter transference can present a clinical obstacle.

Some counselors from middle-class backgrounds may not be equipped to deal with the multiple challenges and life problems that characterize some of their low-income clients' lives, such as homelessness, pregnancy, appalling living conditions, hunger, mistreatment by the police and schools, crime, transience, and chronic violence or the threat of violence (Boyd-Franklin, 2003).

Another middle-class bias in counseling identified by Sue and Sue (1990) is the 50-minute counseling session. Neither the American Psychological Association (APA) nor the American Counseling Association (ACA) ethics codes dictate 45- or 50-minute therapy sessions. Some clients have work schedules that fluctuate from week to week (e.g., waitresses, nurses). This fluctuation disallows having a fixed day and time for therapy weekly. For example, a client may work the 11:00 p.m. to 7:00 a.m. shift at a gas station one week. The next week, his or her work schedule might be from 3:00 p.m. to 11:00 p.m. Pulling double shifts is a way for people to make overtime—the cost is seen in disordered sleep, which disturbs wakefulness and circadian rhythm regulation. For some workers, their schedules may not be posted until a few days prior to the beginning of a new shift.

To accommodate each unique client, particularly in the absence of third-party reimbursement schedules that are rather strict in their requirement of 45-or 50-minute sessions, 90-minute sessions every other week might be preferable and could be offered if it is consistent with the clinician's schedule. A flexible schedule applies to a variety of clients across socioeconomic groups, from highly paid physicians on call to shift workers receiving minimum wage.

Which privileges are professionals willing to relinquish to better accommodate a diverse clientele? Wachtel (2002) stated, "It is extremely difficult to be successful in therapeutic work with patients outside the White middle class if one maintains traditional notions about 'the frame'" (p. 205).

Class issues may not be discussed in counselor training largely because the context in which class occurs is normative and reflective of an American value. An implicit expectation that clients have jobs and conventional work hours based on standard work fuels this oversight. What about clients who do not own cars, live in towns where reliable public transportation is nonexistent, are unable to leave 15 minutes early from their jobs without being docked, or spend an entire afternoon catching and waiting for public transportation and having to walk as well? Some clients experience obstacles in their efforts to receive therapy as a direct result of the ways class shapes people's lives, including our own. Do we subtract the time from the client's hour, even if another client is not scheduled immediately, because of the middle-class cultural adage that "time is money"?

As mental health professionals, we need to make a living. Recruiting full-paying clients with insurance to balance those who are on a sliding scale may be a way to make our professional services more accessible to all people. Conversely, if clients drive up for their appointments in expensive cars and wear expensive clothing, how are we affected by these indicators of wealth or debt? Components of class include art, music, tastes, religion, food, and furniture (Bourdieu, 1984). When high-status clients appear, how self-conscious do we become of our work environments and other indicators of our proximity to middle-class status? How might our personal reactions, feeling intimidated or impressed, affect our ability to extend our best professional services to wealthy clients? Counselors need to look beneath the glamour of socioeconomic class and privilege to avoid being blinded by its allure. There are clients with financial means who come to therapy with clinical wounds.

The Fluidity of Class

Acquiring middle-class status or suddenly becoming low-income in one's life does not erase the effects of early conditioning. Middle-class persons can move into a lower income level because of unemployment, physical and mental illness, violence, divorce or loss of another significant relationship, disability, death of the primary provider, or traumatic event. Class is fluid, and this issue can be overlooked if it is assumed that clients and their counselors have had similar and consistent class socialization experiences from childhood to adulthood. A change in income does not translate into a loss of values to which one has become accustomed.

Middle-Class Bias and Ethical Standards

The roots of a middle-class cultural bias are reflected in the official documents used to standardize the profession and provide its membership with rules and guidelines for professional practice. For example, the ACA Code of Ethics (Section A.10.d) approaches bartering for services with caution. Yet, it has become flexible in its position from nearly 20 years ago when it stated that counselors "refrain from accepting goods or services in return for counseling services because such arrangements create inherent potential for conflict, exploitation, and distortion of the professional relationship" (1995, Section A.10.c). The ACA (2014) section A.10.e ethical code reads as follows:

> A.10.e. Bartering. Counselors may barter only if the bartering does not result in exploitation or harm, if the client requests it, and if such arrangements are an accepted practice among professionals in the community. Counselors consider the cultural implications of bartering and discuss relevant concerns with clients and document such agreements in a clear written contract.

In rural, cultural/ethnic, and/or agricultural communities, money may not be as readily available. A woman may not be able to afford $140 an hour for therapy, her 30-dollar co-pay, or a greatly reduced amount based on a sliding scale. However, she may be able to do landscaping, provide fresh eggs from her chickens, or a fresh turkey for Thanksgiving. Granted, these examples sound like bartering and understandably can be problematic.

The APA (2010) Code of Ethics does not refute bartering within the context of psychotherapy. If Section 6.05 states, "Bartering is the acceptance of goods, services, or other nonmonetary remuneration from clients/patients in return for psychological services. Psychologists may barter only if (1) it is not clinically contraindicated, and (2) the resulting arrangement is not exploitative."

In certain contexts, dual relationships may not be readily avoidable and are the "hallmark of interconnected, rural settings" (Zur, 2006, p. 12). In a small town, dual relationships can look like the therapist shopping at a store that a client owns or going to the same church or temple, or children attending the same school. It is a middle-class bias that presumes such avoidance is preferred or even possible. Collectivistic communities are dependent upon overlapping relationships where role diffusion cannot be avoided. Mental health professionals, themselves, may be involved in conflicting roles (Pedersen, 1997). In addition, if there are few licensed mental health professionals who are ethnic, racial, and/or linguistic minorities, it is likely that clients and their therapists will frequent the same churches, community, recreational activities, and may even have the same employer. Thus, the clear division of roles assumes an abundance of resources that are diverse enough so as not to intersect. The assumption is that clients and their counselors function and live their lives in different social and political circles, which is not the case in some rural communities, communities of color, and ethnic communities. For example, the family rabbi might be the marriage counselor and the child's Hebrew tutor.

Professional organizations maintain concern for clients' well-being and mental health professionals by establishing and adhering to ethical codes that have professional integrity. At the same time, APA recognizes the nature of multiple relationships and says in Section 3.05,

a. A multiple relationship occurs when a psychologist is in a professional role with a person and (1) at the same time is in another role with the same person, (2) at the same time is in a relationship with a person closely associated with or related to the person with whom the psychologist has the professional relationship, or (3) promises to enter into another relationship in the future with the person or a person closely associated with or related to the person.

A psychologist refrains from entering into a multiple relationship if the multiple relationship could reasonably be expected to impair the psychologist's objectivity, competence, or effectiveness in performing his or her functions as a psychologist, or otherwise risks exploitation or harm to the person with whom the professional relationship exists. Multiple relationships that would not reasonably be expected to cause impairment or risk exploitation or harm are not unethical.

b. If a psychologist finds that, due to unforeseen factors, a potentially harmful multiple relationship has arisen, the psychologist takes reasonable steps to resolve it with due regard for the best interests of the affected person and maximal compliance with the Ethics Code.

c. When psychologists are required by law, institutional policy, or extraordinary circumstances to serve in more than one role in judicial or administrative proceedings, at the outset they clarify role expectations and the extent of confidentiality and thereafter as changes occur. (APA, 2010, p. 6)

The current ACA Code of Ethics has changed the ethical guidelines to respect healthy and therapeutic interactions between client and counselor.

A middle-class bias is seen in the very basic tenets of therapy, such as confidentiality. Students learn early in their programs that mental health professionals can be sued for violating a client's confidentiality. For example Pedersen (1997) reminded us that in individualistic contexts personal privacy is in essence a commodity; however, in collectivistic cultures, personal privacy might be viewed as being selfish.

Another middle-class bias exists in the expectation that clients will self-disclose. Actually, this expectation is a hallmark of Rogerian counseling, which assumes that after disclosure, people experience a measurable and identifiable benefit and catharsis. Clearly, the roots of positivism are at work. Some clients may find therapy imbalanced due to the unidirectional nature of the exchange. It could be perceived as inconsistent with community, kinship, and mutuality. Another assumption embedded in disclosure is that an individual will be articulate (in Standard English) and be able to match affective experiences to words. It is not uncommon for patients with trauma histories to struggle with identifying and naming their emotions. It is a tall order for some clients to disclose personal details about themselves and their families with a professional stranger. Many low-wage earners, because of limited education and/or immigrant status, do not speak Standard English. To be clear, inability to speak Standard English is not synonymous with illegal status, limited intelligence, or the inability to learn.

❖ STORYTELLING: COMING DOWN THE MOUNTAIN

A small group of Americans was climbing Mt. Kilimanjaro in Tanzania. We were outfitted with our sturdy sneakers—some of us had hiking boots. I had my fanny pack with my water and energy bars, along with my layered, moisture-licking, wool clothing that people pay too much for at outdoor shops. We were enjoying the splendor of our hike—the birds, the flowers, the monkeys. At the same time, we were tired and challenged by the rigor of this uphill climb. All of sudden, two native Tanzanian youth appeared carrying a long and heavy log balanced on both of their shoulders as they came down the mountain. They were wearing flip-flops. They smiled and warmly greeted us as they scampered past. We were sobered at how limber they were and without all of the provisions (water, food, and special footwear) that we privileged Americans had.

An examination of core and dominant cultural values allows one to see why a middle-class bias prevails in the training of counselors. Competition, the Protestant work ethic, and self-reliance all stem from an individualistic and Western culture (Sue & Sue, 1990). Yet some communities are more collective, wherein greater dependence on others is the norm. Perceptions of dependence also seem to be fostered by class status. (See Storytelling: Coming Down the Mountain.) Perhaps it is easier to live without cultivating a relationship with neighbors if one is not financially interdependent on others. The California community in which I was reared was collective and collaborative in orientation. In my neighborhood, neighbors depended on one another for community. We borrowed household flour and sugar from one another and helped raise and watch over each other's children. Class may dictate one's ability to provide for personal material needs independent of others. Having middle-class status, particularly within an individualistic context, may make it easier not to be in relationships with persons in close proximity to oneself. This is most likely different from poor or collectivistic communities (independent of class differences), where value is placed on kinship networks. Within collectivistic contexts seen among many Arab, African, Asian, Native American, Latino, and agrarian and religious white families (e.g., the Amish), an extension of the personal self is part of the culture or tribe.

Classism

The media plays a role in depicting low-income people as invisible and yet responsible for their predicament. They tend to be presented as unworthy and not deserving of more. Being poor in American society and staying poor is not valued. Such a position does not mirror the American values of competition, success, change, progress, rising above one's situation, and controlling one's life. The inability to significantly alter one's station in life is inconsistent with core American values.

Classism is a form of oppression against the poor. Smith (2005) defines *classism* as

> an interlocking system that involves domination and control of social ideology, institutions, and resources, resulting in a condition of privilege for one group relative to the disenfranchisement of another. Members of both dominant and subordinated groups are capable of prejudice, but only dominant groups have the institutional and cultural power to enforce their prejudices via oppression. (p. 688)

APA (2007b) defines classism as "the network of attitudes, beliefs, behaviors, and institutional practices that maintain and legitimatize class-based power differences that privilege middle and higher income groups at the expense of the poor and working classes" (p. 7). Starting out low-income and becoming rich through marriage, promotion, business, or even winning the lottery is admired. The values of hard work and/ or good fortune, pulling oneself up by one's bootstraps, control, and a belief in a just society are all at work as is the ability to, despite the odds, transcend one's situation.

Socioeconomic class is fluid, which means the so-called lines between class groups are not solid. Many working-class families are governed by middle-class values, such as education as a means of self-help, hard work, money management, perseverance, and delayed gratification. Ogbu (1997) reminded us that membership in class groups is transient since people move in and out of class which is an open entity without clear boundaries. Ogbu and the most recent recession, acknowledge that the white-collar worker can quickly become the blue-collar laborer. Newman (1999), an anthropologist and researcher on poverty, said, "The working poor are perpetually at risk for becoming the poor of the other kind; they are one paycheck away from what is left of welfare, one sick child away from getting fired, one missed rent payment short of eviction" (p. xiv).

Implications for Mental Health Professionals

Schnitzer (1996) asks, "How might clinicians best integrate knowledge about the impact of poverty on mental health into their practice" (p. 577). Unraveling the effects of class on one's life is not easy and can be difficult. Dominant discourses within society and particularly within the nation's training programs connect class and self-worth. More often than not, people who are low-income are seen as lazy, unmotivated, and intellectually inferior.

Within the home, there are cultural experiences that assist children in their adjustment to school, such as being read to, seeing people read books, waiting in line, and organizing one's work or play. Bourdieu (1984) referred to such experiences that have middle-class connections as cultural capital. The home environment, along with a host of other agents (e.g., school, church, neighborhood, extracurricular activities), socializes children toward a middle-class perspective. Linguistic structures, styles of interacting, and authority patterns characterize cultural resources that can be turned into highly beneficial and socially lucrative cultural capital.

Kenway (1988) conducted research on privileged girls in private schools in Australia. She was interested in looking at self-esteem within an educational context. In talking with the girls about their experiences, Kenway found they used words such as proper, right, perfect, education, manners, and success to describe their status as upper class and said, "Self-esteem may be bought via the right 'casual-chic' designer label. In the culture of consumption within which private schools are immersed, success also can be bought alongside approval, acceptance, and social honour [*sic*]" (p. 155). Kenway encouraged her readers to see the costs to these young girls in their efforts to maintain an image based on elite class distinctions as measured by an exclusive school environment.

Income and race impact the patient and the therapeutic event, and without cultural competence will adversely impact the therapeutic alliance. For instance, Garcia-Coll (1997) identified that white women may have a difficult time holding black women's anger and will go to great lengths to suppress, deny, and repress expressions of this anger. White women's historical role in the oppression of black women and their enjoyment of present-day privileges as wives to and daughters of white men who occupy top economic and income earning structures discourage black and white women from joining together and bearing witness to one another's anger, resentment, and guilt. Effective therapy and a clinically supportive therapeutic alliance are not possible with a clinician's lack of insight into the effects of class on personal identity construction.

The middle class represent the referents for society. Counselors need to hear the prevalence of class conditioning when listening to their clients' stories and, where necessary, help their clients make important connections between their identity and the effects of class on their lives. For example, an adult client from a working-class family might be reluctant to take certain occupational risks because of socialization experiences that emphasize security, saving for a rainy day, and being practical about the future. Asking, "What is the effect of growing up low-income on your willingness now to change jobs?" or "What kinds of messages did you receive about being poor or taking risks?" could further the client's exploration of the relationship between early family experiences and staying at a job that is unfulfilling.

Anxiety about change and taking risk might be higher among clients who, as children and now as adults, have difficulty meeting basic needs. This is not to say that middle-class clients are prepared to embrace uncertainty or change, but having access to an inheritance, a family home, and other financial safety nets that augment one's existing resources may make it more psychologically comfortable and financially possible to engage in risk-taking behavior. Such resources include, but are not limited to, a trust fund, a family loan, the family business, the beach house, the summer house, the winter house, a 529 plan (which refers to money saved for college), and land.

Addressing the structural, social, and economic issues that affect clients' lives is essential. In doing so, we approach our clients from an ecological perspective. Regarding black and Latino men, Washington (1987) said, "Economic stressors such as unemployment, underemployment, job losses, health catastrophes, loss of personal property, and gross indebtedness also exert an unacceptable level of chronic stress" (p. 194). The stress is tied into not being able to achieve society's clear standards about manhood, which are synonymous with career and material success. At the same time, addiction, for example, can grossly impair one's ability to seek work and maintain positions once offered. A focus on personal relationships and the clients' insights are critical to therapy; however, an ecological view is warranted (Schnitzer, 1996). The questions in Self-Check Exercise 16.1 may encourage introspection about class.

Self-Check Exercise 16.1

Social Capital

1. Was there an event that you did not attend because you did not have the appropriate attire or accessories?

2. Were there sporting events or clubs that you could not participate in because your family did not have the money?

3. Were there friends you did not invite to your home because you were ashamed of where you lived and how your home looked?

4. What are your experiences with low-wage-earning people?

5. Have you consciously downplayed your wealth by dressing in attire or brands that did not display your wealth?

6. Did you choose friends or shun others because of their income or how they looked or what they drove or ate or wore?

7. Have you ever worked hard to convince people that although you had wealth, you were still a kind person?

8. Did you not date a person you were interested in because you did not think he or she would fit into your life because he or she had inadequate resources or did not come from the "right" family?

9. Were you told that you just did not fit in and yet the criteria for fitting in was not related to money but perhaps other dimensions of identity, such as race or sexuality or body size?

Case Study

Class Divide

Nona is a 35-year-old Native (Cherokee and white) single mother of five children. Two of the children in her care are her sister's. Her sister is in a federal prison for murder. Nona is a nurse's aide. She has been in therapy for 8 months and attends faithfully. She and her therapist, Candace, have decided on a sliding scale. Nona does not have health insurance. Several times, Nona was not able to make it to therapy because the car that her boyfriend had purchased for her had been repossessed. Her boyfriend has an unstable work history due to time spent in jail for drug charges. In therapy, Nona wants to strengthen her relationships and be a more involved parent. Nona receives weekly calls from the school regarding her oldest child who is frequently absent, is disruptive in class, and is known to be inappropriate with the teachers (yelling and disregarding their requests). Nona feels that the teachers and counselors do not understand her daughter, and she feels angry after most interactions with them. Nona's mother and sister do not understand why Nona is going to a perfect stranger to discuss private family business. Nona appreciates the time in therapy to work on herself and get a break from all of the care she provides for everyone else around the clock. All of Nona's top teeth are missing due to diabetes. Her challenges are multiple, yet Candace, her therapist, notices her commitment to therapy. Nona says it is one of the only times in her life where she can focus on herself.

Questions

1. What do psychologists and counselors need to understand in their work with clients who are low-wage earning?

2. What are Nona's strengths?

3. How and when do therapists advocate for their clients?

Discussion and Integration

The Client, Nona

Despite the multiple challenges that describe Nona's life—low-income, single parenting, a significant other who has legal problems and a substance use disorder, and a child with behavioral and learning difficulties—tenacity, hope, and commitment to her personal development describe Nona's strengths. Many people who start out low-income as children and remain poor as adults have learned to "roll with the punches," use humor to "keep from crying," and shout up a prayer to God for help in times of trouble. They have also learned to hustle and make do out of a system that often renders them invisible, pathological, and peripheral.

Socioeconomic status is a major component of biological processes, such as higher blood pressure, greater blockage of coronary arteries, and more rapid progression of HIV infection (Anderson, 2003). In short, poverty is detrimental to psychological well-being (APA, 2000). Nona, like many others who are low-income, does not have health insurance.

As do most parents, low-wage-earning people care about their children. Nona, like many other clients dealing with just "one more thing," may react with muted affect or numbing. "Class and racial differences between therapist and client may mean experiences with emotional and physical assault so profoundly variant that the therapist cannot adequately envision the impact on the human psyche" (Schnitzer, 1996, p. 575).

Nona's boyfriend experiences depression, albeit untreated. His frustration with his irregular employment situation exacerbates his feelings of powerlessness and inadequacy. Nona's current relationship with her boyfriend is without physical violence—in the past, others have been fraught with frequent physical and verbal altercations. This relational change in Nona is a strength.

Like Nona, many unskilled parents leave the training and education of their children to teachers while valuing educational success and achievement. Lareau (1997) conducted research on two very different school populations. At the first school, 60% of parents were professionals, compared with 1% at the other. The majority of the professional parents had college degrees, and many fathers had advanced degrees. Parents in the unskilled jobs had either a high school education or had dropped out of high school. Only 1% of parents at the first school were unskilled workers, compared with 23% at the second one. Lareau found that interactions between professional parents and teachers were more frequent and comfortable. Professional parents were also more involved in the academic preparation of their children. Parents at the school at which the majority of parents were semiskilled or unskilled tended to have uncomfortable and infrequent interactions with teachers. Lareau wrote, "In the middle-class community, parents saw education as a shared enterprise and scrutinized, monitored and supplemented the school experience of their children" (p. 712). Children from middle-class families had greater cultural capital than children from lower income families. This is not to say that the family–school relationship among the middle class was better for children in comparison with children from the working class. Lareau stated, however, that "the social profitability of middle-class arrangements is tied to the school's definition of the proper family-school relationship" (p. 713).

Nona reported that her interactions with the school counselor left her feeling worse. It may be helpful for the therapist to attend such a meeting with her client. School counselors need to be aware of the ways in which culture can work against parents' perception of schools as accessible, particularly for working-class parents and their children. What may appear to be apathy from Nona may be feelings of powerlessness and alienation. For Nona and others like her, the quality of interactions with school personnel is linked to the discourses predominant from her educational contexts that were fraught with shame and difficulty. Many low-income parents carry the mental baggage from their negative early school experiences, which detracted from their ability, in some instances, to discuss their children's school experiences (Brantlinger, 1993).

The Therapist

Jackson (2005) makes a distinction between poor women and low-wage-earning women, which she says "helps us to always keep an eye trained on the economic conditions that create and/ or maintain the challenges that many women and their families experience to seek our services" (p. 238). Low-wage-earning people are more vulnerable within institutional structures, including the school, courts, and the police (Robinson, 1999b). For example, interest rates on credit cards are often near 30%. When making the minimum monthly payment, getting out of debt is nearly impossible, although now credit cards indicate on monthly statements the amount that credit card holders are liable for if only the minimum payment is met monthly. An important skill for Candace is the ability to engage in introspection and to ask questions of herself toward gaining insight into the effects of class on her identity. Standards for social class training do not exist about social class yet classism exists in counselor training. Because of this dearth, "counselors in training must seek experiences where they can explore their own social class worldviews and be challenged in a supportive environment" (Liu & Arguello, 2006, p. 9). As an identity construct, class has a significant impact on development. Like culture, people are often oblivious to it.

What is it about interactions with low-wage-earning people that may feel awkward or confining or familiar? What are the indicators of one's own privileged financial position that may be a point of disclosure to Nona, albeit unintentionally? Candace seeks to nurture an egalitarian relationship with all of her clients, yet at the same time, there is an unequal power dynamic. Feelings of guilt or an inability to relate to the client can contribute to a clinician's perceptions of her effectiveness or experience within the therapeutic alliance. It is important that Candace serve and not colonize Nona (Aponte, 1994). Nona has strengths and it is important that Candace help Nona mine these (e.g., commitment to therapy, perseverance, ability to ask for help, self-care) to offset negative social-class perceptions (Liu, Corkery, & Thome, 2010). Nona should neither have to pay nor wait for Candace to work through her unresolved issues that leave Candace feeling uncomfortable and/ or ill-prepared.

It is common for women who are being battered or who have histories with domestic violence not to have adequate social support. In qualitative research with six black and five white women who had survived battering, eight had an earlier experience of abuse (Hage, 2006). Experiences of abuse are a risk factor for further abuse. Fortunately, Nona has decided to be in a relationship free from the violence that characterized her life when her children were very young and when she was a child. Cultural competence for Candace involves awareness of community agencies that provide services to less advantaged populations (Liu et al., 2010).

To facilitate the process of becoming more aware of her own class experiences and worldview, Candace could recall memories from her childhood that were connected to class and that evoked feelings of pride, embarrassment, guilt, superiority, inferiority, and shame. It is important that Candace, regardless of race, class, sexuality, ability, or gender, endorse mutuality, reciprocity, and sensitivity in her work with Nona. She recognizes that Nona has limited resources but also understands the importance of Nona and other patients contributing financially for therapy. Respecting Nona's situation, she asks, "What do you think you would be able to pay for psychotherapy?" There are tables available, based on the client's income and poverty level, that could help therapists calculate a patient's contribution to therapy; however, Candace does not allow such tables to dictate Nona's ability to ponder this question and access therapy. Candace asks Nona to ponder this question until their next session.

It should be noted that as a licensed mental health counselor, Candace would be unable to accept Medicare if Nona were to receive this government subsidized insurance for age, physical, or mental disability. Increasingly states are seeking to connect counselor licensure with graduation from a CACREP (Council for the Accreditation of Counseling Related Educational Programs) program or undergo enhanced evaluation of the student's educational programs (e.g., submission of program syllabi). In addition, starting January 1, 2022, counselors who do not graduate from CACREP-accredited programs will be unable to apply for the National Certified Counselor certificate issued by the National Board of Certified Counselors, the entity that oversees the National Counseling Exam and the National Clinical Mental Health Counseling Exam. These are the primary exams that graduates of counseling programs take in order to become licensed. Moreover, come 2022, New Hampshire will not allow students to become Licensed Clinical Mental Health Counselors (LCMHC) unless they have graduated from a CACREP-affiliated program. Other accreditation options for master-level counseling graduates are available, although ACA-endorsement may or may not be available. The Masters in Psychology and Counseling Accreditation Council has accredited programs under the Masters in Psychology Accreditation Committee standards and the Masters in Counseling Accreditation Committee standards.

Candace shows cultural competence by being aware of state and federal policies and laws that govern her ability to become impaneled with certain health insurance companies in order to receive third-party payment for particular patients and to become licensed in particular states.

Summary

This chapter explored the investigation of class within the literature as a psychosocial variable. The middle-class bias in graduate counseling training programs was discussed at length. Work conducted by sociologists on school inequity was an important link in this discussion. A case was presented of a client from a low-income background with multiple strengths and challenges. Implications for mental health professionals were explored and questions presented for beginning the personal process of interrogating the dynamic of socioeconomic class in one's life. The impact of state and federal policies on the counselor–client relationship with respect to reimbursement from health insurance companies and obtaining professional licensure was briefly discussed.

17

❖

Converging Disability

I f we are fortunate to live long and prosper, disability will visit each of us in some way, shape, or form. This chapter has been influenced by the literature on disability studies and feminist disability theory (Garland-Thomas, 2002; Olkin & Pledger, 2003; Olkin, 2004). The status of the lived body, the politics of appearance, the medicalization of the body, the privilege of normalcy, multiculturalism, sexuality, the social construction of identity, and the commitment to integration are all aspects of a feminist disability theory, which also includes genetics, beauty, health, prosthetics, and reproductive technologies (Garland-Thomas, 2002). (See Storytelling: Wrong Type of Groom.)

Understanding Disability

On July 25, 2012, a report titled "Nearly 1 in 5 People Have a Disability" (U.S. Census Bureau, 2012) was released to coincide with the 22nd Anniversary of the Americans with Disabilities Act, also known as the ADA. In 2010, nearly 19% of the population, or over 56.7 million people from the civilian, noninstitutional population, had some level of disability (Brault, 2012).

Persons with a disability have a physical or mental impairment that affects one or more major life activities, such as walking, bathing, dressing, eating, preparing meals, going outside the home, or doing housework. A disability can occur at birth or at any point in a person's life. Disability encompasses a variety of internal and external conditions, capabilities, and limitations. It can involve the physical (e.g., muscular dystrophy), systemic (e.g., lupus), cognitive (e.g., traumatic brain injury), visual (e.g., blindness), hearing (e.g., deafness), developmental (e.g., autism), psychiatric (e.g., bipolar disorder), or multiple impairment (Olkin, 2004, p. 333).

A person has a disability if any of the following conditions apply: used a wheelchair, crutches, or a walker; had difficulty performing one or more functional activities such as seeing, hearing, walking, and/or grasping; had difficulty with or needed assistance with one or more activities of daily living such as bathing, dressing, eating, and/or toileting; had a developmental delay or learning disability; had difficulty walking, playing, or moving arms; had a specific condition, such as mental retardation, cerebral palsy, or Alzheimer's disease; had a mental or emotional condition that seriously interfered with everyday activities; or had a condition that made it difficult to remain employed.

Difficulty with at least one activity of daily living was cited by 9.4 million noninstitutionalized adults. These activities included getting around inside the home, bathing, dressing, and eating. Of these people, 5 million needed the assistance of others to perform such an activity. About 15.5 million adults had difficulties with one or more instrumental activities of daily living. These activities included doing housework, using the phone, and preparing meals. Of these, nearly 12 million required assistance. Seven million people reported being frequently depressed or anxious to the extent that it interfered with ordinary activities (U.S. Census Bureau, 2012).

Disabilities and Children in Schools

Knowledge of learning disabilities is important irrespective of where mental health professionals work or with whom. As adults, some of our patients continue to personally struggle with learning disabilities and their after effects on relationships, learning, educational attainment, employment, and self-esteem. Some patients parent children who have learning disabilities, which, understandably, are a source of clinical concern for them. Disorders are clearly defined below. (See Definitions Box 17.1: Specific Learning Disability Definition.)

Tremendous heterogeneity exists among the disabled, thus defining this group as a collective is challenging. There are differences in rates of disability according to age. For example, according to Brault (2012), about 12.3 million people aged 6 years and older (4.4%) needed assistance with one or more activities of daily living, known as

❖ DEFINITIONS 17.1

Specific Learning Disability Definition

A disorder in one or more of the basic psychological processes involved in understanding or using language, spoken or written, that may manifest itself in an imperfect ability to listen, think, speak, read, write, spell, or do mathematical calculations.

Source: National Center for Education Statistics (2015).

(ADLs) or instrumental activities of daily living (IADLs). Among people 15 years of age and older, 21% had a disability.

During the 2012 to 2013 school year, a higher percentage of children and youth ages 3 to 21 years of age received special education services under IDEA for specific learning disabilities than for any other type of disability. Enacted in 1975, the Individuals with Disabilities Education Act (IDEA), formerly known as the Education for All Handicapped Children Act (EAHCA), mandated the provision of a free and appropriate public school education for eligible children and youth ages 3 to 21 (National Center for Education Statistics, 2015). (See Knowledge Box 17.1: Percentage Data on Children and Youth Served Under IDEA, 2012 to 2013.)

Knowledge Check 17.1

Percentage Data on Children and Youth Served Under IDEA, 2012 to 2013

1. Specific Learning Disabilities: 35%

2. Speech or Language Impairments: 21%

3. Health Impairments: 12% (including having limited strength, vitality, or alertness due to chronic or acute health problems such as a heart condition, tuberculosis, rheumatic fever, nephritis, asthma, sickle cell anemia, hemophilia, epilepsy, lead poisoning, leukemia, or diabetes).

4. Autism: 8%

5. Intellectual disabilities: 7%

6. Developmental delays: 6%

7. Emotional disturbances: 6%

8. Multiple disabilities: 2%

9. Hearing impairments: 1%

10. Orthopedic impairments: 1%

Source: National Center for Education Statistics (2015).

Population Box 17.1: IDEA Participation by Race/Ethnicity

American Indians/Alaska Natives: 16%

Blacks: 15%

Whites: 13%

Two or more races: 13%

Hispanics: 12%

Pacific Islanders: 11%

Asians: 6%

Source: National Center for Education Statistics (2015).

The data on special education differs according to race. American Indians/Alaska Natives had the highest percent of children and youth served under IDEA, at 16%. Blacks had the next highest percentage at 15%, followed by whites at 13%. Children and youth of two or more races were at 13%, Hispanics at 12%, Pacific Islanders at 11%. Asians had the lowest level of participation, at 6%. Approximately 50% of children and youth, across racial and ethnic diversity who were served under IDEA received services for specific learning disabilities in addition to services for speech or language impairments (National Center for Education Statistics, 2015). (See Population Box 17.1: IDEA Participation by Race/Ethnicity.)

Adults and Disabilities

As with children, there is a tremendous range of disabilities. There are persons with noncongenital or medically defined disabilities. There are people with nonvisible disabilities who do not self-identity or claim to have a disability. There are also people with visible disabilities within a society where stigma is often associated with certain physical and visible disabilities.

Among people 21 to 64, 17% had a disability. Of people in this age group, over 40% with any disability were employed, compared with 79% of those with no disability. Clearly, people without a disability had higher rates of employment, which increase the likelihood of contending with continuous chronic poverty over a 2-year period (Brault, 2012).

Among adults 65 and older, 50% had a disability (Brault, 2012). Of people in this age group, 37% had a severe disability.

According to Brault's (2012) *Americans with Disabilities: 2010* report, the following data exists for people who are 15 and older: (a) 12 million people required the assistance of others in order to perform one or more basic or instrumental activities of daily living, such as bathing, dressing, doing housework, and preparing meals; (b) 8.1 million had a vision impairment; (c) 7.6 million had a hearing impairment, and among people 65 and older, 4 million had hearing impairments; (d) 3.6 million people used a wheelchair, a number that compares with 11.6 million people who used canes, crutches, or walkers; and (e) 2.4 million people had Alzheimer's disease, senility, or any form of neurocognitive disorders (Brault, 2012).

Among people age 15 to 64 with severe disabilities, approximately 11% experienced persistent poverty. Due to advances in technology, some people, including people without disabilities, are able to work from home and earn a living, whereas for others, technology costs are prohibitive. Among people in this same age range with nonsevere disabilities, just under 5% experienced persistent poverty, and just under 4% experienced continuous poverty with no disability (Brault, 2012).

Gender differences exist with respect to disability. Among women, 20% have a disability whereas 17% of males have a disability (Brault, 2012). Gender, race, and the nature of the disability also contribute to the diversity among the disabled. Persons of color with disabilities represent those with the highest poverty and unemployment rates (Marini, 2001). Among Asians, the rate for the presence of a disability was 13%. Asians also had the lowest prevalence, both of a severe disability and of the need for assistance. Black non-Hispanics had the highest rate for the presence of a disability, 20.38%, and the highest rate of a severe disability and the need for assistance. Among non-Hispanic whites, the rate for the presence of a disability was 19.8%, and it was 13.2% among Latinos (Brault, 2012). (See Population Box 17.2: Disability by Race/Ethnicity.)

Adults aged 21 to 64 with disabilities typically earn less than people who do not have disabilities. The median monthly earnings for people with any kind of disability was $1,961 compared with $2,724 for those with no disability (Brault, 2012). Poverty rates increase with the severity of the disability. In 2010, approximately 28.6% of people aged 15 to 64 with severe disabilities were in poverty while 17.9% of adults with nonsevere disabilities, and 14.3% of people with no disability were in poverty (Brault, 2012).

States and the federal government provide a variety of cash and in-kind benefits to offset the poverty and financial hardship endured by people with and without disabilities. These benefits include: (1) Supplemental Security income (SSI); (2) Social

---

Population Box 17.2: Disability by Race/Ethnicity

Blacks: 20.7%

Whites: 19.8%

Hispanics: 13.2%

Asians: 13.0%

Source: Brault (2012)

Security (retirement, survivor, and disability benefits); and (3) other cash forms, such as Temporary Assistance for Needy Families (TANF), Supplemental Nutrition Assistance Program (SNAP) benefits (formerly called food stamps), and public or subsidized housing (Brault, 2012). Despite the assistance of these two programs, persons with disabilities, as previously stated, are more likely to be unemployed and live in poverty. Persons who are blind and visually impaired have unemployment rates that exceed 70% (American Psychological Association [APA], 2007b).

Within the psychology curriculum, graduate students are more likely to receive instruction on race, gender, class, sexuality, and other dimensions of diversity than they are on disability (Olkin & Pledger, 2003; Pledger, 2003). Although disability pervades all aspects of culture 9 years after the passage of ADA, "The modal number of required courses on disability was still zero, as it was in 1989" (Garland-Thomas, 2002, p. 297).

The individualistic frame that represents the majority of mental health professionals in the West tends to focus studies of disability on the individual instead of expanding the scope to include the family, the community, and even a political context. With less of an emphasis on a medical model of disability, mental health professionals are encouraged to collaborate with other disciplines when conducting disability research in order to approach the study from a multidisciplinary perspective (Tate & Pledger, 2003).

Veterans

On November 11, 1919, Veterans Day originated as Armistice Day, which was the first anniversary marking the end of World War I. Congress passed a resolution in 1926 for an annual observance, and November 11 became a national holiday beginning in 1938. President Dwight D. Eisenhower signed legislation in 1954 to change the name to Veterans Day as a way to honor those who served in all American wars. Military veterans are honored with parades and speeches across the nation—a national ceremony takes place at the Tomb of the Unknowns at Arlington National Cemetery in Arlington, Virginia. Despite the honor of Veterans Day, our nation is filled with wounded veterans who have waited too long for medical care and who face homelessness, unemployment, depression, post-traumatic stress disorder (PTSD), and other burdens associated with war.

In 2013, there were nearly 20 million military veterans in the United States (American Community Survey: 2013 (2014). Of these, 1.6 million were female, 11.3% were black, 6% were Latino, 1.4% were Asian, .7% were Native, and 70.3% were non-Hispanic white (American Community Survey: 2013 (2014).

In 2013, there were nearly 4 million (3.6 million) veterans with a service-connected disability rating. Of this number, nearly 1 million (957,504) had a rating of 70% or higher. A disability that is "service connected" is a result of a disease or injury that was incurred or worsened during active military service. Disability severity is scaled from 0% to 100%. Eligibility for compensation depends on one's rating. There are 9.3 million veterans who are 65 years of age and older compared to 1.5 million who are below the age of 35 (American Community Survey: 2013 (2014). During Vietnam, more than 7 million veterans served our country, and 5 million veterans served during the Gulf War. Nearly 59,000 veterans who served in both of these wars are living. Over 1 million veterans served during World War II; 2 million during the Korean War, and nearly 5 million who served in peacetime only (American Community Survey: 2013 (2014).

According to Salamon (2010), seven mental and physical health issues confront veterans: (1) Musculoskeletal injuries and pain: Over half of all veterans' postdeployment health visits include musculoskeletal injuries and pain, involving back, neck, knee, and shoulder pain. Just over half of all veterans' postdeployment health visits address lingering pain in their backs, necks, knees, or shoulders. (2) Mental health issues: In addition to PTSD, one in ten Iraq War veterans contend with serious psychological and behavioral challenges, including violent behavior, depression, and alcohol abuse. (3) Chemical exposure: Exposure to nerve agents such as sarin, which can trigger convulsions and even death on the battlefield, may cause long-term heart damage in Gulf War veterans, such as enlarged left ventricles, heart rhythm abnormalities, or a reduction in the pumping strength of the heart. (4) Infectious diseases: Despite receiving routine vaccinations prior to deployment, veterans contend with and suffer from infections contracted during deployment, for which vaccines are not available. Included are bacterial infections such as brucellosis, which may persist for years; campylobacter jejuni, which causes abdominal pain, fever, and diarrhea; and Coxiella burnetii, which in chronic cases can inflame the heart. Leishmaniasis, a parasitic disease caused by the bite of a sand fly and native to the Middle East, is a severe condition experienced by veterans. Those inflicted experience weight loss, fevers, headaches, muscle pain and weakness, anemia, and enlargement of the spleen and liver. If untreated, this condition can be fatal. (5) Noise and vibration exposure: Hearing loss and impairment also include persistent ringing and buzzing in the ears, also known as tinnitus, are common effects of loud and harmful noise from gunfire, weapons, and noise from engines, engine rooms, and aircraft. In addition, vets who regularly worked with machinery can suffer vibration exposure, which can prompt irreversible or numbness and pain in the hands and fingers, according to the Veterans Affairs (as cited in Salamon, 2010). (6) Traumatic brain injury (TBI) is often the result of a blow or jolt to the head, disrupts the brain's function, and is considered to be the signature wound of involvement in the Iraq and Afghanistan wars. Between 70% and 80% of combat deaths are from blast-related exposure. Blast exposures and other combat-related activities place service members at a higher vulnerability for a TBI compared to the civilian population. Common effects of TBIs include cognitive issues such as shorter attention span, language disabilities, and an inability to process information. In addition to the TBI, veterans can also suffer from lack of motivation, irritability, anxiety and depression, headaches, memory loss, and PTSD. (7) Urologic injuries: Injuries to the bladder, ureters, kidneys, and genitalia often require surgery. Complications often arise since treatment must be delayed for penetrating injuries to the groin sustained during battle in deference to life-threatening injuries that must first be addressed. (See Knowledge Check 17.2: Common Disabilities Among Veterans.)

> ## Knowledge Check 17.2
>
> **Common Disabilities Among Veterans**
>
> 1. Musculoskeletal injuries and pain
> 2. Mental health issues
> 3. Chemical exposure
> 4. Infectious diseases
> 5. Noise and vibration exposure
> 6. Traumatic brain injury (TBI)
> 7. Urologic injuries
>
> *Source:* Salamon (2010).

Disability Studies

Disability studies is an interdisciplinary field that incorporates sociology, history, medical anthropology, politics, law, feminist psychology, and literature (Olkin & Pledger, 2003). Important to the foundation of disability studies is a shift in the paradigm regarding people with disabilities as consumers and as part of the independent living movement. The following components must also be included in disability studies: (1) grounding in the social model of disability that recognizes power, oppression, and economic issues; (2) an understanding that disability is not just a component of identity but "essential to the exploration of humanness" (Olkin & Pledger, 2003, p. 297); and (3) not reproducing the oppressive discourses that exist in the larger culture is included.

This new and emerging field is not without its critics. Thomas (2004) argued that disability studies as a distinct area of study might lead to segregation of people with disabilities from the rest of society. It was also argued that the name—*disability studies*—places emphasis on individuals' disabilities and not on their abilities.

Disability studies have shed light on the traditional theoretical constructions of disability. The biomedical model of disability has predominated. This model is rooted in the scientific method and defined disability in the language of medicine. A focus is on the disability existing within the individual and not on the person's environment, policy considerations, or structural issues. More recently, a sociopolitical model has emerged that defines people with disability as members of a minority group given the prejudice and discrimination that accompany this identity. Smart and Smart (2006) defined three dimensions of this model: (1) definitions about disability must be from an insider's perspective, from persons with disabilities; (2) people with disabilities must advocate for themselves and not allow "experts" to define disability for them; and

> ### Self-Check Exercise 17.1
>
> **Night**
>
> In *Night (Nacht)*, Elie Weisel, survivor of the Holocaust, discussed running with all his speed and strength past the SS (Schutzstaffel). Those considered disabled, slow, old, and/or weak were to be killed. Although Jews of all ages were murdered, passing these tests of physical strength gave people more time to survive. How would you do?

(3) people with disabilities resist the labels that align them and their bodies with deviance and pathology. This work is in support of the sociopolitical model.

One of the outcomes of disability studies is a new and holistic paradigm of disability that emphasizes new models of research. The integration of participatory action research methods and person–environment conceptualization of disability encourages researchers and clinicians to move away from the limitations of medically oriented definitions and measures of disability (Tate & Pledger, 2003). This emerging research paradigm means collaboration with members of the disability community and involving them in research that is accessible. It is important to not use research participants for the purpose of one's research effort and not offer anything back to the community. (See Self-Check Exercise 17.1: Night.)

Olkin (2004) identified several avenues to recruiting research participants from the disability community. She recommended disability magazines and newsletters, independent living centers, support groups, disability events, and disability-specific Internet sites. Survey Monkey is also a way for persons with disabilities to participate in research. An alternative format could also be used such as very large and dark print. Through Survey Monkey, Perkins (2015) found in his research study of male role norms that men who reported a disability scored significantly lower on male role norms than men who did not report a disability, a finding that may realize some advantage given the burden of high masculinity on many men, whether they know it or not.

The Social Construction of Disability

Many of the barriers that people with disabilities face are reinforced through language (APA, 2007a), encouraging human service providers to be mindful of their use of language. For instance, it is less appropriate to refer to people with disabilities as disabled people. Stating that a person uses a wheelchair is different from the statement that a person is confined or bound to a wheelchair. *Disability* is a broad term. Garland-Thomas (2002) critiqued the definition; she said,

> Clusters ideological categories as varied as sick, deformed, crazy, ugly, old, maimed, afflicted, mad, abnormal, or debilitated—all of which disadvantage people by devaluing

bodies that do not conform to cultural standards: its structuring institutions, social identities, cultural practices, political positions, historical communities, and the shared human experience of embodiment. (p. 5)

Our individualistic and capital-driven culture equates normalcy with bodily control and perfection (see Storytelling: Snow Down). Disability is redefined as non-normative, a loss of control, and a departure from an ideal or what is acceptable. Garland-Thomas (2002) saw similarities across marginalized identities and said, "Female, disabled, and dark bodies are supposed to be dependent, incomplete, vulnerable, and incompetent bodies. . . women and the disabled are portrayed as helpless, dependent, weak, vulnerable, and incapable bodies" (p. 7). Having an able body and mind is not just valued in society, but is considered a blessing from God. The ability to control, produce, reproduce, and master nature are constructed as biological capabilities, and for some, evidence of luck, God's grace, or superiority.

❖ **STORYTELLING: SNOW DOWN**

I slipped on the ice/snow (probably should have realized that pulling a fast moving wagon downhill with my children in tow was not a good idea) and landed on my knee that had recently been operated on 2 months prior. After seeing my doctor, I was told that I was fine, but for about a week, I had mobility issues: limping and walking slowly with some difficulty. I saw how impatient people were as I moved slowly to get onto the subway or to exit. Over 30 million Americans have some type of movement impairment, such as difficulty walking or climbing the stairs or need to use a wheelchair, cane, crutches, or walker. This group is the most populated category of disabilities.

Fowler, O'Rourke, Wadsworth, and Harper (1992) said, "When one's physical and/or mental abilities are considered as the primary status for characterizing individuals, the resulting polarity implicitly divides all persons into two groups: the able and the unable" (p. 14). Much like race and gender, physical disability is elevated to and exists as a status-determining characteristic, overriding other dimensions of the self. Even achieved traits are eclipsed by immutable characteristics as a function of birth or acquired through injury or are due to a medical condition. Relationships are often constituted on the basis of similarity, not only with respect to race and class but also with disability.

Dominant discourses associated with disability are that people with disabilities are helpless, childlike, dependent, undesirable, unattractive, asexual, and low-income wage earners. People with visible disabilities encounter hostility in society due to their physical and mental differences that violate deeply held cultural values about productivity, beauty, control, youth, and mastery over nature, time, and aging. Persons with disabilities are discriminated against, stereotyped, ignored, and in many instances, presumed to be biologically inferior, particularly if the disability is congenital as opposed to acquired (Marini, 2001).

Just as physical attractiveness has been linked to assumptions of moral character, intelligence, marital satisfaction, dating frequency, and quality of life (Dion, Berschid, & Walster, 1972; Webster & Driskell, 1983), so has disability. In fact, disability is constructed within the context of physical unattractiveness. (See Table 17.1: Dominant Disability Discourses.) The socialization process equates self-worth with mobility, thinness, beauty, and not being disabled. Hahn (1988a) said, "The most salient features of many disabled persons are bodily traits similar to skin color, gender, and other attributes that have been used as a basis for differentiating people for centuries and without which discrimination would not occur" (p. 26). Zola (1991) stated that preference for specific body types over others represents another societal "ism." In this work, this form of discrimination has been termed *ableism*. Considerable silence surrounds the experiences of those who have disabilities. This silence is particularly evident among some able-bodied persons who assume that lack of membership in the disability community grants them permission not to be informed, yet many of the experts in disabilities studies are themselves not disabled (Olkin, 2007).

Both Wendell (1989) and Zola (1991) maintained that a theory on disability and the body is needed. Because of the strong cultural assumptions of ability and physical attractiveness, such a theory is beneficial to all, regardless of current or temporary physical status. Although our culture privileges those who are mobile, we are an aging society where more and more people will face various forms of disability.

Many people with disabilities experience their bodies through pain. Wendell (1989) stated that persons who live with chronic pain can teach the general public what it means to share space with that which hurts. Crucial questions emerge, such as how a person welcomes pain into his or her life, especially if it is feared. In turn, are people with chronic pain feared and loathed by those who are reminded of their own vulnerability? Feeling the pain, as opposed to medicating it away (Wendell, 1989), meditating on the pain, engaging in visual imagery, and making peace with it are examples of being in, listening to, and embracing one's body for what it is. This

❖ **Table 17.1**   Dominant Disability Discourses

Dominant Disability Discourses
Helpless
Childlike
Desiring not to have a disability
Asexual
Unattractive
Dependent
Low income
A burden

increased consciousness is a gift of pain. Such a gift can move a person to a place of unconditional acceptance of his or her body despite the circumstances.

Writer Audre Lorde (1994) said, "There is a terrible clarity that comes from living with cancer that can be empowering if we don't turn aside from it" (p. 36). It is through the bold and yet humble confrontation of the pain that strength may be found for the journey. Pain, in its various forms, is a feature of living and is independent of physical ability status.

The wisdom among some people with disabilities may benefit persons without disabilities. The tendency to regard people who are different as "other" impedes benefiting from people who do not look normal. "If disabled people were truly heard, an explosion of knowledge of the human body and psyche would take place" (Wendell, 1989, p. 77). Persons with disabilities have much to teach the able-bodied about acceptance, dignity, and empowerment.

There are numerous real-life stories of people experiencing dramatic and sudden changes in their bodies. (See Case Study: Rethinking Manhood at the end of this chapter.) Wendell (1989), for example, wrote powerfully about the sudden overnight process of going from being able-bodied to being disabled as a result of a disabling chronic disease. "In 1985, I fell ill overnight with what turned out to be a disabling chronic disease. In the long struggle to come to terms with it, I had to learn to live with a body that felt entirely different to me—weak, tired, painful, nauseated, dizzy, unpredictable" (p. 63). Waiting to return to her original state was indeed dangerous because the likelihood of this occurrence was remote. In time, Wendell was required to learn how to identify and coexist with her new disabled body, but not without struggle. "I began slowly to identify with my new, disabled body and to learn to work with it" (p. 63). Within a culture where normalcy and disability are regarded as antonyms, she wrote, "Disabled women struggle with both the oppressions of being women in male-dominated societies and the oppressions of being disabled in societies dominated by the abler-bodied" (p. 64).

Alzheimer's

Alzheimer's disease is the most common form of dementia or loss of intellectual function among people aged 65 and older (see Story Telling: Not Going Home). As common as Alzheimer's is, it is not a normal part of the aging process. In the United States, the number of people 15 and older who had Alzheimer's disease, senility, or any form of neurocognitive disorders ranged from 2.4 (U.S. Census Bureau News, 2014) to over 5 million. Alzheimer's disease is progressive, meaning it only gets worse over time. As a degenerative disorder impacting memory, Alzheimer's first attacks neurons (the brain's nerve cells) in the hippocampus. These neurons, which produce the neurotransmitter, acetylcholine, break connections with other nerve cells and die. Language skills, thinking, and judgment decline when neurons die in the cerebral cortex. In time, changes in behavior become evident.

According to the Alzheimer's Foundation of America (2015), two types of abnormal lesions clog the brains of persons with Alzheimer's disease: (1) beta-amyloid plaques—sticky clumps of protein fragments and cellular material that form outside and around neurons, and (2) neurofibrillary tangles—insoluble twisted fibers composed largely of the protein tau that build up inside nerve cells. These structures are characteristic of the disease; however, scientists are not clear whether they cause Alzheimer's disease or if they are a by-product of it (Alzheimer's Foundation of America, 2015).

❖ **STORYTELLING: NOT GOING HOME**

Recently I watched a CNN special about Glen Campbell, a country music singer with Alzheimer's who is now residing in a retirement facility. I knew of him and had heard his music. He is a legend, but I had never really listened to his music and how lovely it was, with its clear pitch and the beauty of his lyrics. I also resonated with his story, having lost my father to Alzheimer's, a condition also known as the long goodbye. Singer Brad Paisley implored the medical community to identify a cure. He talked about both a grandparent having Alzheimer's and his mother. He somberly said, "I am next, and I am only 41 years old." It is not unusual to find women and men in their 40s and 50s who are considered to be the sandwich generation—where they are caring for their own children while caring for their elderly parents—many who have Alzheimer's in addition to other physical ailments. I have witnessed friends' depression and anxiety spike as they seek to work full-time jobs; lift parents; bathe, shop, and cook for their parents; and search for care providers and drivers to doctor's appointments. Policy issues will have to accommodate the increasing numbers of baby boomers who will require this level of care.

Perfection, Beauty, and the Able Body

Despite the valiant and noble efforts of the women's movement, negative body image continues into the 21st century. According to Hutchinson (1982), "Body image is not the same as the body, but is rather what the mind does to the body in translating the experience of embodiment into its mental representation" (p. 59). Birtchnell, Lacey, and Harte (1985) indicated three aspects of body image: (1) *physiological*, which involves the brain's ability to detect weight, shape, size, and form; (2) *conceptual*, which is the mental picture of one's own body; and (3) *emotional*, which refers to the feelings about one's body weight, shape, and size. A survivor of breast cancer (Elder, 2000) spoke movingly about the impact of the disease, but noted the silence around attractiveness and desirability. She worried about her appearance and how the mastectomy would affect her married life. Her husband was more concerned about her than the loss of her breast and yet saw how the loss of her breast changed his wife's perception of herself.

❖ **STORYTELLING: WRONG TYPE OF GROOM**

In Sharon Anderson and Valerie Middleton's *Explorations in Privilege, Oppression, and Diversity*, a young man tells a story of his approaching wedding day. Being Catholic, he approached his priest to marry him and his bride. The priest would not marry the groom. Why? Because he was divorced?

No. The priest would not marry the man because the man had a spinal cord disability. The priest suspected that the man would not be able to reproduce (the purpose of marriage); therefore, the priest questioned the man's purpose of getting married in the first place.

Physicality in the form of an able body as the most valuable commodity that one has is a damning but active message in society (see Storytelling: Wrong Type of Groom). Discourses about the female body's function as a site for others' approval and scorn set girls and women up to have low levels of self-esteem. Adult women are incapable of helping young women celebrate their bodies when they themselves are unable to honor their own bodily desires. The socialization of young girls to see their primary role in life as pleasing others encourages the development of anxiety, depression, and an unhealthy reliance on others for approval. Brouwers (1990) argued that the emotional aspect of body image is at the crux of bulimia, characterized by recurrent episodes of binge eating and subsequent feelings of lack of control. Intense dissatisfaction with body image and strong hatred of one's body is correlated with bulimia.

Dissatisfaction with one's body is reinforced in the face of unattainable standards of perfected beauty. Restricting and denying one's movement and comfort are handicapping and yet this is what women do regularly to appear beautiful to others. Social desirability is aligned with wearing fashions that are uncomfortable, tight, unflattering (muffin top jeans) and inappropriate (exposure of one's anatomy due to pelvic resting jeans), painful, and even harmful to the body. Stilettos are worn because they add height, slenderize the legs, and elongate the body. They also restrict movement and interfere with normal walking. Bunions, corns, and other serious foot problems suffered by millions of women result from the mantra that pain comes with beauty.

More and more women are opting for expensive and risky plastic surgery to achieve the perfect breasts, nose, and buttocks. Garland-Thomas (2002) noted, "The beautiful woman of the 21st century is sculpted surgically from top to bottom" (p. 10). Aging and obesity are big business. The attitude is that beauty is something to be acquired and at any cost (Okazawa-Rey, Robinson, & Ward, 1987). Liposuction, abdominalplasty, facelifts, buttock enhancement, breast augmentation, and other forms of plastic surgery are commonplace. A closer relationship exists among beauty, thinness, success, power, acceptance, and self-worth for girls and women than it does for boys and men. In fact, one study found that overall body dissatisfaction was higher among girls than among boys (Paxton et al., 1991). This finding may explain why 87% of persons undergoing plastic surgery are women (Steinem, 1992).

Billions of dollars are spent annually on products and services in Herculean efforts to beautify, freshen, deny, and defy the aging process. Looking good is not denounced. The maniacal emphasis placed on physical attractiveness as synonymous with having an able body is problematic. Hahn (1988a) discussed beauty power and its association with mate selection and sexual intimacy. She said, "As long as physical beauty determines sexual choices, human relations will be guided by fortuitous pleasing compositions of bone, muscle, and skin" (p. 27). Hahn observed that inner beauty and character will take a back seat in the competition for partners. Perceived as a prized commodity, beauty operates to "snare a mate who can give her the opportunity to live out her biological and social destiny" (Hutchinson, 1982, p. 60). Rockquemore (2002) said it well: "for women, appearances are power in the mating market" (p. 492).

Age is the one identity construct that has the greatest bearing on beauty. *Ageism*, or discrimination against middle-aged and elderly people, differs between men and women. According to Nuessel (1982), "Ageism is distinct from other forms of discrimination because it cuts across all of society's traditional classifications: gender, race, religion, and national origin" (p. 273). Ageism affects women in that in the normal and inevitable maturational process, men mature and become refined; women wilt and wither. The devaluation of women's bodies among a male-dominated medical community cannot be divorced from lucrative and costly hysterectomies and other surgeries for women. The medical community has used estrogen against women to support a belief that this hormone is essential for femininity and youth. Now women are largely discouraged from using hormone replacement therapy unless indicated. Although there are benefits, such as relief from the symptoms of menopause, cancer is a risk.

As women mature and develop a sense of personal power and an internal locus of control, they may come to perceive their beauty differently. Powerful women recognize that responsible self-care and respect for others is healthier than selflessness and that becoming older is a privilege and a responsibility.

Implications for Mental Health Professionals

Mental health professionals have a responsibility to address disability issues in addition to having the psychological skills and expertise to assist the client (Pledger, 2003). Toward this end, APA's Committee on Disability in Psychology is dedicated to (1) promoting the psychological welfare of people with disabilities, (2) promoting the development and implementation of psychological service delivery models responsive to the needs of people with disabilities, (3) promoting the awareness of disability issues in psychological research as well as specific research activity in disability areas, and (4) promoting inclusion of knowledge about disabilities and disability issues in education, training programs, and professional development of psychologists.

Helping professionals are not exempt from attitudes that favor attractive children and adults over those regarded as unattractive (Ponzo, 1985). Guidance counselors need to be particularly mindful of the power of words in shaping children's constructions of themselves. Lerner and Lerner (1977) wrote, "Evidence suggests that when compared to the physically attractive child, the unattractive child experiences rejecting peer relations, the perception of maladjustment by teachers and peers, and the belief by teachers of less educational ability" (p. 586).

Mental health professionals are also encouraged to ascertain their own beliefs about body image and physical attractiveness. Some may be more inclined to gravitate toward able-bodied and attractive clients. This behavior is biased and discredits a profession that should be oriented toward empowerment and respect. Due to worldview, gender, culture, and/or individual differences, some clients may not value and thus not strive for independence or mastery over their environments. Refusing to do so is not a form of pathology, but such attitudes have to be examined in the context of culture (Marini, 2001).

Mental health professionals need to assess the impact of the culture's messages about beauty, perfection, and disability on their self-esteem and on their perceptions, favorable and otherwise, of others. Smart and Smart (2006) warn, "If the counselor views disability as a tragic inferiority, then he or she will more likely experience a negative, emotional response to the client with a disability" (p. 37). Knowledge about a client's disability and accompanying functional limitations is part of multicultural competence (Marini, 2001).

To improve compliance with ADA and to serve the needs of individuals with disabilities, it is recommended that counselors do the following:

1. Do not deny services to a client with a disability.

2. Do not provide unequal service to clients with disabilities. Different service to respond effectively to a client's needs is not the same as unequal.

3. Provide auxiliary aids such as large print materials, Braille, notepads, and pencils.

4. Evaluate the structural and architectural environment (ramps, curb cuts, elevator control buttons) to ensure access into the building.

5. Involve the services of a contractor when building a new office so that ADA requirements can be followed (APA, 2007a).

Case Study

Rethinking Manhood

Drew is a 24-year-old white male from a low-wage-earning family. At the age of 14, he joined a gang and eventually became a person with a VASCI (violence-acquired spinal cord injury). During a gunfight with a rival gang, Drew was shot two times in the back. One of the bullets nicked his spinal cord. Drew survived the gunshot blasts and is now a quadriplegic. The brush with death was sobering for him and has allowed him to redirect his life. He is now going through peer mentoring training, has a stable relationship with his fiancée, and looks forward to starting college someday in the near future. Part of Drew's role as a peer mentor is to discuss sex following a spinal cord injury. Drew realizes he needs help in addressing these issues and receives assistance from his mentor. Drew's counselor is Lewis. Lewis is a licensed clinical mental health counselor. He is able to provide services to Drew, who receives Medicare, under the supervision of a psychologist. Although Drew is very young, he receives Medicare due to his physical disability. Currently Medicare is the largest health care program in the country and is the nation's flagship health care program, covering more than 40 million people. Medicare does not reimburse professional counselors for outpatient behavioral health services, such as mental health counseling. Medicare currently recognizes psychiatrists, psychologists, clinical social workers, and psychiatric nurses to provide outpatient mental health services (National Board of Certified Counselors, 2015).

Questions

1. How can a mentor assess where Drew is in his own recovery?
2. How does Drew's status as a quadriplegic affect his masculinity and his sexuality?
3. Could a female mentor demonstrate cultural competence with Drew?

Discussion and Integration

The Mentor, Drew

Disability intersects with gender. In a society where masculinity is equated with virility, strength, sexuality, and self-reliance, it is understandable that men with physical disabilities may be culturally perceived by some as contradictions to hegemonic masculinity. Gerschick and Miller (1994) stated that "men with physical disabilities are marginalized and stigmatized because they undermine the typical role of the body in United States culture . . . Men's bodies allow them to demonstrate the socially valuable characteristics of toughness, competitiveness, and ability" (p. 35). To arrive at a place of acceptance of one's body, there has to be (1) a confrontation of the societal standard that maintains that masculinity is not only narrowly defined but also in contradiction to the disabled man's body, (2) repudiation of this socially constructed norm, and (3) affirmation of the self through a recognition that the norms and discourses, and not the person, are problematic (Collins, 1989). From this perspective, the man is able to reconstruct, for himself and for others, alternative gender roles and practices (Gerschick & Miller, 1994).

Myers et al. (1991) stated that, in society today, with all of its isms, "the very nature of the conceptual system is itself inherently oppressive and that all who adhere to it will have a difficult time developing and maintaining a positive identity" (p. 55). A suboptimal system operates when self-worth is attached to factors separate from the self. Optimally, self-worth is intrinsic to the self. Accidents and illness suddenly change the ability and control over one's body.

Values core to the United States: Protestant work ethic, individualism, capitalism, and self-reliance—are inextricably bound to notions of physical attractiveness, power, mobility, strength, control, and dominance over one's body. Vulnerability and uncertainty simply do not coexist well in a society that values domination and conquest. The belief is that illness and subsequent disability are a result of the individual's doing. Wendell (1989) stated, "The demand for control fuels an incessant search for the deep layered explanations for causes of accidents, illness, and disability" (p. 72).

A client who experiences a traumatic loss needs time and space to mourn and process. Drew's life after being shot can be meaningful; first, however, he has to redefine some of the dimensions of manhood, such as success, attractiveness, masculinity, sexual activity, and function. Because "a disability carries sufficient conceptual power to stereotype an individual, regardless of whether the disability was present at birth or acquired later in life" (Fowler et al., 1992, p. 102), Drew's conceptualization of self across multiple identities has shifted. Part of this shifting self-conceptualization encompasses what it means to be a man.

A multiculturally competent mentor is not reluctant to explore the violence in Drew's past and how he makes meaning of it in the present. Had Drew fallen asleep at the wheel of a car and hit a tree, a different set of events would be represented than someone perpetrating violence on his life. Where is Drew with feelings of anger and fantasies of retaliation? In Hernandez's (2005) qualitative study with 16 men with newly acquired spinal cord injury from gunshot trauma, she found three main themes: (1) disability was viewed as a wake-up call or blessing, (2) disability was viewed as a turning point, and (3) disability was viewed as identity transforming.

Drew does not have a disease. His disability is from a violent injury, and he is healthy within the context of his disability. Seeing Drew as sick does not encourage the mentor to view him as active, able, and alive—words that tend not to be associated with the experience of having a disability (APA, 2007a). Garland-Thomas (2002) identifies resistance to claiming a disability identity as partly influenced by limited ways to talk about disability that are not oppressive.

At the appropriate time, the mentor can help Drew critique traditional and oppressive notions of masculinity for all men, regardless of ability or disability. Boys are socialized to believe that masculinity is synonymous with being a protector, provider, and worker. Athleticism and body strength create the basis for virility. Men with physical disabilities struggle with internalized notions of masculinity that are inconsistent with the presence of disability. Men with disabilities are not perceived by society as strong because a large part of this strength and manhood equation is having an able body, which is synonymous with the ability to achieve an erection. There are different types of strength, physical as well as character, that are not typically identified by society.

Asking for psychological help is a form of self-reliance and control (Roberts, Kiselica, and Fredrickson, 2002). Research has shown that supportive social networks are associated with psychological well-being and adjustment to one's disability (Belgrave, 1991; Swanson, Cronin-Stubbs, & Sheldon, 1989). Families for people of color with disabilities tend to have more experience with sharing ethnicity and/or race. Because the person with the disability may be the only one in the family, he or she can feel lonely, particularly if the family is prejudiced, feels that the person sinned and is paying for his or her sins, or not encouraging the family member with the disability to spend time with others who are also disabled (Olkin, 2007).

Prior to the accident, Drew had a very active life, albeit dangerous, involving the full use of his legs. Although Drew's mobility has been improved by his wheelchair, which is controlled by mouth, a measure of Drew's healing is his physical, social, and mental activity. Lewis, Drew's counselor, would want to know what Drew's identity means to him, particularly as he will be helping men who are grappling with changes to and losses of identity. A reflection of Lewis's cultural competence is familiarity with the disability community's preferred language. Crippled, a word that Drew's mother uses on a regular basis, is not acceptable. Other problematic words include handicapped, the disabled, and differently abled (Olkin, 2007). Although licensed and no longer a clinical intern, Lewis participates in collaborative groups where he can benefit from consultation with other licensed mental health professionals. He wants to avoid feeling clinical panic in his work with Drew. Clinical panic describes the clinician's inability to effectively assess or treat the patient (Catalano, 1985).

Recently, Drew has noticed his ability to move two of his fingers on his right hand. This change in functional limitation gives him hope that he will be able to do more in the future. Drew's ability to perform is by no means static and fluctuates across situations and environments—this variation in function is known as the enablement/disablement phenomenon (Pledger, 2003).

Through journaling, small group work, social activism, and by providing assistance to others, Drew can continue to unravel the strongholds of socially constructed notions of desirability, attractiveness, and worthiness that have had an enormous impact on his self-concept. Drew's mentor reframes meanings of strength, realizing that Drew can exhibit strength through his lived experiences of dignity, interdependence, competitiveness, and wisdom.

Many of the issues Drew and other men grapple with are related to sexual impotence. A woman could be an appropriate mentor to the extent that she is comfortable with the client's transference and is able to discuss sex frankly. Moreover, cultural competence asks that professionals become knowledgeable of how their gendered presence shows up in the room. When possible, clients could be asked if they have preferences with respect to the therapist–patient dyad. Patients should neither have to contend with a counselor who remains uncomfortable with intimate conversations that the client needs as part of their recovery nor should patients have to contend with a provider who contributes to their discomfort. Understandably, Drew has major concerns about his sexual activity and its expression, given his inability to achieve an erection. How will he experience sexual gratification? How will he provide sexual pleasure? A series of technological devices are available that assist couples with achieving satisfying sex lives in the event of spinal cord injuries, medication-induced impotence, and other barriers to erection. Penile implants made of silicone or polyurethane can be surgically installed. One type consists of two semirigid but bendable rods; the other type consists of a pump, fluid-filled reservoir, and two cylinders into which the fluid is pumped to create an erection. Vacuum devices can also be used to increase blood flow to the penis. Problems have been reported with both vacuum and inflatable devices (Balch, 2006, p. 509).

Drew's body, mind, spirit, and heart are sources of giving and receiving intense pleasure. Notions of what constitutes a normal sex life had to be altered for Drew to find the meaning that is now a part of his life. Genital sex is one way to give and receive pleasure, but he has learned that it is not the only way.

Finally, it is crucial to remember that what is perceived as attractive is a social construction perpetuated and reproduced. Society, however, can deconstruct and revise what it construes. What would it mean for some religious communities to, as do many Native Americans, not regard disability as punishment for having sinned but embrace people as wonderfully made (Marini, 2001)?

Summary

This chapter examined the culture's fascination and preoccupation with physical attractiveness. A case study examined able-body-ism in a male client who had become disabled as a result of gang violence. Implications for counselors were discussed with respect to the convergence of physical attractiveness, race, age, ability, disability, and gender. Demographic data were presented on the number of Americans with disabilities.

18

❖

Converging Spirituality

Definitions of spirituality and religion are provided. Spirituality as a component of diversity, as an identity construct, and as an integral part of the therapy process are discussed.

Spirituality and Religion Defined

Religion and spirituality are interrelated, but important differences exist. Religion comes from the Latin root *religio*, which means a "bond between humanity and the gods" (Ingersoll, 1995, p. 11). "Religion is the practice of one's beliefs with respect to a higher being. Involved are behaviors, rituals, and routines related to the worship experience" (Robinson & Watt, 2001). Spirituality is understood as the "outward expression of the inner workings of the human spirit" (Swinton, 2001, p. 20).

Age impacts religious identity and affiliation. About two thirds of young people (68%) say they are members of a Christian denomination, and 4% describe themselves as Protestants. Among adults, 81% of adults 30 and older associate with Christianity, and 53% are Protestants. Older people are more likely to be involved religiously and to identify themselves as Christians. Young adults do not pray as often as their elders, yet the number of young adults who state that they pray daily is comparable to the proportion reported among young people in prior decades (Pew Research Center, 2010). The majority of people who reside in America identify as Christian; however, this group is shrinking based on declines reported from 2007 to 2014. (See Population Box 18.1: Changes in Religious Affiliation, 2007 to 2014.)

According to the Pew Research Center (2010), one in four members of the millennial generation, those who were born after 1980 and came of age at the beginning of the 21st century, are not affiliated with any particular faith. They described their religion as "atheist," "agnostic" or "nothing in particular." This tendency compares with less than one fifth of people in their 30s (19%), 15% of people in their 40s, 14% of those in their 50s, and 10% or less among those 60 and older (Pew Research Center, 2010). (See Population Box 18.2: Religious Affiliation by Age.) Overall, millennials are much less affiliated than older generations were at a comparable point in their life

Population Box 18.1: Changes in Religious Affiliation, 2007 to 2014

	2007	2014	%Change
Christian	78.4%	70.6%	-7.8%
Protestant	51.3%	46.5%	-4.8%
Catholic	23.9%	20.8%	-3.1%
Non-Christian	4.7%	5.9%	+1.2%
Muslim	0.4%	0.9%	+0.5%
Hindu	0.4%	0.7%	+0.3%
Other Faiths*	1.2%	1.5%	+0.3%
Unaffiliated	16.1%	22.8%	+6.7%

The "other faiths" category includes Unitarians, New Age religions, Native American religions, and a number of other non-Christian faiths.

Source: Pew Research Center (2015).

Population Box 18.2: Religiously Unaffiliated by Age Group

Total	18-29	30+	30-39	40-49	50-59	60-69	70+
16%	25%	14%	19%	15%	14%	10%	8%

Source: Pew Research Center (2010).

cycle (e.g., 20% of Generation X'ers were unaffiliated in the late 1990s and 13% of Baby Boomers were unaffiliated in the late 1970s). Compared with their elders, young adults attend religious services less often and compared with elders, fewer young people report that religion is very important in their lives (Pew Research Center, 2010). (See Storytelling: Never Been to Church.)

According to the Pew Research Center (2015), the unaffiliated group has risen, from 16% to 22.8%. This more recent Pew study clearly shows that those persons who are religiously characterized as "nones" represent the one largest destination of movement across religious boundaries. For each person who leaves the unaffiliated category and identifies with a religious group more than four others have joined the religious nones (Pew Research Center, 2015).

There are age differences with respect to religion. The religious groups that reflect growth tend to be relatively young and are getting younger. A different picture emerges among religious groups that are shrinking; these groups tend to be relatively old and are getting older. The median age of religiously unaffiliated adults is 36. The median age among self-identified atheists and agnostics is 34.

Muslims and Hindus are relatively young, with a median age of 33, whereas the median age of Jews, Catholics, and Protestants is closer to 50. Put differently, 21% of Christians have reached the traditional retirement age of 65, compared with 9% of the religiously unaffiliated, 5% of Muslims, and 4% of Hindus (Pew Research Center, 2015).

❖ **STORYTELLING: NEVER BEEN TO CHURCH**

When I first started teaching in the south during the late 80s, I do not recall any students requesting to attend a church service for their cross-cultural experience. Within the last 13 years, particularly in the northeast, I have encountered more students who indicate having never been to a church of any kind and ask if they can attend a religious service (e.g., church, mosque, synagogue, temple) as part of their cross-cultural experience. My story is consistent with the data concerning the declining significance of religious affiliation among young people.

While "religion is defined as a set of practices and beliefs (e.g., dogma) that are shared by a community or group" (Halbert et al., 2007, p. 282), spirituality is associated with a transcendent and sacred dimension (Robinson-Wood & Braithwaite-Hall, 2005), a process of finding meaning in one's life (Halbert et al., 2007), and includes a "capacity for creativity, growth, and development of a value system" (Young, Wiggins-Frame, & Cashwell, 2007, p. 48).

Ingersoll (1995) identified spirituality as having seven dimensions:

1. One's conception of the divine or a force greater than oneself

2. One's sense of meaning or what is beautiful and worthwhile

3. One's sense of a relationship with Divinity and other beings

4. One's tolerance or negative capability for mystery

5. Peak and ordinary experiences engaged to enhance spirituality (may include rituals or spiritual disciplines)

6. Spirituality as play or the giving of oneself

7. Spirituality as a systemic force that acts to integrate all the dimensions of one's life (p. 11)

It is possible to be spiritual and not religious and to be religious and not spiritual (Burke & Miranti, 2001). Religion is often associated with an institutionalized set of beliefs "by which groups and individuals relate to the ultimate" (Burke et al., 1999, p. 252). It is defined as the specific organized and codified form through which individuals may express their spirituality (Young et al., 2007, p. 48). Miller and Thoresen (2003) conceptualized religion as associated with the social phenomenon and spirituality understood at the level of the individual; nonetheless, spirituality and religion overlap and are related constructs in that they share some characteristics and do not share others.

Hall and Pargament (2003) caution against the polarization of religion and spirituality, which "ignores the fact that all forms of spiritual expression unfold in a social context and that virtually all organized faith traditions are interested in the ordering of personal affairs" (p. 64). These authors also site other consequences associated with a bifurcation of religion and spirituality:

1. There is a risk that spirituality emerges as good and religion as bad. The truth is that there are helpful and harmful aspects related to each.

2. Most people experience spirituality within a religious context and frankly do not see a distinction between the two.

3. The polarization could lead to duplication of concepts and measures used in research.

Spirituality, Therapy, and Cultural Considerations

Effective therapy does not deny differences between client and therapist but respects completely the multiple identities that comprise the self. Multiculturally competent therapy emphasizes an ecological framework wherein the person and environment interaction is considered along with culture, ethnicity, family, structural issues, history, and spirituality, which is seen as fundamental to who the client is in therapy (Robinson-Wood & Braithwaite-Hall, 2005). Spirituality is a core dimension of life, along with friendship, love, work, and self-regulation (Witmer & Sweeney, 1992), but there are barriers to an inclusion of spirituality into therapy.

The lack of training about spirituality within therapeutic contexts is a key issue for many therapists, particularly given that spirituality has emerged as a dimension of multiculturalism (Hall, Dixon, & Mauzey, 2004). Unresolved religious issues in the therapist's life, lack of clarity about spirituality as a mysterious and deep phenomenon, and fear of imposing values are some of the factors that may contribute to a therapist's silence about spiritual and religious matters. The misguided belief that spirituality cannot and should not be studied has contributed to its absence in research (Miller & Thoresen, 2003). (See Storytelling: Actively Listening to Talk That Shouldn't Be Spoken.)

❖ STORYTELLING: ACTIVELY LISTENING TO TALK THAT SHOULDN'T BE SPOKEN

I use the following case study in class to discuss the intersections of religion, sexuality, gender, and ethnicity.

Miriam is a 26-year-old, physically healthy Lebanese woman living in a medium-sized city in South Carolina with her husband, Samuel. He is also Lebanese. They have been in the United States for 17 years. They came to the United States with their families. They are Arabs, Muslims, and heavily involved in their mosque. They have been married 6 years and have two small children. Samuel is the primary breadwinner and is an engineer. Miriam is a homemaker and is taking classes at the community college. She spends one evening a week studying late. Sam and Miriam's love-making has become infrequent, and it is clear to Samuel that the relationship has changed. When she is home, Miriam spends quite a bit of time on her computer. She said she is studying with a classmate. Samuel suggests they speak with their Imam, the spiritual leader of their Mosque. Miriam told Sam she could not

speak to him. When Sam asked why, Miriam confessed she was having a sexual relationship with her female classmate—and that she has had feelings for women before they married. She prayed these feelings would go away, but they did not. Miriam would prefer to speak with the Imam's wife. Although she is close to her family, Miriam believes she cannot talk with them about this topic. Miriam makes an appointment with Jane, the college counselor. Jane is a white American. The following dialogue occurs during their first encounter:

Jane: *Hi Miriam. My name is Jane. Thank you for coming to see me today. What would you like to talk about?*

Miriam: *It is very hard for me to be here. I have always felt different from other Lebanese women.*

Jane: *Where exactly is Lebanon?*

Miriam: *It's in the Middle East between Israel and Syria. It borders the Mediterranean Sea.*

Jane: *Were you born in Lebanon?*

(Continued)

❖ **STORYTELLING: ACTIVELY LISTENING TO TALK THAT SHOULDN'T BE SPOKEN** (Continued)

Miriam: *I've lived in the United States since I was 9.*

Jane: *Your English is very good.*

Miriam: *I spoke three languages when I arrived in America: English, French, and Arabic.*

Jane: *So you speak Arabic, but you are not from Saudi Arabia. Are you Muslim?*

Miriam: *I am Muslim. I am also Arab but not from Saudi Arabia. Some day, I would like to return to Lebanon and see my extended family.*

Jane: *You said earlier you have always felt different from Lebanese women.*

Miriam: *(Long Pause) I've been having a sexual relationship with another woman in my class.*

Jane: *Do you think you're gay?*

Miriam: *I'm not sure.*

Jane: *How long have you had feelings for women?*

Miriam: *I've been sexually attracted to women since I was a teenager.*

Jane: *Sexual behavior and sexual identity are not the same.*

Miriam: *I don't think I am just experimenting—I enjoy being with this woman, but I feel my behavior is very wrong.*

Jane: *Do you think your feelings for this woman are based on a choice?*

Miriam: *I have prayed that my struggles with same-sex feelings would go away. I feel they are shameful.*

Jane: *What does it mean to you that your feelings for women seem to be a constant in your life?*

Miriam: *My feelings scare me and make me question not only my sexuality, but also my integrity.*

Jane: *What do you mean?*

Miriam: *I think I am bisexual, but it goes against everything I am: a devoted Muslim and follower of Allah—a wife to a good man, and mother to beautiful children.*

Jane: *I hear the enormity of your struggle.*

Miriam: *This keeps me up at night (Miriam begins to cry). I can't concentrate—I have not been eating well. I feel guilt and shame for hurting my husband, but alive when I am with this woman.*

Jane: *Our time is up, but I'm glad you came in today. There are lots of conflicting feelings and emotions you are experiencing, but I believe we can create a place in therapy that provides you with the safety and clarity you need to listen to yourself and come to some resolve.*

Miriam: *I feel better already.*

Jane: *I look forward to seeing you next time. Just remember, as a woman, only your sense of what it means to live in the world is all that matters.*

Miriam: *I was not raised in this manner. In my family, it is not this way—we do what is right and good for the collective—there are pillars to live by.*

Jane: *You may need to be selfish and be your own woman.*

Miriam: *Selfish? My own woman? I don't know what this means as a Lebanese.*

Miriam leaves the counseling session and returns for therapy that next week with Jane.

That evening, Jane talks to a friend of hers: "I had a client today—a really fascinating women from Saudi Arabia or was it Lebanon?—somewhere in the Middle East. She is sure she is bisexual but struggles with what is appropriate for her as a Muslim, wife, and mother. In situations like this, I just want to shake these downtrodden women and say, 'This is your life. No one has the right to live it for you or tell you what you should do. Be your own person.'"

This case that includes diverse identities, allows students to review for the

❖ STORYTELLING: ACTIVELY LISTENING TO TALK THAT SHOULDN'T BE SPOKEN

application of basic clinical skills, including active listening to the patient (as opposed to provide Jane with geographic information), empathy, reflecting, and summarizing (which Jane does not do at the end but instead abruptly announces that they are out of time).

Jane appears to be lacking in multicultural competence as it relates to race, ethnicity, and cultural knowledge. She does, however, seem to exhibit greater comfort with Miriam's sexual identity than with these other dimensions of her identity. An example of this is her statement regarding the difference between sexual behavior and sexual identity. At the same time, there are sexuality discourses (e.g., that gay can be prayed away) that could facilitate Miriam's understanding of her feelings and behavior (e.g., sadness that her prayers to eliminate same-sex feelings are not working). From an individualistic perspective, Jane encourages Miriam to be selfish and to be her own woman. Miriam was confused by Jane's words, particularly since Miriam does not subscribe to individualism, hence her enormous conflict, guilt, and shame. Miriam's culture has fostered collectivism and group interests over individual interests. Jane does not seem to be cognizant of this difference in worldviews. She also does not seem to detect that she is imposing her values onto Miriam by encouraging a feminist perspective.

Jane lacks basic geographic knowledge. When speaking with her friend, she did not know which country Miriam was from and confused speaking Arabic, a language, with being from the country, Saudi Arabia. Jane seems not to understand the press of collectivistic orientations on individual behavior.

This lack of information will make it hard for Jane to implement appropriate intervention strategies for Miriam. Dictating womanhood for another woman is not reflective of the use of appropriate strategies but reflects ethnocentrism and insensitivity to cultural difference.

According to Sabry and Vohra (2013), consultation with an Imam (a Muslim religious leader), a Muslim social work professional, or another respected community member could be helpful when working with Muslim patients. More specifically, they may be able to help identify concepts, which are consistent with Islam, as well as language from Islamic teachings such as *halal* and *haram*, concepts in Islam, which mean what is allowed and what is prohibited, respectively.

There are benefits to a clinician being culturally competent. When clients perceive their therapists as having a multicultural orientation, they are likely to view the therapist as having more credibility. Owen, Tao, Leach, and Rodolfa (2011) examined whether 176 clients' perceptions of their clinicians' multicultural orientation were associated with their psychological functioning, working alliance, and real relationship scores. The researchers also tested whether clients' perceptions of the working alliance and the real relationship served to mediate the relationship between clients' perceptions of their psychotherapists' and psychological functioning. It was found that clients' perceptions of their psychotherapists' multicultural orientation were positively related to working alliance, real relationship, and psychological functioning. Clients' strong alliance was facilitative of improvement in psychological well-being.

The connections between spirituality and therapy are strong. "Both psychological growth and spiritual conversion draw the person out of old ways of being, through the deaths such letting go requires, and into liberation forms of life consistent with one's true self" (Berliner, 1995, p. 113). Both spirituality and therapy are oriented to helping the client do the following:

1. Learn to accept himself or herself in relationship to the environment and with the people in one's environment.

2. Forgive oneself and others. Sometimes not forgiving others makes sense, thus allowing the client to release toxic and debilitating resentment and hurt.

3. Acknowledge personal shortcomings and those of others as part of the human experience.

4. Confront corrective and destructive guilt.

5. Modify patterns of thinking, behaving, and feeling that are self-destructive and contribute to a lesser life. (Burke & Miranti, 2001)

It is impossible to help clients explore anxiety-producing issues around spirituality, death, and sexuality if we, as mental health professionals, have not begun this narrative personally, intrapsychically (Robinson-Wood & Braithwaite-Hall, 2005). When people's belief system fails to provide hope, meaning, and purpose, a crisis of faith is said to result. Professionals need to first assess their own cultural and spiritual faith and belief systems to help clients navigate this uneven terrain.

Braithwaite-Hall (2011) found in her research with 106 African American Christian women that 71% had scores indicating the presence of depressive symptoms, whereas 29% (n=36) had scores that indicated clinical levels of depression. Contrary to the researcher's hypothesis, there was a high prevalence of depression in the sample. Among some Christians, there is a belief that faith in God means not having to succumb to depression, which can be problematic for Christians who experience the very human depths of depression at some point in life.

This cultural interpretation of behavior should not be confused with psychopathology. For example, during times of loss, grief, and stress (Schoulte, 2011), it is not unusual for African Americans to speak to the dead or to believe that the mind, body, and soul are connected in that what affects one affects the other (Sutherland & Moodley, 2010).

Among many people across religious diversity, faith helps them cope with stress while making meaning in life, particularly when seeking to answer questions such as, "What will become of me?" or "What am I going to do?" Spirituality provides hope, particularly in the face of distress and uncertainty, and can give some a sense of meaning and purpose in life (Ganje-Fling & McCarthy, 1996).

One of the significant contributions of multicultural counseling and psychology has been to transition from a narrow focus on the individual to viewing the self in relation to a broader cultural context (Wiggins-Frame & Braun, 1996). Concerning racial and ethnic minorities, Wiggins-Frame and Braun (1996) said, "This shift has prompted recognition of spiritual and healing systems indigenous to racial-ethnic American cultures . . . standards for multicultural counseling competencies all include a call for practitioners to be knowledgeable about and to use religious and spiritual healers and leaders" (p. 22).

Diverse Healing Strategies

Essential as relationships are to well-being, they can be stressful. Each of us could benefit from therapy. The majority of people, however, will not seek the services of a counselor and/or psychologist. There are mental health professionals who will not seek the assistance of a therapist. Church, temple, synagogue, and community groups, in consultation with mental health professionals, can and do offer paraprofessional sensitivity training to leaders. Individuals, couples, or groups who are experiencing transition and need support can benefit greatly from these low-cost, highly effective services. Training can also review when to refer people if and when problems exceed the paraprofessional's scope of training. As people confront and recover from various emotional and psychological trauma, the support of healthy communities may be helpful.

hooks (1993) said that if places of healing do not exist to help people process their grief, they must be created because "bottled-in-grief can erupt into illness" (p. 104). In healing, balance and harmony are restored (Shore, 1995). "Home psychoanalysis" (hooks, 1993), or informal spaces where people feel free to share their stories and receive nonjudgmental support, is not inconsistent with professional help when necessary. Authentic spaces need to be created so that people may heal and move forward, catch their breaths, regain and create new rhythms, and reclaim their voices. Granted, therapists and counselors provide valuable service to people in need, but other havens can and do promote healing.

Effective Lay-Led Healing

Toward strengthening intrapersonal and interpersonal relationships, the following may be helpful:

- *Book and film circles* describe the gathering of people, not just to talk about the books and films they are reading and seeing, but to think reflectively about the connections between the written texts and the motion pictures and their lives and the lives of others. Feelings of isolation are also minimized, and people can see their life stories mirrored in others'.
- *Storytelling* allows people to think of their own personal stories or those told by another person and reflect on their meaning and importance. Alice Walker tells the story of growing up in a family where there were limited financial resources. Although it seemed like there was nothing to eat in the house, her mother, with creativity and care, would prepare the most delicious and nutritious food in beautiful blue bowls. It is empowering for clients to realize that they can author their own lives and live the stories they choose.
- *Affirmations* written on a daily basis provide ritual and rhythm to life while promoting positive thinking. Shinn (1989) offers wonderful examples: (1) my supply is endless,

inexhaustible, and immediate and comes to me under grace in perfect ways; (2) rhythm, harmony, and balance are now established in my mind, body, and affairs; and (3) infinite Spirit, give me wisdom to make the most of my opportunities. Never let me miss a trick.

- *Poetry*—others and one's own. Iyanla Vanzant's (1998) poem, "Yesterday I Cried," is a story about a woman who cried over losses and disappointment. She ends the poem on a triumphant note, embracing her wisdom, resistance, and power.

- *Kitchen table talk* is an informal gathering of friends around the kitchen table to eat and to talk about whatever is on people's minds. An adaptation of this activity can take place in therapy.

- *Burning bowls*. I used to participate in this on New Year's Eve at my church. The minister would direct each of us to write down on a piece of paper that which we did not want to take into the new year. Problems with money, relationships, health, and work were areas to consider. We would then place the pieces of paper in a bowl and burn them. People do not have to wait for the end of the year to participate in this activity of literally incinerating the pieces of paper that reflect what is no longer desired. Patients could be encouraged to think about what they do not want to take with them into the next day, or the next hour. Vanzant (1998) identified several "lessons" one could burn: (1) making decisions in fear, (2) being afraid to say no (or yes), (3) believing you should not get angry, (4) being afraid to trust yourself, (5) not asking for help when you need it, (6) not telling the truth, (7) being afraid to make a mistake, and (8) feeling afraid that you want too much.

- *Letters to oneself*. I have asked my students to write a letter to themselves at an earlier point in their lives. In this letter, they need to offer support, forgiveness, understanding, and wisdom to the younger person they are. A graduate student once wrote to herself as a high school student. She had made a decision to attend a college closer to her home to accommodate her boyfriend who had moved to another state to attend college. He expected her to stay home (as did her mother and sister) in order to receive him during holidays and breaks, thus not wanting her to attend the college of her choice several states away. As a graduate student, she came to realize that she forfeited her desires for his and had been encouraged to do so by both women and men alike.

- *Massage* is a loving way to affirm oneself, relax, and experience soothing human touch.

- *Latin and swing dancing* are high touch, and the music is soulful and stirring.

- *Yoga*: Stretching, calming, reaching, releasing, and receiving.

- *Metaphor* can be very therapeutic with clients who may have a difficult time naming and articulating intense feelings. A client who has a conflicted relationship with her mother could be asked, "What color is the relationship you have with your mother?" "What shape is it?" "Is it a tsunami, an ocean, river, pond, stream, or gutter?" "How does it sound?" and "Who are its friends?" Such questions enable the client to externalize the pain and conflict but to increase their cognitive awareness of how deep their emotion is.

- *Tell me when to stop* is an activity that I have done with clients who have a difficult time clarifying their feelings around conflicting issues. I have asked them to tell me to stop when the width of my hands arrives at a point that represents the depth of their feelings. I had one client who told me that my arms were not wide enough to describe how angry she was at her husband. It was not until that moment that she became aware of the extent of her rage at his infidelity during her pregnancy.

Other Approaches

Other approaches that are instrumental in healing include physical exercise, prayer, meditation, yoga, journaling, aromatherapy, and hydrotherapy. There are times when drug therapy or antidepressants under the careful supervision of a psychiatrist, medical doctor, or nurse practitioner are warranted and can assist people along their journeys. A potential disadvantage is that some patients are unable to cry when they desire due to the effect of antidepressants.

Creative Arts

Creative arts can be very helpful to the therapeutic event. According to Gladding (1997), "Creative arts refers to any art form, including visual representations (paintings, drawings, sculpture), poetry, drama, and music, that helps individuals become more aware of themselves or others" (p. 354). The National Coalition of Art Therapies Association is an interdisciplinary organization that supports all art therapies. Drawings, photography, cartooning, drama, cinema, games, poetry/metaphor, bibliotherapy, working with sand, writing, and music and movement all fall under the umbrella of creative therapies. It helps for counselors to understand the importance of the creative process as a part of the healing taking place. Shore (1995) said, "When clients become artists they have tools for activating their own compost and fertilizing their inner lives" (p. 93).

Wellness

To encourage healing, whether using creative therapies or more traditional ones, a holistic and multidimensional approach in which mind and body are seen as one is essential. Myers, Sweeney, and Witmer (2001) proposed a Wheel of Wellness. Five life tasks for healthy functioning are depicted and include spirituality, self-direction, work and leisure, friendship, and love. There are additional components for self-direction such as sense of humor, physical fitness, sense of worth, and cultural identity. This ecological model interacts dynamically with other life forces including religion, education, family, and community.

Implications for Mental Health Professionals

The first psychiatric hospital in the world was in Baghdad, Iraq, in 705 CE by al Razi (one of the greatest Islamic physicians). Al Razi believed that mental disorders were medical conditions, and could be treated by the use of both psychotherapy and drug treatments (Sabry & Vohra, 2013). The world has contributed to our understanding of psychological disorders and approaches to treating them.

Effective psychotherapy can be a gift in that it has helped people move toward wisdom, peace, and balance following tragedy, loss, change, and crises. For example, in a study by Dilworth-Anderson, Boswell, and Cohen (2007), 303 African American caregivers stated that their spiritual beliefs helped them when providing care to others.

Spiritual beliefs helped caregivers endure, experiencing a sense of reciprocity in giving back to those who had helped them, faith, and gratification to foster positive feelings about giving care.

Psychologists need to expand the subject of spirituality and religion to ascertain its relevance in the client's life (Boyd-Franklin, 2010). For instance, among many black Americans, from civil rights organizing to social activism in the form of feeding programs, prison ministries, and educational centers (Adkison-Bradley, Johnson, Sanders, Duncan, & Holcomb-McKoy, 2005), the black church has been a beacon of hope and light.

Therapists who are able to usher spirituality into the therapy room and critique cultural patterns about religion and gender allow clients to experience the healing benefits of spirituality within therapy. At the same time, mental health professionals can find themselves surprised that for many people, therapy is seen as antispiritual (Boyd-Franklin, 2010).

What mental health professionals-in-training are being taught about spirituality represents a gap in the research (Young et al., 2007). Toward the articulation of competencies that mental health professionals need in their work with spirituality, nine competencies identified during an initial Summit on Spirituality are provided for both counselors-in-training and seasoned practitioners:

1. The ability to explain the relationship between religion and spirituality, including similarities and differences.

2. The ability for the counselor to describe religious and spiritual beliefs and practices within a cultural context.

3. Personal exploration of one's religious and spiritual beliefs.

4. An understanding of various models of religious/spiritual development across the lifespan.

5. Sensitivity to and acceptance of a variety of religious and spiritual expressions in the client's communication.

6. An ability to identify the limits of one's understanding of a client's spiritual expression and demonstrate appropriate referral skills.

7. The ability to assess the relevance of the spiritual domains in the client's therapeutic issues.

8. Sensitivity to and respect of the spiritual themes in the therapeutic process.

9. The ability to use the client's spiritual beliefs in the pursuit of the client's therapeutic goals.

Case Study

Crises of Faith

Tim is a 36-year-old European American man. He has been married for 6 years to Geri, also 36. They met while they were in college and are both from the Northwest. They reside in Seattle,

Washington. They regularly enjoy a variety of outdoor activities throughout the year: cross-country skiing, horseback riding, and marathons. Tim is a youth pastor and feels that his work with troubled teenagers is a calling from God. Geri is the director of music at the church. Tim had noticed a mild ache in his lower abdomen and pain in his genital area. He figured it was due to a rigorous weekend of cross-country skiing, as well as simply getting older. When the pain did not go away, he stopped doing strenuous exercise for a while. Geri noticed that Tim was limping slightly and was more reluctant to have intercourse. Geri pleaded with Tim to go to the doctor, but he was resistant and embarrassed. Once the pain increased, Tim could not ignore it any longer.

Tim had a physical, and during the exam, Dr. Wilson noticed that Tim's left testicle was enlarged. Tests confirmed the doctor's suspicions. Tim was diagnosed with advanced testicular cancer. The doctor recommended the use of radioactive rods and chemotherapy in order to give Tim the highest chances for survival. This technique did not eliminate the cancer, and the removal of both testicles was recommended. After much prayer, and second and third opinions, Tim decided to proceed with the procedure, a bilateral orchiectomy.

Six months later, Tim is cancer free and is back to work as a minister. He does not have the same passion for the ministry as he once did. He feels lost when talking with the teens about dating, marriage, and sexuality. As a result of the surgery, Tim is unable to have an erection and is on testosterone replacement therapy to avoid a feminizing direction to his body: weight gain, loss of muscle tone, and an upward shift in voice pitch. Dr. Wilson encourages exercise that requires less risk of bodily injury, such as walking, gardening, and cycling. He has also recommended medical techniques that would assist Tim and Geri sexually. Tim is turned off at doing something that was meant to be natural. In the last year, Tim has struggled with depression, irritability, and overwhelming feelings of inadequacy. Because they desire children, Geri has suggested they pursue adoption. Based on tests done prior to surgery, Tim was not a good candidate for sperm banking. Tim is not interested in contemplating adoption. On a weekly basis since the surgery, Geri has heard Tim ask, "What have I done that God would treat me like this?" On the advice of his senior minister, Tim reluctantly goes for counseling. His counselor is Michael Grant, a licensed social worker who specializes in men's issues. He is Jewish.

Questions

1. How can Michael integrate Tim's spirituality into the therapy?
2. What are the implications for Michael's spirituality on his cultural competence?
3. How do mental health professionals address crises of faith within therapy?

Discussion and Integration

The Therapist, Michael

Tim's faith seems key to his identity and recovery. Michael understands that spirituality is a salient identity for Tim. At the same time, he is clear about the essential quality of being an attentive listener. In one study, cancer survivors described helpful communication as empathic listening, allowing the client to talk and weep without interjecting helpful advice or cheerleading and offering gentle encouragement. Unhelpful communication included admonishing people to overcome their illness, avoidance, and forced cheerfulness (Curtis & Juhnke, 2003). As a leader in his role as a youth pastor, Tim feels enormous guilt for not being a man of greater faith. The cathartic process of being listened to and speaking one's truth without censor or judgment helps Tim. Over time, he sees the pressure he put on himself to accept his cancer and surgery as God's will, which exacerbated his feelings of powerlessness and rage.

Michael is familiar with "prayer as an integral part of the process for relieving the pain and suffering often associated with their everyday life experience" (Adkison-Bradley et al., 2005). One of Tim's therapy goals is to restore his relationship with God. Michael demonstrates skillful questioning that conveys his understanding of some of the basic principles of Christianity. To facilitate a discussion of spirituality, Michael asks Tim the following:

1. Has religion failed you?
2. How has spirituality helped you in the past?
3. Would you perceive God as answering your prayers if you did not have to have an orchiectomy?
4. How do you make spiritual sense of your cancer-free diagnosis?
5. Do you experience God's presence during prayer and worship?
6. Does your faith affect the way you look at your suffering?
7. Does Jesus's suffering help you make sense of your suffering?
8. How does the orchiectomy affect your sense of your manhood as a complete man of God?

Michael displays multicultural competence by integrating appropriate interventions into the therapeutic event. He is comfortable with the use of Christian scripture in therapy, the therapeutic benefit of Tim sharing his prayers for a miracle of healing, and Tim's conclusion that his earnest prayers went unanswered. Michael's cultural competence and multicultural orientation will be reflected in his ability across several areas, including knowledge of cancer, the integration of cancer surgery in Tim's crises of faith, the intersections of gender and faith, and the ability to engage in candid discussions of sex.

Michael realizes that although cancer-free and post-surgery, Tim is undergoing a crisis of faith. And although such a crisis can lead to spiritual growth and personal transformation, it is disorienting and painful, nonetheless. Having visited a variety of Christian churches on several occasions, Michael understands the crucial role of the church across racial, ethnic, and class diversity.

Parker (1985) saw faith and development as integrated: "The idea that active participation and struggle is necessary is common not only to discussions of religious development but to discussion of other forms of cognitive growth and change" (p. 45). Tim and Michael have ethnic and religious differences between them. Michael's multicultural competence has equipped him with the ability to consider Tim's cultural worldview. Michael is mindful that Tim presents with spiritual issues related to a surgical procedure to treat his cancer.

As a multiculturally competent clinician, Michael considers Tim's cancer diagnosis and surgery and the cumulative impact on him, not only as a man but also as a young man who has not yet fathered children. At the same time, Michael is mindful of the press of dominant discourses on himself and Tim. One of these discourses is that manhood and virility are synonymous. Tim's religious beliefs are gendered in nature as well. Part of his depression is feeling that he has failed Geri by not giving her children. Tim is also concerned that as a result of his operation, his wife looks at him differently, with less desire and less passion. Michael interprets this projection as a reflection of how Tim feels about himself and clearly understands that Tim's sexual self-esteem has been deeply wounded by his cancer surgery, perhaps more so than the actual cancer diagnosis. Tim feels gutted, broken, and abandoned.

Tim thinks of his deceased father and has dreams of him. This information could be a source of clinical insight for Michael. Tim's own existential issues of life and death press upon him. Thus, if Tim were to find comfort in speaking with the dead, including his deceased parents, Michael needs to interpret this behavior within a cultural (religious) context.

In their first session, Michael discloses that he is Jewish (Reform; see Chapter 11, "People of Jewish Descent") and does not go to temple regularly but that his faith is important to him. Wiggins-Frame and Braun (1996) wrote of the importance of mental health professionals clarifying their values and religious beliefs in order to deal with such issues successfully in therapy. Michael tells Tim that he is comfortable discussing religion and that many of his clients are not Jewish but Christians, Protestants, and Muslims, and some are atheists.

Through the process of Michael's skillful questioning, Michael asks Tim to describe his spirituality. Through this process, Tim became aware that he had subscribed to a belief that punishment came to those who had strayed from God's will and had shown disobedience.

Michael, although competent in understanding spirituality and religion to heal and to oppress, consulted with a minister via phone in another state to add to his knowledge about appropriate interventions and to be discreet within the community. Michael communicates to Tim that surrendering to a situation is not the same as condoning it. This difference was a critical one for Tim, who saw that many of the ministers in his spiritual community took the stances that his cancer was God's will, that his survival was a manifestation of God's faithfulness, and that Tim needed to approach God the Father with a grateful heart.

Tim's crisis of faith, although understandable, can have adverse implications for his well-being and quality of life. According to research by Hamilton, Powe, Pollard, Lee, and Felton (2007), many cancer survivors believe that God is with them, healing and protecting them, and is ultimately in control of their lives. Spirituality can play a role in moderating health and well-being (Miller & Thoresen, 2003); however, the converse seems true. In their review of nine hypotheses about the link between religion or spirituality and mortality, morbidity, disability, or recovery from illness, Powell, Shahabi, and Thoresen (2003) concluded, "Religious people who become upset by the belief that God has abandoned them or who become dependent on their faith, rather than their medical treatment for recovery, may inadvertently subvert the success of their recovery" (p. 50).

To join with his client, Michael acknowledges that Tim's disappointment in and doubts about God's provision and care have been expressed through the ages by the Old Testament prophets, Jesus himself, and other people of faith across religions.

Unpacking religious teachings is hard and daunting work. Messages such as "don't question God" or "just pray about it and the problem will take care of itself" do not encourage people to get underneath the emotions that contribute to their crises of faith and extreme disappointment in God. Tim feels deprived of God's grace, which, if present, would have meant healing of his cancer. Michael asks Tim to consider if people can pray for healing, die, and yet still be whole, healed, and benefactors of God's grace?

In time, after rapport and trust have developed and Michael has been instrumental in helping to alleviate Tim's depressive symptoms, he might introduce gender through a question such as, "What is the effect of the surgery on your sense of God's oversight and protection? Do you think God sees his role as healer and provider in the same way that you do?"

Michael asked Tim if he feels forsaken by God? Tim agrees and wonders what he did to be treated in this way. Michael asked Tim, "What did Jesus do to be nailed to the cross?" Michael validates the meaning of spirituality in Tim's life and realizes that it is critical to the lifting of Tim's clinical depression as he slowly makes meaning of his situation (Nichols & Hunt, 2011).

Michael had a clinical hunch that Tim held fast to some religious beliefs that were a source of oppression and did not contribute to his experiencing God's protection in his life (Robinson & Watt, 2001). Tim was characterized by this belief system. From his vantage point, he was deliberate about cultivating a physically active lifestyle and maintaining a spiritual connection with God. Tim, prior to the cancer diagnosis, was a peaceful man. Because he saw himself as faithful to God's call on his life to pursue a divinity degree, commit his life to the ministry, and marry Geri, his wife, he felt lost in his ability to make sense out of the tragedy that had befallen him.

Rather than interpret Tim's difficulty with cognitive restructuring as pathological, Michael understood that Tim's position was largely influenced by his religious beliefs and his cancer diagnosis. Michael's understanding of Christianity, along with his awareness of the overlap between Judaism and Christianity, aided him in disentangling spiritual themes from pathology in Tim's life (Schultz-Ross & Gutheil, 1997). Michael also can hear, feel, and see Tim's clinical depression—his sorrow, disappointment, abandonment, powerlessness—his literal castration.

Michael helps Tim with boundary setting with respect to Geri and her role as caretaker. Again, Michael is familiar with relevant literature. In a study by Ussher and Perz (2010), both men and women who were caregivers (carers) of loved ones with cancer tended to self-silence themselves. Women saw self-silencing as a requisite for coping, as they connected their caregiving with the natural place of being a woman. Women caregivers also had high levels of anxiety and depression. Thus, it may be critical that Geri seek therapy for herself as a form of self-care as she provides care to her husband.

One of the helpful interventions that Michael suggested to Tim was bibliotherapy—reading books, particularly autobiographies of people who have survived medical challenges in life, might reduce his feelings of aloneness. Another possible intervention for Tim was to consider the relevance of a support group comprised of men who had survived prostate and testicular cancers. Because Tim is a private man, he is not open to being part of a support group. Michael introduces this topic at a future time

Another example of Michael's cultural competence is his knowledge of psych-oncology, which is a multidisciplinary field concerned with the psychological and social aspects of cancer (Nicholas, 2013). The psychosocial focus emphasizes caregiving, community response, and the families' adjustment to cancer, mental health issues, such as depression and anxiety, and cancer-related symptoms such as nausea, hair loss, fatigue, and insomnia. Background information on the normal cell cycle and gene mutation, types of cancer, cancer staging and what this means for treatment (surgery, radiation, chemotherapy, bone marrow, stem cell transport), prevalence, survivorship data, and mitosis.

Cultural Competence in Integrating Spirituality and Psychotherapy

Michael demonstrates cultural competence through his ability to integrate spirituality and psychotherapy through Michael's knowledge of the following:

1. Tim's beliefs related to religion and spirituality.

2. The various treatments (e.g., hands on prayer, fasting, baptism, holy water, oil) in the Christian tradition.

3. The context in which major counseling and psychological theories have arisen and how these theories may conflict with Tim's cultural values (e.g., Christian acceptance of God's will and the U.S. value of positivism and making logical links between process and outcome).

4. Tim's discussions with his deceased father are not psychopathological.

5. Being a man of God meant for Tim that: a) God would heal his cancer without the need for his surgery, b) he was especially chosen by God to lead others through service, and c) that Tim's surgery was not a reflection of an answered prayer from a loving and powerful God.

6. Tim feels he has failed in his calling as a man and as a minister given his inability to sire children for his wife and to uphold his calling to serve troubled youth.

7. Resources within the community that could assist Tim's recovery.

8. Policies and beliefs that are a source of oppression and psychological hardship for Tim (e.g., some of Tim's minister colleagues do not agree with Tim seeing a therapist, especially one who is Jewish).

9. The right time to consult with spiritual leaders.

10. The necessary training to engage in and interpret assessment.

11. The therapeutic process, goals, expectations, the patient's mental health bill of rights, and his theoretical approach to therapy.

12. His prejudices and biases around spirituality and religion, both positive and negative.

13. Familiarity with the various literature regarding spiritual experiences.

14. Tim's spiritual beliefs in the pursuit of Tim's therapeutic goals (Cashwell & Young, 2004; West, 2000).

Summary

This chapter examined trends in religious affiliation that reflect recent change and change according to age. A distinction between religion and spirituality was provided by way of definition to avoid treating these terms as synonyms or bifurcations. Multicultural competencies for mental health professionals when seeking to integrate spirituality with other domains of identity were highlighted, as were spiritual approaches to health and recovery. A European American Christian man's crises of faith following testicular cancer diagnosis, surgery, and the aftereffects were presented in a case study. His therapist was also a male and Jewish. The clinician's cultural competence is demonstrated through a knowledge of self, Christianity, cancer, depression, and the role of gender.

19

Converging Social Justice in Diversity Practice ❖

TOPICS COVERED IN THIS CHAPTER

- **Social Justice and Empowerment**
- **Power and Powerlessness**
- **Social Justice and the Therapeutic Process**
- **Feminist Therapy and Social Justice**
- **Patient Navigation: Social Justice Example**
- **Implications for Mental Health Professionals**
- **Case Study**
- **Summary**

Several professional organizations across multiple disciplines have implicated racism, sexism, and other forms of oppression as deleterious to health and well-being. An expansion of mental health professionals' roles includes being active change agents against structural inequalities that foster inequity across race, gender, class, and other sources of identity. Not only in patients' lives but also in our own do the consequences of social inequalities manifest. Social justice is oriented to an understanding of clients' situations as well as to the transformation of the very conditions that press down on people's lives (Vera & Speight, 2003). This transformative work, and to the extent that it is done, describes a social justice framework.

Social Justice and Empowerment

At its core, social justice is concerned with a just and equitable distribution of resources, advocacy, and empowerment as well as a scrutiny of the processes that lead to inequality (Vera & Speight, 2003). Fairness extends to all people, across race, sexuality, physical makeup, religion, and ability and commits to change in systems, policies, and practices that perpetuate inequality (Fouad, Gerstein, & Toporek, 2006). Thus, social justice is concerned with restructuring, outreach, education, and empowerment (Ivey & Collins, 2003). In addition, social justice does the following:

1. Encourages full participation in society.

2. Facilitates awareness of structural forces that contribute to disease.

3. Advocates for people to grow in their awareness of social responsibility.

4. Unifies people with others who are similarly situated and marginalized.

Warren and Constantine (2007) capture social justice as investment and involvement in interpersonal relationships wherein there is unification with "oppressed, marginalized, and disenfranchised groups in various social justice struggles" (p. 232). Warren and Constantine (2007) also discuss the importance of creating environments where people feel physical and psychological safety, resistance to authority, and systemic change. Millions of low-income people (disproportionately people of color) reside in physically and psychologically unsafe areas. Peaceful resistance among some people (e.g., visible people of color) may not be interpreted as peaceful among more powerful others (e.g., the police). Thus, strategies of resistance must be considered with knowledge of this difference otherwise loss of freedom and life can occur.

According to Comstock et al. (2008), relational cultural theory is focused on respecting the quality of relationships that marginalized groups have across the life span that are inextricably linked to race, gender, and social identities. They contend that psychotherapy that does not emanate from a multicultural, social justice paradigm is vulnerable to reproducing the systems of subjugation, shame, and oppression that describe the daily lives of many stigmatized groups. Cultural competence among mental health professionals is connected to knowledge of the ways in which cultural oppression and the myriad forms of social inequity contribute to humiliation and isolation among people who are from devalued groups. (See Storytelling: United Work.)

❖ **STORYTELLING: UNITED WORK**

In my research with highly educated black women and their experiences with microaggressions, all 17 women, in their 20s to 50s, stated that microaggressions had occurred in their lives and were chronic. The three researchers, too, ethnically diverse and highly educated black women, had our own experiences with microaggressions. Some of the

---

❖ **STORYTELLING: UNITED WORK**

study participants were in counseling programs where they experienced microaggressions from other students and faculty. I do not know of any faculty or underrepresented graduate student of color who does not contend with regular microaggressions, which are a source of psychological and physical stress. In others words, all of the faculty and students that I know who are from underrepresented groups contend with regular microaggressions. Do microaggressions reflect social injustice? I believe they do, yet why do they exist? More specifically, what can mental health professions do toward changing and restructuring academic and work environments that produce and perpetuate microaggressing behaviors? Dr. Chester Pierce wrote about microaggressions during the 1980s, when I was a graduate student at Harvard. I write about them 30 years later. Are things

better? In 1982, I arrived in Cambridge for graduate school without a cell phone or laptop (such technology was not accessible to me, if readily available). There were .25 cent public phones and computer labs. More than three decades later, technology is a different world regarding how we write our manuscripts and communicate with others in the states and abroad. With all of our guidelines, cultural competencies, ethical codes (which were debased by APA's involvement with torture as noted in the Hoffman Report), benchmarks, and accreditation commissions, where will counselors, psychologists, and social workers stand with social justice change in 30 years? What kind of change will we see, feel, and recognize with racialized microaggressions, particularly those that occur within our professional organizations, academic departments, and work environments?

Toporek and Williams (2006) conceptualized differences among advocacy, social action, and social justice. In their view, advocacy is a variety of roles that the counseling professional adopts in the interest of clients and includes empowerment, advocacy, and social action. Social action is described as action taken by the counselor external to the client to "confront or act on behalf of client groups" (p. 19). Empowerment is viewed as one goal of counseling and psychotherapy and is often in the service of a social justice paradigm.

Pinderhughes (1995) defined empowerment as "achieving reasonable control over one's destiny, learning to cope constructively with debilitating forces in society, and acquiring the competence to initiate change at the individual and systems level" (p. 136). For McWhirter (1991), empowerment is a process wherein people or groups of people who lack power become cognizant of the power dynamics that operate in their lives (e.g., prejudice, discrimination) and as a result are able to acquire reasonable control in their lives without encroaching on others' rights. (See Storytelling: Change and Costs.)

Empowerment involves educating vulnerable people and communities about resources, information, programs, and behaviors that can improve the overall quality of their lives (Helms, 2003). (See Storytelling: Unable to Accommodate That Request.)

Empowerment is a recognition of power disparities and their creation of imbalance, privileging those with the most resources while inferring disadvantage on those who do not have many. Patients who struggle with discrimination, of any kind, need to know that they have a competent clinician who has sociopolitical awareness, which encompasses ethics, social justice, and cultural competence.

❖ STORYTELLING: CHANGE AND COSTS

A dear friend of mine who lives abroad was home over the summer. She said, "There have been so many civil rights changes in America." What she was referring to included the following:

1. Two females, West Point Academy graduates, have completed the elite Army Rangers training

2. The Confederate flag was removed from South Carolina state grounds

3. Same-sex marriage is legal in all 50 states

What she was not referring to included the following:

1. A recent mini documentary by Gandbhir and Foster (2015) where black and white parents' admonitions to their black sons about racial profiling, the inevitability of encounters with police, and strategies for staying alive were chronicled. Black parents spoke of the requirement to have such daunting discussions with their sons, whereas other groups were not. Another documentary referring to black daughters is needed given their negative encounters with police as well.

2. That little has improved in this country's gun laws, even after 26 souls were lost in December 2012 in Sandy Hook School, Newtown, Connecticut.

3. The increasing gap between the wealthiest and the less wealthy.

4. The patriarchal society that produces and perpetuates the objectification of people, across gender, race, nationality, age, and sexuality in the human sex trafficking.

5. The misguided notion that the presence of people of color indicates that power and privilege have been unpacked and discussed.

6. The fact that sexual assault on college campuses is an epidemic.

Failure to recognize patriarchy and classism may contribute to missed opportunities to make organizational changes that encourage equal participation (Hoffman et al., 2005). Mental health professionals are encouraged to identify and have the ability to discuss privileges that they receive in society due to race, class, gender, ability, religion, skin color, accent, and sexuality (Arredondo et al., 1996). This skill supports educating the woman in the following storytelling about resisting people and systems that exploit her and learning to engage in decision making to keep herself and her child safe and secure. In doing so, a social justice paradigm is activated. (See Self-Check Exercise 19.1: Social Justice in Action.)

Self-Check Exercise 19.1

Social Justice in Action

The number of homeless families has increased and now represents 41% of persons who are homeless. Denials for bed requests have also increased (National Coalition for the Homeless, 2014). Victim blaming increases as the problem of homelessness is located intraindividually as opposed to an examination of structural issues, such as the high costs of housing, a minimum wage that encourages poverty, the pathologizing of women who stay in violent domestic situations due to limited choices, patriarchal socialization that encourages women's dependence on men, and the long-term effects of psychological trauma. As you read, there are children in each of our respective towns and cities who are sleeping in cars, on a relative's couch, or in some other makeshift arrangement.

An example of social justice is educating a homeless woman with clinical depression about the resources and programs available to help her and her unborn child, who she wants desperately to keep and raise. Although adoption is an option—sometimes a good one—it is not always the best one due in part to the problematic images of the homeless and poor: "The U.S. has become one of the most dangerous democracies in which poor women and their children can live" (Cosgrove, 2006, p. 201). With a just distribution of resources, fiscal and human, this woman may be able to revamp her life and take care of her child. Social justice is oriented to examining why this woman and others like her are not perceived to be entitled to and not worthy of more.

Questions that arise from this case include the following: How might a mental health professional who is multiculturally competent, and ethnically responsible, with a social justice orientation help mothers avoid homelessness when shelters are full? What is our social justice responsibility as mental health professionals for patient care outside of the office hours? Do current ethical guidelines regarding dual relationships impact the range and scope of advocacy for those in the most need?

Ethical practice (competence, doing no harm, informed consent, professional boundaries) is critical to social justice work. Three recurring constructs appear to be most salient: respect, responsibility, and social action (Fouad et al., 2006). A position of respect is inclusive of deference to the community, abiding by the community's strengths, and a stance of humility. Responsibility speaks to duty to serve, being conscientious regarding the nature of one's service, and not taking advantage of the vulnerability that marginalized communities face. Social action encourages pro bono work and to identify and eradicate practices that are unjust and corrupt (Fouad et al., 2006).

Both short- and long-term advocacy and social action considerations for mental health professionals are mentioned below:

1. Maintain and develop relationships with community agencies that provide care for people in need. Even licensed providers who have a cash only policy and do not accept insurance, which speaks to the wealth of patients and perhaps of the provider, need to be aware of community services.

2. Use the Internet to identify emergency funds available through churches, the Red Cross, the YMCA, and similar community agencies for a hotel stay.

3. Contact shelters in adjoining towns and see if transportation can be made to transport a family to a safe place.

4. Contact the local newspaper to write a story about this issue in order to educate the public.

5. Contact social services, which are often connected to food banks and other resources to provide emergency food and clothing.

6. Contact congressional representatives about the need for policy changes that can lead to more shelters for families. Write letters and encourage others to do so.

7. Collaborate with schools to advocate for meals, coats, and after school care. Tutoring, counseling, and other services may be available to help children who are contending with stressful life situations.

8. Encourage the woman to trust that situations change and things do get better.

9. When basic necessities are met, such as shelter and food, encourage the woman to write her narrative and give voice to her experience. This can be empowering.

10. Do not resist the expression of the woman's confusion, uncertainty, fear, and anger.

11. Encourage and help identify a support group to reduce feelings of isolation.

12. Get support while supporting. Advocacy work is rewarding but also fatiguing as the slow wheels of bureaucracy turn and systems are exposed.

13. Ask patients what they desire.

14. Do not stereotype, project, or distance (Pinderhughes, 1995).

15. Investigate the availability of a patient navigator to help the woman manage and travel to doctor's appointments.

16. Investigate 12-Step programs, family therapy, and other services and referrals to deal with a multiplicity of challenges that arise when people contend with poverty and the trauma of not having a safe place to sleep at night.

17. Receive consultation and in some cases supervision from other professionals about the best course of action.

18. Explore existing coping skills and behaviors (e.g., panhandling for drugs) and their impact on life quality (e.g., exposure to violence).

19. Give the woman examples of where bias is imbedded in institutions and society.

20. Share how others have coped and survived when confronting a similar situation.

❖ **STORYTELLING: UNABLE TO ACCOMMODATE THAT REQUEST**

There are multiple systems that encourage women's resignation and capitulation. Social justice recognizes that assertive, strong women are inconsistent with society's notions of appropriate gendered behavior. Women who have a disability, are nonwhite, large bodied, and speak with a non-European accent pay a price when they push against (e.g., resist) gendered behaviors. Social justice should not require women, across sources of difference, to acquiesce their power in the name of hegemony or white privilege. I had a patient many years ago who had tremendous work stress. She felt powerless in the presence of not only her supervisors but also colleagues, who often asked her to take on their share of the work given her reputation of being nice and efficient. What most people did not know about her was that she felt tremendous resentment when people, in her view, shirked their responsibilities and loaded them onto her. She did not know how to express her feelings and desires without erupting in inappropriate anger or tears. During a session role-play, I asked her to represent one of her colleagues for whom she had a great deal of anger. True to this role, she sounded and looked different from herself as she provided a list of demands. I looked at her and said, "I am unable to accommodate that request." I offered no explanation, no capitulation, and no apologies. She tried this technique at work and was amazed at how effective it was. A boundary had been established. She used this same statement (which was about getting underneath her learned desire to please people and gain their approval) with her family of origin. Why is this story about an individual woman in this chapter on social justice? The woman in this story represents countless women who experience institutional gender discrimination. As a marginalized individual, she experienced occupational disparities, overrepresentation in low paying jobs, and underrepresentation in positions of political and economic power (Israel, 2006).

To Dulany (1990), empowerment "is another term for finding one's own voice. In order to speak, we must know what we want to say; in order to be heard, we must dare to speak" (p. 133). A social justice framework asks, "Whose voices are heard first and/or above the others and why?" Vera and Speight (2003) argue that although a multiculturally competent counselor is trained to look for discrimination and develop sensitivity to oppression, counseling professionals are not directed to advocate for the elimination of oppression or exploitation. *Mandatory ethics*, or action taken to avoid breaking the rules, differs from advocacy. *Aspirational ethics*, conversely, is taking action at the highest possible level or eliminating oppression, which translates into greater emphasis on prevention, not remediation, and less of a focus on the individual and more on sociohistorical contexts. A communitarian model of justice based on collective decision making and community empowerment is advocated.

Helms (2003) contends that the multicultural competencies and its predecessors offer a framework for doing social justice within the existing structure of counseling and psychology. He acknowledges that the reality of social service delivery may not be supportive of a communitarian model of justice that Vera and Speight (2003) advocate.

Power and Powerlessness

Powerlessness is operationalized as the "inability to direct the course of one's life due to societal conditions and power dynamics, lack of skills, or lack of faith that one can change one's life" (McWhirter, 1991, p. 224). It results in persons feeling unable to have any meaningful impact on their lives. Feelings associated with this disempowered state were identified by Pinderhughes (1989) as less comfort and pleasure, less gratification, more pain, feelings of inferiority and insecurity, and a strong tendency for depression.

A disproportionate share of persons in poverty are people of color. Most jobs are stratified by race, ethnicity, and gender, with women of color at the bottom of the occupational hierarchy and white males at the top. Structural and institutional inequities such as racism, higher rates of unemployment, and incarceration among men of color have profound implications on the economic stability and well-being for the women and children in these men's lives. Race-based inequalities in access to (and quality of) health care, along with higher rates of poverty and lack of insurance coverage, contribute to marginalization and vulnerability to illness.

Racism and other sources of discrimination are bad for psychological health. An accumulation of discrimination adversely impacts mental health and is related to negative physiological reactions (Gibbons et al., 2014), lower feelings of belonging (Clark, Mercer, Zeigler-Hill, & Dufrene, 2012), substance use, breast cancer, obesity (Pascoe & Richman, 2009), and hypertension (Williams, Neighbors, & Jackson, 2003). Even perceived discrimination can play an adverse role in increasing internalizing and externalizing behaviors among members of stigmatized groups (Robinson-Wood, et al., 2015).

In the midst of inequality, low-wage-earning people, unemployed people, immigrants, people of color, and disabled people have relied on kinship networks, faith in unseen forces, and cultural and ethnic practices to live their lives with dignity and power (Robinson, 1999b). Acknowledgment of clients' cultural practices and the ability for the counseling professional to change beliefs and think differently and flexibly are critical to empowerment and advocacy skills (Pinderhughes, 1995).

Strategies of coping and resistance to oppression do not suggest that people are not vulnerable or that the structural inequalities are not crushing; indeed they are. Empowerment and social justice seek to disrupt the forces that habituate in people's lives as a function of class and race oppression. When people are asked what makes them feel powerful, they will respond with, for example, being listened to, being in a loving relationship, having money in the bank, getting a good education, and having physical health. These are individually focused forces, hallmarks of an individualistic society that places the self at the center of analysis. A steady gaze at systemic and historical issues and their impact on the personal is part of a social justice orientation.

More power is characterized by less tendency to depression, more pleasure, less pain, and feelings of superiority (Pinderhughes, 1989). Ours is still a society in which white people, the able-bodied, heterosexuals, the wealthy, Christians, and males are the referent point for normalcy. Power is attributed to these identities and reflects a system of white supremacy. There are implications here for curricula and practica restructuring in order to disrupt this orientation. Counseling students in training and professionals need to assess their belief systems. This work cannot be done in a superficial or cursory manner, but in a way that reflects interrogation of socialization processes from parents, religious leaders, and the educational system. Moreover, this work will facilitate an understanding of the experiences of oneself and others within a particular group (Pope-Davis, Liu, Toporek, & Brittan-Powell, 2001).

Gender and race identities do not neatly line up with psychological empowerment or powerlessness (Robinson, 1999a). Power and powerlessness are not mutually exclusive categories in people's lives. Each gender and race has unique feelings of power and powerlessness (Swanson, 1993). People with marginalized identities need not internalize feelings of less power, yet many counseling graduate students confuse marginalization with internalization. Exposure to multicultural topics in the format they are traditionally delivered may not increase competence about these and other dynamics (Pope-Davis et al., 2001).

Social Justice and the Therapeutic Process

Some insurance co-pays are over $40 for each behavioral health weekly visit. When people are trying to pay rent or their mortgages, buy heating fuel, and food, the behavioral health co-pay may not rise to the top as a priority. Sliding-scale fees can make therapy more accessible to many clients. As discussed earlier, social justice paradigm supports pro bono or reduced fee services as necessary and allowable given professionals' need and right to be appropriately remunerated.

Structural elements to the therapeutic relationship exist (Mencher, 1997), and even though the therapist exercises authority and the client moves into a place of vulnerability, empowerment and social justice are central to the process (Jordan, 1997b). Structural elements that define the therapeutic relationship include the following:

1. The formal beginning and ending.

2. The client or insurance company pays, and the therapist is paid.

3. The client asks for help with some clinical distress, and the therapist provides help based on his or her training and expertise.

4. The client shares more information about his or her life than the counselor shares about his or her life.

5. The therapist agrees to keep the information confidential, whereas the client can share this information with whomever he or she pleases.

6. The relationship is dedicated to the growth of the client.

7. Counselors operate within these structures and, in an effort to empower clients, need to respect their clients and the values that clients bring to counseling.

Helping professionals who operate from clients' strengths and believe in clients' abilities to positively affect the quality of their own lives are in a better position to facilitate client empowerment (McWhirter, 1991; Pinderhughes, 1989). Mental health professionals who perceive clients to be victims because of the oppressiveness of the social context and that they and their clients have little hope of transforming existing power dynamics are not instrumental in creating transforming conditions.

Counselors need to be careful about mystifying the counseling event, particularly if it accentuates the power differential between client and counselor. Balancing the power differential between client and counselor requires empathy, a necessary tool. It represents one of the most important themes in therapy or counseling (Pinderhughes, 1989). Therapists are not superior, yet clients experience shame from a therapist's attitude that reinforces a power differential or the feeling that the therapist knows better than the client does about their life.

Power can be abused by fostering client dependence; it can also be used constructively to facilitate growth and insight. *Productive and constructive power* is at the center of a counseling relationship when a counselor creates a holding environment for a client to make passage through a difficult period. *Destructive power* occurs when one has access to resources and dominates another and imposes one's will through threats or the withholding of certain desired rewards despite implicit or explicit opposition from the less powerful.

Accepting the reality of one's powerless position can bring a sense of power (Pinderhughes, 1989). Empowering the client in therapy to reframe or resist a situation while engaged in social action outside of the therapeutic event to advocate for living wages or health care legislation for children and other issues is reflective of social justice.

As an essential component of social justice, empathy supports respectful interactions between the client and therapist. Where appropriate, the counselor advocates on behalf of the client by, for example, making out-of-office interventions. Empowerment, advocacy, and out-reach differ substantially from rescuing.

Outreach refers to large-scale, direct services that are designed to address existing or even anticipated obstacles to psychological growth and occurs within the context of a community (Vera, Daly, Gonzales, Morgan, & Thakral, 2006). Outreach requires that professionals leave their work settings and venture into rural and/or urban communities with people who may be very different with respect to class, language dominance, race, and employment status. The benefit of outreach is that much needed resources are made available to communities through partnerships with a number of agencies, including churches, schools, and community centers.

McWhirter (1991) reminded us that taking responsibility for doing what another person is capable of doing for the self is disempowering. There are some acts that require the presence of another, and although this is not rescuing, it is being with another. This process of "being with" describes mutuality in counseling and represents an intimate space inhabited by two people governed by a professional context.

Feminist Therapy and Social Justice

Feminist therapy differs philosophically from traditional psychotherapy in that it seeks to understand the experiences of women within their social contexts while challenging systematic gender inequality. It is reflective of a social justice orientation in its observation and open critique of injustice and structural inequalities. More contemporary forms of psychotherapy have challenged the premises of Freudian psychology, such as Adler and Rogers (see Corey, 1991). These theorists, however, have often been silent about the social-political contexts in which men and women exist—contexts constructed by gender and race relations, which for many people are oppressive and marginalizing. Karen Horney, for example, was a trailblazer in feminine psychology, and her work, to this day, continues to offer the profession a refreshing look at the development of neurosis and its etiology in one's family of origin.

Devoe (1990) stated that "feminist therapy emphasizes the need for social change by improving the lives of women rather than by helping them adjust to traditional roles in society" (p. 33). Feminist therapy critiques how a male-dominated and patriarchal society deems women as other, inferior, and invisible. Because psychotherapy is largely influenced by dominant cultural values, the mental health system has participated in the oppression of women and people of color by assessing women from a male and white model. One strength of feminist therapy is that it acknowledges the patriarchal and unjust society in which women and men live and thus seeks to educate people while honoring women's anger and men's sadness (Devoe, 1990). A social justice agenda allows us to see that men have been adversely affected under the system of patriarchy and sexism as well (Robinson, 1999a).

Western psychotherapy is influenced by a psychoanalytical framework, European philosophers, and a hierarchical structure based on hegemonic power. More specifically, the therapist, historically most likely a male, is seen as the expert, and the client, traditionally a woman, is recognized as dependent. In therapy and psychiatry, women have been more likely to receive a diagnosis of mental disorder, are more often prescribed psychotropic medication, and take more prescription and over-the-counter drugs than men (Crose, Nicholas, Gobble, & Frank, 1992).

Ethnic minority clients are also more likely to receive inaccurate diagnoses, be assigned to junior professionals, and receive low-cost, less preferred treatment consisting of minimal contact, medication, or custodial care rather than individual psychotherapy (Ridley, 1989, p. 55). Feminist therapy questions this construction of power and injustice. It proposes instead a more collaborative, egalitarian relationship between client and counselor if therapy is to be therapeutic and ultimately empowering.

Devoe (1990) spoke about an egalitarian relationship and the importance of an emotional link between the client and counselor prior to effective therapeutic work occurring. "The counselor must view the client as an equal both in and out of the counseling relationship . . . [T]he personal power between the client and counselor should be equal whenever possible" (p. 35). It means that when our clients ask us about who we are, it is important not to hide behind a mask of professionalism and see therapy as going in only one direction. Certainly some disclosures are inappropriate, but whether we have kids, places of birth, or vacation destinations might describe joining with clients, not excessive and inappropriate disclosure. Nonetheless, some therapists may not approve of this level of disclosure. Personal differences apply and need to be respected.

Social justice encourages an interrogation of power dynamics in therapy. If the therapist's underlying premise is that the patient intuitively knows what is in his or her best interest, then the therapist accepts a different power position. Professional training and years of relevant experience provide insight into mental health issues, but this learned and experiential knowledge does not replace the woman's subjective and constructed knowledge even if she has yet to tap into it. Finally, a feminist perspective allows the therapeutic process to unfold at the pace that is most comfortable for the client.

A substantial number of women and men may not understand the value of psychotherapy in general and feminist or womanist therapy in particular. We may have to explain to some patients why or how meeting with a clinician on a weekly basis and talking about their feelings is associated with the patient's symptom reduction. Participation in movements for social justice can increase gender consciousness, yet some women of color privilege uniting with men of color toward racial equality over increasing gender consciousness with white women (Chow, 1991). From a dialectical perspective, increasing both racial and gender consciousness is crucial because women of color are always, at all times, both female and racial and ethnic beings. Comas-Diaz and Greene (1994) spoke about the intersections of these identities: "Due to the pervasive effects of racism and the concomitant need for people of color to bond together, women of color experience conflicting loyalties in which racial solidarity often transcends gender and sexual orientation solidarity" (pp. 4–5).

Race intersects and thus shapes gender as well (Tatum, 1997). Privilege and oppression conjointly intensify and/or counter each other, and, along with structural effects of sexism, colonialism, and capitalism, leave some clients not only vulnerable but physically and mentally exhausted (Kliman, 2005). Becoming aware of gender issues may be difficult for many women of color who contend with race, class, as well as gender discrimination. It is common for women to feel overwhelmed at the dynamics of multiple layers of oppression. Layers of oppression should not be confused with race and gender. Racism is different from race (from being black), and sexism is different from gender (from being a woman).

Respecting the patient and their personal narrative within a culturally competent and holding environment is social justice work. (Pope-Davis et al., 2001). In an effort to honor the client's cultural, gender, religious, and political backgrounds and the cumulative impact on the therapeutic process, each client must be viewed from her worldview (Arredondo, Psalti, & Cella, 1993). Social justice orientation considers the external and internal factors that affect behavior, prior to and within therapy. Toward this end, Pope-Davis et al. (2001) suggest that more qualitative research needs to be conducted to move away from self-reports, focus on context, and lessen researcher bias. Warren and Constantine (2007) recognize the pressure of getting tenure at some institutions and encourage participatory action research as an example of social justice research efforts. Within participatory action research, participants are empowered to voice their concerns about structural inequalities and its personal impact.

Patient Navigation: Social Justice Example

In 1989, Patient Navigation began as a result of the work of physician Harold Freeman. As he traveled through America, he listened to the stories of poor people diagnosed with cancer. A year later in 1990, the first American Cancer Society Patient Navigation program was initiated in Harlem at the Harlem Hospital Center in New York City. Harlem is a predominantly black and brown community, and many residents live in poverty and have low levels of education. The purpose of this program was to reduce the barriers that poor people encountered while seeking health care. What he found was published in the American Cancer Society's *Report to the Nation on Cancer in the Poor*. Key findings were as follows:

1. Low income people meet significant barriers when they attempt to seek diagnosis and treatment of cancer.

2. Low income people and their families make sacrifices to obtain cancer care and often do not seek care because of the barriers faced.

3. Low income people experience more pain, suffering, and death because of late diagnosis and treatment at an incurable stage of the disease.

4. Fatalism about cancer is prevalent among the poor and prevents them from seeking care.

Patient Navigation is meant to empower people and can be used by counseling professionals when working with overwhelmed and physically ill clients who are negotiating health systems for cancer care and chronic conditions. Counseling professionals with a social justice orientation can work with clients overwhelmed by their interactions with hospitals and imposing health care systems. Patient navigators are trained to help patients move through the health care system by educating patients, ensuring that the patient goes through with the treatment process, and assisting the patient in negotiating obstacles to care, such as consulting with other providers (e.g., nutritionists) or finding additional assistance, such as someone to help with house-cleaning, grocery, shopping, and child care. Obstacles to care include financial and insurance difficulties, emotional concerns, and other barriers mentioned earlier such as transportation problems. Assisting patients with getting their X-rays, test results, and other records; making referrals to community services such as welfare, housing, home care, and transportation; helping the patient deal with health challenges; securing second opinions; and finding hospice care if necessary are all within the scope of navigators' duties (Thomas, 2006).

Implications for Mental Health Professionals

The Guidelines on Multicultural Education, Training, Research, Practice, and Organizational Change for Psychologists (APA, 2003), the *Handbook for Social Justice in Counseling Psychology*, and the comprehensive competencies identified in 1996 by Arredondo et al. articulate social justice within an ecological context. They encourage mental health professionals to engage in culturally competent practice with people across race, ethnic, and class groups. Knowledge of legal issues that affect clients' lives, biases in assessment and diagnostic instruments, and referral sources that can assist clients is deemed critical. Although there has been greater explication of competencies and guidelines in counseling and psychology, these resources, along with others, represent an important social justice intervention (Ivey & Collins, 2003).

Action represents a different level of resistance to oppression and is a core component of social justice. Action includes exercising institutional intervention skills on behalf of a client, recognizing situations in clients' lives and addressing the incident or perpetrator, filing an informal complaint, filing a formal complaint, and so forth, as well as working at an organizational level to address change whereby policies that discriminate and create barriers are eliminated (Arredondo et al., 1996).

Many mental health professionals are inadequately prepared to work with clients who present with concerns, such as worrying about physical and environmental safety levels and confronting sociopolitical barriers to health care and quality housing (Washington, 1987). People of color as well as low-wage-earning white people have been treated poorly by the mental health establishment, which is often insensitive to sociopolitical realities that affect mental and social functioning. In some circumstances, having a one-on-one client–counselor relationship is not possible or even desirable due to lack of access, unavailability of clinicians for a given area, or the client's sense of mistrust about the benefits and aims of therapy. For this reason, alternative healing strategies discussed in Chapter 18 on spirituality may be helpful (see Case Study: The Socially Just and Authentic Counselor).

Moreover, policy changes, (e.g., same-sex marriage), albeit groundbreaking and long fought, do not erase subtle discrimination. Weber (2015) found that among 18 racially diverse sexual minorities, the taxonomy of racial microaggressions identified by Sue et al. (2007) as well as the sexual orientation and transgender microaggressions developed by Nadal, Rivera and Corpus (2010) contributed to the identification of seven themes: (1) Discomfort with/disapproval of LGBT (lesbian, gay, bisexual, transgender) experience, (2) assumption of universal experience, (3) traditional gender role stereotyping, (4) exoticization, (5) ascription of intelligence, (6) assumption of criminality, and (7) denial of personal privacy.

Sherry Watt (2015), a leading voice in higher education and student personnel, has created a theory called authentic, action-oriented framing for environmental shifts

(AAFES) method. The AAFES method describes the process qualities that she regards as essential to transformational multicultural initiatives, which are closely aligned with a social justice framework. There are three core qualities: (1) *authenticity*, which focuses on how you engage with difference rather than concentration on dissecting the difference; (2) being *action-oriented*, which emphasizes contemplative balance between dialogue and taking action for social change; (3) and *framing for environmental shifts*, which appeals to shifting the environment toward inclusion of *Difference* rather than a focusing on ways the marginalized members of a community can survive or cope within dehumanizing systems structurally designed to remain in place. The genius of her model is its oppositional gaze to the status quo while believing in and striving for a paradigmatic shift.

Case Study

The Socially Just and Authentic Counselor

Robert is a 39-year-old man. He is Shoshoni and married with a 10-year-old son. He is a State Trooper. Robert is also a recovering alcoholic. He has not had a drink in 9 years. Through Facebook, he connected with Loren who he met in college over 18 years ago. Loren is married with an 8-year-old daughter and a 12-year-old daughter. She racially identifies as white. A business trip took Lauren to Wyoming where Robert resides. After sitting up and talking all night long, Robert and Loren decide that they should have gotten together in college and decide to start an intimate relationship. Robert is ecstatic with Loren. Their sex life is fantastic; they complete each other sentences, and they like the same music, books, and have similar political views. Within a few weeks, Robert decides to move to Colorado where Loren resides. He discusses this with his therapist, Anita, who is concerned that Robert is moving too quickly and is headed for a fall. Anita is also Native American. Robert has not told Loren he is a recovering alcoholic. In therapy, Anita engages in a series of role plays with the goal of helping Robert to look critically at his new relationship. She asks Robert to think about who else he knows in the state where Loren resides. "What will your evenings and weekends be like when she is unavailable and you are all alone?" Will this move create vulnerability in your life for drinking alcohol to reappear? Robert assures Anita that he and Loren have made a commitment to spend as much time together as possible. Anita asks Robert what he would do if after moving to be near Loren, the relationship sours. Robert is offended by the question and replies that he and Loren are old souls who have made a lifetime commitment to one another. Anita gently confronts Robert and asks him how he will explain to his child that he is leaving and will only see him twice a month instead of every day? Anita asks, "How do you think your son will be impacted by your increased absence?" Upon hearing this question, Robert becomes defensive and leaves the room. He returns after 10 minutes and resumes therapy. Anita observes lability in Robert's moods, which they have discussed in therapy. Robert's father left him and his siblings when he was a child. Robert said he hated his father for this abandonment and does not want his son to hate him. Anita asks Robert what the financial implications are for permanently leaving his job as opposed to taking a leave of absence from his job and separating from his wife (as opposed to divorcing). Robert says that he knows what he wants to do and does not see the point of a leave of absence from his job or separating instead of divorcing. He and Loren are going to marry once their divorces come through. Robert has told his wife about Loren and that he plans to come home twice monthly in order to see his son. Robert finds a new job as a security officer (the state where he moved was not hiring troopers) and rents an apartment to be near Loren. His wife has put their home on the market and is distraught over her husband's decision to leave the family. She is looking for an apartment and additional work to help meet new expenses associated with Robert's departure. Once Robert moved, he and Loren were excited about spending nearly every evening together, even if for just 20 minutes. Soon Robert noticed Loren putting distance between them. She seemed to make excuses for why she could not spend as much time with Robert as he had desired. About 1 month after Robert moved to be near Loren, she told him that it was not a good idea after all for him to move and that although she wants to, she has decided not to leave her husband. Loren's older daughter saw a card that Robert had sent Loren, and she was so upset by this card that she was inconsolable. Loren's husband lives and works in another state. Upon hearing the news from Loren, Robert bought alcohol and drank an excessive amount. He told Loren that he had been dry for years but that he was going to "check out." Filled with guilt and panic, as well as concern for Robert's safety, Loren called the police. They arrive at Robert's apartment to find him inebriated and confused. His firearm was nearby but the safety was on and Robert did not say anything to the officers to suggest he was suicidal or homicidal. Officers did not ask him why his firearm was out. Robert wears a firearm daily and has a concealed license to do so. Still, Robert was taken to a hospital, against his will, and kept for observation. The psychiatrist describes Robert as noncooperative, dangerous, and diagnosed him with Alcohol induced Psychosis and Substance Use Disorder (severe). He gave Robert Seroquel, a powerful antipsychotic medication. In the morning, Robert said he feels like he has been hit by a Mack truck. Upon his release from the hospital a few days later, Robert called Anita and needed a crisis session over the phone. He was nearly incoherent—panicking, hyperventilating, and regretting "ruining his life." Anita spoke with Robert for 45 minutes. They made plans to speak again in a few days. Anita called the insurance agency to inquire about reimbursement for phone therapy. She was told that insurance does not pay for phone therapy, even in emergency situations. Anita decides to continue to conduct phone therapy with Robert through a sliding scale. Robert's new job does not yet provide health insurance, and his personal finances have been strained due to the costs associated with the move. Anita strongly encourages Robert to find a therapist locally who can lay eyes on him. After each session, she e-mails her session notes to herself for risk management and consults with a colleague. Anita knows that Robert is very vulnerable and wants to help him through this crisis and protect herself in the event of a catastrophic event. Anita knows that Robert enjoys tai chi and suggests that he do tai chi to calm his mind and body. She also suggests that he speak to his sponsor that he had years ago when he was drinking on a daily basis.

Questions

1. Do race and gender impact the diagnoses that are given to patients?
2. Could Anita have intervened any differently with Robert prior to his joining Loren?

Discussion and Integration

Why Robert was taken against his will to the hospital needs to be discussed. The Constitution allows people to bear arms and Robert did not say anything to the officers that was overtly problematic. He did tell Loren that he wanted to "check out." Robert made this statement after his girlfriend, for whom he risked everything, said that she could not continue their relationship. Because of this statement from someone whose blood alcohol level was over the legal limit, the police were called.

To best treat Robert, Anita's knowledge of legal issues is critical as are referral information and community resources. Action is a core component of social justice and includes exercising institutional intervention skills on behalf of Robert. With respect to Robert, this action could involve Anita speaking, upon written permission granted by Robert, to a new therapist. It would also be helpful for Anita to speak with the psychiatrist who released Robert from the hospital. The psychiatrist referred to Robert as dangerous and prescribed a powerful antipsychotic drug. The psychiatrist's comments are now part of Robert's medical record. This event is significant for a man who has a career in law enforcement where he is charged with protecting the public from dangerous people. Anita has decided to file an informal complaint with the Medical Board.

It is worthy to note that the ambulance drivers were able to escort Robert to the hospital without his permission because the police gave them permission to do so. In some states, a medical doctor or a police officer can commit people without their permission. We know that Robert has stigmatized identities as a Native American man with a history of alcoholism. His firearm was out and nearby on a table—this fact is concerning. The police did not query Robert as to why his firearm was out. Robert was drunk in the privacy of his home and was not disturbing the peace. He made no statements to the officers about hurting himself or anyone else. When people say that they want to "check out" after receiving devastating news, what do mental health professionals do with that information? While this information should not be ignored and needs to be followed up—the meaning of this statement must be clarified and considered in context with other information.

Racial Inequities and Culturally Inappropriate Interventions

People of color have been treated poorly by the mental health establishment, which has a history of being insensitive to the sociopolitical realities that affect mental and social functioning among people of color. How was Robert's behavior and demeanor affected by the very recent break up with his girlfriend for whom he left his wife, child, home, and job? Robert, as a recovering alcoholic, had been sober for 9 years but consumed so much alcohol that he became inebriated. Is it possible that Robert is dealing with the aftereffects of alcohol poisoning?

Many mental health professionals are inadequately prepared to competently work with certain clients who present with particular concerns. In some circumstances, having a one-on-one client–counselor relationship is not possible or even desirable due to lack of access, unavailability of competent clinicians for a given area, or the client's sense of mistrust about the benefits and aims of therapy.

Perkins (2015) found that psychotherapy among some men has actually been unhelpful (iatrogenic). Robert told Anita that he did not want another therapist and wants to continue therapy only with Anita. Prior to Anita, Robert had a psychologist who was not helpful. Robert is still reeling from his negative encounter with the psychiatrist at the hospital. What does Anita do? Her client, who is in crisis, is in another state but refuses to seek out a new therapist despite Anita's recommendations. Although he is unwilling to find a new therapist, he is committed to speaking twice weekly, by phone, with Anita and is faithful about sending the mutually agreed upon amount for the sessions. Anita, in consultation with a colleague, agrees to speak to Robert on the phone. She asks him when he is planning to return home to visit his child and requests that Robert come in to the office so that she can see him. Anita wants to be able to look her client in the face and see his expressions, listen to the clarity of his speech, see if there are any tremors, and evaluate his hygiene, mood, and any weight gain or loss.

Interventions

There are structural issues that work against Anita's efforts to help her client. Although most insurance companies will not pay for therapy conducted over the phone, the above case study clearly demonstrates what can happen to a patient who is in crisis away from his therapist. As well, what happens to clients' mental health when clinicians are on extended vacations or have moved out of state? Interventions are still needed particularly when patients are in crisis, and yet therapists need to protect themselves. With some insurance co-pays as high as $40 for each weekly visit (after deductibles), money is a factor that hinders vulnerable patients' access to therapy. Sliding-scale fees, which is what Anita is doing, can make therapy more accessible to many clients. Granted she will not be able to make a living seeing all of her patients on a sliding-scale basis, but she realizes that continued psychotherapy with Robert is critical.

Robert has left his home, wife, child, job, and friends to be in a relationship with a woman who has broken up with him just a month into his move. His losses are enormous, and he deeply regrets his actions. Robert will need to rebuild. One task that Anita can assist Robert with is not holding on to what was or could have been and embracing what the reality is in front of him at the present. The following are both short- and long-term interventions that may help Anita help Robert. Given the fragile state that Robert is in, Anita will need to take action initially and make the following contacts as part of her culturally oriented interventions:

1. Anita can contact centers for information about when and where tai chi members hold their meetings.

2. Anita could contact Alcoholics Anonymous to see when the nearest meeting is.

3. Anita could contact men's organizations to see if there are men's groups or divorce care groups.

4. Anita could encourage Robert to cope daily (e.g., get out of bed, take a shower, get dressed, make a hot meal, take a walk, go to work, etc.)

5. Anita cares for herself while providing psychotherapeutic support to Robert. This work is rewarding but also fatiguing.

6. Anita could collaborate with Robert in his own transformation—ask him what he wants.

7. Anita avoids pathologizing Robert. She does not stereotype, project, or distance (Pinderhughes, 1995).

8. Anita could encourage Robert to attend a 12-Step program, individual, and perhaps, in time, family/marriage therapy with his wife/ex-wife.

9. Anita could encourage bibliotherapy where Robert can read how others have coped and survived with difficult situations.

Anita will use a narrative therapy approach with Robert as a useful intervention. The basic theme of narrative therapy is that the person is not the problem; the problem is the problem (Boje, Alvarez, & Schooling, 2001). In this regard, Robert is not the problem. Pursuing an unavailable woman is the problem. Being impulsive and acting out are the problem. Narrative therapy holds that the knowledge and stories (narratives) that emanate from culture, families, and experiences shape persons. Narrative therapy has to do with learning to tell a different story of yourself. Different stories are possible, even with respect to the same events.

Narrative Therapy Related Questions for Intervention:

1. What is the story that Robert might tell to himself about his move to be with Loren?

2. Was it courageous for Robert to want more love in his life?

3. What does Robert's marriage want him to know about his level of happiness?

4. Why did Robert make room for this situation to unfold as it did, such that all is risked?

5. What does this situation tell Robert about his self- regard as a man, husband, and father?

6. What is the clinical relevance of Robert repeating his father's story?

7. What are different stories that Robert could choose that would best describe his life?

8. How does Robert want to live his life? What stories does Robert want to tell about himself?

Once Robert has arrived at a more psychologically stable place, Anita will focus on two different topic areas for psychotherapy.

First, Anita will explore Robert's relationship with his father who abandoned the family when Robert was a young child—it is clear there is conflict between Robert and his father. Therapy could be a place where Robert could begin to heal this soul wound. Anita knows that one task of adulthood is to unlearn many of the negative tapes received during childhood and adolescence and to replace them with messages that affirm the self and reflect who the individual has sculpted himself to be.

Second, she wants to explore any magical thinking that Robert may have. Robert has kept a stable job for decades; he has been married to the same woman for 12 years and has lived in the same house for as long. Anita questions if running away with Loren was an attempt for Robert to undo the deep sadness from his childhood. Anita mines Robert's risk-taking and impulsivity.

Finally, Anita will take action that can have implications for other clients and their clinicians. She plans to write a letter to the Insurance Commissioner and lobby, along with major mental health organizations, to change the current policy that does not provide payment to practitioners with established patients for phone sessions, particularly in emergencies.

Summary

This chapter discussed an expansion of a mental health professional's role to include being an active change agent against structural inequalities that foster inequity across race, gender, and class. Social justice was defined and the relationship between social justice, social action, empowerment, and advocacy was discussed. The relationship between cultural counseling competencies, ethical guidelines, for psychologists, and social justice was made. A case study integrated the elements of competence, advocacy, and social action within a social justice context and examined the nuances of risk management, policy implications, and the impact of discrimination were examined.

Epilogue

As a child growing up, I listened to the Beatles and Sly and The Family Stone a lot. I am glad I did. I dream of a world where people, irrespective of skin color, hair texture, body size, income, age, sexuality, gender, nationality, and ability can live as one.

I have attempted to present a way for the therapeutic event to embrace the multiple, shifting, and simultaneous identities in all of our lives, and it is my hope that as you read the text, you will think critically and talk about the case studies—about the models, the research, the census data, the discourses, the microaggressions, the injustices, the application of competencies, and the stories. I hope you will let me know what resonated with you and helped you to think about your world differently—and what you did not like or agree with or understand. Thank you for letting me be myself. I am grateful.

Sincerely,

Tracy Robinson-Wood

References and Suggested Readings

Abernathy, A. D. (1995). Managing racial anger: A critical skill in cultural competence. *Journal of Multicultural Counseling and Development, 23*, 96–102.

Abrams, L. S. (2002). Rethinking girls "at-risk": Gender, race, and class intersections and adolescent development. *Journal of Human Behavior in the Social Environment, 6*, 47–64.

Abudabbeh, N. (1996). Arab families. In M. McGoldrick, J. K. Pearce, & J. Giordano (Eds.), *Ethnicity and family therapy* (pp. 333–346). New York, NY: Guilford Press.

Abudabbeh, N. (2005a). Arab families: An overview. In M. McGoldrick, J. Giordano, & N. Garcia-Preto (Eds.), *Ethnicity and family therapy* (pp. 423–436). New York, NY: Guilford Press.

Abudabbeh, N. (2005b). Palestinian families. In M. McGoldrick, J. Giordano, & N. Garcia-Preto (Eds.), *Ethnicity and family therapy* (pp. 487–498). New York, NY: Guilford Press.

Abudabbeh, N., & Nydell, M. K. (1993). Transcultural counseling and Arab Americans. In J. McFadden (Ed.), *Transcultural counseling: Bilateral and international perspectives* (pp. 261–284). Alexandria, VA: American Counseling Association.

Adherents.com. (2007). Major religions of the world ranked by number of adherents. Retrieved from http://www.adherents.com

Adherents.com. (2014). Top 10 largest highly international religious bodies. Retrieved October 27, 2015, from http://www.adherents.com/adh_rb.html#International

Adkison-Bradley, C., Johnson, D., Sanders, J. L., Duncan, L., & Holcomb-McKoy, C. (2005). Forging a collaborative relationship between the black church and the counseling profession. *Counseling and Values, 49*, 147–154.

Ahmad, F., & Iverson, S. (2013). *The state of women of color in the United States: Too many barriers remain for this growing and increasingly important population.* Washington, DC: Center for American Progress.

Ahnallen, J. M., Suyemoto, K. L., & Carter, A. S. (2006). Relationship between physical appearance, sense of belonging and exclusion, and racial/ethnic self-identification among multiracial Japanese European Americans. *Cultural Diversity and Ethnic Minority Psychology, 12*, 673–686.

Alba, R. D. (1990). *Ethnic identity: The transformation of white America.* New Haven, CT: Yale University Press.

Alinsky, S. D. (1990). *Rules for radicals: A primer for realistic radicals.* New York, NY: Random House.

Al-Krenawi, A., & Graham, J. R. (2000). Culturally sensitive social work practice with Arab clients in mental health settings. *Health Social Work, 25*(1), 9–22.

Alzheimer's Foundation of America. (2015). Definition of Alzheimer's. Retrieved from http://www.alzfdn.org/AboutAlzheimers/definition.html

American Cancer Society. (1989). A summary of the American Cancer Society report to the Nation: Cancer in the poor. *CA Cancer Journal for Clinicians, 39*, 263–265.

American Community Survey: 2013. (2014). Veteran statistics from the U.S. Census Bureau. Retrieved from http://factfinder2.census.gov/bkmk/table/1.0/en/ACS/13_1YR/B21001

American Counseling Association. (1995). *Code of ethics*. Alexandria, VA: American Counseling Association.

American Counseling Association. (2002). *Code of ethics*. Alexandria, VA: American Counseling Association.

American Counseling Association. (2005). *Code of ethics*. Alexandria, VA: Author.

American Counseling Association. (ACA). (2014). *Code of ethics*. Alexandria, VA: Author.

American Jews and the Holocaust: History, Memory, and Identity. (n.d.). When and why did Jews immigrate to America. Retrieved on July 16, 2015, from http://userpages.umbc.edu/~jonfeng1/thesisproject/ellieginsburg/questions/historians_jewishimmigration.html

American Psychological Association. (n.d.). *Disability and socioeconomic status*. Retrieved http://www.apa.org/pi/ses/resources/publications/factsheet-disability.pdf

American Psychological Association. (2000). Resolution on poverty and socioeconomic status. Retrieved June 3, 2015, from http://www.apa.org/about/policy/poverty-resolution.aspx

American Psychological Association. (2002). *Code of ethics*. Washington, DC: Author.

American Psychological Association. (2003). Guidelines on multicultural education, training, research, practice, and organizational change for psychologists. *American Psychologist, 58*, 377–402.

American Psychological Association. (2006). *Guidelines for psychotherapy with lesbian, gay, and bisexual clients*. Washington, DC: Author.

American Psychological Association. (2007a). *Disability issues in psychology: Enhancing your interactions with people with disabilities*. Washington, DC: Author.

American Psychological Association. (2007b). *Report of the APA task force on socioeconomic status*. Washington, DC: Author.

American Psychological Association. (2010). *Code of ethics*. Washington, DC: Author.

American Psychological Association. (2012). Benchmarks evaluation system. Retrieved from http://www.apa.org/ed/graduate/benchmarks-evaluation-system.aspx

American Psychological Association. (2015). Report of the independent reviewer and related materials. Retrieved on August 18, 2015, from http://www.apa.org/independent-review/index.aspx

American Psychological Association, Board of Educational Affairs & Council of Chairs of Training Councils (2007). *Assessment of competency benchmarks work group: A developmental model for the defining and measuring competence in professional psychology*. Washington, DC: Author. Retrieved January 2013 from http://apa.org

Ancis, J. R., Sedlacek, W. E., & Mohr, J. J. (2000). Student perceptions of campus cultural climate by race. *Journal of Counseling and Development, 78*, 180–185.

Andersen, A. E. (1986). Males with eating disorders. In F. E. F. Larocca (Ed.), *Eating disorders* (pp. 39–46). San Francisco, CA: Jossey-Bass.

Anderson, M. (2015). A rising share of the U.S. black population is foreign born. Retrieved August 10, 2015, from Pew Research Center: http://www.pewsocialtrends.org/2015/04/09/a-rising-share-of-the-u-s-black-population-is-foreign-born

Anderson, N. B. (2003). *Unraveling the mystery of racial and ethnic health disparities: Who, what, when, where, how and especially, why?* Boston, MA: Institute on Urban Health Research, Northeastern University.

Anderson, S. K., & Middleton, V. A. (2004). *Explorations in privilege, oppression, and diversity*. Belmont, CA: Wadsworth.

ANRED. (2006). *Anorexia and related eating disorders*. Retrieved September 28, 2007, from http://www.anred.com/stats.html

Aponte, H. J. (1994). *Bread and spirit: Therapy with the new poor*. New York, NY: Norton.

Appleby, G. A., Colon, E., & Hamilton, J. (2001). Culture, social class, and social identity development. In G. Appleby, E. Colon, & J. Hamilton (Eds.), *Diversity, oppression and social functioning: Person-in-environment assessment and intervention* (pp. 16–34). Needham Heights, MA: Allyn & Bacon.

Aprahamian, M., Kaplan, D. M., Windham, A. M., Sutter, J. A., & Visser, J. (2011). The relationship between acculturation and mental health of Arab Americans. *Journal of Mental Health Counseling, 33*, 80–92.

Arab American Institute. (2006). *Arab Americans*. Retrieved September 15, 2007, from http//www.aaiusa.org

Arab American Institute. (2012). Demographics. Retrieved on November 9, 2015, from http://www.aaiusa.org/demographics

Arab American Institute. (2015a). Anti-Arab bigotry and Islamaphobia. Retrieved November 8, 2015, from http://www.aaiusa.org/islamophobia

Arab American Institute. (2015b). Ralph Johns. *Together we came.* Retrieved from http://www.aaiusa.org/together_we_came_ralph_johns

Arab American National Museum. (2009). *Three faiths with one God: Arab Americans.* Retrieved on November 8, 2015, from Institute of Museum and Library Services: http://www.arabamericanmuseum.org/umages/IMLS_religion_exhibit/3f_islam.html

Arab League. (2015). League of Arab States. Retrieved on August 18, 2015, from http://www.nationsonline.org/oneworld/arab_league.htm

Arbona, C., & Nora, A. (2007). Predicting college attainment of Hispanic students: Individual, institutional, and environmental factors. *The Review of Higher Education, 30,* 247–270.

Arndt, L. M. R. (2011). Warrior spirit: Soul wound and coping among American Indians in law enforcement. *The Counseling Psychologist, 39*(4), 527–569. doi: 10.1177/0011000010389827

Arndt, L., & Davies, A. (2010). Warrior spirit: Soul wound and coping among American Indians in law enforcement. *The Counseling Psychologist, 39(4),* 527–569. doi: 10.1177/0011000010389827

Arredondo, P. (1992). *Latina/Latino value orientations: Tape 1. Cultural considerations for working more effectively with Latin Americans.* Amherst, MA: Microtraining and Multicultural Development.

Arredondo, P., & Arciniega, G. M. (2001). Strategies and techniques for counselor training based on the multicultural counseling competencies. *Journal of Multicultural Counseling and Development, 29,* 263–273.

Arredondo, P., & Glauner, T. (1992). Personal dimensions of identity model. Boston, MA: Empowerment Workshops.

Arredondo, P., Psalti, A., & Cella, K. (1993). The woman factor in multicultural counseling. *Counseling and Human Development, 2,* 1–8.

Arredondo, P., & Rodriguez, V. (2005). Working with contemporary Latino immigrants. *Counseling and Human Development, 38,* 1–12.

Arredondo, P., Toporek, R., Brown, S. P., Jones, J., Locke, D. C., Sanchez, J., & Stadler, H. (1996). Operationalization of the multicultural competencies. *Journal of Multicultural Counseling and Development, 24,* 42–78.

Asi, M., & Beaulieu, D. (2013). Arab households in the United States: 2006–2010 (American Community Survey Briefs No. ACSBR/10-20). Washington, DC: U.S. Census Bureau. Retrieved November 8, 2015, http://www.census.gov/prod/2013pubs/acsbr10-20.pdf

Assaud, R., & Roudi-Fahimi, F. (2007). *Youth in the Middle East and North Africa: Demographic opportunity or challenge?* Washington, DC: Population Reference Bureau. Retrieved December 29, 2011, from http://www.prb.org/pdf07/youthinmena.pdf

Assessment of Competency Benchmarks Work Group. (2007). *Assessment of competency benchmarks work group: A developmental model for the defining and measuring competence in professional psychology.* Retrieved from http://www.ccptp.org/assets/2011-Conference-Resources/benchmark_competencies_document_-_feb_2007.pdf

Atkinson, D. R., & Hackett, G. (1995). *Counseling diverse populations.* Madison, WI: Brown and Benchmark.

Atkinson, D. R., Morten, G., & Sue, D. W. (1983). *Counseling American minorities: A cross cultural perspective.* Dubuque, IA: William C. Brown.

Avakian, M. (2002). *Atlas of Asian-American history.* New York, NY: Checkmark Books.

Avert. (2015). HIV and AIDS in the Middle East & North Africa (MENA). Retrieved on November 9, 2015, from http://www.avert.org/professionals/hiv-around-world/middle-east-north-africa-mena

Awad, G. (2010). The impact of acculturation and religious identification on perceived discrimination for Arab/Middle Eastern Americans. *Cultural Diversity and Ethnic Minority Psychology, 16*(1), 59–67. doi: 10.1037/a0016675

Balch, P. A. (2006). *Prescription for nutritional healing* (4th ed.). Garden City Park, NY: Avery.

Ballentine, B., & Ballentine, I. (1993). *The Native Americans: An illustrated history.* Atlanta, GA: Turner.

Balogun, O. (2015). *Embracing the hottentot Venus: A mixed-method examination of body image, body image ideals, and objectified body consciousness among African women* (Unpublished doctoral dissertation, in progress). Northeastern University, Boston, MA.

Barakat, H. (1993). *The Arab world.* Berkeley: University of California Press.

Basch, M. F. (1992). *Practicing psychotherapist: A casebook.* New York, NY: Basic Books.

Battle, J., Cohen, C. J., Warren, D., Fergerson, G., & Audam, S. (2002). Say it loud. I'm black and I'm proud. *Black Pride Survey 2000.* New York, NY: The Policy Institute of the National Gay and Lesbian Task Force. Retrieved August 8, 2003, from http://www.thetaskforce.org/static_html/downloads/reports/reports/SayItLoudBlackAndProud.pdf

Beals, K. P. M., & Peplau, L. A. (2006). Disclosure patterns within social networks of gay men and lesbians. *Journal of Homosexuality, 51,* 101–117.

Beals, M. J., & Beals, K. L. (1993). Transcultural counseling and the Hispanic community. In J. McFadden (Ed.), *Transcultural counseling: Bilateral and international perspectives* (pp. 213–238). Alexandria, VA: American Counseling Association.

Beauboeuf-Lafontant, T. (2007). You have to show strength: An exploration of gender, race, and depression. *Gender and Society, 21,* 28–51.

Becerra, R. M. (1988). The Mexican American family. In C. H. Mindel, R. W. Habenstein, & R. Wright (Eds.), *Ethnic families in America: Patterns and variations* (3rd ed., pp. 141–159). New York, NY: Elsevier.

Becvar, S. B., & Becvar, R. (1993). *Family therapy: A systematic integration* (2nd ed.). Boston, MA: Allyn & Bacon.

Begley, S. (1995, February 13). Three is not enough. *Newsweek,* 67–69.

Belgrave, F. Z. (1991). Psychosocial predictors of adjustment to disability in African Americans. *Journal of Rehabilitation,* 37–40.

Bell, A., & Weinberg, M. (1978). *Homosexuality: A study of human diversity among men and women.* New York, NY: Simon & Schuster.

Bem, S. L. (1993). *The lenses of gender: Transforming the debate on sexuality inequality.* New Haven, CT: Yale University Press.

Bennett, L., Jr. (1982). *Before the Mayflower: A history of black America.* Chicago, IL: Johnson.

Berliner, P. M. (1995). Soul healing: A model of feminist therapy. In M. Burke and J. Mirant (Eds.), *Counseling: The spiritual dimension* (pp. 113–125). Thousand Oaks, CA: Sage.

Bernardez, T. (1987). Gender-based countertransference of female therapists in the psychotherapy of women. In M. Braude (Ed.), *Women and therapy* (pp. 25–39). New York, NY: Haworth Press.

Berry, J. W., & Kim, U. (1988). Acculturation and mental health. In P. R. Dasen, J. W. Berry, & N. Sartorius (Eds.), *Health and cross-cultural psychology: Toward applications* (pp. 207–236). Newbury Park, CA: Sage.

Berry, J. W., & Sam, D. L. (1997). Acculturation and adaptation. In J. Berry, M. Segall, & C. Kagitcibasi (Eds.), *Cross-cultural psychology* (Vol. 3, pp. 291–326). Boston, MA: Allyn & Bacon.

Berzon, B. (1988). *Permanent partners: Building gay and lesbian relationships that last.* New York, NY: Dutton.

Birtchnell, S. A., Lacey, J. H., & Harte, S. (1985). Body image distortion in bulimia nervosa. *British Journal of Psychiatry, 47,* 408–412.

Black, L. (1996). Families of African origin. In M. McGoldrick, J. Giordano, & J. K. Pearce (Eds.), *Ethnicity and family therapy* (pp. 57–65). New York, NY: Guilford Press.

Black Women's Health Imperative. (n.d.) Retrieved October 26, 2015, from http://www.bwhi.org

Block, J., & Block, J. H. (2006). Venturing a 30-year longitudinal study. *The American Psychologist, 61,* 315–327.

Boje, D. M., Alvarez, R. C., & Schooling, B. (2001). Reclaiming story in organization: Narratologies and action sciences. In R. Westwood & S. Linstead (Eds.), *The language of organization* (pp. 132–175). London: Sage.

Bourdieu, P. (1984). *Distinction: A social critique of the judgment of taste.* Cambridge, MA: Harvard University Press.

Bowman, V. E. (1996). Counselor self-awareness and ethnic self-knowledge as a critical component of multicultural training. In J. L. DeLucia-Waack (Ed.), *Multicultural counseling competencies: Implications for training and practice* (pp. 7–30). Alexandria, VA: Association for Counselor Education and Supervision.

Boyd, H. (2003). *My husband Betty: Love, sex, and life with a crossdresser.* Berkeley, CA: Seal Press.

Boyd-Franklin, N. (1989). *Black families in therapy: A multisystems approach.* New York, NY: Guilford Press.

Boyd-Franklin, N. (2003). Race, class, and poverty. In F. Walsh (Ed.), *Normal family process* (pp. 260–279). New York, NY: Guilford Press.

Boyd-Franklin, N. (2010). Incorporating spirituality and religion into the treatment of African Americans. *The Counseling Psychologist, 38,* 976–1000. doi: 10.1177/0011000010374881

Bradford, J., Barrett, K., & Honnold, J. A. (2002). *The 2000 Census and same-sex households: A user's guide.* New York, NY: The Policy Institute of the National Gay and Lesbian Task Force. Retrieved from http://www.ngltf.org/downloads/Census/CensusFront.pdf

Bradley, C., & Hawkins-Leon, C. G. (2002). The transracial adoption debate: Counseling and legal implications. *Journal of Counseling & Development, 80,* 433–440.

Bradshaw, C. (1994). Asian and Asian American women: Historical and political considerations in psychotherapy. In L. Comas-Diaz & B. Greene (Eds.), *Women of color: Integrating ethnic and gender identities* (pp. 72–113). New York, NY: Guilford Press.

Braithwaite-Hall, M. (2011). *Standing in the need of prayer: Beliefs about depression and treatment held among African American Christian women* (Unpublished doctoral dissertation). Northeastern University, Boston, MA.

Brantlinger, E. A. (1993). *Politics of social class in secondary schools: Views of affluent and impoverished youth.* New York, NY: Teachers College Press.

Brault, M. (2008, December). *Americans with disabilities: 2005 Household Economic Studies Current Population Study.* Retrieved from http://www.census.gov/prod/2008pubs/p70–117.pdf

Brault, M. (2009). *Review of changes to measurements of disability in the 2008 American Community Survey.* Retrieved from http://www.census.gov/hhes/www/disability/2008ACS_disability.pdf

Brault, M. (2012). *Americans with disabilities: 2010: Household economic studies* (Current Population Reports No. P70-131). Retrieved June 9, 2015, from www.census.gov/prod/2012pubs/p70-131.pdf

Brittingham, A., & de la Cruz, G. P. (2004). Ancestry 2000. *Census 2000 Brief.* Washington, DC: U.S. Census. Retrieved November 10, 2015, from, http://www.census.gov/prod/2004pubs/c2kbr-35.pdf

Bronstein, P., & Quina, K. (1988). *Teaching a psychology of people.* Washington, DC: American Psychological Association.

Brookins, C. B., & Robinson, T. L. (1995). Rites of passage as resistance to oppression. *Western Journal of Black Studies, 19,* 172–185.

Brouwers, M. (1990). Treatment of body image dissatisfaction among women with bulimia nervosa. *Journal of Counseling and Development, 69,* 144–147.

Brown, D. (1981). *Bury my heart at Wounded Knee.* New York, NY: Henry Holt.

Brown, L. (1994). *Subversive dialogues: Theory in feminist therapy.* New York, NY: Basic Books.

Brown, L. M. (2003). *Girlfighting: Betrayal and rejection among girls.* New York: New York University Press.

Brown, L. M., & Gilligan, C. (1992). *Meeting at the crossroads: The landmark book about the turning points in girls' and women's lives.* New York, NY: Ballantine Books.

Browning, C., Reynolds, A. L., & Dworkin, S. H. (1994). Affirmative psychotherapy for lesbian women. *Counseling Psychologist, 19,* 177–196.

Brunsma, D. L. (2006). Mixed messages: Doing race in the color-blind era. In D. Brunsma (Ed.), *Mixed messages: Multiracial identities in the "color-blind" era* (pp. 1–11). Boulder, CO: Lynne Reinner.

Brunsma, D. L., & Rockquemore, K. A. (2001). The new color complex: Appearances and biracial identity. *Identity: An international journal of theory and research, 1,* 225–246.

Bryant, A., & LaFromboise, T. D. (2005). The racial identity and cultural orientation of Lumbee American Indian high school students. *Cultural Diversity and Ethnic Minority Psychology, 11,* 82–89.

Budge, S. L., Katz-Wise, S. L., Tebber, E. N., Howard, K. A. S., Schneider, C. L., & Rodriguez, A. (2013). Transgender emotional and coping processes: Facilitative and avoidant coping throughout gender transitioning. *The Counseling Psychologist, 41,* 601–647.

Burck, C., & Speed, B. (1995). *Gender, power, and relationships.* New York, NY: Routledge.

Bureau of Labor Statistics, U.S. Department of Labor, *The Economics Daily,* Forty-nine percent of employed Asians in management, professional, and related occupations, 2012. Retrieved February 5, 2016 at http://www.bls.gov/opub/ted/2013/ted_20131231.htm

Burke, M. T., Hackney, H., Hudson, O., Miranti, J., Watts, G. A., & Epp, L. (1999). Spirituality, religion, and CACREP curriculum standards. *Journal of Counseling & Development, 77,* 251–257.

Burke, M. T., & Miranti, J. (2001). The spiritual and religious dimensions of counseling. In D. Locke, J. Myers, & E. Herr (Eds.), *Handbook of counseling* (pp. 601–612). Thousand Oaks, CA: Sage.

Burnes, T. R., Singh, A. A., Harper, A., Pickering, D. L., Moundas, S., Scofield, T., ... Hosea, J. (2009). The Association of Lesbian, Gay, Bisexual, and Transgender Issues in Counseling (ALGBT) competencies for counseling with transgender clients. Retrieved March 6, 2015, from http://www.counseling.org/docs/default-source/competencies/algbtic_competencies.pdf?sfvrsn=8

Burnett, J. W., Anderson, W. P., & Heppner, P. P. (1995). Gender roles and self-esteem: A consideration of environmental factors. *Journal of Counseling and Development, 73,* 323–326.

Byrd, W. M., & Clayton, L. A. (2003). Racial and ethnic disparities in healthcare: A background and history. In Institute of Medicine (Ed.), *Unequal treatment: Confronting racial and ethnic disparities in healthcare* (pp. 455–527). Washington, DC: National Academies Press.

Callaway, E. (2014). Ancient genome stirs ethics debate: Sequencing of DNA from Native American 'Clovis boy' forces researchers to rethink handling of tribal remains. *Nature, 506,* 142–143.

Cameron, S. C., & Turtle-song, I. (2003). Native American mental health: An examination of resilience in the face of overwhelming odds. In F. Harper and J. McFadden (Eds.), *Culture and counseling: New approaches.* Boston, MA: Allyn & Bacon.

Cao, L., & Novas, H. (1996). *Everything you need to know about Asian-American history.* New York, NY: Penguin.

Carballo-Dieguez, A. (1989). Hispanic culture, gay male culture, and AIDS: Counseling implications. *Journal of Counseling and Development, 68,* 26–30.

Cardemil, E. V., & Battle, C. L. (2003). Guess who's coming to therapy? Getting comfortable with conversations about race and ethnicity in psychotherapy. *Professional Psychology: Research and Practice, 34,* 278–286.

Carpenter, K. M., & Addis, M. E. (2000). Alexithymia, gender, and responses to depressive symptoms. *Sex Roles: A Journal of Research, 42,* 629–638.

Carrigan, T., Connell, B., & Lee, J. (1987). Toward a new sociology of masculinity. In H. Brod (Ed.), *The making of masculinities: The new men's studies* (pp. 63–100). Boston, MA: Allen and Unwin.

Carroll, L., & Gilroy, P. J. (2002). Transgender issues in counselor preparation. *Counselor Education & Supervision, 41,* 233–242.

Carter, R. T., & Parks, E. E. (1996). Womanist identity and mental health. *Journal of Counseling and Development, 74,* 484–489.

Cashwell, C. S., & Young, J. S. (2004). Spirituality in counselor training: A content analysis of syllabi from introductory spirituality courses. *Counseling and Values, 48,* 96–109.

Cass, V. C. (1979). Homosexual identity formation: A theoretical model. *Journal of Homosexuality, 4,* 219–235.

Cass, V. C. (1984). Homosexual identity: A concept in need of definition. *Journal of Homosexuality, 9,* 105–126.

Catalano, S. J. (1985). Crisis intervention with clinical interns: Some considerations for supervision. *The Clinical Supervisor, 3,* 97–102.

Centers for Disease Control. (2011). HIV fact sheet. Retrieved on May 19, 2015 from http://www.cdc.gov/hiv/pdf/native_fact_sheet_508.pdf

Centers for Disease Control. (2013). HIV among Hispanics/Latinos in the United States and dependent areas. Retrieved November 4, 2015, from http://www.cdc.gov/hiv/pdf/risk_latino.pdf

Centers for Disease Control and Prevention. (2015). American Indian and Alaska Native populations. Retrieved from http://www.cdc.gov/minorityhealth/populations/REMP/aian.html

Central Conference of American Rabbis. (1983). *The status of children of mixed marriages.* Retrieved from http://www.jewishvirtuallibrary.org/jsource/Judaism/patrilineal1.html

Chae, D. H., & Walters, K. L. (2009). Racial discrimination and racial identity attitudes in relation to self-rated health and physical pain and impairment among two-spirit American Indians/Alaska Natives. *American Journal of Public Health, 99,* 144–151.

Chae, M. H., & Foley, P. F. (2010). Relationship of ethnic identity, acculturation, and psychological well-being among Chinese, Japanese, and Korean Americans. *Journal of Counseling & Development, 88,* 466–476.

Chalam, Rabbi. (2013). Are there Jewish values? Shalom from Rabbi Chalom. Retrieved on August 2, 2015, from https://hjrabbi.wordpress.com/2013/07/02/are-there-jewish-values

Chan, C. S. (1992). Cultural considerations in counseling Asian American lesbians and gay men. In S. H. Dworkin & F. J. Gutierrez (Eds.), *Counseling gay men and lesbians: Journey to the end of the rainbow* (pp. 115–124). Alexandria, VA: American Association for Counseling and Development.

Chang, E. C. (1996). Cultural differences in optimism, pessimism, and coping: Predictors of subsequent adjustment in Asian American and Caucasian American college students. *Journal of Counseling Psychology, 43,* 113–123.

Chang, J. (2015). The interplay between collectivism and social support processes among Asian and Latino American college students. *Asian American Journal of Psychology, 6,* 4–14.

Chang, J., & Sue, S. (2005). Culturally sensitive research: Where have we gone wrong and what do we need to do now? In M. Constantine & D. Sue (Eds.), *Strategies for building multicultural competence in mental health and educational settings* (pp. 229–246). Hoboken, NJ: Wiley & Sons.

Chang, P. (2000). Treating Asian/Pacific American addicts and their families. In J. Krestan (Ed.), *Bridges to recovery: Addiction, family therapy, and multicultural treatment* (pp. 192–218). New York, NY: Free Press.

Chang, R. S. (2002). Race, Rights, and Reparation: Law and the Japanese American Internment (review). *Journal of Asian American Studies, 5,* 285–288.

Chao, R. C. (2013). Race/ethnicity and multicultural competence among school counselors: Multicultural training, racial ethnic identity, and color-blind racial attitudes. *Journal of Counseling & Development, 91,* 140–151.

Chao, R. C., Wei, M., Good, G. E., & Flores, L. Y. (2011). Race/ethnicity, color-blind racial attitudes, and multicultural counseling competence: The moderating effects of multicultural counseling training. *Journal of Counseling Psychology, 58,* 72–82. doi:10.1037/a0022091

Chase, C. (Writer). (2003). *The child with an intersex condition: Total patient care.* [Video]. Seattle, WA: Intersex Society of North America.

Chen, G. A., LePhuoc, P., Guzman, M. R., Rude, S. S., & Dodd, B. G. (2006). Exploring Asian American racial identity. *Cultural Diversity and Ethnic Minority Psychology, 12,* 461–476.

Chernin, K. (1985). *The hungry self: Women, eating, and identity.* New York, NY: Harper & Row.

Children's Partnership. (2000). *Tomorrow's youth: A changing demographic.* Retrieved December 15, 2003, from http://www.childrenspartnership.org/pub/children2000/children_of_2000.pdf

Chin, J. L. (2003). Multicultural competencies in managed health care. In D. Pope-Davis, H. Coleman, W. Liu, & R. Toporek (Eds.), *Handbook of multicultural competencies in counseling & psychology* (pp. 347–364). Thousand Oaks, CA: Sage.

Choi, C. Q. (2015). Who were the first Europeans? A 55,000 year-old skull holds tantalizing clues. *The Christian Science Monitor.* Retrieved from http://www.csmonitor.com/Science/2015/0129/Who-were-the-first-Europeans-A-55-000-year-old-skull-holds-tantalizing-clues.-video

Choi, Y., Harachi, T. W., Gillmore, M. R., & Catalano, R. F. (2006). Are multiracial adolescents at greater risk? Comparisons of rates, patterns, and correlates of substance use and violence between monoracial and multiracial adolescents. *American Journal of Orthopsychiatry, 76,* 86–97.

Chojnacki, J. T., & Gelberg, S. (1995). The facilitation of a gay/lesbian/bisexual support-therapy group by heterosexual counselors. *Journal of Counseling and Development, 73,* 352–354.

Choudhuri, D. (2005). Oppression of the spirit: Complexities in the counseling encounter. In S. Anderson and V. Middleton (Eds.), *Explorations in privilege, oppression, and diversity* (pp. 127–136). Belmont, CA: Thomson Brooks Cole.

Chow, E. N.-L. (1991). The development of feminist consciousness among Asian American women. In J. Lorber & S. A. Farrell (Eds.), *The social construction of gender* (pp. 255–268). Newbury Park, CA: Sage.

Chow, E. N.-L. (1994). The feminist movement: Where are all the Asian American women? In R. Takaki (Ed.), *From different shores: Perspectives on race and ethnicity in America.* New York, NY: Oxford University Press.

Christian, B. (1989). But who do you really belong to—Black studies or women's studies? *Women's Studies, 17,* 17–23.

Christian, C. M. (1995). *Black saga: The African American experience (a chronology).* Boston, MA: Houghton Mifflin.

Chung, R. C.-Y. (2005). Women, human rights, and counseling: Crossing international boundaries. *Journal of Counseling & Development, 82,* 262–268.

Chusmir, L. H. (1990). Men who make nontraditional choices. *Journal of Counseling and Development, 69*(1), 11–16.

Clark, C. R., Mercer, S. H., Zeigler-Hill, V., & Dufrene, B. A. (2012). Barriers to the success of ethnic minority students in school psychology graduate programs. *School Psychology Review, 41,* 176–192.

Clark, R., Anderson, N. B., Clark, V. R., & Williams, D. R. (2002). Racism as a stressor for African Americans: A biopsychosocial model. In T. LaVeist (Ed.), *Race, ethnicity and health* (pp. 319–339). San Francisco, CA: Jossey-Bass.

Clutter, A. W., & Nieto, R. D. (n.d.). *Understanding the Hispanic culture* (No. HYG-5237-00). Ohio State University fact sheet. Family and Consumer Sciences. Retrieved September 25, 2007, from http://ohioline.osu.edu/hyg-fact/5000/5237.html

Cohn, D., Passel, J. S., Wang, W., & Livingston, G. (2011). Barely half of US adults are married—A record low new marriages down 5% from 2009 to 2010. Retrieved from Pew Research Center: http://www.pewsocialtrends.org/2011/12/14/barely-half-of-u-s-adults-are-married-a-record-low

Cokely, K. O. (2001). Gender differences among African American students in the impact of racial identity on academic psychosocial development. *Journal of College Student Development, 42,* 480–487.

Cokely, K. O. (2005). Racial(ized) identity, ethnic identity, and Afrocentric values: Conceptual and methodological challenges in understanding African American identity. *Journal of Counseling Psychology, 52,* 517–526.

Cole, J. B., & Guy-Sheftall, B. (2003). *Gender talk: The struggle for women's equality in African-American communities.* New York, NY: Random House.

Coleman, E. (1982). Developmental stages of the coming out process. *American Behavioral Scientist, 25,* 469–482.

Collins, J. F. (2000). Biracial Japanese American identity: An evolving process. *Cultural Diversity and Ethnic Minority Psychology, 6,* 115–133.

Collins, P. H. (1989). The social construction of black feminist thought. *Signs, 14,* 745–773.

Comas-Diaz, L. (1993). Hispanic Latino communities: Psychological implications. In D. Atkinson, G. Morten, & D. W. Sue (Eds.), *Counseling American minorities: A cross-cultural perspective* (pp. 245–263). Madison, WI: Brown and Benchmark.

Comas-Diaz, L., & Greene, B. (1994a). Overview: An ethnocultural mosaic. In L. Comas-Diaz & B. Greene (Eds.), *Women of color: Integrating ethnic and gender identities in psychotherapy* (pp. 3–9). New York, NY: Guilford Press.

Comas-Diaz, L., & Greene, B. (1994b). Women of color with professional status. In L. Comas-Diaz & B. Greene (Eds.), *Women of color: Integrating ethnic and gender identities in psychotherapy* (pp. 347–388). New York, NY: Guilford Press.

Comstock, D. L., Hammer, T. R., Strentzsch, J., Cannon, K., Parsons, J., & Salazar, G. (2008). Relational-cultural theory: A framework for bridging relational, multicultural, and social justice competencies. *Journal of Counseling and Development, 86,* 279–287.

Constantine, M. G. (2001). Predictors of observer ratings of multicultural counseling competence in black, Latino, and white American trainees. *Journal of Counseling Psychology, 48,* 456–462.

Cook, D. A. (1994). Racial identity in supervision. *Counselor Education and Supervision, 34,* 132–241.

Cook, E. P. (1987). Psychological androgyny: A review of the research. *Counseling Psychologist, 15,* 471–513.

Cooper, J. (2015, May 31). Grim history traced in sunken slave ship found off South Africa. *The New York Times.* Retrieved November 5, 2015, from http://www.nytimes.com/2015/06/01/world/africa/tortuous-history-traced-in-sunken-slave-ship-found-off-south-africa.html

Cooper, R. (2002). A note on the biological concept of race and its application in epidemiological research. In T. A. LaVeist (Ed.), *Race, ethnicity, health: A public health reader* (pp. 99–114). San Francisco, CA: Jossey-Bass.

Corey, G. (1991). *Theory and practice of counseling and psychotherapy.* Pacific Grove, CA: Brooks/Cole.

Cornell, S., & Hartmann, D. (1997). *Ethnicity and race: Making identities in a changing world.* Thousand Oaks, CA: Pine Forge Press.

Cose, E. (1993). *The rage of a privileged class.* New York: HarperCollins.

Cosgrove, L. (2006). The unwarranted pathologizing of homeless mothers: Implication for research and social policy. In R. Toporek, L. Gerstein, N. Fouad, G. Roysircar, & T. Israel (Eds.), *Handbook for social justice in counseling psychology* (pp. 200–214). Thousand Oaks, CA: Sage.

Cottone, R. R., & Tarvydas, V. M. (1998). *Ethical and professional issues in counseling.* Upper Saddle River, NJ: Merrill/Prentice Hall.

Craddock, K. (2015). *Native Americans. Relational neuroscience, resistance, and microaggressions among Native, Latina, and black college educated women* (Grant proposal submitted to the National Institute for Minority Health Disparities, nonfunded).

Crockett, L. J., Iturbide, M. I., Stone, R. A. T., McGinley, M., Raffaelli, M., & Carlo, G. (2007). Acculturative stress, social support, and coping: Relations to psychological adjustment using Mexican American college students. *Cultural Diversity and Ethnic Minority Psychology, 13,* 347–355.

Crose, R., Nicholas, D. R., Gobble, D. C., & Frank, B. (1992). Gender and wellness: A multidimensional systems model for counseling, *Journal of Counseling & Development, 71,* 149–156.

Cross, W. E. (1991). *Shades of black: Diversity in African American identity.* Philadelphia, PA: Temple University Press.

Cueva, B. M. (2013). Theorizing the racial and gendered educational experiences of Chicanas and Native American women at the Ph.D. level in higher education: Testimonies of resistance, defiance, survival, and hope. *Dissertation Abstracts International Section A: Humanities and Social Sciences, 74*(5-A(E)).

Curtis, R. A., & Juhnke, G. A. (2003). Counseling the client with prostate cancer. *Journal of Counseling & Development, 81,* 160–167.

Dana, R. H. (1993). *Multicultural assessment perspectives for professional psychology.* Boston, MA: Allyn & Bacon.

Dana, R. H. (2000). The cultural self as locus for assessment and intervention with American Indians/Alaska Natives. *Journal of Multicultural Counseling and Development, 28,* 66–81.

Dana, R. H. (2002). Examining the usefulness of DSM–IV. In K. Kurasaki, S. Okasaki, & S. Sue (Eds.), *Asian American mental health: Assessment theories and methods* (pp. 29–46). New York, NY: Kluwer.

D'Andrea, M., & Daniels, J. (1991). Exploring the different levels of multicultural counseling training in counselor education. *Journal of Counseling and Development, 70,* 78–85.

Daniels, J. (2014). White women and Affirmative Action: Prime beneficiaries and opponents. *Racism Review.* Retrieved June 5, 2015, from http://www.racismreview.com/blog/2014/03/11/white-women-affirmative-action

Darity, W., Mason, P. L., & Stewart, J. B. (2006). The economics of identity: The origin and persistence of racial identity norms. *Journal of Economic Behavior and Organization, 60,* 283–305.

Darwin, C. (1859). *The origin of species by means of natural selection.* New York, NY: Modern Library.

Davis, K. S., Henise, S. B., & Galupo, M. P. (2014). Learning from our oppression: What transgender microaggressions can teach us about our friends and each other. Transhealth Conference 2014 Presentation. Towson University.

Day-Vines, N. L., Wood, S. M., Grothaus, T., Craigen, L., Holman, A., Dotson-Blake, K., & Douglass, M. J. (2007). Broaching the subjects of race, ethnicity, and culture during the counseling process. *Journal of Counseling and Development, 85,* 401–409.

de la Cruz, G., & Brittingham, A. (2003). The Arab population: 2000 (Census 2000 Brief No. C2KBR-23). Washington, DC: U.S. Census Bureau. Retrieved from https://www.census.gov/prod/2003pubs/c2kbr-23.pdf

de las Fuentes, C. (2007). Latina/o American populations. In M. Constantine (Ed.), *Clinical practice with people of color: A guide to becoming culturally competent* (pp. 46–60). New York, NY: Teachers College Press.

DeJong, J., & El-Khoury, G. (2006). Reproductive health of Arab young people. *British Medical Journal, 333,* 849–851.

Delpit, L. (1997). The silenced dialogue: Power and pedagogy in educating other people's children. In A. Halsey, H. Lauder, P. Brown, & A. Wells (Eds.), *Education: Culture, economy, society* (pp. 582–594). Oxford, UK: Oxford University Press.

DeNavas-Walt, C., & Proctor, B. D. (2014). *Income and poverty in the United States: 2013* (Current Population Reports No. P60-249). Washington, DC: U.S. Census Bureau.

DeNavas-Walt, C., & Proctor, B. D. (2015). *Income and poverty in the United States: 2014.* Washington, DC: U.S. Department of Commerce, Current Population Reports.

DeNavas-Walt, C., Proctor, B. D., & Smith, J. (2007). *Income, poverty, and health insurance coverage in the United States: 2006* (Current Population Reports No. P60-233). Washington, DC: U.S. Census Bureau.

DeNavas-Walt, C., Proctor, B. D., & Smith, J. C. (2011). *Income, poverty, and health insurance coverage in the United States: 2010.* Washington, DC: U.S. Census Bureau.

DeNavas-Walt, C., Proctor, B. D., & Smith, J. C. (2013). *Income, poverty, and health insurance coverage in the United States: 2012* (Current Population Reports No. P60-245) Washington, DC: U.S. Census Bureau. Retrieved from https://www.census.gov/prod/2013pubs/p60-245.pdf

Devoe, D. (1990). Feminist and nonsexist counseling: Implications for the male counselor. *Journal of Counseling and Development, 69,* 33–36.

Dey, J. G., & Hill, C. (2007). *Behind the pay gap.* Washington, DC: American Association of University Women Foundation.

Diaz, R. M., & Ayala, G. (2002). *Social discrimination and health: The case of Latino gay men and HIV risk.* New York, NY: The Policy Institute of the National Gay and Lesbian Task Force. Retrieved July 31, 2003, from http://www.thetaskforce.org/static_html/downloads/reports/reports/SocialDiscriminationAndHealth.pdf

Dillard, D. A., Smith, J. J., Ferucci, E. D., & Lanier, A. P. (2012). Depression prevalence and associated factors among Alaska Native people: The Alaska education and research toward health (EARTH) study. *Journal of Affective Disorders, 136,* 1088–1097.

Dilworth-Anderson, P., Boswell, G., & Cohen, M. D. (2007). Spiritual and religious coping values and beliefs among African American caregivers: A qualitative study. *Journal of Applied Gerontology, 25,* 355–369.

Dimidjian, S., & Hollon, S. D. (2010). How would we know if psychotherapy were harmful? *American Psychologist, 65,* 21–33.

Dines, G., & Humez, J. M. (2002). *Gender, race, and class in media: A text-reader.* Thousand Oaks, CA: Sage.

Dingfelder, S. (2013). African American women at risk. *Monitor on Psychology, 44,* 56.

Dinsmore, J. A., & England, J. T. (1996). A study of multicultural counseling training at CACREP-accredited counselor education programs. *Counseling Education and Supervision, 36*(1), 58–76.

Dion, K., Berschid, E., & Walster, E. (1972). What is beautiful is good. *Journal of Personality and Social Psychology, 14,* 94–108.

Dobbins, J. E., & Skillings, J. H. (1991). The utility of race labeling in understanding cultural identity: A conceptual tool for the social science practitioner. *Journal of Counseling & Development, 70,* 37–44.

Dominguez, S., & Arford, T. (2010). It's all about who you know: Social capital and health in low-income communities. *Health Sociology Review, 19*(1), 114–129.

Dominguez, S., & Lubitow, A. (2003). Transnational ties, poverty, and identity: Latin American immigrant women in public housing. *Family Relations, 57,* 419–430.

Dominguez, S., & Watkins, C. (2003). Creating networks for survival and mobility among African American and Latin American low-income mothers. *Social Problems, 50*(1), 111–135.

Drake, B. (2013). *Incarceration gap widens between whites and blacks.* Washington, DC: Pew Research Trust.

Dressel, J. L., Kerr, S., & Stevens, H. (2010). White identity and privilege. In J. A. E. Cornish, B. A. Schreier, L. I. Nadkarni, L. H. Metzger, & E. R. Rodolfa (Eds.), *Handbook of multicultural counseling competencies* (pp. 442–474). Hoboken, NJ: Wiley & Sons.

Duerk, J. (1994). *Circle of stones: Woman's journey to herself.* San Diego, CA: Lura Media.

Dulany, P. (1990). On becoming empowered. In J. Spurlock & C. Robinowitz (Eds.), *Women's progress: Promises and problems* (pp. 133–142). New York, NY: Plenum Press.

Durby, D. D. (1994). Gay, lesbian, and bisexual youth. *Journal of Gay and Lesbian Social Services, 1*(3/4), 1–37.

Dwairy, M. (2004). Individuation among Bedouin versus urban Arab adolescents: Ethnic and gender differences. *Cultural Diversity and Ethnic Minority Psychology, 10,* 340–350.

Dwairy, M. (2005). *Culturally sensitive counseling and psychotherapy: Working with Arabic and Muslim clients.* New York, NY: Teachers College Press.

Dworkin, S. H., & Gutierrez, F. J. (1991). *Counseling gay men and lesbians: Journey to the end of the rainbow.* Alexandria, VA: American Association for Counseling and Development.

Efthim, P. W., Kenny, M. E., & Mahalik, J. R. (2001). Gender role stress in relation to shame, guilt, and externalization. *Journal of Counseling & Development, 79,* 430–438.

Elder, P. (2000). An entirely routine test. In M. Clark (Ed.), *Beating our breasts: Twenty New Zealand women tell their breast cancer stories* (pp. 29–35). New Zealand, Auckland: Cape Catley Limited.

Eliason, M. L., & Schope, R. (2007). Shifting sands or solid foundation: Gay, lesbian, bisexual, and transgender identity formation. In I. H. Meyer & M. E. Northridge (Eds.), *The health of sexual minorities: Public health perspective on lesbian, gay, bisexual, and transgender health* (pp. 3–26). New York, NY: Springer.

Ellis, C. M. (2004). Putting race on the table: Counselors addressing race. *Counseling and Human Development, 37*(1), 1–8.

Emmons, L. (1992). Dieting and purging behavior in black and white high school students. *Journal of the American Dietetic Association, 92,* 306–312.

Ennis, S. R., Rios-Vargas, M., & Albert, M. (2011). The Hispanic population: 2010. *Census Briefs.* Retrieved from http://www.census.gov/prod/cen2010/briefs/c2010br-04.pdf

Enns, C. Z. (1991). The "new" relationship models of women's identity: A review and critique for counselors. *Journal of Counseling and Development, 69,* 209–217.

Enns, C. Z. (1994). On teaching about the cultural relativism of psychological constructs. *Teaching on Psychology, 21,* 205–212.

Equal Employment Opportunity Commission. (1991). *Americans with Disabilities Act handbook.* Washington, DC: Government Printing Office.

Erickson, C. D., & Al-Timimi, N. (2001). Providing mental health services to Arab Americans: Recommendation and considerations. *Cultural Diversity and Ethnic Minority Psychology, 7,* 308–327.

Erikson, E. (1968). *Identity: Youth and crisis.* New York, NY: Norton.

Erwin, T. M. (2006). A qualitative analysis of the *Lesbian Connection's* discussion forum. *Journal of Counseling & Development, 84,* 95–107.

Evans, K. M., Kincade, E. A., Marbley, A. F., & Seem, S. R. (2005). Feminism and feminist therapy: Lessons from the past and hopes for the future. *Journal of Counseling & Development, 83,* 269–277.

Evans, L., & Davies, K. (2000). No sissy boys here: A content analysis of the representation of masculinity in elementary school reading textbooks. *Sex Roles: Journal of Research, 42,* 255–270.

Exum, H. A., & Moore, Q. L. (1993). Transcultural counseling from African-American perspectives. In J. McFadden (Ed.), *Transcultural counseling: Bilateral and international perspectives* (pp. 193–212). Alexandria, VA: American Counseling Association.

Falbo, T., & De Baessa, Y. (2006). The influence of Mayan education on middle school students in Guatemala. *Cultural Diversity and Ethnic Minority Psychology, 12,* 601–614.

Falco, K. L. (1991). *Psychotherapy with lesbian clients: Theory into practice.* New York, NY: Brunner/Mazel.

Falicov, A (1996). Training to think critically: A multidimensional comparative framework. Retrieved December 2015, from http://www.aamft.org/Institutes13/Crash_Course/Individual_Documents/6%20Falicov.pdf

Fallender, C. A., Burnes, T. R., & Ellis, M. V. (2013). Multicultural clinical supervision and benchmarks: Empirical support informing practice and supervisory training. *The Counseling Psychologist, 41,* 8–27.

Farrugia, M. K., Sebire, N. J., Achermann, J. C., Eisawi, A., Duffy, P. G., & Mushtaq, I. (2012). Clinical and gonadal features and early surgical management of 45,X/46,XY and 45,X/47,XYY chromosomal mosaicism presenting with genital anomalies (2012). *Journal of Pediatric Urology, 9,* 139–144.

Fauth, J., & Hayes, J. A. (2006). Counselors' stress appraisals as predictors of countertransference behavior with male clients. *Journal of Counseling & Development, 84,* 430–439.

Fawcett, M. L., Briggs, C. A., Maycock, G., & Stine, E. (2010). Multicultural counseling competency development with a Guatemala travel study. *Journal for International Counselor Education, 2,* 1–18.

Fenell, D. L., & Weinhold, B. K. (1996). Treating families with special needs. *Counseling and Human Development, 28,* 1–10.

Ferdman, B. M., & Gallegos, P. I. (2001). Racial identity development and Latinos in the United States. In C. Wijeyesinghe & B. Jackson III (Eds.), *New perspectives on racial identity development: A theoretical and practical anthology* (pp. 32–66). New York: New York University Press.

Fernandes, C. A. (2014). White privilege, colorblind attitudes, and internalization of racism among college educated Latinos (Unpublished doctoral dissertation proposal). Northeastern University, Boston, MA.

Fine, M. (1991). Invisible flood: Notes on the politics of "dropping out" of an urban public high school. *Equity and Choice, 8,* 30–37.

Fine, M. A., & James-Myers, L. (1990). The development and validation of an instrument to assess an optimal Afrocentric worldview. *Journal of Black Psychology, 17*(1), 37–54.

Fischer, A. R., & Holz, K. B. (2007). Perceived discrimination and women's psychological distress: The roles of collective and personal self-esteem. *Journal of Counseling Psychology, 54,* 154–164.

Florida Department of State. (2015). Andrew Jackson. Retrieved from http://dos.myflorida .com/florida-facts/florida-history/florida-governors/andrew-jackson

Fouad, N. A., Gerstein, L. H., & Toporek, R. L. (2006). Social justice and counseling psychology in context. In R. Toporek, L. Gerstein, N. Fouad, G. Roysircar, & T. Israel (Eds.), *Handbook for social justice in counseling psychology: Leadership, vision, and action* (pp. 37–43). Thousand Oaks, CA: Sage.

Fowler, C., O'Rourke, B. O., Wadsworth, J., & Harper, D. (1992). Disability and feminism: Models for counselor exploration of personal values and beliefs. *Journal of Applied Rehabilitation Counseling, 23,* 14–19.

Fowler, J., & Keen, S. (1978). *Life maps: Conversations on the journey of faith.* Waco, TX: Word Books.

Frabutt, J., Walker, A., & MacKinnon-Lewis, C. (2002). Racial socialization messages in African American families: Descriptive analysis and family process correlates. *Journal of Early Adolescence, 22,* 200-217.

Freeman, T. (2015). What is the difference between orthodox, conservative and reform Judaism? Retrieved on July 13, 2015, from http://www.askmoses.com/en/article/175,329/What-is-the-difference-between-orthodox-conservative-and-reform-Judaism.html

Friedman, C., & Leaper, C. (2010). Sexual-minority college women's experiences with discrimination: Relations with identity and collective action. *Psychology of Women Quarterly, 34,* 152–164.

Frisbie, W. P., Cho, Y., & Hummer, R. A. (2002). Immigration and the health of Asian and Pacific Islander adults in the United States. In T. A. LaVeist (Ed.), *Race, ethnicity, health: A public health reader* (pp. 231–251). San Francisco, CA: Jossey-Bass.

Frontline. (2014). Muslims: Frequently asked questions: Common questions about Muslims and the Islamic faith which shed light on some of the misconceptions about Islam. Retrieved from http://www.pbs .org/wgbh/pages/frontline/shows/muslims/etc/faqs.html

Frost, D. M., Lehavot, K., & Meyer, I. H. (2011). *Minority stress and physical health among sexual minorities.* Poster presented at the American Psychological Association, Washington, DC. Retrieved from http://services.law.ucla.edu/williamsinstitute/pdf/Frost,%20Lehavot,%20&%20Meyer%20%28 APA%202011%29%20FINAL.pdf

Fujimura, J. H., & Rajagopalan, R. (2011). Different differences: The use of "genetic ancestry" versus race in biomedical human genetic research. *Social Studies of Science, 41*(1), 5–30.

Gandbhir, G., & Foster, B. (2015). A conversation with my black son. Retrieved on July 6, 2015, from http:// www.nytimes.com/video/opinion/100000003575589/a-conversation-with-my-black-son.html

Ganje-Fling, M. A., & McCarthy, P. (1996). Impact of childhood sexual abuse on client spiritual development: Counseling implications. *Journal of Counseling & Development, 74,* 253–262.

Gans, H. J. (1992, January 8). Fighting the biases embedded in social concepts of the poor. *Chronicle of Higher Education,* p. A56.

Garcia-Coll, C. (1997). Building connection through diversity. In J. Jordan (Ed.), *Women's growth in diversity: More writings from the Stone Center* (pp. 176–182). New York, NY: Guilford Press.

Garcia-Preto, N. (1996). Latino families: An overview. In M. McGoldrick, J. Giordano, & J. Pearce (Eds.), *Ethnicity and family therapy* (pp. 141–154). New York, NY: Guilford Press.

Garland-Thomas, R. (2002). Integrating disability, transforming feminist theory. *NWSA, 14,* 1–32.

Garnets, L., Hancock, K. A., Cochran, S. D., Goodchilds, J., & Peplau, L. A. (1991). Issues in psychotherapy with lesbians and gay men: A survey of psychologists. *American Psychologist, 46,* 964–972.

Garrett, J. T., & Garrett, M. W. (1994). The path of good medicine: Understanding and counseling Native American Indians. *Journal of Multicultural Counseling and Development, 22,* 134–144.

Garrett, J. T., & Garrett, M. W. (1996). *Medicine of the Cherokee: The way of right relationship.* Sante Fe, NM: Bear.

Garrett, J. T., & Herring, R. D. (2001). Honoring the power of relation: Counseling Native adults. *Journal of Humanistic Counseling, Education, and Development, 40,* 139–160.

Garrett, J. T., & Pichette, E. C. (2000). Red as an apple: Native American acculturation and counseling with or without reservation. *Journal of Counseling & Development, 78,* 3–13.

Garrett, M. (1998). *Walking on the wind: Cherokee teachings for harmony and balance.* Santa Fe, NM: Bear.

Garrett, M. T., Garrett, J. T., Torres-Rivera, E., Wilbur, M., & Roberts-Wilbur, J. (2005). Laughing it up: Native American humor as spiritual tradition. *Journal of Multicultural Counseling and Development, 33,* 194–204.

Garrett, M. T., Torres-Rivera, E., Brubaker, M., Portman, T. A. A., Brotherton, D., West-Olatunji, C., & Grayshield, L. (2011). Crying for a vision. The Native American sweat lodge ceremony as therapeutic intervention. *Journal of Counseling & Development, 89,* 318–325.

Gates, G. J. (2011). *How many people are lesbian, gay, bisexual, and transgender.* Los Angeles: Williams Institute, UCLA, School of Law.

Gates, G. J., & Cooke, A. M. (2010). *U.S. Census Snapshot: 2010. Same-sex couples.* Los Angeles: Williams Institute, UCLA, School of Law. Retrieved from http://williamsinstitute.law.ucla.edu/wp-content/uploads/Census2010Snapshot-US-v2.pdf

Genetic research confirms: There's only 1 human race. (2003, July 15). *St. Louis Post-Dispatch.*

George, I., & Ward, J. V. (2013). *More than kin.* Unpublished draft manuscript.

Gerber, J. S. (2009). Sephardi women in the United States. In *Jewish women: A comprehensive historical encyclopedia.* Brookline, MA: Jewish Women's Archive. Retrieved November 11, 2015, from http://jwa.org/encyclopedia/article/sephardi-women-in-united-states

Gergen, K. J. (1985). The social constructionist movement in modern psychology. *American Psychologist, 40,* 266–275.

Gerler, E. R., & Anderson, R. F. (1986). The effects of classroom guidance on children's success in school. *Journal of Counseling & Development, 65,* 78–81.

Gerschick, T. J., & Miller, A. S. (1994). Gender identities at the crossroads of masculinity and physical disability. *Masculinities, 2,* 34–55.

Gertner, D. M. (1994). Understanding and serving the needs of men. *Counseling and Human Development, 27,* 1–16.

Gibbons, F. X., Kingsbury, J. H., Weng, C., Gerrard, M., Cutrona, C., Wills, T., & Stock, M. (2014). Effects of perceived racial discrimination on health status and health behavior: A differential mediation hypothesis. *Health Psychology, 33,* 11–19.

Gibbs, J. T., & Hines, A. M. (1992). Negotiating ethnic identity: Issues for black-white biracial adolescents. In M. P. P. Root (Ed.), *Racially mixed people in America* (pp. 223–238). Newbury Park, CA: Sage.

Gibbs, J. T., Huang, L. N., & Associates. (1989). *Children of color: Psychological interventions with minority youth.* San Francisco, CA: Jossey-Bass.

Gillem, A. R., Cohn, L. R., & Throne, C. (2001). Black identity in biracial black/white people: A comparison of Jacqueline who refuses to be exclusively black and Adolphus who wishes he were. *Cultural Diversity and Ethnic Minority Psychology, 7,* 182–196.

Gillem, A. R., Lincoln, S. K., & English, K. (2007). Biracial populations. In M. G. Constantine (Ed.), *Clinical practice with people of color: A guide to becoming culturally competent* (pp. 104–124). New York, NY: Springer.

Gilligan, C. (1982). *In a different voice.* Cambridge, MA: Harvard University Press.

GLAAD media reference guide: Transgender issues. (2015). Retrieved from http://www.glaad.org/reference/transgender

Gladding, S. T. (1997). *Community and agency counseling.* Upper Saddle River, NJ: Merrill/Prentice Hall.

Gloria, A. M., & Ho, T. A. (2003). Environmental, social, and psychological experiences of Asian American undergraduates: Examining issues of academic persistence. *Journal of Counseling & Development, 81,* 93–105.

Gloria, A. M., & Peregoy, J. J. (1995). Counseling Latino alcohol and other substance users/abusers: Cultural considerations for counselors. *Journal of Substance Abuse Treatment, 13,* 1–8.

Gloria, A. M., & Peregoy, J. J. (1996). Counseling Latino alcohol and other substance users/abusers: Cultural considerations for counselors. *Journal of Substance Abuse Treatment, 13,* 119–126.

Goldberg, N. G., Bos, H. M. W., & Gartrell, N. K. (2011). Substance use by adolescents in the USA. *Journal of Health Psychology,* 1–10. doi: 10.1177/1359105311403522

Goldenberg, I., & Goldenberg, H. (1996). *Family therapy: An overview* (4th ed.). Pacific Grove, CA: Brooks/Cole.

Goldsmith, A., Hamilton, D., & Darity, W. A. (2006). Shades of discrimination: Skin tone and wages. *Skin Tone Discrimination and Economic Outcomes, 96*(2), 242–245.

Goldsmith, A., Hamilton, D., & Darity, W. A. (2007). From dark to light: Skin color and wages among African Americans. *Journal of Human Resources, 42*(4), 701–738.

Goldstein, L. (2013). Poll Shows Major Shift in Identity of U.S. Jews. *The New York Times.*http://www.nytimes.com/2013/10/01/us/poll-shows-major-shift-in-identity-of-us-jews.html?_r=0

Gone, J. (2010). Psychotherapy and traditional healing for American Indians: Exploring the prospects for therapeutic integration. *The Counseling Psychologist, 38*(2), 166–235. doi: 10.1177/0011000008330831

Gonzalez, M., Castill-Canez, I., Tarke, H., Soriano, F., Garcia, O., & Velasquez, R. J. (1997). Promoting the culturally sensitive diagnosis of Mexican Americans: Some personal insights. *Journal of Multicultural Counseling and Development, 25,* 156–161.

Good, G. E., Dell, D. M., & Mintz, L. B. (1989). Male role and gender role conflict: Relations to help seeking in men. *Journal of Counseling Psychology, 36,* 295–300.

Good, G. E., & Mintz, L. B. (1990). Gender role conflict and depression in college men: Evidence for compounded risk. *Journal of Counseling and Development, 69*(1), 17–21.

Good, G. E., Robertson, J. M., Fitzgerald, L. F., Stevens, M., & Bartels, K. M. (1996). The relation between masculine role conflict and psychological distress in male university counseling center clients. *Journal of Counseling and Development, 75*(1), 44–49.

Good, G. E., & Wood, P. K. (1995). Male gender role conflict, depression, and help seeking: Do college men face double jeopardy? *Journal of Counseling and Development, 74*(1), 70–75.

Good, J. J., & Sanchez, D. (2010). Doing gender for different reasons. Why gender conformity predicts positive and negative self-esteem. *Psychology of Women Quarterly, 34,* 203–214.

Good, M. J. D., James, C., Good, B. J., & Becker, A. E. (2003). The culture of medicine and racial, ethnic, and class disparities in health care. In Institute of Medicine (Ed.), *Unequal treatment: Confronting racial and ethnic disparities in healthcare* (pp. 594–625). Washington, DC: National Academies Press.

Gossett, T. (1963). *Race: The history of an idea in America.* New York, NY: Schocken.

Grall, T. (2013). *Custodial mothers and fathers and their child support: 2011.* Washington, DC: U.S. Department of Commerce Economics and Statistics Administration. Retrieved November 19, 2015 from http://www.census.gov/content/dam/Census/library/publications/2013/demo/p60-246.pdf

Grant, J. M., Mottet, L. A., Tanis, J., Harrison, J., Herman, J. L., & Keisling, M. (2011). *Injustice at every turn: A report of the National Transgender Discrimination Survey.* Washington, DC: National Center for Transgender Equality and National Gay and Lesbian Task Force.

Greene, B. (1994). Ethnic-minority lesbians and gay men: Mental health and treatment issues. *Journal of Consulting and Clinical Psychology, 62,* 243–251.

Greene, B., & Herek, G. M. (1994). *Lesbian and gay psychology: Theory, research, and clinical applications.* Thousand Oaks, CA: Sage.

Grieco, E. M., Acosta, Y. D., de la Cruz, G. P., Gambino, C., Gryn, T., Larsen, L. J., … & Walters , N. P. (2012). The foreign born population in the United States: 2010 (American Community Survey Reports No. ACS-19). Washington, DC: U.S. Census Bureau. Retrieved November 3, 2015, from http://www.census.gov/prod/2012pubs/acs-19.pdf

Grubb, H. J. (1992). Intelligence at the low end of the curve: Where are the racial differences? In A. Burlew, W. Banks, H. McAdoo, & D. Azibo (Eds.), *African American psychology: Theory, research, and practice* (pp. 219–228). Newbury Park, CA: Sage.

Grunland, S. A., & Mayers, M. K. (2002). Enculturation and acculturation: A reading for cultural anthropology. Retrieved from http://home.snu.edu/~hculbert/encultur.htm

Gryn, T., & Gambino, C. (2012). The foreign-born from Asia. *American Community Survey Briefs.* Retrieved June 14, 2015, from https://www.census.gov/prod/2012pubs/acsbr11-06.pdf

Gunn Allen, P. (1992). *The sacred hoop: Recovering the feminine in American Indian traditions*. Boston, MA: Beacon Press.

Gunn Allen, P. (1994). Who is your mother? Red roots of white feminism. In R. Takaki (Ed.), *From different shores: Perspectives on race and ethnicity in America* (2nd ed., pp. 192–198). New York, NY: Oxford University Press.

Gushue, G. V., & Sciarra, D. P. (1995). Culture and families: A multidimensional approach. In J. G. Ponterotto, J. M. Casas, L. A. Suzuki, & C. M. Alexander (Eds.), *Handbook of multicultural counseling* (pp. 586–606). Thousand Oaks, CA: Sage.

Hacker, A. (1992). *Two nations: Black and white, separate, hostile, unequal*. New York, NY: Ballantine Books.

Haddock, S. A., Zimmerman, T. S., & Lyness, K. P. (2003). Changing gender norms: Transitional dilemmas. In F. Walsh (Ed.), *Normal family process* (pp. 301–336). New York, NY: Guilford Press.

Hage, S. M. (2006). Profiles of women survivors: The development of agency in abusive relationships. *Journal of Counseling & Development, 84*, 83–94.

Hahm, H. C., Gonyea, J. G., Chiao, C., & Koritsanszky, L. A. (2014). Fractured identity: A framework for understanding young Asian American women's self-harm and suicidal behaviors. *Race Soc Probl, 6*, 56–68.

Hahn, H. (1988a, Winter). Can disability be beautiful? *Social Policy*, pp. 26–32.

Hahn, H. (1988b). The politics of physical differences: Disability and discrimination. *Journal of Social Issues, 44*(1), 39–47.

Haider, R. (1995). *Gender and development*. Cairo, Egypt: American University in Cairo Press.

Halbert, C. H., Bary, F. K., Weathers, B., Delmoor, E., Coyne, J., & Wileyto, O. (2007). Differences in cultural beliefs and values among African American and European American men with prostate cancer. *Cancer Control, 14*, 277–284.

Hall, C. R., Dixon, W. A., & Mauzey, E. (2004). Spirituality and religion: Implications for counselors. *Journal of Counseling & Development, 82*, 504–507.

Hall, P. C., & Pargament, K. I. (2003). Advances in the conceptualization and measurement of religion and spirituality. *American Psychologist, 58*(1), 64–74.

Hall, R. E. (1992). Bias among African-Americans regarding skin color: Implications for social work practice. *Research on Social Work Practice, 2*, 479–486.

Hall, R. E. (2001). Identity development across the lifespan: A biracial model. *The Social Sciences Journal, 38*, 119–123.

Hall, R. E. (2005). From psychology of race to issues of skin color: Western trivialization and people of African descent. *International Journal of Psychology and Psychological Therapy, 5*, 125–134.

Hall, R. E., & Livingston, J. N. (2006). Mental health practice with Arab families: The implications of spirituality vis-à-vis Islam. *American Journal of Family Therapy, 34*(2), 139–150.

Hamilton, D., Goldsmith, A., & Darity, W. A. (2009). Shedding 'light' on marriage: The influence of skin shade on marriage for black females. *Journal of Economic Behavior & Organization, 72*(1), 30–50.

Hamilton, J., Powe, B., Pollard, A. B., Lee, K., & Felton, A. M. (2007). Spirituality among African American cancer survivors: Having a personal relationship with God. *Cancer Nursing, 30*, 309–316.

Hamm, J. V. (2001). Barriers and bridges to positive cross-ethnic relations: African American and White parent socialization beliefs and practices. *Youth Society, 33*, 62–98.

Hammelman, T. L. (1993). Gay and lesbian youth: Contributing factors to serious attempts or considerations of suicide. *Journal of Gay and Lesbian Psychotherapy, 2*(1), 77–89.

Hanna, S. M., & Brown, J. H. (1995). *The practice of family therapy: Key elements across models*. Pacific Grove, CA: Brooks/Cole.

Hardiman, R. (1982). *White identity development: A process-oriented model for describing the racial consciousness of white Americans* (Unpublished doctoral dissertation). University of Massachusetts, Amherst.

Hardiman, R. (2001). Reflections on white identity development theory. In C. Wijeyesinghe & B. Jackson III (Eds.), *New perspectives on racial identity development: A theoretical and practical anthology* (pp. 108–128). New York: New York University Press.

Hare-Mustin, R. T. (1988). Family change and gender differences: Implications for theory and practice. *Family Relations, 37*, 36–41.

Harper, F. E. (1854). The slave auction. *National Endowment for the Arts & Poetry Foundation*. Retrieved January 17, 2008, from www.poetryoutloud.org/poems

Harris, D. R., & Sims, J. J. (2002). Who is multiracial? Assessing the complexity of lived race. *American Sociological Review, 67*, 614–627.

Harris, K. (1995). Collected quotes from Albert Einstein. Retrieved September 1, 2007, from http://rescomp .stanford.edu/~cheshire/EinsteinQuotes.html

Harrison, P. M., & Beck, A. J. (2005). Prisoners in 2004. *Bureau of Justice Statistics Bulletin*. Washington, DC: U.S. Department of Justice, Office of Justice Programs.

Harrison, P. M., & Beck, A. J. (2006, November). Prisoners in 2005. *Bureau of Justice Statistics Bulletin*. Washington, DC: U.S. Department of Justice, Office of Justice Programs.

Hartung, P. J. (1996). Transforming counseling courses: From monocultural to multicultural. *Counseling Education and Supervision, 36*(1), 6–13.

Harvey, R. D., LaBeach, N., Pridgen, E., & Gocial, T. M. (2005). The intragroup stigmatization of skin tone among black Americans. *Journal of Black Psychology, 31*, 237–253.

Hays, D. G., Dean, J. K., & Chang, C. Y. (2007). Addressing privilege and oppression in counselor training and practice: A qualitative analysis. *Journal of Counseling & Development, 85*, 317–324.

Hays, P. A. (1996). Addressing the complexities of culture and gender in counseling. *Journal of Counseling and Development, 74*, 332–338.

Healey, J. F. (1997). *Race, ethnicity, and gender in the United States: Inequality, group conflict, and power*. Thousand Oaks, CA: Pine Forge Press.

Heinrich, R. K., Corbine, J. L., & Thomas, K. R. (1990). Counseling Native Americans. *Journal of Counseling and Development, 69*, 128–133.

Helms, J. E. (1984). Toward a theoretical explanation of the effects of race on counseling: A Black and White model. *Counseling Psychologist, 12*, 153–165.

Helms, J. E. (1990). *Black and white racial identity: Theory, research, and practice*. New York, NY: Greenwood Press.

Helms, J. E. (1995). An update of white and people of color racial identity model. In J. G. Ponterotto, J. M. Casas, L. A. Suzuki, & C. M. Alexander (Eds.), *Handbook of multicultural counseling* (pp. 181–198). Thousand Oaks, CA: Sage.

Helms, J. E. (2003). A pragmatic view of social justice. *The Counseling Psychologist, 31*, 305–313.

Helms, J. E. (2007). Some better practices for measuring ethnic and racial identity constructs. *Journal of Counseling Psychology, 54*, 235–246.

Helms, J. E., & Parham, T. A. (1984). *Racial identity attitude scale* (Unpublished manuscript).

Henderson, L. I., Metzger, L. L. H., Nadkarni, L. I., & Cornish, J. A. E. (2010). An overview of multi-cultural counseling competencies. In J. A. E. Cornish, B. A. Schreier, L. I. Nadkarni, L. H. Metzger, E. R. Rodolfa (Eds.), *Handbook of multicultural counseling competencies* (pp. 1–21). Hoboken, NJ: Wiley & Sons.

Herman, M. (2004). Forced to choose: Some determinants of racial identification in multiracial adolescents. *Child Development, 75*, 740–748.

Hermann, M. A., & Herlihy, B. R. (2006). Legal and ethical implications of refusing to counsel homosexual clients. *Journal of Counseling & Development, 84*, 414–418.

Hernandez, B. (2005). A voice in the chorus: Perspectives of young men of color on their disabilities, identities, and peer-mentors. *Disability & Society, 20*, 117–133.

Hernandez, M. (1996). Central American families. In M. McGoldrick, J. Giordano, & J. Pearce (Eds.), *Ethnicity and family therapy* (pp. 214–224). New York, NY: Guilford Press.

Herring, R. D. (1992). Understanding Native American values: Process and content concerns for counselors. *Counseling and Values, 34*, 134–137.

Herrnstein, R. J., & Murray, C. (1994). *The bell curve: Intelligence and class structure in American life*. New York, NY: Free Press.

Highfield, R. (2002, December 2). DNA survey finds all humans are 99.9pc the same. *The Telegraph*. Retrieved from http://www.telegraph.co.uk/news/worldnews/northamerica/usa/1416706/DNA-survey-finds-all-humans-are-99.9pc-the-same.html

Hill, V. R., Weglicki, L. S., Thomas, T., & Hammad, A. (2006). Predictors of Arab American adolescent tobacco use. *Merrill-Palmer Quarterly, 52*(2), 327–342.

Hines, P. M., & Boyd-Franklin, N. (1996). African American families. In M. McGoldrick, J. Giordano, & J. K. Pearce (Eds.), *Ethnicity and family therapy* (pp. 66–84). New York, NY: Guilford Press.

Hirata, L. C. (1979). Free, indentured, enslaved: Chinese prostitutes in nineteenth-century America. *Signs, Women in Latin America, 5*(1), 3–29.

History. (2015a). Confederate States of America. Retrieved on July 13, 2015, from http://www.history.com/topics/american-civil-war/confederate-states-of-america

History. (2015b). The Enlightenment. Retrieved on July 28, 2015, from http://www.history.com/topics/enlightenment

History. (2015c). *Kristallnacht.* Retrieved on July 21, 2015, from http://www.history.com/topics/kristallnacht

History. (2015d). The 13 colonies. Retrieved on July 11, 2015, from http://www.history.com/topics/thirteen-colonies

History.net. (2015). *The Civil War.* Retrieved August 15, 2015, from http://history.net/civil war

Hixson, L., Hepler, B. B., & Kim, M. O. (2011). The white population: 2010. *2010 Census Briefs.* Retrieved June 3, 2015, from https://www.census.gov/prod/cen2010/briefs/c2010br-05.pdf

Hixson, L., Hepler, B. B., & Kim, M. O. (2012). The Native Hawaiian and other Pacific islander population. *2010 Census Briefs.* U.S. Department of Commerce. Economics and Statistics Administration. U.S. Census Bureau. Retrieved June 12, 2015, from http://www.census.gov/prod/cen2010/briefs/c2010br-12.pdf

Ho, A. K., Sidanius, J., Levin, D. T., & Banaji, M. R. (2011). Evidence for hypodescent and racial hierarchy in the categorization and perception of biracial individuals. *Journal of Personality & Social Psychology, 100,* 492–506.

Hochschild, A. R. (2003). *The second shift.* New York, NY: Penguin Books.

Hochschild, J. L., & Powell, B. M. (2008). Racial reorganization and the United States Census 1850-1930: Mulattoes, half-breeds, mixed parentage, Hindoos, and the Mexican race. *Studies in American Political Development, 22(1),* 59–96. Retrieved November 3, 2015, from http://scholar.harvard.edu/jlhochschild/publications/racial-reorganization-and-united-states-census-1850-1930-mulattoes-half-br#_ednref140

Hochschild, J. L., & Weaver, V. (2007). The skin color paradox and the American racial order. *Social Forces, 86,* 643–670.

Hodges, G. (2015, January). Tracking the first Americans. *National Geographic, 227,* 124–137.

Hoeffel, E. M., Rastogi, S., Kim, M. O., & Shahid, H. (2012). The Asian population: 2010. *2010 Census Briefs.* Retrieved June 10, 2015, from https://www.census.gov/prod/cen2010/briefs/c2010br-11.pdf

Hoffman, M. A., Phillips, E. L., Noumair, D. A., Shullman, S., Geisler, C., Gray, J., … Ziegler, D. (2005). Toward a feminist and multicultural model of consultation and advocacy. *Journal of Multicultural Counseling & Development, 34,* 116–128.

Hoffman, R. M. (2001). The measurement of masculinity and femininity: Historical perspective and implications for counseling. *Journal of Counseling & Development, 79,* 472–485.

Hoffman, R. M. (2004). Conceptualizing heterosexual identity development: Issues and challenges. *Journal of Counseling & Development, 82,* 375–380.

Holcomb-McCoy, C. C. (2000). Multicultural counseling competencies: An exploratory factor analysis. *Journal of Multicultural Counseling and Development, 28,* 83–97.

Hong, G. L., & Domokos-Cheng Ham, M. (2001). *Psychotherapy and counseling with Asian American clients: A practical guide.* Thousand Oaks, CA: Sage.

hooks, b. (1993). *Sisters of the yam: Black women and self-recovery.* Boston, MA: South End Press.

Hoopes, D. S. (1979). Intercultural communication concepts: Psychology of intercultural experience. In M. D. Psych (Ed.), *Multicultural education: A cross-cultural training approach.* LaGrange Park, IL: Intercultural Network.

Horse, P. G. (2001). Reflections on American Indian identity. In C. Wijeyesinghe & B. Jackson III (Eds.), *New perspectives on racial identity development: A theoretical and practical anthology* (pp. 91–197). New York: New York University Press.

Horst, E. A. (1995). Reexamining gender issues in Erikson's stages of identity. *Journal of Counseling and Development, 73,* 271–278.

Howden, L., & Meyer, J. (2011, May). Age and sex composition: 2010. *2010 Census Briefs*. Retrieved November 2011, from http://www.census.gov/prod/cen2010/briefs/c2010br-03.pdf

Hoxie, F. E. (Ed.). (1996). *Encyclopedia of North American Indians: Native American history, culture, and life from paleo-Indians to the present*. Boston, MA: Houghton Mifflin.

Hsu, F. L. K. (1953). *American and Chinese: Two ways of life*. New York, NY: Abeland-Schuman.

Huber, L. P., & Cueva, B. M. (2012). Chicana/Latina testimonies on effects and responses to microaggressions. *Equity & Excellence in Education, 45*(3), 392–410.

Hud-Aleem, R., Countryman, J., & Gillig, P. M. (2008). Biracial identity development and recommendations in therapy. *Psychiatry (Edgmont), 5*, 37–44.

Hughes, D., Rodriguez, J., Smith, E. P., Johnson, D. J., Stevenson, H. C., & Spicer, P. (2006). Parents' ethnic–racial socialization practices: A review of research and directions for future study. *Developmental Psychology, 42*, 747–770.

Hughes, E. C. (1945). Dilemmas and contradictions of status. *American Journal of Sociology, 50*, 353–357.

Humes, K., Jones, N., & Ramirez, R. (2011). Overview of race and Hispanic origin: 2010. *2010 Census Briefs*. Retrieved from www.census.gov/prod/cen2010/briefs/c2010br-02.pdf

Hunt, B. (1993). What counselors need to know about counseling gay men and lesbians. *Counseling and Human Development, 26*(1), 1–12.

Hunt, B., Matthews, C., Milsom, A., & Lammel, J. A. (2006). Lesbians with physical disabilities: A qualitative study of their experiences with counseling. *Journal of Counseling & Development, 84*, 163–173.

Hutchinson, M. G. (1982). Transforming body image: Your body—friend or foe? In *Current feminist issues in psychotherapy* (pp. 59–67). New York, NY: Haworth Press.

Icard, L. (1986). Black gay men and conflicting social identities: Sexual orientation versus racial identity. In J. Gripton & M. Valentich (Eds.), Social work practice in sexual problems [Special issue]. *Journal of Social Work and Human Sexuality, 4*(1–2), 83–93.

Ignatiev, N. (1995). *How the Irish became white*. London, England: Routledge.

Indian Affairs. (2014). 2013 American Indian population and labor force report. Retrieved June 1, 2015, from http://www.bia.gov/cs/groups/public/documents/text/idc1-024782.pdf

Infoplease. (2015). American Indians by number. Retrieved from http://www.infoplease.com/spot/aihm-census1.html

Ingersoll, R. E. (1995). Spirituality, religion, and counseling: Dimensions and relationship. In M. Burke & J. Mirant (Eds.), *Counseling: The spiritual dimension* (pp. 5–18). Thousand Oaks, CA: Sage.

Ingrassia, M. (1993, August 30). Endangered family. *Newsweek,* pp. 17–29.

Inman, A. G., & Tummala-Narra, P. (2010). Clinical competencies in working with immigrant communities. In J. A. E. Cornish, B. A. Schreier, L. I. Nadkarni, L. H. Metzger, E. R. Rodolfa (Eds.), *Handbook of multicultural counseling competencies* (pp. 117–152). Hoboken, NJ: Wiley & Sons.

Institute of Medicine. (Ed.). (2003). *Unequal treatment: Confronting racial and ethnic disparities in healthcare*. Washington, DC: National Academies Press.

Intersexual Society of North America. (2015). Retrieved from intersex.org

Israel, T. (2006). Marginalized communities in the United States: Oppression, social justice, and the role of counseling psychologists. In R. L. Toporek, L. H. Gerstein, N. A. Fouad, G. Roysircar, & T. Israel (Eds.), *Handbook for social justice in counseling psychology* (pp. 149–154). Thousand Oaks, CA: Sage.

Ivey, A. E., & Collins, N. M. (2003). Social justice: A long-term challenge for counseling psychology. *The Counseling Psychologist, 31*, 290–298.

Ivey, A. E., Ivey, M. B., & Simek-Morgan, L. (1997). *Counseling and psychotherapy: A multicultural perspective* (4th ed.). Boston, MA: Allyn & Bacon.

Jackson, A. (1908). Second annual message. In J. D. Richardson (Ed.), *A compilation of the messages and papers of the presidents 1789–1902* (Vol. 2). Retrieved January 10, 2003, from http://www.pbs.org/wgbh/aia/part4/4h3437t.html

Jackson, L. A., Sullivan, L. A., & Rostker, R. (1988). Gender, gender role, and body image. *Sex Roles, 19*, 429–443.

Jackson, V. (2005). Robbing Peter to pay Paul: Reflections on feminist therapy with low-wage earning women. In M. Mirkin, J. Suyemoto, & B. Okun (Eds.), *Psychotherapy with women: Exploring diverse contexts and identities* (pp. 237–246). New York, NY: Guilford Press.

Jacobson, M. F. (1998). *Whiteness of a different color: European immigrants and the alchemy of race*. Cambridge, MA: Harvard University Press.

Jewish Genetic Disease Consortium. (2015). Retrieved on July 3, 2015, from http://www.jewishgeneticdiseases .org/jewish-genetic-diseases

Jews in Africa. (2015). Retrieved August 2, 2015, from *Am I Jewish: Answers and Questions*: http://www .amijewish.info/w/jews-in-africa

Joe, J. R. (2003). The rationing of healthcare and health disparity for the American Indians/Alaskan Natives. In Institute of Medicine (Ed.), *Unequal treatment: Confronting racial and ethnic disparities in healthcare*. Washington, DC: National Academies Press.

John, R. (1988). The Native American family. In C. H. Mindel, R. W. Habenstein, & R. Wright (Eds.), *Ethnic families in America: Patterns and variations* (3rd ed., pp. 325–366). New York, NY: Elsevier.

Johnson, T., & Sergie, A. (2014). *Islam: Governing under Sharia*. Retrieved November 8, 2014, from Council on Foreign Relations: http://www.cfr.org/religion/islam-governing-under-sharia/p8034

Johnson, T., & Vriens, L. (2011). *Islam: Governing under Sharia*. Retrieved January 11, 2012, from Council on Foreign Relations: http://www.cfr.org/religion/islam-governing-under-sharia/p8034

Jones, H. L., Cross, W. E., & DeFour, D. C. (2007). Race-related stress, racial identity attitudes, and mental health among Black women. *Journal of Black Psychology, 33*, 208–231.

Jones, J. (1985). *Labor of love, labor of sorrow*. New York, NY: Vintage Books.

Jones, M. L., & Galliher, R. V. (2014). Daily racial microaggressions and ethnic identification among Native American young adults. *Cultural Diversity and Ethnic Minority Psychology, 21*(1), 1–9. doi: 10.1037/ a0037537

Jones, N. A. (2005). We the people of more than one race in the United States. *Census 2000 Special Reports*. Washington, DC: U.S. Department of Commerce, U.S. Census Bureau. Retrieved from https://www .census.gov/prod/2005pubs/censr-22.pdf

Jones, N. A., & Bullock, J. (2012). The two or more races population: 2010. *2010 Census Briefs*. Retrieved from https://www.census.gov/prod/cen2010/briefs/c2010br-13.pdf

Jones, N. A., & Symens Smith, A. (2001). The two or more races population: 2000. *Census 2000 Brief*. Washington, DC: U.S. Department of Commerce, U.S. Census Bureau. Retrieved from https://www.census .gov/prod/2001pubs/c2kbr01-6.pdf

Jordan, J. (1997a). Relational development: Therapeutic implications of empathy and shame. In J. Jordan (Ed.), *Women's growth in diversity: More writings from the Stone Center* (pp. 136–161). New York: Guilford Press.

Jordan, J. (1997b). A relational perspective for understanding women's development. In J. Jordan (Ed.), *Women's growth in diversity: More writings from the Stone Center* (pp. 9–24). New York, NY: Guilford Press.

Jordan, J. (1997c). Clarity in connection, empathic knowing, desire, and sexuality. In J. Jordan (Ed.), *Women's growth in diversity: More writings from the Stone Center* (pp. 50–73). New York, NY: Guilford Press.

Jordan, J., & Romney, P. (2005). Women in the workplace: An application of relational-cultural theory. In M. Mirkin, J. Suyemoto, & B. Okun (Eds.), *Psychotherapy with women: Exploring diverse contexts and identities* (pp. 198–214). New York: Guilford Press.

Jose de Acosta (1540-1600): Pioneer of the geophysical sciences. (n.d.). Retrieved from http://www.faculty .fairfield.edu/jmac/sj/scientists/acosta.htm

Jourdan, A. (2006). The impact of the family environment on the ethnic identity development of multiethnic college students. *Journal of Counseling & Development, 84*, 328–340.

Kagitcibasi, C. (1997). Individualism and collectivism. In J. Berry, M. Segall, & C. Kagitcibasi (Eds.), *Cross-cultural psychology: Social and behavioral applications* (Vol. 3, pp. 1–49). Boston: Allyn & Bacon.

Kaiser, J. (2011). NIH uncovers racial disparity in grant awards. Retrieved November 13, 2015, from *Center for Genetics and Science*: http://www.geneticsandsociety.org/article.php?id=5823

Kaplan, A. G. (1987). Reflections on gender and psychotherapy. In M. Braude (Ed.), *Women and therapy* (Vol. 6, pp. 11–24). New York, NY: Haworth Press.

Karenga, M. (1980). *Kawaida theory*. Los Angeles, CA: Kawaida.

Karoub, J. (2015). Census Bureau may count Arab-Americans for the first time. *2020 PBS News-hour.* Retrieved from http://www.pbs.org/newshour/rundown/census-bureau-considering-new-category-arab-americans-2020-count

Kashubeck, S., Walsh, B., & Crowl, A. (1994). College atmosphere and eating disorders. *Journal of Counseling and Development, 72,* 640–645.

Kegan, R. (1982). *The evolving self.* Cambridge, MA: Harvard University Press.

Kena, G., Musu-Gillette, L., Robinson, J., Wang, X., Rathbun, A., Zhang, J., … Dunlop Velez, E. (2015). The condition of education 2015 (NCES No. 2015-144). Washington, DC: U.S. Department of Education, National Center for Education Statistics. Retrieved June 1, 2015, from http://nces.ed.gov/pubsearch

Kenway, J. (1988). *High-status private schooling in Australia and the production of an educational hegemony* (Unpublished doctoral dissertation). Murdoch University, Western Australia.

Kerwin, C., Ponterotto, J. G., Jackson, B. L., & Harris, A. (1993). Racial identity in biracial children: A qualitative investigation. *Journal of Counseling Psychology, 40,* 221–231.

Khazzoom, L. (2015). Jews of the Middle East. Retrieved November 11, 2015, from *MyJewishLearning:* http://www.myjewishlearning.com/article/jews-of-the-middle-east

Kich, G. K. (1992). The developmental process of asserting a biracial, bicultural identity. In M. P. P. Root (Ed.), *Racially mixed people in America* (pp. 304–317). Newbury Park, CA: Sage.

Kim, B. (2011). Client motivation and multicultural counseling. *The Counseling Psychologist, 39,* 267–275. doi: 10.1177/0011000010375310

Kim, B. S. K. (2007). Asian American populations. In M. Constantine (Ed.), *Clinical practice with people of color* (pp. 15–32). New York, NY: Teachers College Press.

Kim, B. S. K., Li, L. C., & Liang, C. T. H. (2002). Effects of Asian American client adherence to Asian cultural values, session goal, and counselor emphasis of client expression on career counseling process. *Journal of Counseling Psychology, 49,* 342–354.

Kim, B. S. K., & Lyons, H. Z. (2003). Experiential activities and multicultural counseling competence training. *Journal of Counseling & Development, 81,* 400–408.

Kim, J. (2001). Asian American identity development theory. In C. Wijeyesinghe & B. Jackson III (Eds.), *New perspectives on racial identity development: A theoretical and practical anthology* (pp. 67–90). New York: New York University Press.

Kimmel, M. S. (2006). Masculinity as homophobia: Fear, shame, and silence in the construction of gender identity. In T. E. Orr (Ed.), *The social construction of difference and inequality: Race, class, gender, and sexuality* (pp.133–150). Boston, MA: McGraw-Hill.

King, N. (1988). Teaching about lesbians and gays in the psychology curriculum. In P. A. Bronstein & K. Quina (Eds.), *Teaching a psychology of people: Resources for gender and sociocultural awareness* (pp. 168–174). Washington, DC: American Psychological Association.

Kitano, H. H. L. (1988). The Japanese American family. In C. H. Mindel, R. W. Habenstein, & R. Wright (Eds.), *Ethnic families in America: Patterns and variations* (3rd ed., pp. 258–275). New York, NY: Elsevier.

Kitzinger, C. (1999). Intersexuality: Deconstructing the sex/gender binary. *Feminism & Psychology* (pp. 493–498). New York, NY: Guilford Press.

Klages, M. (2005). Queer theory definition & literary example. Retrieved November 19, 2015, from http://www.sjsu.edu/faculty/harris/Eng101_QueerDef.pdf

Kliman, J. (2005). Many differences, many voices: Toward social justice in family therapy. In M. Pravder, K. Suyemoto, & B. Okun (Eds.), *Psychotherapy with women: Exploring diverse contexts and identities* (pp. 42–63). New York, NY: Guilford Press.

Kluckhohn, F. R., & Strodtbeck, F. L. (1961). *Variations in value orientations.* Evanston, IL: Row, Peterson.

Knott, L. (2014). Ambiguous genitalia. Retrieved from http://www.patient.co.uk/doctor/ambiguous-genitalia

Kocarek, C. E., Talbot, D. M., Batka, J. C., & Anderson, M. A. (2001). Reliability and validity of three measures of multicultural competence. *Journal of Counseling & Development, 79,* 486–496.

Kochhar, R. (2007). *1995–2005: Foreign-born Latinos make progress on wages.* Washington, DC: Pew Hispanic Center.

Kogan, M. (2000, July/August). Course exposes hidden racial prejudices: Students confront their hidden biases to better prepare for psychology practice. *Monitor on Psychology, 31*(7). Retrieved September 1, 2007, from http://www.apa.org/monitor/julaug00/prejudice.aspx

Kreider, R. (2003). Adopted children and stepchildren 2000. *Census 2000 Special Reports.* Washington, DC: U.S. Department of Commerce, Economics and Statistics Administration. Retrieved October 20, 2007, from www.census.gov/prod/2003pubs/censr-6.pdf

Kreider, R. M., & Ellis, R. (2011). Number, timing, and duration of marriages and divorces: 2009 household economic studies (Current Population Reports No. P70-125). Washington, DC: U.S. Census Bureau. Retrieved November 4, 2015, from http://www.census.gov/prod/2011pubs/p70-125.pdf

Krogstad, J. (2014). Census Bureau explores new Middle East/North Africa ethnic category. *Factank: News in the numbers.* Retrieved June 10, 2015, from Pew Research Center: http://www.pewresearch.org/fact-tank/2014/03/24/census-bureau-explores-new-middle-eastnorth-africa-ethnic-category

Ladany, N., Brittan-Powell, C. S., & Pannu, R. K. (1997). The influence of supervisory racial identity interaction and racial matching on the Supervisory Working Alliance and Supervisee Multicultural Competence. *Counselor Education and Supervision, 36,* 284–304.

Ladany, N., Mori, Y., & Mehr, K. E. (2013). Effective and ineffective supervision. *The Counseling Psychologist, 41,* 28–47.

Lago, L. (Producer), & Solás, H. (Director). (2001). *Honey for Ochun* [Motion picture]. Cuba: Maverick – Domestic Video Distributor.

Laird, J. (2003). Lesbian and gay families. In F. Walsh (Ed.), *Normal family processes* (pp. 176–209). New York, NY: Guilford Press.

Lakoff, R. T., & Scherr, R. L. (1984). *Face value: Politics of beauty.* Boston: Routledge, Kegan, & Paul.

Lamb, M. E. (1982). Parental behavior and child development in nontraditional families. In M. E. Lamb (Ed.), *Nontraditional families: Parenting and child development.* Hillsdale, NJ: Erlbaum.

Landry, B. (2007). *Race, gender, and class: Theory and methods of analysis.* Upper Saddle River, NJ: Pearson/Prentice Hall.

Lane, J. M., & Addis, M. E. (2005). Male gender role conflict and patterns of help seeking in Costa Rica and the United States. *Psychology of Men & Masculinity, 6,* 155–168.

Lao Tsu. (1972). *Tao Te Ching* (G. F. Feng & J. English, Trans.). New York: Vintage.

Lareau, A. (1997). Social-class differences in family-school relationships: The importance of cultural capital. In A. Halsey, H. Lauder, P. Brown, & A. Wells (Eds.), *Education: Culture, economy, society* (pp. 703–717). Oxford, UK: Oxford University Press.

Larsen, L. J., & Walters, N. P. (2013). Married-couple households by nativity status: 2011 (American Community Survey Briefs No. ACSBR/11-16). Washington, DC: U.S. Census Bureau. Retrieved November 18, 2015, from http://www.census.gov/library/publications/2013/acs/acsbr11-16.html

Latin America. (n.d.). *The odyssey: World trek for service and education.* Retrieved from http://www.worldtrek.org/odyssey/latinamerica

LaVeist, T. A. (2002). Why we should study race, ethnicity, and health. In T. A. LaVeist (Ed.), *Race, ethnicity, health: A public health reader* (pp. 1–7). San Francisco, CA: Jossey-Bass.

Le, C. N. (2007). Interracial dating & marriage. *Asian-nation: The landscape of Asian America.* Retrieved October 21, 2007, from http://www.asian-nation.org/interracial.shtml

Le, C. N. (2008). Adopted Asian Americans. *Asian-Nation: The landscape of Asian America.* Retrieved January 27, 2008, from http://www.asian-nation.org/adopted.shtml

Leach, M. M., Behrens, J. T., & LaFleur, N. K. (2002). White racial identity and white racial consciousness: Similarities, differences, and recommendations. *Journal of Multicultural Counseling and Development, 30,* 66–80.

Leaper, C., & Brown, C. S. (2008). Perceived experiences with sexism among adolescent girls. *Child Development, 79 (3),* 685–704.

Lee, C. (2001). Defining and responding to racial and ethnic diversity. In D. Locke, J. Myers, & E. Herr (Eds.), *Handbook of counseling* (pp. 581–588). Thousand Oaks, CA: Sage.

Lee, D., & Ahn, S. (2011). Racial discrimination and Asian mental health: A meta analysis. *The Counseling Psychologist, 39*(3), 463–489. doi: 10.1177/0011000010381791

Lee, J., & Beal, F. D. (2007). Reinventing the color line: Immigration and America's new racial/ethnic divide. *Social Forces, 86,* 561–586.

Lee, R. M. (2003). Do ethnic identity and other-group orientation protect against discrimination for Asian Americans? *Journal of Counseling Psychology, 50,* 131–141.

Lemkau, J. P., & Landau, C. (1986). The "selfless syndrome": Assessment and treatment considerations. *Psychotherapy, 23,* 227–233.

Leong, F. T. L., Wagner, N. S., & Kim, H. H. (1995). Group counseling expectations among Asian American students: The role of culture-specific factors. *Journal of Counseling Psychology, 42,* 217–222.

Lerner, R. M., & Lerner, J. L. (1977). Effects of age, sex, and physical attractiveness on child-peer relations, academic performance, and elementary school adjustment. *Developmental Psychology, 13,* 585–590.

Lesiak, C., & Jones, M. (1991). *In the white man's image* (Film). United States, The American Experience Series.

Lester, R., & Petrie, T. A. (1998). Prevalence of disordered eating behaviors and bulimia nervosa in a sample of Mexican American female college students. *Journal of Multicultural Counseling and Development, 26,* 157–165.

Levitt, H., Butler, M., & Travis, H. (2006). What clients find helpful in psychotherapy: Developing prinici-ples for facilitating moment-to-moment change. *Journal of Counseling Psychology, 53,* 314–324.

Library of Congress. (2015). Indian Removal Act. *Primary documents in American history.* Retrieved from http://loc.gov/rr/program/bib/ourdocs/Indian.html

Lin, J. C. H. (1994). How long do Chinese Americans stay in psychotherapy? *Journal of Counseling Psychology, 41,* 288–291.

Lipsitz, G. (2005). The possessive investment in whiteness: Racialized social democracy and the "white problem in American studies." In T. Ore (Ed.), *The social construction of difference and inequality: Race, class, gender and sexuality* (pp. 402–413). Boston, MA: McGraw-Hill.

Liu, W. M., & Arguello, J. L. (2006). Using social class and classism in counseling. *Counseling and Human Development, 39,* 1–9.

Liu, W. M., Corkery, J., & Thome, J. (2010). Developing competency in social class and classism in counseling and psychotherapy. In J. A. E. Cornish, B. A. Schreier, L. I. Nadkarni, L. H. Metzger, & E. R. Rodolfa (Eds.), *Handbook of multicultural counseling competencies* (pp. 350–378*).* Hoboken, NJ: Wiley & Sons.

Liu, W. M., Saba, R. A., Soleck, G., Hopps, J., Dunston, K., & Pickett, T. (2004). Using social class in counseling psychology research. *Journal of Counseling Psychology, 51,* 3–18.

Livneh, H., & Sherwood, A. (1991). Application of personality theories and counseling strategies to clients with physical disabilities. *Journal of Counseling and Development, 69,* 525–538.

Loewen, J. W. (1995). *Lies my teacher told me: Everything your American history textbook got wrong.* New York, NY: Simon & Schuster.

Loiacano, D. K. (1989). Gay identity issues among black Americans: Racism, homophobia, and the need for validation. *Journal of Counseling and Development, 68,* 21–25.

Lorde, A. (1994). Living with cancer. In E. C. White (Ed.), *The black women's health book: Speaking for our-selves* (pp. 27–37). Seattle, WA: Seal.

Lott, B. (1994). *Women's lives: Themes and variations in gender learning* (2nd ed.). Pacific Grove, CA: Brooks/Cole.

Loup, R. E. (2013). Understanding movements in Judaism. *Apples & Honey.* Retrieved on July 27, 2015, from: http://www.mazeltot.org/understanding-movements-judaism

Macartney, S., Bishaw, A., & Fontenot , K. (2013). Poverty Rates for Selected Detailed Race and Hispanic Groups by State and Place: 2007–2011. American Community Survey Briefs. United States Census Bureau. Washington, DC: U.S. Department of Commerce, Current Population Reports. Retrieved September 29, 2015 from http://www.census.gov/prod/2013pubs/acsbr11-17.pdf

Mackun, P., & Wilson, S. (2011, March). *Population Distribution and Change: 2000 to 2010.* U.S. Department of Commerce Economics and Statistics Administration. Retrieved from www.census.gov/prod/cen2010/briefs/c2010br-01.pdf

Maffly-Kipp, L. (2000). *African-American religion in the nineteenth century.* University of North Carolina at Chapel Hill. Retrieved January 15, 2004, from http://www.nhc.rtp.nc.us/tserve/nineteen/nkeyinfo/nafrican.htm

Mahalik, J. R., Lagan, H. D., & Morrison, J. A. (2006). Health behaviors and masculinity in Kenyan and U.S. male college students. *Psychology of Men & Masculinity, 7,* 191–202.

Maranzani, B. (2012). Eight things you didn't know about Catherine the Great. *History in the Headlines.* Retrieved July 27, 2015, from http://www.history.com/news/8-things-you-didnt-know-about-catherine-the-great

Marini, I. (2001). Cross-cultural counseling issues of males who sustain a disability. *Journal of Applied Rehabilitation Counseling, 32,* 36–44.

Martin, J. K. (2007). African American populations. In M. G. Constantine (Ed.), *Clinical practice with people of color: A guide to becoming culturally competent* (pp. 33–45). New York, NY: Springer.

Martin, M. K., & Voorhies, B. (1975). *Female of the species.* New York, NY: Teachers College Press.

Mass, A. I. (1992). Interracial Japanese Americans: The best of both worlds or the end of the Japanese American community. In M. P. P. Root (Ed.), *Racially mixed people in America* (pp. 265–279). Newbury Park, CA: Sage.

Masters, J., & Sergie, M. A. (2014). *The Arab League.* Retrieved May 5, 2015, from Council on Foreign Relations: http://www.cfr.org/middle-east-and-north-africa/arab-league/p25967

Mastria, M. R. (2002). Ethnicity and eating disorders. *Psychoanalysis and Psychotherapy, 19*(1), 59–77.

McBride, M. (1990). Autonomy and the struggle for female identity: Implications for counseling women. *Journal of Counseling and Development, 69*, 22–26.

McCarthy, J. (2005). Individualism and collectivism: What do they have to do with counseling? *Journal of Multicultural Counseling and Development, 33*, 108–117.

McCarthy, J., & Holliday, E. L. (2004). Help-seeking and counseling within a traditional male gender role: An examination from a multicultural perspective. *Journal of Counseling & Development, 82*, 25–30.

McDonald, A. L. (1990). Living with our deepest differences. *Journal of Law and Religion, 8*, 237–239.

McDonald, A. (2015). How the Irish became white. Retrieved June 10, 2015, from http://www.pitt.edu/~hirtle/uujec/white.html

McFadden, J. (1993). *Transcultural counseling: Bilateral and international perspectives.* Alexandria, VA: American Counseling Association.

McIntosh, P. (1988). *White privilege and male privilege: A personal account of coming to see correspondences through work in women's studies* (Working Paper No. 189). Wellesley, MA: Wellesley College Center for Research on Women.

McIntosh, P. (1989, July/August). White privilege: Unpacking the invisible knapsack. *Peace and Freedom,* pp. 10–12.

McIntosh, P. (1990). *Interactive phases of curricular and personal revision with regard to race* (Working Paper No. 219). Wellesley, MA: Wellesley College Center for Research on Women.

McKelley, R. A., & Rochlen, A. B. (2007). The practice of coaching: Exploring alternatives to therapy for counseling-resistant men. *Psychology of Men & Masculinity, 8*(1), 53–65.

McLoyd, V. C., & Wilson, L. (1992). Telling them like it is: The role of economic and environmental factors in single mothers' discussions with their children. *American Journal of Community Psychology, 20*, 419–444.

McWhirter, E. H. (1991). Empowerment in counseling. *Journal of Counseling and Development, 69*, 222–227.

Mencher, J. (1997). Structural possibilities and constraints of mutuality in psychotherapy. In J. Jordan (Ed.), *Women's growth in diversity: More writings from the Stone Center* (pp. 110–119). New York, NY: Guilford Press.

Mercado, M. M. (2000). The invisible family: Counseling Asian American substance abusers and their families. *The Family Journal: Counseling and Therapy for Couples and Families, 8*, 267–272.

Metzger, L. L. H., Nadkarni, L. I., & Cornish, J. A. E. (2010). In J. A. E. Cornish, B. A. Schreier, L. I. Nadkarni, L. H. Metzger, & E. R. Rodolfa (Eds.), *Handbook of multicultural counseling competencies* (pp. 1–21). NJ: Wiley & Sons.

Middle East Institute. (2004). Retrieved September 10, 2007, from www.mideast.org

Miller, W. R., & Thoresen, C. E. (2003). Spirituality, religion, and health: An emerging research field. *American Psychologist, 58*(1), 24–35.

Min, P. G. (1988). The Korean American family. In C. H. Mindel, R. W. Habenstein, & R. Wright (Eds.), *Ethnic families in America: Patterns and variations* (3rd ed., pp. 199–229). New York, NY: Elsevier.

Mindel, C. H., Habenstein, R. W., & Wright, R. (1988). *Ethnic families in America: Patterns and variations.* New York: Elsevier.

Mintz, L. B., & O'Neil, J. M. (1990). Gender roles, sex, and the process of psychotherapy: Many questions and few answers. *Journal of Counseling and Development, 68*, 381–387.

Minuchin, S. (1974). *Families and family therapy.* Cambridge, MA: Harvard University Press.

Minuchin, S. (1984). *Family kaleidoscope.* Cambridge, MA: Harvard University Press.

Minuchin, S. (1991). The seductions of constructivism. *The Family Networker 15*(5), 47–50.

Mio, J. S. (2005). Academic mental health training settings and the multicultural guidelines. In M. Constantine & D. Sue (Eds.), *Strategies for building multicultural competence in mental health and educational settings* (pp. 129–144). Hoboken, NJ: Wiley & Sons.

Miranda, A. O., & Matheny, K. B. (2000). Psycho-sociological predictors of acculturative stress among Latino adults. *Journal of Mental Health Counseling, 22,* 306–317.

Mishkind, M. E., Rodin, J., Silberstein, L. R., & Striegel-Moore, R. H. (1987). The embodiment of masculinity: Cultural, psychological, and behavioral dimensions. In M. S. Kimmel (Ed.), *Changing men: New directions in research on men and masculinity* (pp. 37–52). Newbury Park, CA: Sage.

Miville, M. L., Constantine, M. G., Baysden, M. F., & So-Lloyd, G. (2005). Chameleon changes: An exploration of racial identity themes of multiracial people. *Journal of Counseling Psychology, 52,* 507–516.

Mohatt, G. (2010). Moving toward an Indigenous psychotherapy. *The Counseling Psychologist, 38,* 236–242. doi: 10.1177/0011000009345532

Mohr, J. J. (2002). Heterosexual identity and the heterosexual therapist: An identity perspective on sexual orientation. *The Counseling Psychologist, 30,* 532–566.

Moir, A., & Jessel, D. (1991). *Brain sex: The real difference between men and women.* New York, NY: Delta.

Montalvo, F. F., & Codina, G. E. (2001). Skin color and Latinos in the United States. *Ethnicities, 1,* 321–341.

Moradi, B., DeBlaere, C., & Huang, Y. (2010). Centralizing the experience of LGBT people. *The Counseling Psychologist, 38,* 322–330. doi: 10.1177/0011000009346325

Moradi, B., & Hasan, N. T. (2004). Arab American persons' reported experiences of discrimination and mental health: The mediating role of personal control. *Journal of Counseling Psychology, 51,* 418–428.

Moradi, B., van den Berg, J., & Epting, F. R. (2006). Intrapersonal and interpersonal manifestation of antilesbian and gay prejudice: An application of personal construct theory. *Journal of Counseling Psychology, 53,* 57–66.

Mullins, E., & Sites, P. (1984). Famous black Americans: A three-generational analysis of social origins. *American Sociological Review, 49,* 672.

Murphy, B. C., & Dillon, C. (2008). *Interviewing in action in a multicultural world.* Belmont, CA: Brooks Cole.

Myers, J. E., Sweeney, T. J., & Witmer, J. M. (2001). Optimization of behavior: Promotion of wellness. In D. Locke, J. Myers, & E. Herr (Eds.), *The handbook of counseling* (pp. 641–652). Thousand Oaks, CA: Sage.

Myers, L. J. (1991). Expanding the psychology of knowledge optimally: The importance of world view revisited. In R. Jones (Ed.), *Black psychology* (3rd ed., pp. 15–28). Berkeley, CA: Cobb and Henry.

Myers, L. J., Speight, S. L., Highlen, P. S., Cox, C. I., Reynolds, A. L., Adams, E. M., & Hanley, P. (1991). Identity development and worldview: Toward an optimal conceptualization. *Journal of Counseling and Development, 70,* 54–63.

Nadal, K. L., Rivera, D. P., & Corpus, J. H. (2010). Sexual orientation and transgender microaggressions. In D. W. Sue, *Microaggressions and marginality: Manifestation, dynamics, and impact* (217–240). New York, NY: Wiley & Sons.

Nadal, K. L., Skolnik, K., & Wong, Y. (2012). Interpersonal and systemic microaggressions toward transgender people: Implications for counseling. *Journal of LGBT Issues in Counseling, 6*(1), 55–82.

Napholz, L. (1994). Sex role orientation and psychological well-being among working Black women. *Journal of Black Psychology, 20,* 469–482.

Nassar-McMillan, S. C. (2007). Arab Amercian populations. In M. Constantine (Ed.), *Clinical practice with people of color: A guide to becoming culturally competent* (pp. 85–103). New York, NY: Teachers College Press.

Nassar-McMillan, S. C., & Hakim-Larson, J. (2003). Counseling consideration among Arab Americans. *Journal of Counseling & Development, 81,* 150–159.

National Association of Social Workers. (2001). Standards for cultural competence in social work practice. NASW National Committee on Racial and Ethnic Diversity. Retrieved August 8, 2015, from https://www.socialworkers.org/practice/standards/NASWCulturalStandards.pdf

National Board of Certified Counselors. (2015). Medicare and professional counselors. Retrieved on July 27, 2015, from http://www.nbcc.org/Advocacy/MedicareAndProfessionalCounselors

The National Campaign to Prevent Teen Pregnancy. (2010). Retrieved October 28, 2015, from http://thenationalcampaign.org/data/landing

National Center for Education Statistics. (2015). *Children living in poverty.* Retrieved on November 7, 2015 from http://nces.ed.gov/programs/coe/indicator_cce.asp

National Center for Health Statistics. (2015). *Health United States, 2014: With special feature on adults, aged 55–64.* Hyattsville, MD. Retrieved November 6, 2015, from http://www.cdc.gov/nchs/data/hus/hus14.pdf#064

National Coalition for the Homeless. (2014). Homelessness in America. Retrieved November 25, 2015, from http://nationalhomeless.org/about-homelessness

National Healthy Marriage Resource Center. (2008). Asian and Pacific Islanders. Retrieved November 7, 2015, from http://www.healthymarriageinfo.org/research-and-policy/marriage-facts/culture/asian-and-pacific-islanders/index.aspx

National Humanities Center. (2006). *American beginnings 1492-1690.* Retrieved on July 8, 2015, from http://nationalhumanitiescenter.org/pds/amerbegin/settlement/settlement.htm

National Park Service. (2015). "Muskox." Washington, DC: U.S. Department of the Interior. Retrieved from http://www.nps.gov/bela/learn/historyculture/Muskox.htm

National Science Foundation, National Center for Science and Engineering Statistics. (2015). *Doctorate recipients from U.S. universities: 2013* (Special Report No. NSF 15-304). Arlington, VA: Author. Retrieved from http://www.nsf.gov/statistics/sed/2013/digest/nsf15304a.pdf

Neal, A. M., & Wilson, M. I. (1989). The role of skin color and features in the Black community: Implications for Black women and therapy. *Clinical Psychology Review, 9,* 323–333.

Neal, L. I., McCray, A. D., Webb-Johnson, G., & Bridgest, S. T. (2003). The effects of African American movement styles on teachers' perceptions and reactions. *The Journal of Special Education, 37,* 49–57.

Nelson, H. L. (1997). *Feminism and families.* New York: Routledge.

Nelson, M. C. (1996). Separation versus connection: The gender controversy. *Implications for Counseling Women, 74,* 339–344.

Neville, H., Spanierman, L., & Doan, B. (2006). Exploring the association between color-blind racial ideology and multicultural counseling competencies. *Cultural Diversity and Ethnic Minority Psychology, 12,* 275–290.

Neville, H. A., Lilly, R. L., Duran, C., Lee, R. M., & Browne, L. (2000). Construction and initial validation of the Color-Blind Racial Attitudes Scale (CoBRAS). *Journal of Counseling Psychology, 47,* 59–70. doi:10.1037/0022-0167.47.1.59

Newman, D. M. (2007). *Identities and inequalities: Exploring the intersections of race, class, gender, and sexuality.* Boston, MA: McGraw-Hill.

Newman, J. L., Fuqua, D. R., Gray, E. A., & Simpson, D. B. (2006). Gender differences in the relationship of anger and depression in a clinical sample. *Journal of Counseling & Development, 84,* 157–162.

Newman, K. S. (1999). *No shame in my game: The working poor in the inner city.* New York, NY: Vintage Books and Russell Sage Foundation.

Nhat Hanh, T. (1998). *The heart of the Buddha's teaching.* Berkeley, CA: Parallax Press.

Nicholas, D. R. (2013). On being a psycho-oncologist: A counseling psychology perspective. *The Counseling Psychologist, 41,* 186–215.

Nichols, L. M., & Hunt, B. (2011). The significance of spirituality for individuals with chronic illness: Implications for mental health counseling. *Journal of Mental Health Counseling, 33,* 51–66.

Nicholson, L. (1997). The myth of the traditional family. In H. L. Nelson (Ed.), *Feminism and families* (pp. 27–42). New York: Routledge.

Nicolau, S., & Santiestevan, S. (1990). *The Hispanic almanac.* New York, NY: Hispanic Policy Development Project.

Nisbett, R. (1995). Race, IQ, and scientism. In S. Fraser (Ed.), *The bell curve wars: Race, intelligence, and the future of America.* New York, NY: Basic Books.

Nobles, W. (1972). African philosophy: Foundations for Black psychology. In R. H. Jones (Ed.), *Black psychology.* New York, NY: Harper & Row.

Nora, A., & Crisp, G. (2009). Hispanics and higher education: An overview of research, theory, and practice. In J. C. Smart (Ed.), *Higher education: Handbook of theory of research* (pp. 317–353). New York, NY: Springer Science + Business Media B.V.

Norris, T., Vines, P. L., & Hoeffel, E. M. (2012). The American Indian and Alaska Native population: 2010. *2010 Census Briefs.* Retrieved from http://www.census.gov/prod/cen2010/briefs/c2010br-10.pdf

Novas, H. (1994). *Everything you need to know about Latino history.* New York, NY: Penguin.

Nuessel, F. H. (1982). The language of ageism. *Gerontologist, 22,* 273–276.

Nugent, H. (2007). Race row Nobel scientist James Watson scraps tour after being suspended. Retrieved October 19, 2007, from www.timesonline.co.uk/tollnews/uk/article2694632.ece

Obermeyer, C. M. (2006). HIV in the Middle East. *British Medical Journal, 333,* 851–854.

O'Connor, M. F. (1992). Psychotherapy with gay and lesbian adolescents. In S. H. Dworkin & F. J. Gutierrez (Eds.), *Counseling gay men and lesbians: Journey to the end of the rainbow* (pp. 3–22). Alexandria, VA: American Association for Counseling and Development.

Ogbu, J. U. (1997). Racial stratification and education in the United States: Why inequality persists. In A. Halsey, H. Lauder, P. Brown, & A. Wells (Eds.), *Education: Culture, economy, society* (pp. 765–778). Oxford, UK: Oxford University Press.

Ogunwole, S. U., Drewery, M. P., & Rios-Vargas, M. (2012). The population with a bachelor's degree or higher by race and Hispanic origin: 2006–2010 (American Community Survey Briefs No. ACSBR/10-19). Washington, DC: U.S. Department of Commerce. Retrieved June 10, 2015 from http://www.census.gov/prod/2012pubs/acsbr10-19.pdf

Okazawa-Rey, M., Robinson, T. L., & Ward, J. V. (1987). Black women and the politics of skin color and hair. *Women and Therapy, 6,* 89–102.

Olkin, R. (2004). Making research accessible for people with disabilities. *Journal of Multicultural Counseling and Development, 32,* 332–343.

Olkin, R. (2007). Persons of color with disabilities. In M. G. Constantine (Ed.), *Clinical practice with people of color: A Guide to becoming culturally competent* (pp. 162–179). New York, NY: Teacher's College.

Olkin, R., & Pledger, C. (2003). Can disability studies and psychology join hands? *American Psychologist, 58,* 296–298.

Olson, M. J. (2003). Counselor understanding of Native American spiritual loss. *Counseling and Values, 47,* 109–117.

Omni, M., & Winant, H. (2006). Racial formations. In T. Ore (Ed.), *The social construction of difference and inequality: Race, class, gender, and sexuality* (pp. 19–29). Boston, MA: McGraw-Hill.

Ore, T. E. (2006). Constructing differences. In T. Ore (Ed.), *The social construction of difference and inequality: Race, class, gender, and sexuality* (pp. 1–18). Boston, MA: McGraw-Hill.

Ossana, S. M., Helms, J. E., & Leonard, M. M. (1992). Do "womanist" identity attitudes influence college women's self-esteem and perceptions of environmental bias? *Journal of Counseling and Development, 70,* 402–408.

Ossario, P.N. (n.d.). *Race genes and intelligence.* Retrieved January 23, 2016 from http://www.councilforresponsiblegenetics.org/pagedocuments/xt0uw7svhy.pdf

Owen, J., Tao, K., Leach, M., & Rodolfa, E. (2011). Clients' perceptions of their psychotherapists' multicultural orientation. *Psychotherapy Theory Research Training, 48,* 274–282.

Owen, J., Thomas, L., & Rodolfa, E. (2013). Stigma for seeking therapy: Self-stigma, social stigma, and therapeutic processes. *The Counseling Psychologist, 41,* 857–880.

Pace, C. (1991). *A description of factors affecting attitudes held by mental health professionals and students toward lesbians and gays* (Unpublished master's thesis). University of Florida, Gainesville.

Padilla, A. M. (1984). Synopsis of the history of Chicano psychology. In J. Martinez & R. Mendoza (Eds.), *Chicano psychology* (pp. 1–19). Orlando, FL: Academic Press.

Palmer, P. J. (1999). A vision of education as transformation. In S. Glazer (Ed.), *The heart of learning: Spirituality in education* (pp. 15–32). New York: Putnam.

Parham, T. (Presenter). (1992). *Counseling African Americans* [Video]. United States, Microtraining and Multicultural Development.

Parker, M. S. (1985). Identity and the development of religious thinking. In A. S. Waterman (Ed.), *Identity in adolescence* (pp. 43–60). San Francisco, CA: Jossey-Bass.

Parker, W. M., & Schwartz, R. C. (2002). On the experience of shame in multicultural counseling: Implications for White counselors-in-training. *British Journal of Guidance and Counseling, 30,* 311–318.

Passel, J. S., Livingston, G., & Cohn, D. (2012), *Explaining why minority births now outnumber white births.* Washington, DC: Pew Research Center. Retrieved June 20, 2015, from http://www.pewsocialtrends.org/2012/05/17/explaining-why-minority-births-now-outnumber-white-births/#population-patterns

Passel, J. S., Wang, W., & Taylor, P. (2010). One-in-seven new U.S. marriages is interracial or interethnic: Marrying out. Retrieved from *PewResearchCenter: Social & Demographic Trends*: http://www.pewsocialtrends.org/2010/06/04/marrying-out

Patterson, C. H. (1974). *Relationship counseling and psychotherapy.* New York, NY: Harper Row Books.

Paxton, S. J., Wertheim, E. H., Gibbons, K., Szmukler, G. I., Hillier, L., & Petrovich, J. L. (1991). Body image satisfaction, dieting beliefs, and weight-loss behaviors in adolescent girls and boys. *Journal of Youth and Adolescence, 20,* 361–379.

Pedersen, P. (1990). The constructs of complexity and balance in multicultural counseling theory and practice. *Journal of Counseling and Development, 15,* 16–24.

Pedersen, P. B. (1997). The cultural context of the American Counseling Association code of ethics. *Journal of Counseling and Development, 76,* 23–28.

Peregoy, J. J. (1993). Transcultural counseling with American Indians and Alaskan Natives: Contemporary issues for consideration. In J. McFadden (Ed.), *Transcultural counseling: Bilateral and international perspectives* (pp. 163–191). Alexandria, VA: American Counseling Association.

Peregoy, J. J., & Gloria, A. (2007). American Indians and Alaska Native populations. In M. G. Constantine (Ed.), *Clinical practice with people of color: A guide to becoming culturally competent* (pp. 61–84). New York, NY: Springer.

Perkins, S. (2015). *Hegemonic masculinity and its effect on attitudes toward seeking professional psychological help* (Unpublished doctoral dissertation). Northeastern University, Boston, MA.

Peterman, L. M., & Dixon, C. G. (2003). Domestic violence between same sex partners: Implication for counseling. *Journal of Counseling & Development, 81,* 40–47.

Pew Research Center. (2010). Religion among the millennials. Retrieved on November 4, 2011, from http://www.pewforum.org/2010/02/17/religion-among-the-millennials

Pew Research Center. (2011). *Muslim Americans: No signs of growth in alienation or support for extremism mainstream and moderate attitudes.* Retrieved June 7, 2015, from http://pewresearch.org/pubs/2087/muslim-americans-islamic-extremism-911-attacks-mosques

Pew Research Center. (2012). Median age for Hispanics is lower than median age for total U.S. population. Retrieved November 4, 2015, from http://www.pewresearch.org/daily-number/median-age-for-hispanics-is-lower-than-median-age-for-total-u-s-population

Pew Research Center. (2013). *The rise of Asian Americans.* Retrieved June 15, 2015, from http://www.pewsocialtrends.org/2012/06/19/the-rise-of-asian-americans

Pew Research Center Survey of U.S. Jews. (2013). *A portrait of Jewish Americans: Findings from a Pew Research Center Survey of U.S. Jews.* Retrieved June 28, 2015, from http://www.pewforum.org/files/2013/10/jewish-american-full-report-for-web.pdf

Pew Research Center Survey. (2015). America's changing religious landscape. Christians decline sharply as share of population; unaffiliated and other faiths continue to grow. Retrieved November 23, 2015, from http://www.pewforum.org/2015/05/12/americas-changing-religious-landscape

Phan, T., & Tylka, T. L. (2006). Exploring a model and moderators of disordered eating with Asian American college women. *Journal of Counseling Psychology, 53,* 36–47.

Pharr, S. (1988). *Homophobia: A weapon of sexism.* Little Rock, AR: Chardon.

Phillips, A., & Daniluk, J. C. (2004). Beyond "survivor": How childhood sexual abuse informs the identity of adult women at the end of the therapeutic process. *Journal of Counseling & Development, 82,* 177–184.

Phillips, M. A., & Murrell, S. A. (1994). Impact of psychological and physical health, stressful events, and social support on subsequent mental health help seeking among older adults. *Journal of Consulting and Clinical Psychology, 62,* 270–275.

Phinney, J. (1989). Stages of ethnic identity development in minority group adolescents. *Journal of Early Adolescence, 9,* 34–49.

Phinney, J. (1992). The multi-group ethnic identity measure: A new scale for use with adolescents and young adults from diverse groups. *Journal of Adolescent Research, 7,* 156–176.

Phinney, J. S. (1990). Ethnic identity in adolescents and adults: Review of research. *Psychological Bulletin, 198,* 499–514.

Phinney, J. S. (1997). Ethnic and American identity as predictors of self-esteem among African American, Latino, and white adolescents. *Journal of Youth and Adolescence, 26,* 165–185.

Phinney, J. S., & Flores, J. (2002). "Unpackaging" acculturation: Aspects of acculturation as predictors of traditional sex role attitudes. *Journal of Cross-Cultural Psychology, 33,* 320–331.

Phinney, J., & Rosenthal, P. A. (1993). Ethnic identity in adolescence: Process, context, and outcome. In F. Adams, R. Montemayor, & T. Oulotta (Eds.), *Advances in adolescent development* (Vol. 4, pp. 145–172). Newbury Park, CA: Sage.

Phornphutkul, C., Fausto-Sterling, A., & Gruppuso, P. A. (2000). Gender self-reassignment in an XY adolescent female born with ambiguous genitalia. *Pediatrics, 106,* 135–137.

Pieterse, A. L., & Carter, R. T. (2007). An examination of the relationship between general life stress, racism-related stress, and psychological health among black men. *Journal of Counseling Psychology, 54,* 101–109.

Pinderhughes, E. (1989). *Understanding race, ethnicity, and power: The key to efficacy in clinical practice.* New York, NY: Free Press.

Pinderhughes, E. (1995). Empowering diverse populations: Family practice in the 21st century (CEU Article No. 50). *Families in Society: The Journal of Contemporary Human Services,* 131–140.

Pleck, J. H. (1984). Men's power with women, other men, and society: A men's movement analysis. In P. P. Ricker & E. H. Carmen (Eds.), *The gender gap in psychotherapy: Social realities and psychological processes* (pp. 79–89). New York, NY: Plenum Press.

Pledger, C. (2003). Discourse on disability and rehabilitation issues. *American Psychologist, 58,* 279–284.

Ponterotto, J. G., Alexander, C. M., & Grieger, I. (1995). A multicultural competency checklist for counseling training programs. *Journal of Multicultural Counseling and Development, 23,* 11–20.

Ponterotto, J. G., & Casas, J. M. (1991). *Handbook of racial/ethnic minority counseling research.* Springfield, IL: Charles C Thomas.

Ponzo, Z. (1985). The counselor and physical attractiveness. *Journal of Counseling and Development, 63,* 482–485.

Pope, M. (1995). The "salad bowl" is big enough for us all: An argument for the inclusion of lesbians and gay men in any definition of multiculturalism. *Journal of Counseling and Development, 73,* 301–304.

Pope-Davis, D. B., Liu, W. M., Toporek, R., & Brittan-Powell, C. S. (2001). What's missing from multicultural competency research: Review, introspection, and recommendations? *Cultural Diversity and Ethnic Minority Psychology, 7,* 121–138.

Pope-Davis, D. B., & Ottavi, T. M. (1994). The relationship between racism and racial identity among white Americans: A replication and extension. *Journal of Counseling and Development, 72,* 293–297.

Portman, T. A. A. (2001). Sex role attributions of American Indian women. *Journal of Mental Health Counseling, 23,* 72–84.

Portman, T. A. A., & Garrett, M. L. (2005). Beloved women: Nurturing the sacred fire of leadership from an American Indian perspective. *Journal of Counseling & Development, 83,* 284–291.

Portman, T. A. A., & Herring, R. D. (2001). Debunking the Pocahontas paradox: The need for a humanistic perspective. *Journal of Humanistic Counseling, Education, and Development, 40,* 185–199.

Poston, W. S. C. (1990). The biracial identity development model: A needed addition. *Journal of Counseling and Development, 69,* 152–155.

Powell, L. H., Shahabi, L., & Thoresen, C. E. (2003). Religion and spirituality: Linkages to physical health. *American Psychologist, 58*(1), 36–52.

Prause, M., & Graham, C. A. (2007). Asexuality: Classification and characterization. *Archives of Sexual Behavior 36,* 341–356. doi 10.1007/s10508-006-9142-.3

Priest, N. C., White, F., Walton, J., & Paradies, Y. (2014). Understanding the complexities of ethnic-racial socialization processes for minority and majority groups: A 30 year systematic review. I*nternational Journal of Intercultural Relations, 43,* 139–155. doi: 10.1016/j.ijintrel.2014.08.003

Race and the human genome: Researchers definitely trump the notion of race with DNA research. (2004). Retrieved January 30, 2004, from http://racerelations.about.com/library/weekly/aa021501a.htm

Rampage, C., Eovaldi, M., Ma, C., & Weigel-Foy, C. (2003). Adoptive families. In F. Walsh (Ed.), *Normal family processes: Growing diversity and complexity* (pp. 210–232). New York: Guilford Press.

Rankin, S. (2002). *Campus climate for gay, lesbian, bisexual, and transgender people: A national perspective.* New York, NY: The Policy Institute of the National Gay and Lesbian Task Force. Retrieved August 3, 2003, from http://www.thetaskforce.org/static_html/downloads/reports/reports/CampusClimate.pdf

Rayle, A. D., Chee, C., & Sand, J. K. (2006). Honoring their way: Counseling American Indian women. *Journal of Multicultural Counseling and Development, 34,* 66–79.

Reid, P. T. (2011). Revisiting "Poor women: Shut up and shut out". *Psychology of Women Quarterly, 35,* 189-192. doi: 10.1177/0361684310395917

Rendon, L. I., & Robinson, T. L. (1994). A diverse America: Implications for minority seniors. In W. Hartel, S. Schwartz, S. Blue, & J. Gardner (Eds.), *Ready for the real world: Senior year experience series* (pp. 170–188). Belmont, CA: Wadsworth.

Renzetti, C. M., & Curran, D. J. (1992). *Women, men, and society.* Boston, MA: Allyn & Bacon.

Reynolds, A. L., & Pope, R. L. (1991). The complexities of diversity: Exploring multiple oppressions. *Journal of Counseling and Development, 70,* 174–180.

Rice, V. H., Weglicki, L. S., Thomas, T., & Hammad, A. (2006, April). Predictors of Arab American adolescent tobacco use. *Merrill-Palmer Quarterly.*

Rich, T. R. (2011a). Ashkenazic and Sephardic Jews. Retrieved on July 17, 2015, from http://www.jewfaq.org/movement.htm

Rich, T. R. (2011b). Movements of Judaism. Retrieved on July 17, 2015, from http://www.jewfaq.org/movement.htm

Richardson, T. Q., & Molinaro, K. L. (1996). White counselor self-awareness: A prerequisite for developing multicultural competence. *Journal of Counseling and Development, 71,* 238–242.

Ridley, C. R. (1989). Racism in counseling as an aversive behavioral process. In P. B. Pedersen, J. G. Draguns, W. J. Lonner, & J. E. Trimble (Eds.), *Counseling across cultures* (pp. 55–78). Honolulu: University of Hawaii Press.

Riggs, M. (Producer/Director). (1994). *Black is. . .Black ain't* [Video]. San Francisco: California Newsreel.

Rivera, N. (1999). Why are people staring at me. In P. F. Gaskins (Ed.), *What are you: Voices of mixed-race young people* (pp. 35–37). New York, NY: Henry Holt.

Roberts, S. A., Kiselica, M. S., & Fredrickson, S. A. (2002). Quality of life of persons with medical illnesses: Counseling & holistic contribution. *Journal of Counseling & Development, 80,* 422–432.

Robinson, G. (2000). *Essential Judaism: A complete guide to beliefs, customs, and rituals.* New York, NY: Pocket Books.

Robinson, T. L. (1990). Understanding the gap between entry and exit: A cohort analysis of black student persistence. *Journal of Negro Education, 59,* 207–218.

Robinson, T. L. (1993). The intersections of gender, class, race, and culture: On seeing clients whole. *Journal of Multicultural Counseling and Development, 21,* 50–58.

Robinson, T. L. (1999a). The intersections of dominant discourses across race, gender, and other identities. *Journal of Counseling & Development, 77,* 73–79.

Robinson, T. L. (1999b). The intersections of identity. In A. Garrod, J. V. Ward, T. L. Robinson, & B. Kilkenney (Eds.), *Souls looking back: Stories of growing up Black.* New York: Routledge.

Robinson, T. L. (2001). White mothers of non-white children. *Journal of Humanistic Counseling, Education and Development, 40,* 171–184.

Robinson, T. L., & Howard-Hamilton, M. (1994). An Afrocentric paradigm: Foundation for a healthy self-image and healthy interpersonal relationships. *Journal of Mental Health Counseling, 16,* 327–339.

Robinson, T. L., & Kennington, P. A. D. (2002). Holding up half the sky: Women and psychological resistance. *Journal of Humanistic Counseling, Education and Development, 41,* 164–177.

Robinson, T. L., & Ward, J. V. (1991). A belief in self far greater than anyone's disbelief: Cultivating resistance among African American adolescents. *Women & Therapy, 11,* 87–103.

Robinson, T. L., & Ward, J. V. (1995). African American adolescents and skin color. *Journal of Black Psychology, 21,* 256–274.

Robinson, T. L., & Watt, S. K. (2001). Where no one goes begging: Gender, sexuality, and religious diversity. In D. Locke, J. Myers, & E. Herr (Eds.), *Handbook of counseling* (pp. 589–599). Thousand Oaks, CA: Sage.

Robinson-Wood, T. L. (2009a). Extending culture beyond race and ethnicity. In C. Lee (Ed.), *Elements of culture.* Boston: Allyn & Bacon.

Robinson-Wood, T. L. (2009b). Love, school, and money: Stress and cultural coping among ethnically diverse Black college women: A mixed-method analysis. *The Western Journal of Black Studies, 33,* 77-86.

Robinson-Wood, T. L. (2010a). "Is that your mom?" A qualitative investigation of white mothers of nonwhite children in the United States and New Zealand. *Journal of Qualitative and Ethnographic Research, 22,* 226–238.

Robinson-Wood, T. L. (2010b). Privileging multiple converging identities in counseling and Clemmont E. Vontress. In Roy Moodley and Rinaldo Walcott (Eds.), *Counseling across and beyond cultures: Exploring the work of Clemmont E. Vontress in clinical practice* (pp. 233–246). Toronto, Canada: University of Toronto Press.

Robinson-Wood, T. L. (2011). "It makes me worry about her future pain": A qualitative investigation of White mothers of non-White children in the United States. *Women & Therapy, 34,* 331–344.

Robinson-Wood, T. L. (2013). *The convergence of race, ethnicity, and gender: Multiple identities in counseling* (4th ed.). Upper Saddle River, NJ: Merrill/Prentice Hall.

Robinson-Wood, T. L. (2015). The relevance of non-colorblind talk between white women and nonwhite children: A discussion. *International Journal of Youth and Family Studies, 6,* 646–661.

Robinson-Wood, T., Balogun, O., Boadi, N., Fernandes, C., Matsumoto, A., Popai, A., & Zhang, X. (2015). Worse than blatant racism: A phenomenological investigation of microaggressions among black women. *Journal of Ethnographic & Qualitative Research, 9,* 221–236.

Robinson-Wood, T. L., & Braithwaite-Hall, M. (2005). Spirit matters: Women, spirituality, and clinical contexts. In M. Mirkin, J. Suyemoto, & B. Okun (Eds.), *Psychotherapy with women: Exploring diverse contexts and identities* (pp. 280–296). New York, NY: Guilford Press.

Robinson-Wood, T. L., & Weber, A. (2015). Deconstructing multiple oppressions among LGBT older adults. In Debra A. Harley and Pamela B. Teaster (Eds.), *Handbook of LGBT elders: An interdisciplinary approach to principles, practices, and policies* (pp. 65–82). New York, NY: Springer Press.

Rockquemore, K. A. (1999). Between black and white: Understanding the "biracial" experience. *Race and Society, 2,* 197–212.

Rockquemore, K. A. (2002). Negotiating the color line: The gendered process of racial identity construction among black/white biracial women. *Gender and Society, 16,* 485–503.

Rodriguez, J., McKay, M. M., & Bannon, W. M. (2008). The role of racial socialization in relation to parenting practices and youth behavior: An explanatory analysis. *Soc Work Mental Health, 6,* 30–54.

Roffman, M. (1974). History of labor in Hawai'i. Center for Labor Education & Research, University of Hawai'i—West O'ahu. Retrieved on November 7, 2015, from http://www.hawaii.edu/uhwo/clear/home/HawaiiLaborHistory.html

Rogers, J. A. (1967) *Sex and race.* St. Petersburg, FL: Helga Rogers.

Rogers, R. L., & Petrie, T. A. (2001). Psychological correlates of anorexic and bulimic symptomatology. *Journal of Counseling and Development, 79,* 178–187.

Rollins, A. & Hunter, A. G. (2013). Racial socialization of biracial youth: Maternal messages and approaches to address discrimination. *Family Relations, 62*(1), 142–153.

Root, M. P. P. (1990). Disordered eating in women of color. *Sex Roles, 22,* 525–536.

Root, M. P. P. (1992). Within, between, and beyond race. In M. P. P. Root (Ed.), *Racially mixed people in America* (pp. 3–11). Newbury Park, CA: Sage.

Root, M. P. P. (1993). *Bill of rights for racially mixed people.* Copyright © Maria P. P. Root, PhD. 1993, 1994.

Root, M. P. P. (1998). Experiences and processes affecting racial identity development: Preliminary results from the biracial sibling project. *Cultural Diversity and Mental Health, 4,* 237–247.

Rosenblum, K. E., & Travis, T. C. (2006). *The meaning of difference: American constructions of race, sex, and gender, social class, and sexual orientation.* Boston, MA: McGraw-Hill.

Rothblum, E. D. (1994). "I only read about myself on bathroom walls": The need for research on the mental health of lesbians and gay men. *Journal of Consulting and Clinical Psychology, 62,* 213–220.

Rowley, S. J., Burchinal, M. R., Roberts, J. E., & Zeisel, S.A. (2008). Racial identity, social context, and race-related social cognition in African American middle school children. *Developmental Psychology, 44, 1537-1546.* doi: 10.1037/a0013349

Roysircar, G. (Ed.). (2003). *Multicultural counseling competencies: 2003.* Alexandria, VA: Association of Multicultural Counseling and Development.

Rudolph, J. (1990). Counselors' attitudes toward homosexuality: Selective review of the literature. *Journal of Counseling and Development, 65,* 165–168.

Ruelas, S. (2003). Objectively measured multicultural competencies: A preliminary study. In D. Pope-Davis, H. Coleman, W. Liu, & R. Toporek (Eds.), *Handbook of multicultural competencies & counseling* (pp. 283–300). Thousand Oaks, CA: Sage.

Russell, G. (1994). *A map of American Indian history.* Phoenix, AZ: Thunderbird Enterprises.

Rust, P. C. (2006). Sexual identity and bisexual identities: The struggle for self-description in a changing sexual landscape. In T. E. Orr (Ed.), *The social construction of difference and inequality: Race, class, gender, and sexuality* (pp. 169–186). Boston, MA: McGraw-Hill.

Ryan, C. (2013). *Language use in the United States: 2011* (American Community Survey Reports No. ACS-22). Washington, DC: U.S. Census Bureau. Retrieved on November 9, 2015, from http://www.census.gov/prod/2013pubs/acs-22.pdf

Sabry, W. M., & Vohra, A. (2013). Role of Islam in the management of psychiatric disorders. *Indian Journal of Psychiatry, 55,* 205–S214.

Sadker, M., Sadker, D., & Long, L. (1993). Gender and educational equity. In J. Banks & C. McGee-Banks (Eds.), *Multicultural education* (pp. 111–128). Boston, MA: Allyn & Bacon.

Salamon, M. (2010). After the battle: 7 health problems facing veterans. *My Health News Daily.* Retrieved on July 26, 2015, from http://www.livescience.com/8916-battle-7-health-problems-facing-veterans.html

Salazar, C. F. (2006). Conceptualizing multiple identities and multiple oppressions in clients' lives. *Counseling and Human Development, 39*(1), 1–18.

Sanchez, D., & Davis, C. (2010). Becoming a racially competent therapist. In J. A. E. Cornish, B. A. Schreier, L. I. Nadkarni, L. H. Metzger, & E. R. Rodolfa (Eds.), *Handbook of multicultural counseling competencies* (pp. 267–290). Hoboken, NJ: Wiley & Sons.

Sanchez, D., Del Prado, A., & Davis, C. (2010). Broaching ethnicity competently in therapy. In J. A. E. Cornish, B. A. Schreier, L. I. Nadkarni, L. H. Metzger, & E. R. Rodolfa (Eds.), *Handbook of multicultural counseling competencies* (pp. 93–116*).* Hoboken NJ: Wiley & Sons.

Sanchez, G. J. (2002). "Y tu, que?" (Y2K): Latino history in the new millennium. In M. Suarez-Orozco & M. M. Paez (Eds.), *Latinos: Remaking America* (pp. 45–58). Berkeley: University of California Press.

Sanchez-Hucles, J., & Jones, N. (2007). Gender issues. In M. Constantine (Ed.), *Clinical practice with people of color* (pp. 183–197). New York, NY: Teachers College Press.

Sandhu, D. S. (1997). Psychocultural profiles of Asian and Pacific Islander Americans: Implications for counseling and psychotherapy. *Journal of Multicultural Counseling and Development, 25,* 7–22.

Santiago-Rivera, A. (2003). Latinos values and family transitions: Practical considerations for counseling. *Counseling and Human Development, 35,* 1–12.

Santiago-Rivera, A. L., Arredondo, P., & Gallardo-Cooper, M. (2002). *Counseling Latinos and la familia: A practical guide.* Thousand Oaks, CA: Sage.

Santiago-Rivera, A. L., Talka, K., & Tully, A. W. (2007). Environmental racism: A call to the profession for community intervention and social action. In R. Toporek, L. Gerstein, N. Fouad, G. Roysircar, & T. Israel, *Handbook for Social Justice in Counseling Psychology: Leadership, Vision, and Action* (pp. 185–199). Thousand Oaks, CA: Sage.

Saucier, M. G. (2004). Midlife and beyond: Issues for aging women. *Journal of Counseling & Development, 82,* 420–425.

Sawy, N. E. (2005). Yes, I follow Islam, but I'm not a terrorist. In T. E. Ore (Ed.), *The social construction of difference and inequality: Race, class, gender, and sexuality* (pp. 570–571). Boston, MA: McGraw-Hill.

Schliebner, C. T., & Peregoy, J. J. (1994). Unemployment effects on the family and the child: Interventions for counselors. *Journal of Counseling and Development, 72,* 368–372.

Schlosser, L. Z. (2008). Microaggressions in everyday life: The American Jewish experience. Retrieved on July 5, 2015, from http://www.bjpa.org/Publications/downloadFile.cfm?FileID=5501

Schneider, B., Martinez, S., & Owens, A. (2006). Barriers to educational opportunities for Hispanics in the United States. In *Hispanics and the future of America.* National Academy of Sciences. Retrieved November 4, 2015, from http://www.ncbi.nlm.nih.gov/books/NBK19909

Schnitzer, P. K. (1996). "They don't come in." Stories told, lessons taught about poor families in therapy. *American Journal of Orthopsychiatry, 66,* 572–582.

Schoulte, J. (2011). Bereavement among African American and Latino/a Americans. *Journal of Mental Health Counseling, 33,* 11–20.

Schofield, W. (1964). *Psychotherapy: The purchase of friendship.* Upper Saddle River, NJ: Prentice Hall.

Scholl, M. B. (2006). Native American identity development and counseling preferences: A study of Lumbee undergraduates. *Journal of College Counseling, 9,* 47–59.

Schorsch, I. (2015). *Conservative Judaism: The core values of Conservative Judaism.* Retrieved on August 2, 2015, from https://www.jewishvirtuallibrary.org/jsource/Judaism/conservative_values.html

Schulte, E. (2002). More black men in jail than college. Retrieved September 25, 2007, from http://www.socialistworker.org/2002

Schultz-Ross, R. A., & Gutheil, T. G. (1997). Difficulties in integrating spirituality into psychotherapy practice. *Journal of Psychotherapy Practice and Research, 6,* 130–138.

Schwartz, W. (1998). The identity development of multiracial youth (ERIC Digest No. 137). Retrieved from ERIC database (ED425248): http://www.ericdigests.org/1999-3/identity.htm

Scott, D. A., & Robinson, T. L. (2001). White male identity development: The key model. *Journal of Counseling & Development, 79,* 415–421.

Scult, M. (2012). Mordecai Kaplan, 1881–1983. Retrieved on November 11, 2015 from http://jwa.org/encyclopedia/article/kaplan-mordecai

Sehgal, R., Saules, K., Young, A., Grey, M. J., Gillem, A. R., Nabors, N. A., Byrd, M. R., & Jefferson, S. (2011). Practicing what we know: Multicultural counseling competence among clinical psychology trainees and experienced multicultural psychologists. *Cultur Divers Ethnic Minor Psychol, 17*(1), 1–10. doi: 10.1037/a0021667.

Sharfstein, D. J. (2007). Crossing the color line: Racial migration and the one-drop rule, 1600–1860. *Minnesota Law Review, 91,* 592–656.

Shih, M., Bonam, C., Sanchez, D., & Peck, C. (2007). The social construction of race: Biracial identity and vulnerability to stereotypes. *Cultural Diversity and Ethnic Minority Psychology, 13,* 125–133.

Shih, M., & Sanchez, D. T. (2005). Perspectives and research on the positive and negative implications of having multiple racial identities. *Psychological Bulletin, 131,* 569–591.

Shinn, F. S. (1989). *The wisdom of Florence Scovel Shinn.* New York, NY: A Fireside Book.

Shiraev, E., & Levy, D. (2004). *Cross cultural psychology: Critical thinking and contemporary applications.* Boston, MA: Pearson.

Shore, L. I. (1995). *Tending inner gardens: The healing art of feminist therapy.* New York, NY: Harrington Park Press.

Shreeve, J. (2015). Oldest human fossil found, redrawing family tree. *National Geographic.* Retrieved November 16, 2015, from http://news.nationalgeographic.com/news/2015/03/150304-homo-habilis-evolution-fossil-jaw-ethiopia-olduvai-gorge

Silberschatz, G., Fretter, P. B., & Curtis, J. T. (1986). How do interpretations influence the process of psychotherapy? *Journal of Consulting and Clinical Psychology, 54,* 646–652.

Sime, M. L., Mona, L. R., Cameron, R. P. (2013). Sexual health and well-being after cancer. *The Counseling Psychologist, 41,* 240–267.

Simon, J. P. (1996). Lebanese families. In M. McGoldrick, J. K. Pearce, & J. Giordano (Eds.), *Ethnicity and family therapy* (pp. 364–375). New York, NY: Guilford Press.

Singh, A. A., Boyd, C. J., & Whitman, J. S. (2010). Counseling competency with transgender and intersex persons. In J. A. E. Cornish, B. A. Schreier, L. I. Nadkarni, L. H. Metzger, E. R. Rodolfa (Eds.), *Handbook of multicultural counseling competencies* (pp. 415–441). Hoboken, NJ: Wiley.

Skovholt, T. M. (1993). Counseling and psychotherapy interventions with men. *Counseling and Human Development, 25,* 1–6.

Slater, S. (1997). Contributions of the lesbian experience to mutuality in therapy relationships. In J. Jordan (Ed.), *Women's growth in diversity: More writings from the Stone Center* (pp. 119–126). New York, NY: Guilford Press.

Smart, J. F., & Smart, D. W. (2006). Models on disability: Implications for the counseling profession. *Journal of Counseling and Development, 84,* 29–40.

Smart, R. (2010). Counseling competencies with women: Understanding gender in the context of multiple dimensions of identity. In J. A. E. Cornish, B. A. Schreier, L. I. Nadkarni, L. H. Metzger, E. R. Rodolfa (Eds.), *Handbook of multicultural counseling competencies* (pp. 475–508*).* Hoboken, NJ: John Wiley.

Smith, B. (1982). Toward a black feminist criticism. In G. Hull, P. Scott, & B. Smith (Eds.), *All the women are white, all the blacks are men, but some of us are brave* (pp. 157–175). Old Westbury, NY: Feminist Press.

Smith, J. C., & Medalia, C. (2015). Health Insurance Coverage in the United States: 2014 (Current Population Reports No. P60–253). Washington, DC: U.S. Census Bureau. Retrieved November 20, 2015, from http://www.census.gov/content/dam/Census/library/publications/2015/demo/p60-253.pdf

Smith, L. (2005). Psychotherapy, classism, and the poor. *American Psychologist, 60,* 687–696.

Smithsonian National Museum of Natural History. (2015a). *Australopithecus afarensis.* Retrieved November 16, 2015, from http://humanorigins.si.edu/evidence/Australopithecus-afarensis

Smithsonian National Museum of Natural History. (2015b). Homo erectus. Retrieved November 15, 2015, from, http://humanorigins.si.edu/evidence/human-fossils/species/homo-erectus

Smithsonian National Museum of Natural History. (2015c). Homo floresiensis. Retrieved November 15, 2015, from http://humanorigins.si.edu/evidence/human-fossils/species/homo-floresiensis

Smithsonian National Museum of Natural History. (2015d). Homo habilis. Retrieved November 15, 2015, from http://humanorigins.si.edu/evidence/human-fossils/species/homo-habilis

Smithsonian National Museum of Natural History. (2015e). Homo heidelbergensis. Retrieved on November 15, 2015, from http://humanorigins.si.edu/evidence/human-fossils/species/homo-heidelbergensis

Smithsonian National Museum of Natural History. (2015f). Homo Neanderthals. Retrieved November 15, 2015, from http://humanorigins.si.edu/evidence/human-fossils/species/homo-neanderthals

Smithsonian National Museum of Natural History. (2015g). Homo rudolfensis. Retrieved November 15, 2015, from http://humanorigins.si.edu/evidence/human-fossils/species/homo-rudolfensis

Smithsonian National Museum of Natural History. (2015h). Homo sapiens. Retrieved November 15, 2015, from http://humanorigins.si.edu/evidence/human-fossils/species/homo-sapiens

Smithsonian National Museum of Natural History. (2015i). Human family tree. Retrieved November 15, 2015, from, http://humanorigins.si.edu/evidence/human-family-tree#

Smithsonian National Museum of Natural History. (2015j). What does it mean to be human. Retrieved November 13, 2015, from http://humanorigins.si.edu/evidence/genetics

Smits, S. J. (2004). Disability and employment in the U.S.A.: The quest for best practices. *Disability & Society, 19,* 647–662.

Sodowski, G. R., Wai, E. W. M., & Plake, B. (1991). Moderating effects of sociocultural variables on acculturation attitudes of Hispanics and Asian Americans. *Journal of Counseling and Development, 70,* 194–204.

Sorosoro. (2011). Inuit-Yupik-Aleut languages. Retrieved from www.sorosoro.org/en/eskimo-aleut-languages

Souter, A., & Murthy, R. S. (2006, October 21). Relation between mental health care and general development. *British Medical Journal, 333,* 861. Retrieved on October 2, 2015 from, http://www.bmj.com/content/333/7573/861.1

Soza, A. (2014). *Girls Will Be Girls: Discourse, Poststructuralist Feminism, and Media Presentations of Women.* A thesis submitted in partial fulfillment of the requirements for the degree of Master of Arts in Communication Boise State University. Retrieved on October 21, 2015 from http://scholarworks.boisestate.edu/cgi/viewcontent.cgi?article=1828&context=td

Spanierman, L. B., & Heppner, M. J. (2004). Psychosocial costs of racism to whites scale (PCRW): Construction and initial validation. *Journal of Counseling Psychology, 51,* 249–262.

Spanierman, L. B., Poteat, V. P., Beer, A. M., & Armstrong, P. I. (2007). Psychosocial costs of racism to whites: Exploring patterns through cluster analysis. *Journal of Counseling Psychology, 53*(3), 434–441.

Spanierman, L. B., Todd, N. R., & Anderson, C. J. (2009). Psychosocial costs of racism to whites: Understanding patterns among university students. *Journal of Counseling Psychology, 56,* 239–252.

Spence, J. T., & Helmreich, R. L. (1978). *Masculinity and femininity: Their psychological dimensions, correlates, and antecedents.* Austin: University of Texas Press.

Spencer, M. B. (1985). Black children's race awareness, racial attitudes, and self-concept: A reinterpretation. *Annual Progress in Child Psychiatry and Child Development, 71,* 616–630.

Spickard, P. R. (1992). The illogic of American racial categories. In M. P. P. Root (Ed.), *Racially mixed people in America* (pp. 12–23). Newbury Park, CA: Sage.

Staples, R. (1988). The Black American family. In C. H. Mindel, R. W. Habenstein, & R. Wright (Eds.), *Ethnic families in America: Patterns and variations* (3rd ed., pp. 303–324). New York, NY: Elsevier.

Stavans, I. (1995). *The Hispanic condition: Reflections on culture and identity in America.* New York, NY: Harper Perennial.

Steinberg, S. (1989). *The ethnic myth: Race, ethnicity, and class in America.* Boston, MA: Beacon Press.

Steinem, G. (1992). *Revolution from within: A book of self-esteem.* Boston, MA: Little, Brown.

Steinmetz, E. (2006). *Americans with disabilities: 2002.* Washington, DC: U.S. Department of Commerce, U.S. Census Bureau.

Sterling, A. F. (1992). *Myths of gender.* New York, NY: Basic Books.

Stevens, M. J., Pfost, K. S., & Potts, M. K. (1990). Sex role orientation and the willingness to confront existential issues. *Journal of Counseling and Development, 68,* 47–49.

Stewart, J. C. (1996). *1001 things everyone should know about African American history.* New York, NY: Doubleday.

Stiver, I. P. (1997). A relational approach to therapeutic impasses. In J. Jordan (Ed.), *Women's growth in diversity* (pp. 288–310). New York, NY: Guilford Press.

Storck, L. E. (1998). Social class divisions in the consulting room: A theory of psychosocial class and depression. *Group Analysis, 31,* 101–115.

Suarez-Orozco, M., & Paez, M. M. (2002). *Latinos: Remaking America.* Berkeley: University of California Press.

Sue, D. (Presenter). (1989). *Cultural identity development* [Video]. United States, Microtraining and Multicultural Development.

Sue, D. W. (2010). *Microaggressions in everyday life: Race, gender, and sexual orientation.* Hoboken, NJ: Wiley & Sons.

Sue, D. W., Arredondo, P., & McDavis, R. J. (1992). Multicultural counseling competencies and standards: A call to the profession. *Journal of Counseling and Development, 70,* 477–483.

Sue, D. W., Bernier, J. E., Daran, A., Feinberg, L., Pedersen, P., Smith, C. T., & Vasquez-Nuttale, G. (1982). Cross-cultural counseling competencies. *Counseling Psychologist, 19,* 45–52.

Sue, D. W., Bucceri, J., Lin, A. I., Nadal, K. L., & Torino, G. C. (2007). Racial microaggressions and the Asian American experience. *Cultural Diversity and Ethnic Minority Psychology, 13,* 72–81.

Sue, D. W., Carter, R. T., Caas, J. M., Fouad, N. A., Ivey, A. E., Jensen, M.,. . . Vazquez-Nuttall, E. (1998). *Multicultural counseling competencies: Individual and organizational development.* Thousand Oaks, CA: Sage.

Sue, D. W., Ivey, A. E., & Pedersen, P. B. (1996). *A theory of multicultural counseling and therapy.* Pacific Grove, CA: Brooks/Cole.

Sue, D. W., Rivera, D. P., Watkins, N. L., Kim, R. H., Kim, S., & Williams, C. D. (2011). Racial dialogues: Challenges faculty of color face in the classroom. *Cultural Diversity and Ethnic Minority Psychology, 17,* 331–340.

Sue, D. W., & Sue, D. (1990). *Counseling the culturally different: Theory and practice.* New York, NY: Wiley.

Sue, D. W., & Sue, D. (1995). Asian Americans. In N. Vaac, S. B. Devaney, & J. Witmer (Eds.), *Experiences and counseling multicultural and diverse populations* (3rd ed., pp. 63–90). Bristol, PA: Accelerated Development.

Sue, S., & Zane, N. (2009). The role of culture and cultural techniques in psychotherapy: A critique and reformulation. *Asian American Journal of Psychology, 1,* 3–14.

Sullivan, P. (1998). Sexual identity development: The importance of target or dominant group membership. In R. C. Sanlo (Ed.), *Working with lesbian, gay, bisexual, and transgender college students: A handbook for faculty and administrators* (pp. 3–12). Westport, CT: Greenwood Press.

Sutherland, P., & Moodley, R. (2010). Reclaiming the spirit: Clemmont E. Vontress and the quest for spirituality and traditional healing in counseling. In R. Moodley and R. Walcott (Eds.), *Counseling across and beyond cultures: Exploring the work of Clemmont E. Vontress in clinical practice* (pp. 263–277). Toronto, Canada: University of Toronto Press.

Sutton, C. T., & Broken Nose, M. A. (1996). American Indian families: An overview. In M. McGoldrick, J. Giordano, & J. K. Pearce (Eds.), *Ethnicity and family therapy* (pp. 31–44). New York: Guilford Press.

Suzuki-Crumly, J., & Hyers, L. L. (2004). The relationship among ethnic identity, psychological well-being, and intergroup competence: An investigation of two biracial groups. *Cultural Diversity and Ethnic Minority Psychology, 10,* 137–150.

Swanson, B., Cronin-Stubbs, D., & Sheldon, J. A. (1989). The impact of psychosocial factors on adapting to physical disability: A review of the research literature. *Rehabilitation Nursing, 14,* 64–68.

Swanson, J. L. (1993). Sexism strikes men. *American Counselor, 1,* 10–13, 39.

Swinton, J. (2001). *Spirituality and mental health care: Rediscovering a "forgotten" dimension.* London, England: Jessica Kingsley.

Syme, M. L., Mona, L. R., & Cameron, R. P. (2013). Sexual health and well being after cancer: Applying the sexual health model. *The Counseling Psychologist, 41,* 268–287.

Syzmanski, D. M., & Sung, M. R. (2010). Minority stress and psychological distress among Asian American sexual minority persons. *The Counseling Psychologist, 38,* 848–872. doi: 10.1177/ 0011000010366167

Takaki, R. (1993). *A different mirror: A history of multicultural America.* Boston, MA: Back Bay Books.

Takaki, R. (1994a). *From different shores: Perspectives on race and ethnicity in America.* New York, NY: Oxford University Press.

Takaki, R. (1994b). The myth of the "model minority." In R. C. Monk (Ed.), *Taking sides: Clashing views on controversial issues in race and ethnicity* (pp. 55–61). Guilford, CT: Dushkin.

Tate, D. G., & Pledger, C. (2003). An integrative conceptual framework of disability, *American Psychologist, 58,* 289–295.

Tatum, B. D. (1992). Talking about race, learning about racism: The application of racial identity theory in the classroom. *Harvard Educational Review, 61*(1), 1–24.

Tatum, B. D. (1997). Racial identity development and relational theory: The case of black women in white communities. In J. Jordan (Ed.), *Women's growth in diversity* (pp. 91–106). New York, NY: Guilford Press.

Than, K. (2011). Massive population drop found for Native Americans, DNA shows. *National* Geographic. Retrieved June 8, 2015, from http://news.nationalgeographic.com/news/2011/12/111205-native-americans-europeans-population-dna-genetics-science

Than, K. (2014). Oldest burial yields DNA evidence of first Americans. *National Geographic.* Retrieved on October 29, 2015, from http://news.nationalgeographic.com/news/2014/02/140212-anzik-skeleton-dna-montana-clovis-culture-first-americans

Therrien, M., & Ramirez, R. R. (2001). *The Hispanic population in the United States: March 2000* (Current Population Reports No. P120-535). Washington, DC: U.S. Census Bureau. Retrieved November 3, 2015, from http://www.census.gov/prod/2001pubs/p20-535.pdf

Thomas, A. J. (1999). Racism, racial identity, and socialization. *Journal of Counseling & Development, 77*(1), 35–37.

Thomas, K. T. (2004). Old wine in a slightly cracked new bottle. *American Psychologist, 59,* 274–275.

Thomas, M. B. (2006). Navigators guide patients through the continuum: Barriers include language, finance, transportation. *Hospital Case Management, 3,* 191–194.

Thomason, T. C. (2000). Issues in the treatment of Native Americans with alcohol problems. *Journal of Multicultural Counseling and Development, 28,* 243–252.

Thompson, E. M., & Morgan, E. M. (2008). "Mostly straight young women": Variations in sexual behavior and identity development. *Developmental Psychology, 44,* 15–21.

Todd, N. R., Spanierman, L. B., & Aber, M. S. (2010). White students reflecting on whiteness: Understanding emotional responses. *J DIVERS HIGH EDUC. 3,* 97–110. DOI: 10.1037/a0019299

Tolaymat, L. D., & Moradi, B. (2011). U.S. Muslim women and body image: Links among objectification theory constructs and the Hijab. *Journal of Counseling Psychology, 58,* 383–392.

Toporek, R. L., & Williams, R. A. (2006). Ethics and professional issues related to the practice of social justice in counseling psychology. In R. Toporek, L. Gerstein, N. Fouad, G. Roysircar, & T. Israel (Eds.), *Handbook for social justice in counseling psychology* (pp. 17–36). Thousand Oaks, CA: Sage.

Torres, L., Driscoll, M. W., & Burrow, A. L. (2010). Racial microaggressions and psychological functioning among highly achieving African-Americans: A mixed-methods approach. *Journal of Social and Clinical Psychology, 29,* 1074–1099.

Towle, E. B., & Morgan, L. M. (2002). Romancing the transgender native: Rethinking the use of the "third gender" concept. *GLQ: A Journal of Lesbian and Gay Studies, 8,* 469–497.

Tran, T. V. (1988). The Vietnamese American family. In C. H. Mindel, R. W. Habenstein, & R. Wright (Eds.), *Ethnic families in America: Patterns and variations* (3rd ed., pp. 276–302). New York, NY: Elsevier.

Troiden, R. R. (1989). The formation of homosexual identities, *Journal of Homosexuality, 17,* 43–73.

Trujillo, A. (2000). Psychotherapy with Native Americans: A view into the role of religion and spirituality. In P. S. Richards & A. E. Bergin (Eds.), *Handbook of psychotherapy and religious diversity.* Washington, DC: American Psychological Association.

Tsai, J. L., & Chensova-Dutton, Y. (2002). Models of cultural orientation: Differences between American-born and overseas-born Asians. In K. Kurasaki, S. Okasaki, & S. Sue (Eds.), *Asian American mental health: Assessment theories and methods* (pp. 95–106). New York, NY: Kluwer Academic.

Tsai, M., & Uemura, A. (1988). Asian Americans: The struggles, the conflicts, and the successes. In P. Bronstein & K. Quina (Eds.), *Teaching a psychology of people* (pp. 125–133). Washington, DC: American Psychological Association.

Turner, C. W. (1997). Clinical applications of the Stone Center theoretical approach to minority women. In J. Jordan (Ed.), *Women's growth in diversity: More writings from the Stone Center* (pp. 74–90). New York, NY: Guilford Press.

Twine, F. W. (2010a). White like who? The value of whiteness in British interracial families. *Ethnicities, 10,* 292–312.

Twine, F. W. (2010b). *A white side of black Britain: Interracial intimacy and racial literacy.* Durham, NC: Duke University Press.

Tylka, T. L., & Subich, L. M. (2002). Exploring young women's perceptions of the effectiveness and safety of maladaptive weight control techniques. *Journal of Counseling & Development, 80,* 101–110.

UAF Interior Aleutians Campus. (n.d.). Indian Reorganization Act (1934). In *Federal Indian Law for Alaska tribes.* Retrieved from https://tm112.community.uaf.edu/unit-2/indian-reorganization-act-1934

Uba, L. (1994). *Asian Americans: Personality patterns, identity, and mental health.* New York, NY: Guilford Press.

Udry, J. R., Li, R. M., & Hendrickson-Smith, K. (2003). Health and behavior risks of adolescents with mixed-race identity. *American Journal of Public Health, 93,* 1865–1870.

Umaña-Taylor, A. J. (2004). Ethnic identity and self-esteem: Examining the role of social context. *Journal of Adolescence, 27,* 139–146.

U.S. Census Bureau. (2000a). *America's families and living arrangements.* Washington, DC: U.S. Department of Commerce.

U.S. Census Bureau. (2000b). *The Asian population: 2000.* Washington, DC: U.S. Department of Commerce.

U.S. Census Bureau. (2000c). *Population by age, sex, and race and Hispanic origin: Current population survey.* Washington, DC: U.S. Department of Commerce.

U.S. Census Bureau. (2000d). *Profile of selected social characteristics: Current population survey.* Washington, DC: U.S. Department of Commerce.

U.S. Census Bureau. (2000e). US Summary: 2000. *Census 2000 Profile.* Washington, DC: U.S. Department of Commerce.

U.S. Census Bureau. (2001a). *The Hispanic population in the United States. March 2000.* Washington, DC: U.S. Department of Commerce, Economics and Statistical Administration.

U.S. Census Bureau. (2001b). Labor force participation for mothers with infants declines for first time, Census Bureau reports. *U.S. Department of Commerce News.* Retrieved September 1, 2007, from http://www.census.gov/Press-Release/www/2001/cb01-170.html

U.S. Census Bureau. (2001c). *Poverty in the United States.* Washington, DC: U.S. Department of Commerce, Annual Demographic Supplement.

U.S. Census Bureau. (2001d). The nuclear family rebounds, Census Bureau reports. *U.S. Department of Commerce News.* Retrieved March 12, 2004, from http://www.census.gov/Press-Release/ www/releases/ archives/children/000326.html

U.S. Census Bureau (2002). *Poverty in the United States.* Washington, DC: U.S. Department of Commerce.

U.S. Census Bureau (2006). Americans with disabilities. *Household Economic Studies.* Washington, DC: U.S. Department of Commerce.

U.S. Census Bureau. (2007a). The American community—American Indians and Alaska Natives: 2004. *American community survey reports.* Washington, DC: U.S. Department of Commerce.

U.S. Census Bureau. (2007b). The American community—Asians: 2004. *American community survey reports.* Washington, DC: U.S. Department of Commerce.

U.S. Census Bureau. (2007c). The American community—blacks: 2004. *American community survey reports.* Washington, DC: U.S. Department of Commerce.

U.S. Census Bureau. (2007d). The American community—Hispanics: 2004. *American community survey reports.* Washington, DC: U.S. Department of Commerce.

U.S. Census Bureau (2007f). The American community—Pacific Islanders: 2004. *American community survey reports.* Washington, DC: U.S. Department of Commerce.

U.S. Census Bureau. (2007e). *FactFinder, 2006. American community survey data profile highlights.* Washington, DC: U.S. Department of Commerce.

U.S. Census Bureau. (2011). 2010 census shows black population has highest concentration in the South. Retrieved August 8, 2015 from https://www.census.gov/newsroom/releases/archives/2010_census/cb11-cn185.html

U.S. Census Bureau. (2012). Nearly 1 in 5 people have a disability in the U.S., Census Bureau reports. Retrieved June 20, 2015, from https://www.census.gov/newsroom/releases/archives/miscellaneous/cb12-134.html

U.S. Census Bureau. (2014a). Distribution of the poor, by age and race: 1959 to 2013 [Table 16]. *Current population survey, annual social and economic supplements.* Washington, DC: Author. Retrieved from https://www.census.gov/hhes/www/poverty/data/historical/people.html

U.S. Census Bureau (2014b). Facts for features: American Indian and Alaska Native heritage month: November 2014. In *United States Census Bureau news* (Release No. CB14-FF.26). Washington, DC: U.S. Department of Commerce. Retrieved from https://www.census.gov/content/dam/Census/newsroom/facts-for-features/2014/cb14ff-26_aian_heritage_month.pdf

U.S. Census Bureau. (2014c). Table 1. Household characteristics of opposite-sex and same-sex couple households: American Community Survey, 1 year file. Washington, DC: U.S. Census Bureau. Retrieved November 19, 2015, from http://www.census.gov/hhes/samesex/index.html

U.S. Census Bureau. (2015a). *Millennials outnumber baby boomers and are far more diverse, Census Bureau reports* (Release No. CB 15-113). Retrieved from https://www.census.gov/newsroom/press-releases/2015/cb15-113.html

U.S. Census Bureau. (2015b). [Data derived from population estimates, American Community Survey, Census of Population and Housing, State and County Housing Unit Estimates, County Business Patterns, Nonemployer Statistics, Economic Census, Survey of Business Owners, Building Permits.] *State and county quickfacts*. Retrieved from http://quickfacts.census.gov/qfd/states/00000.html

U.S. Census Bureau. (2015c). *U.S. and world population clock*. Retrieved from https://www.census.gov/popclock

U.S. Census Bureau (2015d). Poverty. Retrieved on January 24, 2016 from https://www.census.gov/hhes/www/poverty/about/overview

U.S. Census Bureau News (2005). Educational attainment. People 25 years old and over by total money earnings in 2004, work experience in 2004, age, race, Hispanic, origin. Retrieved August 1, 2007, from http://pubdb3.census.gov/macro/032005/perinc/new03_004.htm

U.S. Census Bureau News (2007). Household income rises, poverty rate declines, number of uninsured up. Washington, DC: U.S. Department of Commerce.

U.S. Centers for Disease Control and Prevention (2004). *HIV/AIDS among Hispanics: The body*. Retrieved September 1, 2007, from www.thebody.com

U.S. Department of Health and Human Services. (2001). *Mental health: Culture, race, and ethnicity—A supplement to mental health: A report to the Surgeon General*. Rockville, MD: U.S. Department of Health and Human Services, Public Health Service.

U.S. Department of Labor. (2010). *Labor force statistics from the current population study*. Washington, DC: Author.

U.S. Department of the Interior. (2002). *Federal Register*. Washington, DC: Bureau of Indian Affairs.

U.S. Department of the Interior Indian Affairs. (2015). *Alaskan region overview*. Washington, DC: Bureau of Indian Affairs. Retrieved on October 29, 2015, from http://www.bia.gov/WhoWeAre/RegionalOffices/Alaska

U.S. History.org. (2014). Irish and German immigration. *U.S. History online textbook*. Retrieved from http://www.ushistory.org/us/25f.asp

U.S. National Archives and Records Administration. (2015). Transcript of President Andrew Jackson's message to Congress 'On Indian Removal' (1830). Retrieved October 2015 from http://www.ourdocuments.gov/doc.php?doc=25&page=transcript

U.S. Natural Library of Medicine. (2015). Klinefelter Syndrome. Retrieved on October 25, 2015, from http://ghr.nlm.nih.gov/condition/klinefelter-syndrome

Ussher, J. M. & Perz, J. (2010). Gender differences in self-silencing and psychological distress in informal cancer carers. *Psychology of Women Quarterly, 34,* 228–242.

Utsey, S., Walker, R. L., & Kwate, N. A. (2005). Conducting quantitative research in a cultural context: Practical applications for research with ethnic minority populations. In M. Constantine & D. Sue (Eds.), *Strategies for building multicultural competence in mental health and educational settings* (pp. 247–268). Hoboken, NJ: Wiley & Sons.

VanBoven, A. M., & Espelage, D. L. (2006). Depressive symptoms, coping strategies, and disordered eating among college women. *Journal of Counseling & Development, 84,* 341–348.

Vandiver, B. J. (2001). Psychological nigrescence revisited: Introduction and overview. *Journal of Multicultural Counseling and Development, 29,* 165–173.

Vanzant, I. (1998). *Yesterday I cried*. New York, NY: A Fireside Book.

Vasquez, H., & Magraw, S. (2005). Building relationships across privilege: Becoming an ally in the therapeutic relationship. In M. Mirkin, K. Suyemoto, & B. Okun (Eds.), *Psychotherapy with women: Exploring diverse contexts and identities* (pp. 64–83). New York, NY: Guilford Press.

Vasquez, M. J. T. (1994). *Latinas*. In L. Comas-Dias & B. Greene (Eds.), *Women of color* (pp. 114–138). New York, NY: Guilford Press.

Venner, K. L., Wall, T. L., Lau, P., & Ehlers, C. L. (2006). Testing of an orthogonal measure of cultural identification with adult mission Indians. *Cultural Diversity and Ethnic Minority Psychology, 12*, 632–643.

Vera, E., Daly, B., Gonzales, R., Morgan, M., & Thakral, C. (2006). Prevention and outreach with underserved populations. In R. L. Toporek, L. H. Gerstein, N. A. Fouad, G. Roysircar, & T. Israel (Eds.), *Handbook for social justice in counseling psychology* (pp. 86–99). Thousand Oaks, CA: Sage.

Vera, E. M., & Speight, S. L. (2003). Multicultural competence, social justice, and counseling psychology: Expanding our roles. *The Counseling Psychologist, 31*, 253–272.

Verbian, C. (2006). White birth mothers of black/white biracial children: Addressing racialized discourses in feminist and multicultural literature teaching and learning color consciousness in black families. *Journal of the Association for Research on Mothering, 8*, 213–220.

Vernon, I. (2002). *Killing us quietly: Native Americans and HIV/AIDS*. Lincoln, NE: Bison Books.

Vontress, C. E. (1986). Social and cultural foundations. In R. Hayes & J. Lewis (Eds.), *In the counseling profession* (pp. 215–250). Itasca, IL: Peacock.

Vontress, C. E. (2004). Reactions to the multicultural counseling competencies debate. *Journal of Mental Health Counseling, 24*, 74–80.

Wachtel P. L. (2002). Psychoanalysis and the disenfranchised: From therapy to justice. *Psychoanalytic Psychology, 19*, 199–215.

Waldman, C. (2000). *Atlas of the North American Indian*. New York, NY: Checkmark Books.

Walker, A. (1987). Oppressed hair puts a ceiling on the brain. In *Living by the word: Selected writings, 1973–1983*. Retrieved January 27, 2008, from http://www.endarkenment.com/hair/essays/walker.htm

Wall, V. A., & Evans, N. J. (1992). Using psychosocial development theories to understand and work with gay and lesbian persons. In N. J. Evans & V. A. Hall (Eds.), *Beyond tolerance: Gays, lesbians, and bisexuals on campus* (pp. 25–28). Alexandria, VA: American College Personnel Association.

Walters, K. (2010). From Injun Joe to big chief: The relation between microaggression distress and substance abuse [PowerPoint]. Indigenous Wellness Research Institute University of Washington School of Social Work.

Walters, N. P., & Trevelyan, E. N. (2011). The newly arrived foreign-born population of the United States: 2010. (American Community Survey Briefs No. ACSBR/10-16). Washington, DC: U.S. Census Bureau. Retrieved November 18, 2015, from http://www.census.gov/content/dam/Census/library/publications/2011/acs/acsbr10-16.pdf

Wang, W. (2012). *The rise of intermarriage rates, characteristics vary by race and gender*. Washington, DC: Pew Research Center: Social Demographics and Trends. Retrieved June 5, 2015, from http://www.pewsocialtrends.org/files/2012/02/SDT-Intermarriage-II.pdf

Ward, J. V. (1989). Racial identity formation and transformation. In C. Gilligan, N. P. Lyons, & T. J. Hanmer (Eds.), *Making connections: The relational worlds of adolescent girls at Emma Willard School* (pp. 215–232). New York, NY: Troy Press.

Ward, J. V. (2000). *The skin we're in: Teaching our children to be emotionally strong, socially smart, and spiritually connected*. New York, NY: Free Press.

Ward, J. V., Robinson-Wood, T. L. & Boadi, N. (in press). Resisting everyday colorism: Strategies for identifying and interrupting the problem that won't go away. In Carla Monroe (Ed.), *Race and colorism in education*. New York, NY: Routledge.

Warren, A. K., & Constantine, M. G. (2007). Social justice issues. In M. Constantine (Ed.), *Clinical practice with people of color* (pp. 231–242). New York, NY: Teachers College Press.

Washington, C. S. (1987). Counseling black men. In M. Scher, M. Stevens, G. Good, & G. A. Eichenfield (Eds.), *Handbook of counseling and psychotherapy* (pp. 192–202). Newbury Park, CA: Sage.

Waters, M. (1994). Ethnic and racial identities of second-generation black immigrants in New York City. *International Migration Review, 28*, 795–820.

Watt, S. K. (2015). *Designing transformative multicultural initiatives: Theoretical, research, practical applications, and facilitator considerations*. Sterling, VA: Stylus.

Watt, S. K., Robinson, T. L., & Lupton-Smith, H. (2002). Building ego and racial identity: Preliminary perspectives on counselors-in-training. *Journal of Counseling and Development, 80,* 94–100.

Weber, A. (2015). *Subtle and severe: Microaggressions among racially diverse sexual minorities.* Manuscript submitted for publication.

Webster, M. Jr., & Driskell, J. E. Jr. (1983). Beauty as status. *American Journal of Sociology, 89,* 140–164.

Weedon, C. (1987). *Feminist practice and poststructuralist theory.* New York, NY: Blackwell.

Wehrly, B. (1995). *Pathways to multicultural counseling competence: A developmental journey.* Pacific Grove, CA: Brooks/Cole.

Weisman, L. K. (1992). *Discrimination by design: A feminist critique of the man-made environment.* Urbana: University of Illinois Press.

Wells, S. (2002). *The journey of man: A genetic odyssey.* Princeton, NJ: Princeton University Press.

Wells, S. (Host). (2003). *Journey of man: The story of the human species* [PBS home video]. United States: Tigres Productions. Retrieved from www.pbs.org

Wells, S. (2007). Spencer Wells: A family tree for humanity [Video file]. Retrieved August 20, 2015, from https:/// www.ted.com/talks/spencer_wells_is_building_a_family_tree_for_all_ humanity?language=en

Wendell, S. (1989). Toward a feminist theory of disability. *Hypatia, 4,* 63–81.

West, A. E., & Newman, D. L. (2007). Childhood behavioral inhibition and the experience of social anxiety in American Indian adolescents. *Cultural Diversity and Ethnic Minority Psychology, 13,* 197–206.

West, C., & Zimmerman, D. H. (1991). Doing gender. In J. Lorber & S. A. Farrell (Eds.), *The social construction of gender* (pp. 13–37). Newbury Park, CA: Sage.

West, W. (2000). *Psychotherapy and spirituality: Crossing the line between therapy and religion.* London, England: Sage.

Wester, S. R., Kuo, B. C. H., & Vogel, D. L. (2006). Multicultural coping: Chinese Canadian adolescents, male gender role conflict, and psychological distress. *Psychology of Men & Masculinity, 7,* 83–100.

Wester, S. R., Vogel, D. L., & Archer, J. (2004). Male restricted emotionality and counseling supervision. *Journal of Counseling & Development, 82,* 91–98.

Wester, S. R., Vogel, D. L., Wei, M., & McLain, R. (2006). African American men, gender role conflict, and psychological distress: The role of racial identity. *Journal of Counseling & Development, 84,* 419–429.

White-Johnson, R. L., Ford, K. R., & Sellers, R. M. (2010). Parental racial socialization practices: Association with demographic factors, racial discrimination, childhood socialization, and racial identity. *Cultural Diversity Ethnic Minority Psychology, 16,* 237–247.

Wiggins-Frame, M., & Braun, C. (1996). Counseling African Americans: Integrating spirituality in therapy. *Counseling and Values, 41,* 16–28.

Wijeyesinghe, C. (2001). Racial identity in multiracial people: An alternative paradigm. In C. Wijeyesinghe & B. Jackson III (Eds.), *New perspectives on racial identity development: A theoretical and practical anthology* (pp. 129–152). New York: New York University Press.

Wilkinson, D. (1997). Reappraising the race, class, gender equation: A critical theoretical perspective. *Smith College Studies in Social Work, 67,* 261–276.

Williams, D., Gonzalez, H., Neighbors, H., Nesse, R., Abelson, J., & Sweetman, J. (2007). Prevalence and distribution of major depressive disorder in African-American, Caribbean Blacks, and non-Hispanic whites. *Archives in General Psychiatry, 64,* 305–315.

Wilson, T. P. (1992). Blood quantum: Native American mixed bloods. In M. P. P. Root (Ed.), *Racially mixed people in America* (pp. 108–126). Newbury Park, CA: Sage.

Wilson, W. J. (1994). The Black community: Race and class. In R. Takaki (Ed.), *From different shores: Perspectives on race and ethnicity in America* (2nd ed., pp. 243–250). New York: Oxford University Press.

Wiltz, T. (2014). Counting Americans of Middle Eastern, North African descent. *Stateline.* Retrieved June 9, 2015, from Pew Charitable Trusts: http://www.pewtrusts.org/en/research-and-analysis/blogs/ stateline/2014/08/13/counting-americans-of-middle-eastern-north-african-descent

Wise, T. (2005). *White like me: Reflections on race from a privileged son.* Brooklyn, NY: Soft Skull Press.

Witmer, J. M., & Sweeney, T. J. (1992). A holistic model for wellness and prevention over the life span. *Journal of Counseling & Development, 71,* 140–143.

Wiechelt, S. A., & Sales, E. (2001). The role of shame in women's recovery from alcoholism: The impact of childhood sexual abuse. *Journal of Social Work Practice in the Addictions, 4,* 101–116.

Wong, F., & Halgin, R. (2006). The "model minority": Bane or blessing for Asian Americans? *Journal of Multicultural Counseling and Development, 34,* 38–49.

Wong, M. G. (1988). The Chinese American family. In C. H. Mindel, R. W. Habenstein, & R. Wright (Eds.), *Ethnic families in America: Patterns and variations* (3rd ed., pp. 230–257). New York, NY: Elsevier.

Worell, J., & Remer, P. (1992). *Feminist perspectives in therapy: An empowerment model for women.* New York, NY: Wiley.

The World Bank. (2015). Population female (% of total). Retrieved October 21, 2015, from http://data .worldbank.org/indicator/SP.POP.TOTL.FE.ZS

World Health Organization. (2005). *Tobacco free initiative.* Retrieved September 1, 2007, from http://www .who.int/tobacco/en

Worthington, R. L., Dillon, F. R., & Becker-Schutte, A. M. (2005). Development, reliability, and validity of the lesbian, gay, and bisexual knowledge and attitudes scale for heterosexuals. *Journal of Counseling Psychology, 52,* 104–118.

Worthington, R. L., Soth-McNett, A. M., & Moreno, M. V. (2007). Multicultural counseling competencies research: A 20 year content analysis. *The Counseling Psychologist, 54,* 351–361.

Wrenn, C. G. (1962). The culturally encapsulated counselor. *Harvard Educational Review, 32,* 444–449.

Wu, F. (2002). *Yellow: Race in America beyond black and white.* New York, NY: Basic Books.

Yakushko, O., & Chronister, K. M. (2005). Immigrant women and counseling: The invisible others. *Journal of Counseling & Development, 83,* 292–298.

Yeh, C., & Wang, Y. (2000). Asian American coping attitudes, sources, and practices: Implications for indigenous counseling strategies. *Journal of College Student Development, 41,* 94–103.

Ying, Y. (2002). The conception of depression in Chinese Americans. In K. Kurasaki, S. Okasaki, & S. Sue (Eds.), *Asian American mental health: Assessment theories and methods* (pp. 173–184). New York, NY: Kluwer Academic.

Ying, Y., & Miller, L. S. (1992). Help-seeking behavior and attitude of Chinese Americans regarding psychological problems. *American Journal of Community Psychology, 20,* 549–556.

Young, J. S., Wiggins-Frame, M., & Cashwell, C. S. (2007). Spirituality and counselor competence: A national survey of American Counseling Association members. *Journal of Counseling & Development, 85*(1), 47–52.

Zane, N. W. S., & Huh-Kim, J. (1998). Addictive behaviors. In L. S. Lee & N. Zane (Eds.), *Handbook of Asian American psychology* (pp. 527–554). Thousand Oaks, CA: Sage.

Zetzer, H.A. (2005). White out. Privilege and its problems. In S. Anderson & V. Middleton (Eds.), *Explorations in privilege, oppression, and diversity* (pp. 3–16). Belmont, CA: Thomson, Cole.

Zhang, S., & Moradi, B. (2013). Asian American acculturation and enculturation: Construct clarification and measurement consolidation. *The Counseling Psychologist, 41,* 750–790.

Zia, H. (2000). *Asian American dreams: The emergence of an American people.* New York, NY: Farrar, Straus and Giroux.

Zinn, H. (2003). *A people's history of the United States: 1492–present.* New York, NY: HarperCollins.

Zitzelsberger, H. (2005). (In)visibility: Accounts of embodiment of women with physical disabilities and differences. *Disability & Society, 20,* 389–403.

Zola, I. K. (1991). Bringing our bodies and ourselves back in: Reflections on a past, present, and future "medical sociology." *Journal of Health and Social Behavior, 32,* 1–16.

Zollman, J. (2015). Jewish immigration in three waves. *MyJewishLearning.* Retrieved on July 27, 2015, from http://www.myjewishlearning.com/article/jewish-immigration-to-america-three-waves/3

Zuckerman, M. (1990). Some dubious premises in research and theory on racial differences. *American Psychologist, 45,* 1297–1303.

Zur, O. (2006). Therapeutic boundaries and dual relationships in rural practice: Ethical, clinical and standard of care considerations. *Journal of Rural Community Psychology.* Retrieved from http://www.marshall .edu/jrcp

Zwang, J. (2010, November 29). High school graduation rate is increasing, report shows. *eschoolnews*. Retrieved from: http://www.eschoolnews.com/2010/11/29/high-school-graduation-rate-is-improving-report-shows

Zyromski, B., Bryant, A. Jr., & Gerler, E. R. Jr. (2009). Online reflections about relationships at school: Implications for school violence. *The Journal of School Violence, 8,* 301–311.

Zyromski, B., Bryant, A., & Gerler, E. R. (2011). Succeeding in school: The online reflections of Native American and other minority students. *Journal of Humanistic Counseling, Education & Development, 50,* 99–118.

Index